DESTINATION
CISSP

A CONCISE GUIDE

Rob Witcher | John Berti | Lou Hablas | Nick Mitropoulos

Library of Congress Control Number: 202292270
ISBN: 979-8-9874077-0-7
ISBN: 979-8-9874077-1-4 (Ebook)

Because of the dynamic nature of the Internet, web addresses or links contained in this book may have been changed since publication and may no longer be valid. The content of this book and all expressed opinions are those of the authors.

This work does not constitute the authors engaging in the rendering of professional advice or services. Neither the authors nor any associated with the publication process shall be held liable or responsible for any loss or damage allegedly arising from any suggestion or information contained in this work.

Layout designer: Kelly Badeau
eBook designer: Booknook.biz
Cover illustrator: Aleksei Diuzhov
Cover designer: Vinod Kumar Palli

Images: unsplash.com, pexels.com, pixabay.com
Icons: thenounproject.com

Acknowledgments

To you dear reader: I hope this book helps you achieve your goals!

To gyönyörű with whom I have the privilege of sharing my life, and who created our two incredible and wonderful little menaces. To my mom for always being there for me. And to John (that John↓) for introducing and guiding me to the extremely fulfilling profession of teaching.

—Rob Witcher

To my mom and dad for instilling the proper values. To my amazing brother, whom I admire and drives me to be more like him. To my incredible daughters who make me proud every single day. And to my beautiful wife, who makes my life so incredibly amazing. And finally, to Hal Tipton, who inspired my passion and dedication and made me realize how gratifying this would be.

—John Berti

To each member of this book dream team: Bravo, we did it!

To Rob & John: It is an honor and privilege to work with you!

To my parents: Thank you for your selfless love, care, and guidance. I miss you.

To Beth, Madison, and Patrick: Thank you for your love and support — always and especially during the past several years, as this CISSP journey has unfolded and continues to bloom.

—Lou Hablas

To Rob, John and Lou, who have invited me to be a part of this journey. It is an honour to have co-authored this book with them and be part of a truly gifted team giving back to the security community.

To my son, coming into our lives in a few weeks. The world is your oyster little one. Enjoy every minute.

—Nick Mitropoulos

OVERVIEW OF CONTENTS

CONTENTS

WHY THIS BOOK

Welcome to *Destination CISSP: A Concise Guide*. We're glad you've invited us to join you on your journey toward earning the highly coveted Certified Information Systems Security Professional (CISSP) designation. More than joining you, we hope you'll allow us to guide you to success with our cumulative years of practical experience as security professionals and educators.

The goal of this guide is simple: to help you pass the CISSP exam and to provide you with a foundation of security knowledge that will equip you to be a better security professional and benefit you throughout your career.

As a CISSP, you will be viewed as a competent and knowledgeable security professional, a decision-maker, and a leader. The CISSP exam requires candidates to assimilate a vast array of information spread across eight (8) domains that make up the Common Body of Knowledge (CBK) of security. This book was created with one unique goal in mind: to be a concise guide that still has enough information to help readers understand the concepts behind each domain in a simple and digestible manner.

As many people say, the CISSP exam is "a mile wide and an inch deep," and most candidates bring experience and strength in only a handful of the domains. This guide will help you supplement knowledge you lack and enhance your current understanding of concepts to a deeper degree, which is required for success on this very difficult exam.

Who is the CISSP meant for?

The CISSP is ideal for experienced security practitioners, managers, and executives interested in proving their competence and knowledge across a wide array of security practices and principles, including those in the following positions

- High-Level Management
- Chief Information Security Officer (CSO/CISO)
- Chief Information Officer (CIO)
- Director of Security/Risk & Compliance
- IT Director/Manager
- Security Systems Engineer
- Security Analyst

Value of the CISSP certification

The CISSP certification is a gold standard certification that is globally recognized and respected. Earning the CISSP certification tells employers and peers that you are an extremely knowledgeable and competent security professional; additionally, it indicates that you are disciplined and committed to professional security development.

How to best use this book

Everybody learns differently, but for the sake of your exam preparation, our guide may serve as one of your study resources. Based upon our years of teaching experience, we've aligned the guide with the 2021 CISSP Exam outline and included what we believe to be the most relevant and important material that will help you prepare efficiently and confidently. We recommend that you read the material as presented in order to most effectively synthesize the information and concepts pertinent to the exam. Additionally, through our own experience, we've found that reading with a highlighter and notebook in hand can help you identify and retain important information.

What are "Core Concepts" and "Expect to be tested on?"

The "Core Concepts" and "Expect to be tested on" callouts sprinkled throughout the Guide reflect what we believe to be the most important information a student should focus on. By specifically calling out concepts and information, our goal is to help students stay focused and on track.

CORE **CONCEPTS**

- Summary of key concepts in each section

- Refers to specific topics that you might see questions about on the CISSP exam

For purposes of your studies, you should pay particular attention to these items.

ABOUT THE EXAM

The broad spectrum of topics included in the CISSP Common Body of Knowledge (CBK) ensure its relevance across numerous disciplines in the field of cybersecurity. Successful candidates are expected to be competent in the following eight domains:

1. Security and Risk Management

2. Asset Security

3. Security Architecture and Engineering

4. Communication and Network Security

5. Identity and Access Management (IAM)

6. Security Assessment and Testing

7. Security Operations

8. Software Development Security

If you want to review the full CISSP exam outline, you can find it at https://www.isc2.org/CISSP-Exam-Outline.

The CISSP exam tests much more than simply rote memorization. It tests the deep comprehension and application of knowledge. The exam tests understanding and application of concepts, but more importantly, it tests competence; this is why you'll commonly see multiple answers that seem correct for an exam question, but only one of those answers is in fact the correct (best) answer. Another way of putting this is that the exam answers may offer several true statements, but only one will be the most correct answer based on what the question is asking.

Oftentimes, a question will seek the answer that represents the best, least, or most appropriate answer, among the options offered, and usually two or more possible answers will seem to fit the criteria. However, only one answer fits the criteria in the best possible way. Sometimes, no answer may seem correct. This is precisely why deep comprehension of the material is necessary. To be able to answer all questions, no matter how challenging they appear to be.

There are four different types of questions that you may encounter on the CISSP exam:

- **Multiple-choice:** where you will be given a question and four answers, and you must select the BEST answer. The vast majority of questions on the exam will be multiple choice.

- **Scenario-based**: where a scenario will be presented, essentially a few paragraphs of text, and there will be a multiple choice-question pertaining to the scenario.

- **Drag-and-drop**: where two lists—one on the left and one on the right—need to be matched. Terms and definitions are most often used in these types of questions.

- **Hot-spot question**: where you will be asked to click on a spot on a diagram—the hot spot—that represents what the question is asking. For example, a question might ask, "Where's the best place to install a firewall?" and present a network diagram, and you will be asked to select the desired location on that diagram. Hot-spot questions are exceedingly rare.

The exam typically requires at least two to four months of preparation. This timing will heavily depend on your existing skills, knowledge, background, experience, and the training courses you take. Once you achieve your CISSP certification, Continuing Professional Education (CPE) requirements ensure ongoing professional and knowledge development in all the areas covered by the exam.

May 2021 Exam Change Summary

The CISSP exam is constantly being reviewed, and (ISC)[2] typically refreshes the exam outline about every three years to ensure alignment with the ever-evolving security landscape. In the words of (ISC)[2]:

> The content of the CISSP has been refreshed to reflect the most pertinent issues that cybersecurity professionals currently face, along with the best practices for mitigating those issues. The result is an exam that most accurately reflects the technical and managerial competence required from an experienced information security professional to effectively design, engineer, implement and manage an organization's cybersecurity program within an ever-changing security landscape.

The May 2021 refresh resulted in very minor overall changes to the exam. In fact, during a webinar hosted by (ISC)[2] leadership prior to the change going into effect, it was stated that anybody prepared to take the exam using material aligned with the 2018 version of the exam would be equally prepared to take the 2021 version of the exam.

CISSP exam domain weights changed little:

	Domain	2018 Weight	2021 Weight	Change
1	Security & Risk Management	15%	15%	-
2	Asset Security	10%	10%	-
3	Security Architecture & Engineering	13%	13%	-
4	Communication & Network Security	14%	13%	-1%
5	Identity & Access Management (IAM)	13%	13%	-
6	Security Assessment & Testing	12%	12%	-
7	Security Operations	13%	13%	-
8	Software Development Security	10%	11%	+1%

The structure and material in our guide reflect the topics in the 2021 CISSP Exam Outline.

MINDSET

The most important concept to highlight for passing the CISSP exam is adopting a **managerial mindset** when answering questions versus reverting to a deeply technical "fix-it-now" approach.

We highly recommend that you watch our free video on how to **"Think like a CEO"**: dcgo.ca/thinkCEO

Thinking Like a CEO is how we summarize this extremely important mindset for every student in our classes. You need to approach your studies and especially the exam with the right mindset. You must be focused on helping the business achieve its goals and objectives. You must be focused on helping the organization create more value. Essentially, as a security professional, you are an enabler. You must focus on ensuring that the goals and objectives of the security function are aligned with the goals and objectives of the organization. You need to **think like a CEO**

One of the authors of this guide, John Berti, has been involved with (ISC)^2 for over twenty years; in fact, he was one of the authors of the first Official CISSP guidebook, the Official (ISC)^2 Guide to the CISSP Exam ([ISC]^2 Press), in the mid 2000s. According to John, the questions that make it into the exam pool have gone through multiple rounds of vetting and consideration to make them perfect questions that thoroughly test competence. **Finding the best answer to most questions is a lot easier if you think like a CEO.**

Testing science is applied to the creation of real CISSP exam questions, which makes them excellent to test competence. Ultimately, this enhances the value of the CISSP certification as well as the difficulty of the exam. It's not a "study, memorize, and pass" exam; it's an exam requiring competence, experience, and a methodical approach.

ABOUT THE AUTHORS

Rob Witcher

Rob is one of the driving forces behind the success of the Destination Certification CISSP program. He is a technical wizard, directing the creation of the integrated intelligent learning system.

Rob has over twenty years of intense security, privacy, and cloud assurance experience, including:

- Guiding multiple companies in responding to and recovering from (global headline level) security and privacy breaches
- Leading PCI readiness engagements, SOC2 audits, cloud assessments, and security maturity reviews
- Managing the development of multiyear security strategies and enterprise-wide privacy operating models
- Acting as the CIO of a global mining company

Rob has delivered hundreds of CCSP, CISSP, and ISACA classes globally.

Rob is a dedicated security professional and creative instructor who is deeply invested in the success of our students. He brings an entertaining delivery style that is grounded in years of experience and a deep understanding of what is required for success on the CISSP exam.

John Berti

John is the other driving force behind the success of the Destination Certification CISSP program. With over twenty-five years in the field, a wealth of global experience, and an exceptional ability to make complex topics simple, John brings the CISSP concepts to life through out of the box teaching approaches that lead to our industry-high exam success rates.

John is one of Canada's leading Information Security professionals with outstanding credentials:

- Over twenty-five years of Cyber Risk and Security experience in the industry.
- Twenty years of practical involvement in, experience with, and advising to (ISC)[2].
- Coauthored the best-selling CISSP exam preparation guide *Official (ISC)[2] Guide to the CISSP Exam*.
- Relevant involvement in helping (ISC)[2] develop materials for the official CISSP curriculum, the CCSP curriculum, and sample CISSP exam questions.

John has facilitated hundreds of classes worldwide and quite literally wrote the book on CISSP exam preparation.

Lou Hablas

Lou has more than twenty-five years working in the technology industry, with roles that have included:

- Managing the Identity and Access Management function at an Olympic venue during the 1996 Olympic Games

- Network Administrator for the retail securities division of a major Southeastern bank

- Consultant with a leading Microsoft-centric management consulting and technology services firm

- IT Director for a global non-profit

Lou enjoys helping others succeed and is passionate about using written and verbal communication to simplify and convey concepts.

Nick Mitropoulos

Nick has more than fifteen years of experience in security, threat intelligence, data loss prevention, and incident response. He holds numerous accolades and distinctions in the security industry:

- More than thirty-five security certifications (including [ISC]2's CISSP and SSCP)

- Member of the SANS global CISO network, GIAC advisory board, senior IEEE member, Cisco Champion, and EC-Council global CISO advisory board

- Author of McGraw-Hill's *SSCP Systems Security Certified Practitioner Practice Exams* and *GCIH GIAC Certified Incident Handler All-in-One Exam Guide*

- Winner of the CEH Fall of Fame 2021 and United Nations Hall of Fame awards

- Certified (ISC)², CompTIA, and EC-Council Instructor

TECHNICAL REVIEWER

Taz Wake

Taz has worked in a variety of security roles since 1993. Since then, his work has taken him across the globe in a variety of roles for government agencies and private sector organizations. Moving into the private sector, Taz founded Halkyn Consulting as a boutique security and risk management consultancy delivering technical security advice to businesses worldwide. Since forming the consultancy, Taz has developed CISRTs for multinationals, provided expert Digital Forensics and Incident Response services to a range of companies, and regularly provided specialist training to forensic science labs.

- Holds multiple physical and cybersecurity certifications including CPP, CISSP, CISM, CRISC, CEH, GXPN, GCFA, GCFE, GCIH, GCIA, and more

- SANS instructor for FOR508 Advanced Incident Response, Digital Forensics, and Threat Hunting course

- SANS course author for FOR608 Enterprise Incident Response

- SANS "Lethal Forensicator" and multiple challenge coin winner; 2x winner of the Core Netwars tournament

- Regularly active on Hack the Box, Try Hack Me, Immersive Labs, and other CTF platforms.

NOTES ON THE BOOK

What's up with the mixed case in the titles?

As you navigate this guidebook, you might find yourself wondering about the use of mixed case in the titles and headings. For level 1 and 2 titles/headings, we used the exact wording and case as shown in the CISSP Exam Outline published by (ISC)[2]. Titles at levels 3 and 4 reflect our preference and tend to be more uppercase.

Hey! I found a mistake in the book!

We're a small team that worked incredibly hard to create a CISSP guidebook that we hope will be instrumental in helping you pass the CISSP exam. We have devoted a huge amount of effort into making this book and it's gone through multiple rounds of reviews. However, we are only human, and as much as it irks us, we're pretty sure the odd mistake has evaded us. If you find a mistake, we'd greatly appreciate it if you could let us know so that we can fix it: cisspguide@destcert.com

Thanks, and all the very best in your studies!
Rob, John, Lou, & Nick

INTRODUCTION

The role of security has evolved significantly over the years. Simply focusing on protecting data on a server is no longer enough. Threat actors now target an incredibly broad spectrum of assets across an organization, including a variety of devices such as mobile phones, tablets, industrial controllers, and even smart fridges and sensors. The attack vectors have also evolved, and there's a large increase of phishing emails and other social engineering attacks that try to bypass defenses and take advantage of the weakest element in the security chain: people.

Given the evolution of the security field, one of the fundamental questions for any security professional to consider is: **What is the role of the security function in every organization?**

A solid understanding of the answer to this question will not only make you a better security professional but will also make it much easier to pass the demanding and difficult CISSP exam.

Answers to the question "What is the role of the security function in every organization?" will vary, depending on who is answering. Often, answers will include items such as:

- Reduce risk

- Protect information, IT assets, the company, and its reputation

- Preserve confidentiality and integrity

- Manage availability

- Ensure compliance

All the items listed above equate to one phrase that corporate governance focuses on: **Organizational VALUE**.

Security cannot focus solely on protecting data or information, as these are just some of the things that represent value to any organization.

Security must enable and support the organization in achieving its goals and objectives.
Gone are the days where security existed only to minimize risk or tick a box. While it is still necessary to conduct risk analysis and implement controls to address risks, this needs to be done with a top-down approach and direct input from upper management to ensure the security controls that are implemented help the business achieve its goals and objectives.

Security also protects people, hardware, software, intellectual property, concepts, products, services, and corporate reputation—anything of value. It allows an organization to achieve compliance with laws, regulations, and industry standards, and it protects against various risks.

How can security address all these things if it is reporting to Information Technology (IT)?

The CEO (Chief Executive Officer) is accountable for managing the organization in such a way that ultimately allows it to increase its value, through adhering to a set of rules, practices, and processes; this is governance.

In many organizations, the security function is led by the CISO (Chief Information Security Officer). Information is just one example of the important assets of any organization that security needs to protect. Another frequently used title for those leading a security function is CSO (Chief Security Officer). Often enough, the CSO then reports to the chief information officer (CIO), which can hinder the goal of security. **Security nowadays needs to be empowered to protect ALL the assets of the organization and to do that, it needs to report to those who are accountable for the company. That is, either the CEO or the corporate Board of Directors.**

The key takeaway is that to be a better security professional and to pass the CISSP exam, you must first understand security from a management point of view rather than simply a technical one.

As a security professional, you must always focus on helping the organization achieve its goals and objectives. You must be an enabler to the business.

DOMAIN 1

Security and Risk Management

DOMAIN 1
SECURITY AND RISK MANAGEMENT

The first CISSP domain focuses on the fundamentals of security and how to assess and manage risk. You will learn the concepts of the CIA triad, gain insight into core organizational roles and how they relate to security, and understand the important difference between accountability and responsibility, in addition to corporate laws (policies) and key processes like risk analysis. This domain also focuses heavily on the key factors of governance and compliance, and how security helps by being aligned and contributing to each.

1.1   Understand, adhere to, and promote professional ethics

1.1.1   Ethics

> **CORE CONCEPTS**
> - **Ethics are based on doing nothing that is harmful to anyone else**
> - **For organizations to have consistent ethics, they must be codified in corporate laws (policies)**
> - **(ISC)² Code of Ethics**

Ethics are a foundational element to a successful security program and should be adhered to throughout the organization. The success of any security program requires the proper ethical support from every level of the organization and therefore needs to be driven by management and instilled through proper support, direction, and enforcement through high-level management. Proper ethical behavior is based upon one belief: abide by the rules and do nothing that is harmful to anyone else. However, this belief comes in the form of a challenge: Though almost every professional follows some form of ethics, they tend to vary widely due to upbringing, culture, education, life experiences, religious beliefs, and so on. Thus, most people will pursue a course of action—a course of ethical behavior—based upon what they believe is ethically correct. So, although ethical behavior can help promote a good and secure working environment, there are likely a wide variety of ethical lenses forming the work landscape, especially in a large organization. How, then, can ethical behavior be pursued in a consistent manner to ensure that all employees employ the same set of ethics?

Within an organization, the best way to prescribe, promote, and instill consistent ethical behavior is through the use of corporate rules or laws, more appropriately referred to as policies. Policies that promote sound and consistent ethical behavior help make an organization a better place to work and more valuable to shareholders and to the communities where they operate. Policies must be legal, and adherence to and promotion of them must start with senior management and be consistently communicated to every employee.

(ISC)² Code of Professional Ethics

As a CISSP candidate, you are responsible for understanding and complying with the (ISC)² Code of Professional Ethics, which applies to CISSP holders around the globe. In fact, the CISSP exam will most likely ask at least one question on this topic. The Code of Ethics Preamble and Canons are noted below. **It is important that the Preamble and the Code of Professional Ethics Canons be understood fully in the context of corporate and industry application, and the Canons should be memorized and adhered to in the order presented.**

(ISC)² Code of Ethics Preamble

- The safety and welfare of society and the common good, duty to our principals, and to each other, requires that we adhere, and be seen to adhere, to the highest ethical standards of behavior.
- Therefore, strict adherence to this Code is a condition of certification.

Agreement with and strict adherence to this code is a condition of gaining and maintaining the CISSP certification. The (ISC)² Code of Ethics consists of the Canons outlined in Table 1-1.

Wording and order of the (ISC)² Code of Ethics Canons

(ISC)² Code of Ethics Canons	
1	Protect society, the common good, necessary public trust and confidence, and the infrastructure.
2	Act honorably, honestly, justly, responsibly, and legally.
3	Provide diligent and competent service to principals.
4	Advance and protect the profession.

Table 1-1: **(ISC)² Code of Ethics Canons**

In both the Preamble and the Canons, the topics are in order of importance, and again, **all these items should be memorized as presented. Remember, if a scenario is presented in which there's a conflict in the Canons, they need to be applied in order.**

How to apply Ethics Canons in various scenarios and contexts

1.2   Understand and apply security concepts

1.2.1 Focus of Security

CORE CONCEPTS

- Security must support the business in achieving its goals and objectives
- Security must increase the value of the organization

As outlined in the introduction, the role of security has evolved to become more fully integrated with business processes. For example, for many years, the IT or Information Security function didn't consider physical security to be part of their purview. However, there are a lot of physical assets that an organization owns that don't strictly relate to data—like people—that need protection. Security focuses on anything that represents value, better referred to as assets, and implements controls that ultimately increase the value of those assets. Security should not focus only on information, or data, as this is just one example of assets that represent value to organizations and therefore need to be protected based on that value.

In summary, the focus of the security function is to:

1. Allow and enable the organization to achieve its goals and objectives
2. Increase the organization's value

Security, therefore, is in a support role. Through proper security governance, those who are accountable for increasing the value of the organization can be supported and enabled to achieve their goals.

1.2.2 Confidentiality, Integrity, Availability, Authenticity, and Nonrepudiation

CORE CONCEPTS

- **Confidentiality:** Protects and prevents unauthorized disclosure
- **Integrity:** Protects and adds value to assets by making them more accurate, more timely, more current, more meaningful
- **Availability:** Ensures organizational assets are available when required by stakeholders
- **Authenticity:** Proves the source and origin of important valuable assets
- **Nonrepudiation:** Provides assurance that someone cannot deny having done something

Definitions of Confidentiality, Integrity, Availability, Authenticity, and Nonrepudiation

Figure 1-1 depicts a classic security model known as the CIA triad. The CIA triad is a foundational model that helps organizations design, structure, and implement the security function.

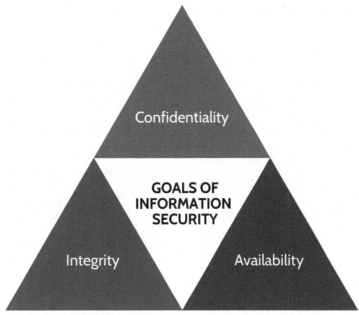

Figure 1-1: **CIA Triad**

The elements of the CIA triad are outlined in Table 1-2:

Confidentiality	Protects assets using important principles such as need-to-know and least privilege; prevents unauthorized disclosure
Integrity	Protects and adds value to assets by making them more accurate, more timely, more current, more meaningful; prevents unauthorized or accidental changes to assets such as information
Availability	Protects critical assets based on value to ensure organizational assets are available when required by stakeholders

Table 1-2: **CIA Triad**

These are the core pillars of security, and, even though referred to as the goals of information security, this is a narrow view of what security needs to focus on today. The goals of the three pillars—Confidentiality, Integrity, and Availability—need to be applied to information and everything else (assets) that represents value to the organization. In other words, security and the core pillars should be referred to as the "goals of asset security" and not just "the goals of information security."

The traditional pillars of security have been increased to include authenticity and nonrepudiation, outlined in Table 1-3:

Authenticity	Proves assets are legitimate and bona fide, and verifies that they are trusted and verified. Proves the source and origin of important valuable assets. Also referred to as "proof of origin."
Nonrepudiation	Provides assurance that someone cannot dispute the validity of something; the inability to refute accountability or responsibility. Also, inability to deny having done something.

Table 1-3: **Authenticity and Nonrepudiation**

1.3 Evaluate and apply security governance principles

1.3.1 Alignment of the Security Function to Business Strategy, Goals, Mission, and Objectives

CORE **CONCEPTS**

- The goal of governance is to enhance organizational value
- Corporate governance is based upon the goals and objectives of the organization
- Security must be managed top down instead of bottom up
- Scoping and tailoring are used to align security objectives with organizational goals and objectives
- Security governance must be aligned with corporate governance

The word *governance* can be defined as the act of governing or overseeing the process of directing something. In other words, governance means to govern properly to allow the organization to achieve its goals and objectives focused on increasing the value of the organization. Those activities can be referred to as corporate governance activities, and examples may include creating new processes, new products, new services, striking new relationships with third parties, improving margins and cash flow, creating new systems and procedures, reducing risk, meeting compliance requirements, and so on. All of these are just a few examples of corporate governance activities that organizations will implement/create to increase value.

Security governance will therefore include all those activities, initiatives, and programs that the security function will drive, initiate, and support, which should always be aligned, focused, and contributing toward those corporate governance activities mentioned above that will ultimately increase the value of the organization. The important point to remember is that this alignment can only be assured in a top-down structure. Those who are accountable for corporate governance activities need to be the ones who drive what security needs to do, to ensure alignment and proper contribution from security to add value and ultimately achieve the goals and objectives of the organization.

Security should be a proactive enabler rather than a reactive function, but this requires senior management to have strong convictions about the need for security. If there is a lack of support, if senior management isn't convicted of the need for security, what do you do? You could educate and convince them of the value of security via an internal champion or perhaps even via the hiring of external consultants.

Security needs to enable the organization's goals and objectives, not just enforce information processes or fix technical issues. Security governance must align with corporate governance, and security's goals and objectives should be driven by the organization's goals and objectives.

To best understand what is meant by the terms *corporate governance* and *security governance*, it is important to first understand what is meant by the term *governance*. At the heart of the word *governance* is *govern*, which means "to lead;" but, for what purpose does governance exist? When officials are elected to government, whether at the local, state, national, or federal level, what are they being elected to do? Ultimately, they're being elected to enhance or increase the value of whatever jurisdiction they will govern by providing better services and better meeting the needs of their constituents. Extending this definition, organizations need people to govern too, with the goal of increasing the value of the organization. Just like every country has officials who are elected to provide for the people and the country itself—in other words, to provide governance—organizations need a similar structure. Who are the members of the governing body of any organization? Typically, this would be the Board of Directors, the CEO, and senior management; their goal is to increase the value—the prosperity, the sustainability, and the viability—of the organization.

Instead of enacting things like local and municipal laws, organizations enact corporate laws called policies that allow the organization and its stakeholders to thrive. The Board of Directors should establish the organizational goals and objectives and set the tone for governance, but it can't necessarily oversee the continuous monitoring and proper implementation of the elements related to these principles. This is why the Board usually appoints an individual to be accountable for corporate governance. This individual—the CEO—therefore becomes directly accountable for corporate governance, or all the activities and initiatives that the organization undertakes to achieve its goals and objectives.

Extending the top-down perspective, it follows that security in any organization is only as good as its leadership; in other words, for security to be effective and for employees to be committed to the need for good security, the Board, CEO, and senior management must adopt, promote, and consistently communicate a security culture.

Security governance can be best aligned with corporate governance when it draws on the knowledge and experience of senior and upper management, HR, Legal, IT, and key functional areas of the organization. Specifically, based upon the expertise from functional areas like Legal, for example, security can know which laws and regulations need to be followed by the organization.

Aligning security governance with corporate governance

The best way any organization can establish and maintain sound organizational governance that aligns with security is through the establishment of an Organization Governance committee, charged with establishing and promoting the top-down governance structure and tone that is critical to an organization achieving its goals and objectives. This committee should meet regularly and include security goals and objectives in its organization. Put simply, the goals and objectives of the security function must be directly aligned with the goals and objectives of the organization.

Scoping and tailoring are important processes to ensure controls are properly aligned with organizational goals and objectives

Scoping and tailoring

Scoping looks at potential control elements and determines **which ones are in scope**—for example, security control elements that could adhere to applicable laws and regulations—**and which ones are out of scope**. In other words, based on the previous example, those security elements that best align with and support the goals and objectives of an organization from a legal perspective would be considered in scope.

Tailoring looks specifically at applicable—in scope—security control elements and further **refines or enhances** them so they're most effective and aligned with the goals and objectives of an organization. This is done from the perspective of each functional area. They should be cost-effective in relation to what they're protecting, and they should ultimately help add value to the organization. When done well, security governance is completely aligned with corporate governance, and the goals and objectives of an organization can be fulfilled in a manner that is cost-effective and adds value.

If the Board of Directors and senior management don't support the security function, security simply becomes a reactive nuisance versus a proactive enabler.

Starting from the top, if the Board and senior management are convicted of the need for robust security that is aligned with the strategy, goals, mission, and objectives of the organization, the security function will be viewed as a great asset and an organizational enabler.

As was mentioned earlier with regards to governance, the CEO is ultimately accountable for guiding the organization and helping it achieve its goals and objectives in order to add value. However, as the roles and responsibilities listed above allude to, accountability can exist elsewhere within an organization. For example, the CFO often is accountable for the accuracy of financial reports, and the Data Controller is accountable for privacy.

1.3.2 Accountability versus Responsibility

CORE CONCEPTS

- Only one person or group or entity must be accountable
- Multiple people can be responsible
- Accountability can never be delegated
- Responsibility can be delegated

At this point, it is important to understand the difference between two very important terms that are sometimes mistakenly used interchangeably: **accountable and responsible**. These two words do not share the same meaning. The word accountable was used earlier very deliberately. How does being accountable differ from being responsible? If someone is accountable for something, that accountability can never be delegated to anyone else. That person will always remain accountable. Responsibility, on the other hand, can be delegated, but the delegator will remain accountable. This explains why security is everyone's responsibility, yet the accountability for security remains with those who are focused on corporate governance—the Board, the CEO and other C-level members, and the owners of assets. If something that negatively impacts value happens in an organization, the CEO is ultimately accountable.

From a functional point of view, delegating responsibilities to the right person or team makes perfect sense and is usually the most effective and efficient means by which an organization achieves its goals and objectives. It's important to know and understand the difference between accountability and responsibility. Table 1-4 highlights the major differences between them:

Accountability	Responsibility
Where the buck stops	The doer
Ultimate ownership and liability	In charge of a task or process
Only one person or group can be accountable	Multiple people can be responsible
Sets rules and policies	Develops plans and implements controls

Table 1-4: **Accountability and Responsibility**

Even if certain functions of the organization are managed by a responsible third party, like a payroll or Cloud Service Provider (CSP), **accountability still resides with the owner of the assets being managed**. To expand on this thought, because it's more and more applicable these days due to the prevalence of cloud-based computing, the owner of any and all data stored in the cloud is accountable for that data. A CSP will often have a contractual-based responsibility for protecting the data, but **the owner of the data is always accountable for the data and therefore liable if there is a data breach.**

Who is ultimately accountable for security? Upper management, the CEO, or the Board of Directors?

Ultimately, the individuals accountable for every single asset in the organization are the Board and the CEO. However, it's not realistic for the CEO to be accountable for every single asset in any large company. So, although you can't delegate accountability, senior management is accountable for the assets that they manage. On the CISSP exam, if a question asks who is ultimately accountable for the finance system, the best answer would be the VP of Finance—but if they aren't listed, the next best answer is the person above them in seniority.

What accountability does the security function hold? The security function is accountable for security governance activities that have been driven, or initiated, by those who are accountable: the Board, the CEO, and other C-suite executives.

1.3.3 Organizational Roles and Responsibilities

CORE **CONCEPTS**

- The role of security is to be an enabler
- The owner/controller is the person that created, bought, or is most familiar with an asset
- The processor is the person, function, or group responsible for data and who do things on behalf of the controller

Who is accountable for what? Who is responsible for what?

Table 1-5 outlines some of the key functions typically found in an organization and their accountabilities and responsibilities from a security perspective.

Role	Accountabilities / Responsibilities
Owners / Controllers/ Functional Leaders / Senior Management	**Accountable** for: ■ Ensuring that appropriate security controls, consistent with the organization's security policy, are implemented to protect the organization's assets ■ Determining appropriate sensitivity or classification levels ■ Determining access privileges
Information Systems Security Professionals / IT Security Officer	**Responsible** for: ■ Design, implementation, management, and review of the organization's security policies, standards, baselines, procedures, and guidelines
Information Technology (IT) Officer	**Responsible** for: ■ Developing and implementing technology solutions ■ Working closely with IS and IT Security Professionals and Officers to evaluate security strategies ■ Working closely with Business Continuity Management (BCM) team to ensure continuity of operations should disruption occur
IT Function	**Responsible** for: ■ Implementing and adhering to security policies
Operator / Administrator	**Responsible** for: ■ Managing, troubleshooting, and applying hardware and software patches to systems as necessary ■ Managing user permissions, per the owner's specifications ■ Administering and managing specific applications and services
Network Administrator	**Responsible** for: ■ Maintaining computer networks and resolving issues with them ■ Installing and configuring networking equipment and systems and resolving problems
Information Systems Auditors	**Responsible** for: ■ Providing management with independent assurance that the security objectives are appropriate ■ Determining whether the security policy, standards, baselines, procedures, and guidelines are appropriate and effective to comply with the organization's security objectives ■ Determining whether the objectives have been met
Users	**Responsible** for: ■ Adherence to security policies ■ Preserving the availability, integrity, and confidentiality of assets when accessing and using them

Table 1-5: **Roles and Accountabilities/Responsibilities**

In **Domain 2 (section 2.3—Provision resources securely)**, additional roles and responsibilities will be covered specific to information security, including: Data Owner/Controller, Data Processor, Custodians, Data Custodian, Data Steward, and Data Subject.

One of the roles described in Chapter 2—**Custodians**—is often confused with **Owners** (mentioned in Table 2-3). Where does the word *custodian* originate? The word *custodian* comes from the word *custody*, and it follows that custodians are people or functions that have custody of an asset that does not belong to them; custodians are caretakers or users. The asset belongs to an owner, but the custodian is entrusted with it and is responsible for protecting the asset while it's in their custody. In this case, *protect* means to ensure that the asset's value is not negatively impacted. For example, related to database access, a custodian is responsible for ensuring that the database is available to the users or applications that need access to it; or, regarding confidential assets, a custodian is responsible for ensuring that information is not divulged that might negatively impact the asset's value.

However, what about a situation where, for example, a custodian is responsible for protecting an asset—data, for instance—and the asset becomes corrupted and unusable? Who is responsible? Who is accountable? Referring back to Table 1-4, the responsibility for the corruption rests with the custodian. However, accountability for the corruption rests with the **asset owner**. In other words, referring to points made earlier, it's critical that owners manage their accountability well and ensure that custodians are equipped to manage their responsibility well. Custodians can only take care of this responsibility if security helps. For a custodian to protect the assets in their custody, the right tools, architecture, security controls, knowledge, and skills must exist and be in place. The asset owner is accountable for ensuring this, and this is achieved through the support that the security function should provide.

Who provides all these tools? The security function. The security function performs two critical tasks: 1) makes it easy for custodians and users to perform their job while accessing assets and 2) security enables and equips owners to protect assets in the most efficient, cost-effective way possible.

Who is specifically responsible for security? Everyone.

Everyone has some degree of responsibility for security in their role; for example, the janitor of a locked building must make sure they're not taking confidential papers off someone's desk and that they're disposing of confidential recycling properly. However, asset owners are accountable for telling people what their responsibilities are. Asset owners are in the best position to know the value of the assets they control, and they can best determine how much security is needed to protect those assets. They also need to communicate what should be protected, who should protect it, and how to do so. Security professionals provide advice, but it's not up to them to secure anything. Security is ultimately everyone's responsibility.

Security frameworks, which will be discussed in more detail later, provide guidelines on how to align the security function with corporate governance. Frameworks like NIST, ISO, COBIT, ITIL, and more will be described more fully. For now, it's important to know that security frameworks provide comprehensive guidance on how to structure security properly.

Before moving to the matter of compliance with laws and regulations, let's examine another key component of security management embodied in two phrases: due care and due diligence.

1.3.4 Due Care versus Due Diligence

CORE **CONCEPTS**

- Due care is the responsible protection of assets
- Due diligence is the ability to prove due care

Table 1-6 details the basic principles surrounding due care and due diligence.

Due Care	Due Diligence
Accountable protection of assets based on the goals and objectives of the organization	**Ability to prove due care to stakeholders— upper management, regulators, customers, shareholders, etc.**
This definition aligns what security should be doing with what the organization should be doing. It aligns accountable protection of assets based on the goals and objectives of the organization. This is what due care means from a security perspective.	Due diligence is what is done to prove due care on a regular basis to organization stakeholders.

Table 1-6: **Due Care vs. Due Diligence**

Consider penetration testing as a representative example. Due care would be the owner of a system requesting that a penetration test be performed and then authorizing the remediation of the vulnerabilities identified by the

Definitions of due care and due diligence

penetration test. Due diligence would then be providing proof that the vulnerabilities were addressed in a cost-effective and efficient way to management and other relevant stakeholders (e.g., customers).

1.4 Determine compliance and other requirements

1.4.1 Compliance with Contractual, Legal, and Industry Standards and Regulatory Requirements

CORE **CONCEPTS**
- Controls should align with compliance requirements
- Legal, privacy, and audit/compliance functions are usually the best sources to determine compliance requirements

Establishing the right security controls isn't just about the internal needs of an organization. There is a plethora of contractual, legal, industry, and regulatory requirements that should inform how different assets are protected—also referred to as compliance requirements. Table 1-7 shows how an organization can determine compliance needs and requirements by defining the most common compliance requirements an organization would need to consider.

Laws	▪ Specific laws that an organization must comply with are based on the assets owned or managed, or the industry, jurisdiction, or country in which the organization operates ▪ Examples of laws: Health Insurance Portability and Accountability Act (HIPAA), Gramm–Leach–Bliley Act (GLBA), Consumer Online Privacy Rights Act (COPPA), Family Educational Rights and Privacy Act (FERPA), General Data Protection Regulation (GDPR), Federal Information Security Modernization Act (FISMA), and Digital Millennium Copyright Act (DMCA)
Regulations	▪ Specific regulations that an organization must comply with are based on the assets owned or managed, the industry, jurisdiction, or country in which the organization operates ▪ Examples of regulations: International Traffic in Arms Regulations (ITAR), Export Administration Regulations (EAR), and Encryption Export Controls
Industry Standards	▪ Specific industries often have associated standards—procedural and technical rules—that help guide the activities of organizations ▪ Examples of industry standards: Critical Infrastructure Protection (NERC CIP), National Institute of Standards and Technology (NIST), and International Organization for Standardization (ISO)
Import/Export Controls	See Domain 1 (section 1.5.3)
Transborder Data Flow Regulations	See Domain 1 (section 1.5.4)
Assets	See Domain 2 (section 2.1)
Personal Data	See Domain 2 (section 1.5.5)
Corporate Policies	See Domain 1 (section 1.7)

Table 1-7: **Compliance Requirements**

The legal, privacy, and audit/compliance functions must work together to ensure compliance, which requires the drive and initiative that security will ultimately design and implement as security controls. The compliance function will monitor compliance, the security function will advise on and enforce controls, and legal and privacy functions will determine organizational compliance needs. As a security professional, it's important to understand what the organization needs to be compliant with and what controls must be in place to adhere to these requirements. This implies that security must know what compliance needs exist, and the best resource to identify and understand these compliance needs is usually the legal function.

Once management understands compliance needs, they can work with security to implement controls. A big part of implementing the right controls is having the right roles and responsibilities defined, to determine who is accountable and who is responsible. Certain people within an organization are going to be accountable for the protection of personal information; many others are going to be responsible for it. Owners need to have clearly defined accountabilities related to compliance, including:

- Defining classification
- Approving access
- Retention and destruction

1.5 Understand legal and regulatory issues that pertain to information security in a holistic context

1.5.1 Cybercrimes and Data Breaches

If not already apparent, information security is a critically important facet of every organization. Every organization should be asking fundamental questions like:

- How is/are our information/assets protected?

- What are the issues pertaining to information security for our organization in a global context?

- What does the current threat landscape look like?

This is important because cybercrime is extremely profitable. This fact explains why most organizations won't admit to being victims or prosecute the perpetrators of cybercrime: the ramifications of doing so, from damaging their reputation to becoming a potential target, are too great. Thus, it's important for organizations to understand the cybercrime threat landscape, especially what the current trends in cybercrime are. Insights gained can help organizations better deploy security and other defense-related resources in the most effective manner. Not every attack can be prevented, but effective security strategies can reduce attacks by making them:

- Not worthwhile

- Too time-consuming

- Too expensive

Bottom line: **Don't be the low-hanging fruit that can be easily picked!**

As a security professional, it's imperative to apply the mandates above and implement effective security measures. Additionally, the security function needs to work with the compliance and legal functions to understand legal and regulatory issues in a global context because these could factor into how security is developed. Security professionals must understand global threats to their organization and respond in a manner that acknowledges them.

1.5.2 Licensing and Intellectual Property Requirements

> CORE **CONCEPTS**
> ▪ The goal of intellectual property laws is to encourage the creation of intellectual goods (inventions, literary and artistic works, designs, symbols, and names) and to protect the same.

Intellectual property is any intangible product (invention, formula, algorithm, literary work, song, symbol, etc.) of the human intellect that the law protects from unauthorized use by others. Intellectual property laws (outlined in Table 1-8) help protect intellectual property assets with the goal of encouraging the creation of a wide variety of intellectual goods. Though intellectual property laws and regulations vary quite a bit from country to country, the basic premises remain the same, as noted below.

What do trade secrets, patents, copyrights, and trademarks protect?

	Protects	Disclosure Required	Term of Protection	Protects Against
Trade Secret	Business information	**No**	Potentially infinite	Misappropriation
Patent	Functional innovations Novel idea/inventions	**Yes**	Set period of time	Making, using, or selling an invention
Copyright	Expression of an idea embodied in a fixed medium (books, movies, songs, etc.)	**Yes**	Set period of time	Copying or substantially similar work
Trademark	Color, sound, symbol, etc. used to distinguish one product/ company from another	**Yes**	Potentially infinite	Creating confusion

Table 1-8: **Intellectual Property Laws**

1.5.3 Import/Export Controls

Import and export controls are country-based rules and laws implemented to manage which products, technologies, and information can move in and out of those countries, usually meant to protect national security, individual privacy, economic well-being, and so on.

The Wassenaar Arrangement

Encryption is a powerful technological tool that can have immense value, but it can also pose a significant threat if it gets into the wrong hands. Cryptography is heavily used in the context of military and government agencies. In the United States, organizations like the National Security Agency (NSA) actively seek to deduce cryptographic keys to decrypt and understand secret communications of governments around the world in an effort to keep the country safe. As a result of the inherent value and potential threat that cryptography represents, global laws and regulations restrict the use of cryptography; and, in many cases, import/export restrictions to certain regions exist. These laws and regulations often pertain to the sales of weapons, but they also pertain to the underlying technology—computers, network infrastructure, and more—that can be used to develop military systems.

The Wassenaar Arrangement was put in place to manage the risk that cryptography poses, while still facilitating trade. It allows certain countries to exchange and use cryptography systems of any strength, while also preventing the acquisition of these items by terrorists.

Participating members can exchange cryptography of any strength, but countries that are not a member are excluded from data exchange.

International Traffic in Arms Regulations (ITAR)

This is a US regulation that was built to ensure control over any export of items such as missiles, rockets, bombs, or anything else existing in the United States Munitions List (USML) (https://www.ecfr.gov/cgi-bin/text-idx?node=pt22.1.121). The responsible agency is the US Department of State, Directorate of Defense Trade Controls (DDTC).

Export Administration Regulations (EAR)

EAR predominantly focuses on commercial-use related items like computers, lasers, marine items, and more. However, it can also include items that may have been designed for commercial use but actually have military applications. The responsible agency is the US Department of Commerce, Bureau of Industry and Security (BIS).

1.5.4 Transborder Data Flow

> CORE **CONCEPTS**
> - Transborder data flow laws restrict the transfer of data across country borders
> - When sharing data across borders, applicable laws must be considered
> - Enforcement of requirements in one country may not apply to other countries

Many countries have enacted laws commonly referred to as transborder data flow, data residency, and data localization laws, which require that specific data remain within the country's physical borders.

Challenges associated with sharing data across international borders

These laws primarily relate to personal data. The idea is to protect a country/state/province/region's citizens' personal data. If an organization is collecting citizens' data, then they are accountable for the protection of that data. As privacy laws and the protection of personal data vary significantly around the world, this has prompted the creation of these transborder data flow laws. If a country/state/province/region has strong privacy laws, then they may wish to prevent personal data from being stored or processed in other countries/states/provinces/regions that may have weaker laws. Hence, transborder data flow laws prevent personal data from leaving the physical borders of a country/state/province/region.

Given these laws, organizations must consider the potential implications of the flow of data across physical borders. This can be very challenging to organizations to keep track of with the proliferation of service providers and global cloud services.

General Data Protection Regulation (GDPR), enacted in May 2018, is a great example of a data residency regulation that specifically requires that personal data of European Union citizens be stored and processed only within the physical borders of the European Union.

1.5.5 Privacy

> ### CORE **CONCEPTS**
> - Privacy is the state or condition of being free from being observed or disturbed by other people
> - Personal data is information on its own or in combination that uniquely identifies an individual

In the context of asset protection and security, it might seem odd to include this topic. In fact, the topic of privacy is very relevant, especially in today's globally connected world. Information that is collected from clients and visitors to websites could be considered very valuable—perhaps as much or more valuable than other organizational assets. If personal information is disclosed as the result of a breach or carelessness, it harms both the individual to whom that personal data refers to and the value of the information itself. Additionally, the organization could face significant fines or damage to corporate reputation. Depending on the nature of the business and industry, the organization may not recover or even survive. Therefore, regardless of the value, it's essential that personal data is well protected to comply with current privacy laws and to protect the value of the information and of the organization itself.

This can become complex for multinational organizations since there's a significant variation around the world in both the definition of personal data and the laws that determine how to protect it. When dealing with personal data, organizations must tread carefully and work closely with their legal departments to identify all the applicable laws and regulations. After consulting with the legal department, it is the security function's responsibility to make sure that the correct controls are in place to achieve privacy. To have privacy, you need security.

Let's consider the topic of privacy. First, what's the definition of privacy? **Privacy is the state or condition of being free from being observed or disturbed by other people.**

Definition of privacy

This is a fundamental concept in privacy laws around the world, based upon the premise that if an organization is allowed to collect personal information, that information might be used in an unauthorized manner or such that causes harm. This explains why privacy laws like Europe's GDPR are becoming more and more common around the globe, and they apply to both government and private business organizations. Generally, privacy laws around the world have, and continue to, become more stringent and more restrictive, requiring the perfect implementation of security controls to ensure compliance.

A very important question that comes to mind is, who and what is impacted if personal data (also referred to as Personally Identifiable Information, or PII) is disclosed? Certainly, the individual to whom the personal data refers is affected. Additionally, the value of the organization that allowed the disclosure is also affected. This could be in the form of significant fines, liability, loss of corporate reputation, or any combination thereof. The organization may not be able to sustain these operations, depending on the industry and sector in which they have activities. For example, imagine how difficult it would be for an incident response company to be able to offer their services after being the subject of a breach. As such, it's essential that personal data is well shielded to comply with current privacy laws and to protect the value of the information and the overall value of the organization itself.

Personal Data

Depending on the location in the world, personal data may be referred to in different ways, and what constitutes personal data can vary significantly. Figure 1-2 contains the various categories of sensitive data types, like PII, PHI, and IP.

Figure 1-2: **Personal Data Types**

The simplest definition of personal data is data that can be used on its own or in combination to identify an individual. Personal data can be referred to as:

- **PI**—Personal Information

- **PII**—Personally Identifiable Information

- **SPI**—Sensitive Personal Information

- **PHI**—Personal Health Information

How is personal data defined in a little more detail? As noted above, the definition of personal data varies quite significantly around the world. In the context of one privacy law or regulation in one part of the world, a telephone number might be considered personal data; in a different context, perhaps not. The same is true for IP addresses, email addresses, and many other types of information. For example, consider the difference between a business and a personal phone. A business phone would need to be known to prospective clients, while a personal phone would not. The same is true for IP addresses, email addresses, and many other types of information. There is no perfect definition of personal data, because it varies significantly around the world, and this points to the notion of direct and indirect identifiers.

Direct identifiers include information that relates specifically to an individual, such as their name, address, biometric data, government ID, or other uniquely identifying number.

Indirect identifiers include information that on its own cannot uniquely identify an individual but can be combined with other information to identify specific individuals, including, for example, a combination of gender, birth date, geographic indicators, and other descriptors. Other examples of indirect identifiers include place of birth, race, religion, weight, activities, employment information, medical information, education information, and financial information.

In general, these definitions clearly describe each type of identifier. However, as a security professional, it's important to communicate with the legal team to be absolutely clear about what constitutes personal data and what jurisdictions and regulations apply. This approach allows everybody in the organization to be on the same page, and for the proper security controls to be implemented. Some examples of direct, indirect, and online identifiers are outlined in Table 1-9:

Direct	Indirect	Online
■ Name ■ Phone number ■ Government ID (e.g. SIN, SSN, driver's license) ■ Account numbers ■ Certificate/license numbers ■ Biometric data	■ Age ■ Gender ■ Ethnicity ■ City ■ State ■ Zip/postal code	■ Email address ■ IP Address ■ Cookies

Table 1-9: **Categories of Identifiers**

1.5.6 Privacy Requirements

CORE **CONCEPTS**

■ **Supervisory authorities are independent authorities in each EU state that investigate privacy complaints**

Privacy Policy Requirements

Everyone deserves a reasonable expectation of privacy. When someone enters personal details at the doctor's reception area or when booking a hotel room and providing credit card details, they expect their data to be adequately protected.

Along the same lines, companies must adhere to agreements and controls that comply with applicable laws and regulations. Table 1-10 contains a summary of the key roles within the privacy realm, while Table 1-11 summarizes some key privacy regulations in different countries.

■ **General Data Protection Regulation (GDPR) principles**

■ **Organization for Economic Cooperation and Development OECD) principles**

■ **Role of supervisory authority**

Data Owners	Owners need to have clearly defined accountabilities including:
	   ■ Defining classification
	   ■ Approving access
	   ■ Retention and destruction
	Different types of owners:
	   ■ Data owners
	   ■ Process owners
	   ■ System owners
	Companies that collect personal data about customers are **accountable** for the protection of the data.

Data Custodians	Need to have clearly defined **responsibilities** Protect data based on input of the owners. Custodians also need tools, training, resources, etc. And who provides all this? Typically the owners.
Data Processors	Need to have clearly defined **responsibilities.** Processes personal data on behalf of the controller / owner.
Data Subjects	Individual to whom personal data relates

Table 1-10: **Data Owners, Custodians, and Processors**

GDPR	▪ A single set of rules will apply to all EU member states
	▪ Each state establishes an independent **Supervisory Authority (SA)** to hear and investigate complaints
	▪ **Data subjects shall have the right to lodge a complaint with a SA**
	▪ Seven principles describe lawful processing of personal data:
	    ▪ Lawfulness, fairness, and transparency
	    ▪ Purpose limitation
	    ▪ Data minimization
	    ▪ Accuracy
	    ▪ Storage limitation
	    ▪ Integrity and confidentiality (security)
	    ▪ Accountability
	▪ **Privacy breaches must be reported within 72 hours**

United States	▪ Gramm–Leach–Bliley Act (GLBA) ▪ Health Insurance Portability and Accountability Act (HIPAA) ▪ Sarbanes–Oxley Act (SOX) ▪ Children's Online Privacy Protection Act (COPPA) ▪ California Privacy Rights Act of 2020
Canada	▪ Personal Information Protection and Electronic Documents Act (PIPEDA)
Argentina	▪ Personal Data Protection Law Number 25,326 (PDPL)
South Korea	▪ Personal Information Protection Act (PIPA)
Australia	▪ Privacy Act ▪ Australian Privacy Principles (APPs)

Table 1-11: **Privacy Regulations in Different Countries**

The list above illustrates just a few of the privacy laws around the world, and the requirements in these laws vary from country to country. You are not expected to be a privacy expert for purposes of the CISSP exam; but as a security professional you should understand that privacy cannot be achieved without security. Security must be involved in implementing the required security controls to achieve the required privacy requirements.

One privacy law that you should have a slightly deeper understanding of is GDPR. The reason is that GDRP is considered by many to be the bellwether for privacy laws in countries around the world. GDPR is one of the most comprehensive privacy laws in the world, and many countries have modeled, or are in the process of modeling their privacy laws on GDPR or plan to in the future. Some of the basic information you should know about GDPR is listed in Table 1-11: Privacy Regulations in Different Countries.

For multinational organizations, it can be quite complex and challenging to keep track of the varying privacy requirements around the world. In response to this problem, the Organization of Economic Cooperation and Development (OECD) has created guidelines that offer a simple set of principles that organizations can use to structure their privacy practices.

OECD Privacy Guidelines

The **Organization for Economic Cooperation and Development (OECD)** is an international organization that is focused on international standards and policies, and finding solutions to social, economic, and environmental challenges. One such challenge that they have been driving for decades is privacy.

Working with its member states, OECD has developed **guidelines** that would help to harmonize national privacy legislation and, while upholding such human rights, would also prevent interruptions in international flows of data. OECD represents a consensus on basic principles that can be built into existing national legislation or serve as a basis for legislation—those countries that do not yet have adequate privacy legislation. These guidelines have consistently been updated to reflect new requirements as technology has advanced.

Are the OECD guidelines mandatory for organizations to comply with? No, usually they're considered a prudent course of action. This is precisely how the OECD Guidelines should be viewed. They are intended as suggestions, as common "best practices" related to privacy and conducting business, regardless of the location around the globe. In other words, the OECD Guidelines can be useful to organizations, as they can provide guidance on how to achieve compliance to privacy requirements. Does this mean a perfectly implemented privacy program, based on the OECD Guidelines, is compliant everywhere? No, but following those guidelines is likely to meet most requirements in a given locale. However, it's not a replacement for reviewing the specific laws and regulations you need to follow. Security professionals can use the guidelines as a starting point for the fundamental security controls organizations should put in place. Once they've done so, it's still necessary to consult with legal experts about the specific laws and regulations they need to comply with, depending on the country in which they are operating. Subsequently, specifics related to that jurisdiction can be considered further for inclusion. OECD's privacy guidelines can be seen in Table 1-12.

Collection Limitation Principle	Limit the collection of personal data to only what is needed to provide a service, obtain the personal data lawfully and, where appropriate, with the knowledge or consent of the data subject
Data Quality Principle	Personal data should be relevant, accurate, and complete, and it should be kept up to date
Purpose Specification Principle	The purposes for which personal data is collected should be clearly specified at the time of collection
Use Limitation Principle	Personal data should only be used based on the purposes for which it was collected and with consent of the data subject or by authority of law; in other words, if an organization says it has collected personal data for a specific purpose, they should only use the personal data for that purpose
Security Safeguards Principle	Personal data should be protected by reasonable security safeguards against loss, unauthorized access, destruction, use, modification, etc. Essentially, security controls must be put in place, because privacy is unattainable without security.
Openness Principle	The culture of the organization collecting personal data should be one of openness, transparency, and honesty about how personal data is being used and in what context.
Individual Participation Principle	When an individual—data subject—provides personal data to an organization, that individual should have the right to obtain their data from the data controller as well as have their data removed. In other words, the individual should have the chance to participate or choose whether to share their personal information or withhold it. The term data subject refers to the individual to whom the personal data pertains.
Accountability Principle	A data controller should be accountable for complying with the other principles. What this basically means is that an organization that collects personal data is now accountable for the protection of that information.

Table 1-12: **OECD Privacy Guidelines**

1.5.7 Privacy Assessments

> CORE **CONCEPTS**
>
> - **Privacy Impact Assessment (PIA) is a process undertaken on behalf of an organization to determine if personal data is being protected appropriately and to minimize risks to personal data where appropriate.**

With the protection of privacy becoming more important with each passing day, requirements calling for privacy and **Data Protection Impact Assessments (DPIA)** have become equally important. In fact, Article 35 of the GDPR legislation includes a provision for Data Protection Impact Assessments (DPIA) and outlines when they're required and how they should be carried out. Additionally, ISO/IEC 29134:2017 describes a process on privacy impact assessments (PIA) and a structure and content of a PIA report. The NIST Technology Innovation Program includes information about PIAs. The European Data Protection Board, other organizations, trade groups, and independent businesses and vendors have and will continue to provide guidance, tools, checklists, and templates.

> - **What is a PIA/ DPIA?**
> - **How often does a PIA/DPIA need to be conducted?**

What is a privacy impact assessment?

A **Privacy Impact Assessment (PIA)** is a process undertaken on behalf of an organization to determine if personal data is being protected appropriately and to minimize risks to personal data as appropriate. Any system that processes personal data could be included in a PIA. Like many other risk management processes, a PIA is not a one-time assessment. Rather, it should be performed each time it's necessary, especially when risk represented by personal data processing operations has changed. Additionally, along with the assessment of risks, accompanying mitigation measures should be included.

Why are they important?

A PIA is performed with a goal to:

1. Identify/evaluate risks relating to privacy breaches
2. Identify what controls should be applied to mitigate privacy risks
3. Offer organizational compliance to privacy legislations

Privacy/Data Protection Impact Assessment Steps

There are no all-inclusive templates for conducting a PIA/DPIA, but the steps outlined in Table 1-13 summarize the core elements of a PIA/DPIA.

> **What are the steps required to conduct a PIA?**

Privacy Impact Assessment Steps

1. Identify the need for a DPIA	Use legislative guidelines, like GDPR, European guidelines, federal and state laws, industry regulations, etc. to determine if a DPIA is required. If any doubt exists, it's best to err on the side of caution and conduct an assessment.
2. Describe the data processing	This involves two steps. The first step answers questions such as: ■ How is data being collected/used? ■ Where is data being gathered from? ■ How much data is being gathered, and how many data subjects are involved? ■ Is this data being stored with any third-party entities? ■ What are the purposes of processing? ■ Are the interests of the data controller legitimate? The second step considers information gathered via questions like those mentioned earlier and further defines the purpose—the what, how, and why—of data processing activities as they relate to the goals of the project.
3. Assess necessity and proportionality	Data processing activities should always correlate with what is actually required for the goals and objectives of a project. The DPIA should confirm this is the case, and this can be done by answering questions such as: ■ Does a legal basis for collected personal data exist? ■ Do data subjects have the right to opt out or in with relation to their personal data? ■ Does a precedent exist for the collecting and processing of data? ■ How are the rights of data subjects protected?
4. Consult interested parties	As part of any DPIA, several key parties should be consulted, including the data protection officer, project stakeholders, and data subjects (or their legal representatives).
5. Identify and assess risks	This step is critically important and likely the most important component of the DPIA, as it involves thoroughly assessing risks to personal data. While some risks might be project dependent, key considerations with any project should include asking: ■ Is data being stored in unsafe locations? ■ Are appropriate access control lists being utilized? ■ What data retention policies are currently in place?
6. Identify measures to mitigate the risks	Once risks associated with a project have been identified, it's imperative that corresponding steps to mitigate those risks be identified and implemented, based upon the cost-effectiveness of doing so. Additionally, this is where a defense-in-depth approach that involves the use of complete controls should be utilized to: ■ protect personal data from unauthorized internal and external access, ■ remove data that is no longer required, via relevant data retention policies and processes, ■ maintain visibility over personal data, ■ automate remediation action when and where possible for the sake of data removal, cleanup, and classification.
7. Sign off and record outcomes	After risks and associated mitigation steps have been identified, all details should be documented and signed off on by relevant parties that could include the data protection officer, senior management, process and project stakeholders, and data subjects.
8. Monitor and review	A PIA should be performed when necessary, especially when risk represented by personal data processing operations has changed. This fact points to the need for ongoing monitoring and review of operations, processes, and all facets of a business that involve handling of personal data.

Table 1-13: **PIA/DPIA Core Elements**

Additionally, Article 35 of the GDPR offers the minimum features of a DPIA:

The assessment shall contain at least:

1. a systematic description of the envisaged processing operations and the purposes of the processing, including, where applicable, the legitimate interest pursued by the controller;

2. an assessment of the necessity and proportionality of the processing operations in relation to the purposes;

3. an assessment of the risks to the rights and freedoms of data subjects; and

4. the measures envisaged to address the risks, including safeguards, security measures, and mechanisms to ensure the protection of personal data and to demonstrate compliance with this regulation considering the rights and legitimate interests of data subjects and other persons concerned.

1.6   Understand requirements for investigation types

See Domain 7 (section 7.1.7).

1.7 Develop, document, and implement security policies, procedures, standards, baselines, and guidelines

1.7.1 Policies, Procedures, Standards, Baselines, and Guidelines

CORE **CONCEPTS**

- Policies = Corporate Laws
- Policies document and communicate management's goals and objectives
- Overarching security policy must come from upper management (tone from the top)
- Procedures = Step-by-Step instructions
- Standards = Specific information related to solutions
- Baselines = Defined minimal implementation levels
- Guidelines = Recommendations or suggestions

Earlier, it was discussed in detail how security must be aligned with organizational goals and objectives. A top-down approach that incorporates a governance committee to help design policies is required. The committee, reporting to the Board of Directors and CEO, should develop an overarching security policy that is aligned with organizational goals and objectives that covers the entire organization and clearly articulates the goals and objectives of the security function. Policies, as we've already briefly touched upon earlier, are corporate laws that reflect the goals and objectives of the organization. They dictate and communicate management's intentions. The overarching security policy is critical, as it sets the tone and helps create the culture necessary for effective organizational security to exist. This policy must be communicated from the CEO, or even the Board of Directors, to be most effective and impactful. It also needs to be consistently communicated and demonstrated by those at the top of the organization.

- Who should write policies and who owns policies?
- How often should policies be reviewed?
- How are policies implemented through standards, procedures, baselines, & guidelines?

The overarching policy should be very simple. It needs to be communicated by the CEO and will clearly spell out how the CEO and organization is accountable for protecting all assets that represent value to the organization—that the CEO and upper management are ACCOUNTABLE, but also that EVERYONE in the organization is RESPONSIBLE for security and protecting the value of assets. The CEO must clearly communicate this and remind the entire organization on a regular basis. If this is done, it creates the proper culture and tone that security needs to be an enabler to the organization. It also ensures that everyone understands the importance of security and that it is everyone's responsibility.

If this is done properly, the security function is seen as an enabler and helper, as opposed to the traditional view of security as an obstacle—where the business goes to be told they can't do something.

Specific functional security policies will flow from the overarching policy. Functional security policies include standards, procedures, baselines, and guidelines that outline how to enact them. While policies don't need to be reviewed every year, standards, procedures, baselines, and guidelines may need to be updated frequently. Any combination of these elements will typically be put in place to support functional policies; together, the compendium of functional policies will be defined, supported, and informed by many standards, procedures, baselines, and guidelines.

Therefore, let's take a close look at a model for creating and maintaining security policies in an organization as depicted in Figure 1-3.

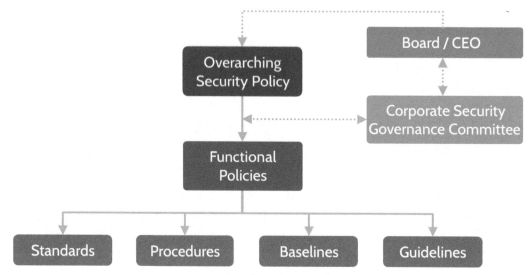

Figure 1-3: **Security Document Hierarchy**

An organization might have a policy, created and owned by the Security Governance Committee, mandating the use of anti-malware software. Functional policies would then need to be developed that dictate exactly how to enact that policy. Those functional policies might include a standard to specify the version of anti-malware software to use, a procedure to outline the steps to install it, and a guideline to suggest ideal goals for anti-malware efforts, such as heuristics in anti-malware software where possible. Each type of supporting document works together to ensure the policy is met.

The success of this model depends on each person performing their role well and supporting functional policies that make sense to the company. If the Board or CEO are unwilling to lead, failure from the top could follow. In our example, this might mean that although an organization would benefit from an anti-malware policy, the Board or CEO may not be working with security to create one. Similarly, if the supporting elements of functional security policies are not considered properly, implementation of security could fail. Thus, it's important that all facets of the model be carefully considered when developing and implementing it.

- **Differences between policies procedures, baselines, and guidelines**
- **Identifying when something provided relates to a procedure, policy, baseline, or guideline**

Many companies have very different definitions of policies, standards, procedures, baselines, and guidelines—but there are industry standards for what each of these documents are meant to be used for. Knowing the precise definition of these standards—outlined in Table 1-14—will help you use them properly.

Policies	<ul><li>Documents that communicate management's **goals and objectives**</li><li>Provide **authority** to security activity</li><li>Define the elements, functions, and scope of security team</li><li>Must be approved and communicated</li><li>Corporate laws</li></ul>
Standards	**Specific hardware and software solutions, mechanisms, and products** Examples <ul><li>Specific anti-virus software, e.g., McAfee</li><li>Specific access control system, e.g., Forescout</li><li>Specific firewall system, e.g,. Cisco ASA</li><li>Published guideline (e.g., ISO 27001) adopted by an organization as a standard.</li></ul>
Procedures	**Step-by-step descriptions on how to perform a task; mandatory actions** Examples <ul><li>User registration or new hire onboarding</li><li>Contracting for security purposes</li><li>Information system material destruction</li><li>Incident response</li></ul>
Baselines	**Defined minimal implementation methods/levels for security mechanisms and products** Examples <ul><li>Configurations for intrusion detection systems</li><li>Configurations for access control systems</li></ul>
Guidelines	**Recommended** or **suggested** actions Examples <ul><li>Government recommendations</li><li>Security configuration recommendations</li><li>Organizational guidelines</li><li>Product/system evaluation criteria</li></ul>(Note: Guidelines allow an organization to suggest something be done without making it a hard requirement and thus cause a negative audit finding)

Table 1-14: **Policies, Standards, Procedures, Baselines, and Guidelines**

1.8 Identify, analyze, and prioritize business continuity (BC) requirements

See Domain 7 (section 7.11).

1.9 Contribute to and enforce personnel security policies and procedures

1.9.1 Personnel Security Controls

> CORE **CONCEPTS**
> - Hiring, onboarding, and terminating employees
> - Employment controls and associated cost-effectiveness

Personnel Security Policies

Companies need clearly documented and communicated personnel security policies that are implemented through procedures, to address the needs related to the use and protection of valuable assets of the organization. Some of the best practices for protecting the business and its important assets are listed below. These best practices all have to do with how people and the organization work together to support the business.

> - **Dealing with potential violations identified in a security assessment**
> - **Dealing with employee terminations and resignations**
> - **Employee duress**

Candidate Screening and Hiring

New personnel represent a risk to security; every organization needs personnel security policies that address and mitigate this risk with the right security controls. Examples of personnel security policies and controls include background checks, access badges, ID cards, what you're allowed to bring in and out of the building, acceptable use policies, code of conduct, employee handbook, and so on.

Employment Agreements and Policies

As part of bringing a new employee into an organization—also referred to as onboarding—company security policies, acceptable use policies, and similar agreements should be reviewed and agreed upon prior to giving a new employee their badge and any system credentials.

Over the course of an employee's time at the company, controls like "separation of duties" and "job rotation" can be used to prevent fraud or violation of organizational policy. In addition to separation of duties and job rotation, two other controls often used are "least privilege" and "need to know." These two access controls are often referred to together, and they help ensure that employees are given only the access they need to perform their job and no more.

Offboarding controls are used when an employee leaves an organization, whether through termination or resignation. Prior to an employee leaving, or in conjunction with it, user system access should be disabled, and the fact that the employee's employment is being terminated should be conveyed to all relevant parties within the organization. Usually, voluntary termination isn't too much of a security risk. However, involuntary termination is a big risk from a security perspective. If a terminated employee becomes hostile, they might be tempted to lash out by stealing or tampering with data. For this reason, involuntary termination usually needs to be handled quite differently than voluntary termination. For example, in some situations, a member from physical security might even be physically present in the HR office while the person is being terminated to escort them out of the building.

Employee Duress

An employee acting under duress may be forced to perform an action or set of actions that they wouldn't do under normal circumstances. For example, consider the scenario of a bank manager threatened by an attacker and told to open the bank's vault while held at gunpoint. In that scenario, the bank manager's life is at risk, so, acting under duress, they may give the attacker what they want. One common practice to handle these stressful situations is to have keywords that denote that an employee is acting under duress. Have you ever watched *The Bourne Identity*? You will notice that at some point one of the field agents calls the CIA headquarters and gives the all clear after inspecting a potentially compromised location. However, the agent in charge does a challenge-response check and expects a specific answer to be provided if the field agent is acting under duress. Training is key in these scenarios so everyone will act calmly and denote they are potentially acting under duress.

Personnel security policies should also be extended to third parties. Third parties include contractors, companies, and anybody that may have access to company assets as part of the service provided to the organization. Table 1-15 provides a list of important personnel security controls, while Table 1-16 summarizes onboarding and offboarding processes.

Personnel Security Controls

Job rotation	Job rotation is quite useful to protect against fraud and provide cross training. It entails rotating staff (especially individuals in key positions), so that an individual can't commit fraud and cover it up. For example, if someone is a loans officer at a major bank and is responsible for approving loans, they can easily defraud the bank by constantly approving loans for known individuals who pass them money as a reward. However, if that individual is rotated to another role, this won't be possible. In addition, this helps the organization to build personnel redundancy. If another staff member learns how to perform the loan officer's job, this can greatly help if that individual decides to leave the company.
Mandatory vacation	Mandatory vacation is a control also used by organizations to detect fraud. Employees are required to go on vacation for a set period of time, during which time another employee can step into the role and determine if any malicious or nefarious activity has taken place or is actively taking place.
Separation of duties	Separation of duties is used to prevent fraud, by requiring more than one employee to perform critical tasks. A good example of this can be found in Accounts Payable/Vendor Management department. For new vendors to be set up to receive payments, at least two people are typically involved: one person to enter the vendor or payment information and another to confirm the vendor or approve the check. This way, a check can't be submitted, reviewed, and processed by a single person, giving them an opportunity to commit fraud.
Need-to-know and Least privilege	Least privilege ensures that only the minimum permissions needed to complete the work are granted to any employee. Need to know ensures that access to sensitive assets is restricted only to those who require the information to complete the work.

Table 1-15: **Personnel Security Controls**

Onboarding	Termination/Offboarding
<ul><li>Identity proofing (ability to identify individuals attempting to access a specific application or service)</li><li>Signoff on policies and agreements</li><li>Access provisioning based on least privilege and Need-to-Know</li></ul>	<ul><li>Timely removal of access</li><li>Involuntary vs. voluntary</li></ul>

Table 1-16: **Onboarding and Offboarding Processes**

1.9.2 Enforce Personnel Security Controls

CORE **CONCEPTS**

- Enforce organizational personnel policies and controls for contractors and vendors
- Contracts, agreements, and NDAs are tools that can be used to enforce personnel security controls
- Attestation and audit are tools that can monitor and show compliance with personnel security controls

Enforcing personnel security controls commences with the hiring process, extends through the employment period, and ends only after the employee has left the organization. Security controls like job rotation, separation of duties, and the others mentioned earlier are important, but policies are the primary means by which these controls are enforced. They often include:

- Company security policies that align with and support organizational goals and objectives
- Acceptable use policies that outline the "do" and "don't" behavior expected by the organization

Additionally, personnel-focused policies are often further supported by things like:

- Nondisclosure agreements (NDA)
- Noncompete agreements (NCA)
- Ethical guideline and requirement questionnaires and agreements
- Vendor, consultant, and contractor agreements and controls

Nondisclosure Agreements (NDAs) are contracts through which the parties agree not to disclose information covered by the agreement. Organizations may require employees to agree to and sign an NDA before the employee is allowed to access sensitive information.

Personnel security policies should also be extended to third parties in the form of contracts and service level agreements (SLAs).

As employee actions and behavior are subject to and enforced by organization policies, third-party vendors should be equally subject to and held responsible for their actions and behavior. Contracts and SLAs, NDAs, attestation, and audit are tools that an organization can use to ensure compliance to organizational personnel policies.

Enforcement of organizational personnel policies and controls for vendors and other third parties are achieved through:

- Contracts/agreements
- NDAs
- Attestation/audit

1.10 Understand and apply risk management concepts

1.10.1 Risk Management

> **CORE CONCEPTS**
> - Risk management is the identification, assessment, and prioritization of risks and the economical application of resources to minimize, monitor, and control the probability and/or impact of these risks
> - Risk management steps: value, risk, and treatment

Every organization (big or small) faces a similar challenge: limited resources are available to protect numerous assets. In those cases, what controls should be used, and what are the most effective ones? How can assets be adequately protected when there are not enough resources present? Risk management aims to answer such questions.

Risk management is the identification, assessment, and prioritization of risks and the cost-efficient application of resources to minimize the probability and/or impact of these risks.

The value of an asset must be understood in order to identify and implement the most cost-effective security controls. If controls are inefficient and not cost-effective, the value of the organization is being eroded. For example, imagine applying a $100,000 security control to a risk that has been calculated to only cost the organization $1,000 per year. That isn't cost-efficient at all.

> - **Risk management and relationship with risk analysis and threat analysis**
> - **Risk management steps**

Table 1-17 provides an overview of the risk management process, and we'll delve into each step in more detail in subsequent sections.

1. Value	The first step is identifying the assets of the organization and ranking those assets from most to least valuable. This process is referred to as asset valuation, and the ranking of assets can be achieved via two methods or, most commonly, a combination of both: ■ Quantitative value analysis ■ Qualitative value analysis
2. Risk Analysis	Determine the risks associated with each asset via the risk analysis process. Risks are identified by determining the specific threats (threat analysis) that could harm the asset, the vulnerabilities (vulnerability analysis) of the asset, what the impact would be if a threat manifests or a vulnerability is exploited, and the expected frequency of the risk occurring. Simple definitions of the four key components that must be identified as part of risk analysis follow: ■ **Threat:** Any potential danger to an asset (could be environment, physical, people, technology). ■ **Vulnerability:** Any weakness that exists that could be exploited by an attacker. ■ **Impact:** The extent to which an asset would be negatively affected. ■ **Probability/likelihood:** The chance that a risk might materialize due to a given threat or vulnerability being present. Based upon the findings from the risk analysis step, the next step is to rank the assets in order of the ones presenting the most risk to those with the least risk, using quantitative or qualitative analysis.
3. Treatment	Once identified, risks must be dealt with (treated), and there are four risk treatment methods: ■ **Avoid** → Don't do whatever the risky thing is (e.g., implementing a certain system, moving to the cloud, jumping off a bridge, etc.) ■ **Transfer** → Purchase an insurance policy (e.g., cyber insurance) ■ **Mitigate** → Implement controls to reduce the risk ■ **Accept** → The owner of an asset accepts a certain level of risk See section 1.10.5 for additional details on risk treatment options.

Table 1-17: **Risk Management Process**

By following the steps outlined above, an organization can come to a full understanding of what comprises its most important and valuable assets as well as the risks associated with each of those assets. Once this understanding has been reached, treatment of risks can be properly evaluated. Since organization's technology, threat landscape, vulnerabilities, and the impact of risks occurring, are constantly changing, risk management is an ongoing and repetitive process.

1.10.2 Asset Valuation

During the first step of risk management, all efforts are focused on identifying the tangible and intangible assets that are of greatest value to the organization. These assets can vary widely: they can be buildings and equipment, critical business processes, the reputation of the company, and many others. Two different forms of analysis can be used to rank the assets of the organization from most to least valuable: qualitative and quantitative. Their main characteristics are depicted in Table 1-18.

Asset valuation

Qualitative Analysis	Quantitative Analysis
Does not attempt to assign monetary value	Assign objective monetary values
Relative ranking system, based on professional judgment	Fully quantitative process when all elements are quantified
Uses words like "Low," "Medium," "High," "1-5," "Probability," or "Likelihood" to express value	
Qualitative analysis is relatively simple and efficient	Purely quantitative is difficult to achieve and time consuming

Table 1-18: **Qualitative and Quantitative Analysis Characteristics**

1.10.3 Risk Analysis

CORE **CONCEPTS**

- Process of identifying threats and vulnerabilities related to an asset
- Identify risks and understand probability/impact of risk occurring

After the asset valuation process, related threats and vulnerabilities must be identified for each asset. Proper risk analysis takes time, effort, and resources. Without the support of senior management and asset owners, risk analysis is not going to be effective. Why? Owners best understand the value of an asset to the organization. Therefore, owners must be deeply involved in the risk analysis process.

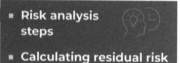

- Risk analysis steps
- Calculating residual risk

Threats and Vulnerabilities

There are three main components to a risk being present:

- **Asset:** anything of value to the organization

- **Threat:** any potential danger; anything that causes damage to an asset, like hackers, earthquakes, ransomware, social engineering, denial-of-service attacks, disgruntled employees, and many others.

- **Vulnerability:** a weakness that exists; anything that allows a threat to take advantage of it to inflict damage to the organization. Examples include open ports with vulnerable services, lack of network segregation, lack of patching, and OS updating.

Table 1-19 contains some examples of threats and vulnerabilities that relate to them.

Risk Type	Threat	Vulnerability
Natural/Environmental	Flood	Building located on a floodplain
Human	Hacker	Employees that haven't been sufficiently trained and are susceptible to social engineering
Operational/Process	Process that's highly susceptible to fraud, e.g., issuing checks	No segregation of duties implemented to prevent fraud
Technical	Malware	Unpatched software
Physical	Power outage	No backup power system

Table 1-19: **Examples of Threats and Vulnerabilities**

Figure 1-4 depicts how risk exposure occurs where there is an asset that is vulnerable, and a threat exists that can exploit the vulnerability.

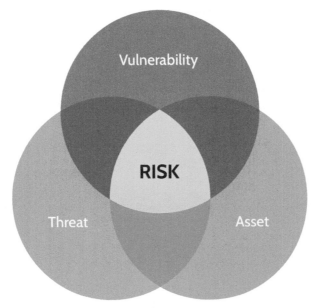

Figure 1-4: **Risk Exposure**

To fully understand each risk for a given asset, two additional pieces beyond threats and vulnerabilities must be considered: impact and probability. The impact is whatever negative consequences there may be to the organization if a risk occurs. Finally, the probability/likelihood is how often a given risk is expected to occur.

Figure 1-5 summarizes how these components fit together and are used to identify the risks for a given asset.

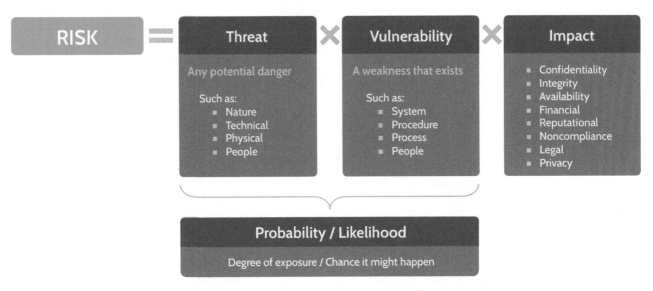

Figure 1-5: **Relationship between Risk, Threat, Vulnerability, and Impact**

Risk Management Terms

Table 1-20 contains a list of core terms used in risk management and how they fit together.

Threat Agent	Entity that has the potential to cause damage to an asset (e.g., external attackers, internal attackers, disgruntled employees)
Threat	Any potential danger
Attack	Any harmful action that exploits a vulnerability
Vulnerability	A weakness in an asset that could be exploited by a threat
Risk	Significant exposure to a threat or vulnerability (a weakness that exists in an architecture, process, function, technology, or asset)
Asset	Anything that is valued by the organization
Exposure/Impact	Negative consequences to an asset if the risk is realized (e.g., loss of life, reputational damage, downtime, etc.)
Countermeasures and Safeguards	Controls implemented to reduce threat agents, threats, and vulnerabilities and reduce the negative impact of a risk being realized
Residual Risk	The risk that remains after countermeasures and safeguards (controls) are implemented

Table 1-20: **Risk Management Core Terms**

Figure 1-6 shows how all the terms mentioned in Table 1-20 interconnect.

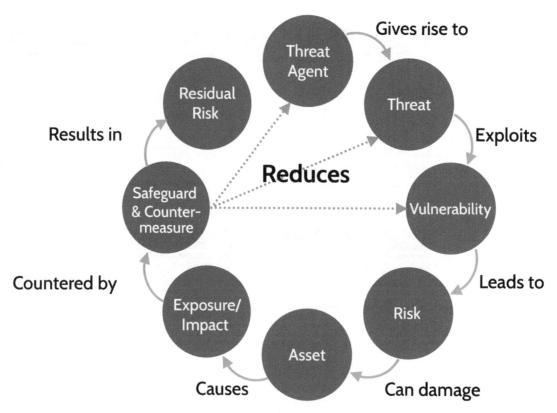

Figure 1-6: **Connections Between Core Risk Management Terms**

1.10.4 Annualized Loss Expectancy (ALE) Calculation

CORE **CONCEPTS**

- ALE = SLE (AV x EF) x ARO

In the section on asset valuation, two ranking methods were mentioned: quantitative and qualitative analysis. Quantitative analysis as part of ranking risks requires calculating how much a risk is expected to cost the organization annually—the Annualized Loss Expectancy (ALE). The ALE can be calculated using this formula:

- **Definitions of ALE, SLE, AV, EF, ARO**
- **Simple calculations using a formula to calculate SLE and ALE**

$$ALE = SLE\ (AV \times EF) \times ARO$$

Definitions of the five components of this formula are as follows, using a CCTV system as an example throughout:

- **Asset Value (AV)**: The cost of the asset in a monetary value, e.g., a CCTV system that costs $2,000.

- **Exposure Factor (EF):** Measured as a percentage and expresses how much of the asset's value stands to be lost in case of a risk materializing, e.g., if the voltage spikes excessively during certain periods of the year, a CCTV might lose three cameras to damage, thus costing $200. This represents 10 percent of the total cost (which is $2,000) and thus makes the EF be 10 percent. The EF will always be a percentage between 0 to 100 percent.

- **Single Loss Expectancy (SLE):** Denotes how much it will cost if the risk occurs once. To calculate the SLE, simply multiply the AV by the EF: SLE = AV * EF, which in this example becomes $2,000 * 10 percent = $200.

- **Annualized Rate of Occurrence (ARO):** Denotes how many times each year the risk is expected to occur. For example, if the voltage spikes excessively three times a year, the ARO is 3.

- **Annualized Loss Expectancy (ALE):** Expresses the annual cost of the risk materializing. To calculate it, use the following formula: ALE = SLE * ARO, which in this example becomes $200 * 3 = $600.

The ALE is a very useful figure, as it shows exactly how much money a given risk is expected to cost the organization per year, and can therefore provide guidance on what controls are cost-justified and should be put in place.

It is not a good business practice to implement controls that cost more than the risk they are meant to mitigate. If the cost of a control is more than the cost of the risk, a good business decision would be to accept the risk. Owners of an asset are best positioned to make this risk acceptance decision.

While the results of the ALE calculation are extremely useful, and quantitative analysis is highly preferred over qualitative analysis, it's extremely difficult to perform this calculation. Most of the numbers you need are quite difficult to assess accurately. Figure 1-7 graphically represents the formulas for the calculations mentioned above.

Figure 1-7: **SLE and ALE Calculations**

1.10.5 **Risk Response/Treatment**

CORE **CONCEPTS**
- **Risk can be managed via four approaches**
- **Risk can never be entirely eliminated**

After the risk analysis process, security should implement the most cost-effective treatments. The right approach depends on the value of the asset and type of risk identified in the previous steps. Figure 1-8 shows the four ways that risk can be managed, using a rather ridiculous diving board as an example.

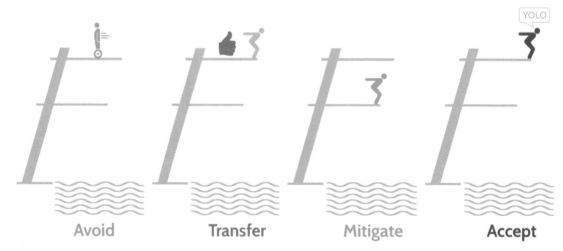

Figure 1-8: **Risk Treatments**

To **avoid** risk means to choose to stop doing whatever exposes the asset to risk. When risk is avoided, significant opportunities might also be lost—opportunity cost. In addition, it may also lead to other risks. For example, avoiding flying may lead to driving across different areas, which may have a higher risk than flying. Risk avoidance is not usually the first choice an organization makes when dealing with risk. The opportunity cost aspect is important. Organizations must always be taking a degree of risk to continue to expand, innovate, and remain relevant. If a risk is avoided, then all the potential upside of the risk is also avoided. Therefore, risk avoidance should be used very selectively.

Using our dividing board example, how do we avoid the risk? **Don't jump.** But of course, the opportunity cost is you miss out on the fun of jumping.

To **transfer** risk means to share some of the risk with another party, usually an insurance company. In this case, the insurer, because of what's called a premium payment, commits to paying the organization if a risk becomes reality. However, even when risk is transferred, ultimate accountability remains with the organization. Responsibility for managing the risk can be transferred, but accountability for the consequences of failing to manage it may never be transferred.

Using our dividing board example, how do we transfer the risk? Get someone else to jump, or at least ensure your life insurance policy is up to date before jumping.

To **mitigate** risk means to implement controls that reduce the risk to an acceptable level. Risk can never be eliminated or reduced to zero. However, it can be reduced enough that residual risk (the risk that remains after controls have been put in place) can be accepted or transferred. Risk mitigation is where organizations typically focus most of their efforts, and types of risk mitigation controls are described in more detail below.

Using our dividing board example, how do we reduce/mitigate the risk? Jump from the lower diving board.

To **accept** risk simply means taking no action or no further action where risk to a particular asset is concerned. This commonly happens when the cost of the control exceeds the value of the asset—the best business decision is to accept the risk. Another example of where an asset owner must accept risk is the residual risk that remains after mitigating controls have been implemented. In any case where risk is accepted, the person to make this decision should **always** be the asset owner or senior management—those who are **accountable**.

And finally using our dividing board example, how do we accept the risk? **Just jump.** Right from the top. Who knows, you might make it!

Note that sometimes various companies choose to ignore a risk. Risk ignorance is not a viable approach to take, nor does it adhere to due care and due diligence. For example, a security analyst mentions to the Chief Security Officer that multiple servers have no AV installed, thus putting them at risk of being affected by malware. If the Chief Security Officer chooses to ignore that risk that was just highlighted, the consequences can be dire for the business and can lead to financial fines and reputational damage.

1.10.6 Types of Controls

CORE **CONCEPTS**

- A complete control is a combination of preventive, detective, and corrective controls

- In defense-in-depth (layered security), a complete control should be implemented at each layer

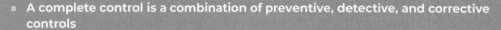

Definitions and examples of the types of controls

Seven major types of controls can be put in place as shown in Table 1-21. Understanding these different types of controls is crucial to carrying out defense-in-depth, which is an approach to security that involves multiple layers of controls. This is also sometimes referred to as layered security.

Directive	Directive controls direct, confine, or control the actions of subjects to force or encourage compliance with security policies. An example is a fire exit sign.
Deterrent	Deterrent controls discourage violation of security policies. An example is a sign warning that a piece of land is private property and trespassers will be shot. Nothing prevents someone from walking past the sign, but it's a good deterrent.
Preventive	Preventive controls can prevent undesired actions or events. For example, a fence that prevents someone from walking onto a private property. Or not having flammable materials around and therefore preventing a fire from starting..
Detective	Detective controls are designed to identify if a risk has occurred. Importantly, detective controls operate after an event has already occurred. An example is a smoke alarm detecting smoke..
Corrective	Corrective controls are used to minimize the negative impact of a risk occurring— minimize the damage. They are used to alleviate the impact of an event that has resulted in a loss and to respond to incidents in a manner that will minimize risk. An example is a fire suppression system activating.
Recovery	Recovery controls are designed to recover a system or process and return to normal operation following an incident. An example is a data backup policy allowing restoration of data on an affected server after an incident has taken place.
Compensating	Compensating controls are typically deployed in conjunction with other controls to aid in enforcement and support of the other controls. However, compensating controls can also be used in place of another control to provide the needed security. An example is deploying a Host Intrusion Prevention System (HIPS) on a critical server, in addition to having a Network Intrusion Protection System (NIPS) operating on that server's subnet. This way, if any offending traffic manages to slip by the NIPS tool, the HIPS on the server may still be able to prevent malware from damaging it.

Table 1-21: **Types of Security Controls**

Remember that detective, recovery, and corrective controls are enforced after an incident is present. However, deterrent, directive, preventive, and compensating controls are applicable before an incident takes place. It is always better to stop something bad from happening than it is to deal with it after it has happened.

A concept that is pervasively used in security is a **complete control**. A complete control is a combination of preventive, detective, and corrective controls at a minimum. The idea being that whenever controls are implemented, ideally the possible preventive control is implemented to prevent risks from occurring, but there is no perfect preventive control, thus detective and corrective controls should also be implemented. This concept of a complete control should be used whenever controls are implemented. At a minimum, ensure that preventive, detective, and corrective controls are implemented at each layer of defense.

1.10.7 Categories of Controls

> ### CORE **CONCEPTS**
> - **Safeguards = proactive**
> - **Countermeasures = reactive**
> - **Categories of controls: administrative, physical, and logical/technical**

A way to categorize the security controls we just reviewed is as safeguards or as countermeasures.

Safeguards are proactive controls; they are put in place before risk has occurred to deter or prevent it from manifesting. Safeguards would be directive, deterrent, preventive, and compensating controls.

> **Safeguards vs. countermeasures**

Countermeasures are reactive controls. They are put in place after risk has occurred and aim to allow us to detect and respond to it accordingly. Countermeasures would be detective, corrective, and recovery controls.

Controls can be further classified in three main categories:

> **Definitions & examples of administrative, technical/logical, and physical controls**

- **Administrative:** Policies, procedures, baselines, and guidelines are all classified as administrative controls. Items like background checks, acceptable use, network policy, onboarding/offboarding policies, and similar things fall in this category.

- **Logical/Technical:** Firewalls, IPS/IDS, AV, antimalware, proxies, and similar tools fall under the logical/technical security controls category.

- **Physical:** Doors, fences, gates, bollards, mantraps, guards, and CCTV fall under the physical security controls category.

Logical/technical controls are typically used synonymously, but there is an important distinction between them. Let's take a physical firewall as an example. To vastly oversimplify, a physical firewall is made up of two major components: the hardware (power supply, CPU, RAM, NICs, etc.) and the software installed and operating on the hardware. The software is the logical component, and the hardware is the technical.

Table 1-22 illustrates various control types and categories that may be implemented in an organization. Note that it isn't exhaustive but provides a good comparison of typically used controls.

	Administrative	Logical / Technical	Physical
Directive	▪ Policy ▪ Procedure	▪ Configuration standards	▪ "Authorized Personnel Only" signs ▪ Traffic lights
Deterrent	▪ Guideline	▪ Warning banner	▪ "Beware of Dog" signs
Preventive	▪ User registration procedure	▪ Login mechanism (security kernel) ▪ Operating system restrictions	▪ Fence ▪ Radio Frequency (RF) ID badges
Detective	▪ Review violation reports	▪ SIEM system	▪ CCTV
Corrective	▪ Termination	▪ Unplug, isolate, and terminate connection	▪ Fire suppression system
Recovery	▪ DR plan	▪ Backups	▪ Rebuild
Compensating	▪ Supervision ▪ Job rotation ▪ Logging	▪ CCTV ▪ Keystroke logging	▪ Layered defense

Table 1-22: **Control Types and Categories**

1.10.8 Functional and Assurance

A good security control should always include two aspects: functional aspect and assurance aspect. Figure 1-9 and Table 1-23 depict and define the functional and assurance aspects.

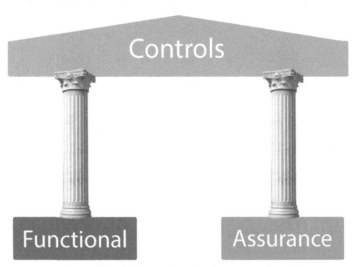

Figure 1-9: **Functional and Assurance**

Functional	Assurance
Control performs the function it was designed to address/does what it is meant to do. For example, a firewall filtering traffic between different subnets.	Control can be proven to be functioning properly on an ongoing basis. Usually proven through testing, assessments, logging, and monitoring, etc.

Table 1-23: **Functional and Assurance**

Anytime a control is implemented, it should include these two aspects. The control should perform some function (e.g., control the flow of network traffic, only allow authorized employees to enter a building, detect smoke from a fire), and there should be some means of verifying/obtaining assurance that the control is working effectively on an ongoing basis.

1.10.9 Selecting Controls

How to determine if a control should be implemented

How much security is enough?

When selecting appropriate security controls, there's a tendency to select the most expensive and top-performing solutions in an effort to provide the maximum level of security to the environment, but this doesn't necessarily make these cost-effective. Security is usually a balancing act between achieving the maximum level of security with the least amount of cost, and at the same time allowing proper functionality.

It is important to remember that implementing any security control has a negative impact on the organization. Security controls make systems more difficult to use, slower, more complicated, and so on. Security for the sake of security must be avoided.

Criteria that should be evaluated as part of deciding what controls to implement include:

- Alignment to organizational goals and objectives—does a control help an organization achieve its goals and objectives, or is the control an impediment?
- Cost-effectiveness—every control must be cost-justified.
- Complete control—a combination of preventive, detective, and corrective controls at a minimum.
- Functional and assurance effectiveness

Measuring Control Effectiveness and Reporting

Once a control, or set of controls, has been decided upon and implemented, it is important to understand how well they're working. One of the best ways to do this is using metrics. To identify the metrics that will matter, the metrics that will be useful to implement and monitor, the target audience must be identified. Further, discussion and research must be done to understand what the target audience need to know – what metrics will provide them with the information they need.

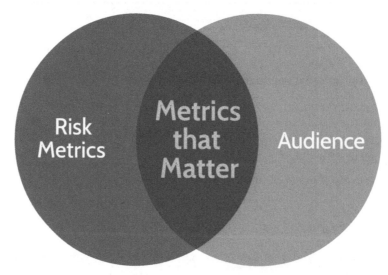

Figure 1-10: **Metrics that Matter**

Different metrics will be valuable to different audiences. For example, senior management will be more interested in "big picture" metrics, while the facilities operations team is more likely to be interested in more detailed metrics that apply directly to their everyday work. Metrics for control status can originate from multiple sources, such as internal monitoring, internal or external auditors, and third-party reports. In addition, the audience can vary and include management, regulators, internal teams, and customers. Figure 1-10 depicts this concept of metrics that matter—metrics that tell the intended audience what they need to know.

Continuous Improvement

The landscape covered by the risk management process is ever-changing—new assets are added, old assets are retired, new threats and vulnerabilities are identified, the impact of a risks occurring changes, etc. —thus making risk management a continuous, arduous, and time-consuming process that needs to be continually updated. The Deming Cycle, sometimes also referred to as Plan Do Check Act (PDCA), shown in Figure 1-11, outlines the cyclical nature of many processes in security, including risk management. The steps of the PDCA/Deming Cycle are defined in Table 1-24.

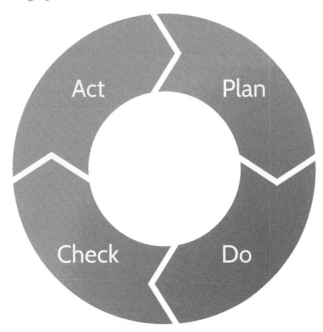

Figure 1-11: **Deming Cycle**

Plan	Determine which controls to implement based on the risks identified
Do	Implement the controls
Check	Monitoring and assurance; are the controls operating effectively?
Act	Based upon findings during the "Check" step, take additional actions as necessary (react), which leads back to planning.

Table 1-24: **Deming Cycle Steps**

Risk management, like many processes in security, must be continually updated and improved. If a new asset is acquired, should a risk analysis be performed? What if a new, significant threat is identified? What if a new vulnerability is identified? What if a new potential impact has been identified? What if new regulations or laws apply? Any and all of these things should trigger an update to an organization's risk matrix.

How often should a risk analysis be conducted?

The perfect answer: as often as necessary. The frequency of risk analysis will depend on the nature of the business and associated risks, and should also be triggered by a change in the value of an asset.

1.10.10 Apply Supply Chain Risk Management Concepts

CORE **CONCEPTS**

- Risk management methodologies should be applied to all vendors, suppliers, service providers

Risk management should also apply to suppliers and service providers to your organization. For example, if an organization is moving to the cloud, that should be factored as an inherent risk into their risk management process. Even though a cloud service provider is responsible for storing data, owners are still accountable for that data. If the organization needs to be compliant with certain laws and regulations, the organization must ensure that their cloud service provider has the required controls in place to meet the organization's compliance requirements. Every organization has security dependencies with external entities—vendors, suppliers, customers, contractors—and risk management should apply to all of them, while including the following items:

- Governance review

- Site security review

- Formal security audit

- Penetration testing

- Adherence to security baseline

- Evaluation of hardware and software

- Adherence to security policies

- Development of an assessment plan

- Identification of assessment requirements and which party will perform it

- Preparation of assessment and reporting templates

In short, owners need to define requirements for suppliers and communicate those requirements to all external suppliers, just as they should do for their processes. Vendors and suppliers perform a significant number of services for many organizations, and this fact should drive external risk analysis as much as internal risk analysis. An organization must be aware of and apply the same risk management process to its suppliers because accountability can't be outsourced. Supply chain risk analysis is as vital and important as any other type of risk analysis.

1.10.11 **Risk Management Frameworks**

CORE **CONCEPTS**

- Risk management frameworks provide comprehensive guidance for structuring and conducting risk management

Imagine you're a newly hired risk manager, tasked with creating a risk management program: identifying all the assets, risks, threats, and vulnerabilities as well as leading the process of developing all the controls. It's a huge and complicated task, and you'd probably search for advice on best practices from someone who's done it before. Frameworks provide just that. They're collections of best practices that give you step-by-step guidance on how to perform certain activities, which controls to implement, and how to implement them. Frameworks allow you to take the collected wisdom of experts and apply it to your organization. The four risk management frameworks in Table 1-25, are some examples of risk management frameworks used to address risks; NIST 800-37 is popular, so more detail on that framework is featured in Table 1-26.

NIST SP 800-37 (RMF)	This guide describes the risk management framework (RMF) and provides guidelines for applying the RMF to information systems and organizations.
ISO 31000	ISO 31000 is a family of standards relating to risk management. The scope of ISO 31000 is to provide best practice structure and guidance to all organizations concerned with risk management.
COSO	COSO provides a definition to essential enterprise risk management components, reviews ERM principles and concepts, and provides direction and guidance for enterprise risk management.
ISACA Risk IT Framework	ISACA's Risk IT Framework contains guidelines and practices for risk optimization, security, and business value. The latest version places greater emphasis on cybersecurity and aligns with the latest version of COBIT.

Table 1-25: **Common Risk Management Frameworks**

NIST SP 800-37 Rev. 2

Though variations of the RMF exist, for purposes of the CISSP exam, NIST SP 800-37 Rev. 2 should be your focus. Understanding the RMF is critical, as it informs and underpins just about every facet of operational security governance within an organization. Table 1-26 lists the seven steps of SP 800-37 Rev. 2.

Steps in the NIST SP 800-37 Risk Management Framework (RMF)

1	**Prepare** to execute the RMF
2	**Categorize** Information Systems In this step, information systems are identified and categorized. It includes questions like "What do we have?"; "How does this system, its subsystems, and its boundaries fit into our organization's business processes?"; "How sensitive is it?"; "Who owns it and the data within it?" The purpose of this step is to determine any potential adverse impacts to the confidentiality, integrity, and availability of organizational operations and assets, thereby informing the organizational risk management process.
3	**Select** Security Controls After a risk assessment has been conducted, select, tailor, and document security controls necessary to protect the information systems. Security controls are management, operational, and technical safeguards or countermeasures embedded into information systems. They protect the confidentiality, integrity, and availability of those systems and the information contained therein; assurance provides evidence that the security controls within an information system are effective.
4	**Implement** Security Controls Activities at this step are based entirely on the controls selected in Step 2 and involve two key tasks: 1) implementing the selected controls in the security and privacy plans and 2) documenting the specific, baseline details of the control implementation. This latter task is critical and allows everybody to understand what controls exist and to understand the controls in the context of the larger operational framework of the organization.
5	**Assess** Security Controls Activities during this step help determine if the security controls are implemented correctly, operating as intended, and meeting the security and privacy requirements for the system and the organization. This step involves formulation of a comprehensive plan that must be reviewed and approved.
6	**Authorize** Information System This step requires senior management to decide whether it's acceptable to operate the system in question, given the potential risk, controls, and residual risk. In addition to determining if the risk exposure is acceptable, Senior Management should review the plan of action related to remaining weaknesses and deficiencies—the residual risk. Finally, this authorization or approval is usually given for a set period of time that is often tied to milestones in the Plan of Actions & Milestones (POA&M), which facilitates tracking and status of failed controls.
7	**Monitor** Security Controls Continuous monitoring of programs allows an organization to maintain the security of an information system over time, adapting to changing threats, vulnerabilities, technologies, and mission/business processes. Milestones from the Authorize step are a key component of the Monitor step, which can also be considered the "continuous improvement" stage. During the Monitor step, questions like "Are the controls still effective?" and "Have new vulnerabilities developed?" are examined. Risk management can become near real-time using automated tools, although automated tools are not required. This helps with configuration drift and other potential security incidents associated with unexpected change on different core components and their configurations.

Table 1-26: **NIST SP 800-37 Rev. 2 Steps**

1.11 Understand and apply threat modeling concepts and methodologies

1.11.1 Threat Modeling Methodologies

CORE **CONCEPTS**

■ **Threat modeling is used to systematically identify, enumerate, and prioritize threats related to an asset**

In order to perform proper risk management, it is important to identify the threats and vulnerabilities associated with each asset. Threat modeling methodologies aid in systematically identifying threats and their severity, which in turn makes risk management more accurate and effective. Figure 1-12 depicts how threat modeling fits in with overall risk analysis.

Purpose of threat modeling

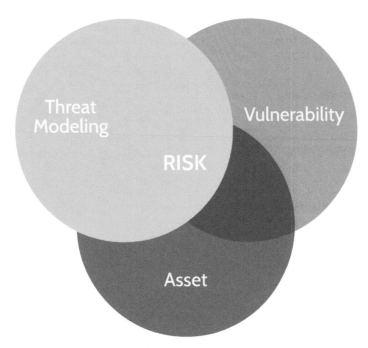

Figure 1-12: **Purpose of Threat Modeling**

Identifying all the threats to a complex asset, like a mobile phone, server, application, network, architecture, function, or process, can be a daunting task. So many possible threats exist, and it can be difficult to decide where to start and how to proceed to ensure a systematic identification and prioritization of threats. This is where threat modeling methodologies can help. They enable: **the systematic identification, enumeration, and prioritization of threats related to an asset.**

Numerous threat modeling methodologies exist, and the primary goal of most is to provide a systematic and deliberate means of identifying and categorizing threats to a given asset. Three of the major threat modeling methodologies you need to know about for the exam are STRIDE, PASTA and DREAD.

STRIDE

STRIDE was developed by Microsoft. Though it was initially developed as a means of assessing threats to applications and operating systems, it can be used in other contexts too. STRIDE is a threat-focused methodology that's less strategic and thorough than PASTA. STRIDE is an acronym as described in Table 1-27.

STRIDE vs. PASTA

	Threat	Violation	Definition
S	Spoofing	Authentication	An attacker pretends to be something or someone to gain unauthorized access
T	Tampering	Integrity	An attacker modifies data at rest (e.g., in a database) or in transit (e.g., over the network)
R	Repudiation	Nonrepudiation	An attacker performs an action on a system that is not attributable to them
I	Information Disclosure	Confidentiality	An attacker can read sensitive information
D	Denial of Service	Availability	An attacker prevents legitimate users from accessing an application/service
E	Elevation of Privilege	Authorization	An attacker gains elevated access rights (e.g., administrative/root access)

Table 1-27: **STRIDE Model**

PASTA

Process for Attack Simulation and Threat Analysis (PASTA), contrary to STRIDE, is an attacker-focused, risk-centric methodology. It is much more detailed than STRIDE and performs threat analysis from a strategic perspective that includes input from governance, operations, architecture, and development. This is done from both business and technical viewpoints.

Stages in PASTA

PASTA is a seven-stage threat modeling methodology, and each stage focuses on a specific set of goals and deliverables that must be achieved as seen in Table 1-28:

1	**Define Objectives**—This considers the inherent application risk profile and addresses other business impact considerations early.
2	**Define Technical Scope**—The philosophy behind this stage is that you can't protect what you don't know. It's intended to decompose the technology stack that supports the application components that realize the business objectives identified from Stage 1..
3	**Application Decomposition**—This stage focuses on understanding the data flows among application components and services in the application threat model.
4	**Threat Analysis**—Reviews threat assertions from data within the environment as well as industry threat intelligence that is relevant to service, data, and deployment model.
5	**Vulnerability and Weakness Analysis**—Identifies the vulnerabilities and weaknesses within the application design and code and correlates to see if it supports the threat assertions from the prior stage.
6	**Attack Modeling**—This stage focuses on emulating attacks that could exploit identified weaknesses/vulnerabilities from the prior stage. It helps to also determine the threat viability via attack patterns.
7	**Risk and Impact Analysis**—This stage centers around remediating vulnerabilities or weaknesses in code or design that can facilitate threats and underlying attack patterns. It may warrant some risk acceptance by broader application owners or development managers.

Table 1-28: **PASTA Stages**

DREAD

DREAD is a threat model primarily used to measure and rank the severity of threats. DREAD is often used in combination with the STRIDE model, where STRIDE identifies the threats, and DREAD is then used to rank the severity of threats. Five key points are considered and a score for each is determined between 1 and 3 (1 being low-risk, and 3 being high-risk). The score from each of the five key points is then tallied up to provide a total score between 5 and 15. This total score is then used to understand the severity or risk of a threat. DREAD is an acronym as described in Table 1-29.

	Key Point	Definition	Score
D	**Damage**	Total amount of damage the threat can cause?	1-3
R	**Reproducibility**	How easily can the threat be replicated?	1-3
E	**Exploitability**	How difficult is it to exploit the threat?	1-3
A	**Affected Users**	How difficult is it to exploit the threat?	1-3
D	**Discoverability**	How easily can the threat be discovered?	1-3

Table 1-29: **DREAD Model**

1.11.2 Social Engineering

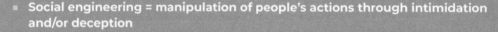

CORE CONCEPTS

- **Social engineering = manipulation of people's actions through intimidation and/or deception**
- **Social engineering is a prevalent means of attack against organizations**

Social engineering can be defined as using deception or intimidation to get people to provide sensitive information that they shouldn't in order to facilitate fraudulent activities.

In most organizations, the biggest security weakness exists between the keyboard and the back of the chair: **employees**. The way attackers persuade employees to do things they shouldn't do is through the use of social engineering techniques. Social engineering is a very prevalent form of attack that exploits the inherent kindness and emotions of people. **It is so prevalent, because it's so effective.**

Common social engineering tactics include **intimidation** (involves inducing fear in order to manipulate someone into a specific course of action), **deception** (involves tricking someone in one manner or another), and **rapport** (building a gradual relationship with a victim in order to take advantage of it down the line).

Definitions of social engineering, phishing, vishing, and smishing

An example of intimidation is blackmail, while lying is one of deception, and pretending to be from the IT team and wanting to help is an example of rapport.

Table 1-30 shows some common forms of social engineering attacks.

Phishing	Phishing is where an attacker sends many emails with the hope that the target will open an email and click on a link or open a file that leads to a malicious action.
Spear Phishing	Spear phishing is a targeted form of phishing that typically focuses on certain individuals or groups of individuals. Through a bit of discovery, the attacker determines what might prompt the targeted individual(s) to click on a link in an email, and the hook is then baited. A classic example is an attacker sending a malicious PDF posing as an invoice to the accounts payable team.
Whaling	Like spear phishing, this is also an email attack and targets the big fish—the whales—in an organization. Typically, people like the CEO, COO, and CFO are the targets of a whaling attack.
Smishing	Smishing is a form of phishing that targets mobile phone users. Typically, an attacker purporting to be from a legitimate company sends a fraudulent text/SMS message to a potential victim, with the hope that the target will click a link in the message. Smishing attacks can be simple, with the hope that a victim will click on a link and then reveal sensitive information, or they can be sophisticated and allow the attacker to control the victim's phone and thereby gain access to bank accounts, corporate resources, and other sensitive material.
Vishing	Vishing is another form of phishing, and the name refers to the way it is typically presented to a potential victim—via voice over IP (VoIP) phone systems (though attacks can take place over mobile phones, landlines, or voice mail).
Pretexting	Pretexting involves the attacker creating a scenario, almost like a script, that very ingeniously and subtly spurs the victim into action. Usually, the pretext will strike an emotional chord—whether it's your "bank" calling with news about suspicious activity related to your account, or a "friend" texting you with news about an unfortunate incident that's left them stranded someplace. Ultimately, a request is made for money, sensitive information, or both.
Baiting	Baiting is a form of social engineering that preys on people's curiosity via the use of physical tools, like USB drives. Usually, the attacker will drop some USB drives in a building parking lot, a hallway, a convention hall, or other crowded area. Then, some employees, hotel guests, or convention attendees will find the device and plug it in to their computer to try and identify the owner and return it.
Tailgating and Piggybacking	Tailgating or piggybacking is the action of following a person who is authorized to enter a restricted area through a door and thus gaining unauthorized access. The difference is that in tailgating the attacker possesses a badge that is fake but looks real. In piggybacking, the attacker doesn't have any badge at all.

Table 1-30: **Social Engineering Attacks**

Mitigating most social engineering attacks can be done most effectively through awareness, training, and education. Strong security policies can also help in this regard. Additionally, there are practical steps that can and should be taken to prevent some of the attacks noted above. Some of the best steps include:

- Requesting proof of identity
- Requiring callback authorization for voice- or text-only requests for network alterations, sensitive information, etc.
- When sensitive information is being requested via email by a purported well-known entity, like a bank, contacting them "out-of-band." In other words, not contacting the entity via any numbers in the email but rather contact them via the entity's website or another confirmed source. Also, not reaching out using random telephone numbers but only valid landline numbers that belong to the legitimate organization in question and can be easily found online.

1.12 Apply supply chain risk management (SCRM) concepts

1.12.1 SLR, SLA, and Service Level Reports

CORE **CONCEPTS**

- Security must be considered for all acquisitions
- Security must be part of procurement process
- Security requirements must be clearly communicated (e.g., SLAs) to suppliers/vendors/service providers
- Security metrics must demonstrate that security controls are operating effectively

Acquisitions are usually made with the goal of adding value to an organization; but they often come with inherent risks, because a product or service from the outside world is being introduced to the organization. Even if the acquisition is of a well-known brand, product, or service, risks exist and must be evaluated as part of the acquisition, or procurement, process. This evaluation should take place as early as possible and include security considerations that minimize the risk that new acquisitions introduce to an organization. Section 1.9 touched on the importance of conducting risk management for suppliers, and this section will provide more detail on exactly how to do it.

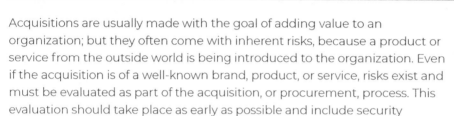

- Security's involvement in procurement
- SLAs
- Why security metrics are used

When an organization looks to acquire a new asset or service, any relevant security requirements must be identified and considered. Security needs to work with the owner to understand the business rationale for acquiring a new asset or service. If security does not understand how the asset will be used, who will access it, and what types of data the asset will store or be transmitted to a service provider, there is no way the right security controls can be identified and evaluated as part of the procurement process.

After business requirements have been identified, they must be validated (confirmed), so the security requirements can be defined. The security requirements are documented in a service level requirements (SLR) document (explained in more detail below). The SLR document is used as part of the procurement process to help the organization evaluate different vendors and/or products against the documented security requirements. For example, a company employing a new credit card processing system might require that the system be PCI compliant; or if they're a health care provider, they might require that a service provider be HIPAA compliant.

Once an organization chooses a vendor or service provider, the requirements in the SLR should be included in the contract with the vendor, with stipulations about how the vendor will continue to meet the requirements on an ongoing basis. These stipulations usually take the form of a contract addendum known as the service level agreement (SLA), also explained below.

Service Level Requirements (SLR)

With the acquisition of a service, additional organizational requirements must be considered, and this is done through a document called an SLR. Specifically, an SLR outlines:

- Detailed service descriptions
- Detailed service level targets
- Mutual responsibilities

The SLR is a very important document during the procurement process, as it defines the security services and service level targets that each potential supplier can be evaluated against. When a winning supplier is selected in the procurement process, the SLR will then be used to inform the requirements that will be documented in the SLA.

Service Level Agreement (SLA)

After a service is acquired, it's imperative that an SLA be put in place between the customer and the service provider. One important note: even though the agreement is between a service provider and a customer, the customer remains accountable for all customer data being processed by the provider. SLAs are addendums to the contract and are therefore enforceable. SLAs often include expectations and stipulations related to:

- Service Levels (performance levels)

- Governance—the customer and the service provider know who is responsible for what

- Security—expected security controls put in place by the service provider that speak to the topic of accountability and responsibility. Accountability can never be outsourced; thus, the security controls needed to protect customer data must be very clearly defined by the customer and put in place to exact specifications by the service provider.

- Compliance with all laws and regulations that relate to the customer's industry or where the customer conducts business

- Liability/Indemnification when any element of the SLA is not met or is below threshold standards

To understand how a service provider is performing on behalf of a customer, and particularly to identify how well expectations defined in the SLA are being met, a service provider will provide service level reports on an ongoing basis.

Service Level Reports

Service level reports are issued by a vendor or service provider to a client and provide insight and information about the service provider's ability to deliver services as defined by the SLA. The service level report compares anticipated and agreed upon service levels with actual service levels and documents the effectiveness of security controls, which allows the customer—the owner—to gain assurance that expectations are being met.

A service level report might contain any of the following components:

- Achievement of metrics defined in the SLA

- Identification of issues

- Reporting channels

- Management

- Third-party SOC reports, which provide independent verification and assurance that the terms of the SLA are being met

There are cases, for example, when considering the acquisition of a cloud-based service, that the acquiring company will not be able to evaluate all facets of the service provider's offering or when a customer wants an outside company to evaluate whether the terms of an SLA are being met. In these situations, third-party assessment and monitoring tools and services can be utilized for the same purposes. Thus, even though a service provider may not allow an organization's auditors onsite to perform an audit, the potential customer can rely on the audit report (usually in the form of a SOC 2, Type 2 report) from a trusted third-party audit firm. This is known as third-party assurance, and it will be discussed in more detail in Section 6.5.2.

1.13 Establish and maintain a security awareness, education, and training programs

1.13.1 Awareness, training, and education

> **CORE CONCEPTS**
> - Everyone is responsible for security; however, they must know what to do
> - The goal of awareness is to change cultural sensitivity to a topic or issue
> - Training provides specific skills
> - Education provides understanding and decision-making capability

Who is responsible for security?

EVERYONE in an organization is responsible for security. However, it's not nearly sufficient to simply say, "Everyone is responsible for security." Employees must understand and know how to execute their security responsibilities. This implies that organizations must provide awareness, training, and education so that everyone knows and understands their security responsibilities.

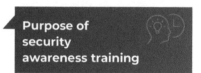
Purpose of security awareness training

Awareness within an organization is fostered with the goal of creating cultural sensitivity to a given topic or issue. Awareness is usually done at an organization-wide level and is designed to get every employee on the

Definition of awareness

same page, so they're all doing things related to security in a similar manner. Examples of awareness include internal phishing campaigns, lunch and learns, and awareness posters hung in visible places.

Training provides specific skills needed to perform tasks related to security. It often focuses on the technical aspects of a role. Examples of training might include a firewall administrator learning how to write firewall rules or a security guard learning how to respond to different situations related to protecting a building and the assets within.

Finally, education helps people understand fundamental concepts and therefore develop decision-making skills and abilities. Table 1-31 contains a comparison between these three.

Awareness	Training	Education
- Raises cultural awareness and sensitivity within an organization - Organization-wide - Less time involved	- More technical - Focuses on specific skills related to security-related task/role	- Focus on fundamental concepts - Develops decision-making skills

Table 1-31: **Awareness, Training, and Education Comparison**

Methods and Techniques to Provide Awareness and Training

The key to engaging awareness, training, and education is to be creative and to use methods that effectively convey the message. Additionally, it's important to speak the audience's language; to talk in terms that will best resonate. In other words, the language used when speaking to members of upper management will be very different from the language used when speaking to members of the IT staff.

Common methods to accomplish this task include:

- Live in-person sessions
- Live online sessions
- Pre-recorded sessions
- Requirements/rewards
- Regular communications/campaigns

Prioritization of Topics

There is never enough time to train everyone on everything, so topics selected for awareness, training, and education should directly align with the organization's goals and objectives. A good source to aid in the identification of topics is the organization's risk register. Risk management identifies the most valuable assets and their associated risks that should help drive awareness, training, and education initiatives.

Periodic Content Reviews

Organizations and the surrounding threat landscape are constantly changing; therefore, awareness, training and education programs and materials should also evolve and be updated accordingly to be most effective.

Metrics to measure effectiveness of a security awareness and training program

Program Effectiveness Evaluation

Speaking of effectiveness, program participants should be surveyed from time to time, and knowledge should be assessed via items like simulated phishing exercises or interactive multimedia presentations that include short quizzes.

Some key metrics that can be used to track effectiveness can be:

- Total number of people completing the awareness program
- Number of people providing feedback in comparison to total attendees
- Number of people reporting suspicious activities after training completion
- Tracking of how well staff members performed. For example, assuming a passing score of 75 percent:
    - Percentage passing with a score of 75 to 85 percent
    - Percentage passing with a score of 86 to 90 percent
    - Percentage passing with a score of 91 percent and above
- Total number of attempts the course was taken by each person

MINDMAP REVIEW **VIDEOS**

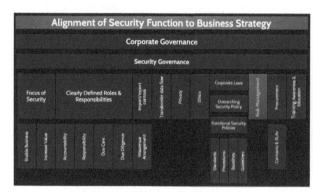

**Alignment of Security Function
to Business Strategy**
dcgo.ca/CISSPmm1-1

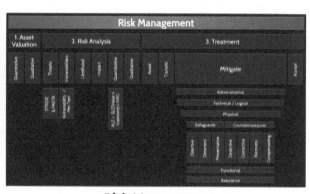

Risk Management
dcgo.ca/CISSPmm1-2

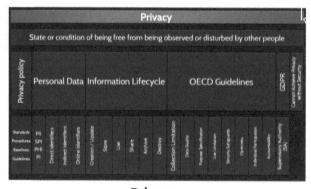

Privacy
dcgo.ca/CISSPmm1-3

CISSP PRACTICE QUESTION APP

Download the Destination CISSP Practice Question app
for Domain 1 practice questions

dcgo.ca/PracQues

DOMAIN 2

Asset Security

DOMAIN 2
ASSET SECURITY

Asset security includes the concepts, structures, principles, and controls aimed at protecting assets—anything of value to the organization.

Security professionals need to be vigilant about asset protection. Even one minor vulnerability can leave a whole system exposed to a security breach, causing an organization to lose money and data, and possibly even compromise the entire company. Good security professionals cover their bases with a systematic approach to asset security: Know what you have, classify it, and protect it based on its classification level, which indicates its value to the organization. You can't protect something if you don't know it's there and the value it represents to the organization.

The concept is simple, but the execution is often incredibly difficult, especially for larger organizations with a lot of assets. Domain 2 gives an overview of the steps involved in asset security to address some of the issues that security professionals often encounter while implementing them.

2.1   Identify and classify information and assets

2.1.1   Asset Classification

CORE **CONCEPTS**

- **Asset classification policies, procedures, and processes help achieve proper protection of assets**

As we learned in Domain 1, protection of assets should always be based on the value of the asset. We also said that the owners of the asset are always in the best position to understand the true value that the asset represents to the organization.

One of the most common problems that organizations face is that they don't know what assets they have or how valuable those assets are. For example, a department manager might have signed up for a cloud service for use by their team, then forgot about it over time, or signed up for the service but never assessed the value of the data stored in it. This leaves the organization vulnerable, particularly if there's valuable data that isn't being protected adequately. Organizational policies, procedures, and processes should be put in place to address the requirement to protect valuable assets. An asset classification program and inventory system would be the starting point that organizations can use to address and properly protect assets. In a large multinational organization, this can be a huge undertaking given the many types of assets within an organization. Additionally, the fact that assets can be created, purchased, rented, or taken over makes the task even more challenging.

In Domain 1, the concept of assets was introduced in addition to balancing the cost of their protection with their value to the organization. In other words, protecting assets should always be based on the value of the asset, and therefore, for security to be an enabler, protecting assets should always be cost-effective. As the value of an asset increases, so does the effort invested in protecting it. Less valuable assets might not warrant costly protection. The first step in asset classification addresses this issue with an asset classification system, a series of classes that represent the level of protection that each type of asset requires. For example, an asset that is classified as "top secret" or "proprietary" is going to have significantly more value than an asset classified as "confidential" or "public." The security team must apply a valid and cost-justified baseline of controls for each level of classification; these controls will be used to create protection baselines for each classification level.

Proper asset classification ensures that assets receive an appropriate level of protection based on the value that they represent to the organization. Asset classification can be defined as ***assigning assets the level of protection they require, based on their value to the organization***.

Value of asset classification

Once assets are captured in an inventory system, the next step is to identify the owners of each asset. Once the asset classification system is in place and asset owners have been identified, security can then work with owners to assign assets an appropriate classification level that determines how the assets are protected. It's important to note that owners are ultimately accountable for ensuring their assets are classified and thus protected appropriately. In fact, it's not uncommon for owners to challenge ownership to avoid being accountable. When this happens, an organization's governance committee must set the tone from the top, stating that owners must own the asset, and the security function is there to support the implementation of suitable controls. In short, assets need to have an accountable owner to ensure proper controls are applied (more on this in section 2.2).

Information Classification Benefits

The information classification process provides several benefits, including:

- Identification of **critical** information: identifies information that the organization considers critical to business success..

- Identification of **sensitivity** to modification: classification helps identify data that must only be modified in specifically authorized ways.

- Commitment to **protect** valuable assets: creates awareness among users that the organization is committed to protecting assets from unauthorized access.

- Commitment to **confidentiality** where applicable: classification helps ensure that sensitive information remains confidential.

2.1.2 Classification Process

CORE **CONCEPTS**
- Asset classification begins with a detailed asset inventory
- Asset owners determine the classification assigned to an asset
- Asset classification is an ongoing process

Data classification ensures that data receive an appropriate level of protection. It sounds simple, but it's a complex process. To be effective, it requires the right tools, procedures, education, and training. As a result, a lot of organizations struggle with optimizing their data classification.

It's not sufficient to just talk about data classification. An organization needs more than just data classification, they need an entire "asset" classification system. An asset can be defined as something that represents value, either quantitative or qualitative, to an organization. When you think about it, data is only one example of an asset that represents value to an organization. Other assets that represent value need to be protected using classification systems, just like data. In fact, progressive companies, especially those that are heavily regulated, have expanded their data classifications systems to include all assets, not just data. They have realized that protecting all valuable assets can be best achieved by using asset classification systems that include all assets regardless of whether they are tangible or intangible.

If we remember the purpose of classification systems, which is to protect assets based on value, we also need to remember that value to assets can be represented through confidentiality (sensitivity), integrity (accuracy and meaningfulness), and availability (criticality). It stands to reason, then, that we need to classify assets based on those three characteristics. Value to assets can be represented in all three (sensitivity, accuracy, and criticality), which means that assets should be classified using three classifications, one for confidentiality, integrity, and availability.

Therefore, one of the other improvements that companies have made is to not only expand data classification systems to encompass all assets, but to also classify assets NOT only based on confidentiality requirements, but also to include integrity and availability. Many asset classification frameworks and industry guidance today will encourage companies to classify valuable assets based on three classifications: one for confidentiality (sensitivity), one for integrity (accuracy), and one for availability (criticality).

For classification to be done properly, it needs to be driven by the owners. A risk with the classification process is that some owners tend to overprioritize their assets during the process. This is a common problem: every asset owner thinks their asset is among the most important. But when the time comes to calculate the costs for the protection of those high-importance assets, owners often take the opposite approach and under classify assets. The solution to this common problem is an asset classification committee or working group, comprised of qualified representatives from different areas of the organization. This committee or working group can provide a more objective classification process.

Another good way to address this problem is for organizations to ensure they have a consistent process to classify assets. This could be achieved through a consistent scoring system that is used by owners to understand the real value that assets represent to the organization. This scoring system and the way it has been used by specific owners in the organization could be vetted and approved by an asset classification board or committee.

Asset classification is ongoing. Because asset classification helps identify the appropriate controls for a given asset, and the nature of assets changes over time, it means that classification levels can change over time too. An asset that is classified as "top secret" today might very well become less valuable to the organization tomorrow, which would warrant a different classification level. Accordingly, the classification of assets must be adjusted over time to ensure the assets are protected based on the value that they represent to the organization.

The classification of an asset also drives archiving and retention requirements. Laws, regulations, industry standards, privacy requirements, company policies, and related guidance might dictate that an asset be retained for a specific number of years, even though it's not being actively used by the organization. Similarly, the same guidance might indicate that the asset should be defensibly destroyed after a set period of time. Thus, the asset life cycle represents a continually changing paradigm that should be monitored and administered on an ongoing basis.

A summary of the asset classification process is depicted in Figure 2-1. The classification process begins with maintaining a continually updated asset inventory.

Asset classification steps

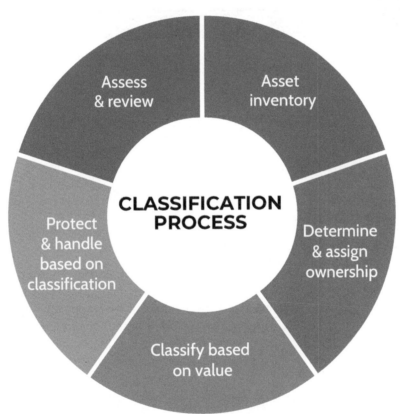

Figure 2-1: **Asset Classification Process**

An organization must know what assets it holds to protect them properly. Every asset must have an asset owner identified, as they are ultimately accountable for the protection of the value of each asset. Asset owners know the value of a given asset better than anybody else and can classify the asset based on this information. Once classified, assets can be properly protected and handled, based upon the assigned classification level, which indicates its value and how to protect it based on that value. Finally, as the value of assets changes—due to age, or to legal, regulatory, or compliance needs, or to any of a number of other reasons—asset classification should be assessed and reviewed periodically. Additionally, since organizations constantly add and remove assets, owners come and go, laws change, and so on, ongoing assessment and review of all steps in the classification process are required.

2.1.3 Classification versus Categorization

CORE **CONCEPTS**

- Classification refers to a system of classes, ordered according to value

- Categorization refers to the act of sorting assets into defined classes

- Ideally, all assets should be categorized into a classification system to allow them to be protected based on value

Now that we've described the concept of classification and how it allows the organization to protect assets based on value, let's look at the difference between classification and categorization. *Classification by itself is simply a system of classes set up by an organization to differentiate asset values and therefore protection levels.* The act of assigning a classification level to an asset is called *categorization*. For example, if an owner says an asset should be assigned the classification "top secret," this is the categorization of the asset. The major difference between classification and categorization is shown in Table 2-1.

Classification	Categorization
System of **classes** ordered according to **value**	The **act of sorting** into defined classifications

Table 2-1: **Difference Between Classification and Categorization**

Classification Examples

- Top secret, secret, confidential, sensitive but unclassified, and unclassified

- Financially sensitive

- Company restricted

- Proprietary

- Trade secret

- Personally Identifiable Information (PII)

Different organizations might use the same classification terminology and labels, but the corresponding value of each classification level in each organization could be completely different. Therefore, it's imperative that the security function educates the owners as well as everybody else within the organization about the value of each classification level, so treatment of assets and understanding throughout the organization is consistent.

2.1.4 Labeling and Marking

CORE **CONCEPTS**

- Labeling refers to the classification of the asset and is system-readable

- Marking refers to the handling instructions of the asset and is human-readable

- Should be consistently applied to all assets within an organization

- Labeling should be cost-effective

Once assets are properly classified and categorized, they should be labeled and marked. Labeling and marking ensure that security operations stay consistent and that users handle and dispose of assets properly as they move through the asset life cycle. In NIST Special Publication 800-53A, labeling and marking are defined as follows:

Organizations can define the types of attributes needed for selected information systems to support missions/business functions. The term security labeling refers to the association of security attributes with subjects and objects represented by internal data structures within organizational information systems, to enable information system-based enforcement of information security policies. Security labels include, for example, access authorizations, data life cycle protection (i.e., encryption and data expiration), nationality, affiliation as the contractor, and classification of information in accordance with legal and compliance requirements. The term security marking refers to the association of security attributes with objects in a human-readable form, to enable organizational process-based enforcement of information security policies.

Though the terms sound similar, they in fact are very different. **Labeling results in output that is system-readable** and is dependent upon security attributes of subjects and objects as determined by security needs specific to the organization. Thus, labeling approaches will vary from one organization to the other. **Marking extends the intent of labeling in a way that can clearly be understood and executed by humans.** Marking refers to specific asset data handling instructions, based on the asset label. Security marking is often used to direct handling of an asset according to external laws and organizational policies. For example, something labeled "top secret" might be marked with instructions not to remove it from the premises. A comparison between the two terms can be found in Table 2-2.

> Main differences between labeling and marking

Labeling	Marking
■ **System-readable**	■ **Human-readable**
■ Association of security attributes with **subjects and objects** represented by **internal data structures**	■ Association of security attributes with objects in a **human-readable form**
■ Enables **system-based** enforcement	■ Enables **process-based** enforcement

Table 2-2: **Comparison Between Labeling and Marking**

As noted, a characteristic of labeling is system-readability. For this reason, labeling often employs one of the following:

- ■ Metadata
- ■ Barcodes
- ■ QR codes
- ■ RFID tags
- ■ GPS tags

Each approach offers pros and cons, and the use of one or another should be predicated upon things like organizational needs, the value of the assets, and the associated approach the organization takes with respect to protecting them. For example, using global positioning system (GPS) tags may be challenging to implement. They are typically only cost-justified in situations where very valuable assets are being moved around and need to be tracked remotely. Radio frequency identification (RFID) tags are lower cost than GPS tags but still much more expensive than QR or bar codes. A cost-effective use case of RFID tags is in warehouses where inventory levels need to be tracked without having to individually handle and scan each item. An RFID reader can just be moved up and down the aisles. Bar codes have minimal cost and can be printed on packaging and are frequently used for scanning groceries in supermarkets. QR codes can hold more information than barcodes, can also be easily printed, and they can be scanned using a smartphone application.

> Cost-effectiveness of different labeling approaches

2.2 Establish information and asset handling requirements

2.2.1 Media Handling

CORE **CONCEPTS**

- Handling requirements are based on the classification of the asset, not the type of media

- Owners determine who may access media, especially sensitive media

Information and handling requirements are another important element to consider when classifying assets. The more valuable the asset, the more controls are needed to restrict who can handle that asset, what they can do with it, and how they should do it. For example, many organizations use offsite storage for some assets but don't want highly classified assets to leave the premises. If those highly classified assets don't have proper handling requirements, they could be mishandled based on value, or they could be sent to offsite storage by mistake; there have been cases of valuable records that have gone missing under these exact circumstances. Asset handling requirements are clear procedures that mitigate risks like these by delineating the proper handling of assets. Handling assets properly, based on value, is an important requirement of any protection scheme.

As part of an asset classification policy, clear procedures for the proper handling of media should be delineated. Whether assets exist on hard drives, tapes, paper, or any other media, the requirements should clearly define and communicate procedures for handling the assets and media, based upon the classification system and storage requirements for each. Based upon policy, asset owners always remain accountable for the protection of their asset, and it is imperative that owners convey the responsibility of using assets to everyone. As such:

- Only designated individuals should have access to sensitive media
- Owners should define who is authorized to access that media

Additionally, handling requirements should ensure that the proper tools and technologies are available—for example, a shredder that would be used for safe document disposal—so users can follow appropriate procedures for the assets they use.

Media Storage

Storage requirements for media are based on the classification of the data. For example, if you're storing top-secret data, then it would be mandated for that to be stored in an encrypted format with a very robust encryption algorithm like AES-256. Additionally, the media itself (e.g., tape, hard drive, etc.) should be stored in a physically secured location safe from unauthorized access, high humidity, and so on.

Media Retention and Destruction

Retention and destruction are based on organizational data classification and data archiving policies. These can be heavily influenced by auditory and regulatory compliance frameworks. For example, PCI DSS requires audit log retention is set for a minimum of one year while it also requires audit logs ranging back ninety days to be available for immediate analysis. When it comes to disposal, PCI DSS requires all credit and payment card information to be destroyed as soon as it is no longer required for business or legal information.

2.3 Provision resources securely

2.3.1 Data Classification Roles and Responsibilities

CORE **CONCEPTS**

■ **Owners are accountable**

■ **Assignment of ownership drives the data classification process**

■ **Data classification roles and responsibilities**

Identifying owners is an essential part of the classification process because they're the ones who are accountable for the assets being protected. Owners are the ones that create or procure the assets and work with them on a regular basis. If owners aren't assigned to assets, then no one is accountable for making sure the controls are in place to protect them. When this happens, security breaches tend to occur. Assets can only be properly classified and protected once owners are identified; every asset needs an assigned owner. Identifying and assigning owners is critical, and this is exactly why the concepts of *owners* and *ownership* exist.

While the CEO and upper management are the owners of an organization, they're not in the best position to protect each asset. They are, however, the most suitable people to promote the need for asset classification and empower the governance committee to set this mandate organization-wide. In turn, owners should understand the importance of following these mandates and the need to classify each asset they're accountable for.

In short, security must work with owners to determine the values of assets and how to protect them, but owners are ultimately accountable for the protection of their assets.

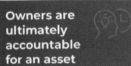

Owners are ultimately accountable for an asset

The owner is:

■ The person who directly interacts with the asset the most. Due to this intimacy, they best understand the asset's value. For example, the HR director might be the owner of an HR database.

■ Even though IT might help manage the underlying systems related to the assets in question, they are only functioning as a custodian.

Owners need to have clearly defined **accountabilities**, including:

■ Classifying and categorizing assets

■ Managing access to assets

■ Ensuring appropriate controls are in place based on asset classification

Owners can delegate *responsibility* for an asset, but they *always remain accountable* for the protection of the asset. In other words, accountability cannot be delegated to anyone else. The owner can delegate the responsibility, but accountability remains with the owner.

Different types of owners exist:

- Data owners

- Process owners

- System owners

- Product owners

- Service owners

- Hardware owners

- Applications owners

- Intellectual property owners

- Etc.

Regardless of the type of asset owned, all owners are accountable for protecting the value of that asset (including its classification and categorization) and approving access to it. The owner retains accountability throughout the asset life cycle, including its retention and end-of-life cycle, which is destruction.

The bottom line is that, regardless of the type of owner, each holds the same accountability, which is:

To understand the value of the assets to an organization and classify them properly and ensure appropriate protection as they progress through their life cycle.

Understand different roles and responsibilities

Table 2-3 summarizes the various roles and responsibilities relating to data protection within an organization.

Data Owner/Controller	**Accountable** for protection of data; holds legal rights and defines policies
Data Processor	**Responsible for processing** data on behalf of the owner/controller (a typical example of a processor is a cloud provider)
Data Custodian	**Technical responsibility** for data (e.g., data security, availability, capacity, continuity, backup and restore, etc.). Data custodians are responsible for custody of systems/databases—not necessarily belonging to them—for any period of time. Additionally, data custodians are responsible for things like network administration and operations, and for protecting assets in their custody.
Data Steward	**Business responsibility** for data (e.g., metadata definition, data quality, governance, compliance, etc.)
Data Subject	Individual to whom personal data pertains

Table 2-3: **Roles and Responsibilities**

2.3.2 Data Classification Policy

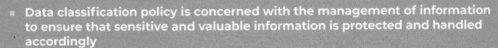

CORE **CONCEPTS**

- Data classification policy is concerned with the management of information to ensure that sensitive and valuable information is protected and handled accordingly
- Data classification policy considers laws, regulations, privacy requirements, customer requirements, cost of creation, operational impact, liability, and reputation

To be effective, asset classification needs to be done consistently, regularly, and thoroughly. When organizations don't follow a proper asset classification system, they will struggle to protect their assets and as a result, they can face fines, data breaches, and reputational impact. Having an asset classification policy formalizes the process so that everyone can follow the set of standards, procedures, baselines, and guidelines necessary to protect the assets as also depicted in Figure 2-2.

Referring to Domain 1 and the perfect model of security, the asset classification policy should be governed by senior management. Because everyone in an organization will own or use these assets, this policy must apply to *everyone*. Like all policies, it should communicate *why* it exists, to *whom* it applies, its importance, who is accountable, who is responsible, who supports, and whatever else needs to be conveyed. The goals and objectives of the organization should drive the policy's structure, which should follow all applicable laws, regulations, and industry standards.

An asset classification policy should:

- Start with an asset policy, which drives the asset classification policy
- Be accompanied by retention, destruction, and archiving policies
- Clearly define accountability and responsibility
- Define varying forms of asset media, such as digital, tape, paper, etc.
- Include all the factors that drive value, which should in turn determine how assets are protected
- Outline asset liability and the consequences of regulatory oversight
- Describe industry standards and how they impact organizational reputation
- Involve security from a consulting and expertise perspective; owners should drive the process

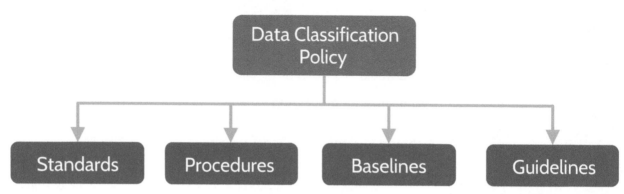

Figure 2-2: **Data Classification Policy**

At the end of the day, it is challenging to quantify the value of all assets, especially intangible assets such as data. This is why qualitative measures like the labels "Top Secret," "Secret," and "Public," among others, are often used. Additionally, organizations will often create data classification boards that can provide an organization-wide perspective and offer asset classification guidance to asset owners.

Though not a complete list, the examples below help organizations determine the value of assets:

1. Laws and regulations
2. Privacy requirements
3. Creation cost
4. Operational impact
5. Liability
6. Reputation

2.4 Manage data life cycle

2.4.1 Information Life Cycle

Information Life Cycle

Data must be protected at each stage of its life cycle. The concept of the information life cycle is founded on the principle that proper controls should be in place at the time of creation and throughout the life cycle. Immediately upon **creation, collection, or update,** information should be assigned a classification (by the owner), which then drives all other activities, such as **storage, use, sharing, archiving, and final disposal or destruction, to protect information throughout its life cycle.** These stages are also highlighted in Figure 2-3, while their definitions are contained in Table 2-4. Also note that each data state might require different protective measures and handling practices. For example, data in use might require one set of procedures, while data in storage requires another. As information moves through each stage of the life cycle, it may increase or decrease in classification or value, and it should be protected at its level.

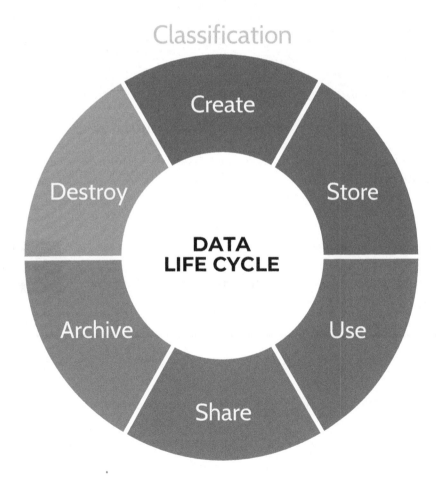

Figure 2-3: **Data Life Cycle Stages**

Create	Generation of new digital content, or the alteration/updating/modifying of existing content
Store	Committing digital data to some sort of storage repository, which typically occurs nearly simultaneously with creation
Use	Data viewed, processed, or otherwise used in some sort of activity, not including modification
Share	Information made accessible to others, such as company users, customers, and partners
Archive	Data leaves active use and enters long-term storage
Destroy	Data is permanently destroyed using physical or digital means (e.g., crypto shredding)

Table 2-4: **Definitions of Data Life Cycle Stages**

2.4.2 Data Destruction

CORE **CONCEPTS**

- **Data remanence** refers to residual representation of information even after attempts to securely delete or remove the data
- **Categories of sanitization—destruction, purging, clearing**
- **Secure removal of data in the cloud**

Depending upon how data is removed from media, remnants of that data typically exist. This means that a significant amount of that data may be recovered by a determined individual. Various methods exist for ensuring the removal of data and the focus these days is toward what is known as "defensible destruction." **Defensible destruction** means being able to prove that there's no possible way for anyone to recover data that has been securely destroyed. Data owners are responsible for ensuring the proper sanitization of the data assets they own.

Three primary data sanitization categories exist: destruction, purging and clearing as also seen in Table 2-5. Every sanitization method fits into one of these categories as also seen in Figure 2-4. **Note that destruction is the most effective.**

Categories of sanitization

Destroy	**Physical destruction of media**; this is the *most effective* means of sanitization.
Purge	Logical/physical techniques used to sanitize; data **cannot** be reconstructed.
Clear	Logical techniques used to sanitize; data **may** be reconstructed. This is the least effective means of sanitization.

Table 2-5: **Sanitization Categories**

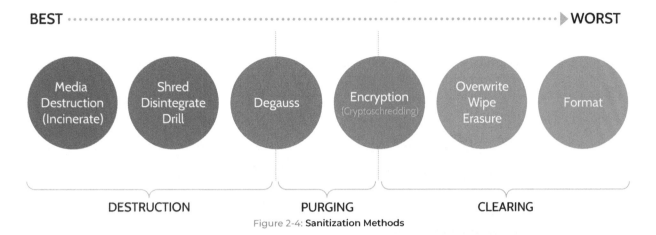

Figure 2-4: **Sanitization Methods**

NIST SP 800-88 revision 1 provides guidelines for media sanitization as outlined in Table 2-6:

Most effective/secure method of sanitization

Media Destruction (Incinerate)	The most effective means by which data can assuredly be removed from media is through physical destruction, ideally in the form of incineration that renders a puddle of metal.
Shred Disintegrate Drill	If incineration is not an option, due to cost or availability, the next best sanitization methods include shredding, disintegrating, or drilling holes in the media. Though effective, these techniques are not foolproof because the right tools in the hands of a skilled and determined attacker could allow some data to be recovered. For example, though drilling a hole (or holes) in a hard drive may render the drive unusable, most of the data on the platters is still very much intact and accessible via different means.
Degauss	Degaussing is the process of applying a very strong magnetic field to magnetic media like hard drives or tapes. The strong magnetic field destroys the underlying data. However, degaussing may also render the media itself unusable. This explains why degaussing sits between destruction and purging in Figure 2-4.
Encryption (Crypto Shredding/ Crypto Erase)	Crypto shredding, or cryptographic erasure, is a technique where data is encrypted using a very strong encryption algorithm, like AES-256, and after that's done, the encryption key is destroyed. By encrypting the data and then sanitizing every copy of the encryption key, the data has been effectively made unrecoverable. Crypto shredding fits between purging and clearing. As long as a copy of the key is never found or brute-forced, or a flaw in the underlying algorithm is never discovered, the data cannot be recovered and has been permanently purged. However, if a copy of the key is found or brute-forced, or the algorithm is compromised, then data may be recoverable and has thus only been cleared.
Overwrite Wipe Erasure	Overwriting, wiping, or erasure all refer to writing all zeroes or all ones or some combination of those to all sectors of a storage device, replacing the original data with this overwritten data. This process can be done multiple times, but even so, research has shown that no matter how many overwrite passes are done, some of the original data may still be recoverable. This explains why it is considered a clearing technique.
Format	The least effective method for destroying data is formatting the hard drive. Depending on the formatting method used it may be relatively easy to recover the data. For example, Windows "Quick Format" simply resets the folder and file address table on the drive; and most, if not all, data remains on the disk until it is overwritten by new information. This means it is possible, although potentially difficult, to recover most or all the data from a formatted drive, using software available from a number of vendors.

Table 2-6: **NIST SP 800-88 Sanitization Guidelines**

Object Reuse

Though the name implies otherwise the term "object reuse" refers to a security methodology that uses *overwriting* to securely remove data from media, as also seen in Figure 2-5. Depending on the number of times data is overwritten, the data may be considered cleared or purged. Object reuse refers to the reassignment of media without the opportunity of data that previously resided on the media to be reconstructed.

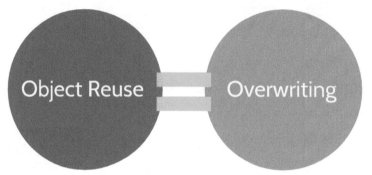

Figure 2-5: **Object Reuse = Overwriting**

Solid State Drive Data Destruction

Solid State Drive (SSD) technology presents potential problems where data remanence is concerned. Unlike traditional hard drives that use magnetic technology, SSDs are hard drives that use flash memory technology to represent ones and zeroes. The data on SSDs cannot be overwritten in the same way as a traditional magnetic hard drive. SSD vendors often provide tools or other means by which data can be securely removed because of this fact. From a security perspective, options available from a given SSD vendor should be the first choice when attempting to mitigate data remanence issues related to SSDs. Otherwise, the best way to mitigate data remanence on an SSD drive is to physically destroy it. To summarize:

- Some manufacturers provide sanitization or crypto erasure capabilities.
- The best option is always physical destruction of media.

Encryption

Crypto shredding (also mentioned in Table 2-6), or crypto erasure, is the best method to use when attempting to remove data from a third-party environment, like that provided by a cloud provider. Crypto shredding encompasses encrypting the data and then securely destroying all copies of the key. After the key is securely destroyed, the data is effectively unrecoverable.

> **Best method for dealing with data remanence in the Cloud**

Physical destruction of media is best but it may be too costly, unavailable or otherwise infeasible.

2.5   Ensure appropriate asset retention

2.5.1 Data Archiving

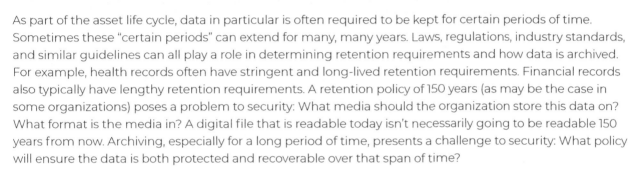

CORE **CONCEPTS**
- Data archiving is part of the asset life cycle
- Data archiving includes requirements for protecting archived data
- Data archiving should be driven by an appropriate retention policy

As part of the asset life cycle, data in particular is often required to be kept for certain periods of time. Sometimes these "certain periods" can extend for many, many years. Laws, regulations, industry standards, and similar guidelines can all play a role in determining retention requirements and how data is archived. For example, health records often have stringent and long-lived retention requirements. Financial records also typically have lengthy retention requirements. A retention policy of 150 years (as may be the case in some organizations) poses a problem to security: What media should the organization store this data on? What format is the media in? A digital file that is readable today isn't necessarily going to be readable 150 years from now. Archiving, especially for a long period of time, presents a challenge to security: What policy will ensure the data is both protected and recoverable over that span of time?

Depending upon the nature of an organization's business, the creation of a subset of classification policies might be necessary. These subset policies would focus on archiving and retention, using standards, procedures, baselines, and guidelines. As with other policies and the supporting elements, legal, regulatory, and possibly industry-related requirements will drive the exact structure of each element. Essentially, data archiving policies answer two questions: How long do we need to keep this for, and how do we achieve that, technically speaking?

Data Archiving

When archiving data, requirements for protecting it must be understood, including:

- Media type
- Security requirements
- Availability requirements
- Retention period
- Associated costs

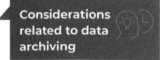

Considerations related to data archiving

Data Archiving Policies

Typically, archiving and retention policies are part of the overall data classification policy. Some important items to keep in mind regarding them are:

Elements of data archiving policies

- Archiving/retention policy are based on laws, regulations, industry standards, and business needs
- Classify records accordingly
- Educate employees and provide them with the right tools

Questions to Consider when Writing a Policy

- Who needs access to the data?
- Do access requirements change over time?
- How long does data need to be kept?
- What are the data disposal requirements?

2.6 Determine data security controls and compliance requirements

What is the best way to ensure data receives appropriate protection based on classification?

In Topic 2.1, we outlined the classification process, noting that specific security requirements and controls exist for each classification used within the classification system. For any given classification, it's important to know what controls are required to protect the asset appropriately. For example, a top secret asset has a different baseline of required security controls than a secret one, and so on. If baselines (minimum levels of security controls) exist for a given classification level, assets can be efficiently and effectively protected.

These baselines vary depending on value but also depend on the state the data is in. Specifically, data can be in one of three states at any given time: data at rest, data in transit, and data in use. The data security controls that protect data may be completely different depending on which of these states the data is in. It is therefore important to understand what security controls are required for each state. For example, one of the ways to protect data in transit is using HTTPS for encryption of data between a client and a server, but that won't be relevant for data in use. While this topic doesn't provide in depth detail about how to protect data in each state (which is something discussed in detail in Domains 3 and 4), it introduces some of the appropriate security controls that can be used as mentioned in Table 2-7.

Data at REST	Data in TRANSIT	Data in USE
Inactive data that is stored (resting) on media: hard disks, tapes, databases, spreadsheets, etc.	Data flowing across a network, such as the internet.	Data being used in computational activities.
Protection:	**Protection:**	**Protection:**
■ Encryption	■ Access Control	■ Homomorphic Encryption
■ Access Control	■ Network Encryption	■ RBAC
■ Backup and Restoration	■ End-to-end	■ DRP
	■ Link	■ DLP
	■ Onion	

Table 2-7: **Data Protection in Each State**

2.6.1 Protecting Data at Rest

> **CORE CONCEPTS**
> ▪ Methods used to protect data at rest—encryption, access control, backup, and restoration

Data at rest refers to data that is stored somewhere. Examples of data at rest include files on a hard drive, a database, and similar states. Data at rest can be protected and secured through access control mechanisms, backups (and restores), and encryption.

Additionally, as more and more organizations are migrating to the cloud, data should first be encrypted locally and then migrated, to best ensure the security and confidentiality of the information being migrated.

> The best way to protect confidentiality of data being migrated to the cloud

2.6.2 Protecting Data in Transit

> **CORE CONCEPTS**
> ▪ Methods used to protect data in transit—end-to-end encryption, link encryption, onion network

Data in transit, also sometimes referred to as **data in motion**, refers to data that is moving across networks, like an organization's internal network or the internet. Like data at rest, methods used to protect data in motion include access controls, encryption, and perhaps redundancy. However, with regards specifically to encryption, two primary options exist to protect data in motion: end-to-end encryption and link encryption. A third option—an onion network—is also described.

End-to-End Encryption

End-to-end encryption means the data portion of a packet is encrypted immediately upon transmission from the source node, and the data remains encrypted through every node—every switch, router, firewall—through which it passes while traveling to the destination node as also depicted in Figure 2-6. Only upon reaching the destination is the packet decrypted. It's a safe way for data to travel among many different nodes without becoming compromised. Though the data is never in plaintext while traversing nodes, routing information is visible—potentially allowing for inferences to be made about the nature of the data. So, the source and destination IP addresses, for example, are in plaintext and visible to anyone, and thus end-to-end encryption does not offer anonymity. This method is particularly useful in the context of virtual private networks (VPNs). In fact, a VPN is a perfect example of end-to-end encryption.

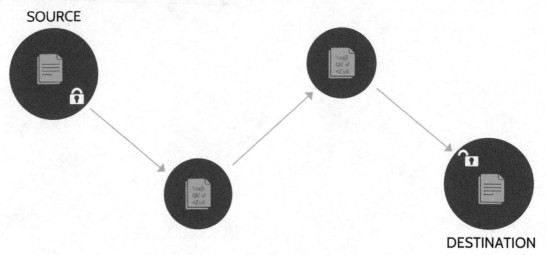

Figure 2-6: **End-to-End Encryption**

Link Encryption

Link encryption means the packet header *and* data are encrypted *between* each node. Encrypting the packet header hides the routing information of packets traversing a network. However, unlike with end-to-end encryption, the header and data are decrypted at each node, so header information and plaintext content are also available at each node. As a result, every node becomes a potential attack or disclosure point.

To better understand how link encryption works, imagine several nodes across a network as depicted in Figure 2-7. At the first node, the routing information determines where the data packet needs to go next, and the entire packet is then encrypted with a key that is shared with the next node and transmitted. At the destination, the entire packet (header information and data) is decrypted using the shared key, and the routing information for the next destination is determined. Again, the entire packet is encrypted using the shared key, and the packet is transmitted. This happens at every node, until the destination node is reached. Along the way, plaintext is available at every node, because the packet needs to be decrypted at every node, so the routing information can be determined prior to re-encryption and transmission. This does not best protect data, because every node is a potential attack point or disclosure point, as information is available in plaintext. The advantage is that routing information can be hidden but only from device to device.

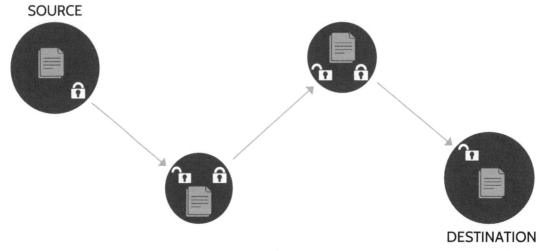

Figure 2-7: **Link Encryption**

As also mentioned in NIST SP 800-12, link encryption is performed by service providers, such as a data communications provider. It encrypts all the data along a communications path (e.g., a satellite link, telephone circuit, T3 line).

In end-to-end encryption, data is encrypted when being passed through a network, but routing information remains visible. End-to-end encryption is generally performed by the end user organization. Some examples of modern usage of end-to-end encryption include Pretty Good Privacy (PGP) and Secure/Multipurpose Internet Mail Extensions (S/MIME) for email. Note that it is also possible to combine both types of encryption.

Onion Network

Compared to end-to-end and link encryption, an onion network describes a very effective method of protecting data in transit, as it essentially provides complete confidentiality and anonymity using multiple layers of encryption. Like the layers of an onion, multiple layers of encryption are wrapped around the data at the first node. As the encrypted data traverses each node, the outermost layer of encryption is removed, which reveals the address of the next node, as also seen in Figure 2-8. This process takes place at every node, until the final node is reached, and the final layer of encryption is removed, revealing the plaintext data. As each node through which the data passes only knows the address of the previous node and the next node, the source and destination addresses remain hidden throughout the transmission.

> An onion network provides anonymity and protection of data

By providing confidentiality of data as well as **anonymity**, an onion network makes it very difficult to determine the sender and receiver while data is in transit. With an onion network, the obvious significant advantage is that each node along the way only knows which node the packet came from and the next node. The source node and destination nodes are unknown, except to the nodes adjacent to each of them. Additionally, each node has no access to the encrypted data within the innermost layer. A perfect example of an onion network is The Onion Router—TOR. The big downside of course is performance, as it slows transmission speeds and requires higher-performance technology to be present to allow decryption to take place efficiently.

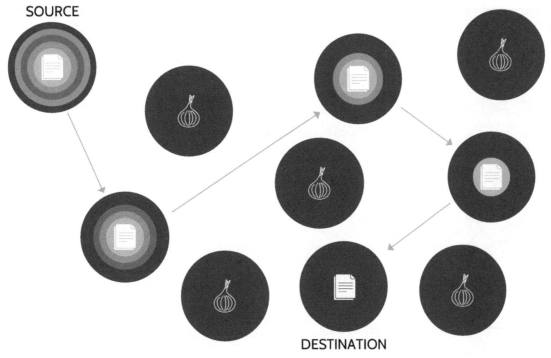

Figure 2-8: **Onion Network Encryption**

2.6.3 **Protecting Data in Use**

Data in use refers to data that is being used in some type of computational activity. One way to protect data in use is through homomorphic encryption, which allows calculations to be performed on data while the data remains encrypted. Homomorphic encryption is ground breaking as it gives an ability to process information while the data is encrypted and doesn't require access to a secret key.

Other ways to protect data in use are role-based access control (RBAC) and digital rights protection (DRP) or data loss prevention (DLP). With RBAC, access to specific data can be controlled to ensure only appropriate entities are able to access and process it based on specific roles and work groups. With DRP and DLP tools we can limit the specific actions someone can take when accessing information.

2.6.4 **Information Obfuscation Methods**

> CORE **CONCEPTS**
> - Obfuscation (or masking) makes something harder to understand
> - Obfuscation methods

To understand what is meant by the term **information obfuscation**, sometimes also referred to as **data masking**, it helps to understand what the word *obfuscation* means. Obfuscation is the action of making something obscure, unclear, or unintelligible; in other words, hiding it.

Obfuscation serves to make something harder to understand, and information obfuscation serves to impair the ability of malicious actors from understanding data, code, and other information. At the same time, information obfuscation can be employed in such a way that the functionality of the system utilizing the technique still functions properly. Information obfuscation may also be used to hide proprietary information, to meet compliance requirements. For example, those outlined in the EU's GDPR legislation offers customers assurance that their information is private and protected. Developers use obfuscation very often in source code to obscure information like a serial number of a product or an application password. A summary of various obfuscation methods is provided in Table 2-8.

Why obfuscation is used

Concealing data	Concealing data, unlike pruning (noted below), completely removes access to sensitive data. Users do not have access, nor do they have visibility and the attribute field does not appear on computer screens and reports.
Information Pruning/Pruning Data	Information/Data pruning primarily takes place in nonproduction environments and involves the removal of sensitive data from attributes. The attribute will still be visible as a field on computer screens and reports, but it will not be populated with data.
Fabricating data	Especially when testing the functionality of a system or in cases where particularly sensitive data exists, fabrication of data is often used. 1. Creating fake data to replace real data facilitates full functional testing. 2. Creating fake data to replace sensitive data prevents unauthorized access and viewing of the actual data.
Trimming data	Trimming data, unlike pruning, removes part of an attribute's value and is typically used for purposes of identification. Common examples of trimming involve Social Security numbers (SSN) and credit card numbers, where only the last four digits are visible and the remaining digits are masked.
Encrypting data	Encryption creates ciphertext of a value and can be done at the attribute, table, or database levels. With access to the proper key, encrypted data can be decrypted, and the ciphertext can be changed to plaintext. Like with trimming, credit card numbers are often encrypted when stored (for example, in a database) or when being transmitted.

Table 2-8: **Obfuscation Methods**

2.6.5 Digital Rights Management (DRM)

> CORE **CONCEPTS**
> - **DRM protects intellectual property (IP) assets and the rights of asset owners**
> - **DRM techniques**
> - **Legal basis for protection in the United States through the Digital Millennium Copyright Act (DMCA)**

NIST SP 500-241 defines digital rights management (DRM) as *"a system of information technology (IT) components and services, along with corresponding law, policies and business models, which strive to distribute and control intellectual property and its rights. Product authenticity, user charges, terms-of-use and expiration of rights are typical concerns of DRM."*

In short, DRM protects assets and the rights of the owners of those assets.

In the context of the NIST definition, intellectual property can include hardware as well as software, and DRM technologies typically focus on limiting the use, modification, and sharing of copyrighted or otherwise proprietary and protected works. Examples of intellectual property typically protected by DRM include:

- Movies and other audio and video works created by publishers

- Video games

- Digital music

- eBooks

- Cable and satellite service providers

In all the examples, DRM is employed to prevent intellectual property from being accessed, copied, or improperly used. It helps copyright holders maintain control over the content and it helps maintain income streams through licensing and rentals.

To achieve these ends, DRM techniques include:

- Licensing agreements that restrict access

- Encryption

- Embedding of digital tags that tie content to specific license holders, theoretically preventing sharing with others

- Use of related technologies that restrict copying or viewing of certain content

Additionally, in 1998, the Digital Millennium Copyright Act (DMCA) was signed into law in the United States and provides legal recourse for violation of DRM protections and the rights of intellectual property holders.

DRM technologies have primarily been used to protect mass-produced media such as songs and movies. The exact same techniques can be used to protect sensitive documents within an organization from unauthorized access and usage. This is referred to as **Information Rights Management (IRM),** a subset of DRM.

2.6.6 Data Loss Prevention (DLP)

CORE **CONCEPTS**

- Data loss prevention focuses on the identification, monitoring, and protection of data.
- DLP data activities take place in three contexts: data in use, data in motion, data at rest.
- DLP takes place for multiple reasons.

Relative to DRM, data loss prevention (DLP) is more all-encompassing. NIST defines DLP as:

A system's ability to identify, monitor, and protect data in use (e.g., endpoint actions), data in motion (e.g., network actions) and data at rest (e.g., data storage) through deep packet content inspection, contextual security analysis of transaction (attributes of the originator, data object, medium, timing, recipient/destination, etc.), within a centralized management framework.

As the definition spells out, DLP focuses on the three specific types of data that were mentioned earlier:

- Data in use
- Data in motion
- Data at rest

In each context, DLP tools attempt to detect and prevent data breaches and potential data exfiltration. For example, in conjunction with acceptable use policies, DLP tools can allow endpoints and portable storage devices to be monitored to protect sensitive data from being used, transferred, or otherwise exposed outside of normal expected usage. Similarly, encryption can be used in a manner that prevents unauthorized access or viewing of things like PII or confidential data. Specific content-aware capabilities of DLP tools can help organizations better monitor data traversing internal and external endpoints in a network. Through content inspection, logging, and development of organizational policies based upon the same, the movement of data that meet certain criteria can be blocked or redirected. Likewise, these capabilities can be used to scan and protect sensitive data stored on employee endpoints and network locations.

Protection of data is important for multiple reasons because it often encompasses more than organizational information, like trade secrets and other proprietary data. Customer, vendor, and employee data are equally important and should be afforded the same consideration and level of protection.

Protection of data has been a long-standing concern, but events over recent years including increasingly stringent regulations, laws, and industry requirements, and an increasingly litigious society, have made the protection of data more important than ever.

MINDMAP REVIEW **VIDEOS**

Asset Classification
dcgo.ca/CISSPmm2-1

CISSP PRACTICE QUESTION APP

Download the Destination CISSP Practice Question app for Domain 2 practice questions

dcgo.ca/PracQues

Security Architecture & Engineering

DOMAIN 3
SECURITY ARCHITECTURE AND ENGINEERING

The Security Architecture and Engineering CISSP domain contains the concepts, principles, structures, and standards used to design, implement, monitor, and secure various architectures such as systems, applications, operating systems, equipment, networks, and those controls used to enforce various appropriate levels of security.

This domain focuses on the key principles and concepts reflecting on the key responsibility of any security professional, which is to design, build, and implement security architectures based on corporate requirements that reflect the goals and objectives of the organization, ultimately to allow the organization to achieve its corporate governance initiatives in the most efficient and cost-effective way possible.

A good way to summarize the content and focus of this domain would be, "The Security Architecture and Engineering domain focuses on the different processes, standards, frameworks, and structures to design and implement secure architectures and how, in order to achieve that, the security function needs to be involved at the start of the engineering life cycle and throughout each of the subsequent phases."

3.1 Research, implement, and manage engineering processes using secure design principles

3.1.1 Security's Involvement in Design and Build

> CORE **CONCEPTS**
>
> - **Security must be involved in all phases of designing and building a product or system; it must be involved from beginning to end.**

Before diving deep into this domain, it's important to understand the meaning behind the title: "Security Architecture and Engineering." What is meant by the word **architecture**? This can relate to a building, design, diagram, structure, or something similar. Really, architecture can mean anything. Items like office buildings, houses, firewalls, and computers can all be considered architectures. Why is that? Because they're all made up of different components. So the word *architecture* implies many components that work together to allow that architecture to be used for the purposes for which it was intended. Consider the example of a laptop. What are the components that make it up? At a high level, they include hardware (e.g., motherboard and processor), software (e.g., the operating system and applications), and firmware (allowing the hardware and software to communicate and operate properly). The user is part of the architecture as well, whenever they're using the laptop.

Now, let's add the word *security*, to make *security architecture*. To secure the architecture, each individual component must also be secured and protected. Using the above example, to protect the prementioned laptop components, the hardware, software, and firmware must all be adequately protected. Security policies, knowledge, and experience must be applied to protect this architecture to the level of value relating to the individual components and to the overall architecture. This is what is meant by the term **security architecture**.

How about if we now add the word **enterprise** to the mix and thus make it **enterprise security architecture**. What does this mean? The word *enterprise* refers to the entire organization, and this now refers to a means by which the entire organization can be protected by breaking the enterprise into different components and protecting each component. What makes up any company or enterprise? Typical components include people, technology, processes, functions, information, hardware, and networks.

So, to protect the entire enterprise, each of these components must be protected based on its value. However, this raises the question: To what level should each component be protected? Some may consist of additional components that also require protection. As always, the level and degree of protection should be based upon value and cost-effectiveness.

Now for the final question: What does the word **engineering** mean?

This commonly points to designing a solution by walking through a series of steps and phases to put the components together so they can work in harmony as an architecture. The building of any architecture requires a corresponding engineering life cycle. That typically starts with a concept, an idea that someone comes up with which then needs to be designed. Once designed, building and implementation can start. Testing also must take place, which happens during the design and build phases and must also be done prior to implementation. Once implemented, it is maintained and, at some point in the future, it is disposed of. These are the steps of the engineering life cycle, and they should be followed anytime something needs to be built.

One of the most important points to highlight is security's role in this process. Security should be involved from the very beginning and should be a consideration throughout the life cycle. Unfortunately, most organizations do not follow this protocol, as security is often not considered at all, or it is an afterthought and pursued at the end. Security considered from the beginning leads to the best outcome, and it is the most cost-effective approach. It leads to what is known as security by design, which means that security should be embedded from the beginning and not just as an afterthought.

3.1.2 Determining appropriate security controls

CORE CONCEPTS

- **Regardless of the framework, model, or methodology used, the risk management process should be used to identify the most valuable assets and risks to those assets, and to determine appropriate and cost-effective security controls to implement this.**

The design and creation of a secure system is not constrained by one framework, model, or methodology. In fact, many security concepts and principles can be applied to its design. A number of secure design principles are noted below, while some of them have been discussed elsewhere in the book (as also referenced).

Examples of Secure Design Principles:

- Threat modeling (discussed in section 1.11.1)
- Least privilege (discussed in section 1.9.1)
- Defense in depth (discussed in section 1.10.6)
- Secure defaults
- Fail securely
- Separation of duties (discussed in section 1.9.1)
- Keep it simple
- Zero trust
- Trust but verify
- Privacy by Design
- Shared responsibility

Secure Defaults

Any default settings a system has should be secured to the extent possible, so no compromise is facilitated. For example, if the operating system allows an administrator account to exist with no password, that will make it easy to launch an attack.

Fail Securely

If a system or its components fail, they should do so in a manner that doesn't expose the system to a potential attack. For example, if a safe has an electronic lock to protect its contents from theft, that lock should remain engaged in the event the electricity fails at the building.

Keep It Simple

Remove as much complexity from a situation as possible and focus on what matters most. In the context of designing and building a secure system, the same thinking applies and results in a number of benefits, including:

- Smaller attack surface

- Less errors and vulnerabilities

- Less complex testing

- Easier and more efficient troubleshooting and problem resolution

If simplicity is ignored, it can lead to the development of complex mechanisms that may not be correctly understood, which makes configuration, implementation, maintenance, and use much more difficult.

In other words, the likelihood of a greater number of vulnerabilities increases as the complexity of the system design and code does.

Zero Trust

With continued advancements in technology and especially with the growth of cloud computing, organizations are more intertwined and interconnected than ever before. As a result, organizations are also more vulnerable than ever before, and this has led to adoption of a security concept known as zero trust. Zero trust essentially means trust nothing, and it is based upon the premise that organizations should not automatically trust anything internal or external to enter their perimeter. Instead, prior to granting access to systems and individuals, those first need to be authenticated and authorized. Network segmentation can greatly be used in this approach, because it allows breaking the network into smaller parts and thus forces users and devices to authenticate each time they move from one network to another. With this perspective, organizations can take steps to adopt a zero trust posture such as those noted below:

- Micro-segmentation of networks

- Granular enforcement of perimeter ingress/egress points, based upon identity, user location, and other data to determine whether to trust the user, device, or application seeking access to enterprise resources.

Additionally, in a zero trust environment, inherent trust should not exist. Simply because a device is connected to a network does not mean the device should have access to anything on the network. Access to network resources should only come as a result of confidence gained through proper authentication, authorization, and accounting (AAA) of users, devices, and services.

Correspondingly, this confidence can only be gained by building trust into the user's identity (user authentication), associated user devices (device verification), and the services they access (service authorization and associated accounting, which is achieved by logging).

Ultimately, for this model to be effective, every connection to a service should be authenticated, and every device and connection should be authorized against a corresponding policy, regardless of the request's origin (internal or external).

To summarize, zero trust's "trust nothing" approach takes security very seriously and recommends the following features (with the zero trust principles being summarized in Table 3-1):

- Strong user authentication
- Authentication of services, which includes the following components:
    - User authentication
    - Device authentication
    - Service authorization
    - Logging and monitoring
- Authorization using a corresponding policy

	Principles for Zero Trust
1	Know your **architecture** (users, devices, and services)
2	Know your user, service, and device **identities**
3	Know the **health** of your users, devices, and services
4	Use **policies to authorize** requests
5	**Authenticate everywhere**
6	**Focus your monitoring** on devices and services
7	**Don't trust any network**, including your own
8	Choose services **designed for zero trust**

Table 3-1: **Zero Trust Principles**

Trust but Verify

In essence, the term is an oxymoron, because complete trust in something implies that no verification is needed. However, complete distrust is also not viable. Locking down architectures, with an eye toward prevention and avoidance, is outdated. Rather, like the concept of zero trust, trust but verify really means being able to authenticate users and perform authorization based on their permissions to perform activities on the network so they can access the various resources. It also means that real-time monitoring is a requirement. In short, focus on employing complete controls that include better detection and response mechanisms. With the cloud and reliance on third-party services becoming more and more ubiquitous, adopting this "complete control" mindset and approach is especially relevant and valuable for an organization.

Additionally, due to the growth in reliance on third-party services, trust should be verified through assurance mechanisms like

- Audits
- Ongoing monitoring
- SOC reporting
- Contracts/agreements, like SLAs and SLRs

Privacy by Design

Privacy by Design is premised on the belief that privacy should be incorporated into networked systems and technologies by default and designed into the architecture. As privacy is achieved through the proper implementation of security controls, the concept of Privacy by Design also means that security becomes an integral part of the design elements of an architecture.

Privacy must be a priority and must become an integral part of organizational and project goals and objectives, design activities, and planning efforts. Privacy should be embedded into every standard, protocol, and process that touches people.

Privacy by Design incorporates seven foundational principles as also depicted in Figure 3-1:

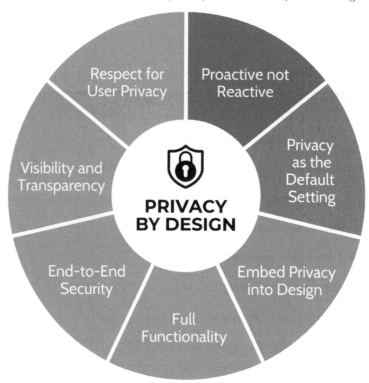

Figure 3-1: **Privacy by Design**

- **Privacy as proactive and preventive, not reactive and remedial.** Privacy by Design (PbD) should anticipate and prevent privacy shortcomings before they occur. PbD does not wait for risks to privacy to arise, nor does it attempt to resolve privacy breaches once they've taken place.

- **Privacy as the *default* setting.** Like many firewalls that include ***explicit deny*** as the default treatment of all traffic, PbD seeks to ensure the automatic—default—protection of personal data in IT systems and business practices. In other words, if an individual takes no action, their privacy is protected as the rule and not as the exception.

- **Privacy embedded into design.** PbD is considered from the inception of a system, application, or process and is included in the architecture, design, and development of the system, application, and process. This approach leads to a result that includes privacy as an essential part of the core functionality being delivered.

- **Full functionality within a given solution.** PbD seeks a "win-win" situation for all parties involved and attempts to accommodate all interests, goals, and objectives rather than demand trade-offs that reduce overall effectiveness.

- **End-to-End Security.** PbD, having been considered from the inception of a system, application, or process, should securely extend through the life cycle of the data involved. Strong security measures—from beginning to end, from cradle to grave—are essential to effective privacy.

- **Visibility and Transparency.** PbD calls for visibility and transparency of all components and processes related to the technology or business practice being used. Furthermore, PbD seeks to assure all relevant parties that whatever components and processes are involved are being operated and used in a manner that is consistent with stated objectives and promises, subject to independent verification.

- **Respect for User Privacy.** PbD ultimately requires the individual to be treated with the utmost respect and care. Regardless of who is designing or working with a system, measures such as strong privacy by default, appropriate notice, and user-intuitive options that allow management of privacy should always be incorporated into the solution. User-centric considerations should always prevail.

Shared Responsibility

As noted already, the ubiquitous nature of the cloud and reliance on third-party services for support of day-to-day operations of organizations around the globe have shifted responsibilities from internal sources to a mix of internal and external sources. With most traditional on-premise IT infrastructure, accountability and responsibility for all facets of the same rests with the organization; with the cloud, depending upon the cloud deployment model being utilized, the same is not true—especially where responsibility is concerned.

Because of increased reliance on third-party services, a corresponding increase in clarity on shared security expectations should exist. The cloud customer and cloud service provider must clearly communicate expectations both ways as well as clearly define related responsibilities. Furthermore, responsibility and accountability in the eyes of the cloud customer must be clearly defined and understood, especially since accountability may never be delegated or otherwise transferred, regardless of the customer–provider relationship.

To this end, consumers and providers must act on these responsibilities and define clear contracts and agreements, which can then be implemented through appropriate policies, procedures, and controls.

3.2 Understand the fundamental concepts of security models (e.g., Biba, Star Model, Bell–LaPadula)

3.2.0 Security Models

CORE **CONCEPTS**

- A model is a representation of something real.
- A security model is a representation of what security should look like in an architecture.

What Is a Model?

A security model is a representation of what security should look like in an architecture being built. Security models have existed and have been used for years. Some of these models include Bell–LaPadula, Biba, Clark–Wilson and Brewer–Nash (also referred to as the Chinese Wall model). These are simple models that provide the basis—the fundamental means—for building confidentiality or integrity into architectures that require these core principles. Like any model, security models represent what security needs to look like. Many people don't value the importance of security models because many of them date back to the early '70s, like Bell–LaPadula; but these still apply today. The conceptual, fundamental ways to address confidentiality that Bell–LaPadula highlights are the same today as they were in the '70s. The way that confidentiality is addressed today is also the same as it was years ago. Technology changes, but the fundamental rules on how confidentiality and integrity are addressed remain the same. It's valuable to understand these models and their underlying rules, as they govern the implementation of the model.

Concept of Security

Here's the bottom line: To ensure the protection of any architecture, it must be broken down into individual components, and adequate security for each component needs to be put in place. Remember that a chain is only as strong as its weakest link. However, note that any system should be broken down and individual components secured to the degree that value dictates doing so.

3.2.1 Enterprise Security Architecture

CORE **CONCEPTS**

- An architecture is group of components that work together.
- Security architecture involves breaking down a system to its components and protecting each component based upon its value.

To implement an enterprise security architecture, frameworks exist to serve as guidelines. Three of the most popular enterprise security architectures are Zachman, Sherwood Applied Business Security Architecture (SABSA), and The Open Group Architecture Framework (TOGAF). Though each differs a bit in structure and terminology, they each basically do the same thing to protect any architecture. Zachman focuses on answering basic question like how, where, who, when, and why by directing those to the various company teams (e.g., designers, owners, architects, strategists, engineers, operators) and acquiring their feedback. However, this is an older model dating back to the '70s and may not necessarily be the most suitable model today, as it merely focuses on classification and organization of enterprise security. SABSA is a newer framework (adopted in 1995) that focuses on security architecture risk and allows security to be embedded in IT functions. It is an open source framework that provides scalability and ease of implementation, facilitates compliance, and can help response prioritization. TOGAF focuses on efficient resource utilization and cost minimization while having a modular structure increasing its adoption, a content framework providing consistency, and a style that allows architectural flexibility.

Security Models

Security models are pretty simple. Essentially, they're the rules that need to be implemented to achieve security. Many security models exist, but most of them are one of two types: lattice-based or rule-based. A good way to envision a lattice-based model is to think of a ladder, where a framework and steps exist that look a bit like layers, going up and down. In other words, a lattice-based model is a layer-based model. It requires layers of security to address the requirements. Two lattice-based models exist: Bell–LaPadula and Biba. Bell–LaPadula addresses one primary component of the CIA triad: confidentiality. Biba addresses another component: integrity. All other models are rule-based, meaning specific rules dictate how security operates. People sometimes argue that lattice-based models also provide rules and ask why they're not considered rule-based. Lattice-based models do include rules, but those rules are confined to layers within the model; hence, the term *lattice-based* is more applicable. Table 3-2 provides a summary of the various lattice-based and rule-based security models.

Layer / Lattice-based Models	Rule-based Models
■ Bell–LaPadula ■ Biba	■ Information Flow ■ Clark–Wilson ■ Brewer–Nash (Chinese Wall) ■ Graham–Denning ■ Harrison–Ruzzo–Ullmann

Table 3-2: **Lattice-Based and Rule-Based Security Models**

3.2.2 Layer-based Models

> ### CORE **CONCEPTS**
>
> ■ **Layer-based security models are also considered lattice-based security models.**
>
> ■ **Bell–LaPadula addresses only confidentiality.**
>
> ■ **Biba addresses only integrity.**
>
> ■ **Lipner implementation is not a model; it is an implementation that combines the best features of Bell–LaPadula and Biba.**

As we mentioned earlier, lattice-based security models, like Bell–LaPadula and Biba, can also be thought of as layer-based security models. Based upon intersecting vertical and horizontal support elements, a lattice structure can be envisioned as having different layers. Extrapolating this concept further, each of the two security models can be viewed as having different layers of security.

Bell–LaPadula

Bell–LaPadula is based on incorporating the necessary rules that need to be implemented to achieve confidentiality. Based upon this query, a lattice-based model was developed as also seen in Figure 3-2.

Bell–LaPadula addresses only confidentiality

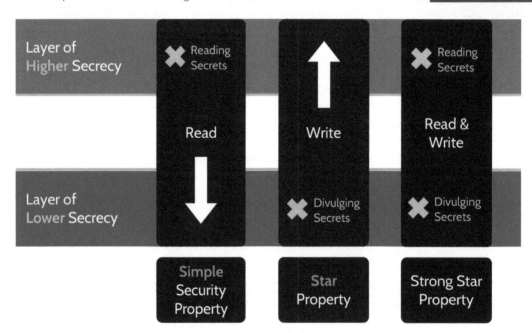

Figure 3-2: **Bell–LaPadula Model**

This model is based on three basic principles:

1. **Simple security property,** also known as "**no read up**" property, relates to reading and denotes that any subject at a particular security level may not read an object at a higher security level.

2. **The star (*) property**, also known as "**no write down**" property, relates to writing and denotes that any subject at a particular security level may not write to an object at a lower security level.

3. **The strong star property** relates to both reading and writing. Having an ability to both read and write means a subject should be able to read and write at their own layer, nothing higher and nothing lower.

Biba

Bell–LaPadula focuses on ensuring data ***integrity*** as shown in Figure 3-3. Integrity could mean things like timely, accurate, relevant, or meaningful, and in fact the words *accurate* or *accuracy* are probably the best for the sake of understanding Biba, as integrity also equates to accuracy of information.

Biba addresses only integrity

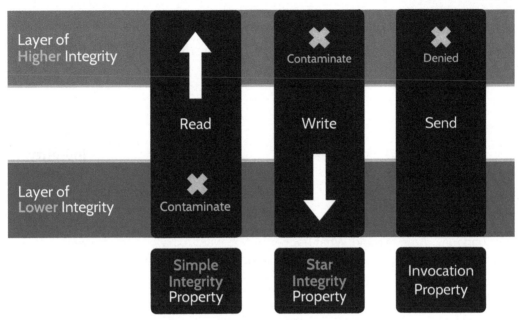

Figure 3-3: **Biba Model**

This model is also based on three basic principles:

1. **Simple integrity property**, also known as the "**no read down**" property, relates to reading and denotes that a subject at a particular level of integrity may not read an object at a lower integrity level.

2. **Star (*) integrity property**, also known as "**no write up**," relates to writing and denotes that a subject at a particular level of integrity may not write to an object at a higher integrity level.

3. **Invocation property** states that a subject can't send information to someone that is rated at a higher layer of information than the current one the subject holds.

Figure 3-4 provides a summary of the abovementioned models, with an emphasis on their two main principles.

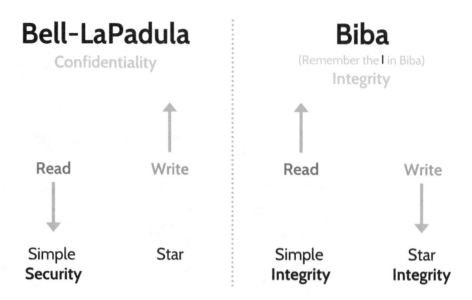

Figure 3-4: **Summary of Bell–LaPadula and Biba**

Lipner Implementation

Now a question may come to mind: What happens if you want to have both confidentiality and integrity? The Lipner implementation, shown in Figure 3-5, is the answer to how you can get the best out of both worlds.

It's simply an attempt to combine the best features of Bell–LaPadula and Biba regarding confidentiality and integrity. As such, *Lipner is not truly a model but rather an implementation of two models.* In theory, Lipner creates great security by combining two lattice-based models but based upon the way Bell–LaPadula and Biba work. Its principle is to separate objects into data and programs and apply sensitivity levels and job categories to subjects.

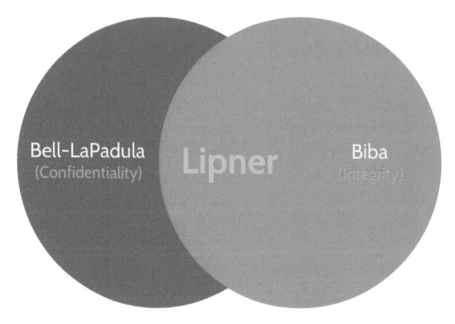

Figure 3-5: **Lipner Implementation**

3.2.3 Rule-based Models

> CORE **CONCEPTS**
>
> - Information flow models track the flow of information and can help uncover covert channels.
> - Covert channels are *unintentional* communications paths; two types exist: storage and timing.
> - Clark–Wilson is an integrity-focused rule-based model that includes three goals and three rules.
> - Brewer–Nash—the "Chinese Wall" model—is designed to prevent conflicts of interest.

At the core of any rule-based model is a set of rules that mediate access between subject and objects. Depending on the model, the number and complexity of rules employed may vary widely, and the focus of the model can also vary. In addition to looking at some specific rule-based models further below, a basic understanding of information flow models and covert channels should first be covered.

Information Flow

Information flow models track the flow of information. If the flow of information can be tracked, this implies it can be tracked throughout its life cycle; in other words, it can be tracked from the point of origin, whether collected or created, to its storage, use, dissemination, sharing with others, and eventually to its end of life (e.g., archival and destruction). Information flow can also help the identification of vulnerabilities and insecurities, like covert channels. Referring to lattice-based models, the information flow model serves as the basis for both Bell–LaPadula and Biba.

Covert Channels

Covert channels are **unintentional** communication paths that may lead to the disclosure of confidential information. The key word is *unintentional*—they're not meant to be there. However, because they're there, the potential for confidential information to be disclosed exists.

A wonderful example of a covert channel occurred in the early '90s and centered around the military operation known as Desert Storm. Some type of military action in the Gulf was supposedly imminent, but Pentagon officials kept exact details and timing under wraps. However, borrowing from something—the "pizza index"—that some people might think of as myth and others fact, journalists and other interested parties kept track of the number of pizzas being delivered to the Pentagon each day. Typically, a small number of pizzas (e.g., three to four) was delivered but just prior to the start of the conflict, a much larger number (like thirty to forty pizzas) was delivered. Based upon the significant change in the number of pizzas being delivered, it was safe to assume or infer that a much larger number of people were working late at the Pentagon. Why? Because, among other things, they were likely helping with the final planning stages of military action. CNN and other news outlets were able to piece together the inadvertent disclosure of sensitive information and predict when military strikes in the Middle East would commence. This is a perfect example of a covert channel—unintentional and inadvertent disclosure of sensitive and confidential information.

Covert channels, also sometimes called *secret channels*, are *unintentional* communications paths, and two types of covert channels exist, as summarized in Table 3-3. Storage refers to when storage capabilities can be exploited in such a way that confidential information is unintentionally disclosed or communicated. *Timing* refers to when the timing capabilities of a system can be exploited in a manner that allows confidential information to be signaled. Looking back at the pizza example, what type of covert channel does it represent? You guessed it—timing—because that's where the weakness is, in the timing mechanism. The number of pizzas ordered in a twenty-four-hour period signaled information that was considered confidential.

> Covert channels are unintentional & may involve storage or timing; when they exist, confidentiality may be compromised

An example of a storage covert channel exists in most technology architectures. On a laptop, sensitive information could be placed in RAM, because a process needs to use it, but when that process finishes, the sensitive information remains present in memory. That could become available to other processes that are placed in memory and can read it. The sensitive information is not meant to be in RAM, but it is in fact there, and it could disclose confidential information. That is an example of a storage covert channel, which represents the majority of covert channels (roughly 99 percent).

Storage	Timing
Process writes sensitive data to RAM, and the data remains present after the process completes; now, other processes can potentially read the data.	An online web server responds to a user providing an existing username within three seconds, while if the username doesn't exist it takes one second. That allows the attacker to perform username enumeration.

Table 3-3: **Covert Channel Types**

Clark–Wilson

Clark–Wilson is an important, rules-based model that focuses only on **integrity**. Unlike, Biba, which only prevents unauthorized subjects from making any changes, Clark–Wilson offers further protection and meets three **goals of integrity**:

1. Prevent unauthorized subjects from making any changes (this is the only of the three that Biba addresses)

2. Prevent authorized subjects from making bad changes

3. Maintain consistency of the system

Biba only addresses #1 and therefore falls short of truly addressing security concerns related to the protection of all integrity, while Clark–Wilson addresses #1 and then further protects integrity through #2 and #3.

> **The goals and rules of integrity found in Clark–Wilson**

Clark–Wilson achieves each of the goals specifically through application of the three **rules of integrity** noted in Table 3-4.

Well-Formed Transactions	Separation of Duties	Access Triple
Good, consistent, validated data. Only perform operations in a manner that won't compromise the integrity of objects.	One person shouldn't be allowed to perform all tasks related to a critical function.	Subject | Program | Object A subject cannot directly access an object, i.e., in a database, access *must* go through a program that enforces access rules.

Table 3-4: **Clark–Wilson Rules**

Brewer–Nash (The Chinese Wall) Model

Brewer–Nash is also known as "The Chinese Wall" model and has one primary goal: *Preventing conflicts of interest*.

An example of where Brewer–Nash might be implemented is between the Development and Production departments in an organization, as the two departments should not be able to influence each other or even allow access between each other. Another example is a big bank, between the Retail Investments and Mergers and Acquisitions (M & A) departments, as knowledge shared from the M&A department could significantly influence activities in the Investments department as also shown in Figure 3-6.

Like Bell–LaPadula, Brewer–Nash primarily addresses issues related to *confidentiality*.

> **Goal of Brewer–Nash**

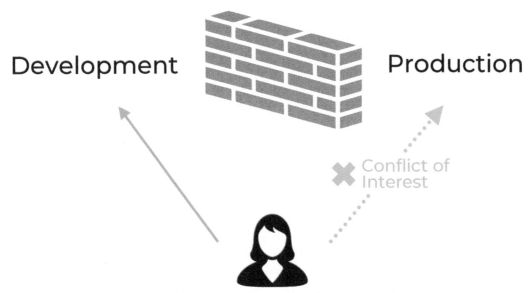

Figure 3-6: **Conflict of Interest between Two Company Departments**

Graham–Denning Model

Graham–Denning is another lesser known, rule-based model that specifies rules allowing a subject to access an object.

Harrison–Ruzzo–Ullman Model

Like Graham–Denning, Harrison–Ruzzo–Ullman is also a rule-based model that focuses on the integrity of access rights via a finite set of rules available to edit the access rights of a subject. It adds the ability to add generic rights to groups of individuals.

Remember that all security models are either classified as lattice-based or rule-based.

3.2.4 Certification and Accreditation

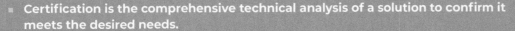

CORE **CONCEPTS**

- **Certification is the comprehensive technical analysis of a solution to confirm it meets the desired needs.**
- **Accreditation is management's official sign-off of certification for a predetermined period of time.**

Evaluation Criteria

This next section deals with what are known as "evaluation criteria systems." The primary thing to remember is they're measurement systems. When architectures—especially security architectures—are built, products are often purchased from vendors. Security today often relies on solutions and mechanisms provided by vendors. This fact introduces a potential problem: How do we know vendor solutions actually provide the level of security we think they provide? Any vendor is going to say they have the best products, the best solutions, the best architectures. For example, if a firewall needs to be purchased, every firewall vendor is going to say their firewall is the best one available and that it will meet our needs perfectly. How can statements like this be confirmed and verified? We would need an independent and objective measurement system that vendors can use for evaluation purposes and companies for purchasing purposes. Such a system could be used by any organization around the globe to make purchasing decisions and not need to rely on vendors themselves. With such a system, similar products from different vendors can easily be compared. If the product requirements are understood—for example, for the firewall noted above—evaluations from multiple vendor firewalls could be compared and the best one chosen. These evaluations, these measurements, could be trusted, because they've been created using an independent, vendor-neutral, objective system. These measurement systems do, in fact, exist and are called "evaluation criteria systems." The most well-known evaluation criteria systems are called Trusted Computer System Evaluation Criteria (TCSEC)—also known as the Orange Book, the European equivalent of TCSEC called Information Technology Security Evaluation Criteria (ITSEC), and the latest one, an ISO standard, called the Common Criteria.

From the description above, it should be clear that vendors and consumers have an interest in using these measurement systems, and this explains why they've become very popular—especially the Common Criteria. Consumers want to shop for and buy products from vendors, and they want to know exactly what security levels the products provide and be able to trust those security capabilities. Likewise, vendors want their products measured and rated, so they'll be more likely to be purchased by customers. For example, if every available firewall is Evaluation Assurance Level 4 (EAL4 indicates a very methodical design, test and review process has been implemented) capable, a firewall that receives a rating of EAL3 is most likely not going to sell very well, as some redesign and other changes will likely need to take place. Evaluation and rating systems like this benefit vendors by giving them confidence that consumers will be interested in the products if the products are rated well. When an independent certified company examines a product using objective and commonly accepted criteria versus a biased entity like the vendor or a related party using subjective and biased criteria, everybody can trust the results. Potential customers can examine the resulting documentation and make informed purchasing decisions, while vendors can examine the results and know exactly how their product compares to the same category of products from other vendors. This is what each of the evaluation criteria systems do, and the Common Criteria, in its third and most recent version, is by far the best one available today.

Certification and **Accreditation** are two related, yet different and very important concepts in security. Their definitions are outlined in Table 3-5.

Certification	Accreditation
Comprehensive technical analysis of a solution or a product to ensure it meets the desired needs	Official management signoff of certification for a set period of time

Table 3-5: **Certification and Accreditation**

Certification is the comprehensive technical analysis of a solution to make sure that it meets your needs. For example, for an organization that needs a firewall, how will the organization easily sift through the likely dozens of firewalls that exist and evaluate the one best suited to meet its needs? Before any decision or recommendation can be made, the requirements of the organization must be understood. Once the requirements are understood, a solution can more easily be identified. Among available

> **Understand the difference between certification and accreditation and what each provides**

firewalls, the one that best meets the requirements will be identified, and a comprehensive technical analysis of each potential solution is the basis for this identification. This is certification.

Accreditation is the official management decision to use a solution. Usually, this is done for a set period of time. One important note, accreditation is not performed by the security function; rather, it's performed by the asset owner or management. They will make the decision to accredit the solution for, let's say, the next eighteen months. Once this time period expires, the certification and accreditation process would be repeated. The same solution that's been in use might still be the best one, at which point management would re-accredit the solution for another set period of time; otherwise, a different solution would be selected.

This is the benefit of some of these evaluation criteria systems, especially of the Common Criteria. Once a vendor's product is evaluated, it becomes available to everybody. In addition, every capability and shortcoming of a given product will be freely viewable. Most vendors commonly publish the results of a Common Criteria assessment on the products section of their website. The collection of products that have been evaluated using the Common Criteria continues to grow, which is great; it requires a massive amount of work, but the output of information is extremely helpful to consumers.

3.2.5 Evaluation Criteria (ITSEC and TCSEC)

> CORE **CONCEPTS**
>
> - **TCSEC, also known as the Orange Book, is the first evaluation criteria system.**
> - **ITSEC followed TCSEC and was developed by Europeans to include elements of the Orange Book and others.**
> - **ITSEC applies to networked environments and measures functional and assurance elements separate from one another.**

Orange Book/Trusted Computer System Evaluation Criteria (TCSEC)

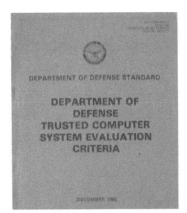

Figure 3-7: **TCSEC Guide**

The first evaluation criteria system created is often referred to as the "Orange Book," depicted in Figure 3-7, due to the fact the cover of the book is orange. It was written as part of a series of books known as the "rainbow series," published by the US Department of Defense in the '80s. Each book in the series deals with a topic related to security, and the cover of each is a different color, thus the nickname "rainbow series." There's one book called the Light Blue Book that deals with password guidelines, while the Red Book deals with network security, and the Orange Book focuses on measuring security products.

The classification levels—the criteria—used in the Orange Book are shown in Table 3-6.

Functional Levels	
A1	Verified Design
B3	Security labels, verification of no covert channels, and must stay secure during start up
B2	Security labels and verification of no covert channels
B1	Security labels
C2	Strict login procedures
C1	Weak protection mechanisms
D1	Failed or was not tested

Table 3-6: **Orange Book Evaluation Criteria**

The Orange Book only measures confidentiality, which reflects the Department of Defense's mission in the early '80s, when confidentiality (especially in the context of the military) was so important. Even by today's standards and when many people say it's obsolete, if you're interested only in confidentiality, there's really no better system than TCSEC. Evaluation criteria goes from D1, which means no security, to A1, which means very robust and mathematically verified security as shown in Table 3-6. Despite the possibility of an A1 rating, most products are typically rated at C2 or B1. Each rating level implies that a given product "inherits" all the characteristics of the previous level.

The Orange Book, however, only measures confidentiality. In addition, it only measures single-box type of architectures; it does not map well to networked environments. This is why a lot of organizations in Europe considered the model from a more current perspective and revamped it. They took what they considered to be a good idea and made it better in what is known as the Information Technology Security Evaluation Criteria (ITSEC).

Information Technology Security Evaluation Criteria (ITSEC)

Unlike the Orange Book, ITSEC measures more than confidentiality, and it works well in a network environment. Also, when ITSEC was created, ways to measure function and assurance separate from each other were incorporated. When a product is considered through the lens of ITSEC, two ratings are given. One rating—the "F" levels—is a functional rating, like the ones used in the Orange Book. The other rating—the "E" levels—was introduced as part of ITSEC and refers to levels of assurance. E levels range from E0 to E6 (as also seen in Table 3-7), with E6 being the top and representing the best level. Obviously, E6 would be a system that provides robust assurance while E0 not so much.

Assurance Levels	
E6	Formal end-to-end security tests + source code reviews
E5	Semi-formal system + unit tests and source code review
E4	Semi-formal system + unit tests
E3	Informal system + unit tests
E2	Informal system tests
E1	System in development
E0	Inadequate assurance

Table 3-7: **ITSEC Assurance Levels (E levels)**

Note that ITSEC improves on the Orange Book by providing:

- Functional measurements (same as the Orange Book)
- Assurance measurements (E levels)

ITSEC was replaced by Common Criteria in 2005.

3.2.6 Common Criteria

CORE **CONCEPTS**

- **Common Criteria evaluation criteria system is the best and most popular system.**
- **Comprised of multiple components that work together and allow a globally recognized rating to be assigned to products.**
- **Common Criteria EAL rating levels**

ISO 15408, better known as the Common Criteria, is the most used of the evaluation criteria systems and is also the most popular; most products are evaluated using it. As such, it's critical to understand Common Criteria components, Evaluation Assurance Levels (EAL), and the ramifications if changes to an EAL-rated system take place.

Like the other evaluation systems, the Common Criteria provides confidence in the industry for consumers and security functions as well as for vendors and others. The Common Criteria is the latest measurement system, and it's also an ISO standard (ISO 15408). It's called the Common Criteria because several countries joined together with a common goal: to create a common measurement system that could be trusted globally. For example, if a German-made product is rated, the rating can be trusted by US-based companies, because the rigorous rating process is independent and objective and globally applicable. To make this possible, globally dispersed, independent, Common Criteria–licensed organizations evaluate

and rate products. A firewall vendor will regularly hire a Common Criteria–licensed company to evaluate and rate their firewall. The licensed organization would use a specific and rigorous process to measure and ultimately rate the firewall with an EAL level that objectively communicates what security it provides. The process also provides documentation that may prove useful to security professionals and other potential consumers of the firewall. Figure 3-8 depicts the Common Criteria components and process flow.

Common Criteria Process

The first component is the **Protection Profile (PP)**. The PP lists the security capabilities that a type or category of security products should possess. For example, there's a Protection Profile for firewalls; it lists the security capabilities that any firewall should contain—for example, two-factor authentication (2FA) capabilities, VPN capabilities, ability to encrypt to 128-bit encryption level, and secure logging, to name a few. Protection profiles exist for different categories of security products and serve to add uniformity to each category; there's one for firewalls, one for access controls, one for IDS systems, etc. This approach provides a consistent framework of capabilities that a specific category of product should possess.

Target of Evaluation (TOE) is the next component. Using the earlier firewall example, if a vendor desires for their firewall to be rated according to the Common Criteria, the firewall would be considered the TOE. The TOE—the Target of Evaluation—is simply a vendor's product that's being rated and being assessed according to the Common Criteria.

> What the Common Criteria Protection Profile (PP) components represent

The next component, the **Security Targets (ST)**, describe—from the vendor's perspective—each of the firewall's security capabilities that match up with capabilities outlined in the Protection Profile. When the firewall is measured, capabilities like VPN, encryption, two-factor authentication, secure logging, and so on are going to be compared against standards listed in the protection profile and tested extensively. For example, the firewall may perform two-factor authentication very well, but it lacks strong VPN capabilities. Security targets are going to be scrutinized, and each will be scrutinized under the dual lens of **functional** and **assurance** security capabilities, the two prementioned pillars of a well-implemented security control.

The evaluation process is the part of the Common Criteria that creates meaningful documentation that becomes available to any interested parties. At the end, after the capabilities of the firewall have been evaluated, an overall EAL level will be assigned to the firewall. An EAL can range anywhere from 1–7, with 7 being the most thorough and exhaustive. The above process steps are summarized in Table 3-8, while the different EAL levels are listed in Table 3-9.

Figure 3-8: **Common Criteria Process**

PP Protection Profile	Specification of functional and assurance requirements for a specific type of security product
TOE Target of Evaluation	The specific product/system to be evaluated
ST Security Targets	Written statement by vendor explaining how functional and assurance specifications of the product meet the protection profile (PP) requirements
Security **Functional** Requirements	Security targets are evaluated from a functional perspective: what features exist and how well they work relative to the desired and expected security behavior.
Security **Assurance** Requirements	Security targets are evaluated from an assurance perspective: that the vendor's claimed security functionality and the CC evaluation process align.
Evaluate	Consider all of the components together
Assign **EAL** (1-7)	See the seven Common Criteria EAL levels below

Table 3-8: **Common Criteria Steps**

EAL7	Formally verified, designed, and tested
EAL6	Semi-formally verified, designed, and tested
EAL5	Semi-formally designed and tested
EAL4	Methodically designed, tested, and reviewed
EAL3	Methodically tested and checked
EAL2	Structurally tested
EAL1	Functionally tested

Table 3-9:**EAL Levels**

Despite the table above illustrating multiple EAL levels, EAL7 is not necessarily the best for the sake of a vendor marketing and selling its product. In fact, most organizations will not purchase a product that is rated above EAL4. Operating systems are typically at EAL3 and firewalls at EAL4.

> EAL level definitions and order

If a product is at EAL7, it could become more vulnerable to compromise, due to being more complex and harder to maintain. Yes, the product might offer more security features and capabilities, but if they require extensive configuration, administrative skills, and maintenance, consumers will likely not use the features. This could ultimately leave an organization at greater risk. Vendors, therefore, must balance the trade-off between functionality and security. Too much of the latter always impacts product speed and administrative overhead, and it might lead to the creation of a very expensive product too. This explains why vendors often produce products that are configurable. Just because a firewall is EAL 4 capable, it doesn't mean it must be operated at EAL4; a customer could very well decide to configure and use it at an EAL3 level.

> The potential negative implications if a product is rated too high

A final thing to note is that, after a product undergoes an evaluation and is assigned an EAL level, the EAL level for that product will remain the same throughout its life span, unless a major change in product functionality is introduced. In other words, when a patch or software update to the product is made, the EAL level remains unchanged.

> If a product is patched or receives software/ firmware updates, the EAL level remains the same

3.3 Select controls based upon systems security requirements

3.3.1 Security Control Frameworks

> ### CORE **CONCEPTS**
>
> - Security control frameworks aid with the control selection process.
> - Security control frameworks provide guidance, based upon best practices.
> - Features from multiple frameworks can be used to meet the needs of an organization.

What Do Security Control Frameworks Provide?

This section focuses on the selection of controls to include in a system. Recall that this domain's focus is building systems and protection mechanisms to secure those systems, which requires breaking the systems down into components and protecting each component. Components should be protected based upon value, which drives the selection of controls. All this activity is predicated on risk management.

As controls are considered, especially mitigating controls, control frameworks can be utilized to aid with the control selection process. Control frameworks provide comprehensive guidance, based upon best practices. For example, a security professional might be pondering how to protect a certain system component, like a storage device, CPU, or piece of memory, and turning to a control framework could offer insight into appropriate controls to consider. Additionally, as control frameworks provide guidance, the best and most applicable elements of multiple frameworks could potentially be utilized as part of the control selection process.

From this perspective, the following section is a reminder of some of the major control frameworks available and how they can be applied. In addition to technical frameworks, many of the ones listed in Table 3-10 focus on overall business processes.

> Understand the major frameworks at a high level, especially ISO 27001/02, which is an internationally recognized framework

COBIT	The Control Objectives for Information Technologies (COBIT) framework is particularly useful for **IT assurance**, such as conducting audits and gap assessments. It was created by Information Systems Audit and Control Assurance (ISACA), for information technology management and IT governance, and therefore it is particularly useful for IT assurance activities.
ITIL	Information Technology Infrastructure Library (ITIL) defines the **processes** in a well-run IT department, from the onboarding process to procurement, change management, configuration management, and access control, to name a few. ITIL defines the processes for IT service management that focuses on aligning IT services with business goals and objectives.
NIST SP 800-53	National Institute of Standards and Technology Special Publication (NIST SP) 800-53 is a set of best practices, standards, and recommendations that help an organization improve its cybersecurity controls.
PCI DSS	The Payment Card Industry Data Security Standard (PCI DSS) is a standard for organizations that **handle credit cards** like VISA, MasterCard, and American Express. The PCI Standard was created by the card brands, and it is administered by the Payment Card Industry Security Standards Council. The standard was created to increase controls around cardholder data to reduce credit card fraud. The volume of transactions processed by a merchant helps determine the method used to validate compliance.
ISO 27001	International Organization for Standardization/International Electrotechnical Commission (ISO/IEC) 27001:2013 specifies the requirements for establishing, implementing, maintaining, and continually improving an information security management system within the context of the organization. It also includes requirements for the assessment and treatment of information security risks tailored to the needs of the organization. The requirements set out in ISO/IEC 27001:2013 are generic and are intended to be applicable to all organizations, regardless of type, size, or nature. **Organizations can be certified against ISO 27001.** **Annex A** of the standard contains the following domains: 1. Information security policies 2. Organization of information security 3. Human resource security 4. Asset management 5. Access control 6. Cryptography 7. Physical and environmental security 8. Operations security 9. Communications security 10. System acquisition, development, and maintenance 11. Supplier relationships 12. Information security incident management 13. Information security aspects of business continuity management 14. Compliance
ISO 27002	ISO/IEC 27002:2013 provides **guidelines** for organizational information security standards and information security management practices including the selection, implementation, and management of controls, taking into consideration the organization's information security risk environment(s). Essentially ISO 27002 provides guidance for implementing the controls in ISO 27001.
COSO	Committee of Sponsoring Organizations of the Treadway Commission (COSO) is a voluntary private sector initiative dedicated to improving organizational performance and governance through effective internal control, enterprise risk management, and fraud deterrence.
HIPAA	Health Insurance Portability and Accountability Act (HIPAA) relates to security controls in the **health-care industry**, and it focuses on the protection of personal health information (PHI) of individuals
FISMA	Federal Information Security Management (FISMA) Act of 2002 requires US federal agencies to develop, document, and implement agency-wide security programs to provide information security for the operations and assets of the agency. FISMA further requires security programs for any other agencies, contractors, or service providers.
FedRAMP	Federal Risk and Authorization Management Program (FedRAMP) provides a standardized approach to security assessment, authorization, and continuous monitoring for cloud products and services. **Any cloud services that hold US federal government data must be FedRAMP authorized.**
SOX	Sarbanes-Oxley (SOX) Act is a direct result of the wild financial fraud at "Enron". The US Congress decided better controls were needed to be in place to prevent similar incidents from happening again, and specifically enacted SOX to prevent financial fraud by public companies and thereby protect the financial interests of shareholders.

Table 3-10: **Security Control Frameworks**

Rationalizing Frameworks

Figure 3-9 illustrates how all these different security frameworks relate to one another.

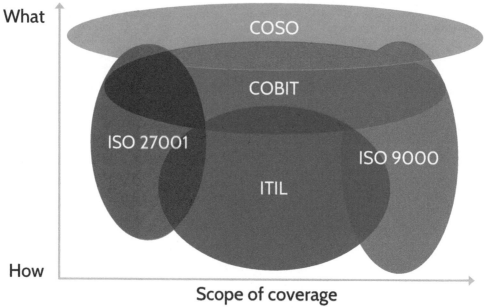

Figure 3-9: **Framework Relations**

Notice that they overlap, which means that frameworks can span contexts, and as also noted earlier, organizations will often choose to use features from multiple frameworks to meet their needs. Consider the example of a hospital, where patients are treated and payments are made. In this context, HIPAA and PCI DSS frameworks should undoubtedly be present, among other frameworks. Most organizations choose to use different ones for various contractual or legal reasons. Then they combine these and attempt to develop one overarching and simplified framework. It doesn't make sense to test a very similar control multiple times. As such, controls are merged, rationalized, and then tested once. This is the approach most organizations take.

3.4 Understand security capabilities of information systems (IS)

3.4.1 RMC, Security Kernel, and TCB

CORE **CONCEPTS**

- Security within information systems always pertains to subjects and objects.

- The Reference Monitor Concept (RMC) is a *concept*.

- *Implementation* of the RMC is known as a security kernel.

- A security kernel should consist of three properties, or characteristics: completeness, isolation, and verifiability.

- The term Trusted Computing Base (TCB) refers to all the protection mechanisms within a system; the TCB is the *totality* of protection mechanisms within an architecture.

Subjects and Objects

Before diving into concepts like the RMC and security kernel, it's important to understand subjects and objects, as defined in Table 3-11, as those concepts are heavily used throughout the following section.

Subject	Object
Active entities	**Passive** entities
A subject is a person, process, program, or anything similar that actively tries to access an object.	An object is anything that is being passively accessed by a subject, like a file, server, process, or hardware component.

Table 3-11: **Subjects and Objects**

Reference Monitor Concept (RMC)

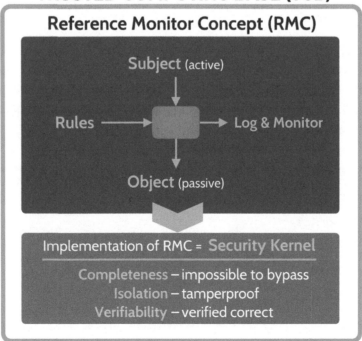

Figure 3-10: **Reference Monitor Concept**

The RMC is simply the concept of a subject accessing an object through some form of mediation that is based on a set of rules, with this access being logged and monitored. This is the "reference monitor concept," depicted in Figure 3-10, which is prevalent throughout security and is a topic often seen on the exam. When a key is put into a door lock, the reference monitor concept is present; when logging on a computer system, the reference monitor concept is there—as a subject is accessing an object—based on a set of rules, and this activity is logged and monitored. This concept is constantly employed in security. There are a few key points to keep in mind about the reference monitor concept. RMC features include:

- Must mediate all access
- Be protected from modification
- Be verifiable as correct
- Always be invoked

It's equally important to remember that the reference monitor concept is just a concept. Unless the RMC is implemented, it's simply some good ideas. The *implementation of the reference monitor concept is known as a security kernel.*

Security Kernel

Here's an important distinction: the security kernel controls access to any asset; the reference monitor concept defines a theory, a concept. *The security kernel is the implementation of the reference monitor concept.* It's important to understand this distinction. Any system that is actually controlling access must be an actual implementation. If it's implemented, it's a security kernel.

When implemented, a viable security kernel should contain three properties.

The first property is known as **completeness**. Completeness means it is impossible to bypass the mediation. If a subject is somehow able to bypass the mediation, there would be no point in having a security kernel. Completeness means it is impossible to bypass the security kernel; the subject must always go through the security kernel when accessing the object.

The next property is known as **isolation**. Isolation relates to the mediation rules and specifically ensures that the mediation rules are tamper-proof. Only authorized individuals should be able to change these rules.

The final property, **verifiability**, relates to the aspect of assurance. It means being able to verify that the security kernel is functioning correctly. How do we do that? This is done through logging and monitoring, including other forms of testing.

Any time a security kernel is implemented, it should demonstrate the three characteristics or properties of the RMC: completeness, isolation, and verifiability, which are also summarized in Table 3-12.

Completeness	Isolation	Verifiability
Impossible to bypass mediation; impossible to bypass the security kernel	Mediation rules are tamperproof	Logging and monitoring and other forms of testing to ensure the security kernel is functioning correctly

Table 3-12: **RMC Characteristics**

Trusted Computing Base (TCB)

Another important concept, another term that encompasses all the security controls that would be implemented to protect an architecture, is known as the trusted computing base, or TCB. This is the term used to refer to all the protection mechanisms within a system, within an architecture; the TCB is the *totality* of protection mechanisms within an architecture. Examples of components that would be within the TCB include all the hardware, firmware, and software processes that make up the security system. For a large organization, things like policies and procedures, onboarding processes, change management, the entire network, security training and awareness programs, and similar things would be part of the TCB. Clearly, the TCB can be huge, and if an entire enterprise is being considered it can be massive.

It's worth highlighting that all components noted below are found in the TCB:

- Processors (CPUs)
- Memory
- Primary storage
- Secondary storage

- Virtual memory
- Firmware
- Operating systems
- System kernel

3.4.2 Processors (CPUs)

CORE **CONCEPTS**

- A central processing unit (CPU) is the brain of a computer; it processes all of the instructions and ultimately solves problems.
- CPU processing involves an ongoing, four-step process: Fetch, Decode, Execute, and Store.
- A CPU operates in one of two states: the supervisor state or the problem state.

A CPU is the component within a computer that processes all the instructions. Essentially, a CPU is the brain of a computer. As shown in Figure 3-11, a CPU constantly iterates through this four-step process:

▸ Fetching instructions and data ▸ Decoding instructions ▸ Executing instructions ▸ Storing results

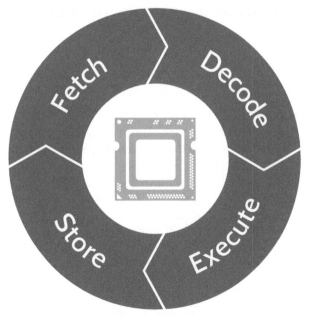

Figure 3-11: **Four-Step CPU Processing**

At their essence, CPUs solve problems.

Processor States

From a security perspective, CPUs operate in one of two processor states: the supervisor or problem state. These states can also be thought of as privilege levels and are simply **operating modes for the processor that restrict the operations that can be performed by certain processes.** A summary of their characteristics is provided in Table 3-13.

Supervisor State	Problem State
<ul><li>Higher privilege level</li><li>Typically, where the system kernel runs, allowing full access to all of the instructions and capabilities of a CPU</li></ul>	<ul><li>Lower privilege level</li><li>Limited access to CPU instructions</li><li>The standard operating mode of a CPU</li><li>Known as "problem" state because fundamentally this is what a CPU does: solve problems</li></ul>

Table 3-13: **Processor States**

3.4.3 Process Isolation

CORE **CONCEPTS**
- **Prevents interactions that could result in negative consequences**
- **Two primary methods: memory segmentation and time-division multiplexing**

If two applications are running on a computer, should one application be able to access the memory of the other application and manipulate it? Not really, unless the applications are specifically designed to allow interaction. If this was allowed, data could be corrupted, and inappropriate access could take place. A worst-case scenario could be one of the running processes accessing the operating system, which is another process. Processes need to be separated.

From a security perspective, process isolation is a critical element of computing, as it prevents objects from interacting with each other and their resources.

In other words, **the actions of one object should not affect the state of other objects.**

Process isolation is often accomplished using either of the two following methods:

- Memory segmentation
- Time-division multiplexing

Time-division multiplexing relates more to the CPU. With time-division multiplexing, process isolation is determined by the CPU. As before, when multiple applications are running, multiple accompanying processes are also running. In this case, the **CPU allocates very small slots of time to each process.** In reality, due to the extremely fast nature of even a slow CPU, being able to run multiple applications at the same time appears seamless. Under the hood, though, each application's process is running in isolation, based upon the CPU's processing time allocation.

Memory segmentation is all about separating memory segments from each other to protect the contents, including processes that may be running in those segments. In many cases it relates more to **Random-Access Memory (RAM)**—the high-speed volatile storage area found in computer systems. When applications are launched, a "loading" or "starting application" message sometimes accompanies that process. What's actually taking place is program code is being moved from the hard drive into RAM, because hard drives tend to be much slower than RAM. With code in RAM, when the CPU makes a request, subsequent processing can happen faster. However, if code from several different applications is loaded into RAM at the same time, one application shouldn't be able to access code from another application.

Memory segmentation ensures that the memory assigned to one application is only accessible by that application. Based upon application needs, segments of memory are isolated and assigned to each application, and no other application should be able to access that particular segment, as depicted in Figure 3-12.

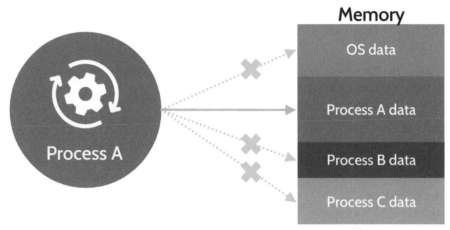

Figure 3-12: **Memory Use**

The process isolation methods are summarized in Table 3-14.

Memory Segmentation	Time-Division Multiplexing
Utilizes RAM and ensures that memory assigned to an application is not accessible by another application	CPU divides time into slices and allocates slots of time to different processes

Table 3-14: **Process Isolation Methods**

3.4.4 Types of Storage

CORE **CONCEPTS**
- **Two types of storage: primary and secondary storage**
- **Primary storage is fast and volatile**
- **Secondary storage is slow and non-volatile**

The topic of storage, briefly mentioned earlier, requires a bit more elaboration. Storage is where data in a computer system can be found. At a high level, two main types of storage exist: primary and secondary storage. Table 3-15 shows the characteristics of each type.

Primary Storage	Secondary Storage
▪ Fast	▪ Slow
▪ Volatile—data is lost when device gets powered off	▪ Non-volatile
▪ Small size	▪ Large size
▪ Examples of primary storage:	▪ Examples of secondary storage:
▪ Cache	▪ Magnetic hard drives
▪ CPU registers	▪ Optical media
▪ RAM	▪ Tapes
	▪ SSD

Table 3-15: **Primary (Volatile) and Secondary (Non-volatile) Storage**

Primary storage is also sometimes referred to as *volatile memory*. With volatile memory, anything stored there is temporary. In other words, if the power goes out, for example, anything stored in volatile memory goes away. With non-volatile memory, if the power goes out, data remains. Examples of volatile (or primary storage) include RAM and cache, to name a couple. If the power to a system gets cut, any data stored in volatile memory goes away. That's a big disadvantage. However, the major advantage is speed; primary memory is extremely fast. Examples of secondary storage (non-volatile memory) include hard drives, tapes, discs (CD/DVD), and similar items.

Another related concept refers to what happens because of RAM filling up when many applications are running at the same time. Data related to each program and running process are loaded into RAM, and if RAM fills up, the system will eventually crash. A way to mitigate this is using what's known as paging, or **virtual memory**, as depicted in Figure 3-13. Even though multiple programs or processes might be running, the operating system keeps track of what is being accessed in RAM and how often. When data stored in RAM is not being used frequently, the operating system proactively moves it out of RAM and onto a portion of the hard drive dedicated for this purpose. This portion of the hard drive is often referred to as the "paging file" or virtual memory. When data stored in the paging file is needed, the operating system pulls it back into RAM. This process can lead to latency and slow performance, but it keeps a system from crashing; it's less of an issue today because RAM is inexpensive.

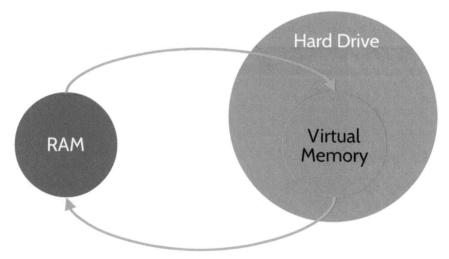

Figure 3-13: **Virtual Memory**

Figure 3-14 depicts the major differences between primary (volatile) and secondary (non-volatile) storage.

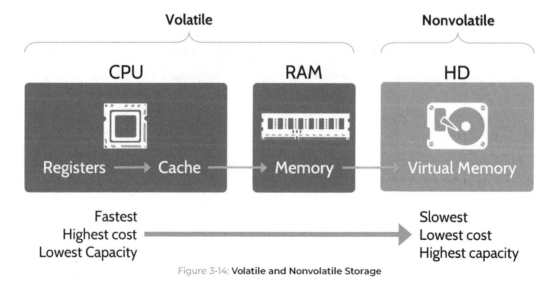

Figure 3-14: **Volatile and Nonvolatile Storage**

3.4.5 System Kernel

CORE **CONCEPTS**

- Core of the operating system that has complete control over everything in the system

- The system kernel and the security kernel are not the same thing.

- Relies on privilege levels for smooth and safe operation

The system kernel is the **core of the operating system** and **has complete control over everything in the system**. It has low-level control over all the fine details and operational components of the operating system. In essence, it has access to everything.

One important thing to note is that **the system kernel and the security kernel are not the same thing**. As noted, the **system kernel** drives the operating system. The **security kernel** is the implementation of the reference monitor concept.

From a security perspective, it's critical to protect the system kernel and ensure that it is operating correctly, and privilege levels aid in this regard.

3.4.6 Privilege Levels

> CORE **CONCEPTS**
>
> - Privilege levels establish operational trust boundaries for software running on a computer.
> - User mode results in lower trust and only allows access to a small subset of system capabilities.
> - Privileged mode, also known as kernel mode, results in higher trust and allows access to more system capabilities.
> - The ring protection model describes a form of CPU layering that is designed to protect critical elements of a computing system.

Figure 3-15 depicts the relation between user and kernel modes.

Subjects of **higher trust** (e.g., the System kernel) can access more system capabilities and operate in **kernel mode**. Subjects **with lower trust** (most applications running on a computer) can only access a smaller portion of system capabilities and operate in **user mode**.

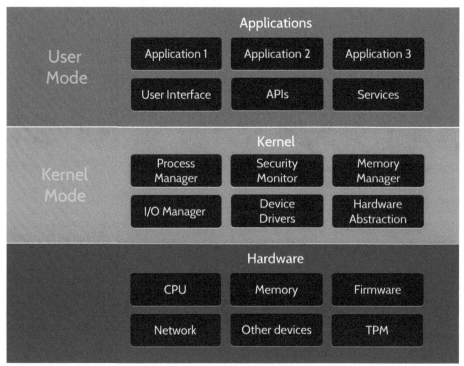

Figure 3-15: **User and Kernel Modes**

Ring Protection Model

The ring protection model, depicted in Figure 3-16, is a form of conceptual layering that segregates and protects operational domains from each other. Ring 0 is the most trusted and therefore the most secure ring. Firmware and other critical system-related processes run in Ring 0. Ring 3 (user programs and applications) on the other hand, is the least trusted and secure level, where the least access exists to protect the kernel from unwanted side effects like malware infecting the machine. The idea behind the model is that each ring communicates with the adjacent ring via system calls, and the outer rings can only communicate with the inner rings via the most trusted system calls.

> Which ring is most critical from a security point of view and would likely support things like firmware and other critical system-related processes

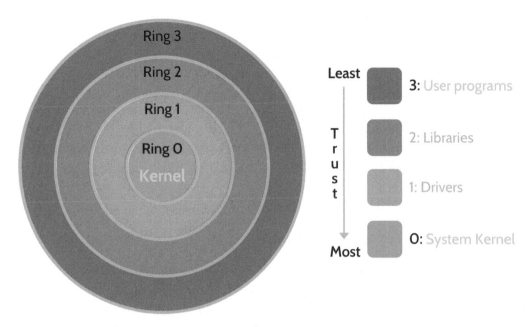

Figure 3-16: **Protection Rings**

Firmware

Firmware is software that provides low-level control of hardware systems; it's the code that boots up hardware and brings it online. One of the challenges with firmware is that it is no longer hard-coded; therefore, it can be updated and modified, which makes it vulnerable to attacks. Changeable, updateable, or modifiable, firmware means that hardware itself is now vulnerable to attacks.

3.4.7 Middleware

> CORE **CONCEPTS**
> ▪ **Middleware acts as an intermediary between two applications.**
> ▪ **Middleware is a layer of software that can speak the languages of two disparate applications and thereby facilitate communication between them.**

The idea of middleware is it's an intermediary; it's a layer of software that enables interoperability (glue) between otherwise incompatible applications. Think of mobile banking as an example. With mobile banking, a mobile device application exists that allows bank balances to be checked, funds transferred, and so on. However, what types of systems do most bank software run on? Most big banks, especially older ones, run on mainframe systems designed decades ago. When those systems were first designed, there wasn't any concept of mobile and web-based banking. A mainframe system doesn't fundamentally understand APIs or things like web-based banking. If an older bank wants to develop a mobile application that can communicate with an underlying mainframe system, something needs to exist between the application and the mainframe to allow that. A translator—middleware—must be present. Middleware is an intermediary that allows disparate applications to communicate with each other. The mobile application speaks one language; the mainframe speaks another. Middleware speaks both languages and can thereby enable communication between two completely different systems that otherwise could not communicate with each other. In Figure 3-17, the middle circle represents the software that acts as middleware, which allows a mobile application (Application A) and a mainframe computer (Application B) to communicate with each other.

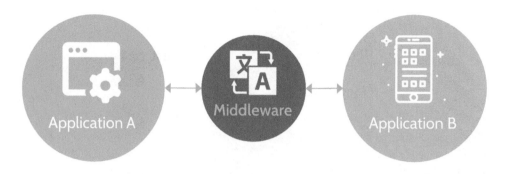

Figure 3-17: **Middleware Representation**

3.4.8 Abstraction and Virtualization

CORE **CONCEPTS**

- Abstraction refers to the underlying complexity and details of a system being hidden.

- Examples of abstraction include driving a car and computing.

- Virtualization extends the computing example further.

Abstraction

Abstraction is a concept that is used extensively in computing. It is an idea that the underlying complexity and details of a system are hidden. Think of driving a car. To the driver, the act of driving involves simple steps that essentially boil down to inserting a key or pushing a button (newer models), putting the car in gear, and driving—using the steering wheel, accelerator, and brakes as necessary. However, while all of this is happening, a significant amount of abstraction is taking place. A driver does not need to worry about how the engine works, or the hydraulic or electrical system, or any other components that ultimately make a car run. All this underlying complexity has been abstracted from the seeming simplicity of hopping in the car and driving away.

Abstraction is also used in programming. CPUs, at their core, understand 1s and 0s. From a human perspective, however, 1s and 0s are very hard to understand, and over the years numerous iterations of programming languages have evolved and abstracted the complexity of computing to human-readable form.

Virtualization

Carrying the concept of abstraction further, **virtualization is the process of creating a virtual version of something to abstract away from the true underlying hardware or software.** Specifically, to facilitate virtualization, a hypervisor is employed. A hypervisor serves as a layer of abstraction between underlying physical hardware and virtual machines (VMs).

3.4.9 Layering/Defense-in-Depth

CORE **CONCEPTS**

- Protection of an asset is best accomplished through the implementation of multiple control layers.

Another important concept is the concept of layered defense or defense-in-depth. What this simply means is the protection of a valuable asset should never rely on just one control. If that control fails, the asset would be unprotected. Instead, multiple control layers should be implemented, and the control at each layer should be a complete control—a combination of preventive, detective, and corrective controls. Let's look more closely at this in the context of an example and while also considering the depiction of defense in depth provided in Figure 3-18.

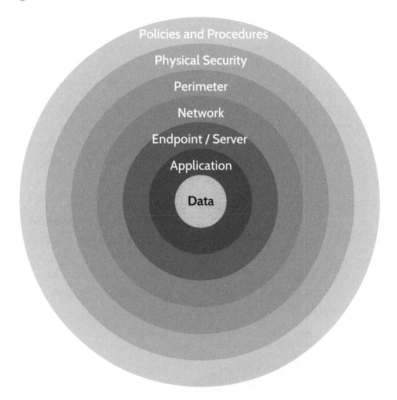

Figure 3-18: **Defense in Depth**

How many layers of defense does a company use to store and protect research and development information? Undoubtedly there's a fence around the building that could be serving as the first layer of defense. In addition, there might be CCTV cameras, and the fence could even be electric. The combination of these controls is preventive, detective, and corrective, thus constituting a complete control. After the fence, guards might be patrolling the area regularly. Next is the perimeter of the building. Similar to the fence, a combination of preventive, detective, and corrective controls exist. Walls, more cameras, and security guards collectively act as another layer of defense. Once inside the building, interior walls and locked doors are in place. Let's imagine that all these controls have somehow been bypassed, and someone reaches the computer system or the server room where highly sensitive data is stored. The system would need to be logged on to, and the related files would need to be identified and then unencrypted. As should be clear, there is a combination of preventive, detective, and corrective controls at each layer. This is the concept of layered security, where multiple layers of controls exist. If there's a failure at one layer, controls at other layers can effectively protect whatever valuable asset, like sensitive research and development data.

3.4.10 **Trusted Platform Modules (TPM)**

CORE **CONCEPTS**

- A trusted platform module (TPM) is a piece of hardware that implements an ISO standard, resulting in the ability to establish trust involving security and privacy.

- A TPM is an independent component of a computing system and functions similarly to a black box.

- Binding and sealing are important elements that help a TPM maintain integrity.

A TPM is a chip that performs cryptographic operations like key generation and storage in addition to platform integrity. For example, when a machine boots the TPM can be used to identify if there has been any tampering of critical system components, in which case the system wouldn't boot. So, a TPM is a piece of hardware—usually installed on the motherboard—that incorporates the international standard denoted by ISO/IEC 11889 on computing devices, like desktop and laptop computers, and mobile devices, among others.

In many ways, a TPM is a black box, meaning that commands can be sent to the TPM, but information stored within the TPM cannot be extracted. TPMs do not rely on an operating system or components external to the device for processing instructions; they have their own internal circuits and firmware. Furthermore, every TPM chip is unique because a unique and secret endorsement key is burned into the chip during production. An endorsement key is a special purpose RSA key that remains hidden and can only be used for encryption, which allows for TPM authentication.

Computers that contain a TPM can create cryptographic keys and encrypt them—using the endorsement key—so only the TPM can be used for decryption. This process is known as **binding**, and it helps protect the key from being disclosed. Computers can also create a bound key that is also associated with certain computer configuration settings and parameters. This key can only be unbound when the configuration settings and parameters match the values at the time the key was created. This process is known as **sealing**, and it refers to associating the key to the TPM. Binding and sealing are particularly important as it relates to maintaining the integrity of the TPM host computing device.

3.5 Assess and mitigate the vulnerabilities of security architectures, designs, and solution elements

3.5.1 Vulnerabilities in Systems

CORE **CONCEPTS**

- A single point of failure is something that, if failure is realized, will result in negative operational impact.

- Redundancy can help alleviate the risk associated with a single point of failure, and it should be implemented where it is cost-justifiable.

- Bypass controls are a potential vulnerability, and their existence creates risks.

- The risks associated with bypass controls can be mitigated using segregation of duties, logging and monitoring, and physical security.

- Time-of-Check Time-of-Use (TOCTOU), also known as a race condition, represents a short window between two events, typically when something is used and when authorization for that use is checked.

- Frequent access or authorization checks can reduce the risk of race conditions.

- Emanations are unseen elements leaking out of systems that might reveal confidential and valuable information if captured and analyzed with the proper equipment.

- Shielding, white noise, and control zones can prevent emanations from being captured.

Single Point of Failure

What does the term *single point of failure* mean? To answer this question, let's examine Figure 3-19.

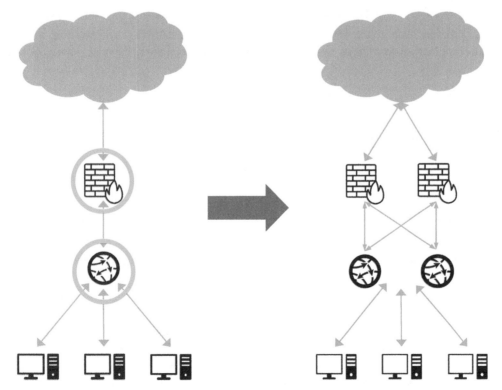

Figure 3-19: **Single Point of Failure**

The cloud represents the internet. Below it, the brick wall with the flame represents a firewall. Next, the ball with arrows pointing at every direction is a router. Finally, below the router are several computer systems. **What are the single points of failure in the diagram?** In this example, the firewall and the router are each considered a single point of failure; if *either* device fails, the connection to the internet is broken. In other words, a single point of failure means that when a single device or connection fails, it impacts the entire architecture.

Reduce Risk of Single Point of Failure

Single points of failure can become very dangerous for any organization and need to be dealt with accordingly, usually by implementing *redundancy*. Looking at the previous example, two firewalls and two routers could be installed to create redundancy and mitigate the risk of single points of failure. Each pair can be configured in what is known as "high availability" so that if firewall 1 fails, traffic can be rerouted through firewall 2; if router 1 fails, traffic can be rerouted through router 2. However, one point that's critical to keep in mind is that redundancy may not be feasible everywhere because it can be very costly. Firewalls and routers are expensive but often necessary. However, a solution like this should only be implemented where doing so is cost-justified.

Bypass Controls

Bypass controls are a potential vulnerability or new source of risk, but *they are intentional*. Let's examine this concept through an example: You need to access the administrative settings of your home router, but for some reason you can't remember the password you set up last time you did this. Being able to perform a factory reset of that device would allow you to enter the configuration utility with default credentials and set up the device from scratch.

The reset process is a bypass control—it's intentional. In the above example, if the primary method of entering the root password fails, it might need to be reset. Bypass controls are intentional for situations just like the one described. They are intentionally built into systems, and they need to be there.

Reduce Risk of Bypass Controls

The addition of bypass controls creates new risks. For example, if someone can gain physical access to a firewall, router, or similar system, they can reset the device. **Bypass controls are needed, and other compensating controls should always be implemented with them to mitigate or prevent their exploitation.** For example, physical security can be leveraged to protect the bypass control from being used. Only authorized people should have physical access to these devices. It's also worth noting that a bypass control isn't a covert channel because a covert channel is *unintentional* while a bypass control is intentional.

Ways to mitigate the risk associated with bypass controls include:

- Segregation of duties
- Logging and monitoring
- Physical security

TOCTOU or Race Condition

What is TOCTOU? This stands for "Time-of-Check Time-of-Use" and essentially represents a short window of time between when something is used and when authorization or access for that use is checked. In other words, in that short time period, something unintended or malicious can transpire. This is also sometimes known as a *race condition*. A user or process attempts to "race in" and make changes to a system before another check to confirm that access is still appropriate. For example, assume there's 2 GB of RAM free and process 1 needs to use 1 GB. It checks and sees that is available. At the same time, process 2 needs 1.5 GB and checks and sees that it is available. A few milliseconds later, process 1 uses 1 GB, and immediately after that process 2 attempts to use 1.5 GB but is unable to, as that's not available anymore, so it unexpectedly crashes. That's an example of a race condition.

Reduce Risk of Race Conditions

To mitigate the risk of race conditions, the frequency of access checks should increase. The more frequent the checks, the greater the frequency of re-authentication, thus reducing the overall risk. However, frequent prompts to re-authenticate could also frustrate users; systems would be very secure, but no work would be accomplished if a user needs to authenticate every fifteen minutes. So, a balance between security and functionality is important.

Emanations

Emanations manifest in the form of unseen things leaking out of systems, like radio or magnetic waves, light, sound, and so on. Examples of radio waves would be Bluetooth and Wi-Fi, to name a couple, while magnetic waves would include waves from hard drives and similar devices.

Emanations represent a valid security concern since any time a device is emanating, valuable data could be available that a properly equipped eavesdropper or system could collect. An example could be something as simple as shoulder surfing, where someone is looking over the shoulder of a user and reading what's on the screen, which is emanating light. Someone can look over the shoulder, see that light, and read what's on the screen. Other much more complicated and advanced ways of doing this exist too. Emanations can potentially be intercepted and unauthorized information gathered as a result. Various ways exist to protect from emanation as described in Table 3-16.

Shielding (TEMPEST)	Proper walls, Faraday cage use, copper-lined envelopes that prevent sensitive information from leaking out or being intercepted; TEMPEST is a specific technology that prevents emanations from a device
White Noise	Strong signal of random noise emanated where sensitive information is being processed
Control Zones	Preventing access or proximity to locations where sensitive information is being processed

Table 3-16: **Emanation Protection**

Shielding is one of the best ways to prevent emanations. Shielding could be as simple as putting up a wall. Walls with no windows could be installed around an office to protect from shoulder surfing or unauthorized access. More complicated shielding is needed when dealing with electromagnetic emanations, radio waves, and similar, and this is usually accomplished through use of a Faraday cage. Examples of Faraday cages could be the sophisticated installations at very secure facilities or something as simple as a copper-lined envelope that prevents emanations from things like RFID cards. These are forms of shielding, which mitigate emanations.

There's one specific type of shielding that is particularly important to know: TEMPEST. This is a specific technology created to protect military equipment from things like electromagnetic pulses and from eavesdropping.

Another way to mitigate or prevent emanations is using **white noise**. White noise is a strong signal of random noise emanated amid offices, where computers might be used to process sensitive information. Most emanations from computer systems are weak, and the stronger signal of random noise prevents the weaker computer signals from being intercepted.

Finally, using **control zones** to prevent access or proximity to a device is another way to prevent emanations from being intercepted. As most emanations are very weak and only are available in a short distance, if someone can't get near the related devices, they can't intercept the signal. So, the last way to mitigate or prevent emanations is using control zones, which are basically just physical security. If different layers of physical security exist that prevent someone from getting near a device, the ability to pick up the emanations is eliminated.

3.5.2 Hardening

> **CORE CONCEPTS**
>
> - Hardening is the process of looking at individual components of a system and then securing each component to reduce the overall vulnerability of the system.

Vulnerabilities in Systems

Let's focus on different vulnerabilities and types of systems. This will be done in the context of mobile devices, desktops, laptops, servers, and so on. However, before moving forward, it's worth taking a step back and focusing on the fact that, at a basic level, all these devices share much in common. They all consist of hardware components (like a CPU and RAM) and all have operating systems and software applications. To protect them, they need to be broken down into components, and each component would need to be secured. Each component within a given device is secured based on value.

Organizational relevance is another term you need to be familiar with, and it indicates how valuable something is to the organization. This is a term you could possibly see on the exam, and you need to remember that it implies value.

Reduce Risk in Client and Server-Based Systems

Examples of hardening include doing things like disabling unnecessary services on a computer system or uninstalling software that shouldn't be there (like an SFTP server running on a user's endpoint). A service represents a small subset of code running on a system for a particular reason. Most computer systems consist of numerous running services, which directly relates to the potential attack surface they have. The more complicated the system and the more running services are present, the greater the attack surface becomes. Contrarily, the simpler and less complex the system, the smaller the attack surface will be, which makes it more difficult for an attacker to find a way into that system. Disabling unnecessary services, updating the operating system, and patching the machines are important parts of system hardening. Other ways to harden systems include:

HARDENING

Disable unnecessary services
Install security patches
Close certain ports
Install anti-malware
Install host-based firewall/IDS
Use encryption
Strong passwords
Backups

- Installation of antivirus software

- Installation of host-based IDS/IPS and firewall

- Perform device configuration reviews

- Implementation of full-disk encryption

- Enforcement of strong passwords

- Obtaining routine system backups

- Implement sufficient logging and monitoring

To make hardening efficient, it's imperative that business requirements be understood. The most important question to ask is, "What is this system meant to do?" That will guide the hardening effort. If a system is supposed to act as a web server, then it shouldn't have fifty different ports open and services installed, as that heavily increases an attacker's chances of breaching it. As most systems contain a significant number of settings and configuration options that need to be considered, hardening checklists should be followed to ensure everything is set properly. Most vendors publish hardening guides for their systems. If a vendor checklist does not exist, Center for Internet Security (CIS) and similar organizations publish hardening guidelines, which are great starting points and can then be customized as needed. Each time a system is deployed, a hardening procedure should be followed, and after each hardening process the resulting configuration should be verified to confirm the system is working as expected. Ideally, the initial and ongoing verification process should be automated (especially for larger environments), but whether manual or automated, it's a critical aspect of the hardening process.

> **What drives hardening decisions?**

3.5.3 Risk in Mobile Systems

CORE CONCEPTS

- Mobile device management (MDM) and mobile application management (MAM) solutions help organizations secure devices and the applications that run on them.
- Mobile device management solutions should particularly focus on securing remote access using a VPN and end-point security as well as securing applications on the device through application whitelisting.

Mobile Devices

Mobile devices are devices like iPhones, Android phones, iPads, and similar. They're small-form factor computing devices that are unbelievably powerful for their size and are typically carried in pockets and purses. The fact that they're small and powerful can allow them to store and access so much data and their mobility presents significant risk to most organizations.

Reduce Risk in Mobile-based Systems

Mobile devices are built in small sizes so their owners can carry them around easily, which is exactly why they are also often lost or stolen. This fact leads most organizations to install additional security controls on them. Mobile Device Management (MDM) and Mobile Application Management (MAM) software help organizations secure devices and the applications that run on them. For example, MDM software allows a security administrator to perform tasks like enforcing different security controls or even wiping a device remotely, and mobile application management (MAM) software can secure applications that interact with corporate data. Note that oftentimes the two are included within a single application.

> **What is the primary difference between MDM and MAM?**

MDM and MAM can be combined with policy enforcement, application of device encryption, and related policies to adequately protect mobile devices if they are lost or stolen.

Policies: One of the best ways to reduce risk related to mobile devices is using policies, like: Acceptable Use, Personal Computers, BYOD/CYOD (Bring Your Own Device/Choose Your Own Device), and Education, Awareness, and Training.

> **What are ways to reduce risk associated with mobile devices and workers?**

Process related to lost or stolen devices: Typically, this involves notification of IT and security personnel as well as a means by which the device can be remotely wiped. Note that remotely wiping is dependent upon the device being connected to the internet and a savvy attacker can easily prevent this from happening.

Remote access security: VPN and 2FA capabilities should be enabled by default, to prevent a mobile device from being used to connect to a remote network in an insecure manner (e.g., when a corporate employee is connecting to the company servers while located in a hotel, airport, or café during a business trip).

What is the best remote access security approach for mobile devices?

Endpoint security: Antivirus/malware, DLP, and similar MDM-provisioned software should be installed on mobile devices just like standard computing equipment. Additionally, the concept of hardening should be employed to minimize the potential attack surface of the devices.

Application whitelisting: Organizations should control which applications users may install on their mobile device through application whitelisting and not allow them to install anything not present on the approved application list.

3.5.4 OWASP Mobile Top 10

> CORE **CONCEPTS**
> - OWASP Mobile Top 10
> - The OWASP Mobile Security Testing Guide is a manual for mobile application security testing and reverse engineering for mobile security testers.

The Open Web Application Security Project (OWASP) Foundation is an organization that is driven by community-led efforts dedicated to improving the security of software, including software and applications that run on mobile devices. Among OWASP's many substantial contributions to the security community are the globally recognized OWASP Top 10 and OWASP Mobile Top 10 lists that conform data from a variety of sources like security vendors and consultancies, bug bounties, and numerous organizations located around the world. The key element collected in every case is the Common Weakness Enumeration (CWE) and associated software or hardware that contain the CWE. In addition to collected data, OWASP surveys members of the community to identify potential new categories for inclusion in the Top 10.

OWASP Mobile Top 10 adheres loosely to OWASP Top 10 methodology, with the focus and categories being on mobile applications. The recent OWASP Mobile Top 10 is listed in Table 3-17.

M1	Improper Platform Usage
M2	Insecure Data Storage
M3	Insecure Communication
M4	Insecure Authentication
M5	Insufficient Cryptography
M6	Insecure Authorization
M7	Poor Client Code Quality
M8	Code Tampering
M9	Reverse Engineering
M10	Extraneous Functionality

Table 3-17: **OWASP Mobile Top 10**

For each identified risk, specific details about it can be found, including threat agents, attack vectors, security weakness, technical impacts, and business impacts, as well as ways to prevent or mitigate the risk. From the perspective of a security professional, this type of information is invaluable, especially as the Top 10 list reflects a large cross section of global organizations and businesses and is updated according to industry feedback about attacks and vulnerabilities.

What are the top vulnerabilities on mobile devices?

In addition to the valuable information provided in the OWASP Mobile Top 10 list, the OWASP Foundation is developing a security standard for mobile applications, which will help in security testing and reverse engineering, which is called the Mobile Security Testing Guide (MSTG). Lastly, another interesting OWASP project is Mobile Application Security Verification Standard (MASVS), which helps identify a security baseline for mobile applications.

What is the OWASP Mobile Security Testing Guide?

3.5.5 Distributed Systems

CORE **CONCEPTS**

- Distributed systems are systems that are spread out and can communicate with each other across a network. The internet is a great example of a distributed system.

- Distributed file systems are systems where files are spread across multiple hosts and made available via sharing across a network.

- Grid systems are interconnected systems that are usually working together to solve a specific and usually very complex problem.

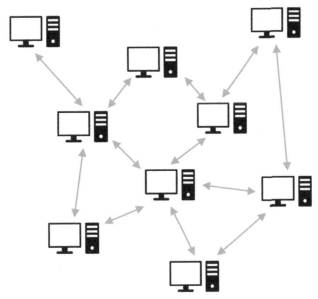

Figure 3-20: **Distributed Systems**

Distributed systems are a number of different systems that are networked together and can communicate with each other as depicted in Figure 3-20. A great example of the world's largest distributed system is the internet. A company network is an example of a distributed system. Although there is significant value in connecting the systems within an organization and then connecting the organization to the internet, there are also significant risks, such as providing a means for potential attackers to gain access to the corporate network and cause mayhem (data breaches, denial-of-service, ransomware, etc.).

What is an underlying risk related to distributed file systems (DFS)?

Distributed file systems (DFS) take the concept of distributed systems a step further by allowing files to be hosted by multiple hosts and shared and accessed across a network. DFS software helps manage the files being hosted and presents them to users as if they're stored in one central location.

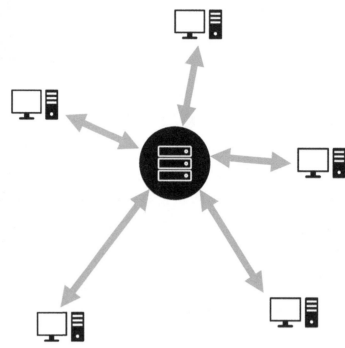

Figure 3-21: **Grid Computing**

Grid Computing

Grid computing, depicted in Figure 3-21, is like distributed systems as it still relates to systems that are connected together, but the thinking behind grid systems is that they're usually connected via a very high-speed connection to serve a greater purpose than simply passing the occasional email or file back and forth. Rather, grid systems are multiple systems working together to solve very complex problems that require more computing power that one system can provide; so, a number of systems are interconnected into a grid and programmed to work in unison to solve difficult problems.

A very interesting example of grid computing is the Search for Extraterrestrial Intelligence (SETI). SETI is a non-profit organization with the stated mission of searching for extraterrestrial life—they were looking for aliens. As a non-profit, SETI does not have access to significant amounts of funding to support their mission. Many years ago, they started a very interesting program based upon short periods of time SETI researchers had access to radio telescopes. When a researcher was done with their research project, there might be a few hours where the radio telescope went unused before another researcher began using it. During the hours of unused telescope time, SETI would point the telescope at a portion of the sky and record significant amounts of data. Not surprisingly, SETI accumulated tons of data, but they had no way to easily process it because high-powered computers are very expensive. Within the data, SETI researchers were looking for signals or patterns that might indicate alien communications. With seemingly no solution to the large data-set analysis needed, SETI solved the problem very creatively. They created a screensaver called SETI at Home, and anybody could download and run it on their computer. When a computer was idle and the screensaver activated, it would download a small chunk of the radio telescope data and process it. While processing, the screensaver displayed a cool visualization depicting what was happening, and the idea quickly resonated with people around the world. Millions of people around the globe downloaded and installed SETI at Home on their home computer and processed these little chunks of data. And in doing so they essentially created the world's largest distributed grid computer.

What's the security risk with grid computing?

Looking at the SETI at Home example, what happens if someone's computer sends inaccurate results? Does this skew a bigger subset of data? So, data integrity and data validation are relevant facets of the concept.

Likewise, inappropriate use of the grid computer is another. Here's an example of misuse: A group of Russian nuclear physicists were working in Siberia and had access to a mainframe system for simulating nuclear explosions and similar scenarios. After some time, they decided to stop using the mainframe for research and switched to cryptocurrency mining. Their new "research" was discovered, likely by a three-letter name Russian agency, which resulted in a permanent move somewhere even more remote than Siberia.

3.5.6 Inference and Aggregation

CORE **CONCEPTS**

- ▪ **Data warehouse**
- ▪ **Big data**
- ▪ **Data mining/analytics**
- ▪ **Inference and aggregation**
- ▪ **Reduce the risk of unauthorized inference and aggregation**

Data Warehouse

Figure 3-22: **Data Warehouse**

The idea behind a data warehouse, depicted in Figure 3-22, is to perform data analytics from a number of different data sets, with the hope of identifying interesting bits of information. Data warehouses are not new and in fact have been around for decades. The problem with them relates to the desire to analyze data from multiple data sets that are stored in different systems; it's challenging to do this, because each data set essentially resides on its own island. A common term related to data warehouses is *data island*, and it's used in the form of a question: "Where are the data islands located?" As this question alludes, the premise of a data warehouse is that all the data from these islands is brought together in one central location. Once in one location, the data is much easier to analyze and to search for trends and other interesting nuggets of information.

What are the security risks related to a data warehouse?

For a couple of reasons, it could be a single point of failure. The first relates to availability. If the data warehouse goes down, access to valuable data insights could be lost. The second relates to the fact that if someone gains unauthorized access to the data warehouses, they could have access to significant amounts of valuable information. So, in addition to some type of redundancy or a good backup plan, access control is an important topic to consider. When data is stored in multiple locations, fine-grained access control is easy. Only the finance people have access to finance data, HR people to HR data, and so on. When data from multiple locations is brought together in one location, managing access control becomes a much more complex issue.

Big Data

Unlike data warehouses, which have been around for some time now, big data is relatively new and has become very popular. The gist of big data is this: data from many different locations is brought into a central repository to be analyzed. On the surface, this sounds very similar to a data warehouse. What's the difference? Three things: variety, volume, and velocity.

Variety means that data can be pulled from a number of different sources. In a data warehouse, only relational data can be stored, only data in a clean table format, with rows and columns. In big data, just about anything can be stored—a text file, an Excel file, a Word document, etc. This fact represents the variety that can be found within a big data repository.

Volume refers to the size of the data sets. With a data warehouse, storage is typically restricted to the storage capacity of a single system; with big data, storage spans multiple systems. Think about this in the context of Google, arguably the best-known big data creator and consumer. When Google first started, what did it do? It indexed the entire internet, and it did so through the creation and use of an open source tool called Hadoop. Google wanted to determine the location of everything on the internet, which resulted in an enormous data set. When a query for anything on the internet was made, Google wanted results to be returned in milliseconds. Google is so proud of query results that it displays the amount of time a search takes. Google invented a number of technologies that enabled them to store vast data sets across many servers and to be able to perform analytic searches across this massive data set very quickly. The technologies built by Google eventually ended up in Hadoop and similar tools. Google wasn't the only one to invent tools like Hadoop, but it's companies like Google that invented ways of dealing with these big data problems. This is the volume part; enormous volume sets can be stored in big data.

Velocity refers to the fact that data can be ingested and analyzed very rapidly in big data—even faster than is possible with data warehouses.

Examples of big data tools include Hadoop, MongoDB, and Tableau.

Data Mining and Analytics

The primary driver behind data warehouses and big data is the desire to identify trends and other interesting insights. Through the analysis of seemingly disparate data, otherwise invisible relationships and little nuggets of valuable information can be gleaned. These insights are typically referred to as *inference* and *aggregation*. Aggregation pulls data into one location. Inference tries to infer things; it tries to identify bits of information in the data. As the rest of this section and the examples will show, **inference, especially unauthorized inference, can create a significant risk to an organization.**
Unauthorized inference can take information from the hands of key decision makers or secure systems and expose it to an entire organization, the competition, or even to the enemy.

Here's a real-life example that helps illustrate. A large retailer had been sending pregnancy-related advertisements and coupons to someone's teenage daughter without that person even knowing their daughter was pregnant. How did they know this fact? It was all about what she had purchased in the previous days and weeks. Basically, they were looking at her buying habits as they employ many data scientists who focus on identifying really interesting nuggets of information based upon consumer buying habits. They look at the massive data sets gathered from all their stores and can figure out trends and, in this case, that a particular consumer was interested in pregnancy-related items. Note that this isn't something illegal, as they were merely analyzing available consumer data. This event made national news, but they didn't stop their practices of mining and analyzing data in order to send targeted advertising; they simply grew more savvy in their approach. Now, instead of a full booklet of pregnancy-related items, a lawn mower, a pool table, and other non-pregnancy-related items are included in the advertisement to better disguise things.

Inference and aggregation can obviously cause problems for organizations. Another example where this can be an even greater issue is in a large bank. Most large banks have multiple divisions, including a brokerage arm—stock traders—as well as a mergers and acquisitions (M&A) arm, which focuses on helping companies raise money in the equities and debt markets, purchase companies, and so on. In this context, the bank's stock traders would love to know what the M&A folks are doing because they could then offer the best trade advice to their customers. But that's not allowed, as it would constitute insider trading. Banks must be very careful to prevent insider trading by preventing employees from inferring things they're not supposed to know. To summarize, Table 3-18 denotes the definitions of aggregation and inference.

Aggregation	Inference
Collecting, gathering, or combining data for the purpose of statistical analysis	Deducing information from evidence and reasoning rather than from explicit statements

Table 3-18: **Aggregation and Inference**

Reduce Risk of Inference and Aggregation

One method to reduce the risk of unauthorized inference is using "polyinstantiation," which allows information to exist in different classification levels for the purpose of preventing unauthorized inference and aggregation (note that more detail about this will be provided in Domain 8).

> **Understand the difference between aggregation and inference and how inference can be mitigated**

3.5.7 Industrial Control Systems (ICS)

> CORE **CONCEPTS**
>
> - Industrial control system (ICS) is a general term used to describe control systems related to industrial processes and critical infrastructure.
>
> - Three primary types of ICSs: Supervisory Control and Data Acquisition (SCADA), Distributed Control System (DCS), Programmable Logic Controller (PLC)
>
> - Due to their inherent complexity and the things they help control/manage, ICS can be quite vulnerable to attack; the best way to reduce risk to ICS is to keep them offline—to "air gap" them from direct or indirect access to the internet.

Industrial control system (ICS) is a general term used to describe control systems (hardware and software) used in industrial processes and critical infrastructure. ICSs are the computer systems and software that control things like power grids, nuclear power plants, automobile manufacturing plants, and similar systems. They are mission critical and very sophisticated with one of the inherent challenges being the specialized software they require. If the software for a power grid or nuclear power plant malfunctions, the consequences can be dire, and it may even result in loss of life. This type of software requires considerable oversight. However, because of the high level of customization an attempt to upgrade the OS, for example, may render the component non-functional. For example, if it was designed to run on Windows XP, an upgrade of that system to Windows 7 could cause the customized software to break. So, a huge challenge with ICS is they are often running on antiquated hardware and software. In addition, nobody wants to tamper with them out of fear that doing so could render them inoperable. As a result, these components that control very important and critical functions can be running on very insecure systems.

Reduce Risk in Industrial Control Systems

One of the best ways to protect ICS is keeping them offline, also known as "air gapping" or creating an "air gap." What this simply means is that ICS devices can communicate with each other, but the ICS network is not connected to the internet or even the corporate network in any way. So, even if someone does try to connect to these ICS systems from the internet or corporate network, they'll be unable to do so.

> **Understand the risk associated with ICS and how best to reduce this risk**

Patching Industrial Control Systems

Industrial control systems by their very nature are difficult to maintain, especially where security is concerned. Often patching of ICS has been avoided, as patching these critical systems may cause unintended consequences and downtime. However, the ubiquitous and far-reaching nature of modern networks (where organizational and ICS networks now often share many of the same pathways, and the use of "smart" technology further blurs the lines and increases potential attack surfaces) requires that ICS be patched when needed. Strong configuration management processes, good patch management and backup/archive plans, and so on should be in place and used when and where possible. When patching ICS systems is not possible (or not possible to the degree needed), additional mitigating steps can be taken to reduce the risk and impact of disruption of critical infrastructure:

> **Understand the implications of patching ICS or alternative ways to mitigate risk if patching is not possible**

- Implement nonstop logging and monitoring and anomaly detection systems to rapidly detect nefarious activities within ICS networks.

- Conduct regular vulnerability assessments of ICS networks, with particular focus on connections to the internet or direct connections to internet-connected systems, rogue devices, and plaintext authentication.

> **Understand each type of ICS at a high level**

- Use VLANs and zoning techniques to mitigate or prevent an attacker from pivoting to other neighboring systems if the ICS is breached.

Additionally, privileged access management and privilege task automation tools can potentially be deployed to help manage risks associated with legacy systems often found within ICS.

The three major types of ICS that should be recognized are described in Table 3-19.

SCADA (Supervisory Control and Data Acquisition)	DCS (Distributed Control System)	PLC (Programmable Logic Controller)
■ System architecture that comprises computers, networking, and proprietary devices as well as graphical interfaces for management of the entire system ■ Used to manage small and large- scale industrial, infrastructure, and facility processes	■ Process control system that monitors, controls, and gathers data from components like controllers, sensors, and other devices typically found in large processing facilities. ■ Unlike SCADA, which includes local and remote management capabilities, DCS is typically controlled locally.	■ Industrial computer, specifically used for the control of manufacturing processes ■ Key features include high reliability, ease of programming and diagnosis of process problems. ■ Often networked with other PLC devices and SCADA systems

Table 3-19: **ICS Types**

3.5.8 Internet of Things (IoT)

> ### CORE **CONCEPTS**
> - Internet of Things (IoT) refers to all the devices, like home appliances, that are connected to the internet.
> - IoT devices, by their nature, are risky. Reducing their risk involves making different purchase decisions, taking every precaution when installing and keeping the technology up to date.

The term *Internet of Things (IoT)* refers to the multitude of devices that are connected to the internet and probably shouldn't be connected to it. IoT is the concept that tiny processing computers, the network cards that allow you to connect a device to the internet, have become so cheap that manufacturers are putting them in everything, including refrigerators, washing machines, dryers, cars, toasters, and so on. It seems that some type of network functionality is being installed in most similar devices these days. What's the risk here? Manufacturers are installing computer and networking technology into the things they build, but the technology being installed is mass-produced; the computer and networking technology is made very cheaply and contains little to no security. After a refrigerator is purchased, how often is built-in technology upgraded? How often is the firmware upgraded on a fridge? The answer to both questions is likely "Never." Nobody thinks about patching their toasters, so the issue persists and grows; very insecure devices are being installed in hardware with a refresh cycle of years. More to the point, very insecure devices are connected to home, and even business, networks. If somebody can remotely connect to one of these devices, they could potentially gain a foothold inside your network and use this access to pivot to bigger targets, like personal and business computers. This is a very real security problem.

Let's briefly touch on the topic of distributed-denial-of-service (DDoS) attack in the context of IoT. A DDoS attack takes place when many computer systems are harnessed together to create what's called a botnet. The botnet can then be used for malicious activities, including those aimed at only one victim. Because so much malicious traffic from so many different sources is aimed at that victim, it is commonly going to be brought offline. In 2016, one of the largest DDoS attacks in history occurred. A bug was found in security cameras and a malicious actor chose to exploit it. Think about it—millions of security cameras have been sold and installed throughout the world; they've been installed in homes, businesses, and anywhere else people might want visibility. Many of these cameras included cheap, mass-produced, highly insecure technology components mentioned earlier; thus, the cameras were IoT devices with zero security. The malicious actor identified a significant vulnerability in the camera IoT technology and proceeded to install malware on millions of cameras around the world; a botnet of massive proportions was created and then used to perpetrate one of the largest DDoS attacks in history. Security cameras and massive DDoS; ironic to say the least, and this highlights the primary problem with IoT devices. They are very insecure and often used in devices that aren't replaced frequently, and owners won't think to upgrade the technology. This is the challenge, and fortunately companies like Microsoft are doing research in this area, specifically focused on building secure chips that can still be mass-produced inexpensively.

Reduce Risk of Internet of Things (IoT)

Reducing the often-inherent risk associated with IoT devices isn't easy. One way would be to not use IoT-enabled devices and equipment unless you absolutely must. If you do, be very thoughtful about their installation, especially where a home or corporate network is concerned. Make sure the technology remains up to date, connect them to a segregated part of the network, and ensure adequate protection is built around it and ensure you scan that network for vulnerabilities and mitigate those accordingly.

3.5.9 Cloud Service and Deployment Models

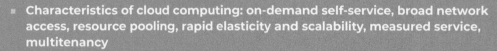

CORE **CONCEPTS**

- Characteristics of cloud computing: on-demand self-service, broad network access, resource pooling, rapid elasticity and scalability, measured service, multitenancy

- Cloud service models: IaaS, PaaS, SaaS, CaaS, FaaS

- Cloud deployment models: Public, Private, Community, Hybrid

- Protection and privacy of data in the cloud should be carefully considered.

Cloud Computing

What does "cloud" entail? A cloud can be private, public, or a hybrid model. It can also allow greater or smaller control to fall on the client or the cloud service provider. It all depends on what the goals are. So many options and variations exist. It is worth noting that regardless of which option you choose from, you are bound to use someone else's infrastructure, which is what the cloud provider does. They offer resources for the clients to use as they see fit.

Some of the most common characteristics of a cloud provider are represented in Table 3-20.

1. On-demand self-service	This means when particular cloud services are needed, they can be provisioned immediately. Whether the service is additional storage, more CPUs, more RAM, and so on, an administrator can add new services as they see fit.
2. Broad network access	This means the cloud can be accessed from anywhere, using various types of devices, like smartphones, tablets, laptops. In fact, most applications in use today are Software as a Service and are accessed through a web browser connected to the internet.
3. Resource pooling	Resource pooling relates to sharing the three primary sources of cloud computing (processors, disk space, and the network). They are almost never directly accessible because of typically being shared—pooled—among multiple users. So, resource pooling describes the relationship between the fundamental hardware that makes up the compute, storage, and network resources—the pool—and the multiple customers that utilize those resources. This is one of the key characteristics of cloud computing that points to significant value and economies of scale for consumers and cloud providers.
4. Rapid elasticity and scalability	Rapid elasticity/scalability follows multitenancy (explained below), and relates to how quickly compute, storage, and network can be increased or decreased in the cloud. Resources can be rapidly provisioned and deprovisioned—usually as quickly as through a few clicks away or automatically.
5. Measured service	Measured service means the cloud provider tracks resource usage very closely, to the point that a cloud customer only pays for resources used measured in very small increments—minutes, or even seconds.
6. Multitenancy	A final characteristic of Cloud computing is multitenancy. Multitenancy means that everybody has access to the cloud—it's open to the public—and cloud resources could potentially be shared with anybody, including malicious third parties being present as tenants on a cloud server. From a security perspective, multitenancy implies significant risk, which places responsibility on cloud providers to implement very strong security controls and isolation between clients.

Table 3-20: **Main Cloud Computing Characteristics**

Note that multitenancy is not always included among the characteristics of cloud computing because many organizations utilize a private cloud. By nature, a private cloud is only accessible by the organization that built it. A public cloud, on the other hand, does reflect multitenancy.

Cloud Service Models

There are three primary service models used in the cloud, depicted in Figure 3-23.

IaaS	PaaS	SaaS
Environment where customers can deploy virtualized Infrastructure storage, and networking components	Platform which provides the services and functionality for customers to develop and deploy applications	Software offered by a Cloud Service Provider which is available on demand, typically via the Internet, for a customer

Figure 3-23: **Cloud Models**

Software as a Service (SaaS) in essence provides access to an application which is rented—usually via a monthly/annual, subscriber-based fee—and the application is typically web-based. A great example of SaaS is Office 365/Exchange 365. Rather than hosting their own email server and dealing with applications like Word and Excel in house, many organizations license the use of these applications by paying Microsoft monthly. This is Software as a Service—simply an application that is hosted in the cloud and accessed through a web browser, usually via monthly subscription.

At the other end of the spectrum is **Infrastructure as a Service (IaaS)**. To understand IaaS, think of it almost like a virtual data center. What is housed in a real data center? Servers, networking equipment, firewalls, switches, routers, storage servers, IDS, IPS, database servers, email servers, and similar devices are found in data centers. With IaaS, all these devices and equipment can be found (in the virtual sense of course). Instead of a physical firewall, IaaS would offer a virtual firewall. Instead of a physical database server, a virtual database server is used to host databases. Essentially, an entire physical data center can be presented virtually through IaaS. Devices can be interconnected, and network segments created, just like in a physical data center. This is Infrastructure as a Service.

In between SaaS and IaaS sits another cloud service: **Platform as a Service (PaaS)**. Let's imagine a customer that wants a custom application. This customer searches the marketplace, but they're unable to find existing software that meets their needs; so, they decide to create their own application and build it from the ground up. Rather than building a development environment too, PaaS provides the infrastructure and platform upon which the application can be developed, tested, and run. Eventually, once the application is live, it essentially looks and functions like SaaS.

Two additional cloud service models that are now pervasively used are **Containers as a Service (CaaS)** and **Function as a Service (FaaS).** Relative to the predominant service models noted above, CaaS and FaaS fit in roughly as shown in Figure 3-24.

Figure 3-24: **CaaS and FaaS added to IaaS, PaaS and SaaS**

To understand **Containers as a Service (CaaS)**, it's first important to understand what is meant by the term container. A container is simply a package of software that contains all the components needed to run the software on any host system. Quite literally, because of this fact, a containerized application can be ported from one system to another and be up and running in a very short period of time. To make this point clearer, CaaS allows for multiple programming language stacks, like Ruby on Rails or node.js, to name a couple, to be deployed in one container. PaaS, on the other hand, requires multiple deployments, with each deployment explicitly supporting one or another stack. With the basic premise of a container being understood, CaaS automates the hosting and deployment of containerized software applications and allows development teams to focus on more important matters. In a world where software testing and updates previously took significantly longer, CaaS environments allow for agile DevOps (ideally SecDevOps) to become reality and to bring more value to customers and to the organizations utilizing this model.

To best understand **Function as a Service (FaaS)**, a couple of other terms should also be understood: serverless and microservices. The word *serverless* is often associated with information technology architectures and implies an architecture without servers. Similarly, microservices are very particular, self-contained services that provide specific business functionality. Due to their self-contained nature, they can be easily and quickly coupled to create stacks of microservices that support a business process or requirements, and they can be decoupled just as easily and quickly. With this understanding, FaaS really describes serverless and the use of microservices to accomplish business goals inexpensively and quickly. Unlike PaaS, FaaS does not require supporting infrastructure to function. PaaS, at its core, requires servers and supporting infrastructure to be available, which costs money, even when idle. FaaS, on the other hand, only requires the underlying microservices to be present, and only when microservices are invoked are costs involved. As with other cloud-based services, FaaS can scale quickly to support growing and shrinking needs. AWS Lambda is one of the earliest examples of FaaS.

Figure 3-25, the shading of boxes denotes cloud provider responsibility while lack of shading denotes customer responsibility.

In every case, in the public cloud, anything related to physical security, physical devices, underlying compute nodes and infrastructure, and hypervisors is going to be managed by the cloud service provider.

Understand cloud service provider and cloud customer responsibilities, depending upon the cloud service model in use

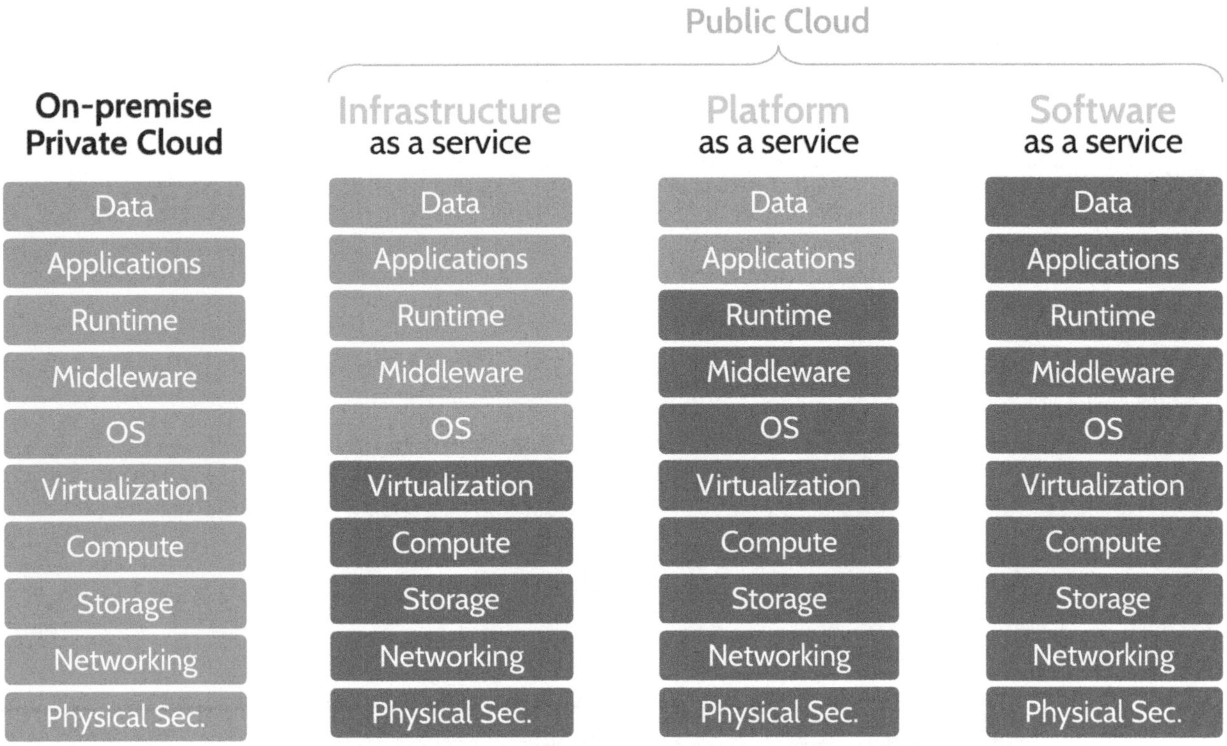

Public Cloud

On-premise Private Cloud	Infrastructure as a service	Platform as a service	Software as a service
Data	Data	Data	Data
Applications	Applications	Applications	Applications
Runtime	Runtime	Runtime	Runtime
Middleware	Middleware	Middleware	Middleware
OS	OS	OS	OS
Virtualization	Virtualization	Virtualization	Virtualization
Compute	Compute	Compute	Compute
Storage	Storage	Storage	Storage
Networking	Networking	Networking	Networking
Physical Sec.	Physical Sec.	Physical Sec.	Physical Sec.

Figure 3-25: **Responsibility between Client and Cloud Service Provider**

Starting from the right, with **Software as a Service (SaaS)**, the purple shading implies that the cloud service provider is responsible for all the items noted in the boxes, so Data, Applications, Runtime, Middleware, and OS are all under the cloud provider's remit. This model provides the client piece of mind as they don't have to deal with any administration and just consume a service, e.g., Google Mail. With **Platform as a Service (PaaS)**, the cloud service provider is responsible for most of the items, but the client is now responsible for their applications and data. With **Infrastructure as a Service (IaaS)**, the client has the greatest degree of control over portions of the cloud environment. The client can create their own network, install their operating systems, and configure the environment exactly as needed.

However, it's important to note that even in cases where the cloud service provider appears to have the most responsibility over the cloud environment, **significant responsibility is still often shared between the cloud service provider and the cloud customer**, and this fact must be considered carefully. Especially where boundaries and therefore potential shared responsibilities exist, the cloud customer and cloud service provider must explicitly clarify who is responsible for what.

One example highlights this fact. In **SaaS**, access control is a shared responsibility. The service provider is responsible for creating the security kernel and all the security-related components that make up the environment, but the customer is responsible for creating user accounts, setting access permissions, and ongoing review and maintenance of those accounts.

Regardless of the nature of shared responsibility, one thing is always constant when talking about the relationship between the cloud service provider and the cloud customer: **the cloud customer is always accountable for their data and other assets existing in a cloud environment.**

Cloud Deployment Models

Several cloud deployment models exist, as depicted in Table 3-21, and these refer to how the cloud is deployed, what hardware it runs on, and where the hardware is located. Most of the deployment models are intuitive and easy to understand.

The first model is **public cloud**, and the name implies who can access it—everybody, the public. A public cloud is in the cloud service provider's data center and consumers are simply accessing it as a service (e.g., Gmail). It's accessible by anyone.

A **private cloud** is only accessible by a paying customer, so it's private to that customer. If it's an on-premises private cloud, this means it's in the customer's own data center; but it can also be in a cloud service provider's data center, where a private, dedicated cloud is provided for use only by the customer. This would be considered an off-premises private cloud.

A **community cloud** is a cloud that is used by a group of users that share common needs or interests, like a group of hospitals, for example. One of the largest community clouds in the world serves interests related to the US government. Representatives of the US government convened with the desire to take advantage of cloud computing, but what they needed had to be FedRAMP compliant. No existing cloud service providers offered FedRAMP-compliant environments, so the government representatives approached Amazon, explained the need, and asked Amazon to build a FedRAMP-compliant community cloud. Now, any US government agency that wants to use the cloud must use this specific community cloud.

The last cloud deployment model is a **hybrid cloud**. A hybrid cloud is any combination of the three previously mentioned, and it is usually a combination of a public and private cloud. For example, many organizations will store their low-sensitivity data in the public cloud, and their high-sensitivity data in their own private cloud.

	Infrastructure MANAGED by	Infrastructure OWNED by	Infrastructure LOCATED	ACCESSIBLE by
Public	Third-Party Provider	Third-Party Provider	Off-Premises	Everyone (Untrusted)
Private / Community	Organization or Third-Party Provider	Organization or Third-Party Provider	On-Premises or Off-Premises	Trusted
Hybrid	Both: Organization and Third-Party Provider	Both: Organization and Third-Party Provider	Both: On-Premises and Off-Premises	Both: Trusted and Untrusted

Table 3-21: **Cloud Deployment Models**

Protection and Privacy of Data in the Cloud

Regardless of the cloud service or deployment model utilized, organizations should take every precaution to ensure that proprietary, personal, and other private information remain protected. In addition to implementing strong access controls, strong encryption practices should be used when and where necessary to properly secure this data. This is especially true when an organization makes the initial decision to move from legacy, on-premises infrastructure to that of a cloud provider. In cases like this, best practices indicate that data should be encrypted and secured locally and then migrated to the cloud.

> What should be a primary concern of an organization considering a move to the cloud?

3.5.10 **Compute in the Cloud**

CORE **CONCEPTS**

- A hypervisor, also known as a virtual machine manager/monitor (VMM), is software that allows multiple operating systems to share the resources of a single physical machine.

- A virtual machine (VM) resembles a computer, but everything is emulated using software.

As noted earlier, one of the characteristics of cloud computing is **resource pooling,** which describes the relationship between the fundamental hardware that makes up the **compute, storage, and network resources** and the multiple customers that utilize those resources. Cloud customers can access compute resources through:

- Virtual Machines (VM)
- Containers
- Serverless

Hypervisors, Virtual Machines (VM), Containers, Serverless

VMs | INSTANCES | GUESTS

VM 1	VM 2	VM 3
App 1	App 2	App 3
Bins/Libs	Bins/Libs	Bins/Libs
Operating system	Operating system	Operating system

Hypervisor

Compute Node

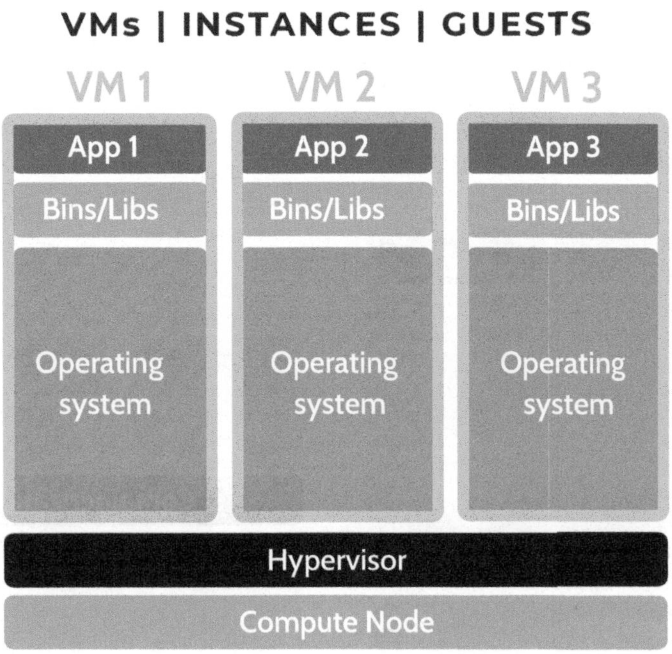

Figure 3-26: **VM and Hypervisor**

As illustrated in Figure 3-26, a **hypervisor is the software that runs directly on hardware or on an operating system and allows multiple operating systems to share the resources of a single physical machine**, also known as a compute node. A hypervisor is often referred to as a **Virtual Machine Manager/ Monitor (VMM)**, and allows administrators to manage virtual machines (VMs)—create, edit, and start/ stop—as well as view VM performance and other statistics. Common hypervisor examples include Oracle VirtualBox and VMware Workstation.

A virtual machine (VM) resembles a computer; however, everything is emulated. Instead of an actual physical machine that contains a CPU, RAM, hard disk(s), and so on, everything is emulated using software. The result is a **VM** that can host an operating system and applications. In an ideal environment, specific functions would be segregated among individual virtual machines, and each virtual machine would be hardened and secured according to the value of the data being processed on the machine. This approach would make a potential attacker's job much more difficult, because multiple virtual machines would need to be attacked and compromised.

Virtual machines are commonly referred by a few different names: **Instances**, Guests and sometimes even Hosts.

From a security perspective, virtual machines are very useful. Business functions can be isolated on a per-virtual-machine basis. In other words, rather than having numerous functions (services) on one machine, they can be separated, with each virtual machine supporting a specific function (e.g., a web server, or a database server, or an FTP server, etc.). This segregation and specialization allows each virtual machine to be very locked down and hardened to a specific function—greatly reducing the attack surface and the blast radius if a machine is compromised.

> **Effective and beneficial cloud environment design considerations**

A useful capability of virtual machines is the ability to create a baseline image of a virtual machine. An **image** is essentially, a pre-built virtual machine ready to be deployed. Once an image has been created it is easy to spin up numerous virtual machines from the pre-built image.

> **The best point of attack to access multiple virtual machines**

Compromising the hypervisor would give an attacker access to the multiple virtual machines it controls, so considerable hardening should be enforced to avoid that.

Virtual Machines versus Containers

Before looking more closely at containers, a quick side-by-side comparison of virtual machines and containers is useful to consider as illustrated in Figure 3-27.

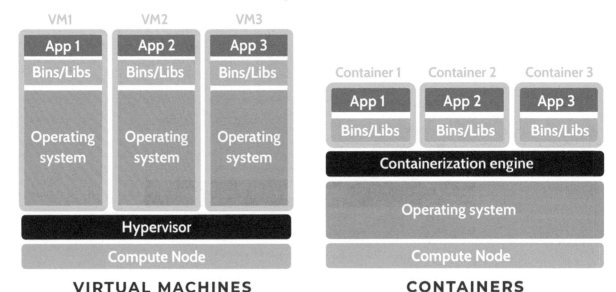

Figure 3-27: **VMs vs. Containers**

Virtual machines are quite "heavy" relative to containers. For every virtual machine being created, an accompanying operating system must also be installed. The hypervisor acts as the layer of abstraction that manages all the underlying physical infrastructure on behalf of each virtual machine. Containers, in comparison, are quite lightweight relative to virtual machines. Multiple containers can be supported by a single operating system, and the containerization engine acts as the layer of abstraction between the containers and the operating system. Relative to each other, containers are more efficient and portable than virtual machines. Virtual machines virtualize an entire computer system; containers only virtualize software and dependent supporting components.

Virtual machines and containers offer advantages and disadvantages relative to one another, some of which are noted in Table 3-24.

	Pros	Cons
Virtual Machines	▪ Isolated security ▪ "Heavy" and effectively function as stand-alone computers and can be treated as such ▪ Requires more administrative overhead	▪ As essentially stand-alone computers, working with VMs can take time in terms of modifying, building, and confirming the functionality of the VM image ▪ VMs can consume significant amounts of storage space on host systems, so initial planning and design of a VM environment must consider this fact
Containers	▪ Lightweight and efficient, as they only include application software ▪ Highly portable, and many containers already exist and are available for download and use in development projects ▪ Allows developers to streamline focus on development efforts	▪ Because containers in a given context share the same operating system and underlying physical infrastructure, a threat to one container is potentially a threat to other containers or the shared resources. ▪ Due to many containers existing in the public domain for download and use, a malicious actor could exploit this fact

Table 3-22: **VM and Container Comparison**

Containers

As noted, containers are highly portable, self-contained applications, with an abstraction layer known as the containerization engine sharing and leveraging resources of that operating system on behalf of each container. As highlighted in Figure 3-28, multiple containers can exist and operate in the context of one operating system. Each container supports one application and contains all the supporting binaries/libraries and other dependent components necessary for the application to run properly and to be easily ported to another system.

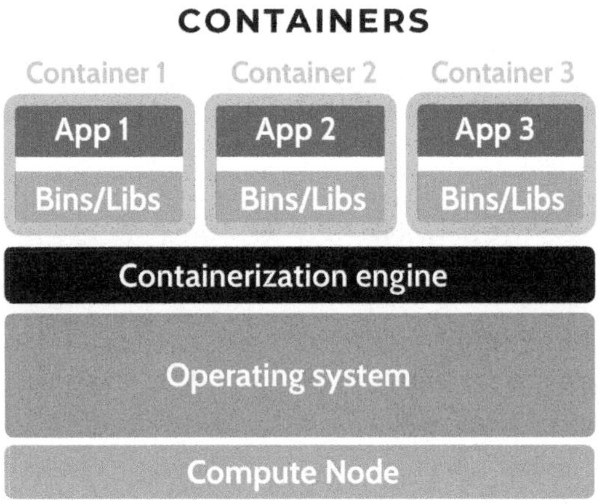

CONTAINERS

Figure 3-28: **Containers**

Dividing Up Services

As shown in Figure 3-29, all functionality of a monolithic application is wrapped together as a single unit, whereas with microservices and serverless, functionality is more defined and self-contained in smaller or individual units.

Monolithic applications typically comprise of a back-end database, an application and a user interface. Correspondingly, this implies a single large code base, and changes to an application may require updates to all three areas. In recent years, application development has trended toward the utilization of microservices, which has been further leveraged via serverless architectures found in cloud computing.

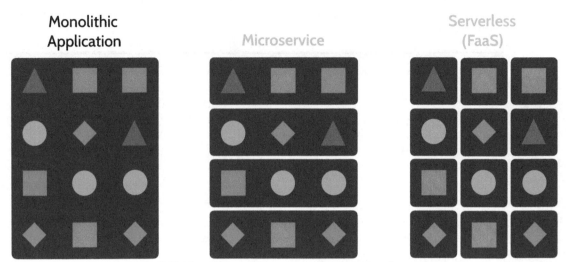

Figure 3-29: **Monolithic vs. Microservices and Serverless Computing**

Microservices

A great way to understand a microservice is to imagine one piece of functionality found in a monolithic application operating as a stand-alone service or small set of related services—a microservice. Compared to a monolithic application that exists and operates as one unit, microservices exist and function as separate units that are loosely coupled via API calls. Due to the loosely coupled nature of these services, all the disadvantages inherent with a monolithic application are mitigated, as each part of application functionality operates as a separate service. If one piece of functionality needs to be scaled, it can be updated and redeployed quickly. The same holds true if new functionality is needed—a new microservice can be built and deployed quickly. The fact that an application is composed of multiple, loosely coupled components allows for better overall understanding of the application, and functional components can be reused across multiple applications. Relative to monolithic application development projects, microservice components can be built more quickly and cost-effectively using much smaller development teams. At the same time that microservices mitigates many of the disadvantages found with monolithic applications, weaknesses of microservices include additional complexity, due to the distributed nature of the architecture. Connections between modules and databases particularly need to be considered, as does testing of components, as an issue with one service could potentially impact a multitude of other services due to the interdependent nature of microservice-based applications.

Function as a Service (FaaS) / Serverless

The term *serverless* takes the basic premise of microservices—hyperfocused, independent pieces of functionality coupled together through APIs—and extends it to the cloud. With serverless, microservices are run in the cloud. AWS Lambda is a perfect example of a serverless environment. With serverless, as the name suggests, the compute service does not involve the provisioning or management of servers. This fact points immediately to cost savings. Rather, when the desired functionality is needed, it can be invoked, and only the actual compute time required is charged. If the serverless functionality goes unused—for whatever reason—there is zero cost. Additionally, and like other potential benefits associated with cloud computing, serverless allows for high availability, scalability, and simple cost management, among others.

3.5.11 Cloud Forensics

> **CORE CONCEPTS**
>
> - **Focus is on the forensic process in cloud computing environments**
> - **Typically, more complex than on-premises forensic investigations**
> - **Virtual disks and VM images are often analyzed as part of cloud forensics**

With any type of investigation that involves on-premises computing equipment, the forensic process is generally straightforward and primarily revolves around securing the scene, not powering the equipment off or on (thus maintaining its original state), capturing data that may reside in volatile memory or storage areas, and making bit-for-bit copies of hard drives and other non-volatile storage devices. Where cloud forensics and investigations are concerned, the forensics process can become much more complex. Because public cloud environments involve multiple customers sharing the same physical infrastructure, including hard drives, physical access to the equipment and storage devices that may contain information relevant to the investigation is typically not possible or allowed.

What types of evidence a cloud forensics investigator might request

In these cases, rather than physical disks and systems, an investigator will most likely request copies—snapshots—of the virtual disk and VM images to obtain evidence and information pertinent to the investigation. A virtual disk is simply a virtual hard drive allocated to a customer from an actual physical hard drive. So, a physical hard drive in a system in a data center might have 1TB of available hard disk space, and one customer might be allocated 250GB of this space for their use. The 250GB of space—the virtual disk—would appear as a stand-alone hard drive to the customer, and it would only be available for their use. Put in bigger context, the virtual disk would be connected to a virtual machine (VM)—the system that appears as a stand-alone system to the organization and utilizes CPU, RAM, and other components of a physical system in a data center. As mentioned above, copies of virtual disks and VMs are known as snapshots. A snapshot is a "snap" of the state and data of a virtual disk or a virtual machine taken at a point in time. In essence, a snapshot is a backup of the disk or the machine. Best practices indicate that snapshot schedules should be set up as part of the host and virtual machine setup and configuration, though snapshots can also be taken on an as-needed basis. Because snapshots capture the state of a virtual machine at the time they're taken, they can prove invaluable for the sake of an investigation. In addition to capturing data stored in non-volatile storage locations, snapshots can also capture evidence that may reside in volatile memory and similar locations on the virtual machine. As with other types of digital evidence, two bit-for-bit copies of a snapshot should be created for purposes of forensic analysis, with the original snapshot and one copy being essentially locked up and untouched and only the second copy actually being examined.

SaaS	▪ Consumer must rely entirely on CSP
PaaS	▪ For underlying infrastructure, consumer must rely entirely on CSP ▪ Consumer is responsible for any application layer code they deployed and application logging
IaaS	▪ Consumers can perform forensic investigations on their VMs ▪ Investigation of network traffic, access to snapshots of memory, or the creation of a hard disk images may require investigative support by the CSP

Table 3-23: **Forensic Data that Can Typically Be Captured by Service Model**

Table 3-25 shows the type of forensic evidence that can be acquired based on the cloud model being used. Cloud forensics presents significant additional challenges relative to those typically found with traditional digital forensics. In fact, NIST published a document in August 2020 entitled "NIST Cloud Computing Forensic Science Challenges" that summarized research in this area by members of the NIST Cloud Computing Forensic Science Working Group. Specifically, members of the research team identified nine challenge categories related to cloud forensics as outlined below:

1. Architecture
2. Data collection
3. Analysis
4. Anti-forensics
5. Incident first responders
6. Role management
7. Legal
8. Standards
9. Training

Within each challenge category, the team further identified subcategories and specific challenges within each subcategory. For example, under the category Architecture there are several subcategories: Data Segregation, Multitenancy, and Provenance. Under the subcategory Data Segregation is a specific challenge noted as Potential evidence segregation. Under multitenancy, three specific challenges are noted: Errors in cloud management portal configuration, potential evidence segregation, and boundaries. Looked at as a whole, sixteen subcategories exist under the nine challenge categories noted above, and within the sixteen subcategories sixty-five specific challenges are identified. Cloud forensics is a complex matter and one that no doubt will continue to pose challenges for years to come as related technologies continue to evolve.

3.5.12 Cloud Computing Roles

CORE **CONCEPTS**

- Multiple computing roles relate to cloud computing: cloud consumer, cloud provider, cloud partner, cloud broker

- The cloud consumer is always accountable for their data stored in the cloud.

- Responsibility can be delegated to other cloud computing roles.

- Data controller = owner of data = cloud customer = accountable

- Data processor = processor of data = cloud provider or other agent of the customer = responsible

Along with the various cloud characteristics and deployment models described earlier, cloud computing involves a number of different roles, as listed in Table 3-22, and it is critically important to have security in the cloud and to understand exactly who is doing what.

> The role that is always accountable for data in the cloud

One of the major roles is **cloud service customer (or consumer).** This is the person or organization purchasing cloud services. When making this purchase, the customer can't outsource accountability for any assets that are being entrusted with the cloud provider. The only thing that can be outsourced is some of the responsibility, and this is done through service level agreements (SLA) agreed upon and signed by the customer and provider. An SLA is a contract and is binding upon all parties involved, but regardless of the terms of the SLA, **accountability always remains with the asset owner.** Akin to a cloud service customer is **cloud service provider**. The provider is the organization that sells cloud services. Both role names and their meaning are intuitive.

Cloud service broker representatives provide service aggregation services to customers. For example, let's imagine a small or medium size company that wants to start moving to the cloud. If the organization wants to adopt the cloud to meet all its needs, it might end up contracting with many cloud service providers because different providers offer different services. For most organizations, managing all the necessary provider relationships would take a lot of work. A cloud service broker handles details like these. They work with individual cloud service providers, and put together packages of services, which they then sell to cloud service customers. They'll aggregate different services from different providers and then offer them as a package. In these cases, rather than having contracts with multiple providers, the cloud customer would only have one contract with the cloud service broker; and the cloud broker will have individual contracts with different providers.

Cloud Service Customer/Consumer	Individual or organization who is accessing cloud services
Cloud Service Provider	Organization that is providing cloud services/resources to consumers
Cloud Service Partner	Organization which supports either the cloud provider or customer (e.g., cloud auditor or cloud service broker)
Broker	Carrier, Architect, Administrator, Developer, Operator, Services Manager, Reseller, Data Subject, Owner, Controller, Processor, Steward

Table 3-24: **Cloud Computing Roles**

A term that relates to cloud service broker is service arbitrage. From a cloud service broker's perspective consider this: Is an individual negotiating and purchasing cloud services on their own going to get a price as good as a broker that goes to a provider on behalf of many customers? Essentially, the broker is getting a volume discount relative to the stand-alone price, and they'll sell the service to their customers for more than what they paid, but less than what an individual customer would likely pay. The broker gets their percentage, the customer still gets a better price, and the provider gets a lot of customers. This is service arbitrage, and this is one way that cloud service brokers earn money.

Two other important roles are controller and processor. In the context of cloud services, the data controller is the cloud customer. The controller defines the rules by which data should be protected. The data processor, on the other hand, is the cloud provider. They're the party that is actually processing the data, based upon the rules defined by the data controller.

Understand the different cloud roles

To simplify, controller = consumer; processor = cloud service provider.

Accountability versus Responsibility

You may be wondering who maintains accountability when organizations outsource data, processes, and systems to the cloud and if accountability can be outsourced. The answer is an emphatic no! Accountability can never be delegated or outsourced as covered in detail in 1.3.2. As a reminder, accountability can't be outsourced or passed down, and it always remains with the owner. Responsibility, on the other hand, can be outsourced, and this often happens to a great extent when working with a cloud service provider. Table 3-23 is the exact same table from 1.3.2 and is here as a reminder of the major differences between accountability and responsibility to help you solidify them in your mind.

Accountability	Responsibility
Where the buck stops	**The doer**
Have ultimate ownership, answerability, blameworthiness, and liability	In charge of task or event
Only one entity can be accountable	Multiple entities can be responsible
Sets rules and policies	Develops plans, makes things happen

Table 3-25: **Accountability vs. Responsibility**

3.5.13 Cloud Identities

CORE **CONCEPTS**

- **Third-party identity provider is a trusted organization that manages user identities and related attributes for purposes of authentication and authorization.**
- **Identity federation involves protocols, standards, practices, and policies that support identity portability and trust relationships among unaffiliated resources and organizations.**
- **SPML enables the automation of adding users to multiple cloud services.**
- **On-premise IAM solutions include Microsoft Active Directory and LDAP based.**
- **Cloud-based IAM solutions include those offered by Amazon, Google, and many other cloud vendors.**
- **Identify as a Service (IDaaS) refers to cloud-based IAM services.**

Identity and Access Management (IAM) in any context can be challenging, and especially so in the cloud, with one of the most significant challenges being that of provisioning users to multiple disparate resources spread across multiple cloud services. Security-related access control principles, like separation of duties, least privilege, and need to know still apply, therefore requiring streamlined and efficient IAM solutions.

For many years, most organizations have used on-premise IAM solutions such as Microsoft **Active Directory (AD)** and **Lightweight Directory Access Protocol (LDAP)**. Active Directory provides numerous functions, such as group and user management, permissions management, and control access to network resources. LDAP is an open and cross platform protocol used to authenticate to directory services, such as AD, and query them.

These traditional solutions served organizations well for years, but as cloud-based applications and the need to use them grew, so too did the pressure (and related challenges) to extend on-premise IAM capabilities outward. To resolve these challenges, **Identity as a Service (IDaaS)** solutions began to emerge that could seamlessly extend traditional IAM services to the Cloud or that could simply manage the IAM process outright. One of their primary advantages is that they provide a centralized, cloud-based system created by experts in the field, which is much easier to rely upon than a potentially decentralized, on-premise solution that requires additional resources to operate. Additionally, many IDaaS solutions offer automated account management and password management requirements are reduced. Utilizing IDaaS allows organizations to focus on their core competencies. At the same time, IDaaS solutions may be more expensive than on-premise solutions, but the trade-off of cost versus man hours and other resources required to maintain an on-premise IAM presence often results in substantial savings for organizations.

> Understand benefits and advantages of cloud-based IAM and FIM solutions over traditional IAM solutions

In the same context as IDaaS is federated identity or federated identity management (FIM). At a high level, federated identity management involves protocols, standards, practices, and policies that support identity portability and trust relationships among disparate resources and organizations; essentially FIM extends the functionality of IDaaS to include multiple resources and organizations. Standards, protocols, and technologies that support FIM include Services Provisioning Markup Language (SPML), Security Assertion Markup Language (SAML), OAuth and OpenID, among others. Table 3-26 provides a summary of the various identity technologies that can be used.

SPML is considered deprecated but still used and was one of the first federated standards to support and manage user access to many cloud-based services. Because SPML is a standard, organizations that utilize it are not locked into a solution, and automation of its capabilities opens the door to a broad spectrum of diverse web-based resources.

SPML (Services Provisioning Markup Language)	SPML is a deprecated XML-based, Organization for the Advancement of Structured Information Standards (OASIS) standard that was developed to allow cooperating users, resource owners, and service providers—the federation—to exchange information seamlessly for purposes of **provisioning**.
SAML (Security Assertion Markup Language)	SAML is an XML-based, OASIS standard that utilizes security tokens that contain assertions about a user. SAML facilitates service requests made by users to service providers in the form of requests to identity providers, which—if the user is authenticated/authorized—result in SAML assertions allowing the user access to the service.
OAuth (Authorization)	OAuth (authorization) is a Federated Identity Management (FIM) open-standard protocol that typically works in conjunction with OpenID (authentication). OAuth provides users and applications with "secure delegated access" via access tokens versus credentials. OAuth enables disparate resources to securely interact in a manner that ultimately allows a client to access data owned by a resource owner.

*Table 3-26: **Identity Technologies***

3.5.14 Cloud Migration

CORE **CONCEPTS**

- Cloud migration involves benefits and risks that should be carefully considered

- One significant risk of cloud migration is vendor lock-in

- Security in the cloud should be understood thoroughly, and organizations should work closely with the cloud service provider to implement security that follows best practices.

More and more organizations have either fully migrated to the cloud already or are exploring options for migrating some or all their operations to the cloud. Benefits of making such a move include shifting costs from a capitalization expense (CapEx) model, where networking and computer equipment is owned by the organization, to an operations expense (OpEx) model, where compute, storage, and networking costs are borne by the cloud service provider and paid for by the organization on an "as needed" basis. This shift, though not necessarily a huge cost-saver, can result in considerable efficiencies gained. Additionally, it's in a cloud service provider's best short- and long-term interest to provide reliable technology and support to its customers. This further shifts the load away from the organization so it can focus on core business activities.

Additionally, moving to the cloud makes applications, services, and data accessible from anywhere, using virtually any type of device, as long as an internet connection is available. This facilitates greater flexibility as well as opportunities for better collaboration among employees, vendors, customers, and other interested parties.

Migration to the cloud also facilitates the centralization of data, which can further facilitate safe storage and backup of data. Depending upon an organization's needs, one of several cloud deployment models could be pursued.

Operating in the cloud requires high-speed access to the internet, potentially from anywhere in the world, as well as reliable backup and recovery options, to ensure ongoing availability of applications and data.

Depending on the cloud deployment model, with the exception of data and potentially of applications or services provided, organizations will have significantly less to zero control over the supporting infrastructure.

One of the most important considerations of cloud migration relates to vendor lock-in—the notion that once migrated, an organization is "stuck" with the cloud service provider and will be unable to move elsewhere. The possibility of this taking place requires an organization to perform significant due diligence and to analyze their needs in relation to what the cloud service provider is offering. One approach larger organizations take to mitigate vendor lock-in is to use multiple cloud service providers to support segments of their business.

Among Cloud migration risk, what is one of the most important things to consider?

Finally, security related to cloud migration must be carefully considered and addressed. Most cloud service providers provide robust security options, and it is imperative that an organization work closely with the cloud provider to ensure best practices are being followed and implemented to secure the organization's valuable assets.

3.5.15 XSS and CSRF

> CORE **CONCEPTS**
>
> - As web-based applications continue to proliferate, so too do instances of cross-site scripting (XSS) attacks
> - Two primary forms of cross-site scripting (XSS): stored/persistent XSS and reflected XSS
> - An XSS attack involves a malicious script that is injected into a trusted website that a visitor's browser then downloads and executes
> - A cross-site request forgery (CSRF) relies on persistence facilitated by cookies in browsers
> - With XSS, the target of attack is the user's browser; with CSRF, the target of attack is the web server

The topic of assessing and mitigating vulnerabilities in web-based systems is important, because the prevalence of web-based applications only continues to grow. Web-based applications are used as a conduit between a client (e.g., a user's browser on their local machine) and an underlying information source (like a SQL database). They are becoming extremely pervasive, not only because of the growth of the cloud, but simply because this is how most organizations now deploy new systems in their environment. With this in mind, let's explore a few major web-based vulnerabilities.

Cross-Site Scripting (XSS)

Cross-site scripting is seen most often in two forms:

- Stored/Persistent/Type I
- Reflected/Nonpersistent/Type II

Stored/Persistent/Type I XSS

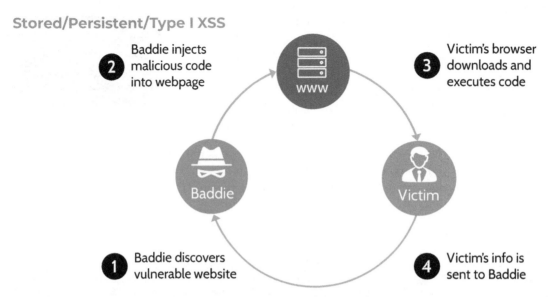

2 Baddie injects malicious code into webpage

3 Victim's browser downloads and executes code

1 Baddie discovers vulnerable website

4 Victim's info is sent to Baddie

Baddie

WWW

Victim

Figure 3-30: **Stored/Persistent/Type I XSS**

Figure 3-30 illustrates what stored XSS looks like. Imagine a user visits a website, like example.com, and sees that a friend has posted a picture of his family. The user comments on the picture, "Wow, what a nice-looking family!" What happens to that comment? It's stored on the website's servers, and anybody with permissions to view that picture can also see the comment. Now, let's imagine that instead of writing a comment, the user writes JavaScript in the comment field. Like a regular comment, the JavaScript is stored on the website's servers, and this time, instead of simply displaying the comment, the web browser of every person who views that picture is going to execute the malicious code that was inserted earlier. When the code executes, something malicious will take place every time that webpage is loaded. This is one form of cross-site scripting (XSS). It requires a vulnerable website that will accept this code. One of the great advantages of this attack is that it literally executes each time a victim visits the vulnerable webpage. The way that this can manifest, as also see in Figure 3-30, is through the following sequence of steps:

1. **Attacker identifies a vulnerable website.**
   The website must be vulnerable to XSS attacks for this to be successful. The attacker will typically use specific tools to examine underlying code related to pages on the website.

2. **Attacker injects malicious code into a page on the website.**
   Based upon #1, the attacker can inject JavaScript on the website. This could be as simple as typing the code into a comment or a form field, with the result that the JavaScript is stored on the web server.

3. **When a victim visits the website, their browser downloads and executes the malicious code.**
   With the JavaScript injected and stored on the website, every subsequent visitor's browser will access the webpage and execute the malicious code.

4. **When the victim's browser executes the JavaScript, information from the victim will be sent to the attacker.**
   Until the malicious code is cleared from the website, many site visitors could be impacted, and a savvy attacker might be able to gain username/password, banking, or other sensitive information because of the JavaScript executing in the browser.

Attackers might use XSS for any of a number of malicious reasons. For example, the JavaScript code could be used to:

- Send a copy of the victim's browser cookies, including session cookies, which could lead to session hijacking and taking over a user's active session to connect to the destination resource.
- Disclose files on the victim's computer system.
- Install malicious applications.

Reflected/Nonpersistent/Type II XSS

Figure 3-31 shows how reflected cross-site scripting works.

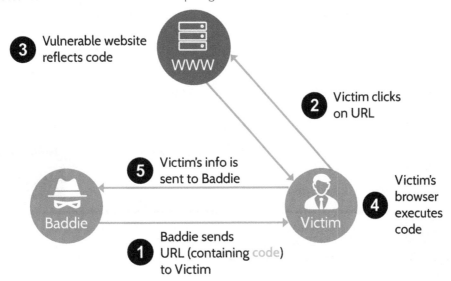

Figure 3-31: **Reflected/Nonpersistent/Type II XSS**

Imagine someone visits example.com, types "cat" in a search window, and selects "submit." The webpage then returns the results of that search query, showing various pictures of cats. Now, let's imagine that an attacker sends a malicious link to the cat lover, and they click on it. This time however, instead of searching for "cat," the URL actually contains a search for a small bit of JavaScript code. So, the cat lover thinks they're searching for "cat," but the URL contains malicious JavaScript code that the web browser is going to execute because of this.

Essentially what is happening in the background is the user is clicking on a URL, which directs them to a website, which then reflects malicious code that was sent to the website back to the victim. This can take place through the following sequence of steps:

1. **Attacker sends a malicious URL to a victim.**
   The URL containing malicious JavaScript code is sent to the victim (commonly via a phishing email).

2. **Victim clicks on URL.**
   Because the URL looks legitimate (or through some other social engineering technique), the user clicks on the malicious link.

3. **The vulnerable website reflects malicious code to the victim.**
   After clicking on the link, the URL that contains the JavaScript code is going to reflect that code back to the victim's browser.

4. **The victim's browser executes the reflected code.**
   Because the malicious code has been reflected back to the victim, their browser is going to execute the JavaScript code.

5. **JavaScript code executes (i.e., sensitive data pertaining to the victim is sent to the attacker).**
   As a result of the JavaScript executing, sensitive data from the victim will be transmitted to the attacker (or any other malicious action the code entails is performed).

It's worth noting that the only person impacted in this scenario is the person who clicked on the malicious URL that was sent by the attacker. The next person to visit example.com and search for something will not receive the same JavaScript code. This is why it's called "reflected," because this attack only "reflects" back to the user who actually clicked on the malicious link. Anyone else who visits the same webpage will not be doing so with the same URL as the victim.

Stored/Persistent and Reflected Cross-Site Scripting Takeaways

From the two examples mentioned above, a few important things should be noted.

- In the first example, malicious code is stored on the web server. This type of cross-site scripting is known as stored or persistent because the malicious code is stored on the server, and every user who visits that webpage is going to fall victim to that attack.

- In the second example, malicious code is reflected back to the victim via a carefully crafted URL. So, unlike the persistent cross-site scripting attack (which leverages multiple victims) reflected cross-site scripting targets one victim—the person who clicks on the provided crafted URL. Anyone else who visits the normal URL will not be impacted.

Which is the most common type of attack? **Reflected is by far the most common and often results when a link in a phishing email is clicked.**

Table 3-27 provides a summary of the types of XSS.

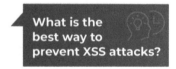

Most common type of XSS attacks

Persistent or Stored	▪ Injected code is stored on the server and embedded in the HTML page sent to all subsequent visitors (victims). ▪ Stored XSS is **persistent**.
Reflected	▪ Injected code is passed to a vulnerable server via URL and reflected to the victim. ▪ Reflected XSS is the **most common** form of XSS.
DOM-based	▪ Client-side Document Object Model (DOM) environment is modified, and malicious code injected. ▪ Can be either persistent or reflected. ▪ DOM-based XSS is intentionally not covered in detail, as this type of XSS attack is far more rare and unlikely to be covered on the exam.

Table 3-27: **Summary of XSS Types**

Regardless of the XSS type, one of the best ways to prevent them is using server-side input validation. Unlike client-side input validation, which could be easily manipulated by an attacker, server-side validation would remove the possibility of manipulation of the data. In addition, a web application firewall (WAF) would be another great way to prevent XSS attacks.

What is the best way to prevent XSS attacks?

Cross-Site Request Forgery (CSRF)

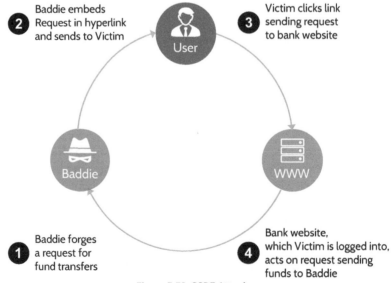

2 Baddie embeds Request in hyperlink and sends to Victim

3 Victim clicks link sending request to bank website

User

Baddie

WWW

1 Baddie forges a request for fund transfers

4 Bank website, which Victim is logged into, acts on request sending funds to Baddie

Figure 3-32: **CSRF Attack**

The success of a cross-site request forgery attack is predicated upon the concept of "persistence" that cookies in browsers facilitate. For example, when a user visits a website frequently, they often tick a box during the login process that says, "Keep me logged in for x number of days." This information is stored in a cookie that is stored in the user's browser. Then, when the user visits the website, e.g., their online banking portal, they're automatically logged in because the cookie sends information to the web server that identifies the user as a legitimate system user. The attack is illustrated in Figure 3-32 and follows the steps below:

1. **Attacker forges a request, e.g., a funds transfer request.**
   The attacker crafts a forged request to make it look legitimate so the victim is fooled into executing it.

2. **Attacker embeds forged request in a hyperlink and sends URL to the victim (e.g., via a phishing email).**
   The forged request could be sent via email, SMS, or another way that appears valid to the victim.

3. **Victim clicks link, sending the request to a legitimate entity, like their bank.**
   Through social engineering or another means, the attacker can entice the victim into clicking on the link.

4. **The legitimate entity, which the victim is logged into, acts on the request as requested by the attacker.**
   Because the victim is already logged into the legitimate entity's online portal (e.g., their bank), the funds transfer request appears valid. As a result, a malicious action can be taken, like transferring funds to the attacker's account, as the bank's web server considers this a legitimate action that is performed by the victim.

With this in mind, the attacker often has a window of time within which to operate, because the CSRF attack does not require the victim to be logged to their bank at the time of the attack. Rather, the persistence of the connection that is facilitated through the cookie can allow the attack to be successful days or even weeks later. By expiring cookies and session tokens more frequently, an attacker's window of opportunity can be considerably reduced.

Another important item to note is that even though the target of the attack appears to be the victim, in fact, **the target of the attack is always the server**. The victim is merely the vector used by the attacker to exploit the vulnerable server.

> Who or what are the target of XSS and CSRF attacks?

XSS versus CSRF

Looking at XSS and CSRF side by side, some key differences exist as highlighted in Table 3-28. **With XSS, the target of attack is the user's browser; with CSRF, the target of attack is the web server.**

XSS	CSRF
▪ Unwanted action performed on the user's browser	▪ Unwanted action performed on a trusted website
▪ User's browser (client) runs malicious JavaScript code	▪ Website (server) executes a command from trusted user's browser
▪ **User's browser is exploited**	▪ **Web server is exploited**

Table 3-28: **XSS vs CSRF**

3.5.16 SQL Injection

CORE CONCEPTS

- Structured Query Language (SQL) is the language used for communicating with databases.
- SQL Injection is a method of attack that utilizes SQL code and commands.
- Input validation is the best method to prevent SQL Injection attacks from being successful.

Understanding SQL Injection should start with an understanding of **Structured Query Language (SQL)**. SQL is a language used for communicating with databases.

SQL Injection is a method of attack that utilizes SQL commands and can be used for modification, corruption, insertion, or deletion of data in a database.

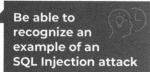

Be able to recognize an example of an SQL Injection attack

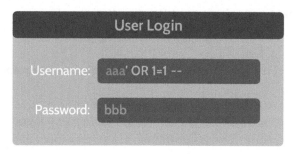

SELECT * FROM users WHERE username = 'aaa' OR 1=1 --' AND password = ' bbb'

SELECT * FROM users WHERE FALSE OR TRUE --' AND password = ' bbb '

SELECT * FROM users WHERE TRUE

Figure 3-33: **SQL injection**

Figure 3-33 illustrates what SQL Injection looks like. In this case, imagine a webserver with a database residing behind it. Further imagine that the website associated with this configuration is a dynamic website, meaning that web pages can be created dynamically using data from the database, based upon user requests and interaction with the website.

Due to the dynamic nature of these websites, a persistent connection to the database is required, but a web user should never be able to directly interact with the back-end database. However, SQL Injection makes that possible.

A simple login screen is used so when a person enters their username and password, the database will be queried for the corresponding information, and if it is valid, the user should be authenticated. Using SQL Injection, however, neither a correct nor incorrect username is entered into the "Username" field; rather, a bit of SQL code is entered as shown in Figure 3-33.

The first part of that—**aaa**—is just text and could be replaced by any other text, same as the entry in the password field. However, everything else following that in the username field (**' OR 1=1 --**) constitutes the SQL Injection string.

Once this information is entered, the web server will formulate the request into SQL code and send it to the database server, asking if this username and password exist in the database. The first SQL statement below the login box shows how this request will be perceived by the back-end SQL database. Because of the apostrophe (') at the end of **aaa**, the database server treats **aaa** as the end of the username and then searches for a username **aaa,** which probably does not exist. Next, **OR 1=1** is treated as a SQL Statement, which when analyzed yields "true." In essence the interpreter executes a logical OR query, which is true if either of the conditions accompanying it are considered true. **aaa** doesn't exist (resulting in a false state); however, 1 always equals 1, so that returns a true state.

Finally, within SQL, the use of "--" is used to signify that everything that follows it is a comment and would be ignored by the SQL interpreter.

So, the result is that based on the above SQL command, the attacker can successfully authenticate and gain access to the system behind the login screen. This example highlights one very important thing: the web server passed unvalidated information directly to the database server.

> **What is the best way to mitigate a SQL injection attack?**

Unvalidated data should never be passed directly from a web server to a database server. **In other words, user input should always be validated, sanitized, or otherwise made to conform to expected formatting standards.** Additionally, the use of things like **prepared statement/parameterized queries** and **stored procedures** can also help protect against SQL Injection attacks. In short, why would you need a -- or = character to be present in a field storing someone's name? The answer is you wouldn't. So, input validation can help you clear the input from any characters that shouldn't be passed on to the back-end SQL database.

The best way to understand a **prepared statement or parameterized query** is to think of a template of SQL code, where variables are used and passed to the query later. The separation helps prevent the intent of a query from being changed, regardless of the variable entered through user input or other means.

Stored procedures essentially operate under the same premise as prepared statements, with the biggest difference being that stored procedures are defined and stored in the database itself and then invoked in the application.

SQL Commands

The SQL commands shown in the table below do not need to be memorized. In fact, a listing of all SQL commands would be significantly longer. These are just examples of some of the most common commands for your awareness—so you can recognize what SQL commands look like.

CREATE	SELECT	GRANT	COMMIT
ALTER	INSERT	REVOKE	ROLLBACK
DROP	UPDATE		SAVEPOINT
TRUNCATE	DELETE		
RENAME	MERGE		
	LOCK TABLE		

SQL Code Examples

Table 3-29 shows you what SQL code looks like—again so you can recognize SQL code. Note that none of these code snippets would be used for SQL injection.

Be able to recognize SQL commands and codes

SELECT * FROM users;	This command would return all of the data stored in the "users" table.
INSERT INTO users (userID, password) VALUES (rob, Pass123);	This command would insert a new record in the "users" table that contains a userID of "rob" with a corresponding password of "Pass123."
DROP accountsReceivable;	This command essentially works like "delete" and results in deleting the table named "accountsReceivable" from the database. Let's hope a working copy of the database backup is handy or else it may become very interesting for the database administrator.

Table 3-29: **SQL Code Examples**

3.5.17 Input Validation

CORE **CONCEPTS**

- No input validation can lead to numerous web application vulnerabilities being exploited.
- Server-side input validation reduces web-based vulnerabilities and the risk of XSS and SQL Injection attacks from succeeding.
- Whitelist input validation only allows acceptable input.

Server-side input validation—checking the contents of input fields—is one of the best ways to prevent XSS and SQL Injection attacks from succeeding. By validating data in an input field on the server side and only allowing data that meets input requirements, SQL code, and commands used in injection attacks can be prevented from running. In addition to standard input validation, which involves clearing input of invalid codes, characters, and commands, another form known as whitelist validation is often used. **Allow list (Whitelist) input validation** only allows acceptable input that consists of very well-defined characteristics, e.g., numbers, character, or both, size, or length, to name a few formats and standards.

What is the best way to mitigate web-based vulnerabilities and what types of attacks can be mitigated or prevented

Another approach is deny list (blacklist) input validation where malicious characters can be discarded as they are considered signs of an attack, i.e., if the = or - characters are met in a "First Name" field, they can be safely discarded as a person's first name wouldn't need to include = or -.

Contrary to server-side input validation, **client-side input validation**—because it's done on the client side—may be bypassed and effectively rendered useless.

What is the risk associated with client-side input validation?

Lack of Input Validation

The more tightly controlled and managed the input, the more secure the application and environment. On the other end of the spectrum, no input validation can lead to serious negative consequences, as numerous web application attacks may be possible**.**

Reduce Risk of Web-Based Vulnerabilities

To reduce the risk of web-based vulnerabilities, hardening steps, like those mentioned in section 3.5.2, should be followed. Note that these may vary depending on organizational requirements as well as the systems being used.

In its simplest form, the goal of hardening is to reduce the potential attack surface of a system, in other words, to reduce risk. The hardening process could involve one or a combination of the following:

- Utilization of a manufacturer's product guide, specifically portions related to security or hardening

- Best practice guidance specific to the organization's industry

- Information gleaned from online sources

With information gained from sources like those noted above, an organization can make informed decisions and customize hardening steps specifically to their environment and security requirements. At the same time, an organization should document their hardening process and keep it updated for purposes of application to newly deployed systems as well as compliance with existing production systems.

3.6 **Apply cryptography**

3.6.1 Introduction to Cryptography

> CORE **CONCEPTS**
>
> - **The history of cryptography spans approximately four thousand years**
> - **The most critical aspect of cryptography is key management**
> - **Cryptographic systems can provide up to five services: confidentiality, integrity, authenticity, nonrepudiation, and access control**
> - **Cryptography is used extensively and is often all around us in many different contexts**

The word *cryptography* is derived from two Greek words—*crypto* and *graphia*; *crypto* means "secret" or "covert" and *graphia* means "writing." So, the foundation and meaning of cryptography is "secret writing"—creating a cipher. Cryptography has existed for thousands of years; some of the earliest examples point to the Egyptians and their use of hieroglyphs. The meanings of the glyphs were often kept secret to give a very small segment of the population an advantage over the general public. Germany has long been a pioneer of cryptography, with one of the best-known examples being the Enigma machine, which was invented in the 1930s. Even by today's standards, the Enigma machine is still an excellent encryption tool if used correctly with good key management.

> **What is the foundation of cryptography?**

Regardless of the encryption method or tool, the most important aspect of cryptography is **key management**; secrecy of the key is paramount to maintaining the effectiveness of any cryptographic system.

Table 3-30 below shows a very brief and high-level overview of the evolution of cryptography, which in itself is not very brief.

Manual	The history of cryptography spans approximately four thousand years, and much time was spent in the manual era of cryptography, where simple rearrangements of letters served to create ciphertext. The **Caesar Cipher** is a perfect example of this type of cryptography. Language and reading comprehension abilities allowed this type of cryptography to be successfully used for years by kings, queens, and other rulers, like Julius Caesar.
Mechanical	As manual cryptography can be a very slow and tedious process, advancements were made that moved it to the mechanical age. Machines were developed that allowed cryptography to be done much more quickly and easily. The Spartan Scytale, perfected by the Greeks, involved the use of rods of various lengths and parchment or papyrus wrapped around a given rod from one end to the other, with the message being written along the length of the writing surface. Once unwrapped, letters would appear randomly everywhere. The only way to read the message would be through use of a rod with the exact same dimensions as the source rod and the writing surface positioned exactly the same way.
Electro-mechanical	As the availability of electricity became more widespread, the mechanical era of cryptography matured into the electro-mechanical era, and devices like the well-known Enigma machine and the lesser-known Japanese cipher machines known as Red and Purple were developed and utilized with great success during World War II.
Electronic	Most current cryptography is electronic, meaning it's driven by software applications better known as cryptosystems. Most cryptosystems support several cryptographic algorithms, and as long as the same system or algorithm is available on each side, two people can communicate securely. A well-known crypto system is PGP, and common algorithms include DES, AES, and RSA.
Quantum	The quantum era of cryptography involves the use of quantum computing techniques that have primarily been focused on key management at present.

Table 3-30: **Cryptography Evolution**

With any cryptographic system, one (or a combination of services) denoted in Table 3-31 can be achieved.

What are the five services that can be achieved using cryptography?

Confidentiality	Confidentiality helps prevent unauthorized disclosure of information and to make data available to only those authorized to view it.
Integrity	Integrity ensures that information has not been manipulated or changed by unauthorized individuals without our knowledge; it helps identify unauthorized or unexpected changes to data.
Authenticity	Authenticity allows verification that a message came from a particular sender.
Nonrepudiation	Nonrepudiation prevents someone from denying prior actions. There are two flavors of nonrepudiation: ■ Nonrepudiation of **Origin**: the sender cannot deny that they sent a specific message. ■ Nonrepudiation of **Delivery**: the receiver cannot deny that they received a specific message.
Access Control	Cryptography enables a form of access control; by controlling the distribution of ciphertext and the corresponding decryption key to only certain people, control over the decryption and therefore access to data can also be controlled.

Table 3-31: **Cryptography Services**

Everyday Uses of Cryptography

Data destruction   Authentication

Electronic Voting

Digital signatures   Secrecy in storage

Secure multi-party computation

Secrecy in transmission

Integrity in storage

Crypto Currencies

DRM

Integrity in transmission   Privacy & anonymity

Whether people realize it or not, cryptography is all around us and used every day in multiple ways. When an online purchase is made, cryptography helps ensure the security and privacy of a customer's credit card details and personal information. When a mobile device or computer downloads security updates from Google, Apple, Microsoft, or another software vendor, cryptography ensures the integrity of the files. Criminals often turn to cryptography to hide communications from law enforcement and government agencies. Organizations that sell movies, video games, music, and similar types of consumable entertainment use cryptography for purposes of digital rights management and antipiracy. Other uses of cryptography include secure electronic voting, digitally signing documents, defensible data destruction in the cloud, cryptocurrencies, and the list goes on and continues to grow.

3.6.2 **Cryptographic Terminology**

CORE **CONCEPTS**

- **Cryptography involves its own nomenclature.**
- **Important terms to be familiar with include: initialization vector (IV)/nonce, confusion, diffusion, avalanche, key space**

At its core, cryptography is the art and science of writing secrets that is accomplished by using an appropriate cryptosystem.

Figure 3-34 shows how cryptography systems work. Plaintext (in this case "CISSP is awesome") is provided as input into a cryptosystem, and a cryptographic algorithm transforms it into ciphertext. The only way this ciphertext can be transformed back into plaintext by a recipient is through use of a compatible cryptosystem and the same cryptographic algorithm.

Figure 3-34: **Cryptosystem Operation**

Table 3-32: Cryptography Terms contains a variety of terms relating to cryptography that you will need to be aware of.

Plaintext	Plaintext, also known as cleartext, is simply data that is readable by anyone.
Encrypt/ Encryption	Encryption is the process of converting plaintext into ciphertext using a cryptographic algorithm and a key/crypto variable.
Key/Crypto variable	A crypto variable is a **string of bits that must be kept secret**. A crypto variable is also referred to as a **key**, and it is the string of bits used to program the cryptographic algorithm. The key determines the specific steps that the cryptographic algorithm will perform to encrypt or decrypt. Encryption takes place when converting plaintext into ciphertext, while decryption is all about converting a ciphertext back to the original plaintext. These two processes are also depicted in Figure 3-35.
Decrypt/ Decryption	Decryption is the process of **turning ciphertext back into plaintext** using a cryptographic algorithm and a key.
Key clustering	Key clustering describes what happens when **two different keys generate the same ciphertext from the same plaintext**. This is something that should be avoided, and effective cryptographic algorithms are designed to minimize or, ideally, eliminate key clustering. Key clustering is bad, because if the two different keys can decrypt the same ciphertext, a brute-force attack can be performed twice as fast, as there will be two different keys that can decrypt the ciphertext. In other words, key clustering effectively reduces your key space (number of keys possible) in half.
Work factor	Work factor is an **estimated amount of time or effort required by an attacker to break a cryptosystem**. The higher the work factor, the more secure the cryptosystem.
Initialization Vector (IV)/ Nonce	An initialization vector (IV), or nonce, is a **random number** that is used in conjunction with the key and fed into a cryptographic algorithm when encrypting plaintext. IVs should only be used once in any session and are used to **prevent patterns** in the resulting ciphertext. In other words, the same plaintext can be fed into a cryptographic algorithm, and even though the same key is used, if a different IV is used, the resulting ciphertext will be different, thus avoiding patterns. When decrypting ciphertext, the same IV used to encrypt the plaintext must be used. If the length of the IV is too short, the resulting ciphertext might be vulnerable to being deciphered. This was the case with Wired Equivalent Privacy (WEP) protocol and effectively rendered WEP useless. *Understand what an initialization vector/ nonce is, how it is used, and potential weaknesses with it*
Confusion	Effective cryptographic algorithms should demonstrate some key properties. The first property is known as confusion, which focuses on hiding the relationship between **the key** and the resulting ciphertext. The confusion property suggests that if one bit of the **key** is changed, then about half of the bits in the ciphertext should change.
Diffusion	Diffusion follows similar thinking as confusion, but is focused on the **plaintext**. It suggests that if a single bit of the **plaintext** is changed, then approximately half of the bits in the ciphertext should change. The diffusion property focuses on hiding the relationship between the **plaintext** and the ciphertext.
Avalanche	To determine the security and effectiveness of an algorithm, the avalanche effect should be studied. The avalanche effect looks at the **degree of confusion and diffusion** that an algorithm provides. The ideal case is that a single bit change to either the key (confusion) or to the plaintext (diffusion) will result in at least a 50 percent change in the ciphertext. Figure 3-36 depicts confusion, diffusion, and avalanche.

Table 3-32: **Cryptography Terms**

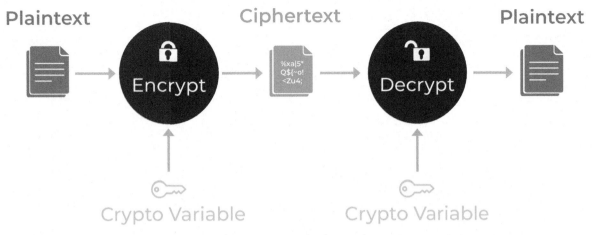

Figure 3-35: **Encryption/Decryption**

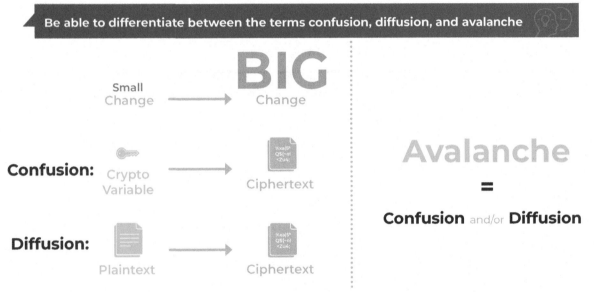

Figure 3-36: **Confusion, Diffusion, and Avalanche**

Key Space

The term *key space* refers to the unique number of keys that is available based on the length of the key. For example, a 2-bit key has a total of four possible, or unique, keys:

Even with the best algorithm, the means to creating strong and effective encryption is to have strong keys.

Data Encryption Standard (DES) uses a 56-bit key, which equates to 2^56 unique keys, or 72,000,000,000,000,000 (15 zeros, 72 quadrillion) unique keys. This is a really large number of keys, but modern computers can brute-force a 56-bit key in a matter of anywhere from a few hours to several days. The amount of time needed to break a key is also known as the *work factor* (as already highlighted in Table 3-29).

To significantly increase the work factor, most symmetric keys in use today are 128- or 256-bit keys, while asymmetric are at least 1024 bits long, with 2048 quickly becoming the norm as computing advances.

3.6.3 Substitution and Transposition

CORE CONCEPTS

- Encryption involves methods known as substitution and transposition.
- Encryption is accomplished through the manipulation of bits—1s and 0s—via synchronous or asynchronous means.
- Patterns must be avoided.
- When implemented and used correctly, one-time pads are the only unbreakable cipher systems.
- Bits are encrypted/decrypted as stream ciphers or block ciphers.

Methods of Encryption

The strongest encryption methods use substitution and transposition as outlined in Table 3-33. If only one round of each method is used, breaking the encryption is fairly easy; thus, with every good method, multiple rounds of substitution and transposition are used. 3-DES, for example, performs forty-eight rounds of substitution and transposition, which provides strong encryption.

Substitution	Transposition
Characters are replaced with a different character	The order of characters is rearranged
GUBBINS > JXEELQV	**GUBBINS > BINBUGS**

Table 3-33: **Substitution and Transposition**

Substitution

Substitution, shown in Figure 3-37, is a method of encryption where every plaintext character is replaced/substituted with a different character to create ciphertext. In the example, all G characters are replaced with J, all B characters are replaced with E, and so on, based on a given key. In this case, GUBBINS is the plaintext, and based upon the key used (a simple shift of three letters to the left), the corresponding ciphertext is JXEELQV.

Plaintext: **GUBBINS**

Ciphertext: **JXEELQV**

Figure 3-37: **Substitution Operation**

Transposition

Transposition, shown in Figure 3-38, is a method of encryption where every plaintext character is shifted around/rearranged based on a given key. Using the prior example, based upon the shifting of characters, the plaintext GUBBINS becomes the ciphertext BINBUGS.

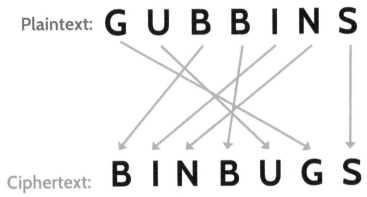

Plaintext: **G U B B I N S**

Ciphertext: **B I N B U G S**

Figure 3-38: **Transposition Operation**

In each example, it should be evident that simple substitutions and transpositions do not hide patterns effectively. The word GUBBINS was specifically used to illustrate this fact. The letter *B* is used twice in GUBBINS, and the resulting ciphertext shows a pattern that reflects this fact. Ultimately, patterns make deciphering the word much easier. In cryptography, patterns should be avoided at all costs, because they significantly undermine the end goal.

> **Understand the inherent weakness of simple substitution and transposition ciphers**

Rail Fence (Zigzag)

Another simple form of transposition is called the *Rail Fence (zigzag) cipher* and is illustrated in Figure 3-39. Basically, the text is transposed by writing it in a table where each row represents a rail, following a zigzag pattern.

Plaintext: **Security through obscurity**

S			R			T			U			B			R		
	E	U	I	Y	H	O	G	O	S	U	I	Y
		C		T			R			H			C			T

Row 1 | S | | | R | | | T | | | U | | | B | | | R | | |
Row 2 | | E | U | I | Y | H | O | G | O | S | U | I | Y |
Row 3 | | | C | | T | | | R | | | H | | | C | | | T |

Ciphertext: **SRTUBREUIYHOGOSUIYCTRHCT**

Row 1   Row 2   Row 3

Figure 3-39: **Rail Fence Operation**

Despite the seemingly more secure-looking output, this form of transposition may still result in patterns being recognizable.

Similarly, transposition ciphers can also be employed using a columnar or a diagonal approach as the key, with the output changing based upon the method used. That is denoted in Figure 3-40.

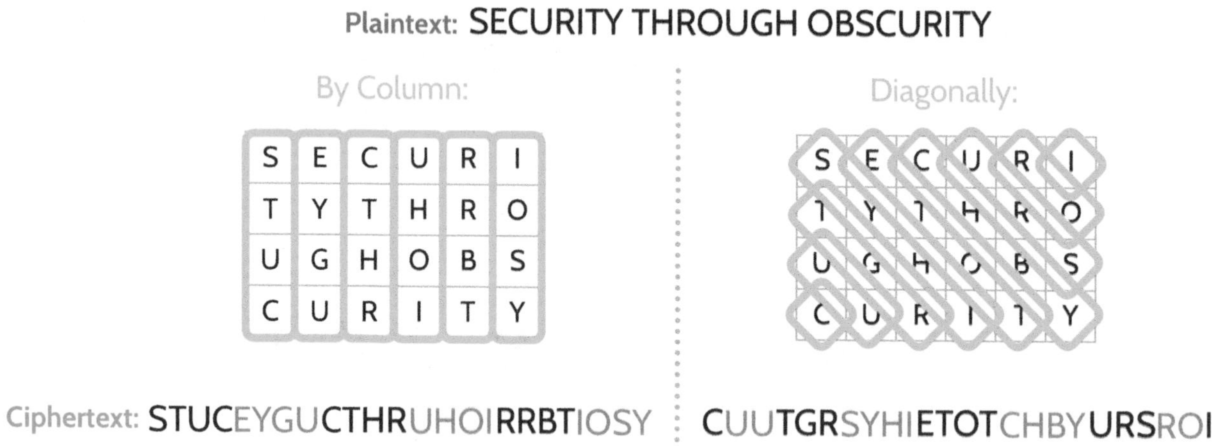

Plaintext: SECURITY THROUGH OBSCURITY

By Column:

S	E	C	U	R	I
T	Y	T	H	R	O
U	G	H	O	B	S
C	U	R	I	T	Y

Diagonally:

S	E	C	U	R	I
T	Y	T	H	R	O
U	G	H	O	B	S
C	U	R	I	T	Y

Ciphertext: **STUC**EYGU**CTHR**UHOI**RRBT**IOSY **CUUTGR**SYHI**ETOT**CHBY**URS**ROI

Figure 3-40: **Columnar and Diagonal Transposition Ciphers**

As highlighted earlier, simple transposition is being used, which means that patterns may still exist in the resulting ciphertext.

Synchronous versus Asynchronous

The examples above could lead a person to believe that cryptography involves the manipulation of actual characters. In fact, cryptography involves the manipulation of bits—1s and 0s—that represent those characters. Cryptography takes the bits that represent, e.g., GUBBINS and manipulates them (using, e.g., substitution and transposition) to create ciphertext.

The bits are manipulated via synchronous or asynchronous methods. Synchronous involves working with bits synchronized through some type of timing mechanism, for example, a clock while encryption/decryption takes place immediately. Asynchronous involves working with collections of bits, and the input is typically dictated by the user or some other element that requires input. A comparison of the two methods is also provided in Table 3-34.

Synchronous	Asynchronous
▪ A timing element is involved ▪ Encryption/decryption requests are performed immediately	▪ Dictated by some other element or entity that requires input ▪ Encryption/decryption requests are processed in batches (queued)

Table 3-34: **Synchronous vs. Asynchronous Encryption**

Repeating Patterns Must Be Avoided

As already mentioned, several times, one of the most important things with any cryptography implementation is the avoidance of patterns. Patterns can severely weaken cryptography, and numerous failures point to key management issues that lead to the emergence of numerous patterns.

To further illustrate, using the English language as an example, common letter usage and patterns exist.

- Most common letter in the English language is **E**
- Most common three-letter word in the English language is **the**
- Most common four-letter word in the English language is **that**

Using this information, a cryptanalyst could examine ciphertext and count all the letters. The one used most often likely would represent *E*. Similarly, the most commonly used three- and four-letter combinations in the ciphertext would likely represent the words *the* and *that*. In the latter case, the word *that* begins and ends with the same letter: *T*. Thus, ciphertext that includes a four-letter combination beginning and ending with the same letter is very likely the word *that*.

The activity of trying to determine keys based upon letter usage patterns is known as **frequency analysis**. Individuals who perform this activity are typically well-trained linguists who deeply understand the language and language statistics related to whatever language is used for encryption.

Substitution Patterns in Monoalphabetic Ciphers

Worth reiterating is that simple substitution and transposition does not hide patterns in monoalphabetic ciphers. Frequency analysis can easily detect patterns in them, as denoted in Figure 3-41, which can then lead to determination of the key.

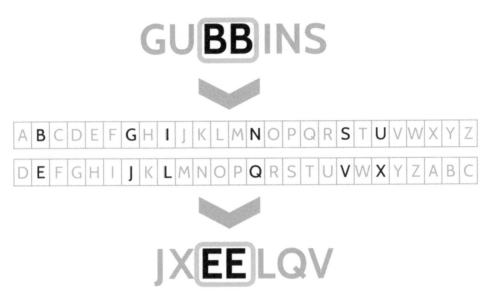

Figure 3-41: **Patterns Indicating Encryption Weaknesses in Monoalphabetic Ciphers**

Substitution—Polyalphabetic Ciphers

By using polyalphabetic ciphers, frequency analysis becomes much more difficult, because patterns are reduced significantly.

The prefix *poly* means *many*, so with polyalphabetic ciphers, multiple alphabets are created and used. Figure 3-42 shows an example of this. The standard alphabet and order can be noted along with the same alphabet in nonstandard format four times. In row 1, the first letter is *Z*, in row 2, the first letter is *Y*, in row 3, the first letter is *X*, and in row 4, the first letter is *W*. Each row number is part of the key, which in this example is 4312.

Based upon the key 4312, the word GUBBINS becomes CRAZEKR. The first letter *G* corresponds to *C* in row 4, the second letter *U* corresponds to *R* in row 3, and so on and so forth. In the case of letter *I*, key usage starts over at row 4, so *I* corresponds to *E*, *N* corresponds to *K* in row 3, *S* corresponds to *R* in row 1. If the word were longer, or a phrase were involved, key usage would repeat in the same manner until the word or message was encrypted.

As can be seen, in this example, no patterns exist. Though *B* is used twice in the plaintext, it becomes *A* and *Z* in the ciphertext because a polyalphabetic cipher was utilized.

Plaintext: **GUBBINS**

Key: 4312

Key	A	B	C	D	E	F	G	H	I	J	K	L	M	N	O	P	Q	R	S	T	U	V	W	X	Y	Z
1	Z	A	B	C	D	E	F	G	H	I	J	K	L	M	N	O	P	Q	R	S	T	U	V	W	X	Y
2	Y	Z	A	B	C	D	E	F	G	H	I	J	K	L	M	N	O	P	Q	R	S	T	U	V	W	X
3	X	Y	Z	A	B	C	D	E	F	G	H	I	J	K	L	M	N	O	P	Q	R	S	T	U	V	W
4	W	X	Y	Z	A	B	C	D	E	F	G	H	I	J	K	L	M	N	O	P	Q	R	S	T	U	V

Ciphertext: **CRAZEKR**

Figure 3-42: **Lack of Patterns in Polyalphabetic Ciphers**

Substitution—Running Key Ciphers

Another cipher that hides patterns very well is known as the running key cipher, which has been used throughout history and especially so after World War II, when distrust between countries was extremely high.

To utilize the running key cipher, the same "book" must exist at both ends of the communication channel. For example, imagine a spy located in one country who needs to communicate with a government located in another country. The spy and the government would both need the same book.

When the spy wishes to communicate with their government, the message that needs to be encrypted is combined with text from the book that appears in a specific location in the book. For example, the spy and government would both know that the starting point is page 32, paragraph 1, sentence 1, or word 5. With this knowledge, the secret message is combined with the corresponding text to create ciphertext. The way the letters are combined is via the numeric equivalent of each letter as shown in Figure 3-43. In this case, the numeric equivalent of each letter in the word *GUBBINS* is combined with the corresponding numeric equivalent of each letter of the text that corresponds with the predetermined starting point from the book, in this case THEQUIC.

So, the value of *G*—7—is combined with the value of *T*—20, which yields 27. As noted in the illustration below, the English alphabet contains only twenty-six letters, so in cases where a combined number is greater than twenty-six, the formula (combined number) – 26 = n should be followed. With the first letter, 27–26 = 1, so the first ciphertext letter is A.

For the second letter, *U* – 21 + *H* - 8 yields 29. Using the formula, 29–26 = 3, so the second ciphertext letter is *C*. Following the same method, the third ciphertext letter is *G*, because *B* (2) and *E* (5) = 7, which corresponds to *G*.

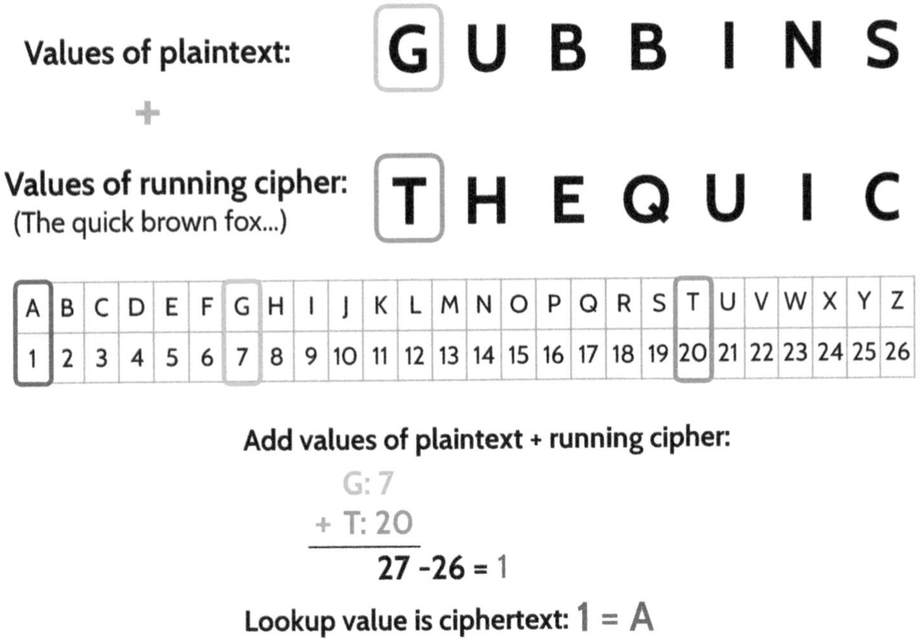

Values of plaintext: **G** U B B I N S

+

Values of running cipher:
(The quick brown fox...) **T** H E Q U I C

A	B	C	D	E	F	G	H	I	J	K	L	M	N	O	P	Q	R	S	T	U	V	W	X	Y	Z
1	2	3	4	5	6	7	8	9	10	11	12	13	14	15	16	17	18	19	20	21	22	23	24	25	26

Add values of plaintext + running cipher:

G: 7
+ T: 20
_____
27 - 26 = 1

Lookup value is ciphertext: 1 = A

Figure 3-43: **Running Key Cipher Operation**

Because a book is used, a very large number of possible keys exist, and each subsequent communication would simply require each party knowing the starting point for purposes of encryption/decryption. As long as a previously used key is not reused, this method of communication can remain very secure. For this reason, spies and their home offices often utilized what's known as a code book. That is a book that has a predetermined starting point acting as the encryption/decryption key for each message. Once a key was utilized, that page in the book would be destroyed, so the key could not be used again.

Substitution—One-Time Pads

With a one-time pad, after every message is encrypted, the key is changed and never reused. Additionally, the key length with one-time pads is always the same length. When implemented and used correctly, **one-time pads are the only unbreakable cipher systems.**

Stream versus Block Ciphers

All symmetric and asymmetric algorithms in cryptography work with bits, not letters. Once a message has been turned into bits, two options exist with regards to how those bits are encrypted and decrypted.

In one case, bits can be worked on one bit at a time as a stream; in the other, bits can be worked on in collections, or blocks of data. So the two types of ciphers that exist are known as **stream ciphers** and **block ciphers.** Variables like speed and where it makes sense to use block as opposed to stream help determine which cipher algorithm to use. To this point, it makes sense to use stream ciphers where data is processed one bit a time, like a computer's hard drive encryption. Block ciphers are typically used in the context of software, like email encryption.

Stream ciphers deal with one bit at a time and are faster, as opposed to block ciphers which work on one block and then must wait momentarily to work on the next block, until all information is encrypted. Stream and block ciphers are summarized in Table 3-35.

Stream	Block
Encrypt/decrypt data **one bit at a time**	Encrypt/decrypt **blocks of bits at a time** (typically 64-bit blocks)

Table 3-35: **Stream vs. Block Ciphers**

Stream Ciphers

When considering stream ciphers a bit further, on the surface it doesn't sound like much can happen with a bit when it is either a 0 or a 1 and can only remain a 0 or a 1. In other words, encryption of only 0 or 1 leaves little to no options. So a bit of creativity needs to be employed to enhance the encryption process.

Look at Figure 3-44.

- **Plaintext** bits that need to be encrypted are combined with bits generated by a **keystream generator**, which is seeded by a crypto variable.

- The bits are combined using a logical operation called **"exclusive or," or XOR**, which helps create the needed confusion and diffusion to make a stream cipher secure.

  - In the XOR process, 0 + 0 = 0, 0 + 1 = 1, 1 + 0 = 1, 1 + 1 = 0 (in other words, the output will be 1 if only one of the inputs is 1).

- The result from each XOR operation becomes the ciphertext.

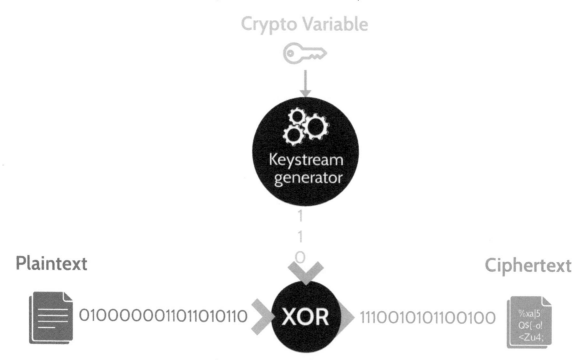

Figure 3-44: **Stream Cipher Operation**

The most commonly used stream cipher is Rivest Cipher 4 (RC4).

Block Ciphers

Block ciphers encrypt data in chunks (called blocks) with a typical block size of 64 bits or multiples of 64-bit blocks, so possibly 128-bit, or 192-bit, or 256-bit blocks. The input and output block sizes remain the same, so a 64-bit block input results in a 64-bit block output. It's also worth noting that most software-based encryption uses block ciphers.

As Figure 3-45 illustrates, instead of bits being encrypted one at a time, they're encrypted in blocks.

- Plaintext blocks, like the letters GUB and BIN, are processed by a block cipher that has been seeded by a crypto variable.

- The output of each operation results in chunks of ciphertext, JXE, ELQ, and the *S* as *V*.

- Each block is processed individually.

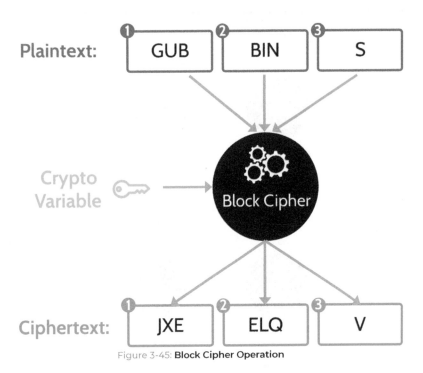

Figure 3-45: **Block Cipher Operation**

Symmetric Block Modes

In cryptography, **stream ciphers provide a clear speed advantage over block mode ciphers, because they work with one bit at a time as opposed to block ciphers that need to fill blocks and do creative operations with those blocks.** This fact that stream ciphers work with one bit at a time makes them especially suitable for encryption across networks and at the hardware level. However, block mode ciphers also provide an advantage, namely, that they have a high diffusion rate and are very resistant to tampering.

> Understand which mode of symmetric cipher is faster/slower

Any block mode cipher, like DES or AES, for example, will support the five modes listed in Table 3-36. Specifics worth noting about each mode are noted in the **"Characteristics"** column. Depending on the need, it might make sense to use one block mode over another. For example, for the encryption of short, nonrepeatable amounts of characters or numbers, ECB works very well, because it is very fast. However, for something like email or text messaging, or anything that might include the same text or numbers, ECB is not very secure. Due to its lack of use of an IV, the same text would result in the same ciphertext being produced, and patterns would emerge, making it susceptible to cryptanalytic attacks and successful deciphering.

For email and longer messages, CBC, CFB, and OFB all work well, because each cipher mode employs an IV as part of the encryption process.

From a speed and security standpoint, however, CTR is likely the best mode to use for longer messages. CTR uses a counter, which is a random initial number that is incremented by 1, 2, 3, and so on during each subsequent encryption pass. CTR is fast, and due to use of a counter, patterns in the ciphertext do not exist. As a result, it is the most commonly used block mode cipher.

Name	Function	Characteristics
Electronic Codebook (ECB)	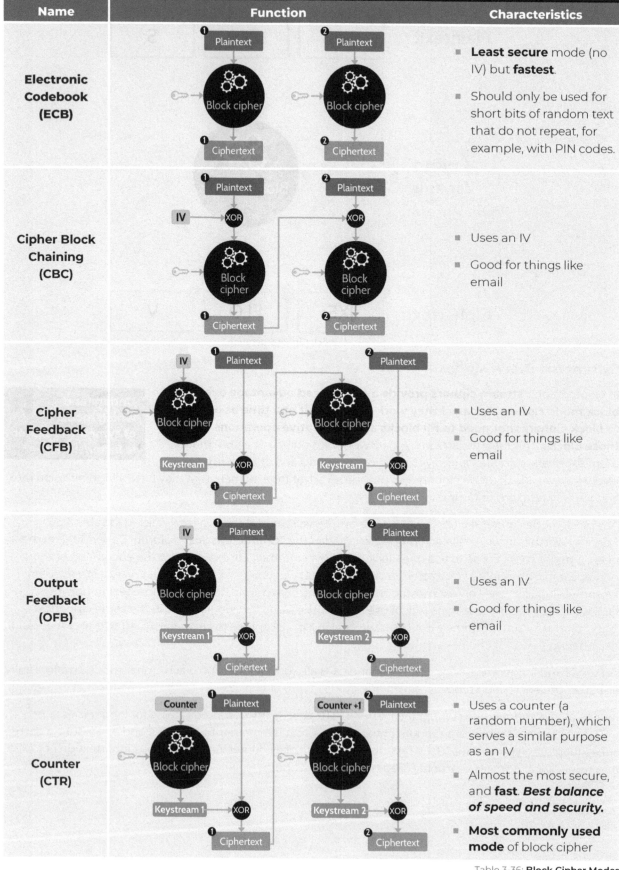	■ **Least secure** mode (no IV) but **fastest**. ■ Should only be used for short bits of random text that do not repeat, for example, with PIN codes.
Cipher Block Chaining (CBC)		■ Uses an IV ■ Good for things like email
Cipher Feedback (CFB)		■ Uses an IV ■ Good for things like email
Output Feedback (OFB)		■ Uses an IV ■ Good for things like email
Counter (CTR)		■ Uses a counter (a random number), which serves a similar purpose as an IV ■ Almost the most secure, and **fast**. *Best balance of speed and security.* ■ **Most commonly used mode** of block cipher

Table 3-36: **Block Cipher Modes**

3.6.4 **Steganography and Null Ciphers**

CORE CONCEPTS

- Steganography is hiding information of a particular type within something else (like a sound file hidden in a picture).
- A null cipher involves hiding a plaintext message within other plaintext.

Steganography and null ciphers are both related to cryptography and used quite extensively. **Steganography** refers to concealing a message within something else, and there are different ways to do this. For example, physical steganography could be as simple as writing a password on a sticky note and hiding the note under a keyboard. Modern steganography implies that technology-driven techniques are used, like hiding a message within an image file, or a music file, or utilizing slack space on a hard drive. **Slack space** is the leftover storage that exists when a file does not need all the space it has been allocated.

Understand the premise underlying steganography and null ciphers

As an example of steganography, another way to hide something within something else is using a null cipher. A **null cipher** hides a message by embedding the plaintext message within other plaintext or noncipher materials. For example, the first letter of each word in a sentence or paragraph could spell the secret message; see Figure 3-46.

Salad embers can ultimately reinvigorate
incessant throat yodelers

Through high rising oceans urchins go hither

Only Brad seemed confident upwind regarding
Italy's third yacht

= Security Through Obscurity

Figure 3-46: **Null Cypher Example**

Steganography and null ciphers are summarized in Table 3-37.

Steganography	Null Cipher
Plaintext is hidden **within something else** (e.g., a picture)	Plaintext is **mixed with a large amount of** **nonciphertext**

Table 3-37: **Stenography and Null Ciphers**

3.6.5 **Symmetric Cryptography**

CORE CONCEPTS

- Symmetric key cryptography is fast.
- Key distribution and scalability are major disadvantages.
- Out-of-band communication can facilitate key distribution.
- Know symmetric algorithms from weakest (DES) to strongest (AES).

Symmetric key cryptography is extremely fast and can encrypt massive amounts of data. In the context of networks—trusted and untrusted—where significant amounts of data need to be encrypted/decrypted quickly, symmetric cryptography tends to be the best solution.

> **Understand advantages and disadvantages of symmetric cryptography**

However, key distribution is a glaring and inherent weakness, especially if the parties involved in communication are separated by any amount of distance. **Out-of-band communication can be used to overcome this weakness**, but this itself is not necessarily the best or most feasible solution. Out-of-band implies that normal communication channels are not utilized to exchange a key, so internet-based solutions would not qualify. Rather, a meeting in person, a voice call, or perhaps an SMS message could be utilized for the purpose of key exchange. In addition to the key distribution problem associated with symmetric cryptography, a problem with scalability also exists. **Scalability** refers to the number of symmetric keys that would be required to support secure communications among a large group of users. For example, if two people want to communicate with each other, only one key is required. However, if three people want to securely communicate with each other, three keys would be required. Four people would require six keys. With each new person added, the number of keys required for secure communication doubles; so, the key requirement grows exponentially. A simple formula can be used to determine the number of keys required for a given number of people to securely communicate with each other:

$$n * (n–1) / 2 = \text{number of keys}$$

$$n = \text{number of people}$$

For example, for 1000 people, 1000 * (1000-1) / 2 = 499,500 keys. That's a tremendous number of keys, and it underscores the key distribution management problem that exists with symmetric cryptography. Table 3-38 shows a summary of advantages and disadvantages of symmetric cryptography.

Advantages	Disadvantages
■ Fast/efficient ■ Strong	■ Key distribution ■ Scalability ■ No authenticity, integrity, or nonrepudiation

Table 3-38: **Advantages and Disadvantages of Symmetric Cryptography**

A number of symmetric key algorithms exist, and several of them are popular and heavily used. For example, Data Encryption Standard (DES), which uses an algorithm called **Data Encryption Algorithm (DEA)** is still used, though its key length of 56 bits leaves it susceptible to brute-force attacks. Knowing the risks associated with shorter key lengths, other algorithms have been developed over the years, including the **International Data Encryption Algorithm (IDEA)**, with its key length of 128 bits—the first symmetric algorithm to use this length. In addition to its longer key length, IDEA is significant, because PGP supported it first. PGP is a cryptosystem that became available in the early 1990s that offers the five services that cryptography can support.

Even with the strength of IDEA due to its 128-bit key length, it never became popular. In fact, the problem with DES's 56-bit key length was addressed by development of 2-DES (Double DES) and 3-DES (Triple DES), which make it more secure and will be discussed further below.

Among the algorithms listed in Table 3-39, AES is one of the most popular and widely used. The US government-sponsored a competition to develop a new algorithm that could be used to protect sensitive government information. An entry named Rijndael was the winner, which became known as AES.

> **Rank symmetric algorithms from weakest to strongest**

Regardless of the algorithm, longer key lengths equate to larger key spaces, which provides better overall key strength and security against brute-force attacks.

Strength	Name	Key Length (Bits)	Block Length (Bits)
Weak	RC2-40	40	64
	DES	**56**	**64**
	RC5-64/16/7	56	128
Medium	RC5-64/16/10	80	128
	Skipjack	80	64
Strong	RC2-128	128	8
	RC5-64/12/16	128	128
	IDEA	**128**	**64**
	Blowfish	128	64
	3DES	**168 = 112**	**64**
Very Strong	RC5-64/12/32	256	128
	Twofish	256	128
	RC6 (derived from RC5)	256	128
	Rijndael (AES)	**128, 192, or 256**	**128**

Table 3-39: **Symmetric Algorithms**

DES/3-DES

DES, 2-DES, and 3-DES all share the same basis, a 56-bit key, sixteen rounds of substitution and transposition, and a 64-bit block size. From a confusion and diffusion perspective, based upon the multiple rounds of substitution and transposition, DES is one of the best algorithms available. As a result of this strength, the cryptography industry has found ways to extend the life of DES by developing variations known as 2-DES and 3-DES. 2-DES works by doubling the number of keys used. So instead of using a single 56-bit key, two 56-bit keys are used. 3-DES works similarly but does not take its name from the number of keys used but rather the fact that three iterations of the algorithm always take place. In fact, 3-DES can use two or three keys. Its characteristics have been summarized in Table 3-40.

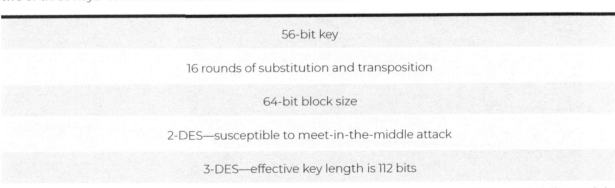

56-bit key

16 rounds of substitution and transposition

64-bit block size

2-DES—susceptible to meet-in-the-middle attack

3-DES—effective key length is 112 bits

Table 3-40: **DES Characteristics**

One thing worth mentioning about DES involves an attack known as "meet-in-the-middle" and pertains to 2-DES and 3-DES. Remember, 2-DES uses two 56-bit keys, so the key length is 112 bits; 3-DES uses three 56-bit keys, so the key length is 168 bits. However, because of the way the meet-in-the-middle attack works, which effectively removes 56 bits of strength, the effective key length of 2-DES is reduced to 56 bits and 3-DES is reduced to 112 bits. Without getting into the technical specifics, a meet-in-the-middle attack works by attacking both ends of the key space and working toward the middle. Once the middle is reached, both keys are known. Take 2-DES for example. In order to encrypt a plaintext with it, like the world CISSP, it first is encrypted with key1 (producing, e.g., 2873!@dOIUD), and that is then encrypted with key2 (producing, e.g., NBDJ029845!@). The attacker will try to generate all possible key1 combinations (2^56) and all key2 combinations (2^56) so they can:

> **Understand why the effective key length of 3-DES (Triple DES) is 112**

1. Take the plaintext (CISSP) and encrypt it with numerous key1 values (generated by all combinations in the 2^56 key space)

2. Take the final ciphertext (NBDJ029845!@) and try to decrypt it with numerous key2 values (generated by all combinations in the 2^56 key space).

3. When the output of #1 matches that of #2, the attacker can successfully decrypt the plaintext.

As a result, 2-DES is really no more secure than DES, and it is not used. On the other hand, even though the **effective key length of 3-DES is 112** and not 168 bits, 112 is still very effective. In fact, any symmetric cryptography key length greater than 90 bits is considered to be adequately strong, and therefore 3-DES is still very effective and widely used.

Rijndael/Advanced Encryption Standard (AES)

As was noted earlier, Rijndael—better known as AES—was the winner of a US government-sponsored competition.

AES is considered a variable key size algorithm, which means key sizes of 128, 192, and 256 are all supported, while the block size is always 128 bits. An interesting side note is that Rijndael supports block sizes of 128, 192, and 256, but the US government did not adopt the extra block sizes.

Out-of-Band Key Distribution

With symmetric key cryptography, one of the biggest challenges is key distribution, because the sender and receiver of an encrypted message must have the same key. Sending the key via the same communication channel used to send the message itself is ineffective, because the key could easily be intercepted and used to read the encrypted message as well as any further encrypted communication.

> **Understand why out-of-band key distribution is necessary**

So, some type of out-of-band—and ideally more secure—key distribution method must be employed to share the key, as also highlighted in Figure 3-47.

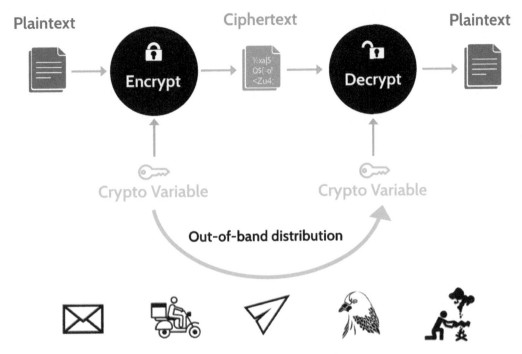

Figure 3-47: **Out of Band Distribution**

Out-of-band distribution might mean the two parties meet someplace and exchange the key, sending a letter, having a phone call, or some other means by which the key can be shared.

3.6.6 Asymmetric cryptography

CORE **CONCEPTS**

- Asymmetric cryptography solves the key exchange problem associated with symmetric cryptography.

- Enables digital signatures, digital certificates, authenticity, and nonrepudiation (of origin and delivery)

- Utilizes key pairs consisting of a public key and a private key

- Two primary types of **hard math problems**: factoring and discrete logarithms

- Popular asymmetric algorithms include RSA (uses factoring) and Elliptic Curve (ECC, uses discrete logarithms)

As discussion about symmetric cryptography explained, it is very fast, but the fundamental problem with key distribution is significant. As a result, cryptologists explored ways to solve the key distribution problem, and in the 1970s two of them—Diffie and Hellman—developed an idea they called "**public key cryptography**." They premised their idea on the fact that symmetric key cryptography requires the sender and receiver to share the same key, and they asked "What if everybody had two keys that were related to each other mathematically, with the mathematical linkage being such that if something is encrypted with one key it can never be decrypted using the same key? Rather, the other key would need to be used." This way, one of the keys can be shared with everybody for communication purposes, and this key can be known as the **public key**. The other key would be retained by the owner and be known as the **private key**; it would not be shared with anybody

Understand advantages and disadvantages of asymmetric cryptography and how these compare to symmetric cryptography

else. Then, if anybody wants to send the owner a secret message, they can encrypt the message using the public key, and because only the mathematically linked key—the private key—can be used to open the message, nobody else would be able to read it.

So the problem with key distribution is solved, because the only key that ever needs to be shared with anybody is the public key, and it can be shared via any and every means available.

Because the linkage between the public and private **key pair** is mathematically based, it's critical that very complex mathematics be utilized to prevent someone from looking at a public key and computing the private key relationship. Thus, because of the mathematical relationship between a public and private key pair, asymmetric cryptography is significantly slower than symmetric cryptography. Furthermore, as processors become faster, asymmetric algorithms need to be strengthened, which means asymmetric cryptography becomes even slower. A perfect example of this is Rivest, Shamir, and Adleman (RSA). RSA is the most commonly used asymmetric algorithm, and its strength has had to continue to increase to mitigate advancements in processing technology. While its strength has increased, its functionality has slowed due to the increased mathematical complexity required to keep the key pair secure.

In addition to solving the key distribution and scalability issues associated with symmetric cryptography, asymmetric cryptography provides some other significant benefits, namely in the form of digital signatures, authenticity (also referred to as proof of origin), and other services. Because of the key pair relationship and the idea that the private key should remain secure and private, if somebody wants to prove to somebody else that a certain message was sent by them, they can encrypt the message using their private key. Anybody with the public key could decrypt and read the message, but this might not matter as much as proving that the sender of the message is who they say they are. This is known as authenticity or proof of origin.

Looking at symmetric and asymmetric cryptography together, it's clear that each offers advantages and disadvantages; yet the disadvantage of one is usually found as an advantage with the other. Thus, both types of cryptography are often used together in what's known as hybrid cryptography, or hybrid mode, which is what SSL/TLS uses. See Table 3-41.

Advantages	Disadvantages
<ul><li>Solves key exchange problem</li><li>Enables digital signatures and other services, like authenticity (proof of origin), confidentiality, and access control</li><li>Solves scalability</li></ul>	<ul><li>Significantly slower</li><li>Requires large key sizes</li></ul>

Table 3-41: **Asymmetric Cryptography Advantages and Disadvantages**

Figure 3-48 shows two uses of asymmetric cryptography. The top part shows how it addresses **proof of origin**, while the bottom part shows how to address **confidentiality**.

To obtain confidentiality, anybody who wants to send you a secret message can encrypt the plaintext message using your public key. Remember, anybody else having access to the public key cannot decrypt that message; only the holder of the private key can decrypt it. Thus, when you receive the message, you'll use your private key to decrypt and read it, which you only have access to.

Whenever confidentiality is desired, the public key of the receiver should be used to encrypt the message; then, only the receiver's private key can be used to decrypt the message.

To obtain authenticity, or proof of origin—identify with certainty who a message came from—a sender should encrypt the message using the sender's private key. Anybody with the sender's public key can decrypt the message and therefore know without a doubt who sent the message, as the sender is the only person having access to their private key. Though this example does not provide confidentiality, it does provide authenticity or proof of origin—knowing the source of the message.

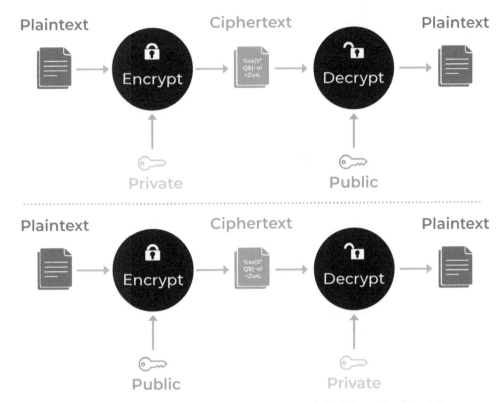

Figure 3-48: **Using Asymmetric Cryptography for Proof of Origin and Confidentiality**

A good example might include situations where software patches are concerned. When Microsoft publishes patches, end users want to know with certainty that the patch is issued by Microsoft. If Microsoft encrypts the patch with their private key, all end users with Microsoft's public key can decrypt it and know with confidence that the patch they're applying to their servers is a valid vendor patch.

Hard Math Problems

Two hard mathematics problems are still primarily used for key generation: factoring and discrete logarithms as denoted in Figure 3-49. Note that for each of the examples below, very small numbers are being used, but in reality, cryptography would use significantly larger numbers.

The idea behind **factoring** is that multiplication can be done very quickly and easily—take two large prime numbers and multiply them to come up with a result. However, with only the result on hand, it is very difficult to determine two numbers that were multiplied together to produce that. If two significantly long prime numbers are multiplied together, determining those numbers based upon only the result could take several years. This is the type of math used by RSA for key generation and helps explain why RSA is so effective for purposes of cryptography.

With **discrete logarithms**, a different type of mathematics is being used by all the other asymmetric algorithms, like Elliptic Curve (ECC) and Diffie–Hellman, to name a couple. In this case, any prime number is raised to the power of another prime number to determine a result. As with factoring, this process can be performed very quickly and easily. However, with only the result on hand, it can be extremely difficult to determine what was the prime number that was raised to the power of another prime number to produce that result.

It should be noted at this point that mention of the use of prime numbers is very specific. A prime number is special in that it can only be divided by itself or by 1. Thus, when factoring is used, there is only one solution to the problem.

Finally, a third hard math problem exists—the Knapsack problem—but it is not used anymore, because attacks have been identified that can break any algorithm that uses it. In other words, attacks can solve the Knapsack problem, which has effectively made any algorithm that uses it insecure and useless. Deprecated algorithms that use the Knapsack problem include Chor Rivest Knapsack and Merkle Hellman Knapsack algorithms.

To summarize:

- Factoring and discrete log asymmetric algorithms depend on using **very large prime numbers.**

- When using such large numbers, it is **very difficult to work backward to determine the original integers.**

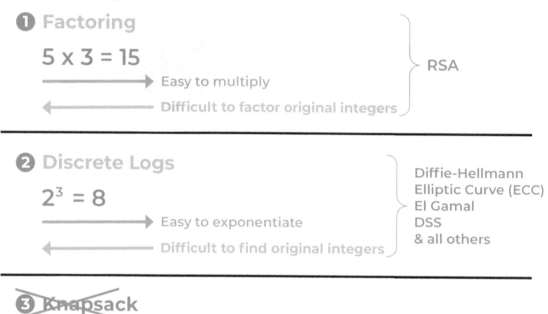

Figure 3-49: **Factoring and Discrete Logarithms Operation**

Asymmetric Algorithms

Table 3-42 contains some of the most popular asymmetric algorithms in use today. Despite having been around since the late 1970s, **RSA**, for example, is still extensively used, because it continues to provide exceptional security. Despite efforts, no significant weaknesses have been identified. This points to the way that hard mathematical problems can be used so effectively and successfully.

> Understand an advantage ECC has over RSA

Elliptic Curve (ECC) was developed in the early 2000s, and it improved upon RSA by allowing for the use of shorter keys to achieve the same level of security. This improvement came because of ECC using discrete logarithm mathematics for key generation instead of factoring. As a result, ECC is faster and more efficient. ECC is particularly useful in situations where bandwidth, computational power, and storage capacity might be limited, e.g., on mobile phones.

Like RSA, the **Diffie–Hellman Key Exchange** was developed shortly before RSA, and it too continues to provide very effective encryption services, though it is almost exclusively used today for the exchange of symmetric keys between parties.

> Understand the two primary types of hard math problems used with asymmetric cryptography and which type is used

Remember that RSA uses factoring of large prime numbers for key generation, while ECC and Diffie–Hellman both use discrete logarithms.

Rivest, Shamir, and Adleman (RSA)	Uses **factoring** mathematics for key generation.
Elliptic Curve (ECC)	Uses **discrete logarithm** mathematics for key generation. ECC uses shorter keys than RSA to achieve the same level of security, which means ECC is faster and more efficient.
Diffie–Hellman Key Exchange	Uses **discrete logarithm** mathematics for key generation is **primarily used for the exchange of symmetric keys between parties.**

Table 3-42: **Common Asymmetric Algorithms**

3.6.7 Hybrid Key Exchange

CORE **CONCEPTS**

- **Diffie–Hellman Key Exchange (uses discrete logarithms) is an asymmetric algorithm used primarily for symmetric key exchange.**

- **Hybrid cryptography blends the advantage of symmetric cryptography—extremely fast—with the advantage of asymmetric cryptography—solves the key distribution problem.**

Diffie–Hellman Key Exchange Protocol

Referring to the early discussion about symmetric and asymmetric key cryptography, it was made clear that symmetric key cryptography is the best, and really only, thing to use when speed and bulk processing are required. It is the only type of cryptography that can host the speeds required for being able to encrypt and decrypt fast enough for the applications that require cryptography today. For example, with a VPN, only symmetric key cryptography can be used to efficiently support the amount of data traversing the network. The fact that symmetric key cryptography is used means that the same key needs to be on each end of the connection, and this presents a challenge—securely communicating the key between a remote user and the corporate network. This challenge is resolved through a bit of mathematical magic, and this method is used by all VPN solutions to generate the same secret at each end for purposes of encryption and decryption during each VPN session. In fact, this is why these keys are called session keys. **Session keys** are symmetric keys that are used for specific sessions—they are only used for one session, and when a new session is started a new session key will be generated. If a given VPN session ends for any reason, the establishment of a new VPN session would include the negotiation of a new symmetric key. For this key to be agreed to, without sending it across the network where it could be intercepted, the Diffie–Hellman Key Exchange Protocol would be utilized. The way this protocol works is described in Figure 3-50.

 The value and use of Diffie–Hellman Key Exchange Protocol

Let's imagine that Alice wants to communicate from a remote location with Bob, who is located at the corporate office.

1. Alice's and Bob's systems each generate a random number, 7 and 3, in this example. The numbers are essentially a secret, as they don't know each other's numbers.

2. On each end, the random number is multiplied by the same number, in this example 2. As a result, Alice's number is now 14 and Bob's is 6. Keep in mind that with a real scenario, the actual numbers used would be much more complex, as would be any applied mathematical computations, which would actually entail one-way operations—in other words, operations that could not be easily reversed by an attacker. The numbers here are simply to help illustrate the concept.

3. At this point, Alice and Bob each have numbers related to each other mathematically. Alice's and Bob's systems send the numbers to each other; Alice's system sends 14 to Bob's system, and Bob's sends 6 to Alice's.

4. At this point, they each relate the number they received back to the original random number through a multiplication operation. So, Alice multiplies the number she received (6) with her original number (7), and Bob does the same (14 x 3).

5. Quick math shows the result of the mathematical operation to be 42—the key—on both sides.

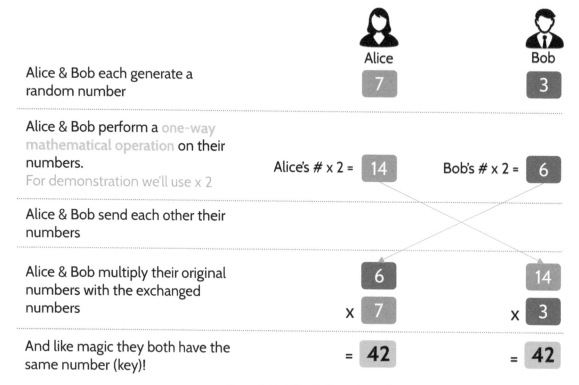

Alice & Bob each generate a random number

Alice & Bob perform a one-way mathematical operation on their numbers.
For demonstration we'll use x 2

Alice & Bob send each other their numbers

Alice & Bob multiply their original numbers with the exchanged numbers

And like magic they both have the same number (key)!

Figure 3-50: **Diffie–Hellman Operation**

Though simple, this example illustrates how a bit of mathematical magic serves to generate the same secret at both ends, which really represents the symmetric session key that can be used for encryption and decryption purposes. This process explains why Diffie–Hellman is referred to as a key management protocol.

Hybrid Cryptography

Hybrid cryptography was mentioned earlier in the context of advantages offered by symmetric and asymmetric cryptography. In each case, the advantage of one often counters the disadvantage of the other, which implies that the use of both types in a hybrid fashion can be particularly effective. Remember that symmetric cryptography is extremely fast, but key distribution is a problem that asymmetric cryptography solves but in a much slower manner.

Hybrid cryptography solutions employ the advantages of symmetric and asymmetric cryptography. Symmetric algorithms are used for bulk processing and speed—for anything that requires frequent encryption and decryption and where both need to be done very quickly. Asymmetric algorithms are used to exchange symmetric keys. Additionally, most hybrid solutions incorporate hashing algorithms for purposes of integrity, the ability to create digital signatures for purposes of nonrepudiation, and other features.

Figure 3-51 illustrates how a simple hybrid solution works. In this case, Alice wants to send Bob a very large message. As a result, she can only use symmetric cryptography, and let's assume she chooses to use 3-DES and picks one of the keys that it uses. Alice knows that for Bob to be able to decrypt the message, he's going to need the exact same symmetric key used by Alice to encrypt the message.

To share the symmetric key securely with Bob, Alice knows that she can encrypt it with Bob's public key and send this to Bob. Because Bob keeps his private key secure and only known to himself, he is the only person who can decrypt the symmetric key sent by Alice. Once decrypted, Bob will then have the same session key, which will allow him to quickly decrypt and read Alice's very large message.

Though simple, this is a great example of hybrid cryptography—a combination of symmetric and asymmetric cryptography.

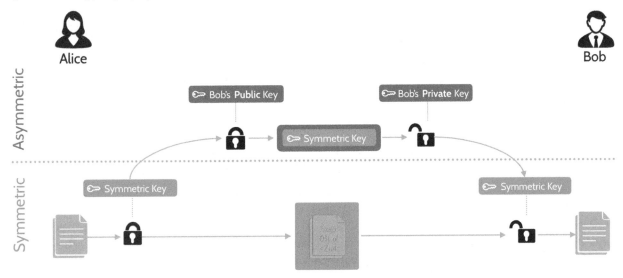

Figure 3-51: **Hybrid Cryptography Operation**

3.6.8 Message Integrity Controls

CORE **CONCEPTS**

- Message integrity checks (MIC) help to ensure the integrity of a message between the time it is created and the time it is read.

- A MIC works by creating a representation of the message, which is sent with the message.

- Message integrity checks are based upon math, some more complex—and therefore more effective—than others.

- The use of simple math can result in a collision, meaning two different messages can result in the same representation.

- Hashing is very effective as a MIC and works the same way, regardless of the length of input; the result is always a fixed length digest, based on the hashing algorithm used.

- The birthday paradox best illustrates how collisions occur and why they should be avoided to maintain integrity.

As a refresher, it has been mentioned that there are five core services that can be provided by cryptography:

- Confidentiality
- Integrity
- Authenticity (proof of origin)
- Nonrepudiation
- Access control

In the context of security and cryptography, integrity means something is intact and unchanged from its original state. **Message integrity checks (MICs) are designed to ensure that messages remain unchanged from the time of creation to the time they're read.** Changes to a message can happen intentionally or unintentionally, and MICs can help identify when changes have occurred, regardless of the cause. Note that message integrity controls and message integrity checks can be used interchangeably.

What is the primary goal underlying the use of message integrity controls (MICs)?

From a cryptographic perspective, if one person sends another person a message, something needs to be done to the message first to create a representation of it. Then, when the message is sent, the representation of the message is also sent. The recipient then takes the message, applies the same integrity algorithm as the sender, and compares the resulting representation of the message with the representation included by the sender with the original message. If the two representations match, integrity of the message is confirmed.

Figure 3-52 shows several types of MICs. Each control is based upon mathematics, which differ between each of them. Cyclical redundancy check (CRC), checksum, and Hash Message Authentication Code (HMAC) controls tend to use very simple math, while the controls based on hashing algorithms use much more complex math. The simple math used by these basic message integrity controls is very susceptible to something known as a collision, meaning two different messages can result in the same representation of each message. Collisions are described in more detail below. **Hashing algorithms, on the other hand, are much more sensitive to small bit changes and much more resistant to collisions, and they are therefore much more effective as integrity control mechanisms.**

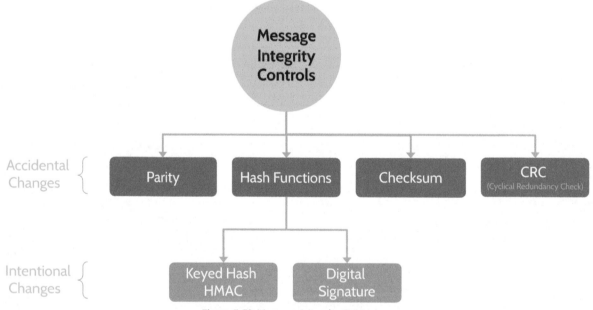

Figure 3-52: **Message Integrity Controls**

Hashing

The key elements that make hashing algorithms so effective are outlined in Table 3-43.

Fixed length digest	A message of any length can be hashed, resulting in a fixed length message digest. For example, a 20-terabyte hard drive or a single sentence email could be run through the same hashing algorithm and the results will be digests (hash values) of exactly the same length. The length of digests for common hashing algorithms are listed below. **Any length input always equals the same length output.**
One-way	Hashing relies on one-way mathematical functions that generate an output – a fixed length message digest (hash value) – that represent the input, but it is NOT possible to go backwards and figure out the original input. In short, **it is not possible to determine the input of a hashing algorithm by inspecting the output.**
Deterministic	If the same message is hashed twice using the same algorithm, the message digest will be exactly the same in each case. **The same input always equals the same output.**
Calculated on entire message	For a message digest to be trustworthy, it must be calculated on the entire message, not simply a portion of it.
Uniformly distributed	A good hashing function should map the inputs as evenly as possible over its output range. In other words, there should be a roughly equal probability of any hash value being generated.
Collision resistant	A collision takes place when two different input values generate the same output. A good hashing algorithm should generate a completely different output even if only a single bit of the input is changed. A hashing algorithm would not be useful to prove integrity if the input could be modified and exactly the same hash value was generated on the original input and the modified input. **It should be very hard to find two inputs that hash to the same output.**

Table 3-43: **Hashing Algorithm Key Properties**

Hashing Algorithms

Several of the most popular hashing algorithms are noted below with the length of their outputs.

- **MD5:** 128-bit digest
- **SHA-1:** 160-bit digest
- **SHA-2:** 224/256/384/512-bit digests
- **SHA-3:** 224/256/384/512-bit digests

MD5 message digests are always 128 bits in length. SHA-1 digests are always 160 bits in length. In the case of SHA-2 and SHA-3, the message digest length is determined by the version used. The longer the digest, the less opportunity for collisions.

Collisions

Collisions occur when the hash values—digests—from two different inputs are the same. As a result, integrity of a message can't be confirmed. In the case of sensitive communication between two parties, imagine if a man in the middle was able to modify a message in such a way that the digest of the original message and modified message were the same. This could potentially lead to serious consequences, as the receiving party would think the message is uncorrupted.

Figure 3-53 illustrates how a collision occurs. Two different messages exist (#1 and #2), which have different content and length. When they're run through the same hashing algorithm, however, they each result in the same message digest. This is a collision.

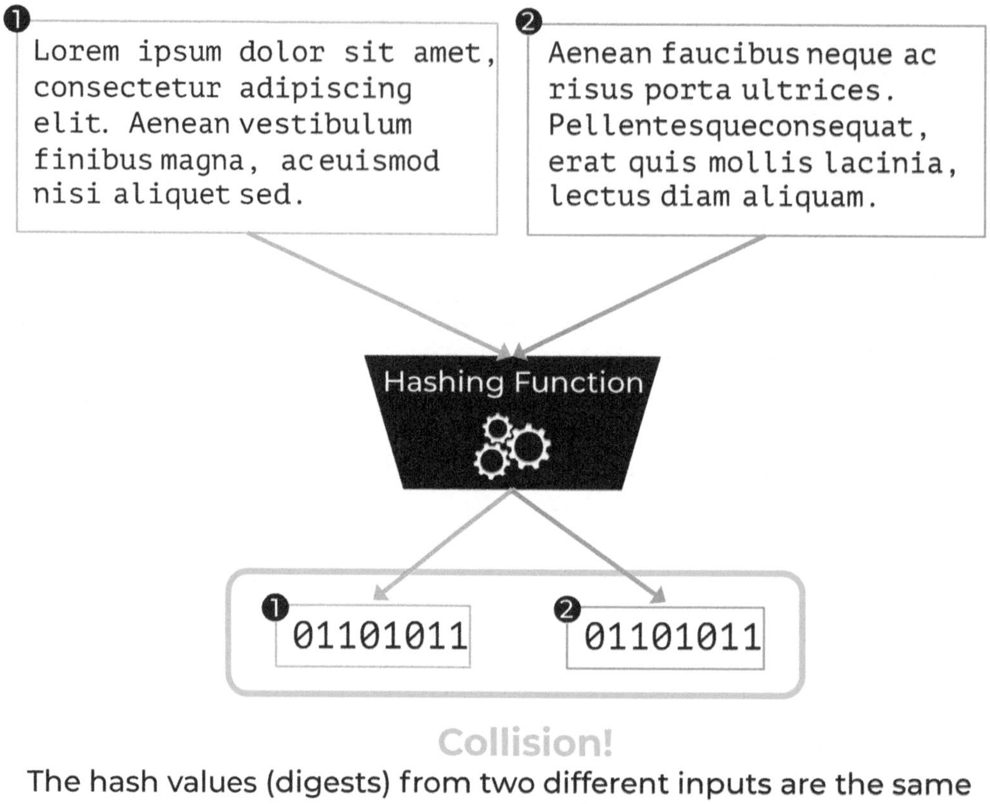

❶
```
Lorem ipsum dolor sit amet,
consectetur adipiscing
elit. Aenean vestibulum
finibus magna, ac euismod
nisi aliquet sed.
```

❷
```
Aenean faucibus neque ac
risus porta ultrices.
Pellentesque consequat,
erat quis mollis lacinia,
lectus diam aliquam.
```

Hashing Function

❶ `01101011`   ❷ `01101011`

Collision!
The hash values (digests) from two different inputs are the same

Figure 3-53: **Collision Example**

Birthday Attack

What's the best way to explain collisions? Something called the "birthday paradox" offers great insight.

As more people enter a room, the chance of any two people having the same birthday (same month and day of birth but not down to the year) grows exponentially. With two people, there's a 1 out of 365 chance of a match. If one more person is added, the probability rises exponentially. Every time one person is added, the probability doubles. By the time twenty-three people are in the room, there's a 50 percent chance that at least two people share the same birthday. To reach 99 percent, only 60 people need to be in the room.

This same concept and mathematics apply to attacking hashing algorithms, where the goal is to identify collisions. In other words, the goal is to find different messages that produce the exact same digest, meaning a collision is then present. This is referred to as the "birthday attack."

3.6.9 Digital Signatures

CORE **CONCEPTS**

- Digital signatures provide three services: integrity, authenticity, nonrepudiation.

- Digital signature uses include having the same legal significance as a written signature, code signing to verify the integrity and authenticity of software, and nonrepudiation (of origin and delivery).

Before diving too deeply into the topic of digital signatures, it's worth thinking about why they are so beneficial and necessary. As discussed, hashing is used to provide **integrity**. However, attaching a hash value to some data, such as an email, that is transmitted across a network is insufficient to prove integrity. Imagine sending an important, unencrypted email across the internet and only attaching the hash digest of the message to prove the integrity of the email. Now, further, imagine that a man-in-the-middle (MITM) intercepted the email before it reached the intended recipient. After reading the message, the MITM altered the contents of the email, removed the original hash digest, calculated, and attached a new digest (based upon the altered message), and sent the email on to the original intended recipient. Upon receiving the message, the recipient would calculate the hash digest of the message, see that it matches with the attached hash digest, and falsely assume that the email has integrity.

This is a huge problem that, thankfully, can be easily resolved with digital signatures, which also provide two additional extremely useful services: authenticity and nonrepudiation.

Digital signatures provide a means by which communication between two parties can be assured to be authentic, have integrity, and be unable to be repudiated later. Specifically, digital signatures provide three services: integrity, authenticity, and nonrepudiation. More details about each service can be found in Table 3-44.

Integrity	To confirm the integrity of a digital signature, the receiver calculates the hash value of the message sent by the sender and then compares this value to the hash value attached in the original message. If the two values match, the receiver knows the integrity of the message that was sent is intact.
Authenticity	Authenticity (or proof of origin) is achieved and confirmed very easily by the sending party encrypting the hash value of the message with their private key and the receiving party being able to decrypt the message with the sender's public key. As soon as the message can be successfully decrypted, authenticity has been achieved and confirmed.
Nonrepudiation	If integrity and authenticity are both achieved, nonrepudiation of origin and delivery has also been achieved. This simply means that the sender cannot deny they sent the message—the receiver knows the sender sent the message (by virtue of use of the sender's private key) and the message has not been altered in any way (by virtue of the hash values matching)—and the receiver cannot deny receiving the message.

Table 3-44: **Digital Signature Services**

Creating Digital Signatures

The process of creating a digital signature is quite easy and fundamentally involves two steps as also shown in Figure 3-54:

1. The sender hashes the message, which produces a fixed length message digest.

2. The sender encrypts the hash value with the **sender's *private* key**.

Note that because a digital signature is basically just an encrypted hash value with an output of 128/194/256/512 bits, digital signatures are very small in size.

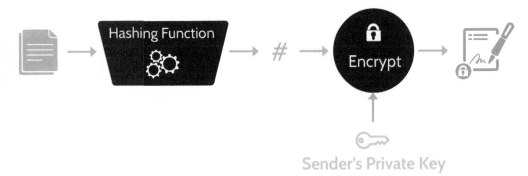

Figure 3-54: **Digital Signature Creation**

Using Digital Signatures

Figure 3-55 shows how Alice and Bob might use digital signatures as part of their communication in order to achieve integrity, authenticity, and nonrepudiation.

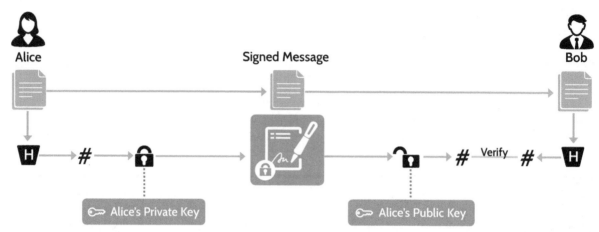

Figure 3-55: **Digital Signature Creation**

Alice wishes to send a message to Bob, and she desires for it to have integrity, authenticity, and nonrepudiation. To that end, she follows these steps:

1. She writes her message, and she hashes it, thus creating a fixed length message digest.

2. She encrypts the hash value (the message digest) using her private key, now producing a digital signature (similarly to what was depicted in Figure 3-54).

3. She attaches the digital signature to the email and sends it to Bob.

Do note that although Alice has produced a digital signature and sent it as part of the message to Bob, if anybody intercepts that, they'll be able to read the message. A digital signature does not provide confidentiality—anybody could potentially read the message, as that content hasn't been encrypted.

Once Bob receives the message from Alice, he needs to reverse the process by the following steps:

1. Decrypt the digital signature with Alice's public key. Once he's able to do that, authenticity has been proven. Bob knows the message came from Alice.

2. Hash the message he received (using the same hash algorithm used by Alice).

3. Compare the hash value he calculated in step #2 with the hash value received from Alice. If the values match, Bob will know that the message was not altered in transit.

With authenticity and integrity verified, nonrepudiation has also been verified. Alice cannot deny that she sent the message.

Uses of Digital Signatures

Digital signatures can be used in numerous ways. They are commonly used for document signing. In fact, compared to traditional signatures that can potentially be forged, a digital signature could not easily be duplicated, because this would require access to the sender's private key. These days, even a whole house can be rented just by electronically signing documents provided by the real estate agent.

> **How digital signatures might be used**

Another common usage of digital signatures **is code signing**, which allows for the authenticity and integrity of code to be verified. For example, when downloading and installing an operating system update on an iPhone, it is important to know that the software update is from Apple (authenticity) and the update wasn't modified in transit (integrity). This can be achieved by Apple creating and attaching a digital signature to a software update. An iPhone will decrypt the digital signature attached to an Apple software update with Apple's public key—if the digital signature decrypts with Apple's public key, that proves authenticity. Next, the iPhone will hash the software update and compare the hash value generated to the hash value contained in the digital signature—if the hash values match, that proves integrity.

Another example of code signing is for a developer to generate and attach a digital signature to code they are uploading to a code repository, and thus the authenticity and integrity of code can be verified.

3.6.10 **Digital Certificates**

CORE **CONCEPTS**

- Digital certificates bind an individual to their public key.
- All certificate authorities conform to the X.509 certificate standard.
- The "root of trust" or "trust anchor" is the foundation of all digital certificates and is represented by a root certificate authority.
- Digital certificate best practices suggest that public/private key pairs be periodically replaced, which means the associated digital certificate is also replaced.
- When a private key has been compromised, a digital certificate should be revoked by the issuing certificate authority.
- With certificate pinning, when a certificate from a web server is trusted, each subsequent visit to the site does not include a request for a new copy of the certificate.

How Can We Be Certain We Have Someone's Public Key?

To confirm with certainty someone's public key, a copy of their digital certificate is needed. Digital certificates bind individuals to their public keys. The issuing **Certificate Authority (CA)** signs an individual certificate with the CA's private key, thereby ensuring the integrity and validity of the certificate and public key being issued.

What does a digital certificate contain?

The process of creating a digital certificate is outlined in Figure 3-56.

1. Alice generates a standardized file that contains information about herself, her company, and her public key.

2. Alice sends the file to a certificate authority, like Entrust, GoDaddy, Network Solutions, or Comodo, to name a few.

3. The certificate authority will first confirm Alice's identity and other information (thus performing identity proofing).

4. The CA will encrypt the information Alice provided with the CA's private key, which creates Alice's digital certificate.

Who can decrypt a given CA's digital certificate? Anybody who has the CA's public key can decrypt the digital certificate, and virtually every web browser and computer operating system include the public keys of the major global certificate authorities. Thus, virtually everybody can decrypt one of the big CA's digital certificates.

When exchanging public keys with others, therefore, the best practice is to do so by sending them a copy of the digital certificate that contains the public key. Doing so ensures that an attacker in the middle, even if they're able to intercept the digital certificate, can't replace the owner's public key with the attacker's public key. Only a certificate authority can modify a digital certificate, because the CA's private key is needed to do so.

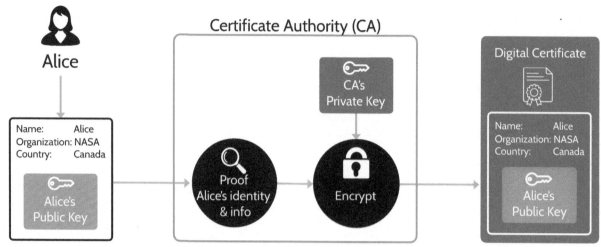

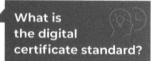

Figure 3-56: **Digital Certificate Creation**

X.509—Digital Certificate Standard

For purposes of interoperability and ease of understanding by browsers, each CA needs to create certificates that are consistent in their formats. As such, all certificate authorities conform to the X.509 certificate standard, which contains fields like certificate version, serial number, encryption algorithm, issuing CA, validity period, and public key value.

What is the digital certificate standard?

Root of Trust

Understand the relationship between root, intermediate, and issuing CAs

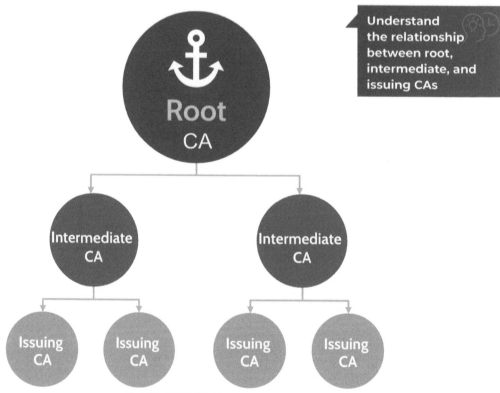

Figure 3-57: **CA Hierarchy**

Root of trust, or the **trust anchor**, is the foundation of digital certificates' integrity. In the case of every digital certificate, ultimately a root CA's key is used to sign the certificate, but oftentimes intermediary CAs (Subordinate CAs) act as proxies and sign and issue digital certificates on behalf of the root CA as seen in Figure 3-57.

From a security perspective, the reliability of the entire system is dependent on the security of the root CA's private key. If this key were ever compromised, significant and far-reaching global damage could take place, and the entire system could fall apart. The best protection against something like this is to keep the root CA offline or inaccessible and to use intermediate CAs to issue certificates.

The Root CA self-signs its certificate, and it is then used to sign subordinate certificates, usually known as intermediate CAs. **Intermediate CAs** can also sign certificates, shown as **Issuing CAs**. These issuing CAs would be the ones used to sign entity-level CAs—those used by organizations when applying for a digital certificate. If one of these CAs is compromised, then the damage can be contained by revoking only the certificates issued by them, which would be far less than those that would be signed by a root CA if it was constantly kept online.

Figure 3-58 shows an example of the root CA, or chain of trust, related to Amazon's digital certificate. That's signed by a subordinate CA (DigiCert Global CA G2), which in turn is signed by the root CA, DigiCert Global Root G2.

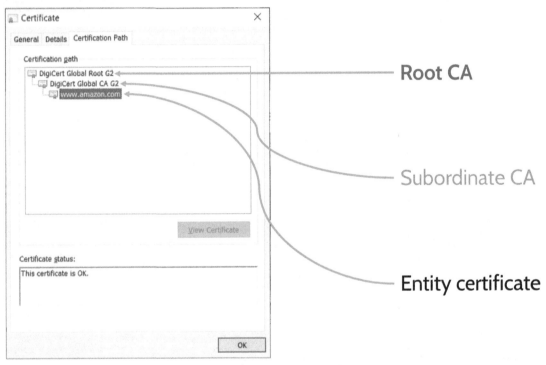

Figure 3-58: **Amazon's Digital Certificate**

Digital Certificate Replacement and Revocation

A best practice related to key management is periodic replacement or rotation of keys, and the same applies to management of digital certificates. If a public/private key pair is being replaced, this means that the accompanying digital certificate would also need to be replaced. As part of normal business, digital certificates are issued with an expiration date, and a given certificate should be replaced on or before the expiry date in order to maintain continuity of operations.

However, in cases where a private key may have been compromised, all trust in the associated public key should cease, and the certificate revocation process should be followed. Certificate revocation involves contacting the issuing CA, explaining the situation, and asking that the digital certificate associated with the key pair be revoked.

Of the two situations, revocation is much worse, because it implies that a private key has been compromised and nobody should trust the public key.

Digital certificate replacement and revocation are summarized in Table 3-45.

Replacement	Revocation
Regular replacement of **expired** certificates	Replacement of certificate when associated private key has been **compromised**

Table 3-45: **Digital Certificate Replacement and Revocation**

Revocation Confirmation Methods

Continuing the discussion from above, once a digital certificate has been revoked by a CA, there are two primary ways to confirm the revocation. The older method for checking involves what's known as the **Certificate Revocation List (CRL)**. In this case, an organization would contact a CA and ask if a particular certificate has been revoked. In turn, the CA would send the organization a list of all revoked certificates from the CA. This list can be quite extensive. Once received, the organization's cryptosystem would search the entire list to determine if the certificate in question has, in fact, been revoked. This is not an efficient process, as it requires a large volume of data to be often transmitted to be able to identify revoked certificates.

> **Understand how the revocation status of a certificate can be checked and the difference between CRL and OCSP**

The better, newer method involves **Online Certificate Status Protocol (OCSP)**. With this method, an organization's system will query the CA, asking if a particular certificate has been revoked, and the CA will reply with a simple yes or no.

This said, even when a certificate has been revoked and a browser indicates the same, users will oftentimes ignore warnings and proceed to a website that may be malicious or compromised. User awareness is still a key component of protecting an organization.

CRL and OCSP are summarized in Table 3-46.

Certificate Revocation List (CRL)	Online Certificate Status Protocol (OCSP)
Client downloads and searches list of serial numbers of all revoked certificates from the CA	Client queries CA for revocation status of specific certificate serial number

Table 3-46: **Revocation Confirmation Methods**

Certificate Life Cycle

A certificate's life cycle includes a number of distinct phases presented in Table 3-47.

Enrollment	To be issued a digital certificate, an entity must first submit a request for certificate to a certificate authority (CA). This request is usually in the form of a CSR, or certificate signing request, that requires certain identifying fields to be completed for the process to move forward. As part of this process, the requesting entity also generates a public/private key pair. The private key is usually stored in the entity's local certificate store, and the public key is included as part of the CSR.
Issuance	Upon receiving a valid CSR, a registration authority follows a process known as **identity proofing,** where the validity of information included in the entity's CSR is confirmed. This process is typically quite thorough, as the CA wants to ensure the legitimacy of the entity requesting the certificate. After completing this process, the CSR will be effectively signed by the root of trust (root CA) private key, following the X.509 standard, and the certificate will be issued by an intermediate/issuing CA. Upon issuance, the entity will store the digital certificate in their certificate store.
Validation	When a certificate is invoked, as part of web browsing or ecommerce transactions, the **validity of the certificate** is typically automatically confirmed with the issuing CA. This process specifically confirms if a certificate has been revoked or is expired, and if either case exists, a warning is issued, and many browsers today will block access to a website or prevent the transaction from proceeding. Validity of a certificate can also be performed manually by checking the CA's certificate revocation list (CRL), a list of digital certificates that have been revoked by the issuing CA) or by using the online certificate status protocol (OCSP), an internet protocol that enables automated lookup of the status of an issuing CA's digital certificates.
Revocation	For any of a number of reasons, a certificate might become invalid and need to be revoked. For example, through improper key management or malicious activity, an entity's private key might become compromised, or the enrollment process could involve incorrect validation of information and issuance. In cases like these and others, a certificate will be revoked and added to the issuing CA's revocation list, which can be queried to verify a certificate.
Renewal	All certificates are issued with an expiration date, typically in increments of twelve months from the time of issuance. Prior to expiration, an entity will receive a notice of expiration, at which time the entity can **renew the certificate**. If an expiration date passes, a warning will be issued to any users who visit the site where the expired certificate is in use. Relative to issuance, renewal of a certificate is a relatively simple process that typically involves confirming the information included as part of the original CSR.

Table 3-47: **Certificate's Life Cycle**

Certificate Pinning

When a user visits a website, like example.com, the web server sends the server's certificate to the browser by virtue of the browser requesting it. However, if a malicious actor is sitting between the web server and the user, the malicious actor might send a spoofed certificate to the user when the browser makes the request. Certificate pinning offers a means by which this possibility can be avoided.

> **What is certificate pinning?**

With certificate pinning, when a certificate from a web server is trusted, each subsequent visit to the site does not include a request for a new copy of the certificate. There are two primary ways to accomplish certificate pinning:

1. When an application is first created, by coding the certificate into the application itself. Thus, if the certificate is already pinned to the application, there is no need to request a copy of the certificate from the server.

2. The very first time a website is visited, the certificate obtained from the initial request is pinned to the browser, and no subsequent requests are required during future visits to the same site.

Fundamentally, certificate pinning involves no key distribution and thus alleviates any concerns relating to it.

3.6.11 Public Key Infrastructure

> **CORE CONCEPTS**
>
> - Public key infrastructure (PKI) is the basis for keys to be distributed and owners of public keys to be verified.
>
> - The standard used to create all digital certificates is X.509.
>
> - PKI consists of several components: certificate authority (CA), registration authority (RA), intermediate/issuing CA, certificate DB, certificate store.
>
> - The root of trust in any PKI is the CA, which ultimately issues certificates.

Public key infrastructure (PKI) is the entire suite of technology systems that allows keys to be distributed and owners of public keys to be verified.

> **Understand the major components of PKI and the certificate life cycle**

Figure 3-59 highlights the major components of PKI, which have also been summarized in Table 3-48.

In the left pane, you see Alice, who desires to have her own public and private key pair. She generates this pair of keys using an application on her computer and stores them in her machine's certificate store. It's especially important that her private key be kept very secure, because Alice is the only person who should ever have access to it. Looking at the lower right pane, we see Bob as the relying party with whom Alice wants to communicate. To communicate with Bob, Alice must send him her public key. However, if she simply sends her public key, there's a risk: her key could be intercepted and replaced with an attacker's public key. Instead, Alice will send her digital certificate.

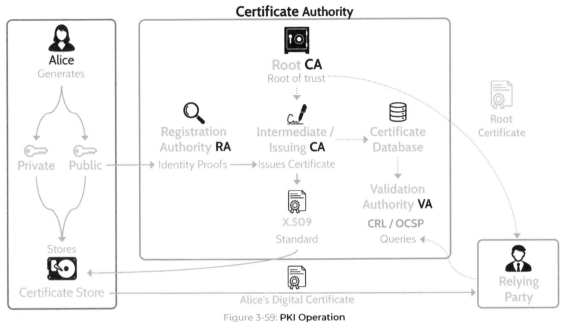

Figure 3-59: **PKI Operation**

To obtain a digital certificate that contains her public key, Alice must utilize a certificate authority (CA). A **Registration Authority (RA)** will ask Alice for some identifying information as well as a copy of her public key and it will "**identity proof**" Alice to confirm she is, in fact, Alice. After this step, Alice's public key will be signed by the root CA's private key. The root CA is known as the root of trust, but the signing process is usually facilitated through an intermediary known as the intermediate or issuing CA. Once signed, the intermediate/issuing CA issues the certificate.

Once issued, Alice can store a copy of the certificate in her Certificate Store, and she can send a copy of the certificate to Bob. As time passes, Bob might want to confirm that Alice's certificate is still valid or learn if it's been revoked. To do this, Bob can query the Validation Authority (VA) entity of the certificate authority via one of two prementioned protocols, CRL or OCSP. Each certificated authority maintains a large database, known as the **Certificate Database**, of all the certificates they have issued, and which have been revoked.

Finally, for Bob to decrypt Alice's certificate, he's going to need the root CA's public key (which can be obtained from the root CA's certificate), which is typically preinstalled in commonly used operating systems and web browsers.

Certificate Authority (CA)	Root of trust
Registration Authority (RA)	Identity proofs on behalf of CA
Intermediate / Issuing CA	Issues certificates on behalf of CA
Certificate DB	List of certificates issued by CA and revocation list
Certificate Store	Repository of certificates and user's private key on user's computer

Table 3-48: **PKI Components**

Note that without a PKI it is still possible to encrypt and send data, but you cannot verify the identities of the other participating parties. In other words, without a PKI, it's impossible to entirely trust the digital identity of another entity or person.

3.6.12 Key Management

As already mentioned, key management is incredibly important. If a key is secure, the underlying cryptographic system is secure. In other words, an attacker can know the ciphertext, the algorithm, the IV, and everything else about the system, and if the key remains secure, the system is secure. This concept was formalized by Auguste Kerckhoffs, a Dutch cryptographer, in the nineteenth century and is known as Kerckhoffs' principle.

Kerckhoffs' Principle

Kerckhoffs' principle states that *a cryptosystem should be secure even if everything about the system, **except the key**, is public knowledge.*

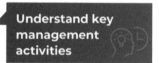
Understand key management activities

Table 3-49 contains numerous key management activities, which are also explained in more detail later.

Key Creation / Generation	The key generation/creation process includes the following attributes:: <ul><li>fully automated process, because a manual process would likely lead to patterns being present</li><li>keys are randomly chosen from the entire available key space, which helps avoid patterns, and pseudorandom number generators are typically employed for this very purpose</li><li>asymmetric keys are much longer than symmetric keys</li></ul>
Key Distribution	Key distribution is the practice of securely distributing keys. Methods used could include: <ul><li>out-of-band distribution (although this is not very efficient)</li><li>key wrapping using key encrypting keys (KEK)</li></ul>
Key Storage	Key storage is one of the most critical—if not the most critical—aspects of securing a cryptographic system. Two types of systems are utilized for key storage: <ul><li>Trusted Platform Module (TPM)</li><li>Hardware Security Module (HSM)</li></ul>
Key Change / Rotation	Key change/rotation refers to how often encryption keys should be replaced.
Key Distribution / Disposition	Key disposition refers to how keys are handled, especially in instances where data in the cloud is concerned. Two primary methods of key disposition/destruction are most often used: <ul><li>crypto shredding</li><li>key destruction</li></ul>
Key Recovery	Key recovery refers to techniques used to recover a key. Three primary techniques exist: split-knowledge, dual control, and key escrow.

Table 3-49: **Key Management Activities**

Key Creation/Generation

Key creation/generation focuses on creating keys. Ideally, this process should be fully automated. In other words, people should not attempt to generate their own keys in order to avoid a significant weakness: patterns. Humans are not very adept at creating true randomness, and anything that contains patterns in cryptography is prone to being deciphered very quickly. Thus, the use of computer systems can help avoid this issue, though even computer systems use what are known as pseudorandom number generators, which are not truly random numbers. However, for purposes of cryptography, a pseudo randomly generated number will not likely demonstrate a pattern for too many years to count.

In addition to utilizing an automated key creation process, keys should be randomly chosen from the entire key space. For example, DES has a key of 56 bits, which gives it a key space of (2^{56}) or approximately 72 quadrillion keys. When choosing a key from that space, it should be chosen in a truly random manner instead of in order of creation or incrementally.

Key Distribution

After keys have been generated, they need to be distributed, and two primary methods of key distribution exist: out-of-band and key wrapping.

Out-of-band refers to the practice of using a different way to communicate the key than the method being utilized to exchange messages. In other words, if people are communicating via the internet, out-of-band could be any of the following, to name a few examples:

- in person
- phone call
- letter

Key wrapping, better known as key encryption keys (KEK), operates just as the name suggests. A key is "wrapped" inside another key. For example, imagine two people (Amanda and John) know they'll be communicating quite a bit over the course of a week, and they want to use a symmetric key to encrypt their communications. Additionally, for extra security, they want to change the symmetric key every hour. Obviously, many keys will be required to meet this requirement. Something like Diffie–Hellman Key Exchange could be used to share the keys, but this would require quite a bit of work. A better solution would be to generate the number of keys needed, about two hundred for this example so extra keys are also available, and then use Diffie–Hellman to generate the same symmetric key on each side. Then this one symmetric key can be used to "wrap" and exchange the two hundred keys. This is key wrapping—many keys are encrypted with another key.

Key Storage

By now, it should be clear that key storage is one of the most critical—if not the most critical—aspects of securing a cryptographic system. Two types of systems are utilized for key storage: the Trusted Platform Module (TPM) and Hardware Security Module (HSM). Table 3-50 summarizes their characteristics.

 Trusted Platform Module (TPM)	A TPM is a tiny microchip installed on the motherboard of laptops and servers that stores encryption keys for the system on which it is installed. In other words, a given system's certificate store is storing the keys in the TPM module. This is important, especially as it relates to full drive encryption, which means the entire hard drive is encrypted. If the keys were stored on the hard drive and somebody stole the drive, they would have access to the ciphertext—the encrypted hard drive—as well as the key to decrypt it. This explains why a TPM module is installed on the motherboard and essentially operates as a self-contained unit for the sake of cryptographic operations related to the device on which it is installed. To summarize, *a TPM is a secure computer chip (crypto processor) built into machines (e.g., laptops), which stores encryption keys and certificates.*
 **Hardware Security Module (HSM)**	Unlike a TPM, which stores encryption keys for a single device, a Hardware Security Module (HSM) stores encryption keys for an entire organization. An HSM essentially looks like a server and is connected to a network, though it is a very hardened device. It's locked down so tightly because its sole purpose is to generate and store encryption keys for an organization. To summarize, *a HSM is a physical device, typically connected to an organization's network, specifically built to securely store and manage encryption keys for the organization.*

Table 3-50: **Key Storage Techniques**

Key Rotation

The concept of *key rotation* refers to how often encryption keys should be replaced. The value of the asset is what commonly dictates the frequency of key rotation. The more valuable the asset, the more frequently the key should be rotated.

Key Recovery

There are three main methods to perform key recovery as noted in Table 3-51.

Split Knowledge	Could be as simple as writing the key out on a piece of paper, cutting the paper in half, or into thirds, and then giving the other pieces to other people. Knowledge of the key is split among two or more parties.
Dual Control	Imagine a scenario that involves a nuclear missile. To launch it, two keys must be turned at the same time. Have you ever seen *Crimson Tide*? Both the submarine captain and the executive officer needed to turn their launch keys for a missile launch to take place. So, there's at least two different controls that must happen at the same time. With encryption keys, this is often implemented using tiny vaults. The backup encryption keys are stored in a vault, which can only be unlocked via the presence of two individuals. This is a form of dual control
Key Escrow	The term *escrow* refers to a trusted third party, usually in the context of significant financial transactions. Anyone who has bought or sold a house has likely dealt with escrow, because the seller doesn't want to give the keys to the buyer until money is in the bank, and the buyer doesn't want to give the money until the keys are in hand. So, a trusted third-party acts on behalf of both parties and accepts the keys and the money on behalf of each party. Once in possession of both, it hands the keys to the buyer and the money to the seller. Key escrow means encryption keys are stored with a trusted third party. It's very commonly used with cloud computing. In some countries, encryption keys must be shared with the government in order to conduct business there.

Table 3-51: **Key Recovery Methods**

Key Disposition

Key disposition, or key destruction, is a very important matter. Let's examine this in the context of cloud, where data is actually stored across multiple servers and hard drives. Imagine that some of this data is sensitive, like PII. Now imagine that the organization storing this data desires to move to a different cloud service provider. After moving the data, say, from AWS to Azure, privacy laws dictate that the data previously stored on AWS must be securely destroyed. Secure destruction means the organization can prove the data has, in fact, been removed from AWS. The best way to securely destroy data is to physically destroy the media used to store the data. This points to things like shredding, melting, or otherwise rendering every part of a hard drive unusable.

However, in this case, simply asking Amazon to delete the data is not enough. You can't be sure the vendor will do that, especially when other customers have data on those same hard drives and that data is likely spread across numerous drives.

Crypto shredding is another key disposition method that can be used, especially if the data is stored in the cloud. You can choose a strong encryption algorithm and encrypt that data and then destroy the key, which would mean that the data is effectively destroyed. Nobody can read it, because it's been strongly encrypted, and the decryption key has been destroyed.

3.6.13 S/MIME

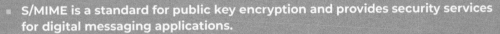

CORE **CONCEPTS**
- S/MIME is a standard for public key encryption and provides security services for digital messaging applications.
- S/MIME requires the establishment or utilization of a public key infrastructure (PKI) in order to work properly.

Secure/Multipurpose Internet Mail Extensions—better known as S/MIME, is a standard for public key encryption and provides a number of security services for digital messaging applications. Basic security services offered by S/MIME are:

- Authentication
- Nonrepudiation of origin
- Message integrity
- Confidentiality

S/MIME also offers optional security services, including:

- Signed receipts
- Security labels
- Secure mailing lists
- Extended method of identifying the signer's certificate(s)

S/MIME's popularity grew out of necessity, as internet email has evolved from a simple platform capable of handling text-based messages to a much more complex platform capable of handling digital images, files, sound clips, and other forms of multimedia. This evolution of internet email technology coincided with a shift in design and use, from a relatively small community of trusted colleagues at universities and government agencies to the global community. Due to the nature of internet email usage during the early years, the need for security was minimal, and it was not designed into solutions.

Understand the basic differences between MIME and S/MIME and the services S/MIME provides

As usage expanded to include millions of users around the world as well as different types of digital information beyond simple text-based messages, Multipurpose Internet Mail Extensions (MIME) was employed. MIME does not address security issues, but security features were developed and added to MIME to create S/MIME.

S/MIME adds features to email messaging, including:

- Digital signatures for authentication of sender
- Encryption for message privacy
- Hashing for message integrity and nonrepudiation of origin

To use these features, a public key infrastructure (PKI) must be in use to support senders and recipients of S/MIME messages.

Putting it All Together

Let's now walk through an example that shows all five services of cryptography in use and demonstrates where it's best to use symmetric cryptography vs. asymmetric cryptography, and digital signatures vs. digital certificates. In this example, Alice and Bob have never communicated before, and Alice wants to send a very large file to Bob. In sending this file, Alice wants to achieve:

- Confidentiality,
- Integrity,
- Authenticity (Proof of Origin),
- Nonrepudiation of origin and nonrepudiation of delivery,
- and Access control

Step 1. Alice and Bob need a copy of each other's public keys. But recall, they can't just send each other their public keys, because they couldn't verify they had received each other's public key. Therefore, the first thing Alice and Bob exchange are their digital certificates to give each other a verifiable copy of their public key, as depicted in Figure 3-60.

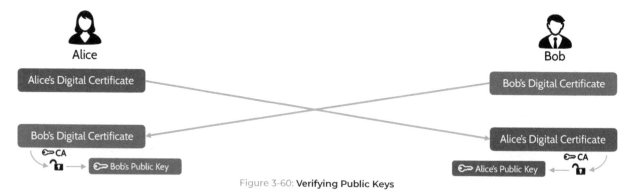

Figure 3-60: **Verifying Public Keys**

Step 2. Alice wants to send a very large document to Bob, and she wants it to remain *confidential*. Thus, she needs to encrypt the file, and because it is a very large file, she needs to use a fast and efficient encryption method. Symmetric key cryptography provides the solution. She needs to encrypt the file using a symmetric encryption algorithm, such as AES. She now faces the Achilles' heel of symmetric algorithms: key distribution. She needs to somehow securely transmit a symmetric encryption key to Bob.

Alice selects a symmetric encryption algorithm and generates a symmetric encryption key. To send this symmetric encryption key with confidentiality to Bob, she encrypts the symmetric key with Bob's public key. This ensures that only Bob's private key can be used to decrypt the copy of the symmetric key and solves the problem of key distribution. Alice can send the encrypted symmetric key to Bob, and the only person in the world that should be able to decrypt is Bob with his private key, as depicted in Figure 3-61.

Figure 3-61: **Symmetric Key Distribution**

Step 3. Alice can now encrypt the file with the symmetric algorithm she selected—the same symmetric key she sent to Bob. Encrypting the plaintext of the file generates a large file of ciphertext that Alice sends to Bob. Bob can then decrypt the file using the symmetric encryption key he received from Alice in Step 2, as depicted in Figure 3-62.

By encrypting the file and sending Bob the ciphertext and the symmetric key in Step 2, Alice has achieved two services of cryptography here in Step 3:

1. **Confidentiality:** the large file was sent encrypted, thus providing confidentiality
2. **Access control:** By Alice choosing who she sends the symmetric key to and the ciphertext, she can control who can decrypt and thus access the file. This is a form of access control as she is allowing Bob to access the encrypted large file.

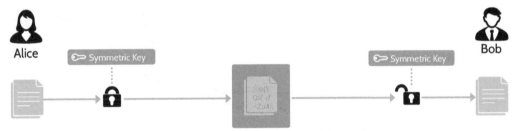

Figure 3-62: **Symmetric Encryption and Decryption**

Step 4. Alice also wants Bob to be able to verify the integrity and authenticity of the file, and she wants nonrepudiation of origin. To achieve these three services, Alice needs to generate a digital signature for the file. To accomplish this, she first hashes the file and encrypts this hash value with her private key, thus generating her digital signature for the file. Next, she sends her digital signature to Bob. Upon receiving Alice's digital signature, he needs to decrypt it with Alice's public key. If Alice's digital signature decrypts with her public key, that proves **authenticity, otherwise referred to as "proof of origin."** Only Alice could have created her digital signature with her private key, and this proves it came from her.

When Bob decrypts Alice's digital signature, he gets a copy of the hash value that Alice generated for the file. Bob now needs to hash the file that he received and compare the hash value from Alice's digital signature to the hash value that he just calculated. If they match, that proves **integrity**. Bob now knows he received exactly the same file that Alice sent.

Additionally, Bob now has nonrepudiation of origin for the file—Alice cannot deny she sent the file. Bob knows the file came from Alice via the **authenticity,** and he knows it was exactly the file Alice sent via the **integrity** and thus **nonrepudiation of origin**, as depicted in Figure 3-63.

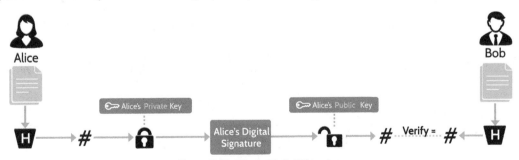

Figure 3-63: **Alice's Digital Signature**

Step 5. The final cryptographic service that Alice wants to achieve is nonrepudiation of delivery. She wants to know that Bob received exactly the file she sent, and she doesn't want him to be able to deny that he received the exact same file. To achieve nonrepudiation of delivery, Bob will need to create and send his own digital signature for the file back to Alice. To create his digital signature, Bob encrypts the hash value for the file he calculated in Step 4 with his private key. He then sends his digital signature to Alice. Alice decrypts Bob's digital signature with Bob's public key and gets a copy of the hash value that Bob generated for the file. If Bob's digital signature decrypts with his public key, that proves **authenticity (proof of origin)**—Alice knows the digital signature came from Bob. The final step is for Alice to compare the hash value from Bob with the hash value for the file she calculated in Step 4. If the hash values match, then she knows Bob received exactly the same file she sent—**nonrepudiation of delivery**, as depicted in Figure 3-64.

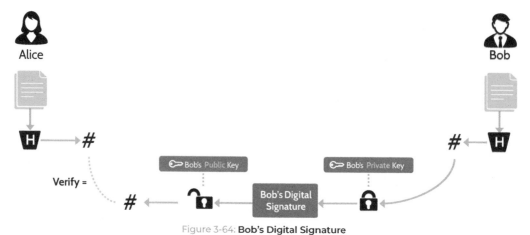

Figure 3-64: **Bob's Digital Signature**

Figure 3-65 illustrates all these steps together to achieve all five services of cryptography: confidentiality, integrity, authenticity (also referred to as proof or origin), nonrepudiation (of origin and delivery), and access control.

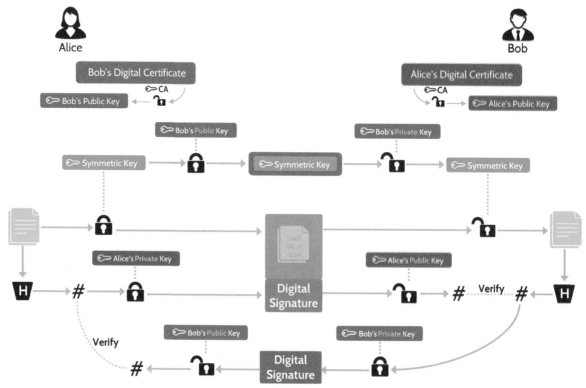

Figure 3-65: **Five Services of Cryptography Depicted**

3.7 Understand methods of cryptanalytic attacks

3.7.1 Cryptanalysis

CORE CONCEPTS

- Cryptanalysis is a multidisciplinary science.
- Two primary types of cryptanalysis attacks exist: cryptanalytic attacks and cryptographic attacks.
- The main purpose of cryptanalysis is to deduce or figure out the key (since in cryptography, everything is known except for the key).

Cryptanalysis is the science of:

- Cracking codes
- Decoding secrets
- Breaking cryptographic protocols
- Finding and correcting weaknesses in encryption algorithms
- Finding or deducing the key

Two main types of cryptanalysis attacks can be defined, as also summarized in Table 3-52, which are going to be analyzed later.

Cryptanalytic Attacks	Cryptographic Attacks
■ Ciphertext only	■ Man-in-the-middle
■ Known plaintext	■ Replay
■ Chosen plaintext	■ Temporary files
■ Chosen ciphertext	■ Implementation
■ Linear and differential	■ Side-channel
■ Factoring	■ Dictionary attack
	■ Rainbow tables
	■ Birthday
	■ Social engineering

Table 3-52: **Cryptanalysis Attack Types**

3.7.2 Cryptanalytic Attacks Overview

CORE CONCEPTS

- The primary goal of a cryptanalytic attack is to determine the key.
- Brute-force attack involves trying every possible key until the correct key is identified; typically not effective unless the key length is very short (56 bits or less).
- Cryptanalytic attacks: ciphertext only, known plaintext, chosen plaintext, chosen ciphertext.
- Linear and differential attacks use complicated math to deduce the key; linear cryptanalysis uses a known-plaintext approach and differential cryptanalysis uses a form of chosen-plaintext attack.
- Factoring attacks attempt to factor a very large prime number, to determine the private key, and are utilized against the RSA algorithm (which uses factoring as the underlying hard mathematical problem).

What is the primary goal of cryptanalytic attacks?

The primary goal of any cryptanalytic attack is to *determine the encryption key*.

Brute-Force Attack

Brute-force attacks are quite simple. The attacker tries every possible key until the correct key is identified. While simple to execute, brute-force attacks are not very effective, because any key length of a reasonable size will increase the attack time exponentially. Table 3-53 illustrates this concept. For clarity, the term *key length* also refers to the number of bits in a key; so, key length = bits. Similarly, the term *key space* also refers to the number of keys available, based upon the key length; so, key space = number of keys available.

The attack times noted in the table apply to a system built in 1999 at a cost of $250,000. The system was called "Deep Crack" and was developed to break DES. Modern computing technology and capabilities would reduce the attack time for a 56-bit length key to minutes and the other key lengths to a fraction of the years required by Deep Crack, but even then, the attack times would not decrease enough to make a significant difference.

Key Length	Key Space	Attack Time
56	7.2×10^{16}	20 hours
80	1.2×10^{24}	54,800 years
128	3.4×10^{38}	1.5×10^{19} years
256	1.15×10^{77}	5.2×10^{57} years

Table 3-53: **Brute-Force Time Relative to Key Lengths**

Additional Cryptanalytic Attacks

Because even with modern computers certain key lengths would require too many years to successfully brute-force, other ways to determine the key can be utilized. A comparison of the most common cryptanalytic attacks can be found in Table 3-54.

> **Understand the different cryptanalytic attacks**

Known by Cryptanalyst

Attack	Algorithm	Ciphertext	Plaintext	Device	Details
Ciphertext only		✓			Most difficult attack
Known plaintext		✓	✓		The plaintext/ciphertext pair is available
Chosen plaintext	✓	✓	✓	✓	All elements except the key are known, and the plaintext is attacked
Chosen ciphertext	✓	✓	✓	✓	All elements except the key are known, and the ciphertext is attacked

Table 3-54: **Cryptanalytic Attack Comparison**

From the four types of attacks in Table 3-54, some may be more effective than others. A **ciphertext-only attack is the most difficult, because the attacker ONLY has access to the ciphertext**. In other words, the attacker has no real way to determine the actual plaintext except through enormous and timely effort.

With a **known-plaintext attack, the attacker has access to both the ciphertext and plaintext,** and both sources of information can be used to determine the key. More importantly, once the key is determined, two things can happen. One, other pieces of ciphertext can be easily decoded, and two, the key can be used to forge messages.

By far, **the easiest cryptanalytic attacks are chosen plaintext and chosen ciphertext. In each case, everything except the key is known, which makes determining it much easier.** In the case of a chosen-plaintext attack, the attacker can feed plaintext into the device and examine the resulting ciphertext to determine the key; in the case of a chosen-ciphertext attack, the opposite happens, and ciphertext is fed into the machine with the resulting plaintext being scrutinized. It's important to note that even with access to a device and the algorithm, the actual key must still be deduced through examination of the resulting outputs.

In addition to the attack types noted above, other attacks exist, like:

- **Linear and differential cryptanalysis**

  Both types of attacks **use complicated math to deduce the key**. In each case, multiple iterations of the attack are conducted to determine probability values of a given key being the key used for encryption. Differential cryptanalysis employs a form of chosen-plaintext attack, while linear cryptanalysis uses a known-plaintext attack approach.

- **Factoring cryptanalysis**

  In this attack, the attacker is **trying to factor a very large number to determine the private key**. In other words, the equation used to create the key is fairly easy to perform in one direction—multiplying two very large prime numbers together—but the reverse is not true; going from the very large number to the two original numbers is virtually impossible and could likely only be accomplished over a very long period of time. **This type of attack is specifically focused on the RSA algorithm, which uses factoring as the underlying hard math problem.**

3.7.3 Cryptographic Attacks

> CORE **CONCEPTS**
> - The goal of cryptographic attacks can vary.
> - Multiple types of cryptographic attacks, including popular ones like man-in-the-middle, replay, side-channel, social engineering, and ransomware.

As noted above, the goal of cryptanalytic attacks is to deduce the key. With cryptographic attacks, the same is not always true, as will be discussed in the various cryptographic attacks noted in the rest of this section.

Man-in-the-Middle Attack

In this attack, denoted in Figure 3-66, the attacker pretends to be both parties in relation to the communication. The attacker places themselves in the middle of the conversation between Alice and Bob. When Alice sends a message to Bob, she's really communicating with the attacker, who will respond and act as if he's Bob; likewise, if Bob initiates the communication, the attacker will pretend to be Alice. Via this type of attack, the attacker can control the flow of information very carefully and potentially learn valuable information that can be used in other attacks.

Understand the different cryptographic attacks and key characteristics of each

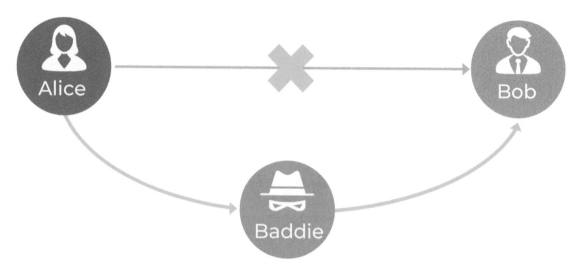

Figure 3-66: **Man-in-the-Middle Attack**

Replay Attack

A replay attack, also presented in Figure 3-67, is like a man-in-the-middle attack, as the attacker is again able to monitor traffic flowing between two or more parties. However, this time the attacker aims at capturing useful information (like session identification details or authentication information) and then "replaying" it later to gain access to a target system. An example of that can be when a user logs into a system, and the password is hashed for security purposes; so, the username and hashed password are sent across the network, and if the hashed password matches what is stored in the system, the user will be successfully authenticated, commonly establishing a session with a specific identifier.

An attacker performing a replay attack can obtain a copy of that session identifier as it was communicated via the network and try to replay it to the server to denote the legitimate user.

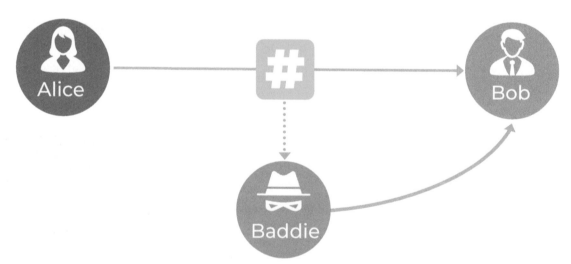

Figure 3-67: **Replay Attack**

Pass-the-Hash Attack

The goal of the attacker during this attack is to gain access to valid password hashes that can then be used to bypass standard authentication steps and authenticate to a system as a legitimate user. Since the attacker doesn't know a valid password for a user, they can try to intercept the password hash and then, instead of brute forcing that to try and obtain a password, they can present the hash to a target resource in the hope that it will be tricked into thinking that the attacker is the legitimate user to which this hashed password relates.

Temporary Files Attack

For any decryption or encryption activity to take place on a system, certain things must be present on the system, like the plaintext or ciphertext, as well as the algorithm and the encryption/decryption key. During the encryption or decryption process, the key might be obtained from a secure storage area and temporarily stored in RAM or another volatile memory location to facilitate quick decryption/encryption calculations. At this point, if an attacker can gain access to the system, they might be able to read the memory space and gain access to the key, which could then be used for much broader purposes.

Implementation Attack

Implementation attacks focus on an inherent weakness in how an algorithm is implemented rather than a weakness with the algorithm itself. An example of this is WEP, which is fundamentally broken. The algorithm underpinning WEP—RC4—is actually a great algorithm, but in the case of WEP, RC4 is implemented very poorly. Specifically, there is a problem with the initialization vector (IV), among other things, that allows RC4 to be cracked very easily and quickly. The IVs used are too short, and due to that, they're repeated too often.

So the issue is not the algorithm itself, but rather the way the algorithm is implemented, which makes WEP inherently insecure.

Side-Channel Attack

Side-channel attacks are very sophisticated attacks and are therefore only used by equally sophisticated organizations, like intelligence agencies, advanced persistent threat groups, and security researchers.

With a side-channel attack, the target is not the system or the algorithm itself. Rather, using complex tools, a system's operations can be monitored and measured. Based upon these observations and measurements of items like timing (the length of time to perform an activity), power used (how much power is consumed during an activity), and radiation emissions (emissions made by all devices and systems), significant insight can be gleaned.

Table 3-55 summarizes the different types of side-channel attacks.

Timing	Radiation Emissions	Power
Focuses on the **length of time** of an activity	Focuses on the **emissions** made by all devices and systems	Focuses on **how much power is consumed** during an activity

Table 3-55: **Side-Channel Attacks**

Dictionary Attack

The goal of a dictionary attack is to determine somebody's password. Rather than trying every possible combination of letters and numbers, an attacker will utilize a much **more efficient method** and **try the most likely possibilities/combinations of words** to determine a password. In the past, actual dictionaries were used. Now, these attacks can be enhanced by using databases of leaked passwords that exist and are available on the internet as the result of past breaches.

Rainbow Tables

Passwords should never be stored as plaintext in a system database. Rather, the hashed value of the password should be stored, so in case of a system breach, an attacker would only have hashed values instead of actual passwords. From the perspective of an attacker, a rainbow table anticipates such a situation and is a **precomputed table of hash values, based upon the most popular passwords used in the world and the most popular hashing algorithms.**

Essentially, a rainbow table is a big database that contains passwords and hash values, and it can be used to quickly determine specific hash values used for authentication. An attacker can steal a password file (which contains hashed passwords) and use the rainbow table to identify matches of those hashed representations.

Reducing the Risk of Rainbow Tables

The best way to reduce the risk related to rainbow table attacks is to use what's known as "salt." Salt is a random value appended to a password, which is then hashed. A rainbow table attack will not work against a database that has been salted because now instead of just the password being hashed, there's a random string appended to it before hashing takes place. This also has the added advantage that it doesn't allow the attacker to identify two users who have the same password. If both Alice and Bob set a password of "password123," then a random salt will be appended to each password before getting hashes, thus resulting in two totally unrelated hashing representations. Each user is assigned their own unique random salt value.

Random text concatenated to a password

Peppers serve a similar purpose as salts, but instead of having a unique random value for each user, the same pepper (the same random value) is used for all users in a system. Salts are therefore considered to be more secure than peppers.

Birthday Attack

A birthday attack is used to identify collisions in hashing algorithms. Remember the birthday paradox statistics mentioned earlier, denoting that in a group of twenty-three people there's 50 percent chance of two of them having the same day and month of birth. That fact could represent a collision. **Collisions, hashing, integrity, and birthday attacks typically point to each other.**

Social Engineering

In addition to the more tech-centric attacks noted above, social engineering attacks can be used to obtain a cryptographic key as well. Two such attacks are: **purchase key attack** (bribing someone to obtain a copy of the key) and **rubber hose attack** (use of duress or torture to obtain the key).

Kerberos Attacks

Kerberos exploitations may take on several different forms, and each involves a password hash related to specific elements of Kerberos. One such exploitation is actually an extension of the pass the hash attack noted above. In this case, after an attacker uses a stolen password hash to authenticate as a legitimate user, the password hash is then used to create a valid Kerberos ticket.

Other Kerberos attacks involve what are known as golden and silver tickets. In the former case, an intruder who can obtain the KRBTGT account password hash has access to what's known as a golden ticket. The KRBTGT account is the Kerberos Key Distribution Center (KDC) service account and is responsible for encrypting and signing all Kerberos tickets. Through this access, an intruder can forge ticket granting tickets (TGT), which means any account in the active directory can be exploited. With a golden ticket and through interaction with the KDC, an intruder can request ticket granting service (TGS) tickets, which give access to system-specific resources, like a SQL server or an application server.

The latter case involves the forging of Kerberos TGS tickets, by virtue of an attacker gaining access to the password hash of a target service account, for example, for a service like SharePoint, MSSQL, and so on. In this context, TGS tickets are known as silver tickets, because the scope of access is limited compared to the access of a golden ticket—the KRBTGT service account password hash. Silver tickets only allow for access to a particular resource, including the host system. However, the ability to forge silver tickets also means that an attacker can create TGS tickets undetected, because interaction with the KDC is not required.

Ransomware Attack

Ransomware exploits have grown significantly in recent years, and one reason has been the corresponding growth in popularity of cryptocurrency. By nature, cryptocurrency is shrouded in secrecy, which aligns perfectly with the goal of actors involved in ransomware attacks—to remain anonymous or untraceable. Ransomware actors could be acting on behalf of nation-states or simply cybercriminals seeking to enrich themselves, and the target of attack could be anything from critical infrastructure to valuable intellectual property, and anything in between that could lead to a significant ransom being paid. When victim files are encrypted, sadly even paying the ransom doesn't guarantee the victim will get access, as that totally depends on the attacker's whim. Also, sometimes the file decryption may not work, which means that file access can't be restored. Lastly, various victim companies hire third parties to negotiate ransom and get file access back for them or work with law enforcement and security companies to see if they can identify any encryption vulnerabilities that would allow them to identify the encryption key and obtain their coveted files.

Fault Injection Attack

Fault injection is a technique that can be used to determine where vulnerabilities might exist. Typically, fault injection involves deliberately injecting a fault into hardware or software to modify its normal behavior, which then allows identified vulnerabilities to be corrected. Fault injection is often used during hardware and software testing. With a fault injection attack (FIA), however, an attacker is attempting to change normal behavior in order to exploit something, for example, an access control mechanism. Fault injection attacks are sometimes used in conjunction with side-channel attacks (like a differential power analysis) where the fault injection attack can be used to reduce countermeasures, and then the differential power analysis attack can take place.

3.8 Apply security principles to site and facility design

3.8.1 Intro to Physical Security

CORE **CONCEPTS**

- Physical security seeks to protect an organization from the outside to the inside.
- The primary goal of physical security is the safety and protection of human life.
- Physical security goals
- Threats to physical security

Goals of Physical Security

Physical security, like logical security, ultimately focuses on increasing the value of an organization by providing protection from outside the perimeter to all assets within, including protection related to confidentiality, availability, and integrity as depicted in Figure 3-68. For example, let's consider availability. Physical security is responsible for things like ensuring that the building's temperature is consistent and that there is a good clean supply of electricity.

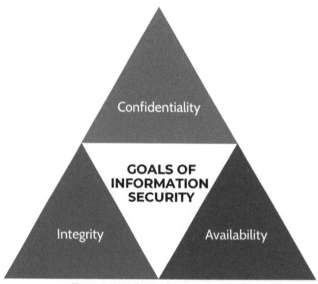

Figure 3-68: **Information Security Goals**

Computer systems can't be up and running and provide good availability without proper physical security controls in place. Physical security is about protection of the organization from around the building all the way to the inside and with the same overarching goals of providing confidentiality, integrity, and availability.

Like logical security, physical security employs several controls, but the names are slightly different. With logical security, preventive, detective, and corrective controls are used; with physical security, deter, detect, and correct are used. Deterrence is focused on preventing. Detecting is focused on identifying something. Assessing and responding is focused on correcting. More detail on these can be found in Table 3-56.

> **Know the primary goal of physical security**

Primary Goal of Physical Security

Safety and protection of human life is the most important goal and focus of physical security, and this fact drives many of the decisions related to physical security. In simple terms, this simply means that the implementation of any physical security control should never put people in danger.

Deter/ Prevent	This type of control serves to deter or prevent an intruder from taking certain action. A sign in front of someone's property stating "All trespassers will be shot" or a sign stating "Danger: Mines" is a great example of a deterrent. A fence is a good example of a preventive control. The overall idea with preventive/deterrent controls is to try to prevent an attacker from attacking. While it would be ideal to prevent an attack from being successful, this is not a reasonable expectation, as all controls can be defeated.
Delay	Delay controls function to hinder activity being pursued by an intruder. Locks are a great example of delay controls; they serve to delay an intruder's activities. As such, they should never be counted upon by themselves and should be used in combination with other controls such as cameras to detect an attacker attempting to pick a lock and security guards who can assess and respond.
Detect	Detective controls help detect or alert to an intrusion. A barking dog is a good example of detective control; when the dog is quiet, all is well, and when the dog is barking, something might be amiss and needs to be investigated. A CCTV camera is another good example of a detective control, as it can detect and capture activity and help drive a proper response.
Assess	Assessment can lead to a proper response to a given situation. Assessment functions in the same manner as a corrective control.
Respond	Aligned with "assess" is "respond," which also functions in the same manner as a corrective control and denotes taking appropriate action to an event that has taken place.

Table 3-56: **Physical Security Controls**

Threats to Physical Security

Threats to physical security might take any of a number of forms, and a list of them could grow very long. Below are a few examples:

- **Theft:** The attacker steals items from the premises of the target.
- **Espionage:** Usually sensitive or proprietary information (like a new drug research) is targeted by the attacker, who aims to obtain that and sell it to a competitor or on the dark web for monetary gain.
- **Dumpster diving:** Inspecting a company's trash to obtain sensitive information that might not have been disposed in a secure manner.
- **Social engineering:** Leveraging the human element and trying to persuade a company employee to perform an action or provide information to an unauthorized individual.
- **Shoulder surfing:** A form of social engineering where the attacker is standing over someone's shoulder as they perform an activity (e.g., logging in to a sensitive resource) in the hope to gain sensitive information.
- **HVAC:** Compromise the heating, ventilation, and air conditioning system for either access or damaging company equipment.

3.8.2 Layered Defense Model

CORE CONCEPTS

- The best physical security involves a layered, or defense-in-depth, approach.
- Physical security must always consider the safety and protection of people.

One of the main concepts applied in physical security is the concept of layered defense. Essentially, this is defense-in-depth. Multiple layers of defense are put in place, starting outside the building of an organization. A typical first layer of physical security defense could be a fence. Then the next layer would be the perimeter of the building. But remember that human life is always at the forefront of any security system. Let's consider a question in relation to that. What's the optimal number of doors to have on a building's perimeter? The most optimal number of doors from a security standpoint is zero; however, this is not functional. So what's the next best answer? The next best number would be one, but that may impact personnel safety because buildings need to have multiple egress points so people can easily exit the premises in case of emergency. So that makes the ideal answer "as close to zero as possible."

3.9 Design site and facility security controls

3.9.1 Security Survey

> **CORE CONCEPTS**
>
> ■ Security, or site, surveys are an extension of risk management and involve: threat definition, target identification, and facility characteristics.
>
> ■ **Crime Prevention Through Environmental Design (CPTED)** is a specific professional practice that outlines guidelines and best practices regarding the design of buildings and surrounding structures, considering the environment as well as nearby infrastructure and facilities.

How do we decide which physical security controls to put in place?

First, the most valuable assets and their associated risks must be identified; then, risk treatments can be evaluated and the most appropriate—based upon value—can be put in place. Because the focus is physical security, the risk management process is sometimes called a **security survey** or site survey; still, the goal remains the same: identify the most valuable assets and then consider risk treatments, based upon the vulnerabilities and threats to those assets.

This is the process in security, or site, survey: threat definition, target identification, facility characteristics. Then, based on survey findings, site planning can be conducted. Remember that when identifying appropriate controls, the goal of site planning is to protect people.

Though not specifically mentioned above, one of the primary driving questions behind physical security is "What and where are the most valuable areas?" Inside a building, for example, what's a wiring closet? Inside every office, hotel, hospital, there are rooms—often one on each floor and usually a main room—where network cables are pulled and other network equipment, like switches and routers, are housed. Should people have access to these areas? Of course not, unless they're specifically authorized to access these areas, because they're considered sensitive or high-value areas. The point is this: high-value areas within a facility or campus need to be identified and appropriate, and cost-effective controls to protect these areas should be implemented. Some key terms surrounding security surveying and high-value areas have been provided in Table 3-57 and Table 3-58.

Threat Definition	This is where applicable threats are identified. These could be any type of threat that might impact the site.
Target Identification	What are the assets that might be targeted by threats (identified as a result of "threat definition")?
Facility Characteristics	Identify each asset's vulnerabilities.
Life	This is the number one priority of physical security—to protect life, to protect people.
Property	Closely aligned with the number one goal of protecting life is the goal of creating a safe physical work environment that anticipates ideal working conditions as well as conditions that might exist in the event of a disaster. This includes exterior and interior elements and should support the top priority of protecting people.
Operations	Items like an organizational Business Continuity Plan (BCP) and Disaster Recovery Plan (DRP) should be developed and utilized for this purpose.

Table 3-57: **Security Survey**

Wiring Closets	Typically found on each floor in a building, where wires and other important networking equipment might be located
Media Storage	The area where physical/digital media that store sensitive and value assets is located
Evidence Storage	The area where important evidence is stored
Server Rooms	The room(s) where the most important and valuable network assets and infrastructure are located
Restricted Work Areas	Any work locations that require additional security, due to the nature of the work being performed, the people performing the work, or any combination thereof

Table 3-58: **High-Value Areas**

3.9.2 Perimeter

CORE **CONCEPTS**

- Perimeter controls are an important element of physical security, including things such as landscaping, grading, fences, gates, and bollards.

- Like access points (doors) to a building, the less access points through a fence, the better the security of the perimeter.

A few specific controls that can be placed around the perimeter of a building for protection include things like landscaping. **Landscaping** is actually a very important control. Things like trees and bushes can be placed around a building in such a manner to prevent close access to certain parts of the building and to direct how people move around the exterior of the building. Large trees should not be directly adjacent to a building, because people could potentially use them as cover. The same applies to dense foliage, which could block CCTV sightlines. With the proper landscaping and other well-placed perimeter controls, like lighting, around a building, people with bad intentions will have a very difficult time achieving their goals.

Grading is another control and refers to the slope of the ground. Does it make sense to slope the ground away from or toward a multimillion-dollar data center? Away, so if a massive rainstorm hits and causes flooding, the data center remains bone dry.

Bollards are another great physical security control. They're pop-up barriers, about the size of a thick pipe, that prevent cars from driving on certain streets or into restricted areas at certain times; they're also stationary and are often found in front of office buildings and especially in front of US State and Federal government buildings as well as in front of military base entry points. Stationary bollards in front of these buildings are usually quite large, and they are positioned in a manner to prevent vehicles, even large ones, from driving straight into the building or past a checkpoint and blowing up, which is what happened in the past at the FBI office in Oklahoma and resulted in significant loss of life. Many organizations that employ bollards will use large concrete flower planters around their buildings—this has the effect of looking attractive and defeating vehicle-based attacks.

3.9.3 **Closed-circuit TV (CCTV)**

CORE **CONCEPTS**

- CCTV cameras serve primarily as a detective control.
- CCTV cameras also deter and monitor, and it can be used for security audits.

Closed-circuit television cameras, better known as CCTV cameras, **serve primarily as a *detective* control**, though they also function as a deterrent and can be used for security audits. **A few things to consider related to camera systems:** First, ***placement***. Cameras should cover major entrance and exit ways

What primary type of control are CCTV cameras?

as well as other areas of importance, and they should be placed and positioned in a manner that allows a person's face and other important distinguishing features to be captured. Second, ***image quality***. It's imperative that the quality of the captured images be considered, whether those images are captured during the day or at night and in any conditions. If the cameras are placed correctly, but the quality of the image is such that people are unrecognizable, then the system is worthless. Third, ***transmission media***. Among other things, you must identify how will the images be transmitted back to the monitoring stations and recording systems, if there are people watching the camera feeds 24x7x365 or, if everything is going to be captured to tapes/hard drives, how long will the recordings be kept before being archived. Also note that local law may dictate some of these decisions, as in many areas of the world, strict privacy laws define for what purpose and how long images may be kept, who may view them, what areas the cameras cover, and whether they are recording public areas, and so on.

3.9.4 **Passive Infrared Devices**

CORE **CONCEPTS**

- A passive infrared device is a motion sensor that detects motion by picking up on infrared light.
- Passive infrared devices are very sensitive to temperature changes.
- Passive infrared devices must continually recalibrate themselves based on ambient temperature.

What's a passive infrared device? It's a **motion detector**, and the way it detects motion is by picking up on infrared light. It's essentially a low-resolution camera that's able to detect infrared light by taking a picture of a room on a continual basis and then comparing the pictures. Human beings are usually warmer than a room, because they give off heat; so, when someone enters a room, the

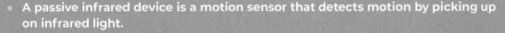
How a passive infrared device works

passive infrared device is comparing one image to the next. Very quickly, the device will see that the image has changed and send an alert, if programmed to do so, or otherwise make note of the presence of the person in the room. Passive infrared devices are very sensitive to temperature changes, and even in a manner contrary to the way most people would consider, especially in places, for example, like Texas. Texas temperatures often get warmer than the temperature of the human body. Once it's too hot outside, many passive infrared devices will note the change of something cooler instead of something hotter. As a result of this fact, passive infrared devices must constantly recalibrate themselves based on ambient temperature so they can detect what's happening.

3.9.5 Lighting

CORE **CONCEPTS**

- External lighting serves as a deterrent and as a safety precaution.
- External lighting allows camera systems to have better visibility of the surrounding area.

External lighting is a very good security control, especially as a deterrent. If a building is well lit, it's very hard to sneak around it at night. It's also good from a safety perspective. A well-lit exterior allows people to see where they're walking, and statistics show that attacks are far less prevalent in a well-lit parking lot. So external monitoring/lighting helps keep people safe, and it also allows camera systems to work optimally and to detect things.

3.9.6 Doors and Mantraps

CORE **CONCEPTS**

- Door composition and frame construction impact security of doors significantly.
- Mantraps typically consist of a double set of doors or a turnstile and prevent tailgating/piggybacking.

On the surface, the topic of doors does not typically receive much acclaim. However, in the realm of security and controls, there are a few things about doors that deserve attention. One of them concerns the composition of the door. In other words, how the door is made, as its composition makes a very big difference as to its security. The construction of the door makes a difference, and so does the construction of the frame. If the world's most secure steel door is hung on a wooden frame, what is an intruder going to do? They're going to bust the frame and kick in the door. So the door frame also matters. The final thing that needs to be considered is the location of the hinges. If the hinges are on the outside and accessible, the pins can be knocked out and the door easily removed. Many exterior doors on buildings have exterior hinges. Does this make the door more or less secure? It makes it less secure, but why are the hinges on the outside? For the safety of people, so when the door is pushed it swings outward. Unfortunately, there have been tragedies at places like night clubs when a fire breaks out or another emergency occurs, and everybody runs to escape and hit doors that open inward. Even though it's less secure, for the safety of people in places like nightclubs or movie theaters, doors should hinge outward.

What do mantraps prevent?

A **mantrap**, on the other hand, is usually one of two things: a double set of doors, with space for one or two people in between, or, a turnstile, with enough room usually for one person. In either case, a mantrap is designed to prevent **tailgating—an unauthorized person following an authorized person into a building or other secure location.** In the case of a double set of doors, the authorized person enters the first door, and after the first door closes, the second door will open. Usually, two forms of authentication are involved: a badge to enter the first door and perhaps biometrics to open the second. If a tailgater somehow makes it through the first door, they'll immediately be noticed and will be trapped in the room. The other type of mantrap, a turnstile, is quite common in buildings around the world and only allows one person at a time. The person steps into a small chamber and the walls move around the person, giving them access to the inside.

3.9.7 Locks

CORE **CONCEPTS**

- Locks are a delay control; they do not prevent access.

- Two types of locks: mechanical and electronic.

- Biometric locks are more prevalent, but employees may not desire to use them due to privacy concerns.

- The security of a combination lock is dependent on the complexity of the combination.

What pieces of hardware are usually found on doors and door handles or around doors? Locks, like the traditional keyed lock, or, more likely in an office setting, some type of electronic lock—card reader, keypad, or biometric. **Regardless of the type, locks are a delay control.** Given enough time, just about any lock can be defeated; thus, they delay versus prevent.

Depending upon the type of lock in use, a few precautions should be noted. Some locks are susceptible to shoulder-surfing, others to brute-force attacks, and many to multiple types of attack. Take a standard combination lock, for instance, where a dial is turned in alternating directions and stopped at a specific number at the end of each turn. Depending on the number of internal mechanisms, locks like this are often easily defeated. Furthermore, if the composition of the metal making up the lock is weak, it can easily be compromised. Keypad locks, where the digits are typically easy to see, can

> Understand inherent weaknesses with some types of locks and precautions that should be taken

easily be shoulder-surfed. In cases like this, it makes sense to install some type of cover or shield to prevent others from seeing what code combination is being entered. And in cases where the keypad code is shared among people, the code should be changed, and access privileges reviewed frequently. Another means by which access to or within a building can be granted is using biometric systems. They're another way of gaining physical access.

Types of Locks

Table 3-59 contains some of the most common lock types. Each type of lock, whether mechanical or electrical, can be extremely complex and multiple variations can exist.

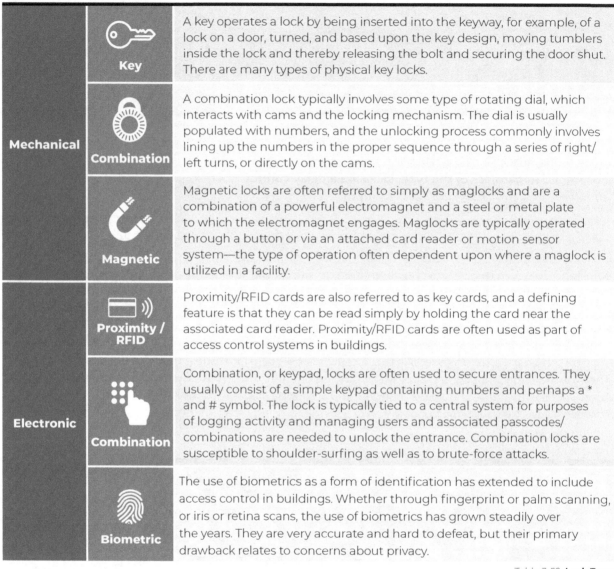

Mechanical	**Key**	A key operates a lock by being inserted into the keyway, for example, of a lock on a door, turned, and based upon the key design, moving tumblers inside the lock and thereby releasing the bolt and securing the door shut. There are many types of physical key locks.
	Combination	A combination lock typically involves some type of rotating dial, which interacts with cams and the locking mechanism. The dial is usually populated with numbers, and the unlocking process commonly involves lining up the numbers in the proper sequence through a series of right/left turns, or directly on the cams.
	Magnetic	Magnetic locks are often referred to simply as maglocks and are a combination of a powerful electromagnet and a steel or metal plate to which the electromagnet engages. Maglocks are typically operated through a button or via an attached card reader or motion sensor system—the type of operation often dependent upon where a maglock is utilized in a facility.
Electronic	**Proximity / RFID**	Proximity/RFID cards are also referred to as key cards, and a defining feature is that they can be read simply by holding the card near the associated card reader. Proximity/RFID cards are often used as part of access control systems in buildings.
	Combination	Combination, or keypad, locks are often used to secure entrances. They usually consist of a simple keypad containing numbers and perhaps a * and # symbol. The lock is typically tied to a central system for purposes of logging activity and managing users and associated passcodes/combinations are needed to unlock the entrance. Combination locks are susceptible to shoulder-surfing as well as to brute-force attacks.
	Biometric	The use of biometrics as a form of identification has extended to include access control in buildings. Whether through fingerprint or palm scanning, or iris or retina scans, the use of biometrics has grown steadily over the years. They are very accurate and hard to defeat, but their primary drawback relates to concerns about privacy.

Table 3-59: **Lock Types**

With one type of lock in particular—combination—security is dependent upon one thing: *the complexity of the combination.* If the combination consists of only a few numbers or characters, it can easily be determined. By requiring a longer combination, complexity is increased exponentially and the possibility of a brute-force attack succeeding drops significantly.

What determines the security of a combination lock?

3.9.8 Card Access/Biometrics

CORE **CONCEPTS**

- Card access control systems are inexpensive, relative to biometric access control systems.
- Card access control systems are more prone to abuse and are not foolproof.
- Biometric access control systems are very accurate, but employees may not desire to use them due to privacy concerns.

In the realm of physical security, card access and biometric security control mechanisms are often used and quite helpful with regards to automating passage of people through security checkpoints, doors, elevators, and other physical barriers. Often enough, card access control systems require a card to be read upon entry to a building or space and again on exit. These movements are typically logged by the access control system and can provide a level of safety for employees by being able to determine who may still be in a building and potentially their location, in the event of an emergency.

> How card access/badge systems can be used to ensure people's safety

With card access, whomever possesses an authorized card would be able to gain access to secured areas, so in and of themselves, they may not be the most secure form of access control. Cards can be lost, an employee may loan their card to a colleague, and so on. Coupled with biometrics, however, access can be much more strictly enforced, and biometric access control can be used very successfully by itself. Biometric checks of this type often involve facial recognition, a palm scan, or a retina or iris scan.

Relative to each other, biometric access control systems are significantly more expensive than card access systems. Additionally, as privacy is more and more a topic of concern around the world, employees may not be comfortable with the use of biometric access control systems. Thus, they are best used where security is most important and the cost benefit of doing so makes sense.

3.9.9 Windows

CORE **CONCEPTS**

- Windows often represent a major point of vulnerability in a structure.
- Shock and glass break sensors can help detect window breaches.
- Sensors that detect sound and frequencies are useful in quiet environments.
- Shock and glass break sensors detect vibrations related to glass breaks and are useful in noisy environments.

Another important physical security control topic is windows. Most people love having lots of windows in their homes and at their place of work. They allow for wonderful views, lots of natural light, and fresh air. But windows represent a major weak point.

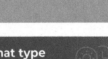

> What type of sensor is effective in a noisy environment?

To mitigate that weakness, shock or glass break sensors can be used. **Shock sensors** must be installed on each pain of glass and are designed to detect the vibrations related to glass breaking. **Glass break sensors** are different, they are essentially microphones that are tuned to listen for the sound of glass breaking. The advantage of glass break sensors is typically less sensors are required as one glass break sensor could be listening for the sound of multiple windows breaking in a room.

Shock sensors are particularly useful and effective in noisy environments, as they can effectively detect glass breaking in loud occupied rooms (e.g., if there is a loud party).

3.9.10 **Walls**

CORE **CONCEPTS**

- The composition and height of walls is important for the sake of strong physical security.

Walls are another important aspect of physical security. Like doors, the **composition** of walls is the primary concern. A standard wood or steel frame wall is fairly easy to breach. Along with the composition, the **height** of a wall also contributes to its security. Does it extend from the floor to the ceiling? If so, is the ceiling a drop ceiling, where—in most cases—the wall ends at the drop ceiling? To ensure a secure room, the wall should extend from the floor to the true ceiling, not to a drop ceiling or anything similar. Similarly, in data centers, raised floors are often found, because this supports the flow of cool air from the HVAC system and routing of electric cables; in this case, walls should extend from the actual floor to the true ceiling.

3.9.11 **Automated Teller Machine (ATM) Skimming**

CORE **CONCEPTS**

- Skimming utilizes disguised technology to steal debit and credit card information from people.

- Automated teller machines (ATM) and gas station pump card readers are frequently targeted for placement of a skimmer.

- Antitampering technology is the best way to prevent skimmers from being placed on card readers, like those used on gas pumps and ATMs.

Skimming is the act of placing cleverly disguised technology at a point of sale—gas station pumps and Automated Teller Machines (ATM) are two frequent targets—and capturing debit and credit card information from unsuspecting customers. Gas station pumps, especially newer ones, include card reader technology that allows people to pay for gas at the pump, instead of going inside a building or otherwise needing to interact with an attendant. Similarly, ATMs can often be found outside of banks, inside convenience and grocery stores, and other places where people often need cash. ATMs bring the convenience of banking to each of these locations and allow people to withdraw cash, check balances, and even make deposits to checking and savings accounts without stepping foot inside a bank or interacting with a teller. As a result of the convenience and widespread use afforded by these card reader technologies, they're often the target of hackers and criminals.

Oftentimes, the skimming technology looks and functions like the real technology. The stolen information can be stored on the skimmer device, and more frequently it is transmitted to criminals via real-time methods that utilize mobile data or wireless connections. Even though skimmers look like the real thing, they can be detected by a few methods:

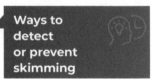
Ways to detect or prevent skimming

1) Pull on the keypad or card insert/reader mechanism to see if it detaches easily. Card readers in any location—gas pump, ATM, retail check-out, and so on—should be tamperproof. **Ideally, readers include antitampering protection to prevent the placement of skimmers.**

2) Look at the spelling on the device itself. Many criminals do not have strong command of the English language, and misspellings are often indicative of something amiss.

3) If errors occur during the transaction process, this could be a sign that a skimmer is in use. Usually, a gas pump reader or ATM will indicate an unavailable system at first glance. If the system appears to be available and then throws errors after a card has been entered and PIN code entered, a skimmer may have just captured the information.

Infrastructure Support Systems

The term "infrastructure support systems" refers to the three major services or utilities that are always a focus of physical security; they're often referred to as power, ping, and pipe. Power is pretty obvious—electricity. Ping refers to the internet. Pipe refers to cooling water and how it is piped into a facility. Most buildings, especially data centers, have a significant cooling water need; without it, buildings would quickly overheat, leading to equipment failure and disgruntled people. Physical security is concerned with providing a good, clean, consistent supply of all three utilities.

3.9.12 Power

Within any organization, disruptions in electrical power can seriously impact the business. The goal is clean, steady power. Two of the major systems used to provide clean, consistent power are Uninterruptible Power Supply (UPS) systems and generators.

What's a **UPS**? Essentially, it's a giant battery—it could be one battery or multiple batteries linked together—and it is designed to provide power when regular electrical power goes out. However, most UPSs are designed to only provide power for a short period of time lasting in minutes. UPSs also provide power conditioning, which simply means the power that enters the UPS is cleaned up—there are no sags, dips, or other power issues with what is flowing to important devices.

Generators are typically large diesel engines hooked up to an alternator to produce electricity. Generators can run for long periods of time, depending upon the supply of fuel. When the power fails, a signal is sent to the generators to turn on, but they can take some time—maybe up to a minute—to become fully functional. UPSs provide short-term power in the interim, while the generator engine becomes fully operational to provide long-term-power.

Within the area of power, situations can arise where there is no power available, not enough power, or too much power. The various types of power degradations and disruptions are summarized in Table 3-60.

	Short period of time (Milliseconds)	**Long period of time (Seconds, minutes, hours, days)**
No Power	Fault	Blackout
Not enough power (e.g., low voltage)	Sag / Dip	Brownout
Too much power (e.g., high voltage)	Spike	Surge

Table 3-60: **Power**

3.9.13 Heating Ventilation and Air Conditioning (HVAC)

CORE **CONCEPTS**

- An important element of physical security is temperature and humidity control, for the sake of people, equipment, and areas of a building that may require specific temperature and humidity settings.

- Air quality is an equally important consideration.

- Positive pressurization helps ensure that contaminants do not enter a building, room, or space.

As mentioned earlier, one aspect of physical security is the maintenance of correct temperatures within a building. People, equipment, and other areas of a building all require optimal temperatures in order to function most effectively and efficiently. Heating, ventilation, and air conditioning (HVAC) systems provide air that is the right temperature, the right humidity, and the right air quality. Variations in any or all these variables can significantly impact a work environment.

The American Society of Heating, Refrigeration, and Air-Conditioning Engineers (ASHRAE) Technical Committee 9.9 created widely accepted guidelines for optimal temperature and humidity set-points in data centers, and these guidelines are summarized in Table 3-61.

	Low	**High**
Temperature	64.4°F / 18°C	80.6°F / 27°C
Humidity	**40%** Relative humidity	**60%** Relative humidity

Table 3-61: **ASHRAE Temperature and Humidity Guielines**

If the temperature is too hot or cold, people get cranky, and equipment may not function correctly. If the humidity is too low, static electricity can develop and potentially cause electrical shots; if humidity is too high, condensation can develop, which may cause corrosion and shorts as well. Air quality, especially in data centers, is also important, as this is the air used to cool servers. If the air is filled with dust and debris, over time, servers and other equipment will become filled with the same things. This can lead to overheating and eventually failure. So, air should be filtered, and contaminants removed.

One term related to air quality is "positive pressurization." **Positive pressurization** refers to air that is pumped into a server room or data center at a slightly above ambient pressure. It's not much, but when higher than the ambient pressure and a door to the server room or data center opens, clean air will rush out of the room rather than potentially dirty air rushing in. Even if

> Description of "positive pressurization" and the benefit it provides

cracks exist in the walls or someone cracks a window, with positive pressurization all that will happen is clean air will flow out - preventing dirty air from infiltrating. In summary, the reason to use positive pressurization is to **keep the air in the data center cleaner – free of contaminants** that would collect inside equipment causing it to overheat and fail.

The above recommendations are summarized in Table 3-62.

Temperature	**Humidity**	**Air Quality**
Avoid too hot or too cold	Too low = static electricity	Clean air; contaminants should be filtered out
	Too high = condensation may develop and lead to corrosion or shorts	Positive pressurization

Table 3-62: **HVAC Recommendations**

3.9.14 **Fire**

CORE **CONCEPTS**

- Fire requires fuel, oxygen, and heat—if any of the three are removed, the fire goes out.

- Fire and the risk of fire should be prevented via a complete control of prevention, detection, and correction.

- Fire detectors—flame, smoke, and heat

- Water-based fire suppression systems—wet pipe, dry pipe, pre-action, deluge

- Gas-based fire suppression systems—INERGEN, Argonite, FM-200, Aero-K

- Fire extinguishers

- CO_2 is noncorrosive, but must be used with caution if people are around.

Think of fire as a three-legged stool. If one of the legs is removed, the fire—like the stool—fails; it goes out. The three legs of the fire stool are: fuel, oxygen, and heat. All three are required for a fire to burn. Take any one of the three away, and the fire goes out. This is where it makes sense to think about fire as a risk. When mitigating any risk, preventive, detective, and corrective controls should be put in place. Ideally, where fire is concerned, the goal is prevention, and one of the best ways to prevent fire is not to have combustible materials in the vicinity of what is being protected.

> **Understand types of fire detection systems and the most effective for early detection**

If fire can't be prevented, it should be easily detected. And once fire is detected, it should be possible to immediately correct it, in other words, to quickly extinguish it. This is where fire detection systems as well as water-based and gas-based fire suppression systems come into play.

Even in the best-case scenarios, fires will still happen, and in those cases it's critical that they can be quickly detected. Three primary types of fire detection systems exist: flame, heat, and smoke, as also seen in Table 3-63.

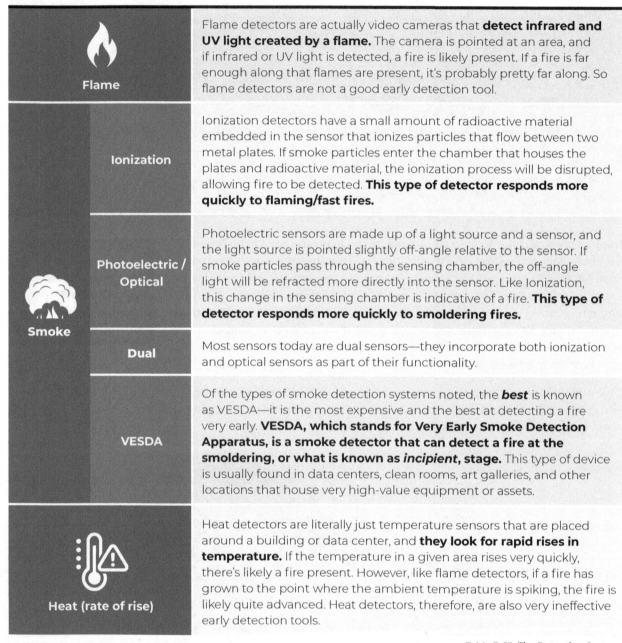

Flame	Flame	Flame detectors are actually video cameras that **detect infrared and UV light created by a flame.** The camera is pointed at an area, and if infrared or UV light is detected, a fire is likely present. If a fire is far enough along that flames are present, it's probably pretty far along. So flame detectors are not a good early detection tool.
Smoke	**Ionization**	Ionization detectors have a small amount of radioactive material embedded in the sensor that ionizes particles that flow between two metal plates. If smoke particles enter the chamber that houses the plates and radioactive material, the ionization process will be disrupted, allowing fire to be detected. **This type of detector responds more quickly to flaming/fast fires.**
	Photoelectric / Optical	Photoelectric sensors are made up of a light source and a sensor, and the light source is pointed slightly off-angle relative to the sensor. If smoke particles pass through the sensing chamber, the off-angle light will be refracted more directly into the sensor. Like Ionization, this change in the sensing chamber is indicative of a fire. **This type of detector responds more quickly to smoldering fires.**
	Dual	Most sensors today are dual sensors—they incorporate both ionization and optical sensors as part of their functionality.
	VESDA	Of the types of smoke detection systems noted, the **best** is known as VESDA—it is the most expensive and the best at detecting a fire very early. **VESDA, which stands for Very Early Smoke Detection Apparatus, is a smoke detector that can detect a fire at the smoldering, or what is known as *incipient*, stage.** This type of device is usually found in data centers, clean rooms, art galleries, and other locations that house very high-value equipment or assets.
Heat (rate of rise)	Heat (rate of rise)	Heat detectors are literally just temperature sensors that are placed around a building or data center, and **they look for rapid rises in temperature.** If the temperature in a given area rises very quickly, there's likely a fire present. However, like flame detectors, if a fire has grown to the point where the ambient temperature is spiking, the fire is likely quite advanced. Heat detectors, therefore, are also very ineffective early detection tools.

Table 3-63: **Fire Detection Systems**

Best Way to Prevent or Limit Damage from a Fire

As already mentioned, the best way to prevent a fire is to minimize combustible materials in proximity to valuable assets. For example, in a data center, where server and other network equipment is routinely added and removed, the new pieces of equipment should be unpacked and unboxed on the loading dock, leaving all the combustible cardboard and other material there and only transporting the bare metal hardware into the room. However, as noted above, in the event a fire does occur, the best way to limit damage is through early detection, and the best way to do this is through implementation of a VESDA smoke detector that is capable of detecting fire at the incipient stage.

Fire Suppression

After a fire has been detected, the goal is to correct it, or put it out. Fire correction systems fall into two categories: water-based and gas-based. Water-based systems use water to extinguish the fire. They remove the heat from a fire, which causes it to cease burning.

Water-Based Fire Suppression Systems

Four **primary types of water-based systems** exist: **wet pipe, dry pipe, pre-action, and deluge**, as described in Table 3-64. Water-based fire suppression systems work by removing heat from the fire equation. Relative to gas-based systems, they are much less expensive, and they are much simpler to operate. However, a major disadvantage of water-based systems is that they use water, which could potentially destroy millions of dollars of equipment in the event of a fire. So water-based systems are not typically found in data centers or other areas where their use would cause significant damage. This is where gas-based systems come into play, though they are significantly more expensive than water-based systems.

> Understand the pros and cons of water-based and gas-based suppression systems and which type is best for a data center and places where expensive equipment and other items are housed

Wet Pipe	Wet pipe means the pipes in a sprinkler system are "wet"—filled with pressurized water at all times. In the event of activation, water will flow until the water source is shut off. This can result in significant excess water after a fire has been extinguished. Though inexpensive, wet systems include some significant disadvantages: • risk of leaks • when used in locations where freezing is a possibility, pipes can freeze and burst—water expands when frozen—and once thawed, flooding will occur
Dry Pipe	Dry pipe systems appear very similar to wet-based systems, with the big difference being that dry pipe systems do not always have pressurized water in the pipes. They're dry and typically filled with some type of pressured gas (e.g., air or nitrogen). Dry pipe systems are often combined with some type of **pre-action system** (defined below) that, when triggered, activates a valve that allows water to fill the pipes very quickly and extinguish the fire.
Pre-action	Pre-action means the fire suppression is armed when something happens. For example, in the context of a dry pipe system, a pre-action system—which incorporates a detection system—will only activate valves that release water when a fire is detected. Many pre-action systems are tied to the primary "standpipe"—the main water pipe—in a building. A standpipe is tied to piping on each floor, with a corresponding valve off the standpipe on each floor. With a pre-action system in place, if a fire is detected on the third floor, for example, the system will activate the valve connected to the piping on the third floor, releasing water only to that floor. Additionally, only the sprinkler heads that have been activated by heat on the that floor will shower water. This type of system offers great advantages: • due to the detection system, concerns of water damage due to false activations can be eliminated • water is held back until detectors in the area are activated; thus, in the example above, other floors would not be showered with water
Deluge	A deluge system involves massive amounts of water flowing at once. With it, all sprinkler heads are in the open position. Thus, if a fire is detected, when the pre-action system activates the water valves, water will immediately flood the pipes and flow out of every sprinkler head. A deluge system should only be used where immediate extinguishment of a fire is required, like in a fireworks or explosives factory, where a fire could cause a catastrophic explosion.

Table 3-64: **Water-Based Fire Suppression Systems**

Gas-Based Fire Suppression Systems

Gas-based systems are more expensive to install and more expensive to maintain, among other things, but they possess one significant advantage: they don't use water. Instead, they use various types of gases, and these gases are specifically selected because they don't typically damage expensive equipment. Gas-based systems extinguish fires by one of two means: they remove the oxygen from the impacted location or interrupt the chemical process that the fire consists of. Note that care must be taken with gas-based systems because although they're great at putting out a fire they can also kill everybody in a room. Typically, prior to a gas-based system deploying, an alarm sounds, emergency lights blink, and people are provided with ample time to evacuate the area before the gas is released.

Gases most commonly used in gas-based systems are INERGEN, Argonite, FM200, and Aero-K, as shown in Table 3-65. **One gas that used to be popular but is now illegal is Halon; it should never be used in a gas-based system and was outlawed because of its significant negative impact on the environment, specifically on the ozone layer that protects the Earth's atmosphere**.

INERGEN	INERGEN is a gas-based system that became popular in the early 1990s in response to the banning and subsequent replacement of Halon-based systems. INERGEN works like CO_2 in that it reduces the oxygen concentration where a fire exists, thus helping extinguish it. At the same time, and unlike CO_2-based systems, the use of INERGEN still allows for a breathable atmosphere, which is critical for the sake of personnel who may still be in the area when an INERGEN system is discharged.
Argonite	Argonite is a gas-based system consisting of a mixture of argon and nitrogen. Similar to INERGEN, its use does not endanger human life, and it too is safe for the environment and therefore a suitable replacement for Halon.
FM-200	Like INERGEN and Argonite, FM-200 is considered a "clean agent," meaning it does not endanger human life when used, and it does not leave residue, which makes it safe for high-value computing equipment and other hardware typically found in a data center.
Aero-K	Aero-K is a fire suppression system that disperses an ultrafine, potassium-based aerosol that can quickly suppress a fire. Additionally, the aerosol mist remains suspended in the air for a period of time, which allows it to prevent reignition of the fire as well as to disperse naturally and not leave a residue on equipment. It too is considered environmentally friendly and a safe alternative to Halon.

Table 3-65: **Gas Fire Suppression Systems**

Fire Extinguishers

Because different types of fire exist, different types of fire extinguishers also exist, as shown in Table 3-66. Fire extinguishers are denoted by "class," and different class extinguishers put out different types of fire:

- Class A extinguishers are used for putting out fires fueled by common combustibles
- Class B extinguishers put out liquid-based fires, like those fueled by gasoline
- Class C extinguishers put out electrical fires
- Class D extinguishers put out fires fueled by combustible metals; they use dry powder as a suppression agent
- Class K extinguishers are usually found in commercial kitchens, and they use wet chemicals as suppression agents.

Class	Type of Fire	Suppression Agents
A	Common combustibles	Water, foam, dry chemicals
B	Liquid	Gas, CO2, foam, dry chemicals
C	Electrical	Gas, CO2, dry chemicals
D	Combustible metals	Dry powders
K	Commercial kitchens	Wet chemicals

Table 3-66: **Fire Extinguisher Types**

CO₂

CO2, better known as carbon dioxide, is something commonly found in nature and is also commonly used as a suppression agent. More importantly, it's not corrosive to expensive equipment. Some other suppression agents corrode equipment. *However, the one caveat with CO2 is this:* **if too much is used, and people are present, those people might die, because it removes oxygen from the air.** If using a gas-based system, a better alternative would be one of the systems that utilizes the gases noted above, like Aero-K, FM-200, Argonite, or INERGEN.

> **Understand why CO2 is an effective suppression agent**

MINDMAP REVIEW **VIDEOS**

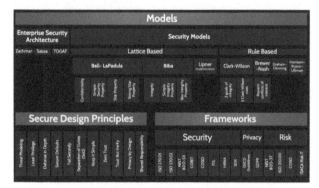

Secure Design, Models and Frameworks
dcgo.ca/CISSPmm3-1

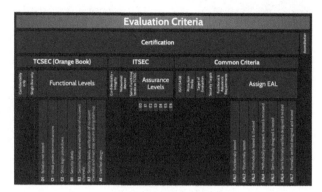

Evaluation Criteria
dcgo.ca/CISSPmm3-2

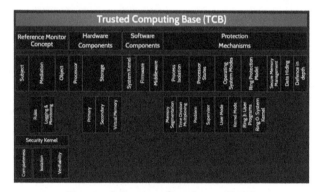

Trusted Computing Base (TCB)
dcgo.ca/CISSPmm3-3

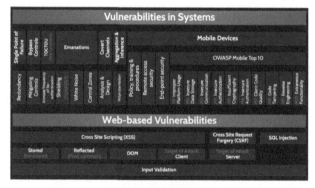

Vulnerabilities
dcgo.ca/CISSPmm3-4

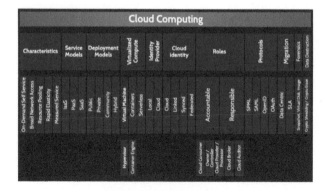

Cloud Computing
dcgo.ca/CISSPmm3-5

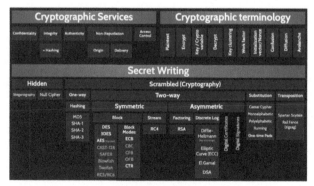

Cryptography
dcgo.ca/CISSPmm3-6

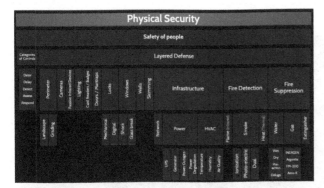

Digital Certificates and Signatures, PKI, and Key Management
dcgo.ca/CISSPmm3-7

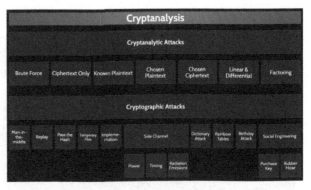

Cryptanalysis
dcgo.ca/CISSPmm3-8

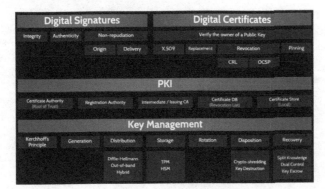

Physical Security
dcgo.ca/CISSPmm3-9

CISSP PRACTICE QUESTION APP

**Download the Destination CISSP Practice Question app
for Domain 3 practice questions**

dcgo.ca/PracQues

DOMAIN 4

Communication & Network Security

4.1   Implement secure design principles in network architectures

4.1.1 Open System Interconnection (OSI) Model

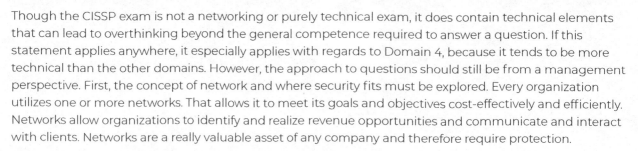

CORE **CONCEPTS**

- Open System Interconnection (OSI) and TCP/IP models
- General understanding of what happens at each layer
- General understanding of common devices and protocols found at each layer
- Concepts of encapsulation and decapsulation

Though the CISSP exam is not a networking or purely technical exam, it does contain technical elements that can lead to overthinking beyond the general competence required to answer a question. If this statement applies anywhere, it especially applies with regards to Domain 4, because it tends to be more technical than the other domains. However, the approach to questions should still be from a management perspective. First, the concept of network and where security fits must be explored. Every organization utilizes one or more networks. That allows it to meet its goals and objectives cost-effectively and efficiently. Networks allow organizations to identify and realize revenue opportunities and communicate and interact with clients. Networks are a really valuable asset of any company and therefore require protection.

What Is a Network?

A network is at least two devices that are connected to each other. Like people, in order to communicate, these devices must be able to speak a common language (which is what a protocol does), and common rules of communication must be followed.

What Is a Protocol?

The common rules of network communication are called protocols. A protocol is simply a standard set of rules that are understood, conformed to, and abided by so that two or more devices on a network can communicate. Protocols allow messages to be sent and received, interpreted, and acted upon, and all of this takes place in the context of what's known as the Open System Interconnection (OSI) model.

OSI (Open System Interconnection) Model

Many people know the OSI model as simply a seven-word mnemonic that corresponds to its seven layers as depicted in Table 4-1. It's important to know the seven layers, what happens at each of them, and where security fits in. OSI stands for Open Systems Interconnection, which implies that the OSI model is about open systems that can interconnect and communicate with each other, using protocols. The OSI model is a structured, layered architecture comprising seven layers. Because it is a layered architecture, think of the seven layers of the OSI model as team members. Each member has responsibilities that allow the ultimate goal of communication to be accomplished. No layer can work on its own and accomplish this ultimate goal.

Although a lot of people simply refer to every type of information as "packets," that is actually incorrect. Information within the uppermost three OSI layers (Application, Presentation, and Session) is referred to as "data." When that reaches the Transport layer it is referred to as "segments." At Layer 3 (Network), the term "packets" or "datagrams" is commonly used. Layer 2 (Data Link) uses the term "frames" while at Layer 1 (Physical) everything is just referred to as bits (or 0s and 1s).

7	Application	
6	Presentation	Data
5	Session	
4	Transport	Segments
3	Network	Packets/Datagrams
2	Data Link	Frames
1	Physical	Bits

Table 4-1: **OSI Layers**

Now, you may be wondering how you will be able to remember these seven layers. The two most commonly used mnemonics for OSI are: **A**ll **P**eople **S**eem **T**o **N**eed **D**ata **P**rocessing and **P**lease **D**o **N**ot **T**hrow **S**ausage **P**izza **A**way. The first mnemonic refers to the OSI model from a top-down approach (Layer 7 to Layer 1). The second mnemonic refers to the OSI model from a bottom-up perspective (Layer 1 to Layer 7). Both are depicted in Figure 4-1.

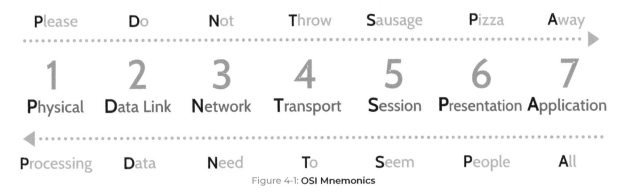

Figure 4-1: **OSI Mnemonics**

It's very important to know what security-specific features exist at different layers of the OSI model. The higher the layer, the more functional the security features become, and more comprehensive controls can be implemented; the lower the layer, the opposite is true. However, at the higher layers, the functionality is accompanied with complexity, which has an expense at speed and efficiency. Similarly, at the lower layers, where complexity is minimized, speed and efficiency are a given. At the lowest layer—the Physical layer—no intelligence exists. This is simply the layer that interconnects devices, and it is extremely fast.

Something else that should be kept in mind is that some types of devices—firewalls, for example—can be found at multiple layers in the OSI model. Firewalls can exist at three of the seven layers—Network, Session, and Application—and functionality at each layer varies significantly. At the Network layer, packet filtering firewalls can be found. Decision-making here is very limited, but processing efficiency is high. On the upper end, at the Application layer, application or application proxy firewalls can be found. They offer significant decision-making capabilities, but at the cost of substantial overhead and processing efficiency.

Clearly, the technology industry long-ago recognized that making security decisions requires striking a balance between functionality and efficiency. This explains the importance of security protocols, and why so many exist and operate at different layers of the OSI model.

Let's relate this and take it a step further. The OSI model is exactly that—it's a model, and a model is simply a representation of something and the accompanying rules. The OSI model is a representation of communication rules and to work the OSI model must be implemented. The actual implementation is through TCP/IP. The internet protocol suite (TCP/IP) consists of many protocols—a family of protocols. TCP and IP and the other members of the protocol family run at different layers of the OSI model to support the underlying tasks of a given layer.

For example, the Network layer is primarily responsible for taking information and routing that, breaking it—fragmentation—into manageable chunks called **datagrams** and providing addressing so those chunks can be communicated across a network using a logical addressing scheme called IP addresses.

The Transport layer is responsible for transporting information that is being exchanged between devices. Think of it as the truck that carries information between two people. To provide reliable transportation, a road should be built that facilitates ordered flow of traffic, including consistent reporting of road conditions. Within the family of protocols mentioned above, TCP is the protocol that provides ordered and reliable transport service.

Conversely, unordered, and unreliable transport services can also be provided by simply pointing the trucks toward the destination and not relying on a specific road. In this case, the trucks are simply loaded, and the drivers are told to go find the destination. The drivers will likely follow different routes, arrive in different order, and some may not arrive at all. All the trucks may travel quickly, but otherwise they'll be completely unreliable. Within the family of protocols, UDP is the protocol that operates in a similar manner—unordered and unreliable, but very quick, transport.

Let's consider this from the perspective of two people connected by devices across a network. If one person wants to send the other an email, an application like Outlook will be used to compose and send the message. Once ready to go, the person will hit "send." At this point, the Application layer will take the message, perform certain activities, and then pass it to the next layer, the Presentation layer. This process will continue all the way down to the Physical layer, which is where devices actually connect and bits (0s and 1s) are encoded as voltage and sent across the wire. Seemingly magically, those bits will travel the wire until they reach the other person's device via the Physical layer. At this point, the Physical layer will perform certain functions and pass the information up to the next layer, the Data Link. This process will continue all the way up to the Application layer, at which point the other person can read the email.

The description above describes two processes known as **encapsulation** and **decapsulation**. As information moves down, from the Application layer to the Physical layer, encapsulation is taking place. Each layer will add its own header and trailer information to the existing data and then pass it down to the next layer. On the other side, when the fully encapsulated information arrives, a process called decapsulation takes place, where the header and trailer information is removed layer by layer all the way up to the Application layer.

Note that although the OSI model consists of seven layers, the TCP/IP implementation consists of four layers as shown in Table 4-2. Like the OSI model, rules must still be followed, but just a bit differently. For instance, the top three layers of the OSI model are handled by the Application layer of the TCP/IP model. The Transport layer is the same in both models. The OSI Network layer is called the internet layer in TCP/IP and then the bottom two layers of the OSI model are handled by TCP/IP's link layer.

> **What happens and what protocols are found at each layer?**

OSI	Description	Devices & Protocols	TCP/IP
7 Application	Identify capabilities of applications and resource availability	Application Firewall HTTP/S, DNS, SSH, SNMP, FTP	**4 Application**
6 Presentation	Formatting of data	XML, JPEG, ANSI	
5 Session	Interhost communication and session management	Circuit Proxy Firewall	
4 Transport	End-to-end connection with error correction and detection	TCP/UDP, iSCSI (SAN)	**3 Transport**
3 Network	Logical addressing, routing and delivery of datagrams	Routers, Packet Filtering Firewalls, IP addresses, ICMP, NAT	**2 Internet**
2 Data Link	Physical addressing, and reliable point-to-point connection	Switches, bridges, MAC addresses, L2TP, PPTP	**1 Link**
1 Physical	Binary transmission of data across physical media (wire, fiber, etc.)	Hubs, NICs, Network media	

Table 4-2: **OSI vs. TCP/IP**

4.1.2 Layer 1: Physical

CORE **CONCEPTS**

- **Data at Physical layer exists as bits—0s and 1s**
- **Transmission media—wired, wireless, and so on**
- **Network topologies: Bus, Tree, Star, Mesh, Ring**
- **Collisions and collision avoidance; CSMA**
- **Transmission methods: unicast, multicast, broadcast**
- **Layer 1 devices: hubs, repeaters, concentrators, network interface cards (NICs)**

Layer 1, the Physical layer, focuses on how devices interconnect as well as encoding the bits, the 0s and 1s, that Layer 1 understands. Devices can connect using wired or wireless technologies. For now, let's focus on wired technologies, with the three most used media being *twisted pair*, *coaxial*, and *fiber optic*. The use of one versus another should focus first and foremost on security and then speed and cost, although different organizations may have a varying approach on this. Table 4-3 summarizes the major types of wired and wireless transmission media.

> Understand what happens at Layer 1 and how the primary wired transmission media types differ from one another

Wired	Wireless
■ Twisted Pair	■ Radio Frequency
■ Coaxial	■ Infrared/Optical
■ Fiber Optic	■ Microwave

Table 4-3: **Transmission Media**

Twisted pair cable refers to the fact that it is a pair of wires twisted together in a specific way that creates a magnetic field, which allows the signal traveling across the wire to remain within the magnetic field. Additionally, twisted pair cable can be shielded (STP) or unshielded (UTP), with shielded twisted pair offering additional protection from cross talk and interference.

Whether they realize it or not, most people are familiar with **coaxial cable**. This is the cable often used by cable companies to bring television, telephone, and high-speed internet access to homes. Coaxial cable consists of a single strand of copper wire sheathed in a protective coating, and a technology called multiplexing allows the wire to provide all the services mentioned. Multiplexing allows the information carried along the wire to be split into different frequencies, waves, and time slices at the same time, and it does so at incredible speeds.

Unlike twisted pair and coaxial cable, which use voltage for communication, **fiber optic** utilizes light pulses to represent 0s and 1s. Both speed and security are great advantages of using fiber optic. Among other things, twisted pair and coaxial cable are both subject to what's known as **cross talk**—interference—because copper, by design, conducts electricity. Thus, nearby electrical equipment, lightning, and deliberate signal scrambling can severely disrupt communications. Additionally, each type of cable can be tapped to intercept or eavesdrop the signal. These types of issues can impact the integrity of communications as well as confidentiality of information being passed along the wires. Though fiber is not immune to issues like tapping, it's certainly not as easy. Using security requirements as the primary decision driver, fiber is the best choice among the three. In addition to security, other criteria that should also be considered when choosing among transmission media options include bandwidth, distance, geographic location, interference levels, cost, and so on. For example, relative to twisted pair and coaxial cable, fiber optic cable offers significantly better signal quality over long distances.

Cabling is one part of the equation; another part relates to **topologies**, or how the cables are laid out. The most used network topologies are depicted in Figure 4-2.

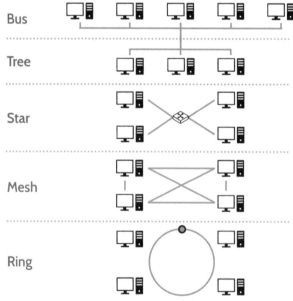

Figure 4-2: **Network Topologies**

The most common network topology is known as a **bus topology**. Bus simply means all devices are connected to a central wire, called a bus. One great advantage of the bus topology is that the failure of one node does not affect the rest of the network; all other devices can still communicate with each other. So a bus topology allows for node failure. From a security point of view, a bus topology has several weaknesses. For one, the bus represents a single point of failure. For another, all devices are connected to a single wire, so by default every device can intercept all the information being transmitted across the wire. These transmissions are known as broadcasts. As the network grows, adding more devices to the network is as simple as extending the bus, but doing so leads to an issue known as attenuation. Attenuation is a loss of signal strength over distance, but this can be mitigated using signal boosters and repeaters. Looking back at broadcasts for a moment, another disadvantage of a bus topology is that when two or more devices send information at the same time, something called a collision can occur.

Another topology is known as a **tree topology**, which somewhat resembles a tree with different branches. By virtue of this structure, one of the immediate benefits is that transmissions can be isolated to certain branches of the tree, thereby limiting transmissions from being seen by the entire network. In addition, if any of the tree leaves become damaged or unavailable, the issue doesn't affect the whole network, as that node can be easily repaired or removed.

One of the benefits of these topologies is that they can be mixed and matched when building out networks. By doing so, functional and security needs can be achieved. This is one reason why a bus topology is the most implemented topology, because it easily supports other topologies and can be combined with them.

A **star topology**, as the name suggests, resembles a star. All devices are connected to a central device, like a switch or a hub. One significant disadvantage of a star topology is that the central device represents a single point of failure. If that device goes down, communication between all devices is effectively halted. However, if switches are being used, functionality exists that allows network segmentation to be implemented by connecting certain devices to certain ports. Segmentation allows a network to be segmented based on value, which leads to the creation of a more sophisticated network, as elements of a bus topology are expanded to include elements of other topologies, like tree and star. Though more complexity is introduced, additional functionality and security are added too.

A **mesh topology** interconnects every device with every other device. This is excellent for purposes of redundancy—if one device goes down, communication with other devices is not impacted. Mesh topologies can be implemented as full (where every device is connected to every other device) or partial (where only the most critical devices are connected to each other for purposes of redundancy).

A **ring topology** looks like a ring. Devices are connected to a closed loop, and in a sense the loop is still essentially a bus, which can lead to issues like collisions. However, particular ring topology implementations (like a token ring) can include a mechanism called a token that is designed to prevent collisions. The token is passed around the ring from device to device, and when the token is in possession of a device, the device can send information. This approach mitigates the issue of collisions, but it also introduces one particular problem, which led to the demise of token ring networks. Namely, if any node in the ring went down, it prevented the token from being passed to the next node. The direction of travel of the token could be reversed, but the problem of one node impacting the entire network remained. That's why specific implementations use a redundant ring, which can replace the primary ring in the event it becomes unavailable.

Dealing with Collisions

As described, being able to mix and match different topologies can provide significant functionality and security benefits. However, one of the major problems found in all the topologies except token ring is collisions. Three primary methods exist to handle collisions.

1. **Token-based collision avoidance:** A token is passed from device to device, and only the device holding the token can transmit information. This is what token ring networks use.

2. **Polling:** Interconnected devices poll each other to learn if any information needs to be transmitted. This method obviously implies a significant amount of network traffic, which explains why it is not popular or used often, if at all.

3. **Carrier Sense Multiple Access (CSMA)**: Modern networks use what's known as Carrier-Sense Multiple Access. Devices are connected to the same carrier, the same wire, and therefore each device can sense the wire to identify if another device is transmitting. To send information, the wire must be available, and devices can sense this availability based upon what travels across the wire—voltage. Voltage represents 1s and 0s. +5 volts = 1 and -5 volts = 0. To send information, no voltage should be on the wire. Once the wire is free, data can be transmitted, which should then be acknowledged by the receiving device. If the acknowledgment comes back in a reasonable amount of time, everything is okay. If not, information might need to be resent.

Even with CSMA, collisions are still going to occur. For example, in the case of a wireless network, there's no media to sense if there's someone already transmitting, which makes it rather difficult to use. In addition, CSMA tends to require larger transmission times due to its operation and as such can cause delays. This is why two flavors of CSMA exist—CSMA with **Collision Avoidance** (CSMA/**CA**) and CSMA with collision detection (CSMA/CD). CSMA/CA completely avoids collisions. CSMA/CA is used in the context of wireless networks and employs the use of two lanes of communication. One lane is used to receive information, and the other is used to send information. When a device communicates with a wireless access point, CSMA/CA is used.

Wired networks, like Ethernet networks, use the other flavor of CSMA. That's CSMA/**CD – Collision Detection**, which detects collisions after information has been transmitted. Think about it this way: when data is transmitted, voltage is running across the wire. If there's a spike in voltage after transmission, it means a collision has likely occurred. Thus, the information that was just transmitted would likely need to be sent again. All wired networks use CSMA/CD.

Transmission Methods

As a quick review, a network is two or more devices that are connected to each other. How these devices communicate is through transmission methods. One method is one-to-one, which is called *unicast* and is used when a specific device needs to be reached. Another method is one-to-many, which is called *multicast* and is used when a group of devices need to be reached. The final method, *broadcast*, is one-to-all and is used when all the devices, e.g., on a specific subnet, need to be reached. From a security perspective, unicast is the most secure method, because communication is limited to a specific destination device.

In addition, Table 4-4 contains a summary of the various transmission methods that can be used to communicate.

Unicast	Multicast	Broadcast
One-to-**One**	One-to-**Many**	One-to-**All**

Table 4-4: **Transmission Methods**

Layer 1 Devices

Several important devices operate at Layer 1, among them hubs, repeaters, and concentrators. Because they operate at Layer 1, they're very fast, but they're also not considered intelligent devices, as they don't possess any decision-making abilities. Table 4-5 contains a list of all of those.

Hubs	A hub is a Physical layer device with multiple ports and is used to connect multiple devices in a network. A hub is a very simplistic, passive device, which receives a data frame at one port and broadcasts that to all the other ports on the hub. Hubs are very "noisy" as a result, and data collisions often occur since they are a part of the same collision domain.
Repeaters	A repeater is a Physical layer device that is sometimes referred to as a signal booster and is often used to mitigate the issue of signal attenuation when data is being transmitted over a long distance. A repeater regenerates the signal and then sends it along to the destination..
Concentrators	Concentrators are like hubs in that both devices deal with multiple signals. However, while hubs repeat signals to all connected devices, concentrators *combine* all signals for transmission down a single line—they concentrate signals together.

Table 4-5: **Layer 1 Network Devices**

4.1.3 Layer 2: Data Link

CORE **CONCEPTS**

- Data at the Data Link layer exists as frames.
- Physical addressing via MAC addresses uniquely identifies devices on a network.
- Two types of networks: circuit-switched and packet-switched
- Common location to implement link encryption
- Layer 2 devices: bridges and switches
- Layer 2 protocols: L2TP, PPTP, ARP

Looking at the OSI model, Layer 2—the Data Link layer—acts as a conduit between Layer 1—the Physical layer—and Layer 3—the Network layer. The Physical layer only works with bits, and the Network layer works with datagrams. Between them, the Data Link layer takes datagrams from the Network layer and formats them in a manner that allows the Physical layer to work with them as bits. Likewise, the Data Link layer takes bits from the Physical layer and formats them in a manner that allows the Network layer to work with them as datagrams.

Physical Addressing

Layer 2 is also the layer where devices that operate across a network are physically and uniquely identified and separated from each other. This makes sense, because for a network to work, the devices on it need to have unique physical addresses. This unique physical address exists and is known as a **Media Access Control (MAC)** address. A MAC address is simply bits—0s and 1s—that uniquely identify and distinguish every device on a network, and this unique identifier is specified via a device's network card. To ensure unique MAC addresses, an industry standard was adopted that specifies that each address should comprise 48 bits of information, with the first set of bits being specific to the vendor (first 24 bits or 3 bytes, which constitute the Organizational Unique Identifier, OUI), and the remaining bits (last 24 bits or 3 bytes) being specific to the device and assigned by its manufacturer, as shown in Figure 4-3. Note that, based on this information, duplicate MAC addresses should never exist under normal circumstances.

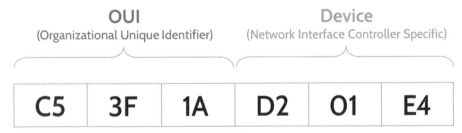

Figure 4-3: **MAC Address**

Networks work by virtue of logical address schemes that facilitate communication between devices. This is done at Layer 3 and is known as IP addressing, which can take IP addresses and convert them to MAC addresses and vice versa. Specifically, two protocols handle these needs: **Address Resolution Protocol (ARP)** and **Reverse Address Resolution Protocol (RARP)**. ARP allows IP addresses to be mapped to physical addresses, while RARP allows physical addresses to be mapped to IP addresses.

ARP poisoning is a topic that will be examined in more detail later, but it's good to introduce now. ARP poisoning is a spoofing or masquerading type of attack, where one or more devices on a network pretend to be other, legitimate devices. Then information intended for a legitimate device will be sent to the device masquerading as the legitimate one. ARP poisoning can be accomplished quite simply, because every device contains an ARP table, which facilitates request resolutions. The ARP table can be modified to point to a rogue device, thus spoofing and masquerading the legitimate device. DNS, routers, and switches all use tables as well and could therefore be subject to unauthorized modification too.

In networking, there are two types of network communications that mainly exist: circuit-switched and packet-switched networks.

Circuit-Switched Network

A great example of a circuit-switched network is the **Public Switched Telephone Network (PSTN)**, which has been in existence for many, many years. Connecting across the PSTN requires another person's telephone number, which can then be dialed, and a series of devices that comprise the PSTN will establish the circuit—the connection, as shown in Figure 4-4. Thus, the name circuit-switched network. Parties on each end of the circuit can speak and hear at the same time, which illustrates the fact that full-duplex transmission is in place. With a circuit-switched network, a *connection is established permanently or on demand and is maintained between switches in order to route traffic to the correct destination.*

Circuit-Switched Network

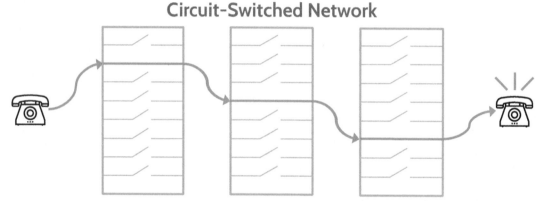

Figure 4-4: **Circuit-Switched Network**

Transmission of Digital Data over Analog Connections

When telephone communication was first being envisioned, scientists and engineers determined that because the human voice is analog, analog frequencies should be used for telephone communication. However, as technology advanced and data demands grew, the need for better communication technology also increased. Data doesn't travel well over analog frequencies, though a temporary fix came in the form of modems. A modem, which stands for modulator/demodulator, takes data and converts it to analog, so that it can be transmitted across the analog telephone network. Once it arrives at its destination, the analog signal is converted back to data by the receiving modem as depicted in Figure 4-5. As was already noted, data does not travel well across analog networks, and part of the issue lies in the fact that regardless of the surrounding technology, communication speed over analog networks is limited to 65,000 bits per second. This explains why separate data networks were built, including the global network known as the internet. Data networks were built for speed and bandwidth, and it wasn't long before voice communications using data transmission was perfected. We know this as Voice over IP, or VoIP or IP telephony, which *encapsulates the internet protocol to enable transmission of **digital data** over **analog connections.*** Though the ability to do telephony across data networks offers several advantages, it also presents a number of security risks.

Analog Network

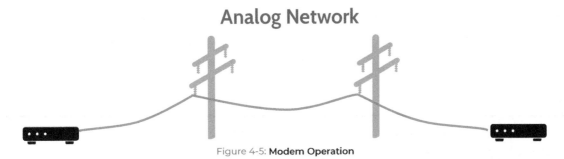

Figure 4-5: **Modem Operation**

Packet-Switched Network

Packet-switched networks function by taking data that needs to be communicated from one device to another and breaking it into datagrams or packets. Each data packet contains information, such as addresses and sequence numbers. As Figure 4-6 illustrates, the datagrams may travel along different routes to the final destination, and they might even arrive in a different order than how they were sent. Switches switch the packets to the final destination, based on the header information and network conditions. Some datagrams might not even arrive, as there is no guarantee of delivery with data networks.

Packet-Switched Network

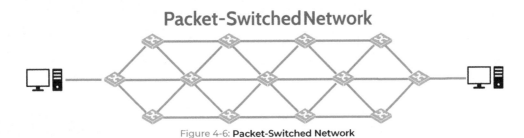

Figure 4-6: **Packet-Switched Network**

Layer 2 Protocols

Table 4-6 outlines Layer 2 protocols that are of the TCP/IP family of protocols. The first three are tunneling protocols, which are required to create virtual private networks (VPN), which are encrypted tunnels.

L2F	Layer 2 Forwarding tunneling protocol
PPTP	Point-to-Point Tunneling Protocol. Uses three distinctive authentication protocols: 1. Password Authentication Protocol (PAP): Simplest but least secure of the three. Uses a static plaintext password for authentication. 2. Challenge Handshake Authentication Protocol (CHAP): More secure than PAP, as password is encrypted before being sent over the wire. 3. Extensible Authentication Protocol (EAP): Considered the most robust of the three due to its increased level of flexibility, allowing it to be combined with other protocols.
L2TP	Layer 2 Tunneling Protocol
SLIP	Serial Line Internet Protocol—an older protocol used for remote access via serial ports and modem connections
ARP **IP to MAC**	Address Resolution Protocol—used to map IP addresses to MAC addresses
RARP **MAC to IP**	Reverse ARP—used to map MAC addresses to IP address

Table 4-6: **Layer 2 Protocols**

Layer 2 Devices

Significant devices that operate at Layer 2 are bridges and switches, as also depicted in Table 4-7. Like Layer 1 devices, Layer 2 devices are efficient and fast, with just a bit more functionality, like for example the ability to form VPNs. Switches have a bit more functionality, because they have ports that can be used to create network segments.

Bridges	Connect different networks together, with no concern for what traffic is going across the bridge
Switches (Layer 2 switches)	Connect multiple network devices together. A packet sent to the switch is forwarded only to the intended recipient, based on the destination MAC address in the packet header

Table 4-7: **Layer 2 Network Devices**

4.1.4 Authentication Protocols

> ### CORE **CONCEPTS**
>
> - **As remote authentication needs have matured, authentication protocols have also matured to meet those needs.**
>
> - **Extensible Authentication Protocol (EAP) is the best authentication protocol available, and its capabilities have been extended as Protected Extensible Authentication Protocol (PEAP).**

To understand the topic of authentication protocols, it's important to understand a bit about how the need came to be. Not too long ago, the only way for an organization to host remote access was with the use of modems. Larger organizations would typically have modem banks—a bunch of modems in a room, connected to the network. Employees would dial a phone number, and if a modem was available, a remote connection to the network could be

Understand the basic difference between PPP, PAP, CHAP, and EAP

made. Of course, this was before the internet grew to what it is today, and VPN solutions became the rule rather than the exception. So, the PSTN was used and a protocol that allowed TCP/IP to run across dial-up networks needed to be created. This led to **Serial Line Internet Protocol (SLIP)** being developed. Though SLIP worked, it didn't work well, and as remote access grew in popularity, a better protocol called **Point-to-Point (PPP)** replaced it.

PPP is a Layer 2 protocol that is used to allow remote access, typically via VPN solutions today. With the advent of PPP and knowing that remote communication most often supported people, the creators of PPP determined that including authentication protocols made sense. As a result, three authentication protocols were developed as part of PPP—PAP, CHAP, and EAP—with each protocol achieving different levels of popularity and each offering different degrees of functionality and security. These are depicted in Figure 4-7.

Password Authentication Protocol (PAP) simply prompts for a user ID and password when establishing a connection. Sadly, passwords are transmitted in plaintext, and the user will never be prompted to change their password, as it will be static in nature.

As a result of the issues with PAP, **Challenge Handshake Authentication Protocol (CHAP)** came to the foreground. CHAP is an improved version of PAP. Passwords are encrypted during transmission, while challenges are sent in regular intervals behind the scenes to ensure that an intruder has not hijacked or otherwise compromised a session.

The most robust and flexible authentication protocol of the three is **Extensible Authentication Protocol (EAP)**. The word *extensible* means being able to be extended or designed to allow new capabilities and functionality to be added. EAP allows vendors to adapt the latest authentication technologies, like smart keys and digital certificates, to their products. In fact, due to its inherent strengths, EAP can also be embedded into other things, like wireless security, where it's used with WPA2 for purposes of connecting to wireless networks and authenticating users at the same time.

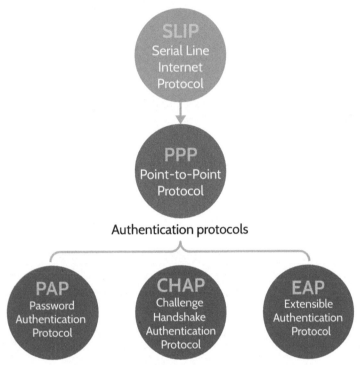

Figure 4-7: **SLIP and PPP Protocols**

Protected Extensible Authentication Protocol (PEAP)

Note that PEAP is a more improved version of EAP, as it encapsulates EAP within an encrypted and authenticated **TLS tunnel** as seen in Figure 4-8. A comparison between the most common types of EAP can be seen in Table 4-8.

> What differentiates PEAP from EAP?

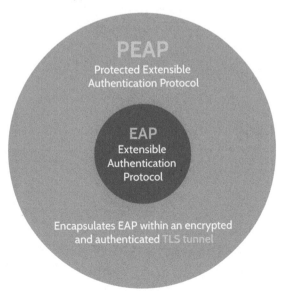

Figure 4-8: **PEAP**

Understand what type of authentication (client, server, or both) each type of EAP provides

Type	Client Authentication	Server Authentication	Security	Industry Support	Proprietary
EAP-TLS	**Certificate**	**Certificate**	**High**	**High**	**No**
EAP-TTLS	ID & Password	**Certificate**	Medium	Medium	Yes (Funk Software & Certicom)
EAP-PEAP	ID & Password	**Certificate**	Medium	**High**	Yes (Cisco, RSA, & Microsoft)
LEAP	ID & Password	ID & Password	Low	**High**	Yes (Cisco)
EAP-MD5	ID & Password	–	Low	Low	**No**

Table 4-8: **EAP Types**

4.1.5 Layer 3: Network

CORE **CONCEPTS**

- Data at the Network layer exists as packets/datagrams.

- Logical addressing is used to map IP addresses to MAC addresses—ARP; Reverse ARP (RARP) maps MAC addresses to IP addresses.

- Route selection, including alternate routes to avoid congestion or node failure

- Layer 3 devices: packet filtering firewalls, routers, and Layer 3 switches

- Layer 3 protocols: ICMP, IGMP, IPsec, and routing protocols, including OSPF

The Network layer handles two very basic but important responsibilities—fragmentation and IP addressing. Fragmentation provides the ability to take data and break it up into datagrams or packets—chunks of data—and then allow those datagrams to be delivered to their destination via IP addressing. The IP protocol within TCP/IP specifically handles most of the responsibilities found at the Network layer. In this context, ARP and RARP are heavily relied upon. If data is leaving the network, the sending device's MAC address is mapped to an IP address; if data is entering the network, the IP address is mapped to the receiving device's MAC address.

Layer 3 Protocols

Layer 3 is home to several significant TCP/IP protocols. In addition to the already discussed IP protocol, IGMP, IPsec, and routing protocols BGP, OSPF, and RIP operate at Layer 3 as also seen in Table 4-9.

ICMP	Internet Control Message Protocol is used for messaging and specifically provides feedback about problems in the network communication environment. Ping and traceroute are two important commands that utilize ICMP. Ping attempts to see if a host device is reachable; traceroute tries to map the path of traffic. Together or alone, both command tools can provide significant information about a network.
IGMP	Internet Group Management Protocol is used to establish and manage group memberships for hosts, routers, and similar devices.
IPsec	IPsec is a tunneling protocol that supports authentication of other Layer 3 devices as well as encryption. It's discussed in more detail in section 4.3.2.
OSPF	Open Shortest Path First is a routing protocol used by routers to manage and direct network traffic properly and efficiently. OSPF includes security features that make it a more secure routing protocol than others.

Table 4-9: **Layer 3 Network Protocols**

Internet Group Management Protocol (IGMP) is used to establish and manage group memberships for hosts, routers, and similar devices. One important thing to note is that authentication in this context does not mean access control authentication. Rather, it refers to authentication of other devices that operate at Layer 3, like routers and Layer 3 switches.

Routers are the most important devices that operate at Layer 3. They route data based on information included in the header portion of the datagram, and those routing decisions are based upon a routing protocol. A routing protocol is simply a language and set of rules that routers understand and use to make decisions about routing. **Border Gateway Protocol (BGP)**, Open Shortest Path First (OSPF), and Routing Internet Protocol (RIP) are common routing protocols.

In addition to the Layer 3 protocols mentioned above, **Internet Control Message Protocol (ICMP)** is another very significant Layer 3 protocol. ICMP is used for the messaging aspects of networking and acts as a helper protocol by facilitating reporting issues over ICMP messages. For example, an ICMP "destination host unreachable" message denotes that the packet destination couldn't be reached. However, note that ICMP can also be used maliciously. An attacker can use the ping utility to identify if a host is "alive" and reachable in any given network. Traceroute is a utility that maps the hosts between a source and destination and provides the traffic path taken. Both commands are often utilized as part of the reconnaissance phase of an attack, and this explains why it is standard practice for organizations to filter incoming ICMP packets at the firewall.

> **What protocol is often used to quickly determine if network communication problems exist?**

Layer 3 Devices

Several significant devices operate at the Network layer, Layer 3. The most obvious are routers, but Layer 3 switches can also be found at the Network layer. In relation to the exam, unless a question specifically mentions a Layer 3 switch, assume that this refers to a Layer 2 device.

In addition to routers and **Layer 3 switches**, packet filtering firewalls also operate at Layer 3. Firewalls help protect networks from a number of different types of malicious activity, and they can operate at three of the seven layers of the OSI model. As was previously mentioned, the speed and efficiency of devices is inversely proportional to their intelligence as you go up the OSI model. Layer 3 firewalls are still fast, but they possess only limited decision-making capabilities. In fact, Layer 3 firewalls are only able to interpret the header portion of a datagram. Simple concepts like source and destination IP addresses and ports (which equate to services) can be used to make decisions. If source IP addresses from certain countries are listed as malicious, the packet filtering firewall can be instructed to drop the packet and not allow it to traverse the network. Additional intelligence exists in firewalls operating at higher OSI layers (like the Application layer, where application proxy firewalls can filter traffic based upon web content, deep packet inspection, stateful inspection, antivirus, intrusion detection signatures, and so on). Of course, this increased intelligence and functionality comes with a price: slower processing speed and increased device cost. Table 4-10 contains an indicative summary of Layer 3 network devices.

Packet Filtering Firewalls	Devices that make decisions based upon the header portion of a datagram, such as the source and destination IP addresses. Due to low processing overhead, they are very fast..
Routers	Devices that connect and route network traffic between networks, based upon IP information included in received data packets. Routers utilize routing protocols and typically dynamically maintain routing tables to determine the optimal route for data packet forwarding.
Switches (Layer 3 switches)	Layer 3 switches function very similarly to routers and are often used to connect devices on the same virtual local area network (VLAN).

Table 4-10: **Layer 3 Network Devices**

> **Know what layer routers operate at and what layers routers operate between**

4.1.6 Logical Addressing

CORE **CONCEPTS**

- Internet protocol datagrams consists of data, also known as the payload.

- IPv4 = 32 bits divided into four groups of 8 bits each versus IPv6 = 128 bits divided into eight groups of 16 bits

- Private versus public IP addresses; private IP addresses are not routable on the internet

- Network classes (subnetting) allows for the creation of networks of varying sizes.

IPv4 addresses are comprised of four numbers separated by dots, e.g., 192.168.1.254. The IP address is a 32-bit value, and each number represents an 8-bit octet. The valid range for each of them is 0–255, with .0 used to denote a specific network, e.g., 192.168.1.0, and .255 to denote a network's broadcast address.

Each packet header contains routing details, like source and destination IP addresses. These fields can each hold 32 bits of information, which are divided into four groups of 8 bits (known as bytes). This is why IPv4 addresses consist of four decimal numbers. If every bit in a given octet is turned on, the highest number that can be achieved is 255. This fact points to a limitation with IPv4 addresses—the highest number in any octet can only be 255.

With a bit of math, it can quickly be seen that the number of valid, unique 32-bit IP addresses is limited. In fact, the number is just under 4.3 billion—2^{32}. When this was originally put into production, no one imagined we would need more addresses. However, with the rapid expansion of the internet and our need to be constantly connected, the IPv4 address space quickly wasn't enough. To allow for better addressing consumption and management, Network Address Translation (NAT) came into effect. Take the example of your home network, which has a router provided commonly by your ISP. That router has a publicly known routable address, provided by your ISP, but when you connect multiple devices to your local network (like your internet TV, tablet, mobile phone, laptop, and others) they all get private addresses assigned to them. NAT is what your router uses to change all those internal IP addresses to that single publicly routable ISP address each time traffic leaves your network and is directed externally. The fact that internal IP addresses are changed is also a great security feature because it allows internal IP addressing schemes to be hidden. This prevents attackers from being able to easily perform reconnaissance and gather information about a potential target.

LAN Technologies

Institute of Electric and Electronic Engineers (IEEE) is an organization of very bright individuals who meet regularly to discuss and ratify technologies, especially new ones. Through the ratification process, standards and parameters can be stipulated, resulting in uniformity and use of the technologies by vendors. For example, different Wi-Fi standards and parameters are defined by the IEEE 802.11 family of standards, which over time grew from 802.11 to 802.11a, b, and g. Then n and ac came along, and now 802.11ad is at the helm. Table 4-11 summarizes three common IEEE standards from the 802 family.

Wired	Wireless	Virtual LAN (VLAN)
IEEE 802.3 defines a collection of communication standards for physical connections on a wired, Ethernet network.	IEEE 802.11 is a collection of communication standards specific to the implementation of WLAN communication.	IEEE 802.1Q defines the standard for virtual local area networks. VLANs are used to create isolated networks for purposes of security and to minimize broadcast traffic on a network.

Table 4-11: **LAN Technologies**

Internet Protocol (IP)

IP is the principal communications protocol for **addressing and routing packets** of data, so that they can travel across networks and arrive at the correct destination.

Internet Protocol v4 Datagram

Figure 4-9 depicts the IPv4 header. As can be seen, several fields besides the source and destination IP addresses exist in it. The significance here is the 32-bit source IP address and the 32-bit destination IP address, which means IPv4 is limited to a maximum number of 4.3 billion IP addresses. NAT, discussed earlier, mitigated the issue of IP addresses running out while experts in the industry who recognized the onrushing problem developed IPv6.

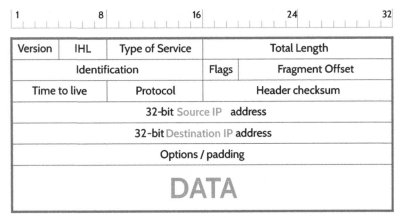

Figure 4-9: **IPv4 Header**

Internet Protocol v6 Datagram

IPv6 (shown in Figure 4-10) expands IP addressing to 128 bits, and using the same math noted with regards to IPv4 points to the IPv6 address space being significantly larger—staggeringly so—as 2^{128} is a very big number. Additionally, unlike the four decimal numbers separated by dots that represent IPv4 addresses, an IPv6 address is represented in hexadecimal format, with each group separated by colons.

One benefit of IPv6 is backward compatibility, which explains why some organizations are still using IPv4 at the same time as they move to incorporate IPv6 more fully into their networking environment. At some point, all organizations will only be using IPv6, and experts have predicted that the IPv6 address space will never be exhausted. But they likely said the same thing about IPv4.

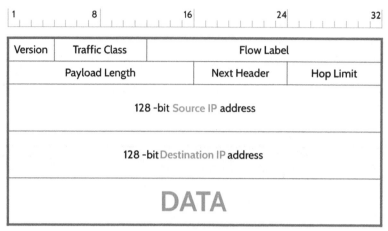

Figure 4-10: **IPv6 Header**

IPv4 versus IPv6

Table 4-12 contains a comparison between IPv4 and IPv6. Back in the day, nobody ever imagined the need for IP addresses would grow the way it did. With the introduction of IPv6, hopefully the need for IP addresses will never be exceeded again. One other thing that's important to note is that security, in the form of the protocol IPsec, is built into IPv6.

	IPv4	IPv6
Address Size	32-bit (4 bytes)	128-bit (16 bytes)
Address space	2^{32} = **4,294,967,296**	2^{128} = **340,282,366,920,938,463,463,374,607,431,768,211,456**
Address format (example)	10.0.0.1	0000:0000:0000:0000:0000:ffff:0a00:0001
IPsec	Optional	Mandatory feature of IPv6—using IPsec is not mandatory

Table 4-12: **IPv4 and IPv6 Comparison**

Private IPv4 Addresses

Earlier, when NAT was mentioned, the concepts of public and private IP addresses were also discussed. Unlike public IP addresses, private addresses may be used by any organization or individual and are commonly used for local area networks in the context of large and small organization network environments as well as in home networks. Private IP addresses are non-routable, which means their use within corporate or home networks provides a layer of security between public-facing internet devices and internal devices. In fact, because private IP addresses are non-routable, two businesses next door to one another could use the exact same private IP range for their internal networks. And using NAT, conceivably an organization with thousands of computers and peripherals could connect to the internet through a single router configured with one public IP address. Table 4-13 lists the private IPv4 IP address ranges (according to RFC 1918), which are not to be used on public networks (like the internet).

From	To
10.0.0.0	10.255.255.255
172.16.0.0	172.31.255.255
192.168.0.0	192.168.255.255

Table 4-13: **Private IPv4 Address Ranges (RFC 1918)**

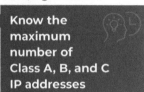

Be able to differentiate public IP address from private IP addresses

Network Classes (Subnetting)

In its simplest form, subnetting allows for the creation of networks with more logical host limits versus the limitations imposed by specific IP addressing classes. Looked at another way, if networks were limited to only Class A, B, or C ranges, every network would have only 254, 65,534, or 16+ million IP addresses for host devices, and these limitations could create huge inefficiencies, potential security issues, significant administrative overhead, and potential network-related performance and congestion issues. Through the use of subnetting, which reflects awareness of the current environment and planning for the future, the proper-size logical host environment can be architected and deployed and can mitigate many, if not all, of the issues noted. Table 4-14 summarizes the subnet classes and related IP address ranges.

Know the maximum number of Class A, B, and C IP addresses

	# of addresses
Class A	16,777,216 (2^{24}) = **16,777,214**
Class B	65,536 (2^{16}) = **65,534**
Class C	256 (2^{8}) = **254**
Class D	Multicast address
Class E	Reserved

Table 4-14: **Subnet Classes and Related IP Address Ranges**

4.1.7 Layer 4: Transport

CORE **CONCEPTS**

- **TCP and UDP are two transport protocols that reside at Layer 4.**

- **TCP three-way handshake: SYN, SYN-ACK, ACK**

- **Ports equate to services that provide specific functionality.**

- **Layer 4 protocols: TCP, UDP, SSL/TLS**

TCP and UDP

As previously mentioned, Layer 4 (the Transport layer) is like a truck that transports information between devices. Delivery services can come in the form of reliable, ordered transmission (using TCP) or in unreliable, unordered transmission (using UDP). Many people refer to UDP as a "send and pray" protocol. This said, both protocols are still heavily relied upon, and each serves a purpose. For reliable, perhaps a bit slower, transmissions, TCP is the clear choice. However, UDP is fast, and for things like video streaming, which requires speed, as well as handling DNS requests, UDP is very efficient.

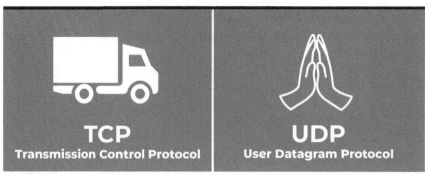

Table 4-15: **TCP and UDP**

TCP versus UDP Headers

Figure 4-11 illustrates the differences between UDP and TCP headers. As you can see, the UDP header contains much less information than the TCP header, which makes it much easier and faster to process. The additional information contained in the TCP header provides the reliability needed for certain applications, which, however, requires considerable processing time.

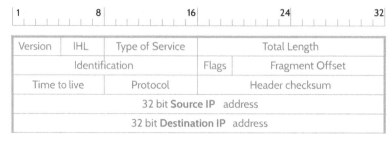

| 1 | | 8 | | 16 | | 24 | | 32 |

Version	IHL	Type of Service		Total Length		
Identification			Flags	Fragment Offset		
Time to live		Protocol		Header checksum		
32 bit **Source IP** address						
32 bit **Destination IP** address						

UDP Header

Source Port	Flags
Length	Header & Data Checksum

OR

TCP Header

Source Port		Flags	
Sequence Number			
Acknowledgement Number			
Data Offset	Res	Flags	Window Size
Header & Data Checksum		Urgent Pointer	

DATA

Figure 4-11: **UDP and TCP Headers**

TCP Three-Way Handshake

Out of the entire family of protocols, TCP is the only one that provides reliable, ordered, sequenced transmissions. This reliability, however, comes at a cost. Looking back at the truck analogy, for this reliability to be realized, a road first needs to be built. What's known as the TCP three-way handshake is the building of the technological road to reliably connect hosts across a network. Let's examine this more closely through an example depicted in Figure 4-12.

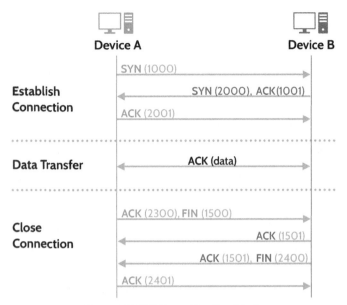

Figure 4-12: **TCP Three-Way Handshake**

Imagine two devices, A and B. Device A is initiating communication, and Device B is the receiving device. This is the sequence of steps that follows:

1. Device A first sends what's known as a synchronization (SYN) request along with a random session ID or synchronization number (in this case 1000). The session ID number is random in order to prevent an attacker from predicting the number, which if known could allow the session to be hijacked.

2. The receiving device is going to acknowledge the synchronization request by sending a packet with the ACK (acknowledge) flag set (in which it's going to increment the session ID it received in step #1 by one, making this 1001). In addition, because the goal is two-way communication, the receiving device will also send its own synchronize (SYN) request and random session ID number (in this example, 2000) to the initiating device. That means that the packet Device B sends in step #2, will have two flags set, SYN and ACK.

3. Device A sends a final packet with the ACK flag set, including an incremented session ID number (2001, which is incrementing the SYN value of 2000 that it received earlier by one). So the full final sequence is SYN, SYN – ACK, ACK.

Here's where the reliability of TCP comes in.

Each transmission must be acknowledged by the receiving device, and in the three earlier steps, a full-duplex connection is established; thus, the term three-way handshake. Communication in both directions can take place and all transmissions are acknowledged.

Additionally, the synchronization number allows each party to know that all data has been received. If a synchronization of 1000 is sent, the number received in reply should be 1001. If something other than 1001 is received, it means one or more packets are missing and retransmission would then be requested. This functionality further ensures the reliability for which TCP is known.

To close the connection, finish requests and acknowledgment of them takes place. That is done in a pair of FIN-ACK packets. If a graceful disconnection is to take place, Device A can send a FIN request, to which Device B would respond with an ACK. In the same regard, Device B may then send a FIN request, to which Device A would respond with an ACK. As such, we would have two pairs of FIN-ACK sequences to gracefully terminate the session.

For all its inherent advantages, the TCP three-way handshake can also be exploited for malicious purposes. Consider this example: When a synchronize request is received, the receiving device tries to acknowledge it by sending an ACK, and the session ID incremented by one. What if many synchronize requests from different hosts are arriving at the same time? Of course, the receiving device will attempt to acknowledge each request. However, if the requests are coming faster than can be handled, the receiving device's process or connection queue is going to fill up faster than it's emptying. Eventually, the queue is going to fill up, and the system may crash and/or become unresponsive. This is how a SYN flood attack works. To handle something like this, it's best to offload the processing of SYN requests and utilize hardware or software at the Application layer to handle the load. At the Application layer, some type of SYN proxy will be more intelligent and able to handle the incoming requests. It can determine very quickly that a SYN flood is present and simply drop the incoming requests, and the host continues to operate normally.

Ports

Ports equate to services, and services are small applications that provide specific functionality. For example, for the common web service, HTTP, port 80 is used by default. Some of the services associated with different ports are used quite extensively, while others are hardly used. Additionally, some of the most popular or most functional services are also the most often exploited services. Some examples of commonly used ports are denoted in Table 4-16.

If a service is not needed, especially ones that are dangerous, the associated port should be closed, and techniques like packet filtering can be used to block datagrams that reference the associated ports in the header. The use of packet filtering in this sense is part of a process called *hardening*. In addition to using packet filtering, hardening might also involve shutting down services—effectively shutting down the ports—on host machines or within applications or architectures inside a network, because services in those contexts might also provide a communication channel that malicious actors can exploit. If security is needed across a network, hardening can be used to enforce the use of more secure versions of services, like HTTPS or SFTP, instead of HTTP and FTP (which are plaintext protocols). And in cases, where a service cannot be made more secure, a tunneling and encryption protocol like SSH can be used to protect the data transmission. Hardening focuses on security, whether through the removal of or disabling of services, blocking services, or applying patches and upgrades to address known vulnerabilities in an architecture or application.

Among the 65,535 available TCP and UDP ports, three classes exist, also shown in Figure 4-13:

1. **Well known:** Used by specific system services like HTTP, HTTPS, SMTP and similar ones

2. **Registered:** Internet Assigned Numbers Authority (IANA) assigned ports after a specific request is submitted (e.g., UDP 4244 used by the famous Viber, which is a VoIP application)

3. **Dynamic/Private/Ephemeral:** These high ports are dynamically assigned and are often used by applications and other services. For example, when a host machine sends a SYN request to initiate a connection, the source port might be something like 52,367.

Figure 4-13: **Port Ranges**

21	File Transfer Protocol (FTP)
22	Secure Shell (SSH) (remote login protocol)
23	Telnet (remote command line protocol)
25	Simple Mail Transfer Protocol (SMTP)
80	Hypertext Transfer Protocol (HTTP)
443	Hypertext Transfer Protocol Secure (HTTPS)

Table 4-16: **Common TCP Ports**

> **Be familiar with port ranges and common ports and the services they provide**

Layer 4 Protocols

Table 4-17 lists some of the most common Layer 4 used protocols.

TCP	Transmission Control Protocol—provides reliable, ordered, connection-oriented, sequenced services. The cost of TCP's reliability is speed; it's a slower protocol. When reliability is needed, TCP is the protocol of choice.
UDP	User Datagram Protocol—unreliable, "I'll try my best, but there are no guarantees . . ." services. "Send and pray" is a phrase often attributed to UDP. UDP's unreliability also results in it being a much faster protocol. For streaming and for things like DNS requests, UDP is good.
SSL/TLS	Secure Socket Layer (SSL)/Transport Layer Security (TLS) are essentially the same thing—TLS is simply the name for the newest version of SSL, and the name was changed to remove confusion about what layer of the OSI model the protocol runs at: the Transport layer. SSL/TLS is the most used security protocol across the Internet, and it facilitates secure connections between, for example, a browser and a secure server located anywhere in the world.

Table 4-17: **Layer 4 Protocols**

4.1.8 Layer 5: Session

CORE CONCEPTS

- Supports interhost communication and coordinates dialogue between cooperating application processes

- Maintains a logical connection between two processes on end hosts

- Ideal place for identification and authentication

- Layer 5 protocols: PAP, CHAP, EAP, NetBIOS, RPC

- Layer 5 devices: circuit proxy firewall (also referred to as circuit level gateway)

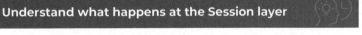

> **Understand what happens at the Session layer**

Layer 5 (the Session layer) is responsible for establishing and maintaining connections. It can perform functions like establishing, maintaining, synchronizing, and tearing down a connection.

Layer 5 Protocols

Some of the protocols in the table below have already been mentioned. PAP, CHAP, and EAP are the authentication protocols that support the PPP protocol found at Layer 2, which as you may remember facilitates remote connections that are ultimately established at Layer 5, the Session layer. RPC and NetBIOS are additional protocols found at Layer 5, and they also help facilitate remote access. These have been listed in Table 4-18, including the prementioned PAP, CHAP, and EAP as reminders.

PAP	Password Authentication Protocol simply prompts for a user ID and password when establishing a connection. However, passwords are transmitted in plaintext, and the user will never be prompted to change their password as it will be static in nature.
CHAP	Challenge Handshake Authentication Protocol was developed because of PAP's vulnerabilities. CHAP is an improved version of PAP. Passwords are encrypted during transmission, and challenges are routinely sent behind the scene to ensure that an attacker has not replaced the original client.
EAP	The best authentication protocol is called Extensible Authentication Protocol. The word *extensible* means being able to be extended or designed to allow new capabilities and functionality to be added. With this understanding, EAP allows vendors to adapt the latest authentication technologies, like smart keys and digital certificates, to their products. In fact, due to its inherent strengths, EAP can also be embedded into other things, like wireless security, where it's used with WPA2 for purposes of connecting to wireless networks and authenticating users at the same time.
NetBIOS	Network Basic Input/Output System is a legacy communications protocol that allows computers within a local network to communicate with each other and with various peripheral devices, like file shares and printers.
RPC	Remote Procedure Call is a communications protocol that facilitates communications between clients and servers to execute procedures.

Table 4-18: **Layer 5 Protocols**

Layer 5 Devices

The primary type of security device found at the Session layer is known as a circuit proxy firewall or gateway. Unlike other firewalls found at the Application layer, circuit proxy firewalls do not filter individual network packets; rather, they monitor and track traffic to determine if it is legitimate by inspecting TCP packet handshakes and sessions. One benefit of circuit proxy firewalls is that they hide details of an internal network from external users through the use of network address translation (NAT), so all outgoing traffic shows only the gateway IP address.

4.1.9 Layer 6: Presentation

CORE **CONCEPTS**

- Formatting and encryption of data for end users
- Ensures compatible syntax in how the information is represented for exchange by applications
- Provides translation, encryption/decryption, and compression/decompression

Layer 6, the Presentation layer, focuses on the visual elements of data. It focuses on graphics, character conversions, codecs, and other elements that relate to how data is actually presented to users at the Application layer. Codecs are a particularly interesting topic in this context. Codecs are small software programs that enable different types of video files to be viewed on a computer. Users are usually alerted to the need for a codec by their multimedia application, at which point the user will use Google, for example, to search for, download, and install the codec. Unfortunately, malware writers often use codecs to deliver malicious software too, so consumers should be very careful to confirm that a given codec is free from malware.

Like modem standing for modulator/demodulator, codec stands for coder/decoder, or better, compression/decompression, that represent a multitude of ways that digital media is handled. Digital media often entails very large files, and delivering these large files from a media source to consumers requires significant bandwidth and some technical wizardry—like compression/decompression—to assist. This is where codecs came into play. However, because one codec standard was not adopted, a multitude of codecs were developed to support the multitude of video formats. As vendors wanted their video format to grow in popularity, supporting codecs were often made freely available and shared on the internet, and they became a hotbed of malware as a result. Today, content distribution networks (CDNs) handle the bulk of media distribution around the world. Vendors locate servers around the globe specifically to host things like YouTube videos closer to consumers.

4.1.10 Layer 7: Application

> ### CORE **CONCEPTS**
>
> - **Layer where most functionality resides, also the layer where most security breaches and attacks occur**
> - **Provides a user interface through which a user gains access to communication services**
> - **Ideal place for end-to-end encryption and access control**
> - **Layer 7 protocols: HTTP/S, FTP, DNS, Telnet, SSH, SMTP, SNMP**
> - **Layer 7 devices: gateways and application firewalls**

Layer 7 (the Application layer) is the layer where most functionality resides. For this reason, it's also the layer where most security breaches and attacks occur. Think about it: applications are created to provide functionality, and this often requires significant amounts of coding. In fact, this points to another CISSP domain that focuses entirely on software development and application security (Domain 8).

Be familiar with what happens at Layer 7

Layer 7: Protocols

Among a number of protocols, or services, that run at the Application layer, those listed in Table 4-19 (along with their default ports) are some of the most popular. As can be seen, many of these protocols come in two versions: standard (HTTP) and secure (HTTPS).

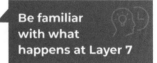

Be familiar with common Layer 7 protocols and their uses

HTTP/S	**Hypertext Transfer Protocol (HTTP)** using TCP port 80 is essentially the language of the web and allows for communication between web browsers and web servers. However, it's not inherently secure. Thus, **Hypertext Transfer Protocol Secure (HTTPS)** using TCP port 443 was developed to meet the needs of situations where secure web communication is required. HTTPS incorporates SSL/TLS for purposes of tunneling and therefore protecting traffic from interception across the internet.
FTP/FTPS/ TFTP	**File Transfer Protocol (FTP)** using TCP ports 20 and 21 is heavily utilized by companies, but it is also one of the most vulnerable services. Thus, a more secure version of FTP—**Secure FTP (SFTP)**, also referred to as SSH FTP using TCP port 22—was developed, so companies can transmit and retrieve files securely. Note that **Trivial File Transport Protocol (TFTP)** using UDP port 69 is highly insecure, and most companies tend to ban and disable this service as a result.
DNS/DNSSEC	Domain Name Service (DNS) using TCP and UDP port 53 maps hostnames to IP addresses. Surprisingly, DNS includes very little built-in security, and an initiative has been under way for a number of years to better protect DNS services through the use of Secure DNS (DNSSEC). DNSSEC provides for better protection of DNS data itself, so it can't be easily spoofed or otherwise misused.
Telnet	Telnet (using TCP port 23) is one of several protocols that allows a user to remotely connect from one computer to another computer on the same network. As it stands, it's a very insecure protocol, and it's best used in conjunction with something like Secure Shell (SSH), which protects the transfer of data between devices.
SSH	Secure Shell (SSH) using TCP port 22 is a network protocol that utilizes public-key cryptography for purposes of secure connections to a remote computer. Some uses of SSH include login to a shell on a remote server, execution of commands on a remote host, and securing file transfer protocols, among many others.
SMTP/POP3	Simple Mail Transport Protocol (SMTP) using TCP port 25 is the protocol used for sending email over the internet, while Post Office Protocol (POP3) using TCP over port 110 is the one used for receiving email.
SNMP	Simple Network Management Protocol (SNMP) using UDP ports 161 and 162 is a protocol most often used by network administrators to collect, organize, and manage information related to devices on a network. Over the years, SNMP has been revised, and earlier versions (1 and 2) are considered highly vulnerable. SNMPv3 is the latest and recommended version.

Table 4-19: **Layer 7 Protocols**

Layer 7 Devices

Adding security at Layer 7 typically involves deploying gateways and firewalls. Essentially, a firewall can be a software or hardware solution and is used to filter traffic between two (or more) networks. A firewall can be as simple as a router that makes filtering decisions on packets based on an access control list, or it can be an extremely sophisticated, specifically purposed device that looks at traffic headers and/or payload to make complicated decisions. Two common Layer 7 devices are summarized in Table 4-20.

> Be familiar with common Layer 7 devices and their uses

Gateways	Gateways are simply connections between domains or networks.
Firewalls	At Layer 7, firewalls are known as application-proxy firewalls. At this layer, they're extremely sophisticated and therefore able to make the most informed and intelligent decisions. Because of this fact, application-proxy firewalls tend to have more processing overhead, and they're typically slower than firewalls found at lower layers.

Table 4-20: **Layer 7 Devices**

4.1.11 Network Administrator

CORE **CONCEPTS**

- The term network administrator is often used interchangeably with system administrator.
- Network administrators are primarily responsible for technical matters related to a network.

A network administrator, sometimes also referred to as system administrator, is usually a member of the IT department. Among their responsibilities, they help support information systems and resources and the CIA triad through proper

- configuration of the network, servers, desktop and mobile computers, and other computing devices,
- patch and software update management, and
- vulnerability management.

4.1.12 Convergence and Voice Over IP (VOIP)

CORE **CONCEPTS**

- Convergence refers to the ability of native IP networks to carry non-IP traffic via what are known as converged protocols.
- Popular converged protocols include Fibre Channel over Ethernet (FCoE), Internet Small Computer Systems Interface (iSCSI), Voice over Internet Protocol (VoIP)
- VoIP Protocols: SRTP (Secure Real-time Transport Protocol) and SIP (Session Initiation Protocol)
- Vishing is a specific type of attack that takes place in VoIP environments

Convergence

In recent years, data networks have been tasked with carrying multiple types of traffic in addition to data traffic. Now it's very common for a network to carry data, voice, multimedia, and other types of traffic. This ability is referred to as IP convergence, as depicted in Figure 4-14.

Recall the earlier discussion about SCADA and ICS. Typically, those systems use non-IP means of communication, which then requires their traffic to be tunneled across IP networks. This points to IP convergence or the ability of native IP networks to carry much more than only IP data. For example, telephony is not a native part of an IP network. IP telephony requires data networks to be able to support IP telephony protocols like H.323 and SIP. This is IP convergence.

From a security perspective, functionality is being added to the basic requirements of a data network, and anytime functionality is added, more potential vulnerabilities and security concerns are also added.

Important converged protocols include Fibre Channel over Ethernet (FCoE), Internet Small Computer Systems Interface (iSCSI), and Voice over IP (VoIP).

Each type of converged protocol serves a purpose, but because data networks do not include native security, carrying a different protocol across a data network poses risks. If confidentiality is a need, encryption can be used, which adds latency because data needs to be encrypted and then decrypted during transit.

Figure 4-14: **Convergence**

Three commonly used converged protocols are noted in Table 4-21.

FCoE	Fibre Channel over Ethernet
iSCSI	Internet Small Computer Systems Interface
VoIP	Voice over Internet Protocol

Table 4-21: **Converged Protocols**

FCoE enables Fibre Channel protocol traffic to be encapsulated and carried over Ethernet networks. iSCSI enables the use of SCSI commands across a network, particularly in the context of storage-related activities like backups. VoIP, which many people refer to as IP telephony, enables data networks to carry voice traffic using protocols such as H.323 and SIP. With each of these examples, security is not a built-in component, and adding it often results in lowered functionality and efficiency. Other common terms relating to voice are summarized in Table 4-22.

> **Be familiar with VoIP, common VoIP protocols, and the types of attack that takes place in VoIP environments**

PBX	A private branch exchange is a private telephone network that supports internal communications, usually in the context of an organization or a place like a hotel.
PSTN	A public switched telephone network is essentially the traditional, copper-wire-based telephone network that allows people and businesses to communicate with each other.
VoIP	Voice over Internet Protocol allows people and businesses to communicate via an internet connection, instead of a traditional copper-wire-based phone line.

Table 4-22: **Common Terms Related to Voice**

Considering the way that IP networks operate—with data being broken up into packets and sent across the network, where they might travel in different directions and arrive in a different order than they were sent—it follows that supporting voice communications in the fundamentally same manner is not as easy. For this reason, specific protocols were developed to ensure smooth and secure VoIP sessions and to mitigate problems that might otherwise result if voice and video session packets were treated the same as ordinary data packets. Two main VoIP protocols are summarized in Table 4-23.

Secure Real-time Transport Protocol (SRTP)	**Session Initiation Protocol (SIP)**
This is the secure version of RTP, which supports encryption, authentication, integrity, and replay attack protection. Note that RTP is mainly used for streaming voice and video over IP, with no existing security in it. SRTP also provides good bandwidth optimization, low resource requirements, and is independent from underlying protocols. The full description of its operation is described in RFC 3711.	SIP is responsible for initiating, maintaining, and terminating voice and video sessions. It can also support a direct connection between PBX and public telephony networks.

Table 4-23: **VoIP Protocols**

Vishing

Vishing is a form of phishing (**v**oice ph**ishing**) that specifically takes place in the context of VoIP environments. The attacker can easily spoof known or familiar numbers and then obtain information that a victim might not otherwise provide. Note the difference between vishing and smishing. Vishing entails the attacker calling the victim and trying to obtain valuable information or make them perform a certain action (e.g., click on a URL). Smishing, on the other hand, relates to the attacker sending SMS messages to the victim (**SM**S ph**ishing**).

4.1.13 Network Security Attacks

CORE **CONCEPTS**

- Network attacks resemble network assessments in terms of the steps/phases that each follows, with the exception of assessments including an exploitation phase.

- Passive attacks do not change the environment or information; active attacks can change information.

- SYN scanning is an active attack that abuses the way the normal three-way TCP handshake operates and helps an attacker determine what services might be running on a target machine.

- SYN flooding abuses the normal three-way TCP handshake by rapidly "flooding" a target machine with multiple SYN requests that ultimately exhaust the target machine's resources, causing it to crash.

- A Denial-of-Service (DoS) attack is any attack that attempts to impede or completely deny functionality of a system—one machine is being used to cause the loss of functionality. A distributed-denial-of-service (DDoS) attack involves multiple machines acting in unison.

- A man-in-the-middle attack is any attack that originates in between two connected devices.

- Spoofing and masquerading are essentially the same thing—pretending to be someone or something else.

- ARP poisoning involves a malicious user modifying their ARP table to direct network traffic meant for another device to their device.

- ARP uses tables to map IP addresses to physical addresses—the MAC addresses—of a device. Every device on a network has a physical address and an ARP table.

With an understanding of the OSI model, relevant protocols and devices found at each layer, and a sense of the importance of security at each layer, let's dive a bit deeper and examine how to best prevent and defend against network attacks. With any attack, a series of steps or phases will be executed.

Understand how a network attack differs from a network assessment

Network Attack Phases

Network attacks and network assessments (including penetration tests) are very similar. In fact, at a high level, they include identical steps. The main difference is that an attacker will not care if they inflict damage on the target network when they are launching an exploit, while the penetration tester will do that in a more controlled manner and while respecting the scope and rules of engagement.

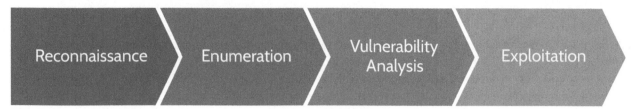

Figure 4-15: **Attack Phases**

In virtually all cases, any successful attack will sequentially go through the phases outlined in Figure 4-15. From a security perspective, making each of these phases very difficult or impossible to achieve should be the goal. Preventing attacks is practically impossible, which is why organizations should focus on making potential attacks time consuming, expensive, and not worth the effort, so attackers will look elsewhere.

With any attack, **reconnaissance** will first be performed. Reconnaissance is the initial gathering of valuable information that will aid the attacker. IP address ranges used by an organization, domain names, services that are running on devices, or operating system in use are all things an attacker might seek as part of the reconnaissance phase.

From a security perspective and with this in mind, one of the best things an organization can do to minimize the amount of information an attacker might discover during the reconnaissance phase is to not publish things like IP address ranges or domain names. Additionally, much information about an organization can be gleaned from social media, from sites like LinkedIn, or from technical forums, where people from around the globe often convene to learn from and help each other. Individually, these bits and pieces of information might not mean much, but when gathered together by a determined attacker, they could very well become the key that opens the door. So, limiting publicly available information is one part of the equation, and creating policy and awareness for the sake of staff is another.

The phase that follows reconnaissance is known as **enumeration**. Usually before account enumeration, the attacker will perform scanning to look for open ports, especially open ports for interesting services like FTP or HTTP servers, and other software versions of interest. Once those are identified, the attacker will try to enumerate the target for active accounts that can be used to gain access.

During **vulnerability analysis,** the attacker will look for vulnerabilities that can be exploited. That's why it's so helpful for an organization to have a vulnerability management program, as they can use the same tools as attackers and perform similar vulnerability analyses to identify vulnerabilities and gaps and implement controls to make it very difficult for an attack to be successful.

During **exploitation,** the attacker attempts to exploit the vulnerabilities identified during the vulnerability analysis phase. An organization can put detection mechanisms in place to provide alerts if some type of breach or attack does take place during exploitation. For example, if an attacker tries to perform brute-force password cracking against the administrator account, an alert can be generated to signify this activity.

In addition to understanding the network attack phases, it's important to understand the difference between passive and active attacks. In general, a **passive attack** means the attacker is passively performing an activity (e.g., intercepting traffic and inspecting it) without directly interacting with the target. However, during an **active attack**, the attacker will directly engage with target, e.g., during a Denial-of-Service attack.

Passively Eavesdropping

Passive attacks leave the environment unchanged, and the target has no idea that anything has taken or is taking place. Eavesdropping is a great example of a passive attack. Information is being reviewed, but nothing is changing, and the information gained can be used for purposes of exploitation later in the attack. Monitoring or reviewing information traveling across a network is another form of eavesdropping. This is also known as sniffing the network or network sniffing, as shown in Figure 4-16. Data intended for others is intercepted, but no other action is taken.

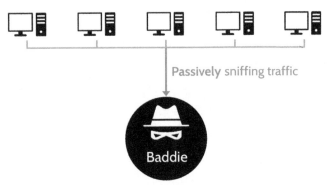

Figure 4-16: **Passive Traffic Sniffing**

Actively Scanning

Unlike passive attacks, active attacks change packet content. Masquerading and denial-of-service attacks are examples of active attacks. During scanning, the target gets alerted of the activity as there's interaction with it, so it's considered an active attack. A classic scanning tool for that is Nmap, and it only supports active operating system fingerprinting, because it sends specific packets and waits for responses to be provided by the target system, which are then reviewed to identify what the target OS may be.

> **Understand how SYN scanning and SYN flooding abuse the normal three-way TCP/IP handshake**

SYN Scanning

Tools like Nmap can easily perform SYN scanning, which consists of the following steps and is also depicted in Figure 4-17.

1. A client sends a SYN packet to a target machine's specific port (e.g., TCP port 80) to try and identify if it's open or closed.

2. Possible responses are:

   a. If the port is open, the target replies with a SYN-ACK packet, and then the client responds with a final ACK packet, and the session is established.

   b. If the port is closed, the target responds with a RST packet, and the session is terminated.

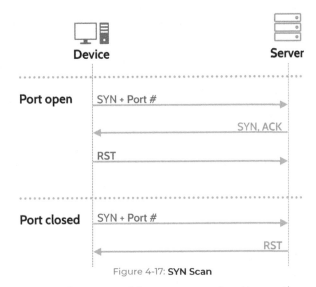

Figure 4-17: **SYN Scan**

Note that if the attacker wants to perform a stealth scan, e.g., using Nmap, they can do so by sending a RST packet at the third step of the three-way handshake and thus never sending the final ACK and formulating a full connection. This is known as a stealth or half-open scan.

SYN Flooding

As noted, with a normal three-way handshake, each open connection consumes a small amount of system resources. SYN flooding, depicted in Figure 4-18, takes advantage of this fact when multiple SYN requests are sent in rapid succession to a target machine, which responds with a SYN-ACK packet, considering these valid connection requests (parts of the first step of the three-way handshake). However, as the volume increases, the target machine is unable to acknowledge new requests fast enough, as its connection table is now filled. Eventually, the target machine's system resources and ability to respond are exhausted, and the machine crashes or stops responding entirely. SYN floods are active attacks, because they impact the host by degrading its performance or bringing it down altogether.

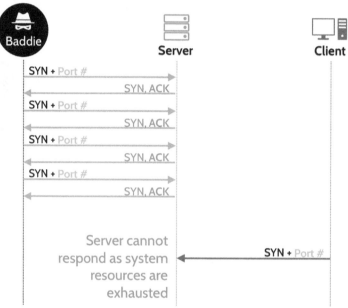

Figure 4-18: **SYN Flood**

One of the best ways to protect against SYN attacks is using a proxy, which acts on behalf of the devices on a network. The proxy has the ability and intelligence to understand whether a SYN scan or flood is taking place and then act accordingly to block the attack. Firewalls and IPS devices are also quite good at detecting SYN flood attacks and dropping offending traffic.

IP-Based Attacks

A number of IP-based attacks exist, like SYN flooding, eavesdropping, overlapping fragment, and teardrop attacks, all depicted in Table 4-24.

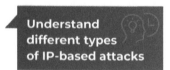

Understand different types of IP-based attacks

Fragment attacks	**Overlapping fragments**	This attack uses overlapping fragments in an attempt to bypass firewalls and IDS/IPS tools to gain access to a target system. Part of the attack pattern is sent in fragments, along with other data that can pass through the firewall. The goal of the attacker is to pass the attack sequence through any security tools, and when reassembly takes place (at the destination resource) to have the attack sequence created for it to execute.
	Teardrop	With this UDP attack, the attacker sends fragments of packets of differing sizes, out of order, and with fake fragment sequence numbers to a target system. The target system cannot reassemble the packets, causing it to consume its resources and degrade its performance and even crash, thus causing a denial-of-service attack.
IP Spoofing attacks	**Smurf**	A Smurf attack is executed following steps below: 1. Attacker spoofs their IP address to match the victim's 2. Attacker sends multiple ICMP echo request packets to intermediary network devices 3. Those devices respond with ICMP replies, which are directed to the victim (since the attacker spoofed their IP address to match the victim's in step #1) This causes a denial-of-service attack to take place at the victim's device, which is inundated with ICMP reply traffic.
	Fraggle	Like a Smurf attack, a Fraggle attack is also a denial-of-service attack that begins with IP spoofing. The attacker then sends a massive amount of UDP packets to the target system (destined to ports 7 and 19). Historically these ports relate to the Character Generator Protocol (CHARGEN) service. If either of these ports is open on a target, once they receive a request they will start generating a sequence of characters that will be directed to the victim thus overwhelming it with traffic. *Note that both the Smurf and Fraggle attacks are considered old attacks, and it's unlikely to see them used today.*

Table 4-24: **Fragment and IP Spoofing Attacks**

DoS and DDoS

In the context of discussion about IP-based attacks, Denial-of-Service was mentioned. Let's examine this concept a bit more, including what's known as a Distributed-Denial-of-Service attack. Both types can be seen in Figure 4-19.

> **Understand DoS and DDoS, man-in-the-middle, and spoofing attacks**

A **Denial-of-Service (DoS)** attack is any attack that attempts to impede or completely deny functionality of a system or network. In this sense, one machine is being used to cause the loss of functionality. A **Distributed-Denial-of-Service (DDoS)** attack involves multiple machines acting in unison. In this case, what first must happen is that a number of hosts must be compromised by a threat agent. Once this is accomplished, the compromised hosts can be programmed to work as one, aiming all their processing power and bandwidth at the target, resulting in a Distributed-Denial-of-Service attack.

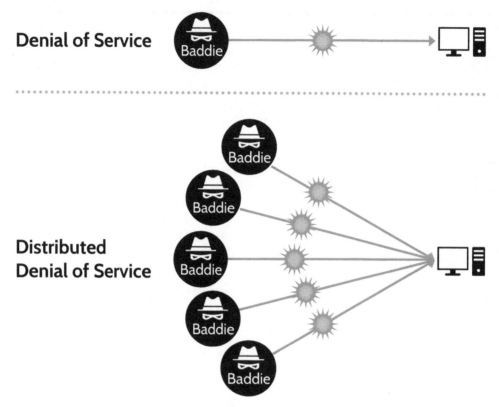

Figure 4-19: **DoS and DDoS Attacks**

Man-in-the-Middle

A man-in-the-middle attack, depicted in Figure 4-20, manifests when the attacker inserts themselves in the communication path of two entities and thus has an opportunity to intercept and manipulate traffic between them.

Figure 4-20: **Man-in-the-Middle Attack**

Spoofing

Spoofing and masquerading, mentioned earlier, are essentially the same thing. Spoofing is pretending to be someone or something else, because that someone or something usually possesses more privileges or has access to a resource. For example, an attacker may spoof their IP address to bypass an access control list that only accepts traffic from a certain IP address. In that case, the attacker may assume a different IP to send offending traffic to a target. It's really important to remember that when an IP address is spoofed by the attacker, although they can send traffic to a target resource, they won't be able to accept something in response. Any response will be directed to the legitimate holder of that IP address.

Spoofing is not limited to one area of focus. Email, DNS entries, user IDs, IP and MAC addresses, and even biometrics can be spoofed. Really, anything that might prove valuable or useful can be spoofed.

Common Tools and Protocols

Table 4-25 summarizes some common tools and protocols that attackers use to take advantage of networks.

Ping	Ping is a TCP/IP-based utility that is used to determine if a network host is "alive" or available and to measure response time. It can be a very useful and quick network troubleshooting tool. However, because of the way it functions, it can also be a very useful reconnaissance tool, by allowing an attacker to identify potential targets.
Traceroute	Traceroute, like ping, is a TCP/IP-based utility that takes ping a step further and actually maps a network connection from one host to another. Its usefulness comes in that it shows every hop traversed between the two locations. An attacker can take advantage of that to map a target network.
ICMP	ICMP stands for Internet Control Message Protocol and supports TCP/IP utilities like ping and traceroute, among others. ICMP messages come as different types that are differentiated by types and associated codes (think of them as subtypes). For example, when using the ping utility to see if a host is alive, ICMP might return a type 3 code 1 "Destination Unreachable" message. Type 3 means the destination is not reachable, while code 1 shows that this is due to the host not being reachable in particular. For example, a code 0 would indicate the target network was unreachable. This can be valuable information for an attacker..
DHCP	Dynamic Host Control Protocol is used to assign a valid IP address to a device when it first connects to a network. Whether at home, on a corporate network, or anywhere else, if a connection to a network is made a valid IP address is assigned to the connecting device. DHCP does this automatically. An attacker can use a tool to make them seem like they are a legitimate DHCP server on the network and thus trick victims into getting connection information, which may include setting up the attacker's machine as their default gateway. In that regard, the attacker would then be able to intercept all network traffic, as it would pass through their machine.
Ipconfig	Used mainly in Windows systems to display TCP/IP network configuration values and can refresh Dynamic Host Configuration Protocol and Domain Name System settings.
WHOIS	A query and response tool that is widely used for querying databases that store the registered users or assignees of an internet resource, such as a domain name, an IP address block, or an autonomous system public domain registration information.
Dig	A network administration command-line tool for querying the Domain Name System (DNS).
Putty	A free and open source terminal emulator, serial console, and network file transfer application. It supports several network protocols, including SCP, SSH, Telnet, rlogin, and raw socket connection.
Nmap	A free and open source network scanner used to discover hosts and services on a computer network by sending packets and analyzing the responses.
John the Ripper	John the Ripper (JtR) is an open source password cracking tool and is available for many operating systems.
Netstat	A command-line network utility that displays network connections for TCP and UDP (both incoming and outgoing), routing tables, and a number of network interface (network interface controller or software-defined network interface) and network protocol statistics.
Nslookup	A network administration command-line tool used for querying the Domain Name System (DNS) to obtain domain name or IP address mapping or other DNS records.

Table 4-25: **Common Tools and Utilities Attackers Leverage**

ARP Poisoning

We already mentioned how ARP works earlier. An attacker can try to leverage the protocol's operation to intercept traffic destined for a legitimate designation as depicted in Figure 4-21. A switch has a content addressable memory (CAM) table, which holds mappings of MAC addresses and which ports the respective devices are connected to. When traffic for a device for

Understand what ARP tables do and ARP poisoning

which the switch doesn't have an entry reaches it, it will send a broadcast message that essentially asks, "What MAC address belongs to this IP address?" All of the devices will look at their ARP tables, and the device associated with that IP address will reply back, "That's me, here's my MAC address," at which point the switch will send the request to that device. It's actually quite simple, and this fact explains why it's equally simple for someone to modify their ARP table to direct network traffic meant for another device to their device. There's no authentication or security built into ARP tables, and the same holds true for many other devices and protocols that utilize tables. As such, if the attacker were to send an ARP reply to the switch denoting a specific MAC address, then the switch would consider that legitimate and log it in its ARP table.

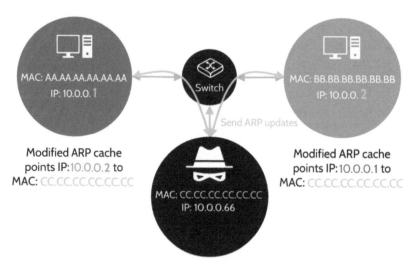

Figure 4-21: **ARP Poisoning**

Monitoring of activities across network segments is one of the best ways to prevent ARP poisoning. This holds true with regards to DNS too, though in recent years, DNSSEC has been developed and employed by many organizations to prevent DNS poisoning. With all these vulnerabilities, if good preventive or detective controls don't exist, good compensating controls should be implemented. This typically means more logging and monitoring, depending on the value of the asset in question.

4.1.14 **Wireless**

CORE CONCEPTS

- IEEE 802.11 specifications define wireless standards.
- Wireless authentication requires an authenticated key exchange mechanism.
- Temporal Key Integrity Protocol (TKIP) was designed to replace WEP without requiring the replacement of legacy hardware, due to a significant flaw found in WEP.
- To protect any wireless communication, four things are needed: access control, authentication, integrity protection, and encryption.

The radio frequency spectrum (which supports wireless technologies) does not have built-in security. Bluetooth, Wi-Fi, and similar technologies contain no native security features. Regardless of the wireless technology in use, one of the easiest ways to introduce security is through segregation. In other words, especially with Wi-Fi, different networks can be set up. Guests can be segregated to their own network, employees to an internal network, and vendors or external visitors to yet another network, with each network segment containing security appropriate to the need. All of this points to a network architecture as illustrated in Figure 4-22.

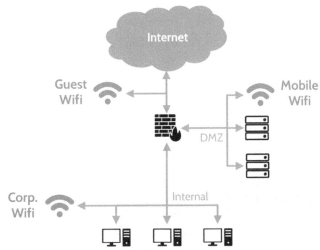

Figure 4-22: **Network Architecture**

Radio Frequency Management

Radio frequency management refers to the placement of devices that broadcast wireless traffic. For example, the placement of Wi-Fi access points within a building should carefully consider how far out wireless signals extend outside the building. If the signal extends to the parking lot, somebody could sit in a car for hours and attempt to break into the network. Ideally, access points are located in such a way that authorized individuals can utilize the Wi-Fi service and untrusted people cannot.

Managing Wi-Fi signals is called radio frequency management, which can prove quite challenging at times as there are an abundance of different devices operating at different areas of the radio spectrum, as also seen in Figure 4-23. In addition to Wi-Fi, other technologies like Bluetooth, cellular, and RFID, can be found. Despite

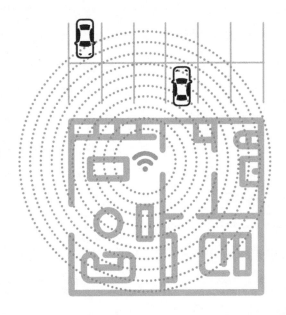

the differing technologies, they all share a common feature. They're all examples of emanations. Though a number of frequencies exist, three of them—2.4 GHz, 5 GHz, and 900 MHz—are of particular interest. These are unlicensed radio frequencies, which means that anybody can create a technology or device that operates within those frequencies. From a security standpoint, this means that if a Wi-Fi device operates at 5 GHz, there are very likely other devices that operate at 5 GHz too and can therefore pick up those Wi-Fi signals. However, there's no security built into any of them. To secure them, some features needed to be added.

WIRELESS RADIO SPECTURM

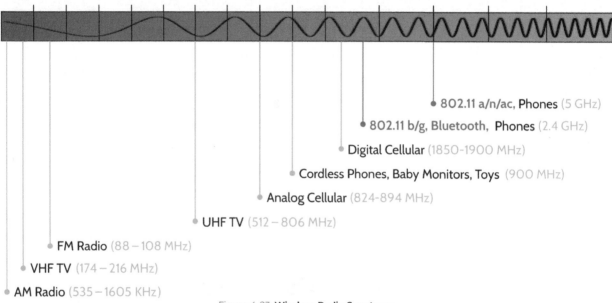

- **802.11 a/n/ac, Phones** (5 GHz)
- **802.11 b/g, Bluetooth, Phones** (2.4 GHz)
- **Digital Cellular** (1850-1900 MHz)
- **Cordless Phones, Baby Monitors, Toys** (900 MHz)
- **Analog Cellular** (824-894 MHz)
- **UHF TV** (512 – 806 MHz)
- **FM Radio** (88 – 108 MHz)
- **VHF TV** (174 – 216 MHz)
- **AM Radio** (535 – 1605 KHz)

Figure 4-23: **Wireless Radio Spectrum**

Wireless Technologies

As noted in Figure 4-23, the wireless radio spectrum includes a number of wireless technologies, some of which are summarized in Table 4-26. In its most basic form, wireless refers to communication without using the physical medium of wires or cables. It is the transmission of data over the air—via channels encompassed by the wireless radio spectrum.

Wi-Fi	Wi-Fi, described in more detail below, follows standards outlined by IEEE 802.11 specifications. Wi-Fi is used in many contexts, from printing to connecting to network resources and turning a mobile phone into a Wi-Fi hot spot for use by a computer or other devices.
Bluetooth	Bluetooth is a wireless technology that supports devices in close proximity. For example, many people today use Bluetooth keyboards and mice with their computers instead of wired versions. Similarly, most modern automobile audio systems include Bluetooth, which allows a similarly equipped mobile phone to connect and play music stored on the phone through the automobile speakers.
Cellular	Though the terms Wi-Fi and cellular are often used interchangeably, cellular refers more specifically to wireless protocols and standards used in the context of mobile phones. Within this spectrum, **Code Division Multiple Access (CDMA)**, **Global System for Mobiles (GSM)**, 3G, 4G, and now 5G all represent the specific ways the devices are designed to communicate with cellular networks.
 **RFID**	RFID, also known as Radio Frequency Identification, refers to a specific type of wireless system that is made up of readers and some type of Wi-Fi-enabled tag, chip, or label. The reader emits radio waves and receives signals back from the Wi-Fi-enabled object. The tag, chip, or label can be used for any of a number of purposes, such as asset management, inventory control, or similar type of tracking. RFID technology allows otherwise mundane tasks to be automated as well as to reduce errors that might otherwise occur when processes are performed manually.

Table 4-26: **Important Wiireless Technologies**

802.11 Wireless Protocol Family

Table 4-27 outlines different IEEE 802.11 specifications, starting with 802.11 and progressing to one of the latest: 802.11ac. This is essentially a look down wireless memory lane. Each variation of wireless is noted, along with the frequency range(s) a given specification covers as well as the maximum achievable speed. However, as noted above, each specification shares the same security concern—security is not native to any of them.

Type	Frequency	Top speed
802.11	2.4 GHz	2 Mbps
802.11a	5 GHz	54 Mbps
802.11b	2.4 GHz	11 Mbps
802.11g	2.4 GHz	54 Mbps
802.11n	2.4 GHz & 5 GHz	72 – 600 Mbps
802.11ac	5 GHz	422 – 1300 Mbps
802.11ax (Wi-Fi 6)	2.4 GHz & 5 GHz	10 Gbps
802.11ad (WiGig)	60 GHz	7 Gbps

Table 4-27: **802.11 Protocol Family**

802.11 Security Solutions

To secure wireless communication, four (4) security services are required: access control, authentication, encryption, and integrity protection. Over the years, different bundled security protocols have been developed that provide these services, and they're represented by three main standards in the wireless industry: 802.1X, WPA, and WPA2. It's worth noting that WPA3 has been released but is still not widely implemented.

> **Understand common wireless standards, from weakest to strongest, and elements of each**

Table 4-28 outlines how each of the security services are implemented. For example, WPA2 uses a pre-shared key (PSK) or 802.1X for access control. It also uses EAP or PSK for authentication, CCMP (which is essentially AES Counter Mode) for encryption, and CCMP-AES plus **Message Authentication Code (MAC)** to ensure integrity.

	802.1x Dynamic WEP	Wi-Fi Protected Access (WPA)	Wi-Fi Protected Access 2 (WPA2)	Wi-Fi Protected Access 3 (WPA3)
Released	1997	2003	2004	2018
Access Control	802.1X	802.1X or Pre-Shared Key	802.1X or Pre-Shared Key	802.1X or Pre-Shared Key
Authentication	EAP methods	EAP methods or Pre-Shared Key	EAP methods or Pre-Shared Key	EAP methods or Pre-Shared Key
Encryption	WEP	TKIP (RC4)	CCMP (AES Counter Mode)	CCMP or GCMP (Galois Counter Mode Protocol)
Integrity	None	Michael MIC	CCMP	CCMP or GCMP

Table 4-28: **WEP and WPA**

Wireless Authentication

There are three main ways used to authenticate to a wireless network:

- Open authentication (a device can connect by using the network's SSID, with no security enabled).
- Shared key (a pre-shared network key is used, which is shared across any device that needs to connect to the network).
- EAP is used (authentication requires an authenticated **key exchange** mechanism), which can lead to one- or two-factor authentication:
  - **One-factor**: EAP-MD5, LEAP, PEAP-MSCHAP, TTLS-MSCHAP, EAP-SIM
  - **Two-factor**: EAP-TLS, TTLS with OTP, and PEAP-GTC

Note that to achieve robust authentication in wireless networks, it's ideal to have mutual authentication enforced, which means that the client is asserted of the access point it's connecting to, and the access point can be assured that the client is valid.

Wireless Encryption

The main encryption technologies are:

- Temporal Key Integrity Protocol (**TKIP**): Was instituted as a fix of the WEP vulnerabilities and was used in WPA (with an RC4 stream cipher and 128 bit per-packet keys) but is vulnerable to attacks mainly due to the WPA requirement to support hardware compatibility with WEP.
- Counter-Mode-CBC-MAC Protocol (**CCMP**): Uses Advanced Encryption Standard (**AES**) with 128-bit keys, which is used in WPA2.

Wireless Integrity Protection

Main methods for integrity protection are:

- TKIP uses a Message Integrity Code called "Michael."

- WPA2 uses CCMP (which uses AES in CBC-MAC mode).

A short summary of TKIP is provided below:

- Designed to **replace WEP** without requiring the replacement of legacy hardware

- Required due to significant flaw found in WEP—specifically, the use of a weak IV that allowed WEP to be easily cracked

- Sends each new packet with a unique encryption key (key mixing)

- TKIP is no longer considered secure and is superseded by AES

TKIP is an interesting protocol, as it served as a stopgap when significant flaws and vulnerabilities were discovered with WEP. Immediately, attempts were made to mitigate the vulnerabilities with WEP. TKIP, which uses a 128-bit key size symmetric stream cipher known as RC4, was developed. A better version of TKIP was developed, a counter mode version, that uses stronger encryption known as AES.

To protect any wireless communication, four things are needed: access control, authentication, integrity protection, and encryption. TKIP implements a **Message Integrity Check (MIC)**, often referred to as "Michael." The details about how it works are not necessary for the sake of the CISSP exam; it's enough to know that it provides integrity control, like a hashing algorithm. Additionally, TKIP was implemented in a manner almost as if applying a patch. Technology that already used WEP would still work, and the more secure encryption protocol TKIP would handle encryption needs.

4.1.15 **VLAN and SDN**

> ### CORE **CONCEPTS**
>
> - **VLAN = Virtual Local Area Network, which allows local networks to be created using hardware devices, like Layer 3 switches, and other technologies and software. A VLAN reduces the need for physical wiring.**
>
> - **IEEE 802.1Q is the standard that supports VLANs on networks.**
>
> - **SDN = Software-Defined Networks, which refers to networks created and managed using software.**
>
> - **SDN architecture includes application, control, and data planes.**
>
> - **Communication between application and control planes is facilitated by northbound APIs; communication between data and control planes is facilitated by southbound APIs.**

Virtual Local Area Network (VLAN)

Virtualization technologies are the underpinnings of cloud computing. Though virtualization is more well-known now, virtualization capabilities have been around since the early days of computing. Mainframe computers could actually be broken up into virtualized environments, with each environment having its own operating system, devices, peripherals, and so on. From a

security perspective, isolating things through this type of separation creates a more secure environment. Since the days of mainframe computers, virtualization has matured significantly, to the point where cloud computing is now at the forefront of most often used technologies.

Virtualizing networks is separating networks by creating segments that are separate from each other. Through this isolation, a more secure environment can be created.

VLAN stands for virtual local area network, and a VLAN can be created using devices, technologies, and software. A VLAN **reduces the need for physical rewiring by creating virtual tunnels through physical networks to connect devices**. VLAN segments should be created and used based upon the value of those segments. Typically, a Layer 3 switch can be used to create VLANS, based upon needs and value. Figure 4-24 shows a simple example of two VLANS (VLAN 1 and VLAN 2) that were created across two switches. Specific ports are configured to support a given VLAN, and any devices connected to those same ports will be on the same VLAN.

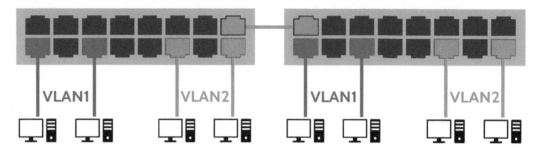

Figure 4-24: **VLAN Operation**

Software-Defined Networks (SDN)

As the name suggests, software-defined networking (SDN) is basically creating and managing a network using software. Software applications can be written that are very intelligent and function to the point that they mimic hardware devices, like routers, switches, and firewalls. Of course, as has been discussed, this software-based functionality comes at the cost of potential vulnerabilities that can be exploited.

> **Understand how a SDN differs from a traditional wired network**

Figure 4-25 illustrates a traditional network and a software-defined network (SDN). In the latter, applications provide the functionality provided by hardware devices found in a traditional network. With a software-defined network, some traditional physical network elements—like cabling—are still required; otherwise, the primary network elements are virtualized, and the network functions exactly as if everything were hardware based.

A SDN provides abstraction from the underlying physical network to enable rapid reconfiguration with centralized control. The abstraction is accomplished in the context of "planes"—areas where certain processes are executed.

With a SDN, two primary planes are found—the data plane and the control plane. Looking closely at Figure 4-25, there is one control plane for the SDN. The **control plane** acts as the "brain" of the SDN and understands everything about the network. More specifically, it is the part of the SDN that determines how the routing of packets across the network should take place. Based upon this information, it follows that routing tables and routing protocols would be part of the control plane.

Based upon *how* the control plane determines packets should be forwarded, the **data plane** handles the actual forwarding of packets to the proper destination.

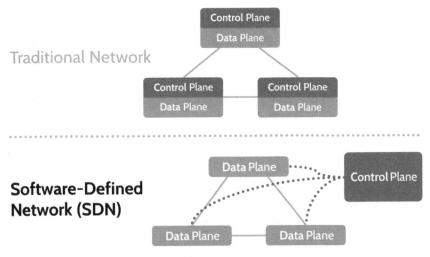

Figure 4-25: **Traditional vs. SDN Network**

SDN Architecture

Figure 4-26 further illustrates the architecture of an SDN and brings to light another plane—the Application plane, as well as two more terms: Northbound and Southbound APIs.

> **Understand the basic components, including flow, of an SDN**

The **Application plane** in an SDN hosts the applications and services that make network function-related requests from the control plane via northbound APIs. Application plane applications and services could include things like firewall and other security functionality, reporting, and network management, to name a few examples. Northbound APIs only pertain to communication between the Application and Control planes.

Similarly, **Southbound APIs** only pertain to communication between the Data and Control planes. The southbound interface facilitates communication between the SDN controller and the physical networking hardware.

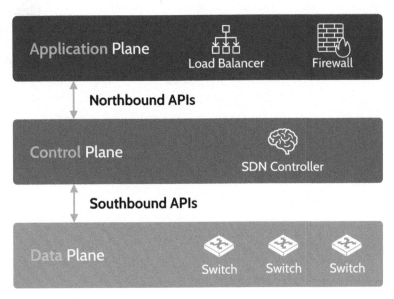

Figure 4-26: **SDN Architecture**

IEEE 802.1Q

IEEE 802.1Q refers to the IEEE standard that supports VLANs and SDNs. Among other things, the standard defines a system of what is known as "VLAN tagging" for network traffic as well as how bridges and switches should handle tagged frames. In effect it ensures that traffic destined for a specific VLAN, e.g., VLAN1, is able to only reach that VLAN and no other one.

Know the IEEE standard that supports VLANs and SDNs

4.1.16 Wide Area Networks (WAN)

CORE **CONCEPTS**

- WANs connect LANs through technologies such as: dedicated leased lines, dial-up phone lines, satellite and other wireless links, and data packet carrier services.

- WAN protocols include: X.25, Frame Relay, Asynchronous Transfer Mode (ATM), and Multi-Protocol Label Switching (MPLS)

To understand what constitutes a Wide Area Network (WAN), it helps to understand what constitutes a Local Area Network (LAN). A LAN is traditionally considered as a network that is confined to a small, local area, like a building. A WAN therefore is a network that extends far beyond a single location and usually involves connecting devices across wide geographical boundaries, like different cities or even different countries. Certain technologies enable these connections, and they're often sold or leased to consumers by service providers, like AT&T, Verizon, Sprint, among others. These providers have engineered WAN packet-switching networks that enable connectivity between locations, for example, a LAN in Texas to a LAN in Washington, DC, and they charge for things like data and bandwidth needs as well as for varying levels of quality of service (QOS). As the name implies, QOS focuses on error handling and the ability to provide services like IP convergence.

Of course, these technologies have evolved over the years. Original WAN technologies connected devices across telecommunications networks—PSTN—using modems. Satellite and microwave-based technologies were also quite prevalent years ago. Today, however, data packet carrier services are most often used. These services include things like Frame Relay, ATM, and MPLS, and are procured through service providers as noted above.

Know common WAN protocols and key features of each

Table 4-29 outlines some of the key evolutions of WAN technologies.

X.25	X.25 is one of the pioneers of WAN packet-switching protocols. In fact, it's still highly regarded for its error correction capabilities. At the same time, X.25 is not efficient and creates high overhead.
Frame Relay	Frame Relay followed X.25, and unlike X.25's focus on quality of service and error correction, Frame Relay's focus is on speed of transmission. In the context of Frame Relay, two types of circuits can be found: permanent virtual circuits (PVCs) and switched virtual circuits (SVCs). PVCs support end-to-end links over a physical network, and SVCs are similar to circuit-switched networks, like PSTN.
Asynchronous Transfer Mode (ATM)	ATM builds on many of the best features of Frame Relay and can support very high-speed transmission needs. ATM is connection-oriented and works through the creation of a virtual circuit between endpoints prior to data being exchanged. ATM virtual circuits can be permanent or on-demand.
Multi-Protocol Label Switching (MPLS)	MPLS is at the forefront of current WAN connectivity solutions, because it offers network connectivity that includes built-in security. Using features like forwarding tables and labeling schemes, MPLS providers can guarantee that customer's data transmissions cannot be touched by anybody else while traversing the MPLS provider network. However, even with this guarantee, the provider networks are still untrusted networks, right? Just because AT&T can guarantee that an organization's data transmissions will be safe while traveling across AT&T's network, somebody within AT&T could still access and read those transmissions. It's their network, so they can potentially access all data traveling within it. This explains why many organizations, even when using MPLS technology, will still encrypt their data—to prevent potential data snooping from the MPLS provider itself.

Table 4-29: **WAN Technologies**

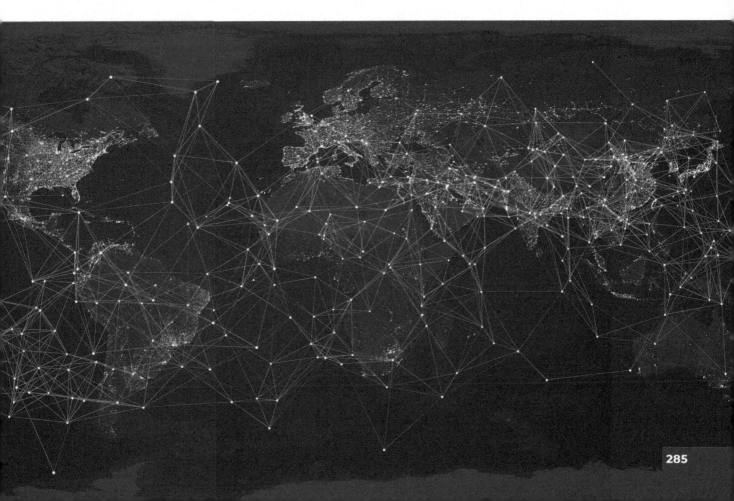

4.2 Secure network components

4.2.1 Network Architecture

CORE CONCEPTS

- Network architecture includes employing concepts such as defense in depth, partitioning, a well-protected network perimeter, network segmentation, and bastion hosts.

- Partitioning and network segmentation refer to the same concept where visibility of certain network traffic is limited through the use of networking devices, like switches and routers, and firewalls.

- Proxies are devices that act on behalf of someone else.

- NAT and PAT are examples of proxies that facilitate wide scale access to the Internet and serve as a layer of protection against eavesdropping of internal network structures.

Good network architecture can provide many benefits and help prevent and protect an organization if attacked by malicious outsiders or insiders. Key elements of network architecture include the concepts noted below.

> **Understand what is meant by the term "network architecture" and key elements of a good network architecture**

Defense in Depth

The concept of defense in depth refers to combining multiple layers of security controls to protect a network. Think of defense in depth as multiple layers of circles, with items like policies and procedures being the outermost layer, environmental considerations being the next, physical infrastructure next, followed by operating systems, and finally software configurations. Put another way, the outermost layer consists of people and processes, then architecture controls, then cabling and switching, and finally operating system controls and things like firewall configurations.

Partitioning

Partitioning is the practice of controlling the flow of traffic between segments. Refer to the earlier network topology example of a bus (depicted in Figure 4-2), where all devices are connected to the same wire—each device can see all the traffic traveling across the wire.

To protect this traffic, partitioning—also known as network segmentation—can be utilized. Some areas of a network might require a higher level of security than others. Partitioning can be used to prevent traffic from those areas from being seen across the entire network. Switches, routers, and firewalls can all be used to create partitions, or segments, and then rules implemented to control the flow of traffic between segments.

By far, the most important partition to create is the one that separates an organization network from externally connected networks. The best example of an external network is the internet. Organizations do want, and often need, to be connected to the internet, but they also want to block certain network traffic—in both directions. Incoming traffic should certainly be scrutinized and confirmed to be legitimate, but outgoing traffic should also be scrutinized for purposes of things like data loss prevention and identification of any malicious traffic destined to the outside world. So, firewalls and devices that sit between the main network and the internet can enforce rules that look at incoming and outgoing traffic.

Network Perimeter

The network perimeter is the last point any organization can control. Like physical security, where controls should comprise preventive, detective, and corrective capabilities, the same should hold true for the network. Controls at the perimeter should comprise preventive, detective, and corrective capabilities. Similar to a physical perimeter, where the ideal number of entrance and exit points is exactly zero, a network perimeter should be equally hard to breach. Ideally, only one entrance and exit point should exist. Otherwise, like a building with multiple entrances and exits, monitoring the flow of traffic can be extremely difficult. Limiting the ingress and egress point of a network to one creates a **choke point**—a point where devices and technologies that enforce rules can be placed to ensure all incoming and outgoing traffic is analyzed. Figure 4-27 depicts two choke points in a simple network, the first between the public network and the non-sensitive private network, and a second choke point that any traffic must pass through to access the sensitive private network.

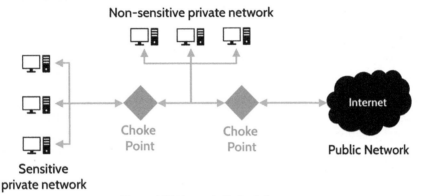

Figure 4-27: **Network Choke Points**

Network Segmentation

Referring to Figure 4-27, consider the public network to be the internet and the devices to the left to be an internal network (named sensitive private network). Access to the internet is important for so many reasons—to connect with clients, business partners, to market products via a website, and to exchange email, just to name a few. To make these connections and accomplish these goals, specific applications hosted on specific devices would need to be in place. For instance, if customers want to order products, an e-commerce application would need to exist. If anybody wants to send or receive an email, an email application would need to be running. With this in mind, does it make sense for these applications to be hosted on the internal network? From a security perspective, this would be very unwise, because people from the public network—from the internet—would then be on the inside, and everything would be at risk.

Bastion Host

This risk can be mitigated through the creation of a subnetwork, usually referred to as a **Demilitarized Zone (DMZ)**, where services and applications that require public access can be segregated. The DMZ is not part of the internal network nor is it part of the internet, it sits in between the two and it can be controlled by the organization. As alluded to above, any service or application that requires access from the outside—like web applications, email, DNS, and remote access—can be placed in the DMZ. Because the

> Understand what is meant by the term "bastion host" and where a bastion host might typically be found in a network architecture

organization controls the DMZ, it can also provide necessary protection for each application. In this context, devices and applications within a DMZ are often referred to as **bastion hosts** and bastion applications. The word *bastion* is French and loosely translates to "fortress," readied and strengthened for attack. Within the DMZ, hosts and applications that have been hardened and strengthened to protect against exploits and attacks are referred to as bastions. Between the DMZ and the Internet is a boundary router. The simplest form of a firewall is a router which sits between two networks and controls the flow of traffic by analyzing each packet header for source and destination IP addresses and ports. A router used in this role is often referred to as a **boundary router**, as shown in Figure 4-28.

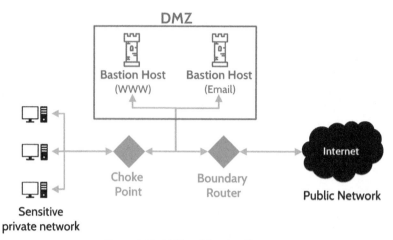

Figure 4-28: **DMZ and Bastion Hosts**

Proxy

One way to provide strong security across a network is through the utilization of what are known as proxies. A proxy is a device that acts on behalf of something else, commonly a user or application. In the context of a network, as shown in Figure 4-29, a proxy helps facilitate the connection between a client and a server, because it is better equipped to manage and direct outgoing and incoming traffic. *A proxy or proxy server is an intelligent application or hardware that acts as an intermediary and is placed between clients and a server.* As a result of the inherent intelligent nature of proxies, they're usually found at Layer 7—the Application layer—of the OSI model. In Figure 4-29, the client perceives the connection as being direct to the server, though the server perceives otherwise—the connection is from the server to the proxy. In reality, the actual connection in both cases is from the client to the proxy and from the server to the proxy. All decision requests are routed through the proxy, which has the intelligence and ability to make decisions, enforce rules, and otherwise manage requests.

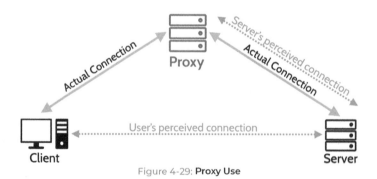

Figure 4-29: **Proxy Use**

This provides enhanced security because devices like web proxies are used to filter requests and discard any traffic that resolves to a known malicious destination. That can help keep the environment secure because if that proxy wasn't there to perform filtering, the user would have easily navigated to a malicious domain.

NAT and PAT

An example of NAT was already mentioned in section 4.1.6, where the home router scenario was discussed. As a refresher, NAT is the mechanism that allows us to translate private IP addresses to public ones and vice versa. PAT  is another mechanism that can be used, which helps us perform port translation, in the same notion as IP address translation is performed. At the same time, NAT and PAT provide a layer of security to organizations by masking internal networking schemes, which can hinder reconnaissance efforts of attackers. NAT and PAT are summarized in Table 4-30.

Network Address Translation (NAT)	Port Address Translation (PAT)
In its simplest form, NAT changes IP addresses to other IP addresses. For example, a private, internal, and non-routable IP address to a routable IP address.	PAT is an inherent part of NAT, and it helps keep track of individual internet requests using unique port assignments for each request.

Table 4-30: **NAT and PAT**

An example of NAT/PAT operation is depicted in Figure 4-30.

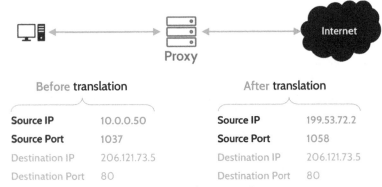

Before **translation**		After **translation**	
Source IP	10.0.0.50	**Source IP**	199.53.72.2
Source Port	1037	**Source Port**	1058
Destination IP	206.121.73.5	Destination IP	206.121.73.5
Destination Port	80	Destination Port	80

Figure 4-30: **NAT/PAT Operation**

It's easy to see that NAT is used to change the source IP address from 10.0.0.50 (a private, non-routable address) to 199.53.72.2, which is a publicly routable IP address that allows access to internet-based resources. At the same time, PAT is used to change the source port from 1037 to 1058, which is a unique port assigned only to the connection in this example. If other connection requests existed, the source IP after translation would likely be the same, but the source port would be different—it would be unique for each connection. Because of this uniqueness, when request results are returned, the proxy server can easily track and route those results to the device from which the original request was made.

4.2.2 Firewall Technologies

CORE CONCEPTS

- A firewall is a concept that enforces security rules between two or more networks.
- Firewall technologies include: simple packet filtering firewalls, stateful packet filtering firewalls, circuit-level proxy firewalls, and application-level firewalls.
- Simple and stateful packet filtering firewalls operate at Layer 3
- Circuit proxy firewalls operate at Layer 5
- Application proxy firewalls operate at Layer 7

What is a firewall?

A firewall is a *concept* that enforces security rules between two or more networks by performing traffic filtering. A firewall could be as simple as a router or as complex as a set of applications that work together to protect a network. In network security, a firewall either allows or blocks traffic, based upon predefined rules. Firewalls are typically found between an internal network and the Internet, but they're also frequently used internally to protect different network segments from each other and they are preventive controls.

Understand the different firewall technologies and pros/cons of each

Firewall Technologies

Table 4-31 summarizes the different firewall technologies in use today.

Packet Filtering	■ Examines packet headers to either block or pass packets ■ Uses access control lists (ACLs) that allow it to accept or deny access
Stateful Packet Filtering	■ State and context data are stored and updated dynamically ■ Provides information for tracking connectionless protocols; e.g., Remote Procedure Call (RPC) and UDP-based applications where source/destination ports and IP addresses are used to track state
Circuit-Level Proxy	■ Create a circuit between client and server without requiring knowledge about the service ■ Have no application-specific controls ■ An example is a SOCKS server
Application-Level Proxy	■ Able to inspect packet payload ■ A different proxy is needed for each service ■ Can be a performance bottleneck

Table 4-31: **Firewall Technologies**

Additionally, with the functionality described above, it makes sense that firewall technologies exist at different layers of the OSI model. Recall from earlier discussion that efficiency and intelligence vary at each layer of the OSI model. At the lower layers, intelligence is very low, but efficiency is very high; at the higher layers, intelligence is very high, but efficiency is much lower. Table 4-32 breaks down where firewalls live in the OSI model and key characteristics of each firewall technology.

> **Understand where different firewall technologies are found in the OSI model and implications of the same**

Simple Packet Filtering	Stateful Packet Filtering	Circuit Proxy	Application Proxy
OSI **Layer 3** Network	OSI **Layer 3 & 4**	OSI **Layer 5** Session	OSI **Layer 7** Application
Simplest	Complex	More Complex	Very Complex
Fastest	Fast	Higher latency	Highest latency
Filters based on source and destination IP address and port	Maintains state table and filters based on pattern matching	Filters sessions based on rules	Filters based on data (Payload)

Table 4-32: **Firewalls and OSI Layers**

Context-Based Access Control (CBAC)

CBAC is a feature of firewall software that intelligently filters TCP and UDP packets based on application layer protocol session information. It allows for deep traffic inspection and filtering to take place, that is, it's able to detect potential DDoS attacks or provide advanced statistics about the various connections and protocols used.

4.2.3 Firewall Architectures

With advancements in firewall technologies, firewall architectures have also evolved and become more sophisticated. Firewall architectures specifically focus on how firewall technologies can best be utilized and deployed to provide robust security for an organization.

Packet Filtering

A packet filtering firewall architecture, depicted in Figure 4-31, is the simplest one. The internal network is represented by the computer icons, and a simple router is placed between the internal network and the internet or another untrusted network. The router, which operates at Layer 3, can only make decisions based upon information that exists at Layer 3—the header portion of the datagram, which contains information like source IP, destination IP, service being requested, and so on. Thus, decision-making capabilities are very limited, but efficiency and speed of decision-making is very high.

Figure 4-31: **Packet Filtering Firewall**

Dual-Homed Host

A dual-homed host improves upon a packet filtering router by replacing it with a more intelligent computer or host that contains two network cards. The host can understand *all* layers of the OSI model and can therefore support all types of firewall technologies described above. As a result, the host can make simple to very complex decisions. This architecture is depicted in Figure 4-32.

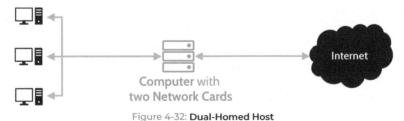

Figure 4-32: **Dual-Homed Host**

Screened Host

By combining the architectural elements of a packet filtering and dual-homed host firewall, a screened host firewall architecture results as shown in Figure 4-33. The router can handle the first level of decision-making related to incoming packets, and any packets that are allowed through can then be further examined by the bastion host, which can be any type of firewall technology. In addition to providing initial filtering services, the packet filtering router can act as a screening device for the bastion host. In other words, before an attacker could target the bastion host, they would first need to compromise the router. This is why this type of firewall architecture is known as a screened host firewall architecture.

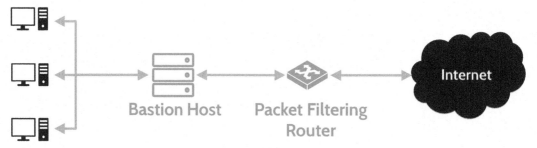

Figure 4-33: **Screened Host**

Screened Subnet

Figure 4-34 shows a screened subnet architecture, where two firewalls are used and between them a subnet, such as a DMZ, can be created. Traffic from the outside can be specifically directed to the DMZ and thereby protect the internal network from potential attacks. Screened subnet architectures are expensive as two firewalls are required; however, a potential advantage is that the two firewalls could be purchased from different vendors. Thus, if a vulnerability is discovered in one firewall, the same vulnerability is unlikely to exist in another vendor's firewall.

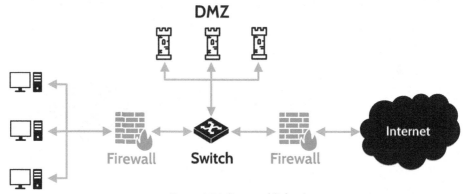

Figure 4-34: **Screened Subnet**

Three-Legged Firewall

Figure 4-35 depicts a three-legged firewall, by virtue of the three connection points, although any number of connection points could really exist. This is dependent on the needs and creativity of the organization. Any number of firewall technologies can be utilized in the context of this type of firewall, and the choices made in this regard should directly reflect the security needs of the organization and the assets being protected.

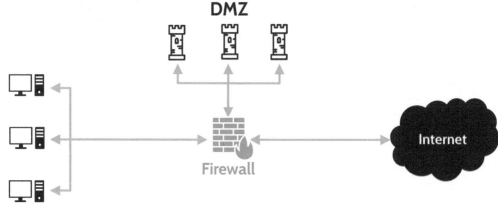

Figure 4-35: **Three-Legged Firewall**

4.2.4 IDS and IPS

> CORE **CONCEPTS**
>
> - Data inspection involves monitoring and examining data.
> - Intrusion Detection System (IDS) performs data inspection and detects, logs, reports, and sometimes triggers other devices to take corrective action.
> - Intrusion Prevention System (IPS) performs data inspection and additionally prevents or takes corrective action.
> - Two types of IDS/IPS systems: network-based and host-based.
> - Mirror/span/promiscuous port refers to setting a specific port on a network device (e.g., switch) to receive ALL traffic transiting the network device for monitoring purposes.
> - Two IDS/IPS detection methods: pattern and anomaly.
> - Ingress and egress monitoring refers to the specific flow of traffic; ingress = incoming traffic, and egress = outgoing traffic.
> - Whitelisting and blacklisting: whitelisting refers to specifically allowed IP addresses—all others are blocked; blacklisting refers to specifically blocked IP addresses—all other IP addresses are allowed by default.

Considering that firewalls are preventive controls, but a complete control encompasses prevention, detection, and correction, it follows that other systems should be in place and work with firewalls to provide the most protection to an organization. Specifically, these systems should provide detection and correction capabilities, and at the network level this involves data inspection.

Data Inspection

At a high level, data inspection involves monitoring and examining transmitted data and taking appropriate action if not allowed by security rules. Drilling down a bit, data inspection includes the activities summarized in Table 4-33.

Virus scanning	Files are scanned against known signatures for malware.
Stateful inspection	Dynamic state/context table is maintained to track and analyze communications between systems.
Content inspection	Content of mobile code is scanned and inspected for compliance with specific security rules.

Table 4-33: **Data Inspection Activities**

IDS and IPS

> **Understand the similarities and differences between IDS/IPS**

Drilling even further, data inspection can be accomplished using devices created specifically to examine the header and data (or payload) portions of a packet.

An **Intrusion Detection System (IDS)** is just as the name suggests—a detection system. An IDS examines traffic at the network level or the host level, specifically looking for malicious activity, policy violations, or other signs of suspicious activity and can alert and/or log those events. An IDS does not take direct action against malicious activity; however, the activity could trigger the corrective steps that need to happen, for example, by being tied back to a firewall, the firewall could take corrective action like filtering packets or blocking IP addresses.

An **Intrusion Prevention System (IPS)**, on the other hand, can prevent, detect, and take corrective action when necessary. When an offending pattern is identified, the IPS can, for example, block the source IP address or terminate a connection.

IDS and IPS systems are summarized in Table 4-34.

Intrusion Detection System (IDS)	Intrusion Prevention System (IPS)
Monitors a network or host for malicious activity or policy violations and **reports events**.	Monitors a network or host for malicious activity or policy violations, **reports events**, and **attempts to block**.

Table 4-34: **IDS and IPS**

Network-Based versus Host-Based

There are two types of IDS and IPS systems: network-based and host-based.

Network-based IDS/IPS require strategically placed sensors across a network and monitor network traffic to ensure that rules are applied. Host-based IDS/IPS run as agents on specific devices, like servers and other mission-critical systems, and do the same thing. From the perspective of which type of device provides the best protection, a combination of both types offers the best means of protection, detection, and correction for a network and associated critical systems. Network-based versus host-based IDS/IPS systems are summarized in Table 4-35.

> **Understand the pros and cons of network-based vs. host-based IDS/IPS**

Network-Based IDS/IPS	Host-Based IDS/IPS
Monitors network traffic transiting a **network segment**.	Installed on a host (server) and **monitors only that host**.

Table 4-35: **Network-Based vs. Host-Based IDS/IPS**

IDS/IPS Network Architecture

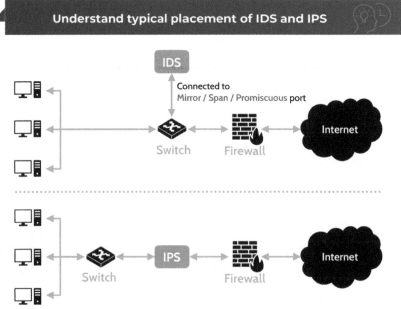

Figure 4-36: **IDS/IPS Architecture**

The sole purpose of an IDS is to detect, and to gain the benefits of a complete control, the IDS would need to be coupled with something else that could provide the additional capabilities of prevention and correction. As shown in the top half of Figure 4-36, an IDS is connected to a network via a mirror or span port (also known as promiscuous port). This allows the IDS to get a copy of all network traffic. If potentially malicious traffic is identified, the IDS can communicate with the firewall, which can then take preventive and corrective actions.

In the lower half of Figure 4-36 the IPS is placed in line with the network traffic, because it has the capability to detect, prevent, and correct. As traffic comes into the network, it passes through the IPS. If a rule is triggered for malicious activity, the IPS can act and prevent that from traversing the rest of the network.

IDS & IPS devices can potentially be placed in numerous locations across a network depending on where detection and correction capabilities are desired. Typically, an IDS/IPS device needs to be placed in each network segment to be monitored. The pink boxes in Figure 4-37 very roughly depict some of the potential IDS/IPS locations in a basic network architecture. The exact placement and selection of IDS or IPS devices is a complicated topic beyond the scope of the CISSP exam.

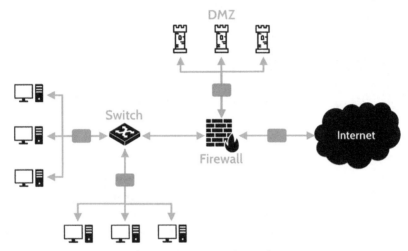

Figure 4-37: **The Need for IDS/IPS**

Mirror/Span/Promiscuous Port

When a port on a network device (e.g., switch) is described as **mirror**, **span**, or **promiscuous** it's meant that traffic passing through that device is copied to that port and any device connected to it, like an IDS, can obtain a copy of it for inspection. When you install Wireshark (one of the most common packet analyzers in the industry), at some point of the installation process it warns you that the network card will now be set in promiscuous mode so that the machine can capture surrounding network traffic.

> **Understand what is meant by any term that uses the words *mirror*, *span*, or *promiscuous* with the word *port***

Setting a device port to this mode allows broadcasts from any device on the network to be monitored, which can then allow the IDS/IPS to work most effectively.

IDS/IPS Detection Methods

Two types of analysis engines are used with IDS/IPS: pattern-based and anomaly-based, both depicted in Table 4-36.

> **Understand the two types of IDS/IPS analysis engines and how each works**

Pattern-based engines focus on known types of attacks and use this information to build a database of patterns for detection purposes. Anomaly-based engines look for unusual, abnormal, and out-of-the-ordinary patterns, which implies they understand what is normal and predictable. Anomaly-based engines therefore go through a learning process that involves monitoring user activity and understanding what is considered normal, and anything that is out of the ordinary will be triggered as an anomaly.

Pattern	Signature analysis	Detection method where IDS/IPS looks for specific patterns (signatures), such as byte sequences in network traffic, or known malicious instruction sequences. Like antivirus/antimalware applications, in order for a pattern-based analysis engine to be most effective, it's important that signatures be kept up to date.
Anomaly	Stateful matching	Looks for anomalies in the context of a stream of traffic (state) or overall behavior rather than the individual packets
	Statistical anomaly	Compares traffic to typical, known, or predicted traffic profiles to look for statistically significant anomalies from the norm
	Protocol anomaly	Identifies anomalies based on network protocols, i.e., abnormal sequence numbers, fragment offsets, etc.
	Traffic anomaly	Identifies anomalies in expected pattern and behavior of network traffic transmitted within a session

Table 4-36: **IDS/IPS Detection Technologies**

Ingress and Egress Monitoring

The terms *ingress* and *egress* refer to the direction of flow or, in this case, network traffic, as shown in Figure 4-38. Ingress is the act of going in or entering; egress is the act of going out or exiting. It follows that **ingress monitoring** is monitoring all traffic entering a network; **egress monitoring** is monitoring all traffic exiting a network. The best protection involves both types of monitoring. Ingress monitoring can help prevent malicious traffic from entering a network; egress monitoring can help prevent data loss, denial-of-service, and other types of malicious activity from originating from the corporate environment. It's important that IDS/IPS monitor traffic in both directions.

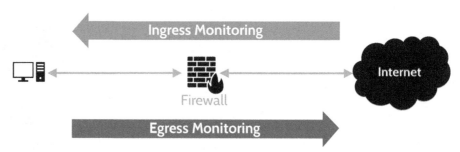

Figure 4-38: **Ingress and Egress Monitoring**

Allow List and Deny List (Whitelisting and Blacklisting)

A technique that IDS/IPS devices can use to detect and potentially block suspicious traffic is allow lists and deny lists.

> **Understand the difference between the terms "allow list (white list)" and "deny list (black list)"**

Allow and deny lists are lists of IP addresses and specifically determine what action may or may not be performed with respect to the IP addresses in a given list. With an allow list, network traffic to listed IP addresses is allowed. Any other IP address is blocked by default. Deny lists are the exact opposite; any traffic to listed IP addresses is specifically blocked. Any other IP address is allowed by default.

Note, that "allow lists" and "deny lists" are much better terminology, and these terms are becoming more pervasively used in the industry. However, you may still see references to whitelists and blacklists, including on the exam, which is why we have noted this terminology.

Allow lists and deny lists are summarized in Table 4-37.

Allow List (Whitelist)	Deny List (Blacklist)
The following IPs may be visited. **All other addresses are NOT permissible.**	The following IPs may NOT be visited. **Any other address is permissible.**

Table 4-37: **Allow List and Deny List**

4.2.5 Sandbox

CORE **CONCEPTS**

- A sandbox is a safe area where untrusted code can be isolated and run.
- Four possible alert scenarios: true/false-positive, true/false-negative.
- False-negative is a worst-case scenario.

When an IDS/IPS identifies potentially malicious activity, something called a sandbox can be activated. A sandbox is a safe area, where unknown or untrusted code can be isolated and run and tested and determined to be malicious or not. Being able to run **potentially malicious software** in a sandbox environment is one of the corrective actions that an IDS/IPS can take. In addition, sandboxes are used quite often by malware analysts who run malicious code in them and try to identify indicators of compromise and gain an in-depth understanding of how malware operates.

Alert Statuses

Table 4-38 illustrates the possible conditions of alerts that may be received by security tools. These outcomes are quite important and can denote if tools are working optimally or if tuning is required to maximize efficacy.

Understand false-positives and false-negatives and the worst possible outcome

1. **True Positive:** An attack is taking place and the security tool raises an alert to denote that fact. This indicates appropriate operation is in effect.

2. **True Negative**: No attack is present, and no alert is generated by a security tool. This indicates appropriate operation is in effect.

3. **False Positive:** An alert is generated by the security tool; however, there's no actual attack taking place (e.g., a suspicious login alert was generated for a user logging in from Colombia who had never logged in before from that location, but that person is legitimately there for work for the next three months). This is indicative of tuning required to eliminate unnecessary alerts from flooding the security team.

4. **False Negative:** An attack is ongoing, but the security tool failed to raise an alert. This is the worst scenario, since the security team isn't aware of malicious activity actually taking place in the environment. New rules being applied, policy redesigns, and new attack signatures are usually some of the things analysts use to resolve this issue.

	True	False
Positive	**True-Positive** Alarm is generated and attack is present	**False-Positive** Alarm is generated but **no attack** is taking place
Negative	**True-Negative** No alarm is generated and no attack is taking place	**False-Negative** No alarm is generated but an attack is actually taking place

Table 4-38: **Possible Alert Statuses**

4.2.6 Honeypots and Honeynets

CORE CONCEPTS

- Honeypots and honeynets are technical detective controls.

- Honeypots are individual computers and devices set up to appear as legitimate network resources.

- Honeynets are two or more networked honeypots.

- Honeypots and honeynets contain vulnerabilities that entice intruders into exploring further.

- Enticement is legal and pertains to situations where an intruder has already broken into a network.

- Entrapment is illegal and pertains to situations where somebody is persuaded to break into a network.

Honeypots are individual computers (usually running a server OS posing as interesting targets for an attacker), but they contain no real data or value to the organization employing them. **Honeynets** are two or more honeypots networked together, and a sophisticated honeynet will also employ the use of routers, switches, or gateways. Honeypots and honeynets invariably always contain vulnerabilities—usually unpatched systems, applications, open ports or running services—that aim to entice potential attackers into exploring further. This exploration can then be detected. Honeypots and honeynets are usually located within the DMZ, or within a separate subnet and are usually built using virtualized systems.

> What type of control do honeypots/honeynets represent?

Purpose of honeypots and honeynets

Honeypots and honeynets, depicted in Figure 4-39, can serve a number of purposes, including:

- Detecting sophisticated cyberattacks, such as **Advanced Persistent Threats (APTs)**, where an attacker gains access to a network / system and stays there undetected for a long period of time. APTs are difficult to detect with traditional detective controls like an IDS system, as the attacker is very intentionally minimizing any activities that could be detected. For example, the attacker will use passive monitoring and data gathering techniques vs. actively scanning the network or systems.

- Helping trace how an attacker has traversed or moved through a network

- Distracting attackers away from valuable systems or resources

- Gathering valuable information that may help a security team better define their organization's security plan

- Conducting research by companies that serve the cybersecurity community

However, honeypots, and honeynets come with risks, including:

- Attackers might be able to leverage access to the honeypot or honeynet and gain access to real hosts or network resources, depending on the underlying architecture.

- If employed incorrectly, legal action against the company using the honeypot or honeynet could be the result, which is known as entrapment.

In either case, the ultimate responsibility for damages or monetary liability would rest upon the shoulders of senior management.

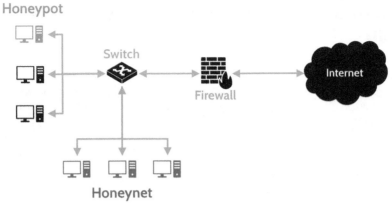

Figure 4-39: **Honeypot and Honeynet**

Enticement and Entrapment

As noted above, when working with honeypots and honeynets, an organization must be careful to avoid entrapment of a potential attacker, which is illegal. Table 4-39 provides the definitions of enticement and entrapment, including their core difference.

> **Difference between enticement and entrapment**

Enticement	Entrapment
Legal activity of persuading someone to commit a crime that they were already planning to commit.	**Illegal activity** of persuading someone to commit a crime that they would not otherwise have committed

Table 4-39: **Enticement and Entrapment**

4.2.7 Endpoint Security

CORE CONCEPTS

- Endpoint security focuses on protection of devices found on corporate networks and seeks to minimize the attack surface and thereby prevent or minimize attacks.

- Network access control (NAC) solutions seek to unify endpoint security technology, user authentication, and overall network security.

Endpoint security refers to the specific protection of client devices (endpoints) commonly found in corporate networks. Laptops, tablets, mobile devices, printers, IoT devices, and wireless devices are common examples of endpoints that are also potential attack points and paths to corporate networks. Endpoint security strives to minimize the attack surface and narrow the path to the corporate network as much as possible.

> **Primary focus of endpoint security and where commonly found**

In the past, endpoint security was mainly accomplished through antivirus software. Today, endpoint security has evolved and become much more robust. In addition to antivirus software, many organizations deploy comprehensive device management policies and enforcement applications, endpoint data leak prevention (DLP), **Network Access Control (NAC)** solutions to restrict access (e.g., if an endpoint does not pass a health check) and platforms focused on endpoint threat detection, response, and monitoring.

> **How network access control (NAC) solutions complement endpoint security**

4.3 Implement secure communication channels according to design

4.3.1 Tunneling and VPNs

CORE **CONCEPTS**

- Remote access is connecting to resources over an insecure network.
- Tunneling is the process of taking a datagram and placing it inside the data portion of another datagram.
- Split tunneling allows disparate remote resources to be used at the same time.
- Generic Routing Encapsulation (GRE) is a tunneling protocol that can be used to encapsulate a variety of protocols.
- VPNs are encrypted tunnels.
- PPTP and L2TP are Layer 2 tunneling protocols; L2TP is typically used in conjunction with Internet Protocol Security (IPsec).
- SSL/TLS, SOCKS, and SSH are tunneling protocols that include encryption capabilities.

Remote Access

Implementing secure communication channels is an important component of network security. In other words, putting protections in place to support network connections—especially remote access—is critical. Remote access is connecting to corporate resources over an insecure network (internet). Due to this fact, a method to protect traffic across that untrustworthy network must be utilized, and the best method is usually a VPN solution.

Tunneling

Before we can understand VPN solutions in depth, the concept of tunneling (depicted in Figure 4-40) must first be examined, because tunneling is the precursor to establishing a VPN. ***VPN is tunneling plus encryption; without encryption, it can only be called a tunnel.*** Tunneling is simply the process of taking a datagram and placing it inside the data portion of another datagram. If the header and data portion of one datagram are placed into the data portion of another datagram, a tunnel is created. Some people also refer to this as encapsulation. The header and data from the one datagram become the data portion of the other datagram.

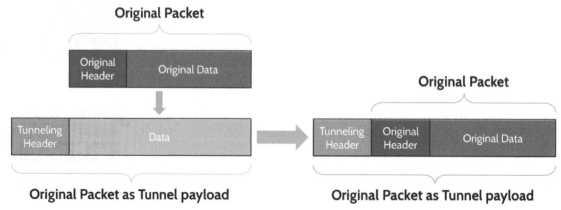

Figure 4-40: **Tunneling Operation**

This **encapsulation** process does not hide anything. It's simply placing the original datagram inside the data portion of another one. If the information needs to be hidden, to be protected, encryption of the data portion of the new datagram must take place. This results in tunneling plus encryption.

Why is tunneling used? The premise behind tunneling is that the encapsulated datagram is being forced along the path specified in the header of the host datagram. So, whatever path might be specified in the header of the encapsulated datagram, the header of the host datagram will dictate the actual path both datagrams follow. However, the encapsulated datagram can still be read because no encryption is used.

Tunneling protocols exist at several different layers of the OSI Model. This starts at Layer 2 and can go all the way up to Layer 7. At each layer, different functionality is available, and it's important to remember that the higher the layer, the bigger the trade-off between functionality and performance. At lower layers, performance is very efficient, but functionality is more limited. At higher layers, functionality is considerably enhanced, but performance is slower. Decisions about which tunneling protocol to use should take these factors into account.

Generic Routing Encapsulation (GRE)

In a sense, Generic Routing Encapsulation (GRE), depicted in Figure 4-41, is a tunneling protocol that can encapsulate a variety of protocols and route them over IP networks. GRE can transport traditional IPv4 traffic as well as multicast and IPv6 traffic, and it provides a means by which traffic can be exchanged between two networks using a network like the internet. GRE works by encapsulating the original packet—the payload that needs to be delivered—inside an outer packet. Once the receiving endpoint is reached, the GRE packet is removed and the original packet—the payload—is forwarded to the ultimate destination. Unlike IPsec, which can use ESP to provide encryption and secure a payload, GRE is not considered a secure protocol, because it provides no encryption, just encapsulation.

> **Pros and cons of GRE and how it works**

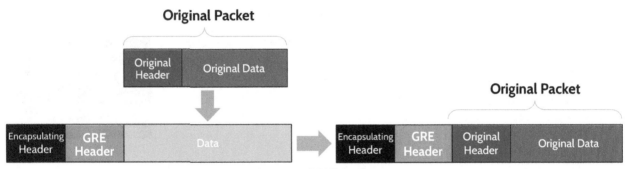

Figure 4-41: **GRE Tunneling**

Split Tunneling

Split tunneling allows a user to access disparate resources—the internet and a LAN, for example—at the same time, without all the traffic passing through the VPN. In the example shown in Figure 4-42, in the upper half of the diagram, access to a corporate LAN can be achieved through use of a VPN (encrypted tunnel) established through a hotel network, while noncorporate resource access, illustrated in the lower half of the diagram, is achieved through a direct connection from the user's computer to the hotel network. It's important to note, however, that running internet traffic directly from the user's computer through the hotel network can bypass organizational security controls, which can create significant risk for the organization.

> **Understand what a split tunnel is and what its inherent weaknesses are**

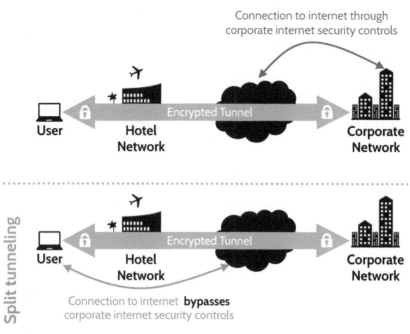

Figure 4-42: **Split Tunneling Operation**

At the same time, split tunneling helps reduce network bandwidth and resource consumption. For example, if the user is browsing to a publicly accessible resource, like Google drive, then there's no point in having that traffic traverse the corporate VPN tunnel and then be redirected to Google's servers. It could just be directed there to begin with, thus optimizing resource consumption. On the other hand, if a company file server is being accessed, the VPN tunnel can be used.

Virtual Private Network (VPN)

VPNs are one of the most reliable and cost-effective ways to securely connect two networks together.

> **Know the most reliable and cost-effective way to securely connect two networks**

To create a VPN, tunneling plus encryption is needed. A number of solutions exist that utilize SSL/TLS or IPsec VPN technologies. Layer 2 and Layer 3 VPN solutions typically provide both the functionality and efficiency required to host a VPN.

Tunneling and VPN Protocols

PPTP, L2F, and L2TP are Layer 2 tunneling protocols. They're efficient but don't provide much in the way of functionality and security. Moving up layers allows these needs to be met, and much more functionality can be gained. For example, SSH—at Layer 7—can be used to host command line utilities that would normally contain zero security. Telnet, FTP, and similar protocols don't contain security, but they become very secure when utilized in the context of an encrypted SSH tunnel. Remember, a VPN requires a tunnel and encryption.

> **Know the most common Layer 2 protocols and understand the differences between PPTP and L2TP**

Table 4-40 illustrates commonly used tunneling protocols that include encryption capabilities, with one exception: L2TP. The protocols that contain encryption capabilities can be used to create VPNs. In the case of L2TP, it is often deployed in conjunction with IPsec, which adds the needed encryption element to create a VPN.

	Protocol	Tunneling	Encryption	OSI Layer
SSH	Secure Shell	✓	✓	7 – Application
SOCKS	Socket Secure	✓	✓	5 – Session
SSL/TLS	Secure Sockets Layer/Transport Layer Security	✓	✓	4 – Transport
IPsec	Internet Protocol Security	✓	✓	3 – Network
L2TP	Layer 2 Tunneling Protocol	✓		
L2F	Layer 2 Forwarding Protocol	✓	✓	2 – Data Link
PPTP	Point-to-Point Tunneling Protocol	✓	✓	
GRE	Generic Routing Encapsulation	✓		Encapsulation at multiple layers

Table 4-40: **Common Tunneling Protocols**

4.3.2 IPsec

CORE **CONCEPTS**

- IPsec is preferred for establishing a VPN and is embedded in IPv6 as a default feature.

- IPsec offers authentication via Authentication Header (AH) and encryption via Encapsulating Security Payload (ESP).

- IPsec works in one of two modes: transport or tunnel.

- Internet Key Exchange (IKE) is used to generate the session key shared at each end of the VPN.

- Security Associations (SA) are used to establish components in each direction for an IPsec-based VPN. One SA is needed for each component in each direction.

Of the tunneling and VPN protocols listed in Table 4-40, IPsec is the preferred method for establishing a VPN. One thing to remember about IPsec is that it is natively supported in IPv6 and is therefore becoming a standard component of networking. IPsec offers two advantages over other protocols from a security perspective. It adds authentication of devices as well as encryption. Authentication is added through AH and encryption through ESP. AH provides integrity, data-origin authentication, and replay protection. ESP provides all the functions AH does, in addition to ensuring confidentiality, as it provides payload encryption.

Think of each as subprotocols or elements of IPsec.

Additionally, IPsec can be utilized in two different modes: transport mode and tunnel mode. Transport mode uses the header of the original datagram, whereas in tunnel mode the header of the new datagram encapsulates and encrypts the AH or ESP header and original IP header in the data, or payload, portion of the new datagram. Recall from earlier that the original datagram was encapsulated in the data portion of a new datagram. Now, a choice exists: the header and payload of a datagram can be encrypted inside the new data portion. One encrypts only the payload; the other encrypts the header and the payload. Tables 4-41 and 4-42 and Figure 4-43 summarize the IPsec modes.

> **Understand elements and modes of IPsec and services provided by each mode**

IPsec Modes

Authentication Header (AH)	Encapsulating Security Payload (ESP)
Provides integrity, data-origin authentication and replay protection	Provides integrity, data-origin authentication, replay protection, and **confidentiality** through **encryption of payload**

Table 4-41: **Authentication Header (AH) and Encapsulating Security Payload (ESP)**

Transport Mode	Tunnel Mode
Use header of original packet, followed by the AH or ESP header, then the payload	New header encapsulates the AH or ESP header and the original IP header and payload

Table 4-42: **IPsec Modes**

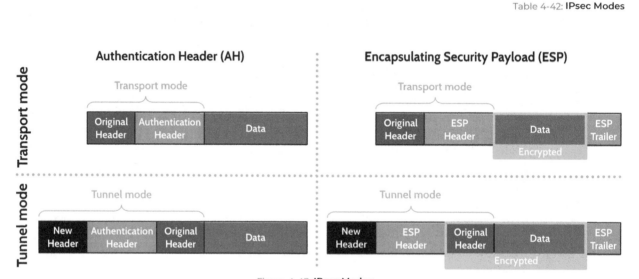

Figure 4-43: **IPsec Modes**

Internet Key Exchange (IKE)

To create a VPN, two things are required: tunneling plus encryption. The only type of encryption that can be used for a VPN is symmetric, meaning the same key is utilized at each end of the VPN connection. This implies that all VPN solutions must include a key management protocol that allows the same secret to be generated at each end. In the context of IPsec, the key management protocol used is known as Internet Key Exchange, or IKE. IKE is essentially a version of Diffie–Hellman and is used by IPsec to generate the same session key at each end of a VPN.

> **What protocol is used to exchange keys with an IPsec VPN?**

Security Association (SA)

IPsec tunnels are established through a Security Association (SA). *SA is a* **one-way** *establishment of attributes at the start of communication between two entities.* Imagine two people who want to connect and communicate. To do so, security associations would need to be established. Because an SA is one-way form of communication (like walkie-talkies), where only one person can communicate at a time, in order for two people to communicate, an SA would need to be established in each direction. If IPsec AH and ESP components are needed, SAs are needed in each direction for each component. So, if both AH and ESP are needed, a total of four SAs is required—two SAs in each direction.

Attributes include:

- Authentication algorithm
- Encryption algorithm
- Encryption keys
- Mode (transport or tunnel)
- Sequence number
- Expiry of the SA

4.3.3 SSL/TLS

CORE CONCEPTS

- **Secure Sockets Layer/Transport Layer Security (SSL/TLS) provide secure client to server connections; the two names refer to the same thing, but TLS is now the proper standard and most current version, as SSL is obsolete.**

- **DROWN attack is a major threat to SSLv2.**

- **SSL/TLS connection steps: client hello, server hello, creation and sharing of session key, establishment of secure session.**

- **Asymmetric cryptography is used to encrypt the symmetric session key created by the client.**

- **Unencrypted SSL sessions can exist, where a browser and server authenticate to one another, but the communications channel is not encrypted.**

Over the years, Secure Sockets Layer (SSL) has been instrumental as a means of securing communications channels. Of course, like most technologies, it's been revised over the years, with the latest revision being SSL 3.0. In 1999, SSL was revised yet again, but this time, to remove confusion about where this protocol operates in the OSI model, it was renamed to Transport Layer Security (TLS), and the most recent revision of TLS was released in 2018 as TLS 1.3.

SSL/TLS is used extensively; in fact, most websites that require secure connections between a browser and a web server utilize SSL/TLS. And even though TLS is the proper name, many people still refer to it as SSL. Naming conventions aside, the key is that the latest version is being used, as use of SSLv2—even when used for purposes of backward compatibility—could result in what is known as the **DROWN attack** exploiting a specific vulnerability in SSLv2. If successful, a DROWN attack could result in a session being compromised, and sensitive information—passwords, credit card numbers, proprietary and other valuable data—could be read or stolen. Because disabling backward compatibility can be somewhat complicated, the best defense against DROWN is for server owners to ensure their private keys are not utilized with web, email, and other servers that allow SSLv2 connections.

SSL/TLS provides secure client to server connections; for instance, when managing your bank account via the bank's online portal, or when looking at your insurance or medical information from providers of those services. A secure connection can be established between your browser and a secure server anywhere in the world, and the secure connection protects transmission of sensitive information and transactions from eavesdropping. A secure connection can be established in four relatively simple steps, as outlined in Figure 4-44.

Understand the foundational reason for using SSL/TLS

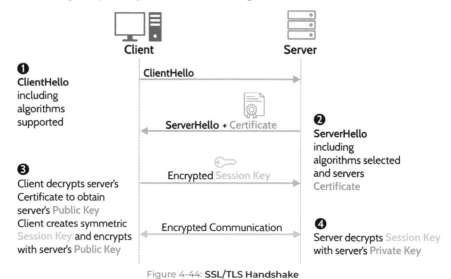

Figure 4-44: **SSL/TLS Handshake**

Figure 4-44 shows an example of an SSL/TLS handshake.

You want to purchase something online from Amazon.

Initially, you'd visit Amazon's website by typing www.amazon.com in your browser's address bar. This establishes the initial connection, and at the same time Amazon's server and your browser understand that a secure connection is required, which activates the SSL/TLS handshake process.

Understand the SSL/TLS handshake process and how asymmetric and symmetric cryptography both play a role in establishing a secure session

1. The client, your browser, will first send a client hello message to the server, which allows the server to determine whether it understands the client, the browser. If all is well, the server will essentially respond with a message saying it understands the browser. Otherwise, if the browser is outdated or doesn't have a compatible version of SSL/TLS installed, the server will respond with some type of error warning.

2. After the initial "hello," the second step requires the server to do something similar and send a server hello message to the client. However, with the hello message, the server will also send its certificate, which contains Amazon's public key.

3. With Amazon's public key, the client's browser understands what certificate authority issued Amazon's certificate. For this example, let's assume that VeriSign issued the certificate. The browser knows this because one of the fields on the certificate is the issuer ID, which the browser uses to look up the issuer, in this case, VeriSign. With this information and built-in functionality, the browser fetches VeriSign's public key and decrypts the certificate. If the certificate decrypts properly, the public key on Amazon's certificate can be trusted and, in fact, Amazon's server has been authenticated. You know your browser is connected to Amazon's server and not a server pretending to be Amazon. Otherwise, to spoof Amazon, VeriSign's certificate would've first needed to be spoofed, which would require access to VeriSign's private key. And only VeriSign has access to its private key.

4. With the first three steps complete, step four involves the creation of a symmetric key (session key) that will be utilized from this point forward for the session. Again, utilizing functionality built into the browser, a session key is created and encrypted using Amazon's public key and then sent back to Amazon, where Amazon's private key will be used for decryption. At this point, the client's browser and Amazon will each hold the same session key, which will be used for further communication. Now safe transmission of authentication information, credit card numbers, and other sensitive information can take place, because only the client and Amazon have access to this specific session.

From the example above, let's highlight some key takeaways.

- There's always a need for the client to authenticate the server. In this case, it's much more important for the client to ensure it has authenticated to Amazon. Or when banking, it's vital to know that the client has authenticated to the actual bank. There's really no need for Amazon or the bank to authenticate the client—whether the client is at home or somewhere around the world, the server really doesn't care. However, if this functionality was needed, it's built into SSL/TLS and is known as mutual authentication. In this case, the server can also authenticate the client, which would require the client to have a certificate too.

- Only the client can create the session key, which is then sent back to the server encrypted with the server's public key.

The SSL/TLS handshake process happens all the time and very quickly. Once complete, a small lock in the browser address bar will appear, and the URL will begin with HTTPS, which signifies a secure HTTP session is now enforced.

TLS VPN versus IPsec VPN

> **Understand high level differences between TLS VPN and IPsec VPN, including the layers where they operate and which one provides encryption by default**

Both TLS and IPsec VPNs provide secure communication channels, but they do so a bit differently from one another. A comparison is provided in Table 4-43.

TLS VPN	IPsec VPN
- Operates at the Transport layer and above	- Operates at the network layer
- Can be used to encrypt traffic sent between any **processes** identified by port numbers	- Can be used to encrypt traffic between any **system** that can be identified by an IP address
- Encrypts connections by default	- The use of IKE provides a layer of data authentication via an external protocol
- Easier to establish and manage and has more granular configuration options available	- Does not encrypt connections by default
- A successful attack could lead to compromise of specific systems and applications	- Can be more complicated to establish, configure, and manage
	- A successful attack could lead to compromise of an entire network

Table 4-43: **TLS vs. IPsec VPN**

Choosing one type of VPN over another is very dependent upon the requirements of the organization and the specific goals and objectives that relate to security of information being communicated internally and externally. Factors like performance, security, data authentication, and others should be considered in this vein. The approach that might work for one organization could be completely wrong for another organization.

4.3.4 Remote Authentication

> CORE **CONCEPTS**
>
>
>
> ▪ Remote authentication protocols include: RADIUS, TACACS+, Diameter.
>
> ▪ RADIUS was originally developed to support dial-in networking and provides authentication, authorization, and accounting.
>
> ▪ TACACS+ uses TCP and encrypts all packets.
>
> ▪ Diameter is the successor to RADIUS and includes much-improved security, including EAP.

One important consideration related to remote access is that a simple VPN connection does not prove who is sitting behind the VPN. If a company uses SSL/TLS for VPN capabilities, the VPN only protects the traffic between the device on one end and the server or device on the other end. Most organizations also want to know who is using the computer or browser and will therefore use some type of authentication—usually two-factor—for this purpose. Authentication protocols like RADIUS, TACACS, TACACS+, and Diameter, summarized in Table 4-44, are typically the most used for this purpose.

Understand the importance and use of remote authentication protocols and their similarities and differences

Remote Authentication Protocols

RADIUS	Remote Authentication Dial-In User Service is an application-layer protocol that allows a user to connect to and access network resources. RADIUS was developed to support dial-in networking and provides authentication, authorization, and accounting (AAA).
TACACS+	Terminal Access Controller Access Control System Plus was developed by CISCO as an extension of TACACS and an improvement over RADIUS. Unlike RADIUS (which uses UDP) TACACS+ uses TCP and encrypts all the transmitted packets, while RADIUS only poorly obfuscates user passwords.
Diameter	Diameter is the successor to and an enhanced version of RADIUS. Diameter adds improved security features, such as EAP, which provides a much more secure and robust authentication of users.

Table 4-44: **RADIUS, TACACS+, and Diameter**

MINDMAP REVIEW **VIDEOS**

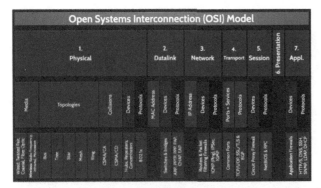

OSI Model
dcgo.ca/CISSPmm4-1

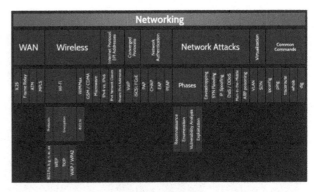

Networking
dcgo.ca/CISSPmm4-2

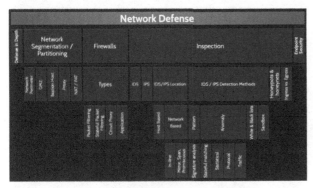

Network Defense
dcgo.ca/CISSPmm4-3

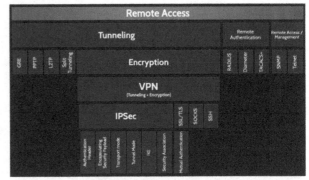

Remote Access
dcgo.ca/CISSPmm4-4

CISSP PRACTICE QUESTION APP

Download the Destination CISSP Practice Question app for Domain 4 practice questions

dcgo.ca/PracQues

DOMAIN 5

Identity
& Access
Management

5.1 Control physical and logical access to assets

5.1.1 Access Control

CORE CONCEPTS

- Access control is the concept that refers to the collection of mechanisms that work together to protect organizational assets while simultaneously allowing controlled access to authorized subjects.

- Fundamental access control principles include: need to know, least privilege, separation of duties.

- Access control is applicable at all levels of an organization and covers all types of assets.

What is access control?

*Access control is the collection of mechanisms that work together to protect the **assets** of an organization and, at the same time, **allow controlled access to authorized subjects.***

Access control enables management to:

- Specify which **users** can access the system

- Specify what **resources** they can access

- Specify what **operations** they can perform

- Provide individual **accountability**—know who is doing what

Access Control Principles

The fundamental access control principles denoted in Table 5-1 are important to understand because they are applied everywhere within access control. Individually and together, they help protect organizational assets by limiting what individuals can do with an asset in order to perform their job, and nothing more.

Need to Know	Least Privilege	Separation of Duties
Defending sensitive assets by restricting access to only required personnel who require access	Defending sensitive assets by granting only the minimum permissions required by the user or system	Defending sensitive assets by requiring more than one person to complete a task, to ***prevent errors and fraud***

Table 5-1: **Access Control Principles**

Need to know: The concept of *need to know* can be applied in many ways. Imagine a law enforcement agent being undercover and investigating a case. Their true identity doesn't need to be known to anyone apart from their direct supervisor and a handful of agents involved in the case. In short, only who needs to know will know to maintain operational security.

> **Understand the fundamental access control principles and how they might be applied**

Least privilege: A classic example of overprivileged accounts exists in a variety of companies today where several people (if not the whole company) just have local administrator permissions on their machines. This goes against least privilege. Most people in a company don't need to have local administrator permissions, and hence to apply least privilege, a group policy should state that everyone has standard accounts configured, apart from a handful of administrators.

Separation of duties and responsibilities: Separation of duties and responsibilities refers to the concept that one person should not be responsible for all aspects of a process. Separation of duties is often employed in areas of an organization where money is received or disbursed. For example, when a new vendor is added to an accounts payable system, one person might enter the vendor information and another person might confirm the validity or accuracy of the information. These two steps can help prevent fake vendors from being created in a system. In addition, when the vendor is paid, one person might enter the invoice and payment information, another person might generate the check, and yet another actually confirms the check amount against the invoice and then signs it. Another example relates to developers, they should not be the same people who push applications to production. There needs to be a separation of duties in place, so proper testing, validation, and approval can be conducted to prevent errors. *Separation of duties helps prevent fraud.*

Access Control Applicability

Access control includes *all aspects and levels* of an organization and covers all types of *assets* including:

- Facilities
- Systems/Devices
- Information
- Personnel
- Applications

Access Control System

- The focus of access control is controlling a subject's access to an object through some form of mediation.
- Mediation is based upon a set of rules.
- All activity is logged and monitored to provide accountability and gain assurance that things are working properly.

Fundamentally, the above point to the use of the RMC, or Reference Monitor Concept, where some type of rules-based decision-making tool is placed in between subjects and objects to mediate access, and all activity is logged and monitored for the sake of accountability and assurance. Any implementation of the RMC is known as a security kernel. Figure 5-1 depicts the RMC and its various components.

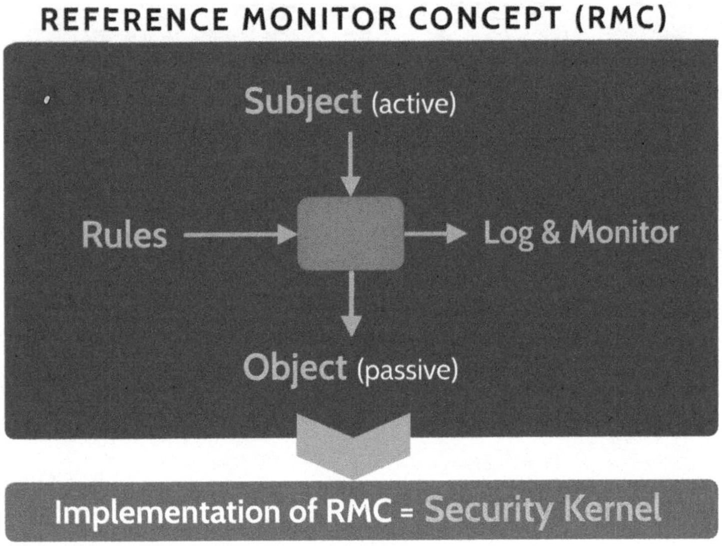

REFERENCE MONITOR CONCEPT (RMC)

Figure 5-1: **RMC Components**

Logical Access Modes

- Access control is more granular than simply allowing subjects to access objects.

- Access control rules allow the access control mechanism to be much more granular.

- Specific access rules allow precision with regards to what subjects can access what objects and exactly what those subjects can do with those objects.

- Access should be based on the use of concepts like *need to know* and *least privilege*.

Access rules and related subject rights will vary from system to system, but in general, the following logical access modes can be found in most systems:

- Create

- Update

- Read

- Read/Write

- Execute

- Delete

5.1.2 Administration Approaches

CORE **CONCEPTS**

- **Access control administration often takes one of two approaches: centralized or decentralized, and many organizations also utilize a hybrid approach.**

- **Each approach offers pros and cons.**

Access Control Administration Approaches

When administering access control, two primary approaches are often taken: centralized or decentralized, although more and more organizations are now also utilizing a hybrid approach that incorporates elements of centralized and decentralized approaches. All of these are depicted in Table 5-2.

Understand access control administration approaches and pros and cons of each approach

Centralized	Hybrid	Decentralized
- One central system controls access to remote systems - One username and password in the central system used to access all systems - Central administrative point represents a single point of failure and potential target of attack	- Approach taken by most organizations, and it means access control utilizes both approaches (centralized and decentralized) - This is often due to legacy systems in an organization that can't be integrated with newer, more modern, access control systems	- Control is granted to the people closer to the resource - Access requests are not processed by one centralized entity; separate usernames and passwords exist on each resource - Lack of standardization, overlapping rights and security holes may exist - Peer-to-peer relationship

Table 5-2: **Centralized, Decentralized, and Hybrid Access Control**

Centralized Administration

Some advantages of a centralized approach are much easier administration, lower overhead, cost reduction, and greater flexibility. However, a major disadvantage is that the central administrative point represents a single point of failure as well as target of attack.

Decentralized Administration

Likewise, an advantage of a decentralized approach is the ability to manage access control at much more granular levels, though a corresponding disadvantage is that this ability creates much more administrative overhead. Another advantage is that decentralized administration of access control minimizes the risks associated with a single point of failure, as found with centralized administration. If one system goes down or is compromised, other systems remain viable.

5.2 Manage identification and authentication of people, devices, and services

5.2.1 Access Control Services

CORE **CONCEPTS**

- Access control services consist of: identification, authentication, authorization, accountability.
- Identification refers to the assertion of a user's identity or a process to a system.
- Authentication refers to the verification of an identity through knowledge, ownership, or characteristic.
- Authorization refers to the level of access defined for the identified and authenticated user or process.
- Accountability refers to proper identification, authentication, authorization that is logged and monitored.
- Accountability is also known as the Principle of Access Control.

Access control and related services are fundamental elements of organizational security. Assets and users can best be protected and held accountable for their actions. In fact, this latter point—the notion of accountability—is the fundamental driver behind Access Control Services. As a security professional, it's imperative to understand the implications of nonexistent or weak and ineffective access control, especially as it relates to the Principle of Access Control.

The components of Access Control Services are depicted in Figure 5-2 and explained in detail in the following section.

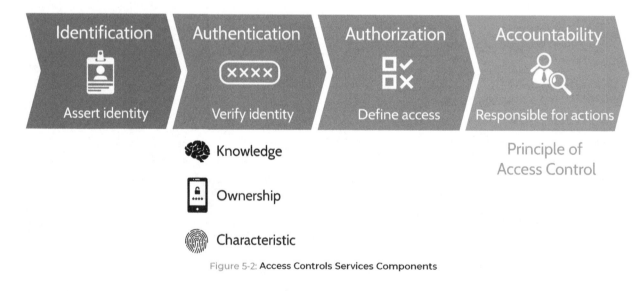

Figure 5-2: **Access Controls Services Components**

5.2.2 Identification

The notion of identification is simple: To gain access to a system, a *unique* identity should be presented, which can then be used to trace activity to an individual. Shared user accounts potentially allow circumvention of the Principle of Access Control and therefore should not be used.

Identification as the first component of Access Control Services, identification methods and guidelines

A few examples of identification methods include a user's ID (for example, first name, last name, both, etc.), account ID, access card, biometrics.

User identification needs to be

- **Unique** (relating to one individual or process)
- **Nondescriptive of role** (e.g., admin accounts should not include the word "admin," or finance-related user accounts should not point to a role or job related to the same)
- **Issued and used securely** (e.g., use a password manager to generate and store user passwords rather than writing them down to a notepad)

As it pertains to **authentication**, there are three factors of authentication that can be used to verify a user's identity, which are summarized in Table 5-3.

Authentication by Knowledge	Authentication by Ownership	Authentication by Characteristic
Something you **know**	Something you **have**	How you behave or your physiology; something you **are**

Table 5-3: **Factors of Authentication**

5.2.3 Authentication by Knowledge

Authentication by knowledge, or also known as something you know, simply means that a person uses a password, a passphrase, or a response to one or more security questions to authenticate to a system. A password could be as simple as "password" or something more complex, like "m{BLB9FF#6h`J#U$." Complex passwords aren't easy to remember, which is why many people write down their passwords on sticky notes and place them under their keyboard or on their monitor. A passphrase is typically as complex as the password example and much easier to remember. The thinking here is that a sentence or lyric from a song or book can be used to authenticate. A phrase is longer and can be as or more complex than a standard password. Finally, one or more security questions can be presented to a user, and upon answering them correctly the user is authenticated. The questions are usually chosen by the user, and the corresponding correct answers should be details that only the user knows. These are

Authentication by knowledge as one type of authentication

often known as cognitive questions. In addition, note that answers to these questions don't have to be true. For example, if a question asks, "What's your maiden name?" you can still answer "3487487glkjgokjo!(*&" (good luck pronouncing that!), but the point is that the answer doesn't have to be true. This makes security questions impossible to guess from an attacker's point of view.

Different forms of authentication by knowledge

Ideally, whether a password, passphrase, or questions are used, each should be unique to the user and not easily guessed or otherwise determined.

5.2.4 Authentication by Ownership

CORE CONCEPTS

- Authentication by ownership is the component of Access Control Services that refers to verification of an identity through something a user possesses.

- One-Time Passwords (OTP) are generated via a synchronous or asynchronous process.

- Soft tokens refer to software-based applications, like Google Authenticator, that generate one-time passwords.

- Hard tokens refer to small physical tokens, like RSA's SecureID device, that generate one-time passwords.

- Smart cards are typically credit-card-size plastic cards with an embedded semiconductor chip that stores, accepts, and sends information; they work in collaboration with a smart card reader.

- Memory cards are typically credit-card-size plastic cards with a narrow magnetic strip on the back of that card that contains information related to the card owner, issuing bank, account number, PIN, etc.

One-Time Passwords (OTP) are exactly what the term says, they are passwords that can be used one time. Additionally, one-time passwords are *dynamic* in that they expire after being used, or they expire after a certain period of time. One-time passwords can be generated via a **soft token**, a software app (like Google's Authenticator app), or they can be generated via a **hard token**, a dedicated hardware device (like RSA's SecureID device).

Authentication by ownership as another type of authentication

One-time passwords can be generated via an asynchronous or synchronous process as depicted in Figure 5-3. Of the two processes, asynchronous is much less common, as it involves a fair amount of complexity with regards to the synchronization elements involved between the authorization server and the user and system they're accessing. This complexity often comes with a hefty price tag, though it does offer a more robust layer of security. Relative to the asynchronous process, the synchronous one-time password authorization process is much more straightforward and less complex.

> **Understand the difference between asynchronous and synchronous password generation**

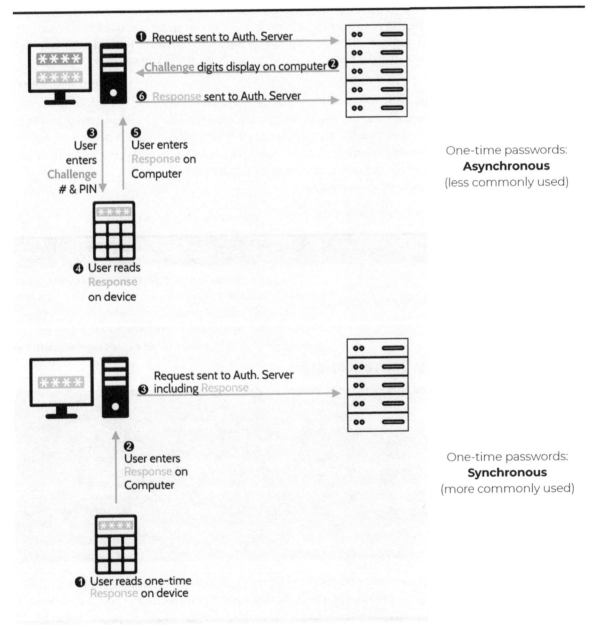

Figure 5-3: **Synchronous and Asynchronous One-Time Passwords**

Smart/Memory Cards

Both smart and memory cards consist of an authentication factor by ownership, as you have a smart or memory card in your possession. Both cards store information about the card holder. Smart and memory cards are summarized in Table 5-4.

Understand the differences between smart and memory cards

Smart Card	Memory Card
Called smart cards because they contain a small embedded integrated circuit (IC) chip that can perform calculations and generate unique authentication data with each transaction.	Implies a form of memory stored on a card, typically on a magnetic strip on the back of the card. The same data is read from the magnetic strip with every transaction.

Table 5-4: **Smart and Memory Cards**

A memory card will have a magnetic stripe on the back of the card, which is where the information is stored. Older cards were typically just memory cards, and this fact led to widespread growth of credit card fraud—specifically skimming (covered in 3.9.11). Newer cards (especially modern debit and credit cards) tend to be a combination of smart and memory card as they contain a chip (smart) and a magnetic strip (memory). The chip in smart cards can act as a processing engine for them to accept, store, and send information as they communicate with a card reader.

There are two main methods that smart cards can communicate with a reader as noted in Table 5-5.

Contact Smart Cards	Contactless Smart Cards
The chip in the card needs to contact the reader for the chip to be powered and allow transactions to be processed.	The reader sends out signals that are powerful enough to communicate with and power the chip in a smart card, allowing it to perform some calculations and wirelessly send a response to the reader.

Table 5-5: **Smart Cards' Communication Methods**

5.2.5 Authentication by Characteristics

CORE **CONCEPTS**

- **Authentication by characteristics refers to physiological and behavioral biometric types.**

- **Biometric device accuracy can vary and is not always 100 percent accurate.**

- **The use of biometric devices must consider: processing speed, user acceptance, protection of biometric data, accuracy.**

- **Crossover Error Rate (CER) represents the intersection between Type 1 (false reject) and Type 2 (false acceptance) errors, and it measures the accuracy of a biometric system.**

The various physiological and behavioral authentication types are shown in Table 5-6. Remember that physiological relates to the physical attributes of a person, while behavioral relates to how a person behaves.

Physiological Characteristics	Behavioral Characteristics
fingerprints	the way a person writes
hand geometry	the way a person walks—their gait
facial features	the way a person speaks—their voice
eyes (retina and iris)	the way a person types—keyboard dynamics

Table 5-6: **Physiological and Behavioral Authentication Types**

Biometric Device Considerations

Due to the nature of how biometric authentication works, factors like the ones noted below must be considered:

- Processing Speed
- User Acceptance
- Protection of Biometric Data
- Accuracy

Biometric systems can be much slower than other types of authentication systems. Because of this fact, users may be less willing to accept the implementation and use of biometric authentication, and because of the inherent uniqueness of biometric data, its protection is of paramount importance. Finally, the accuracy of biometric systems must be carefully considered.

Biometric Device Accuracy/Types of Errors

Unlike other types of authentication systems, biometric systems are not 100% binary. In other words, they're not always 100% accurate. With a traditional username/password authentication system, for example, the username and password must be 100% correct for a user to be authenticated to a system. The same cannot be said of a system that uses physiological or behavioral attributes for authentication.

> **Biometric error types and which is worse**

When considering biometric systems and their accuracy, two primary types of errors need to be understood as summarized in Table 5-7.

Type 1—False Rejection	Type 2—False Acceptance
▪ A **valid user** is **falsely rejected** by the system	▪ An **invalid user** is **given access** to a system ▪ Much more serious and potentially dangerous situation

Table 5-7: **Metrics for Biometric Systems Accuracy**

With Type 1 errors, the result is usually just frustrated users that can't authenticate to the system. However, with Type 2 errors, a malicious individual could gain access to the environment, as the tool falsely thinks they are legitimate. Hence, **Type 2 errors are much more dangerous than Type 1 errors**. Also note the terms False Rejection Rate (FRR), which expresses the Type 1 error rate, and False Acceptance Rate (FAR), which expresses the Type 2 error rate.

An interesting feature of biometric systems is that these error rates are inverse to one another, which relates to the system's tuning. In other words, by tuning a system and reducing Type 2 errors, Type 1 errors tend to increase. On the other hand, by reducing Type 1 errors, Type 2 errors will increase. This inverse relationship is depicted in Figure 5-4.

Crossover Error Rate (CER)

As Figure 5-4 depicts, when Type 1 (false reject errors) are low, Type 2 (false accept errors are high) and vice versa. The intersection of the two error plots is what's known as the Crossover Error Rate (CER). The crossover error rate is a useful metric for biometric systems, because it's a way to measure the overall accuracy of the system. No system is going to have a CER of zero, but a number closer to zero means the system is more accurate. CER is often used when looking for and comparing biometric systems and their functionality and effectiveness.

> **Crossover error rate and what it represents**

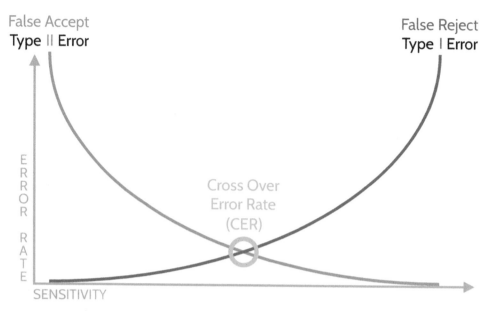

Figure 5-4: **FAR, FRR, and CER**

Biometric Templates

As noted above, the protection of biometric data is extremely important. If someone's biometric data is exposed, the consequences are much more severe than, for example, their password being exposed. The reason is obvious: if someone's password is exposed, they can just change their password and memorize the new password. However, if their biometric data is exposed, they can't just grow a new finger or a new eyeball.

Accordingly, raw, or original biometric data should never be stored, such as a simple picture of a fingerprint. Instead, good biometric systems will use one-way mathematical functions to create a representation of the features or characteristics from the source data – this digital representation is called a **template**. A template is essentially a digital representation of someone's unique biometric features.

Templates can be used in two major ways as summarized in Table 5-8

1 : N for Identification	1 : 1 for Authentication
Imagine someone walks up to a locked door and places their finger on a biometric scanner to unlock the door. The scanner has no idea who this person is before they place their finger on the scanner. The scanner is capturing the person's biometric data, generating a new template, and then searching through a database of existing templates to try to find a reasonably close match to identify the person.	Imagine a user logs into their laptop by typing in their username and password. As a second factor of authentication, the laptop then asks the user to place their finger on the built-in biometric scanner. The scanner will capture the user's biometric data, generate a template, and because the user has already been identified with their username, the system will look up the user's existing template in a database and compare the user's existing template to the newly generated template. If the templates reasonably match, then the user is authenticated.
A 1 : N scan of biometric templates is used for identification	**A 1 : 1 comparison of biometric templates is used for authentication**

Table 5-8: **Uses of Biometric Templates**

Biometric Devices

As can be seen in Table 5-9, biometric devices vary and focus on different characteristics.

Physiological	**Fingerprint**	Fingerprint scanners examine a fingerprint. These are very common, especially on devices like computers and mobile phones, and they're reasonably accurate. They're also often used at border crossings, for example, between the United States and Canada.
	Hand geometry	Hand geometry scanners are rarely used, but often portrayed in movies. The scanning device could be a small machine, with an outline of a hand and guideposts that help position the hand and fingers for scanning; or, the device could be a futuristic-looking screen upon which a user places his or her hand, and the geometry is read. Some devices scan the ridges of the hand, while others examine the geometry.
	Vascular pattern	Vascular pattern scanners examine veins in a hand and are often used in testing centers, like the ones where CISSP and other exams are administered. The scan allows biometric information of the exam candidate to be captured prior to the exam, and if a break or visit to the restroom is needed, the hand can be rescanned and the results compared to the original. This ensures that the exam candidate remains the test taker, and not somebody else.
	Facial	Facial scanners examine an individual's facial features and pattern.
	Iris	Iris scanners examine the colored ring around an individual's eye.
	Retina	While iris scanners examine the colored ring around an eye, retina scanners look at the back of the eye and specifically at the vein pattern of the retina. **Retina scanners are very accurate; in fact, they're the most accurate type of biometric system.** They're also controversial. For one thing, they're invasive, due to the way they operate, and this explains why they're rarely used. In use, an individual has to place their eye to a rubber eye cup, and a bright light is flashed as part of the scan. Most people find this process unpleasant. Additionally, and more to the point of controversy, retina scans can lead to privacy issues, because the results of a retina scan can reveal medical issues related to the individual.
Behavioral	**Voice**	How a person speaks.
	Signature	How a person writes.
	Keystroke	How a person types on a keyboard.
	Gait	How a person walks.

Table 5-9: **Biometric Authentication**

Biometric device types and least/most accurate

5.2.6 Factors of Authentication

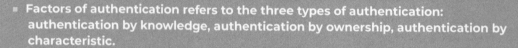

CORE **CONCEPTS**

- **Factors of authentication refers to the three types of authentication: authentication by knowledge, authentication by ownership, authentication by characteristic.**

- **Single-factor authentication refers to any one of the three types of authentication being used.**

- **Multifactor Authentication (MFA) refers to two (or more) of the three types of authentication being used.**

Refer back to the three types—factors—of authentication:

- Authentication by knowledge—something you know

- Authentication by ownership—something you have

- Authentication by characteristic—something you are (physiological or behavioral)

Each of these families on its own can be thought of as a type of single-factor authentication. If an authentication system uses any number of authentication types but all falling within a single factor (e.g., all belong "to something you are"), then single-factor authentication is in place. However, two (or more) of these factor families used in combination can be considered as multifactor authentication (e.g., using any authentication type from "something you are" and another belonging to "something you have"). Single-factor versus multifactor authentication are summarized in Table 5-10.

> Understand the difference between single-factor authentication and multifactor authentication and what constitutes each type

Single-factor Authentication	Multifactor Authentication
One (1) factor of authentication used by itself	Two (2) or more **different** factors used in combination

Table 5-10: **Factors of Authentication**

If a user logs in to a system using only an RSA ID key and a Microsoft token, they've authenticated using a single factor. However, if the authentication process involves entering a password and an RSA token, then two factors of authentication have been used, and therefore this would be considered multifactor authentication.

Also, consider this question. If a username/password combination *and* a challenge question is used, is this single-factor or multifactor authentication? Before you answer, consider what type of authentication each represents. A username/password is authentication by knowledge; likewise, so is a challenge question. So, in fact, even though two authentication objects are utilized, only a single-factor of authentication has been employed (something you know). It's important to understand the different factors of authentication and to be able to distinguish them from each other.

5.2.7 Credential Management Systems

Credential management systems allow organizations to effectively manage—at scale—access to assets by ensuring that all personnel, processes, and devices have unique credentials. Credential management systems are designed to manage (grant and revoke) and issue credentials, typically using strong two-factor authentication that incorporates public key infrastructure. Credential management systems include the programs, processes, technologies, and personnel used to create trusted digital identity representations of individuals and nonperson entities (processes) and bind those identities to their credentials.

5.2.8 **Single Sign-on (SSO)**

CORE **CONCEPTS**

- Single sign-on refers to authenticating one time and being able to access multiple systems.
- A disadvantage of single sign-on is the implication of centralized administration, which represents a single point of failure.
- Kerberos is one of the major single sign-on protocols, and it provides accounting, authentication, and auditing services.
- SESAME is an improved version of Kerberos, but it has not been widely adopted due to Kerberos being built into Microsoft Windows operating systems by default.
- Kerberos disadvantages include that it only supports symmetric encryption, and it is vulnerable to TOCTOU attack.

The concept of Single Sign-On (SSO) is best illustrated through an example. From the perspective of a user, single sign-on takes place when the user types in their username and password, or username and Microsoft Authenticator code, for example, and is then authorized to access multiple systems. The user logs in one time and is authorized to access multiple systems.

> **Understand the underlying premise and pros and cons of single sign-on**

Users typically love it, and one immediate advantage is they'll be more likely to use one stronger password to log in once versus using a bunch of weaker passwords to access multiple systems.

A big disadvantage of SSO was mentioned in the section about administration approaches. SSO implies centralized administration, and centralized administration represents a single point of failure from both an availability and a confidentiality perspective. If a SSO system is compromised, an attacker potentially has access to everything. Contrarily, if the system goes down, users have access to nothing.

At a high level, the single-sign-on process is depicted in Figure 5-5.

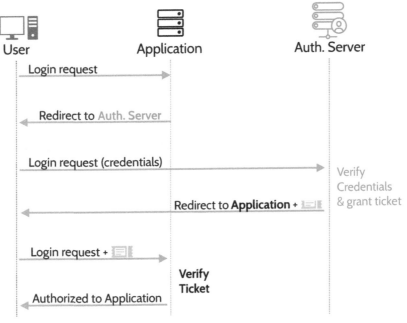

Figure 5-5: **Single Sign-On Process**

1. A user sends a login request to an application.

2. If the user has not already logged in or authenticated, the application will essentially say, "I don't know who you are right now," and redirect the user back to the authentication server, saying, "You're not currently authenticated, I don't know who you are, you need to go and authenticate."

3. The user will identify themselves to the authentication server and authenticate via knowledge, ownership, or characteristic, or a combination of two or more types. Once authenticated and authorized, the user will be given some type of ticket or token.

4. The user is directed back to the application, and the ticket or token is presented for authorization to the application.

5. If the application grants authorization, the user will be able to access the application.

Pros and Cons of Single Sign-On

The pros and cons of single sign-on are summarized in Table 5-11.

Pros	Cons
<ul><li>User experience</li><li>Users may create stronger passwords</li><li>Timeout and attempt thresholds enforced</li><li>Centralized administration</li></ul>	<ul><li>Single point of failure for compromise and availability</li><li>Inclusion of unique/legacy systems</li></ul>

Table 5-11: **Pros and Cons of Single Sign-On**

Kerberos

One of the major SSO authentication protocols is known as Kerberos. As a side reference, the name Kerberos stems from Greek Mythology and refers to the three-headed dog, Cerberus, that guarded the gates of Hell. Drawing from the myth, Kerberos protects access to resources and provides three primary functionalities:

> **Understand how Kerberos works as well as specific components of Kerberos**

- Accounting

- Authentication

- Auditing

Kerberos is an old and complicated protocol, and thankfully you do not need to be an expert on how the protocol works for the exam. Figure 5-6 provides a simplified depiction of the major steps in the Kerberos authentication process. Alice is the client who wants to access a service. If Alice does not currently have a valid ticket, she must first be authenticated by the Kerberos service before she can access the desired service.

- Alice, the **Client**, sends a couple of initial messages to the Kerberos **Authentication Service (AS)**.

- The Authentication Service will verify that Alice is a valid user and, if so, will send a few messages back to Alice. One message is encrypted with Alice's password as the encryption key, and another message is the **Ticket Granting Ticket (TGT)**—a message that Alice cannot decrypt as it is encrypted with the **Ticket Granting Service's (TGS)** key.

- When Alice receives the messages from the authentication service, she decrypts one of the messages with her password as the encryption key. This is the way that Kerberos verifies that the user knows their password without having to send the user's password across the network. If the user knows their password, they can use it to decrypt one of the messages and can therefore proceed with the process. If the user doesn't know their password, they can't decrypt the message and obtain the information they need to proceed.

- Assuming Alice knows her password and decrypts the message, she will create a couple of new tickets and send them along with the still encrypted TGT to the Ticket Granting Service.

- When the Ticket Granting Service receives the messages from Alice, it performs a number of verification steps, and if everything looks good, it will create some new messages to send back to Alice including the encrypted **Service Ticket** (encrypted with the service's key).

- When Alice receives the messages from the Ticket Granting Service, she creates some new messages and sends them to the **Service** along with the still encrypted service ticket.

- When the service receives the messages from Alice, it does a final few verification steps, and if everything looks good, the service will finally grant Alice access.

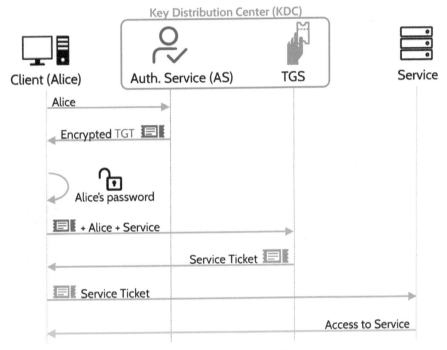

Figure 5-6: **Kerberos Operation**

This is a very incomplete description of all the various messages that are sent, the data they contain, and all the verification steps performed at each stage; however, it should provide a sufficient overview of the critical messages (TGT and Service Ticket), and the major services of Kerberos—the Authentication Service and the Ticket Granting Service—both of which are components within what is known as the **Key Distribution Center (KDC)**.

Despite Kerberos's inherent strengths, including that it enables single sign-on, some significant disadvantages exist too. For one thing, Kerberos only supports symmetric encryption (e.g., RC4, DES, AES), which automatically implies symmetric key distribution challenges. For another, Kerberos only issues one major ticket, which is used to gain access to a system. As a result of using only one ticket, a system is vulnerable to a Time Of Check Time Of Use (TOCTOU) attack, which can be mitigated by increasing the frequency of authentication. In other words, to minimize the risk associated with a TOCTOU, or session hijacking, attack, users should be re-authenticated more frequently, especially if the system is a high-value system. Re-authentication means expiring the ticket, which means the user must login again. The point is this: for users accessing low-value systems all day, forcing them to re-login frequently, because of a high-value system in the environment, can create a significant burden and end-user resistance. In this scenario, it would be better to isolate the high-value system(s) and allow users to have longer-life-span tickets for the rest.

SESAME

Secure European System for Applications in a Multi-Vendor Environment, better known as SESAME, is an improved version of Kerberos. Like Kerberos, SESAME is a protocol for enabling single sign-on. Additionally, one of the big advantages of SESAME over Kerberos is that it supports symmetric and asymmetric cryptography, so it naturally solves the problem of key distribution, and it issues multiple tickets, which mitigates vulnerability to attacks like TOCTOU.

Even though SESAME is a better protocol, Kerberos is by far the more prevalent, because it's built into many prevalent systems including the Windows operating systems, MacOS, and various Linux and Unix distros. Remember that to use Kerberos in a Windows environment, Active Directory must be enabled.

5.2.9 CAPTCHA

> CORE **CONCEPTS**
>
> - CAPTCHA is a security measure that works by asking a user—typically a visitor to a website or portal—to complete a simple test to prove they're human and not a robot or automated program.
>
> - CAPTCHA is used to prevent automated account creation, spam, and brute-force password decryption attacks.

When accessing a website, vendors often employ the use of what is known as Completely Automated Public Turing test to tell Computers and Humans Apart (CAPTCHA) as a security measure to protect against automated account creation and to protect users from spam and brute-force password decryption attacks. CAPTCHA works by asking a user to complete a simple test to prove they're human and not a robot or automated program trying to access or break

Understand what CAPTCHA is and why it is most often used

into a protected account or area of a website. In its simplest form, CAPTCHA works by presenting a website visitor with an image of distorted letters and numbers and asking the user to type those letters and numbers into an empty field on the page. If the information is typed in correctly, the visitor gains access to the protected area; if not, the visitor is typically given another opportunity to do so. Bottom line: CAPTCHA is used to prevent bots from creating multiple accounts on systems, spam, and unauthorized access.

5.2.10 Session management

> CORE **CONCEPTS**
>
> - Session management refers to management of sessions created through a successful user identification, authentication, and authorization process.
>
> - A session represents the connection and interaction between a user and a system.
>
> - Session hijacking is a risk where no session management exists.
>
> - Session termination and re-authentication is the best way to prevent or mitigate session hijacking.

Session management refers to sessions, and a **session** is what's created as the result of a successful user identification, authentication, and authorization process as shown in Figure 5-7. Upon a user being authorized by a system, a session is created, and the session represents the connection and interaction between the user and the system. Until the user logs out—manually or automatically—a session remains intact. Session management is focused on managing sessions effectively and securely for the entire duration.

Figure 5-7: **User Successful Authentication**

Session Hijacking

Session management is very important, because without it a major risk exists: session hijacking (shown in Figure 5-8). In other words, through simple carelessness or sophisticated technical means, somebody other than a legitimate user could gain access to a session and use it for malicious purposes. The preventive measure for session hijacking is session termination, which is an important component of session management.

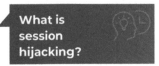

What is session hijacking?

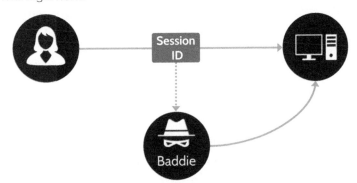

Figure 5-8: **Session Hijacking**

How do you prevent session hijacking?

As noted, session hijacking can be mitigated through session termination, and several major ways exist to terminate a session. The primary and best way to prevent session hijacking is through frequent re-authentication. Many VPN solutions include continuous re-authentication as part of their security package. Session encryption keys are established at the beginning of a VPN session and then re-established in the background at certain time intervals. Additionally, a user is continually re-authenticated by the system in a manner that is transparent to the user. That makes it much more difficult for an attacker to compromise a user's active session.

How can session hijacking be prevented?

Session Termination

In addition to continuous authentication, other major ways to terminate a session are outlined in Table 5-12.

Schedule Limitations	Schedule limitations refers to a system administrative control that logs all users out of a system at a set time, for example, at 5 p.m. every evening, or perhaps the system does not allow logins during a weekend.
Login Limitation	Login limitation refers to preventing more than one simultaneous login using the same user ID. In other words, an account may not be shared and used at the same time by different people (or even the same person).
Time-outs	If there's inactivity, or after a set period of time, a session expires (it's timed out).
Screensavers	Screensavers are another popular session-management tool. After a screensaver pops up on a computer, typically the only way to gain access is through re-authentication.

Table 5-12: **Session Termination Methods**

5.2.11 Registration and Proofing of Identity

CORE **CONCEPTS**

- Identity proofing—registration—is the process of confirming or establishing that somebody is who they claim to be.

- Identity proofing is a component of provisioning in the identity life cycle.

Identity proofing, also sometimes called registration, is simply the process of confirming or establishing that somebody is who they claim to be before they are given access to a valuable resource or asset. Remember, for example, what happens before a certificate authority (CA) issues a digital certificate to somebody.

> **What is identity proofing, and when does it take place?**

The registration authority (RA) proofs the identity of the certificate applicant. Similarly, prior to beginning employment and issuing an employee badge, account credentials, etc., an organization will proof the identity of a new employee. Using some type of government issued ID, a driver's license, or other form of identification unique to an individual, the company will confirm that the person is who they claim to be.

5.2.12 Authenticator Assurance Levels (AAL)

CORE **CONCEPTS**

- Authenticator Assurance Levels (AAL) refer to the strength of authentication processes and systems.

- AAL levels rank from AAL1 (least robust) to AAL3 (most robust).

With regards to digital identities, the National Institute of Standards and Technology has produced a suite of documents that can be found here: https://pages.nist.gov/800-63-3/. One document, NIST SP 800-63B, entitled "Authentication and Lifecycle Management," contains information about the AAL levels, which has been summarized in Table 5-13.

> **Understand AAL ratings and elements of each**

AALs measure the robustness of the authentication process. The higher the number, the more robust the strength of the service provided.

AAL1	<ul><li>Some assurance</li><li>Single-factor authentication</li><li>Secure Authentication protocol</li></ul>
AAL2	<ul><li>High confidence</li><li>Multifactor authentication</li><li>Secure Authentication protocol</li><li>Approved cryptographic techniques</li></ul>
AAL3	<ul><li>Very high confidence</li><li>Multifactor authentication</li><li>Secure Authentication protocol</li><li>"Hard" cryptographic authenticator providing proof of possession of key and impersonation resistance</li></ul>

Table 5-13: **AAL Levels**

5.2.13 Federated Identity Management (FIM)

CORE **CONCEPTS**

- Single sign-on refers to one-time authentication to gain access to multiple systems in one organization; federated identity management (FIM) refers to one-time authentication to gain access to multiple systems, including systems associated with other organizations.

- Federated Identity Management (FIM) relies on trust relationships established between different entities.

- FIM trust relationships include three components: principal/user, identity provider, relying party.

- Principal/user = the person who wants to access a system.

- Identity provider = the entity that owns the identity and performs the authentication.

- Relying party is also known as the service provider.

In comparison to single sign-on (SSO), where a user authenticates one time and gains access to multiple systems in the context of an organization, federated identity management (FIM) allows a user to authenticate one time and gain access to multiple disparate systems. In other words, a user gains access to company-owned systems as well as systems outside of the organization's control.

> Understand the basis of Federated Identity Management (FIM) and the three components that make up any federated access system

Microsoft's Active Directory is one example of the type of system used within an organization to provide SSO services.

Let's take a closer look at federated identity management, sometimes referred to as federated access, through an example. When a person travels via airplane, they must go through a security checkpoint before proceeding to the departure gate. Passing through this checkpoint means the traveler is in a secure zone. After traveling to another location, the person is still in a secure zone, because the new airport trusts the security check that was performed at the original airport. This fact highlights one of the most important and foundational aspects of federal access—*trust relationships between different entities*. In this example, the two airports are owned and operated by different organizations, but they share a trust relationship.

Let's look at federated access in the context of the logical world. With many websites today, when creating an account, two or more options are often available. One option is to create an account using a unique username and password; another option is to create an account using an already existing Facebook, Google, or account from a similar platform. For this example, imagine a user prefers to use their Google account, and they want to create an account on Pinterest, but Google doesn't own it. So the user visits Pinterest, and they're given the option to create an account or log in with Google (among several choices). They choose to log in via Google, and a small window pops up asking them to provide their Google username and password. Google is authenticating the user, but because a trust relationship exists between Google and Pinterest, Pinterest is trusting the authentication being performed by Google. This is another, real-world example of federated access in the logical world.

With any federated access system, three major components exist as depicted in Figure 5-9. First is the **user**, also referred to as the **principal**. The user or principal is the person who wants to log in or access the system. Second is the **identity provider**. The identity provider is the entity that owns the identity and performs the authentication. In the example above, Google is the identity provider. Third is the **relying party**, sometimes called the **service provider**. In the example noted above, Pinterest is the relying party. Federated identity management—federated access—relies on a trust relationship between the three entities.

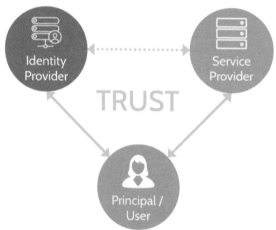

Figure 5-9: **Federation Components**

5.2.14 Federated Access Standards

CORE CONCEPTS

- **Key Federated Access protocols include: Security Assertion Markup Language (SAML), WS-Federation, OpenID (for authentication), OAuth (for authorization).**

- **SAML is frequently used in Federated Identity Management (FIM) solutions and provides authentication and authorization.**

- **OpenID and OAuth are open-standard federated access protocols that provide authentication via OpenID and authorization via OAuth.**

- **SAML assertions are written in a language called XML, or Extensible Markup Language. XML is a way of communicating in a manner that is machine and human-readable.**

Several major protocols enable federated access, with Security Assertion Markup Language (SAML) being one of the most important to understand. WS-Federation, OpenID, and OAuth are the others that should be known at a high level. Figure 5-10 depicts these four federated access standards and whether they provide authentication or authorization services or both.

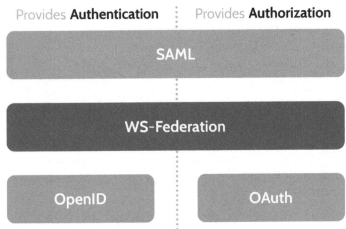

Provides **Authentication**   Provides **Authorization**

Figure 5-10: **Federated Access Standards**

WS-Federation (like SAML) offers authentication and authorization functionality. Like most federated access standards, the primary goal is enabling identity federation authentication and authorization. WS-Federation was created by a consortium of companies, including IBM, Microsoft, and Verisign, and it was codified as a standard by **OASIS**.

OpenID and OAuth are complementary protocols that often work together. **OpenID** provides the authentication component, and **OAuth** provides the authorization component to a federated access solution. In its simplest form, OpenID allows a user to use an existing account to identify and authenticate to multiple disparate resources—websites, systems, and so on—without the need to create new passwords for each resource. With OpenID, a user password is given only to the user's identity provider—Microsoft, for example—and the identity provider confirms the user's identity to sites the user visits. OAuth is the protocol or standard that allows users to gain access—to be authorized—to resources. Both OpenID and OAuth are open standards. While they can work independent of each other—especially OpenID—they're often deployed together, because of the richer functionality they provide as a unit.

Security Assertion Markup Language (SAML)

SAML's operation is depicted in Figure 5-11.

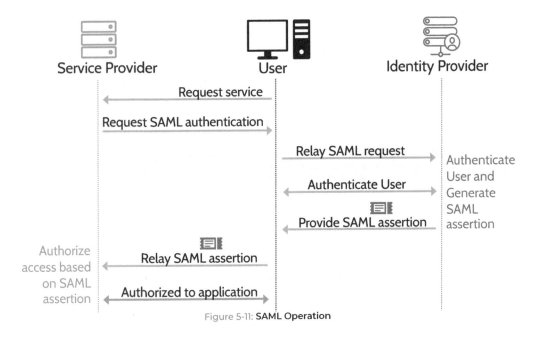

Figure 5-11: **SAML Operation**

SAML provides two capabilities: authentication and authorization.

1. First, the user (**principal**) must authenticate via the identity provider. If the user is not logged in and requests access to a service (offered by the service provider), the request will get bounced to the identity provider, where the user can authenticate.

2. The **identity provider** will authenticate the user through the process of identification and authentication, at which point the user will be issued a SAML assertion ticket. One critical fact to note here: the SAML assertion ticket does not contain the username and password of the user. Rather, as the name suggests, the ticket contains assertion statements that the service provider—the relying party—can use for authorization purposes or to determine the level of authorization granted to the user.

3. Once the SAML assertion ticket is provided to the user, the user will pass it on to the **service provider**. The relying party is going to read the assertion statements contained within the SAML ticket and make an authorization decision. Similar to Kerberos, SAML uses tickets or tokens, usually denoted as SAML assertion tickets or tokens. The words are used interchangeably, and the critical thing to note is that assertions or statements about the user—username, role, level of access, etc.—are contained within them.

The four major components of SAML are summarized in Table 5-14.

Component	Function
Assertion	Authentication, authorization, and other attributes
Protocol	Defines how entities request and respond to requests
Bindings	Mapping of SAML onto standard communication protocols (ex: HTTP)
Profiles	Define how SAML can be used for different business use cases (ex: Web SSO, LDAP, etc.)

Table 5-14: **SAML's Key Components**

In addition to the above, it's important to remember two key characteristics of SAML.

- SAML uses assertion tickets or tokens.
- Assertions are written in a language called **Extensible Markup Language (XML)**, which is a way of communicating in a manner that is machine and human-readable.

5.2.15 Accountability = Principle of Access Control

CORE CONCEPTS

- **Accountability = the Principle of Access Control.**

The Principle of Access Control refers to accountability.

In order to achieve accountability, several things need to happen:

1. Users must be uniquely identified
2. Users must be properly authenticated
3. Users must be properly authorized
4. All actions should be logged and monitored

With all these components in place, then, and only then, can the Principle of Access Control be achieved.

5.2.16 Just-in-time (JIT) Access

CORE **CONCEPTS**

- Just-in-time access refers to the elevation of user privileges to an authorized user for a short period of time, so a user may complete necessary, but infrequent, tasks.

- Just-in-time access mitigates the need for long-term elevation of privileges, which minimizes potential security risks.

The term "just-in-time" is often used in the context of just-in-time delivery, meaning an organization—a manufacturer, for example—receives components needed for production at the time production commences. One of the huge benefits of this type of arrangement is that the manufacturer can focus on what it does best and not need to worry about managing and storing inventory. If they know they're going to produce 100,000 widgets, they'll get enough components (and some extra, just in case) to produce those 100,000 widgets at the time needed.

Just-in-time access works in a similar fashion, albeit from a security perspective. Imagine a user that needs to access a sensitive part of a database once a month to run a report. At a high level, just-in-time access allows the user to gain elevated privileges during this monthly time window to run the report. Just-in-time access mitigates the need for long-term elevation of privileges, and the way it is set up and administered oftentimes allows for the access to be granted in an automated fashion versus a manual process. In other words, it minimizes potential security risks, and it does so in a manner that is efficient and effective.

5.3 Federated identity with a third-party service

5.3.1 Identity as a Service (IDaaS)

CORE CONCEPTS

- Identity as a Service (IDaaS) refers to the implementation or integration of identity services in a cloud-based environment.

- Risks of IDaaS include those related to availability of service, protection of critical identity data, and trusting a third party with potentially sensitive or proprietary information.

Understand the basic premise underlying Identity as a Service and why it might be used as well as associated risks

Identity as a Service (IDaaS) is the implementation or integration of identity services in a cloud-based environment. In other words, identification, authentication, authorization, accounting, and federated access all take place in the cloud. IDaaS has a variety of capabilities, which are:

- Provisioning

- Administration

- Single Sign-on (SSO)

- Multifactor authentication (MFA)

- Directory Services

- On premises and in the cloud

It also supports multiple types of identities/accounts as listed in Table 5-15.

	Account Stored	Authentication by
Cloud Identity	Created and managed **in the cloud**	Cloud service
Synced Identity	Created and managed in local store (e.g., active directory) and **synced/copied** to cloud or vice versa	Either local or cloud
Linked Identities	**Two separate accounts** which are **linked**. For example: one account in local store and second account in cloud service	Either local or cloud
Federated Identity	Identity Provider	Identity Provider

Table 5-15: **IDaaS Identities**

Identity and Access Management Solutions

Identity and Access Management (IAM) solutions can use any of the three models listed in Table 5-16.

On Premise	▪ Systems controlled by a private organization ▪ They are not reliant on the internet to function ▪ Are typically very secure
Cloud	▪ Service and systems provided by a cloud service provider ▪ Through the use of Federated Identity protocols (like SAML), organization user identities and credentials can be used ▪ Can be subject to availability risk as well as security risks due to the multitenant nature of the public cloud
Hybrid	▪ Hybrid IAM solutions combine the best features of on premises and cloud, and offer the most flexibility for dynamic and growing organization

Table 5-16: **IAM Models**

IDaaS Risks

Potential risks relating to IDaaS include the following:

- **Availability of the service:** If the cloud service provider suffers an outage or the service is otherwise unavailable, the users will be unable to access systems.

- **Protection of critical identity data:** PII and other sensitive data will be in the control of the cloud service provider. That means adequate protection of data is based on protection mechanisms the provider has available.

- **Entrusting a third party with sensitive or proprietary data:** Based upon the identity data shared with the cloud service provider, other information about the organization might also be gained. Protections need to be in place to protect against this information from being leaked or shared with any unauthorized parties.

5.4 Implement and manage authorization mechanisms

CORE CONCEPTS

- Discretionary Access Control (DAC) means an asset owner determines who can access the asset; access is given at the *discretion* of the owner.

- Rule-based access control is based upon rules and can be utilized in a very granular manner, though it is very administrative-heavy as a result.

- Role-based access control is based upon roles or job functions, and users can be assigned to one or more roles that include authorizations to perform duties.

- Attribute-based access control is very granular and is based upon user attributes, such as job function, type of device, working hours, asset classification, and so on.

- Other access control approaches include: context-based access control and risk-based access control. Context-based access control typically looks at the context (internal or external) of an initiating connection and is usually enforced via firewall rules. Risk-based access control looks at elements of a user connection—IP address, time of access request, and so on—to determine a risk profile associated with the request. Based upon the result, further authentication challenges may be presented to the user before access is granted.

- eXtensible Access Control Markup Language (XACML) is one tool that defines and enables attribute-based access control.

Within the realm of **authorization**, a number of different philosophies and methodologies exist, and these can be broadly categorized as:

- Discretionary
- Mandatory
- Non-discretionary

Each of these categories are analyzed in detail in the following section. They're also illustrated in Figure 5-12, while their main characteristics are listed in Table 5-17.

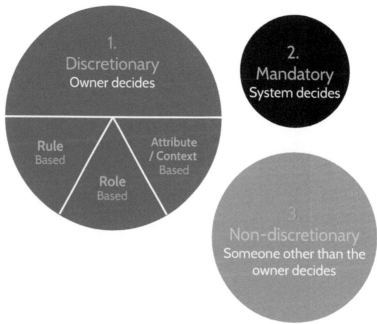

Figure 5-12: **Access Control Types**

Access Control Summary

Discretionary Access Control (DAC)	▪ **Owner** determines access rules
Role-Based Access Control (RBAC)	▪ Access to resources is based on **user roles** (e.g., firewall administrator, or accounts payable clerk)
Rule-Based Access Control	▪ Access to resources is based on a **set of rules** (e.g., an Access Control List, ACL)
Attribute-Based Access Controls (ABAC)	▪ Access to resources is based on user **attributes** (e.g., OS, browser version, IP address)
Mandatory Access Control (MAC)	▪ **System** determines access rules based on **labels**
Risk-Based Access Control	▪ Considers elements of a user connection (IP address, time of access request) to determine a risk profile associated with the request. Based upon the result, further authentication challenges may be presented to the user.

Table 5-17 : **Main Characteristics of Access Control Types**

With this foundation, let's explore each of these authorization mechanisms further.

5.4.1 Discretionary Access Control (DAC)

CORE **CONCEPTS**

- ▪ Discretionary Access Control (DAC) means an asset owner determines who can access the asset; access is given at the *discretion* of the owner.

- ▪ Three primary types of DAC exist: rule-based access control, role-based access control, and attribute-based access control.

> Understand the premise of discretionary access control and the three primary types of DAC

Discretionary Access Control (DAC), as the word *discretionary* implies, means *somebody* determines who can access an asset. That *somebody* is the owner. *The defining characteristic of DAC is that access is given, based upon the owner's discretion* as also shown in Figure 5-13. That's considered a great security best practice, since owners are accountable for and are therefore in the best position to determine who should access those assets.

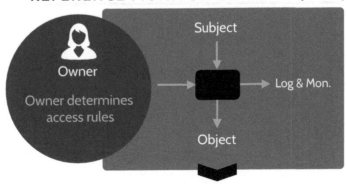

REFERENCE MONITOR CONCEPT (RMC)

Implementation of RMC = Security Kernel

Figure 5-13: **DAC Operation**

Within the realm of discretionary access control, three primary types of DAC exist:

1. **Rule-Based Access Control**: Access to an object by a given subject is based upon one or more rules, determined by the owner.

2. **Role-Based Access Control (RBAC)**: Access to an object by a given subject is based upon the role, or job function, and related authorizations needed to perform duties.

3. **Attribute-Based Access Control**: Access to an object by a subject is much more granularly controlled and based upon attributes, such as job function, type of device being used to access the object, time of day, classification of the asset, and so on.

> **Understand primary types of discretionary access control and their differences, why each might be used, and pros and cons of each**

Rule-Based Access Control

Rule-based access control is simply a set of rules assigned to users. Look at Table 5-18. The ruleset governs access to the numerous objects. As such, if a subject requires access to an object, a rule will be present to allow or deny that. For example, there's a rule in place to only allow Alice read access to Bob's directory and nothing more while she has both read and write access to her home directory.

User	Resource	Read	Write	Execute
Alice	24th floor printer			✓
Alice	Alice's home directory	✓	✓	
Alice	Bob's home directory	✓		
Alice	Historical finance data	✓		
Alice	Finance database	✓	✓	✓
Alice	CRM	✓		
Bob	24th floor printer			✓
Bob	Bob's home directory	✓	✓	
Bob	Marketing data	✓	✓	
Malory	Alice's home directory	✓		
Malory	Bob's home directory	✓		

Table 5-18: **Rule-Based Access Control**

Note that while rule-based access control offers much more granular control, it also requires much more administrative effort.

Role-Based Access (RBAC)

With role-based access control, users can be assigned to one or more roles and access is determined by a given role. The significant advantage gained by role-based access control is simplified and more manageable user and permissions administration. Instead of managing permissions at the user level, only permissions at the role level need to be considered, and then users with appropriate needs simply need to be assigned to the role or roles. Typically, RBAC roles will mirror the structure or organizational chart of an organization and, based upon this fact, the use of RBAC is often considered a "best practice." For example, in an organization with five hundred people who provide call center services, access needs are likely the same for each person. The use of RBAC in this case can eliminate much redundant and administrative overhead. Contrarily, in a more complex environment, where many more roles and cross-functional needs exist, an organization could easily end up with more roles than users and therefore much more complex RBAC needs.

Figure 5-14 shows an RBAC operation example, but the primary point to take away from this is that RBAC provides the ability to assign privileges to users with minimal administrative overhead.

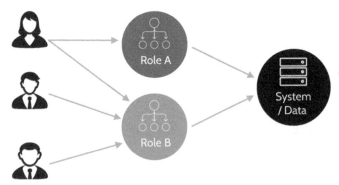

Figure 5-14: **RBAC Operation**

Implementing Full-RBAC across an entire organization is often very difficult and counterproductive. One of the main reasons to implement RBAC is to reduce access administration burden. When Full-RBAC is implemented across an entire organization for every system, it is common to end up with more roles than employees. Hence, Full-RBAC may increase the access administration burden.

This is one of the reasons most organizations implement Limited or Hybrid-RBAC, depicted in Figure 5-15.

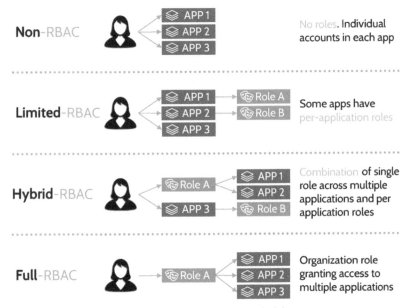

Figure 5-15: **Different RBAC Models**

Attribute/Context-Based Access Control

Attribute- or context-based access control is interesting and becoming quite prevalent. The premise behind the increased usage of attribute-based access control is the need to do a better job of authenticating user access with regards to the cloud, as most cloud-based applications are web applications. One of the defining characteristics of cloud computing is broad network access, which implies the ability to access cloud applications from anywhere with any type of device. If a company develops a web-based application and hosts it in the public cloud, is it protected by the corporate firewall and hidden inside the corporate network? No, it's on the public internet and potentially accessible by anybody. Because of this fact and because so many companies are moving to the cloud and hosting important applications there, the need for better authentication and authorization to those applications is imperative. ABAC's operation is shown in Figure 5-16, where a user needs to access a particular resource, and for that to happen, the authorization engine has to check the policy and match that against a variety of attributes that relate to the user and their environment.

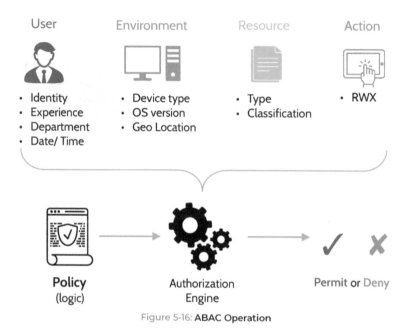

Figure 5-16: **ABAC Operation**

eXtensible Access Control Markup Language (XACML)

One of the tools that defines and enables attribute-based access control is a standard known as eXtensible Access Control Markup Language—XACML. This standard defines an attribute-based access control policy language, architecture, and processing model that allows attribute-based access to be implemented and utilized in a standardized manner.

Understand the purpose of XACML

Risk-Based Access Control

Risk-based access control looks at elements of a user connection, like the IP address, time of access request and more, to determine a risk profile associated with the request. Based upon the result, further authentication challenges may be presented to the user before access is granted.

5.4.2 Mandatory Access Control (MAC)

CORE **CONCEPTS**

- Mandatory Access Control is very rare to see in use, and only typically used in government organizations, where confidentiality is often of primary importance.

- Mandatory Access Control requires every asset in an organization to have a classification and every user to be assigned a clearance level.

- A Mandatory Access Control system determines access based upon clearance level of the subject and classification, or sensitivity, of the object.

The key distinguishing feature of MAC (depicted in Figure 5-17) is that access is determined by a system, and most MAC systems are designed to protect confidentiality related to assets and information. The system itself makes access control decisions, based upon the classification of the objects being accessed and the clearance of the subject requesting access. In a MAC environment, every single object should be classified with a specific classification label, e.g., public, secret, top secret, and so on. Correspondingly,

> Understand defining characteristics of mandatory access control and where and why it is typically used

all users should have a security clearance that aligns with the classification system used for objects. Within this framework, access will then be granted or denied accordingly. For example, if a user with "Public" clearance attempts to access an object that is classified as "Secret," the system will deny the request. Note that MAC isn't often implemented in private companies because in a typical organization it's very rare to find employees with clearly defined levels of clearance and every asset with a clearly defined classification level. This explains why one or a combination of the previously discussed access control systems is used. However, in the context of government (specifically the military), MAC might be easily used. Even here, though, it's not a given.

REFERENCE MONITOR CONCEPT (RMC)

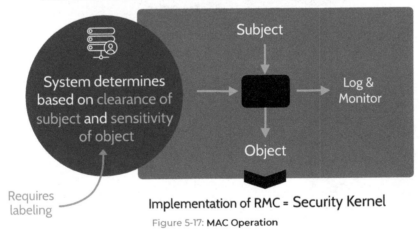

Figure 5-17: **MAC Operation**

5.4.3 Non-discretionary Access Control

CORE CONCEPTS

- Non-discretionary Access Control means that somebody other than the asset owner determines who gets access.
- Non-discretionary Access Control should be avoided, if possible.

Contrary to Discretionary Access Control (DAC) is **Non-discretionary Access Control** (depicted in Figure 5-18). If DAC means the owner decides who can access an asset, Non-discretionary Access Control means someone *other* than the owner determines access. Although this isn't a security best practice, it's an existing working practice in many companies and leads to someone in the IT department, for example, creating a user account and granting access to numerous assets, whether access is needed or not. One reason is that an identified owner does not exist for a system; therefore, Discretionary Access Control can never be exercised. Additionally, situations may exist where the owner (accountable) delegates responsibility of access control to areas like IT, but then the owner doesn't offer input with regards to who should be given access. Rather, that's left up to the IT folks and therefore is another example of Non-discretionary Access Control being exercised.

REFERENCE MONITOR CONCEPT (RMC)

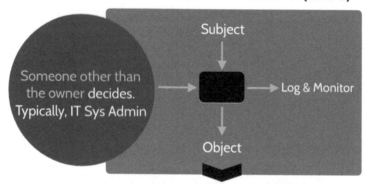

Someone other than the owner decides. Typically, IT Sys Admin

Subject

Log & Monitor

Object

Implementation of RMC = Security Kernel

Figure 5-18: **Non-discretionary Access Control**

5.5 Manage the identity and access provisioning life cycle

5.5.1 Vendor Access

CORE CONCEPTS

- Vendor identity and access provisioning for systems and data should be considered with the same or more care than employee identity and access provisioning.

- Vendor provisioning might also include a security review component that includes a deeper review of the vendor or inspection of a vendor's facilities, systems, and other relationships.

With any organization, certain functions and critical relationships require vendor access to some systems and data. Outsourced functions and relationships can vary and might include things like IT services, marketing, finance and accounting, and supply chain suppliers, to name a few. As a result, third-party vendor relationships can represent significant risk to an organization, and identity and access provisioning for these relationships should be considered with as much or more care as identity and access provisioning for employees. In addition to normal provisioning, review and revocation activities, vendor access provisioning might include a security review of the vendor or even an onsite inspection of the vendor's facilities and systems.

5.5.2 Identity Life Cycle

CORE CONCEPTS

- Identity Life Cycle is composed of three parts: provisioning, review, revocation.

- Provisioning = upon hire of new employee and when employee changes roles

- Review (also known as user access review) = should take place as often as necessary, and more frequently for higher privilege accounts

- Revocation = upon voluntary or involuntary termination

The Identity Life Cycle is simple in concept and refers to the creation or provisioning of user access, the periodic review of that access, and eventually the revocation of that access. The three steps of the Identity Life Cycle are depicted in Figure 5-19.

Understand the identity life cycle and what happens at each stage

Figure 5-19: **Identity Life Cycle**

Provisioning activities include things like background checks, confirming skills, and identity proofing, among other things.

Periodically, this access should be **reviewed** to ensure continued appropriate access. Assets and systems to which a user has access should be reviewed by the asset or system owner to determine if ongoing access is necessary or if access should be modified. Timeliness of access reviews is dependent on a few variables, the most important being as often as necessary, based upon the value of the asset or system in question. Different assets and systems have different values to an organization and different risk profiles. This fact ultimately drives the need for more frequent or less frequent access reviews. Additionally, different types of user and system accounts also drive the timing of access reviews. High value accounts—system/admin/root—should be reviewed much more frequently than lower value accounts.

Eventually, and when necessary, an account should be *revoked*, or deprovisioned. **Revocation** typically takes place when an employee leaves the organization, through voluntary or involuntary separation, but it can also take place when an employee changes roles. This is very important to note. Otherwise, if an employee changes roles, they may gain additional privileges and rights as well as maintain existing privileges and rights, which can lead to increase in actual appropriate access. So, sometimes it is appropriate to revoke access for an employee and provision again, based upon new needs as set forth by the appropriate asset and system owners.

5.5.3 User Access Review

CORE **CONCEPTS**

- Account access review is an ongoing process, regardless of the type of account (user, system, service).

- Account access review frequency should be based upon the value of resources and associated risks.

- Privileged accounts should be reviewed more frequently.

Why access reviews should be conducted

Once an account has been registered for a user, and the user is granted access to facilities, systems, and other resources, that doesn't mean that the access should remain forever. All user access should be reviewed on a periodic basis by the owner of the asset, because the owner is in the best position to conduct this review and confirm that continued user access is appropriate. Additionally, user access reviews can mitigate access or privilege creep.

How often should access reviews be performed?

The fact that user access should be reviewed at least annually raises additional questions. What about if a user changes role, leaves the company, or you're concerned about admin or "super user" roles? How often should reviews take place in these cases?

How often should access reviews be conducted?

In the case of a user changing roles, their access should be reviewed at the time of the change. New access should be granted, as needed, and any access that is not needed should be removed. Of course, access should always be reviewed and approved by the owner. When someone leaves the company (through voluntary or involuntary termination) that user's access should be reviewed, and in most cases, all access should be removed. In the case of administrative and "super user" accounts, because they grant broader and more powerful access, access might need to be reviewed more frequently than annually; perhaps these reviews should occur as often as weekly.

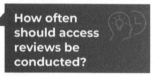

Which accounts should be reviewed most frequently?

In every case, the value of the resources and the associated risks should drive access review timing. As noted above, it might be fine to review some user access annually, while other reviews might need to take place more frequently.

Privilege Escalation

In addition to more frequent reviews of privileged accounts, a recommended security practice is for system administrators (users with admin, root, and similar privileges) to only use their privileged accounts when strictly necessary.

Privileged users should utilize two accounts. They should use a standard user account for regular business purposes, such as checking email, participating in meetings, and so on, and they should use a separate account with elevated privileges only when performing administrative tasks that require a higher level of access. A good example of this approach on Unix/Linux systems is the command sudo ("superuser do"). An administrator can use a standard user account when logged into a system and only run specific commands or programs that require elevated privileges with the sudo command.

This way, when an administrator is performing activities that are most likely to compromise their account, such as checking email, browsing the web, and so on, they are using their standard user account. The likelihood of their privileged account being compromised and used for malicious purposes is greatly reduced.

5.6 Implement authentication systems

5.6.1 Authentication Systems

CORE **CONCEPTS**

- **Authentication systems are used to prove or verify an identity or system assertion.**

- **Popular authentication systems include: OpenID Connect (OIDC), Open Authorization (OAuth), Security Assertion Markup Language (SAML), Kerberos, Remote Authentication Dial-In User Service (RADIUS) and Terminal Access Controller Access Control System Plus (TACACS+).**

As has been previously discussed, the implementation of authentication systems helps protect an organization, its users, and its critical assets from unauthorized access. At its core, authentication is the act of proving, or verifying, an identity or system assertion.

A number of authentication systems exist, and some of the more popular ones include:

- OpenID Connect (OIDC)/Open Authorization (OAuth)

- Security Assertion Markup Language (SAML)

- Kerberos

- Remote Authentication Dial-In User Service (RADIUS) and Terminal Access Controller Access Control System Plus (TACACS+)

RADIUS, TACACS+, SAML, and Kerberos were both discussed in this chapter and in Domain 3. OIDC and OAuth are briefly discussed below:

- **OpenID Connect (OIDC)/Open Authorization (OAuth)—OAuth** is an access delegation standard that target applications can use to provide client applications with secure delegated access over HTTPS. It authorizes devices, APIs, servers, and applications with access tokens rather than credentials. **OpenID Connect (OIDC)** is an identity layer built on top of the OAuth 2.0 framework. It allows third-party applications to verify the identity of the end user and to obtain basic user profile information. While OAuth 2.0 is about resource access and sharing, OIDC is about user authentication.

MINDMAP REVIEW **VIDEOS**

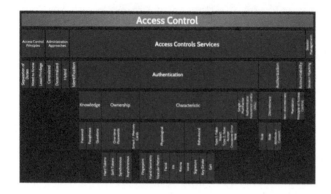

Access Control
dcgo.ca/CISSPmm5-1

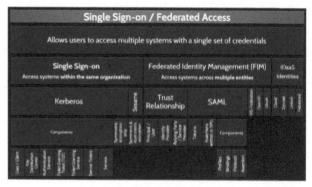

Single Sign-on/Federated Access
dcgo.ca/CISSPmm5-2

CISSP PRACTICE QUESTION APP

Download the Destination CISSP Practice Question app
for Domain 5 practice questions

dcgo.ca/PracQues

DOMAIN 6
Security Assessment & Testing

6.1 Design and validate assessment, test, and audit strategies

Purpose of Security Assessment and Testing

Domain 6 focuses on security assessment and testing of architectures, assets, and systems. Information covered in earlier domains underscored the importance of every control to address security from the perspective of the two pillars—functional and assurance—that should support every control. Security assessment and testing specifically focuses on the latter—providing assurance to stakeholders, how security is contributing to goals and objectives, and that the right level of security is built into any architecture that provides value to the organization. In other words, *the purpose of security assessment and testing is to ensure that security requirements/controls are defined, tested, and operating effectively*. Additionally, security assessment and testing apply to the development of new applications and systems as well as the ongoing operations, including end-of-life, related to assets.

Consider this question for a minute: How many architectures and systems do we interact with daily and simply take for granted they will work? Think about all the planes in the sky, traffic control infrastructure in a major city, computer systems, and mobile phones, to name a few examples. Though an imperfect measuring tool, the number of lines of computer code required to run and manage each of those systems can offer a glimpse as to their complexity, and some of these systems require millions or even billions of lines of code.

It is estimated that a modern operating system can contain something like fifty million lines of code. That's a massive number. Is there a chance that maybe a mistake or two exist in those fifty million lines of code? Yes, it's pretty much guaranteed that many mistakes, bugs, unknown exploits, and vulnerabilities may reside in fifty million lines of code. With each passing day, systems in use around the globe are becoming ever more complex. The more complex, the more opportunity and likelihood for errors to exist. Furthermore, not only are systems becoming more complex, but our dependence upon them is becoming more critical and pervasive, like planes using avionics systems with millions of lines of code. Most planes today can fly themselves, with very little manual intervention. However, air crashes still happen because of fatal errors. Obviously, these architectures are incredibly important, and it's imperative that they run well to ensure as much safety and order as possible. Rigorous testing and assessments must be done, and it's very important to understand that it's not just about the initial development of a system. Once deployed to production, a system should be monitored and tested consistently for a number of reasons, i.e., making sure regulatory requirements are being met. When updates to a system are made, it should be tested to ensure the updates did not break something or create vulnerabilities. Even when a system is retired, testing and assessment should be done to confirm that data has been migrated to a new system properly and has been defensibly destroyed on the old.

6.1.1 Validation and Verification

> **CORE CONCEPTS**
>
> - **Validation answers one fundamental question: Are we building the right product?**
> - **Verification follows validation and asks a related and equally important question: Are we building the product correctly?**

> **Understand validation & verification and the difference between the two**

Two very important terms related to testing are: *validation* and *verification*. Both terms underscore the necessity and importance of early and ongoing testing, not simply testing after a product has been built.

Validation is the process that begins prior to an application or product being built. Validation is concerned with answering one fundamental question: *Is the right product being built?* From the start, it's imperative that requirements are understood and documented correctly.

Verification follows validation and is the process that confirms an application or product is being built correctly. Like validation, verification answers another fundamental question: *Is the product being built correctly?* Domain 6 focuses a significant amount of attention on testing to ensure that an application or product is functioning properly, is secure, and is meeting business requirements. Testing can never offer 100 percent confidence that an application is working perfectly. However, verification testing can be used to develop a level of confidence, and the desired level is typically directly proportional to the organizational relevance and value of the application or system. Level of confidence is another way of saying "level of care" about how well the application or product is working. A high level of confidence would be desired regarding a plane's avionics systems but not about the workings of a company wiki.

> Understand when verification should be performed/stopped and what helps determine the stopping point

Included with verification are three terms that deserve further examination: *completeness, correctness, and consistency* (also known as the 3 Cs).

- Completeness means ensuring all the use cases of an application, based upon all defined requirements related to functionality, have been covered.

- Correctness refers to each "use" case representing what's supposed to be built.

- Consistency speaks to functionality being specified consistently in all areas.

These three words capture the essence and philosophy of application and system development.

Validation and verification are summarized in Table 6-1:

Validation	Verification
Are we building the **right product**?	Are we building the **product right**?
Develop a level of confidence that business requirements are clearly understood and have been validated with the business owner. Cannot build the right product if it is not clearly understood what the owner wants.	Develop a level of confidence that whatever is being built Is meeting all the defined requirements. The product is being built correctly based on the requirements defined during the validation stage.

Table 6-1: **Validation and Verification**

6.1.2 Effort to Invest in Testing

CORE CONCEPTS

- **The purpose of security assessment and testing is to provide assurance regarding the architecture, application, or system being assessed and tested.**

- **Assurance is provided through validation and verification.**

- **The effort to invest in testing should be proportionate to the value the application or system represents to the organization.**

- **Testing strategies include: internal, external, third party.**

- **The role of a security professional is to: identify risk and advise testing processes to ensure risks are appropriately evaluated.**

As with all things related to security in an organization, the time and effort invested in testing should be proportional to the value it represents to the organization. Value drives security, including the testing done to prove to stakeholders that security is contributing. Testing strategies flow from this value/security relationship.

How much testing is enough?

Testing Strategies

As noted earlier, testing strategies are used to provide assurance and can be considered from three broad contexts: *internal*, *external*, and *third party*. Each can be used alone or in combination, based on the type/level of assurance sought.

Internal testing (or assessments) are conducted by someone internal to the organization, in other words, by an employee.

External testing or assessments can be defined in two different ways, and both should be noted.

On one hand, a company that uses a certain application, for example, Microsoft Azure, might use a team of employees to look at Azure's hosting environment, which is external to the company. So, a company essentially audits or examines the environment of an external service provider.

On the other hand, imagine a company building an application using its own development team. Internal testing has been conducted, but the company also wants independent testing performed as a means of providing objective assurance that the application is well designed and working properly. To meet this need, the company hires a major consulting firm to come in and audit the application. This consulting firm is external to the company that is building the application.

Third-party testing, as the name suggests, means three parties are involved in the process: the customer, the vendor, and then perhaps a consulting or similar company. Third-party testing is very prevalent in the context of cloud computing. For example, imagine a customer is interested in cloud computing, and they engage Amazon to provide one or more services offered by Amazon Web Services (AWS). The customer, rightly so, wants to know if AWS is secure. To provide independent and more objective assurance about the security of their services, Amazon may engage a consulting firm to come in, test their environment and service offerings, and produce reports about their findings. Then, when a company asks Amazon about the security of their services, Amazon can point to the independently produced report to assure the customer. Thus, three parties—the consumer, the service provider, and the external auditor—make up third-party testing.

Testing strategies and implications of each

All three strategies are depicted in Table 6-2 and can be used in combination based on the type/level of assurance sought.

Internal Audit	External Audit	Third-party Audit
Testing conducted by somebody internal to the organization	Testing via either of two scenarios: - somebody internal to the organization examining an external service provider's controls, or - an organization asking somebody external from the company to come in and provide an unbiased examination of an application or system	Three parties are involved: customer, vendor, independent audit firm

Table 6-2: **Testing Strategies**

Role of Security Professional

As might make sense, based upon everything written to this point, testing should include all relevant stakeholders. However, the role of security professionals is to do three things:

- Identify risk

- Advise testing processes to ensure risks are appropriately evaluated

- Provide advice and support to stakeholders

The security team should not actually perform the testing alone; however, security should advise, provide assurance, monitor, support, and evaluate results.

> **Understand the role of a security professional**

6.2 Conduct security control testing

6.2.0 Testing Overview

CORE **CONCEPTS**

- Security control testing typically includes steps that align with the phases of the application and systems development process.
- Software testing includes several types of testing that build upon one another: unit testing, interface testing, integration testing, system testing.

Examples of Testing Performed

Figure 6-1 provides a high-level overview of some of the required software testing throughout the system life cycle, and Table 6-3 summarizes the testing performed at each phase. This is not an official framework and accordingly shouldn't be memorized. It is simply meant to provide an overview and highlight that testing is required during every stage of a system's life cycle from the start and throughout.

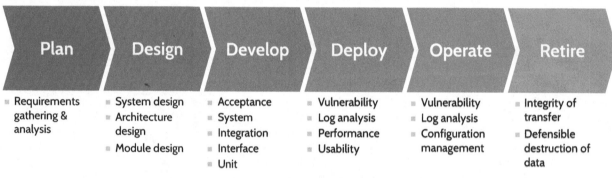

Plan	Design	Develop	Deploy	Operate	Retire
▪ Requirements gathering & analysis	▪ System design ▪ Architecture design ▪ Module design	▪ Acceptance ▪ System ▪ Integration ▪ Interface ▪ Unit	▪ Vulnerability ▪ Log analysis ▪ Performance ▪ Usability	▪ Vulnerability ▪ Log analysis ▪ Configuration management	▪ Integrity of transfer ▪ Defensible destruction of data

Figure 6-1: **Software Testing Phases**

Planning	Capture related requirements to a system before any design takes place and validate the requirements have been accurately captured.
Design	The security team can provide advice on what types of controls the system should have to protect fundamental security principles, like confidentiality, integrity, and availability. Test to confirm all required controls have been included in the system design, architecture design and module, and so on.
Develop	Numerous types of testing must be performed during the development stage to confirm all the required controls are being implemented correctly: unit testing, integration testing, system testing, acceptance testing, vulnerability assessments, and so on.
Deploy	Moving an application from a quality assurance/preproduction/testing environment to the actual production environment. Numerous types of testing must be performed during deployment: usability testing, performance testing, reviewing logs for errors and anomalies, vulnerability assessments, and so on.
Operate	Configuration management reviews can be performed to ensure the product is working as intended without its security being compromised. Vulnerability management and log analysis can continue being performed for that very purpose.
Retire	Testing and ensuring that data has been migrated into the new system in a secure manner in addition to safely disposing it from the old one.

Table 6-3: **Software Testing Phases**

Software Testing Overview

Most software development projects comprise multiple teams, with each team responsible for developing specific aspects of functionality that are then brought together as a complete software product. Software testing should be a comprehensive process that examines everything from the individual functional components to the integrated functional system, and the process is outlined in Table 6-4.

Unit Testing	Examines and tests **individual components** of an application. As specific aspects (units) of functionality are finished, they can be tested.
 **Interface Testing**	As more and more individual components are built and tested, interface testing can take place. Interfaces are standardized, defined ways that units connect and communicate with each other. Interface testing serves to **verify components connect** properly.
 **Integration Testing**	Integration testing focuses on testing **component groups** (groups of software units) together.
 **System Testing**	System testing tests the *integrated system* **(the whole system).**

Table 6-4: **Software Testing Stages**

6.2.1 Testing Techniques

CORE **CONCEPTS**

- Testing techniques are broken down broadly into two categories: manual and automated.

- Manual testing is performed by a person.

- Automated testing is performed by an automated tool.

- Static application security testing (SAST) looks at the underlying source code of an application while the application is not running; SAST is considered white box testing, because the code is visible.

- Dynamic application security testing (DAST) examines an application and system as the underlying code executes; DAST is considered black box testing, because the code is not visible.

- Fuzz testing is a form of dynamic testing and is premised upon chaos, to see how an application responds to complete randomness.

- Code review is considered from two perspectives: black box (zero knowledge about the code is available) and white box (full knowledge about the code is available).

- Test types include: positive (tests a system from a normal usage perspective), negative (tests a system from the perspective of normal errors), misuse (tests a system from the perspective of a malicious user or attacker); all three test types are valuable.

- Equivalence partitioning is testing, where specific input values are used to test from a grouping perspective (partitions of values and possible inputs).

- Boundary value analysis is testing from a bounds perspective (lower and upper bounds of groups or partitions).

Methods/Tools

When developing an application or other software, several testing techniques can and should be utilized, and they can be done via manual or automated means.

Manual testing means a person or team of people is performing the tests. They might be following a specific process, but they're actually sitting in front of a computer, looking at code, testing a form by entering input, and so on.

Automated testing means that test scripts and batch files are being automatically manipulated and executed by software. Thorough testing employs both approaches to produce a multitude of outcomes and achieve the best results.

Manual and automated testing are summarized in Table 6-5.

Manual Testing	Automated Testing
Done by a person—hands on keyboard	Done by an automated tool, like code scanning or vulnerability assessment software

Table 6-5: **Testing Methods/Tools**

Understand the key differences between SAST, DAST, and fuzz testing

Runtime

Runtime specifically refers to whether an application is running.

With **Static Application Security Testing (SAST)**, an application is not running, and it's the underlying source code that is being examined. Static testing is a form of white box testing, because the code is visible.

With **Dynamic Application Security Testing (DAST)** testing, an application is running, and the focus is on the application and system as the underlying code executes. As opposed to static testing, dynamic testing is a form of black box testing, because the code is not visible. The entire focus is the application itself and how it behaves, based upon inputs.

Fuzz testing is a form of dynamic testing. The entire premise behind fuzz testing is chaos. In other words, fuzz testing involves throwing randomness at an application to see how it responds and where it might "break." Fuzz testing is quite effective, because application developers and programmers tend to be very logical people, and the software they develop tends to reflect this fact. By testing from an illogical perspective—by throwing chaos at an application—issues not previously uncovered can be identified.

There are two major types of fuzz testing as defined in Table 6-6.

Mutation (dumb fuzzers)	Generation (intelligent fuzzers)
The input to an application is **randomly changed** by flipping bits or appending/replacing additional random input.	**New input** to an application is **generated from scratch** based on an understanding of the file format or protocol.
This is often referred to as **dumb fuzzing** as the fuzzer has no understanding of the input structure	This is often referred to as **smart / intelligent fuzzing** as the fuzzer must understand the input structure

Table 6-6: **Mutation and Generation Fuzzers**

The three major types noted are summarized in Table 6-7.

Static (SAST)	Dynamic (DAST)	Fuzz
▪ White box ▪ Examines code	▪ Black box (no access to code) ▪ Examines application itself	▪ Form of dynamic testing ▪ Premise is chaos

Table 6-7: **SAST, DAST, and Fuzz Testing**

Understand the difference between black box and white box testing

Code Review/Access to Source Code

Code review and access to source code can be considered from two perspectives when testing:

- No access to the source code exists (also known as black box testing)

- Access to the source code does exist (also known as white box testing)

Extrapolating further, the concepts defined above can be mixed and matched. For example, automated static white box testing means a tool is used to automatically examine the available source code, looking for common errors, undefined variables, and similar types of problems. Automatic dynamic black box testing, on the other hand, is like how vulnerability scanners operate. A vulnerability scanner does not have visibility or access to the underlying source code. Instead, it performs dynamic testing that seeks to identify common vulnerabilities and other issues with an application. Both types of testing provide value and can be mixed and matched as needed to provide comprehensive results.

> **Be able to differentiate between test types— positive, negative, and misuse**

Test Types

When a system is running, it's possible to test it as if a user was using it. Specifically, the system can be tested a few different ways—via positive testing, negative testing, or misuse testing. These testing types are explained in Table 6-8.

Positive Testing	Focuses on the response of a system, based upon normal usage and expectations. For example, under normal circumstances, if a login page requires a username and password, and the correct username and password are provided, the system should complete the log-in process. This is positive testing, checking if the system is working as expected and designed.
Negative Testing	Focuses on the response of a system when normal errors are introduced. Using the example above, if the incorrect username or password are entered, the system shouldn't crash. It simply should not log the subject in and should instead issue some type of error indicating an incorrect username or password was entered. This is normal, expected behavior, under negative testing.
Misuse Testing	Unlike positive and negative testing, misuse testing is a bit more devious. With this type of testing, the perspective of someone trying to break or attack the system is applied. If a system can be tested and understood from the standpoint of normal expected usage (when everything is done correctly, or when errors are made), it should also be understood from the viewpoint of somebody who wants to break into or otherwise abuse the system in order to gain further access.

Table 6-8: **Positive, Negative, and Misuse Testing**

> **Understand the difference between equivalence partitioning and boundary value analysis**

Equivalence Partitioning and Boundary Value Analysis

These two testing techniques are designed to make testing **more efficient**.

Let's use the following example, which is also depicted in Figure 6-2. An application provides a user with a password input box, which instructs them to enter a password between eight and sixteen characters. An inefficient way to test would be to test passwords of a set number of characters one by one:

- A password of 0 characters should be **rejected**
- 1 character should be rejected
- 2, 3, 4, 5, 6 and 7 characters should all be rejected
- 8 characters should be **accepted**
- 9, 10, 11, 12, 13, 14, 15 and 16 characters should all be accepted
- And 17 characters and above should be **rejected**

To test this password input box more efficiently, boundary value analysis could be used. **Boundary value analysis** requires first identifying where there are changes in behavior—these are called boundaries. In the given example, there is a change in behavior between 7- and 8-character lengths—7 should be rejected, and 8 should be accepted. There is a second boundary between 16- and 17- character lengths—16 should be accepted and 17 should be rejected. Once the boundaries have been identified, **testing can be focused on either side of the boundaries**, as this is where there are most likely to be bugs.

Equivalence partitioning starts with the same first step of boundary value analysis—identifying the boundaries, and then goes a step further to identify partitions. Partitions are **groups of inputs that exhibit the same behavior.** Based on the example, there are three partitions:

1. Partition I: Password consisting of zero to seven characters (all rejected)
2. Partition II: Password consisting of eight to sixteen characters (all accepted)
3. Partition III: Password consisting of seventeen or more characters (all rejected)

Once the partitions have been identified, some testing can be performed within each partition.

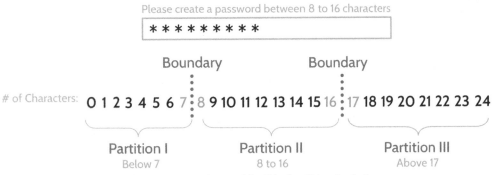

Figure 6-2: **Boundary and Partitioning Value Analysis**

A summary of equivalence partitioning and boundary value Analysis can be seen in Table 6-9, while Figure 6-3 contains some testing examples to demonstrate different types of testing just discussed.

Equivalence partitioning	Inputs are divided (partitioned) into **groups that exhibit the same behavior** with test cases covering each partition.
Boundary value analysis	**Focus on testing data at the boundaries** with test cases covering extreme ends of the input values.

Table 6-9: **Equivalence Partitioning and Boundary Value Analysis**

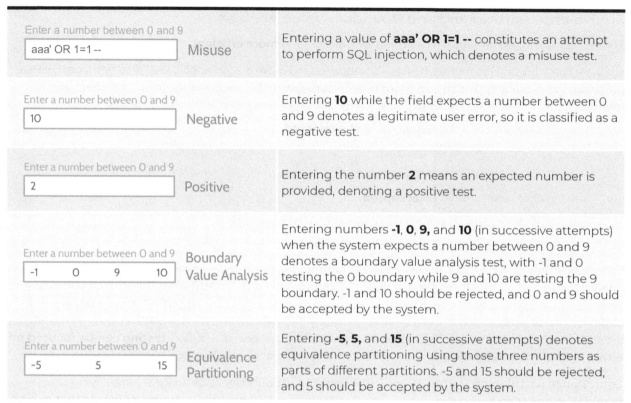

Figure 6-3: **Testing Examples**

Table 6-10 summarizes a couple of additional types of testing that can be performed in specific scenarios

Decision Table Analysis	Different **input combinations** and their corresponding system behavior/output are captured in a table (useful for complex software testing and requirements management).
State-Based Analysis	A set of **abstract states** that a unit of software can take are defined, and then tests compare its actual state to the expected state (useful for testing GUIs and communications protocols).

Table 6-10: **Decision Table and State-based Analysis**

Test Coverage Analysis

Test coverage analysis or simply "coverage analysis" refers to the relationship between the amount of source code in a given application and the percentage of code that has been covered by the completed tests. Test coverage is a simple mathematical formula: amount of code covered/total amount of code in application = test coverage percent. To illustrate using a simple example, if an application contains one hundred lines of code and fifty lines have been tested, the test coverage would be calculated as follows: amount of code covered/total amount of code in application = 50/100 or 50 percent.

6.2.2 **Vulnerability Assessment and Penetration Testing**

> CORE **CONCEPTS**
>
> - **Vulnerability testing techniques tend to be automated and can be performed in minutes, hours, or a few days; penetration testing techniques tend to be manual and can take several days, depending on the complexity involved.**
>
> - **Testing stages include: reconnaissance, enumeration, vulnerability analysis, exploitation, reporting.**
>
> - **Testing perspectives include: internal (inside a corporate network) and external (outside a corporate network).**
>
> - **Testing approaches include: blind (tester knows little to nothing about the target) and double-blind (tester knows little to nothing about the target and internal security teams do not know the test is coming).**
>
> - **Testing knowledge includes: zero, or black box (similar to blind approach, where tester knows nothing about a target), partial, or gray box (tester has some information about a target), full, or white box (tester has significant knowledge about a target).**

Purpose of Vulnerability Assessment

Vulnerability assessments and penetration testing (better known as pen testing) are important topics when discussing vulnerabilities and threats, and this points back to the more general topic of risk analysis. As a quick review, a vulnerability can be defined as *a weakness that exists in a system*, while a vulnerability assessment is an attempt to identify vulnerabilities in a system.

> **What is the purpose of vulnerability assessment?**

With any risk analysis, it is important to first know what assets exist. Next, the threats these assets face must be identified, which can happen through threat modeling. Two well-known and often-used threat modeling methodologies are STRIDE (Spoofing, Tampering, Repudiation, Information disclosure, Denial-of-Service, Elevation of privilege) and PASTA (Process for Attack Simulation and Threat Analysis). Finally, to understand the full breadth of risk that exists, vulnerabilities must also be identified.

> **Understand the difference between vulnerability assessment and penetration testing**

Vulnerability analysis helps in this regard, and two primary methods are used to identify vulnerabilities: vulnerability assessment and pen testing.

Vulnerability Assessment versus Penetration Test

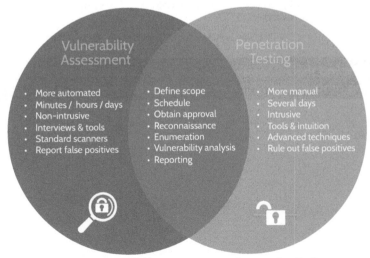

Figure 6-4: **Vulnerability Assessment vs. Penetration Testing**

Figure 6-4 shows a comparison between vulnerability assessment and penetration testing.

Both processes start the same way, as they each seek to identify potential vulnerabilities. However, with a **vulnerability assessment**, once vulnerabilities are noted, no further action is taken apart from a report of findings being produced. A **penetration test** goes a very important step further: after the identification of vulnerabilities, an attempt is made to exploit each vulnerability (breach attack simulations).

Various common characteristics exist between vulnerability assessments and penetration tests. A scope of what is being examined needs to be defined. Furthermore, an activity schedule needs to be set. In either case, if activity takes place without prior knowledge of the owners of the systems or network, alerts may unnecessarily be triggered, and a response set in motion. In other words, with either a vulnerability assessment or pen test, business impact can be a possible result (especially with a pen test). There is not an insignificant chance that production systems can be negatively impacted (e.g., knocked offline) because of these tests. Thus, a very clearly defined scope, schedule, and approval of activity must be in place.

However, some core differences between vulnerability analysis and penetration also exist.

For one, vulnerability analysis tends to be more automated. Tools like Nessus, Qualys, and InsightVM can be run and automatically gather significant information about vulnerabilities in a system or network. Pen tests, on the other hand, tend to be more manually driven, although pen testers will often use automated scanners. With a pen test, manual attempts to exploit vulnerabilities and breach a system are made. The quality of results is often directly proportional to the skill level and experience of the pen tester.

Additionally, whereas a vulnerability assessment can be performed quickly (minutes, hours, or a handful of days usually), a pen test can take significantly longer (commonly several days), depending upon the complexity of the identified vulnerabilities and targets being exploited. Finally, it's worth noting that during a pen test, confidential or sensitive information might be accessed or identified. Along with the likelihood that a pen test could cause impact, this fact further underscores the need for approval and perhaps even something like an NDA being in place before taking any type of assessment or action against a network.

When performing a vulnerability assessment or a penetration test, a series of steps are followed, which are shown in Figure 6-5.

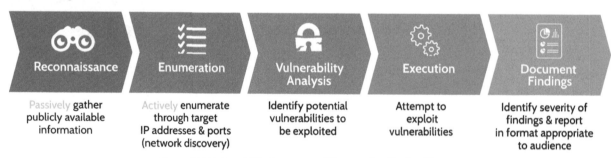

Figure 6-5: **Vulnerability Assessment/Penetration Testing Phases**

Understand the vulnerability assessment and penetration testing process and which key step differentiates the two

1. **Reconnaissance:** Involves gathering publicly available data via activities like Domain Name System (DNS) and WHOIS queries, browsing social media sites like LinkedIn, browsing job listings on sites like Indeed or forum sites like Google Groups, where sensitive company information might be inadvertently posted by somebody looking for help with an issue. With just a small amount of effort, a large amount of publicly available information about a company can be gleaned, and the company won't know that this information is being sought nor that it is being compiled. Thus, *reconnaissance is considered a* **passive activity** because the target doesn't know any activity is taking place or can't detect that this information is being gathered, as there's no direct interaction between the tester and target.

2. **Enumeration:** Unlike reconnaissance, where information is passively gathered, *enumeration is considered an* **active activity** because the target can detect the scans. Typically, items enumerated are IP addresses, ports, hostnames, and user accounts. If reconnaissance indicates that an organization has control of a certain IP range, enumeration will involve identifying which IP addresses and ports specifically are being used and potentially open. Ports equate to services, and 65,536 TCP and UDP ports exist (0–65,535) and can be enumerated. If a port is open, this means a service is running. For example, if port 80 is open, there's likely a web server running, assuming default ports are being used. Enumeration focuses on identifying a system and services behind a given IP address. Knowing this information can point to potential vulnerabilities specific to the system. A web server will be vulnerable to certain things that don't apply to a database or other type of server. Enumeration helps determine and narrow down this information. In addition, enumeration focuses on identifying hostnames and active user accounts on the various targets, which can be leveraged for access later.

3. **Vulnerability analysis:** This phase follows enumeration and helps determine which vulnerabilities exist within a target network or machine. However, this stage also represents a fork in the road where vulnerability and penetration tests are concerned. If a vulnerability test is being performed, attempts to exploit are not conducted, and the next step is documentation of findings and compilation into a report.

4. **Execution/Exploitation:** *If a penetration test is being performed*, an attempt will be made to exploit the identified vulnerabilities and therefore confirm, definitively, if the vulnerability can be exploited and is a true-positive. The execution step is only performed as part of a Penetration Test

5. **Document findings/Reporting:** This is where it all comes together, regardless of whether this is a vulnerability assessment or a penetration test. The tester will use a report to compile all their findings and provide a detailed record of all the techniques tested, which worked, and which didn't, associated tools, identified vulnerabilities, and most importantly mitigation steps required to be taken by the organization. Some vulnerabilities might require immediate attention, while others can be considered informational and less serious. It's important to clearly define and prioritize these vulnerabilities, so proper attention can be given to the most critical vulnerabilities first. Additionally, another important facet of documentation is trying to eliminate and remove as many false-positives as possible. Otherwise, a vulnerability report that should be twenty pages in length is more likely to be two hundred pages, and the critical data is buried in a sea of otherwise non-essential information. As much as anything, compiling findings in a clear, concise, and relevant manner are as or more important than the efforts that preceded the documentation process.

Testing Techniques

Vulnerability assessments and penetration testing can be quite nuanced, and several variables come into play with each. These variables include: perspective, approach, and knowledge.

Perspective

Perspective refers to the perspective from which the assessment or test is being performed. Is the assessment or test coming from an internal (inside the corporate network) or from an external (out on the internet) perspective? Table 6-11 explains the difference between internal and external testing.

Understand testing technique perspectives, approaches, and knowledge types

Internal Testing	External Testing
The test is being performed **from inside the corporate network**. This is important because threats can originate from inside a network (like a disgruntled employee or attacker already inside the network), and an internal test can help pinpoint exactly what an insider threat can access or what may have already been compromised.	Testing **from an external perspective**, where threats from outside the network can be considered and tested. Note that an outsider may need to circumvent multiple layers of defences (defense in depth) in order to access a resource which might be easily (or even directly) accessible if they were positioned internal to the network.

Table 6-11: **Internal vs. External Testing**

Approach

In addition to testing from an internal or external perspective, testing can be approached differently. One approach is known as blind and the other as double-blind. Table 6-12 explains the difference between blind and double-blind testing.

Blind Testing	Double-Blind Testing
The **assessor is given little to no information** about the target being tested. It might simply be the name of the company or an IP address provided; otherwise, the assessor is blind to network details and must use reconnaissance and enumeration techniques to gain more visibility about the target. With a blind approach, members of the target company's IT and Security Operations teams will likely know that some type of test is coming and can be better prepared to respond to alerts.	A double-blind approach goes one step further. In addition to the accessor being **given little to no information** about the target company, the target company's IT and **Security Operations teams will not know of any upcoming tests**. This type of approach tests the assessor's ability to identify vulnerabilities and other weaknesses as well as the target's internal team ability to respond. In this case, and to prevent the notion that hacking or anything illegal is taking place, usually only senior management will be aware of upcoming tests, because they commissioned the double-blind test.

Table 6-12: **Blind vs. Double-Blind Approach**

Knowledge

Knowledge pertains to how much insight or information an assessor has about a target. Table 6-13 explains the difference between zero, partial, and full knowledge testing.

Zero Knowledge (black box)	Partial Knowledge (gray box)	Full Knowledge (white box)
The assessor has **zero knowledge**—same as the blind approach noted above.	The assessor is given **some information** about the target network but not the full set that a white box test would have. It lies somewhere in between a white and black box test.	The assessor is given **full knowledge** (including items like IP addresses/range, network diagrams, information about key systems, and perhaps even password policies).

Table 6-13: **Zero, Partial, and Full Knowledge**

6.2.3 Vulnerability Management

CORE **CONCEPTS**

- **Vulnerability management is the cyclical process of identifying, classifying, prioritizing, and mitigating vulnerabilities**

Vulnerability management is a critical element of the risk management process that aids with the determination and implementation of appropriate controls related to identified vulnerabilities. At its core, vulnerability management is the ongoing process of identifying vulnerabilities, understanding the potential organizational impact as part of risk analysis, and ensuring that vulnerabilities are mitigated.

The steps of vulnerability management

At a high level, an effective vulnerability management process should include the following steps noted below.

- An understanding of all assets in an organization, which requires an accurate **asset inventory.**
- Identifying the **value of each asset** in the inventory, which requires:
    - A data/asset classification and categorization structure.
    - Identified owner for each asset.
    - Assigned classification and categorization for each asset.
- Identifying the **vulnerabilities for each asset** and remediation of identified vulnerabilities via patching, updating, and other means necessary to eliminate the vulnerabilities or reduce their risk (all remediation activities should be done as part of a patch or remediation management process, which is part of change management).
- **Ongoing review and assessment** of all steps to ensure the asset inventory is kept up to date, and new vulnerabilities are identified and remediated.

Always remember that vulnerability management is a cyclical and ongoing process, because organizational assets are constantly being added and removed and new vulnerabilities are constantly being identified.

6.2.4 Vulnerability Scanning

CORE **CONCEPTS**

- Automated vulnerability scanning can help identify vulnerabilities from an organizational perspective as well as from the perspective of an attacker.

- Two primary types of vulnerability scans: credentialed/authenticated scans and uncredentialed/unauthenticated scans.

- Banner grabbing is a process used to identify a system's operating system, applications, and versions.

- Fingerprinting works to identify the unique characteristics of a system through examination of how packets and other system-level information is formed.

- Interpretation and understanding of scan results is often achieved with the help of two tools: CVE and CVSS.

- CVE, also known as Common Vulnerability & Exposures dictionary, is "a list of records—each containing an identification number, a description, and at least one public reference—for publicly known cybersecurity vulnerabilities."

- CVSS, known as Common Vulnerability Scoring System, reflects a method to characterize a vulnerability through a scoring system considering various characteristics.

- Two types of alerts: false-positives and false-negatives.

- False-positives: the system claims a vulnerability exists, but there is none.

- False-negatives: the system says everything is fine, but a vulnerability exists; false-negatives are bad.

Automated Vulnerability Scanners

Most vulnerability scans are performed using automated tools, like Nessus, Qualys, OpenVAS, InsightVM, or Retina. These tools can scan entire networks or individual machines, and even specific applications for *known* vulnerabilities. They can also perform two significantly different types of scans: credentialed or non-credentialed scans.

> **Understand the different ways automated vulnerability scanning can be used and implications of each approach**

When run as a credentialed scan, the vulnerability scanner is given a username and password to log into the system it is scanning. Being able to authenticate allows Nessus to scan at a much deeper level and report more detailed information as a result. Additionally, credentialed scans often help eliminate false-positives (where the system claims a vulnerability exists but there is none), because specific configuration settings and similar details can be considered. Finally, credentialed scans can help ensure that all systems are configured correctly relative to baseline configuration for a given system. Variances can easily be noted and addressed.

Non-credentialed scanning means the vulnerability scanner is *not* given the ability to login and connect to the network, system, or application being scanned. Used in this manner, the tool will help identify especially glaring vulnerabilities and weaknesses but without being able to perform deep scanning (due to the lack of credentials). False-positives may be identified in a larger volume, and they will need to be addressed with the appropriate teams. Both types of scans should be used, as each serves specific purposes that when combined can prove very insightful and useful.

Credentialed versus uncredentialed scanning is summarized in Table 6-14.

Credentialed/Authenticated	Uncredentialed/Unauthenticated
■ Automated scanning tool given username/password in order to authenticate to the system being scanned ■ Helps prevent false-positives	■ Scanning tool is used from perspective of a hacker ■ May lead to false-positives

Table 6-14: **Credentialed vs. Uncredentialed Scanning**

An important thing to note is that a vulnerability scanner can only identify *known* vulnerabilities. These tools depend upon up-to-date catalogs or databases of all known vulnerabilities in order to identify them in the systems being scanned. As one might imagine, these catalogs and databases are continuously evolving and in constant need of updating. When Nessus scans a system, it compares details about the system with known vulnerabilities about it in the database. If a vulnerability is not known and therefore not in the database, the tool will report nothing.

Banner Grabbing and OS Fingerprinting

An important consideration when assessing a computer system is knowing exactly what operating system and version of the software is running. Is it a Linux system, or Windows 7, or Windows 10, and, if Windows 10, exactly what build of the OS? Knowing the operating system and exact version can help identify specific vulnerabilities. Vulnerabilities that apply to one operating system and version likely differ from vulnerabilities that apply to other operating systems and versions.

Banner grabbing and fingerprinting are methods whereby active or passive techniques are used to **identify** *a system's specific operating system, applications, and associated versions.*

The more information that can be gained about a system, the easier it is to protect it or, conversely, attack it. **Banner grabbing** helps identify software and versions, while **fingerprinting** looks a bit more specifically at the way a packet is formed and similar attributes to identify the unique characteristics of a system—similar to the ridges of a person's fingerprint that make it unique.

Interpreting and Understanding Results

Closely coupled with identifying and reporting results from activities like vulnerability scanning, banner grabbing, and fingerprinting is identifying the severity and exact nature of the results. This is done using two tools: CVE and CVSS, which are explained in Table 6-15.

> **Understand the difference between CVE and CVSS and how they are used together to evaluate vulnerabilities**

 **CVE (Common Vulnerability & Exposures) Dictionary**	CVE, also known as Common Vulnerability and Exposures directory, is a list of security flaws and vulnerabilities that are publicly disclosed for awareness and risk mitigation. Security and technology-related firms around the world keep an eye out for vulnerabilities in their products, services, and elsewhere. Whenever a new vulnerability is discovered, the company that made the discovery typically tends to publicize it and give the vulnerability a unique name. This can be challenging, because another company may identify the same vulnerability using a different tool set, and thus—on the surface—the same vulnerability may be identified using different names. The CVE mitigates this duplication by serving as a clearinghouse to **ensure that each vulnerability is only identified and recorded one time**. Through the use of a standardized and unique identification number as well as description for each vulnerability, companies around the world can be on the same page.
CVSS (Common Vulnerability Scoring System)	CVSS, known as Common Vulnerability Scoring System, is a framework that uses common vulnerability metrics and characteristics to provide an average **score of how severe a vulnerability is**. It assigns a number between 0 and 10 to any vulnerability; the higher the number, the more severe and critical the vulnerability. When a company identifies a new vulnerability, a scoring methodology will be followed to determine a score and then reported for inclusion in the CVSS database.

Table 6-15: **CVE vs. CVSS**

When a vulnerability scanner is used to run a scan, a detailed report of findings will be generated. For each identified vulnerability, CVE and CVSS information will be included—the CVE identifying the vulnerability, and the CVSS scoring the severity of the vulnerability.

False-Positives and False-Negatives

With any type of monitoring system, two types of alerts often show up. One type, a false-positive, indicates a vulnerability exists, but in fact there is no vulnerability. The other type, a false-negative, indicates everything is fine, but in fact a vulnerability is lurking. While false-positives can create a lot of "noise" and administrative overhead, false-negatives can potentially lead to serious harm and damage. Of the two, false-negatives are much worse, as they don't allow us to identify specific vulnerabilities within the network.

False-positives versus false-negatives are summarized in Table 6-16.

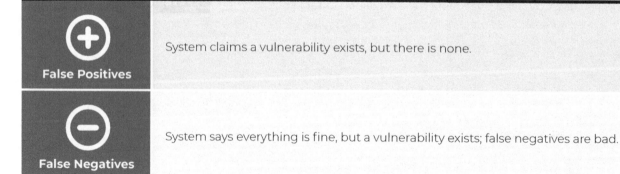

False Positives	System claims a vulnerability exists, but there is none.
False Negatives	System says everything is fine, but a vulnerability exists; false negatives are bad.

Table 6-16: **Possible Alert Statuses**

6.2.5 Log Review and Analysis

Understand the importance of timely log review and analysis

Review and analysis of log files is a best practice and can help an organization know if systems deployed in production are working properly. This said, as most systems can generate significant amounts of logged data, it's important that the points noted in Table 6-17 be considered.

 Log what is **relevant**	Most systems produce a wealth of information, but not all of it is relevant. Using risk management as a guide, risks to assets can point to ways to detect if a risk were to occur. This in turn points to what is relevant to log.
 **Review** the logs	Whether done via automated or manual means, logs must be reviewed. In today's typical environments, an automated system (like a SIEM tool) is going to best facilitate the review of hundreds, thousands, or even millions of logged events.
 Identify errors/ anomalies	As log review is undertaken, focus on identifying errors or anomalies that may indicate attacks or suspicious activities. Examples include: • **Errors:** Unexpected errors that might indicate a system is not working properly. • **Modification:** Modification to a system, especially if unauthorized. This is usually a significant red flag and may indicate a breach. • **Breach:** Actual penetration of a system or network that may lead to significant damage—monetary, reputation, or worse.

Table 6-17: **Log Review and Analysis**

Log Event Time

Ensuring consistent time stamps of log entries is very important. If an organization has deployed multiple servers and other network devices—like switches and firewalls—and each device is generating events that are logged, it's critical that the system time, and therefore the event log time, for each device is the same. Otherwise, if a breach occurs, for example, trying to correlate activities as an attacker moves through a network becomes extremely difficult. Consistent time stamps mean all system and device clocks are set to the exact same time, and this is done by use of **Network Time Protocol (NTP)**. With most networks, at least one network device (and usually two or more, for purposes of redundancy) is synchronized with a publicly available nuclear clock managed by a government agency, like NIST. Then all other network devices are synchronized with the one device, therefore ensuring consistent time stamps across a network.

Log Data Generation

As already noted, log data is generated by virtually every system operating in an organization. Logging and monitoring processes go deeper and include:

- Generation
- Transmission
- Collection
- Normalization
- Analysis
- Retention
- Disposal

These topics will be covered in more detail in Domain 7.

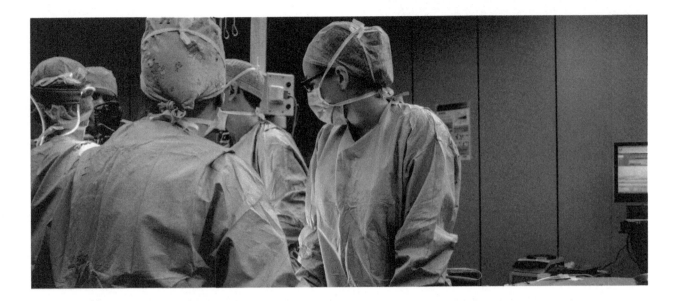

6.2.6 **Limiting Log Sizes**

CORE **CONCEPTS**

- **Log file management is important.**

- **Two log file management methods are used: circular overwrite and clipping levels.**

- **Circular overwrite limits the maximum size of a log file by overwriting entries, starting from the earliest.**

- **Clipping levels focus on when to log a given event, based upon threshold settings, and log file sizes are limited as a result.**

Log file management in any organization is important, especially with regards to log file sizes, and two methods are often utilized for this purpose: *circular overwrite and clipping levels*. The purpose here to ensure that log files only contain relevant information and are not full of massive meaningless information.

> Understand the difference between circular overwrite and clipping levels and which could potentially provide more valuable information

The first method—**circular overwrite**—works as the name suggests. For example, if the log file size is set to 100 MB or perhaps ten thousand logged events, enabling circular overwrite means that once the log file reaches the maximum size or length, log entries start being overwritten, from the earliest to the most recent. Thus, the maximum file size or number of entries will never be exceeded. If disk or memory space is limited, circular overwrite can be very useful and potentially prevent a disk from filling up or the system from crashing.

The other method—**clipping levels**—is a bit more interesting and potentially more informative. Rather than logging every bit of activity, clipping levels focus on *when* to begin logging. For example, logging every failed login attempt due to a wrong password makes no sense, as people mistype passwords all the time. However, what if the wrong password is typed fifty times, or twenty-five times, or even fifteen times? This could indicate a system-related problem or password cracking attempt. This is where clipping levels can be effectively used. A threshold can be set to only allow logging of any activity once that threshold is met. So, clipping levels is another way to limit log file sizes and to narrow down the focus of logging to the most pertinent and meaningful details. Unlike circular logging, though, clipping levels do not actually delete data. So, if an organization is interested in identifying something like security breaches, using clipping levels is a better approach, because relevant information can be logged and preserved. If circular logging is used, breach-related log entries might be overwritten and deleted due to file size or number of entries limitation.

6.2.7 Operational Testing—Synthetic Transactions and RUM

CORE **CONCEPTS**

- Operational testing occurs while a system is operating.
- Operational testing techniques include: Real User Monitoring and Synthetic Performance Monitoring.
- Real User Monitoring (RUM) monitors user interactions and activity with a website or application.
- Synthetic performance monitoring examines functionality as well as functionality and performance under load.

Operational testing is performed when a system is in operation. Within the context of operational testing, two testing techniques are often employed.

- **Real User Monitoring** is a passive monitoring technique that monitors user interactions and activity with a website or application. Log files are often examined in real-time, and performance measures might also be fed from the website or application into a Real User Monitoring tool for more detailed analysis.

- **Synthetic Performance Monitoring** is a bit more complicated and more interesting. The word synthetic can also be referred to as fake, phony, or counterfeit, and so "synthetic performance monitoring" means making up transactions and subjecting them to an architecture or system to see how it reacts. Let's look at an example to illustrate. Imagine a bank that operates an online banking system. Bank customers can log in to the system, check account balances, pay bills, transfer funds, and perform other related actions. The online banking system provides a lot of functionality, and to best serve customers it's important that this functionality be available whenever a customer desires to use it. Thus, ongoing testing of the system's functionality is important. Testing can be done manually, but this can be a slow and painful process, and it might miss some tests. A better solution is using automation. Test scripts for each type of functionality can be created and then run at any time. This is what synthetic performance monitoring describes.

Along with these functional tests, synthetic performance monitoring can also test functionality and performance under load. What happens if thousands of the tests noted above were conducted simultaneously? Of course, this would indicate how well the system can handle load and speaks to the performance side of things. So, synthetic performance monitoring considers the functional and performance aspects of a system.

For sake of accuracy, the best environment to perform synthetic testing in is production. However, prior to testing in production, significant QA and related testing must be done in a test environment. Cyber Monday, Black Friday, and similar online events place enormous loads on retail e-commerce environments, and retail organizations will often perform major functionality and load tests using their production environment prior to these big events.

Real user monitoring and synthetic performance monitoring are summarized in Table 6-18.

Real User Monitoring	Synthetic Performance Monitoring
Monitoring user transactions in real time for usage, performance, and errors	**Running scripted transactions** to monitor functionality, availability, and response times

Table 6-18: **Real User Monitoring and Synthetic Performance Monitoring**

6.2.8 **Regression Testing**

> **CORE CONCEPTS**
>
> - **Regression testing is the process of verifying that previously tested and functional software still works after updates have been made.**
> - **Regression testing should be performed after enhancements have been made or after patches to address vulnerabilities or problems have been issued.**
> - **Results of regression testing should be captured and communicated in a manner that is specific and relevant to the party reading the results—this is done using "metrics that matter."**

Regression testing is the process of verifying that previously tested and functional software still works after updates have been made. Updates can be in the form of enhancements or similar changes, or in the form of patches to address vulnerabilities or problems. Regression testing is used to verify that the software still works and that nothing else is broken.

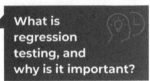

Additionally, regression testing of a complex application can take time and might involve a significant number of tests. Once this testing is complete, the results need to be compiled and reported. If thousands of tests have been run, is it likely that the CEO is going to be interested in hearing or reading about all the details? No, of course not. The CEO is likely only going to be interested in a high-level summary report. However, the development team would likely be very interested in all the details contained in the results. This information could prove very useful.

As noted and coupled with things like regression testing and the related reporting of results, it's critical to consider who your audience is and what they need to see. This points to the need to build reports using "metrics that matter." For senior management, the report should include metrics that enable them to make informed decisions from an organizational perspective; for members of an application development team, the report should include metrics that include detailed information regarding the application and the development process. As such, the points below should be considered when creating these reports:

- Objective pass/fail decisions
- Include the right detail for the right audience
- Metrics that matter

6.2.9 **Compliance Checks**

With everything noted above about security control testing in mind, it's imperative that compliance checking be an integral and ongoing part of the security control testing process. Through review and analysis of implemented controls and their output to confirm alignment with documented security requirements, compliance can be confirmed.

Furthermore, compliance checking can confirm that testing and controls are aligned with organizational policies, standards, procedures, and baselines, and it can effectively put a bow on all the activities described in this section.

6.3 Collect security process data (e.g., technical and administrative)

6.3.1 Key Risk and Performance Indicators

CORE **CONCEPTS**

- Key risk and performance indicators help inform goal setting, action planning, performance, and review, among other things.

- Key risk indicators (KRI) are forward-looking indicators and aid risk-related decision-making.

- Key performance indicators (KPI) are backward-looking indicators and look at historical data for purposes of evaluating if performance targets were achieved.

- SMART metrics are: Specific, Measurable, Achievable, Relevant, Timely.

The term *SMART metrics* has been around for some time and refers to data points that can be used for goal setting, taking action, and so on. More to the point, they should be specific, measurable, achievable, relevant, and timely.

- Specific—Result clearly stated and easy to understand?

- Measurable—Result can be measured/have the data?

- Achievable—Results can drive desired outcomes?

- Relevant—Aligned to business strategy?

- Timely—Results available when needed?

Oftentimes, SMART metrics are found in the context of employee performance and reviews. They can also be used in the context of security, and these metrics should be specific to the audience—what do they want to see, what do they need to know, etc.

In this context, two types of metrics are very important: KPIs—Key Performance Indicators and KRIs—Key Risk Indicators.

KPIs are backward looking. They look at historical data and indicate whether performance targets were achieved. KRIs are forward looking. They help with decision-making about things like risk exposure, operational risk, and so on.

How do you decide what to focus metrics on?

This said, not everything can be measured. Organizations make decisions on which metrics to focus on based on their business goals and objectives, denoting what's most important to the organization.

Example Areas for Metrics

- Account management
- Management review and approval
- Backup verification
- Training and awareness
- Disaster recovery (DR) and business continuity (BC)

A closer look at these areas would show account management metrics to likely focus on user activities that might take place in the context of a help desk on things like "mean time to resolution," "average response time," and "number of support emails" as they relate to service tickets. Account management metrics might also focus on details related to user accounts in a system, like last log-on time, status of account, and time of last password change.

> **Understand the difference between KPIs and KRIs and metrics that represent each type**

Management review and approval metrics typically focus on products and processes, including the review and approval process itself. Things like "time to resolve defects," "number of defects identified," "defect detection effectiveness," "average cost per defect," "deliverables," and "process used by reviewers" might be metrics included as part of management review and approval, along with many other metrics.

Backup verification refers to the process of verifying that backed up data is valid and accessible. This typically involves routine restores of subsets of data to confirm the availability and integrity of all information. It should also include a more thorough exercise from time to time that assumes a worst-case scenario, where significant amounts of data have been lost, that requires the restoration of that data from multiple sources. Related metrics might include "number of backups verified," "time between backup verification exercises," "number of verified files or total amount of data verified."

Training and awareness metrics examine things like "number of employees who completed training" as well as results from phishing-related exercises, like "number of times phished" and "phishing emails reported."

Finally, DR and BC metrics include things like Recovery Time Objective (RTO) and Recovery Point Objectives (RPO), and they might also include others, like "total plans that cover each critical process," "actual time required to restore a process," and "time between plan updates," to name a few examples.

A comparison between KPIs and KRIs can be found in Table 6-19.

Key Performance Indicators (KPIs)	Key Risk Indicators (KRIs)
- **Backward** looking metrics	- **Forward** looking metrics
- Metrics that indicate the **achievement of performance targets**	- Metrics that indicate the level of **exposure to operational risk**
- Provide insights about risk events that have **already affected the organization**	- Help to better monitor **potential future shifts in risk conditions or new emerging risks**

Table 6-19: **KPI vs. KRI**

6.4 Analyze test output and generate report

6.4.1 Test Output

CORE CONCEPTS

- Results of security assessments and testing should include steps related to: remediation, exception handling, and ethical disclosure.

As part of security assessments and testing, it is important to note what steps will be taken to address issues and vulnerabilities identified during the assessment and testing. It is equally important to note what steps might *not* be taken and why this is the case. Finally, as is becoming more the rule, it's important that newly discovered vulnerabilities be disclosed and shared with others. These activities are summarized in Table 6-20, and details from each activity should be incorporated into a report.

Remediation	Based upon assessments and testing, remediation steps for all identified vulnerabilities should be documented.
Exception handling	If an identified vulnerability will not be remediated, this should be documented too, including the reason why that's the case. For example, perhaps remediation would cost too much relative to the value of the asset at risk or the chance of the risk being realized. Regardless of the reason, exceptions should be carefully considered and noted.
Ethical disclosure	Some identified vulnerabilities might be new discoveries and point to significant flaws and weaknesses in widely used software and hardware. In this context and for the sake of other users, customers, and vendors, it's very important that newly discovered vulnerabilities be shared to the extent necessary to protect anybody who may be exposed to the same vulnerabilities.

Table 6-20: **Test Output**

6.5 Conduct or facilitate security audits

6.5.1 Audit Process

CORE **CONCEPTS**

- Audit approaches include: internal, external, and third party.
- Internal audits involve employees focused on organizational processes.
- External audits involve employees focusing on vendor processes.
- Third-party audits involve independent auditors focusing on vendor processes.
- Audit plans typically include: defining the audit objective, defining the audit scope, conducting the audit, and refining the audit process.

Assessments and third-party audits are an integral part of operations and the security assessment and testing strategy of an organization. Audits consist of internal, external, and third-party efforts, and oftentimes a hybrid approach is utilized. The security function needs to support the audit process. Regardless of the type of audit, most audit plans include the following steps:

> **Understand components of an audit plan**

- Define the audit objective
- Define the audit scope
- Conduct the audit
- Refine the audit process

To the last point, a typical audit process might include:

- Determining audit goals
- Involving the right business unit leader(s)
- Determining the audit scope
- Choosing the audit team
- Planning the audit
- Conducting the audit
- Documenting the audit results
- Communicating the results

Expanding upon the types of audits, internal audits involve an organization's own employees examining the organization's own systems; external audits could be a company's employees examining a vendor's systems or external auditors, for example, an independent audit firm's auditor looking in and providing an independent assessment of a company's controls. Third-party audits involve an independent auditor examining the operations and governance of a service provider. The service provider pays the independent auditor to conduct the audit and produce a report. The service provider can then provide this report to their customers. As a reminder, the different audit approaches were listed in Table 6-2.

> **Understand the different audit approaches and what each approach entails and how the security function needs to support the audit process**

6.5.2 System Organization Controls (SOC) Reports

> ### CORE **CONCEPTS**
>
> - Audit standards have matured over the years from SAS70 → SSAE 16 → SSAE 18.
> - ISAE 3402 is the international standard in assurance engagements and is quite similar to SSAE 16/18 standards, with slight variations.
> - SOC 1 reports are quite basic and focus on financial reporting risks.
> - SOC 2 reports are much more involved and focus on the controls related to the five trust principles: security, availability, confidentiality, processing integrity, and privacy.
> - SOC 3 reports are stripped down versions of SOC 2 reports—typically used for marketing purposes.
> - Type 1 reports focus on a point in time (SOC 1 and SOC 2).
> - Type 2 reports focus on a period of time, covering design, and operating effectiveness (SOC 1 and SOC 2).

Over the years, audit standards have evolved. Years ago, SAS 70 was the gold standard. It was superseded by SSAE 16, which in turn has been superseded by SSAE 18. In each case, the standard outlines how to conduct third-party audits. In the United States, the American Institute of Certified Public Accountants (AICPA) is the governing body that oversees and refines these standards that essentially say, "Anyone who is going to conduct audits should ensure that the following details are included." The SSAE 18 standard defines three types of Service Organization Controls (SOC) reports:

> **Understand the difference between SOC 1, SOC 2, and SOC 3 reports and what each report entails**

SOC 1 reports focus on **financial reporting risks**.

SOC 2 reports focus on what are known as the **five trust principles: security, availability, confidentiality, processing integrity, and privacy**. A SOC 2 report will cover controls related to security, availability, and confidentiality. Coverage of controls related to processing integrity and privacy are optional, and it therefore may or may not be included in the report. SOC 2 reports can be quite detailed documents that contain information about an organization's controls and how they operate as well as details about an organization's systems. In fact, SOC 2 reports often contain a fair amount of confidential information about an organization, and they should be protected from accidental disclosure or disclosure to unauthorized people. However, certain information contained within a SOC 2 report would be valuable for new prospective customers to know. This is where SOC 3 reports can be very helpful.

Essentially, a **SOC 3** report is a stripped down and sanitized version of a SOC 2 report. It's a **marketing tool** that potential customers or interested parties can read to gain a basic understanding of a service provider's controls.

As security professionals, the most meaningful among available SOC reports are SOC 2.

It's important to also understand that two types of SOC 1 and SOC 2 reports exist. These are known as Type 1 and Type 2, also known as Type I and Type II.

> **Understand the difference between Type 1 and Type 2 SOC reports and which is more comprehensive**

A **Type 1** report focuses on the **design of controls at a point in time**. To conduct a Type 1 audit, an auditor will come into an organization and focus on paperwork (policies, procedures, baselines, and so on). The auditor is essentially evaluating whether a process is properly designed on the day they looked at it. Do policies and procedures exist? Are they documented? Do they contain expected information?

This examination is done from the perspective of a point in time, and just speaks to whether a control appears to be appropriately designed at that point in time. A Type 1 audit does not provide any indication as to whether controls are operating effectively.

A **Type 2** report examines not only the design of a control but more importantly the **operating effectiveness over a period of time**, typically a year. A Type 2 report covers everything in a Type 1 report and then goes much deeper to confirm that controls are operating effectively. Looking at change management, for example, the auditor would confirm that a change management policy exists as well as associated procedures—that the controls are properly designed. Then the auditor would examine a "population" of changes—perhaps all the changes that occurred during the past year. From that population, the auditor would choose a subset of changes and examine them closely. Did the control operate effectively? Was testing, including regression, performed? Was the change management review board involved? Did the appropriate stakeholders approve the change? Were the changes documented? The auditor is going to dig much deeper and confirm the operating effectiveness related to all samples examined, and again, this operating effectiveness will cover a period of time.

From the types of reports defined, it should be clear that **SOC 2, Type 2 are the most desirable reports for security professionals,** as they report on the operating effectiveness of the security controls at a service provider over a period of time.

A Type 1 report would usually be used during the first year that a service provider begins having a third-party audit conducted. If a company is just ramping up and undergoing audits, they're likely to have issues with their controls that need to be rectified, especially for the sake of long-term customer perceptions and credibility. By pursuing a Type 1 audit first, the auditor can identify gaps, missing controls, and other problems, with the expectation that the organization will reconcile everything during the coming months and that a Type 2 audit will be conducted the next year. So, SOC 2, Type 1 reports typically are used in the first year and SOC 2, Type 2 reports then become the norm in order to show operational control continuity and compliance. The various SOC report types are depicted in Figure 6-6.

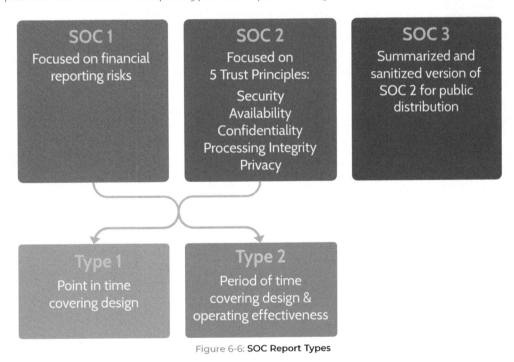

Figure 6-6: **SOC Report Types**

6.5.3 Audit Roles and Responsibilities

CORE **CONCEPTS**

- Audit roles include: executive (senior) management, audit committee, security officer, compliance manager, internal auditors, and external auditors.

- Audit responsibilities vary based upon the audit role.

It's important that executive (senior) management understand that the tone must be set from the top, and this applies to assurance as well. Yes, auditors are doing the work, but executive management must clearly articulate that assurance is important and that the process is supported and a priority for the organization.

At the same time, the Audit Committee, which is made up of key members of the Board as well as senior stakeholders from across the organization, should provide oversight and direction to the audit program. The Chief Security Officer's (CSO) or Chief Information Security Officer's (CISO) role is to advise on security-related matters. Compliance managers are usually responsible for an audit function, scheduling audits as necessary or required, ensuring that auditors are hired and trained, among other things. Internal auditors work for the organization they audit and provide assurance that corporate internal controls are operating effectively. External auditors work outside the organization—typically for an independent organization—and come inside to examine an organization's controls. A summary of these roles can be found in Table 6-21.

> **Understand audit roles and responsibilities**

Executive (Senior) Management	Sets the proper tone from the top, promotes the audit process, and provides support where needed
Audit Committee	Composed of members of the Board/senior stakeholders to provide oversight of the audit program
Security Officer	Advise on security related risks to be evaluated in the audit program
Compliance Manager	Ensure corporate compliance with applicable laws and regulations, professional standards, and company policy
Internal Auditors	Company employees who provide assurance that corporate internal controls are operating effectively
External Auditors	Provide an unbiased and independent audit report as they are independent of the entity being audited

Table 6-21: **Audit Roles**

MINDMAP REVIEW **VIDEOS**

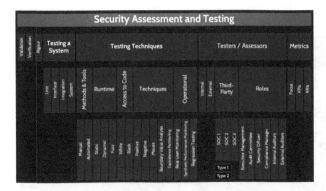

Security Assessment and Testing
dcgo.ca/CISSPmm6-1

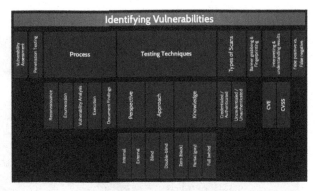

Identifying Vulnerabilities
dcgo.ca/CISSPmm6-2

Log Review and Analysis
dcgo.ca/CISSPmm6-3

CISSP PRACTICE QUESTION APP

Download the Destination CISSP Practice Question app
for Domain 6 practice questions

dcgo.ca/PracQues

DOMAIN 7

Security Operations

DOMAIN 7

SECURITY OPERATIONS

Domain 7 is where the rubber meets the road and focuses on integrating security within organizational operations. Oftentimes, this integration is in the form of processes that are put in place and configured to ensure that systems remain secure. Essentially, security operations are the day-to-day activities that the security function performs to support the entire organization in achieving its goals and objectives.

7.1 Understand and comply with investigations

7.1.1 Securing the Scene

> CORE **CONCEPTS**
>
> - Securing the scene is an essential and critical part of every investigation.
>
> - Securing the scene might include any/all of the following: sealing off access to the area where a crime may have been committed, taking photographs, documenting the location of evidence, and avoiding touching anything—computers, mobile devices, thumb drives, hard drives, and so on—that may have been used as part of the crime.

One facet of security operations is investigations. Imagine you're a very experienced and capable investigator. To conduct a proper investigation, evidence needs to be secured in the appropriate manner. Security professionals may need to support the entire investigation process and do it correctly. **The bottom line: investigators need to be able to conduct reliable investigations that will stand up to scrutiny and cross-examination.**

As an experienced and capable investigator, imagine that your organization has been breached and you've managed to track the hacker back to their criminal lair—their parents' basement. As you descend the stairs, you discover the scene from where the crime was perpetrated, and you quickly make note of the computer that was used. Are you going to walk up to it and start moving the mouse around or typing on the keyboard to start gaining insights about what this person did? Of course not, because experience has taught you that doing so might contaminate the scene. In fact, the first thing you'll do is **secure the scene** to prevent contamination from taking place. That might involve blocking off the area where the crime took place, taking photographs, documenting the location of evidence in the scene, taking snapshots of the system, and so on. With forensic computer investigations, the exact same concept applies. Otherwise, **once evidence has been contaminated, it can't be decontaminated.** *It's imperative to employ the right process and approach from the beginning.*

7.1.2 Evidence Collection and Handling

CORE CONCEPTS

- The forensic investigation process should include, among other things, the identification and securing of a crime scene, proper collection of evidence that preserves its integrity and the chain of custody, examination of all evidence, further analysis of the most compelling evidence, and final reporting.

- Evidence collection should be guided by early establishment and maintenance of the chain of custody.

- The chain of custody focuses on who handled what evidence, when, and where, and its primary focus is control, which implies integrity.

- Sources of information/evidence include: oral/written statements, written documents, computer systems, visual/audio recordings, photographs, surveillance footage, and so on.

- MOM = motive, opportunity, means.

Forensic Investigation Process

The need to perform digital forensics exists within any organization that uses computer systems, networks, and the multitude of electronic devices currently available in the marketplace. Whether in response to a crime or incident, a breach of organizational policy, troubleshooting system or network issues, or a number of other reasons, digital forensic methodologies can assist in finding answers, solving problems, and, in some cases, successfully prosecuting crimes.

> **Understand the steps of the forensic investigation process and what happens at each step**

As the term *methodologies* implies, digital forensic processes can vary; but, certain digital forensic science practices and standards are typically consistent, regardless of context. First among them relates to identifying and securing the scene, which is focused on protecting potential evidence from being touched, removed, or otherwise contaminated until it can be properly examined. This step also marks the beginning of the chain of custody, which is critical where a crime may have been committed and for the sake of all evidence that may ultimately be admissible as part of a trial. After a scene is identified and secured properly, the formal collection of evidence can take place. Whether dealing with physical or digital evidence, proper care must be taken to protect the integrity of whatever is collected. Forensic policies, standards, and procedures can aid with the collection process to ensure the integrity of the evidence collected as well as establish the chain of custody.

Once collected, evidence and data can be examined and analyzed via automated and manual means to determine what might be of consequential interest for the sake of building a case, identifying a culprit, or otherwise moving further along with an investigation.

Finally, as noted further below, results of the analysis should be compiled in a report. The report should describe every facet of the investigative process, from beginning to end, as well as action items to be completed, recommendations for improvement, and anything else that may prove valuable. Additionally, because multiple audiences may exist, the report may need to be compiled in different formats or with varying levels of detail for the sake of a given audience.

Sources of Information and Evidence

Sources of information and evidence as part of a computer security investigation often include oral and written statements, documents, audio/visual records, and of course, computer systems. For purposes of Domain 7, the primary focus will be computer systems, networks, and network devices. Possible sources of information are noted in Table 7-1.

Oral/written statements	Statements given to police, investigators, or as testimony in court by people who witness a crime or who may have information deemed pertinent to an investigation.
Written documents	Handwritten, typed, or printed documents such as checks, letters, wills, receipts, or contracts, to name a few, that may be relevant for the sake of an investigation.
Computer systems	In the context of an investigation, a computer system could include the unit that houses the CPU, motherboard, and other system-related components that might store data in a non-volatile manner, as well as the storage devices—SSD, HDD (external/internal), USB device, and so on—and any other peripheral that may have been connected to a computer while a crime was committed.
Visual/audio	As part of a computer security investigation, visual and audio evidence could include photographs, video and taped recordings, surveillance footage from security cameras, and so on.

Table 7-1: **Sources of Information and Evidence**

In addition to sources of information, you also need to take numerous types of evidence into account. Those have been noted in Table 7-2.

Real evidence	Real evidence is tangible **physical objects** (e.g., hard drives, SSDs, USB drives)—not the data on them. Real evidence can be physically held, touched, and inspected, and this type of evidence is often very important in a case. It is often used to prove or disprove a factual issue in a trial.
Direct evidence	Direct evidence speaks for itself and **requires no inference** (e.g., eyewitness accounts, confessions, a smoking gun). Direct evidence directly proves a fact being discussed. An example of direct evidence is video footage showing a defendant breaking into the computer storage area and walking out with two laptops.
Circumstantial evidence	Also referred to as indirect evidence, circumstantial evidence suggests a fact by **implication or inference** and can prove an intermediate fact. An example of circumstantial evidence is a witness testifying that the defendant was near the computer storage area after it had been broken into.
Corroborative evidence	Corroborative evidence supports facts or elements of the case, not a fact on its own, but **supports other facts.** Corroborating evidence can be very powerful, as it serves to uphold and confirm testimony of witnesses and other forms of evidence.
Hearsay evidence	Hearsay evidence is testimony from **witnesses who were not present**. No firsthand proof of accuracy or reliability exists, but the content is being offered to prove the truth of the matter at hand. Hearsay evidence is usually inadmissible in a court, unless an exception to hearsay rules is made.
Best evidence rule	The best evidence rule essentially states that **original** evidence rather than a copy or duplicate of the evidence should be entered as evidence.
Secondary evidence	Secondary evidence is a **reproduction** of, or **substitute** for, an original document or item of proof (e.g., print out of log files). In cases where original evidence no longer exists, a court may allow secondary evidence to be presented in a trial.

Table 7-2: **Evidence Types**

Motive Opportunity Means (MOM)

Another concept often employed while conducting investigations is what's known as MOM. MOM stands for motive, opportunity, and means, and it serves as a guide when conducting an investigation. In other words, what might have motivated the suspect? Did the suspect have the opportunity to perpetrate the crime? Did the suspect have the means?

7.1.3 Locard's Exchange Principle

CORE **CONCEPTS**

- Locard's exchange principle: with every crime, something is taken and left behind

A simple yet effective method for identifying where to look for evidence is the notion that, whenever a crime is committed, something is taken and something is left behind. This explains why pictures are taken, carpets are vacuumed, fingerprints lifted, and crime scenes are otherwise meticulously examined. An eighteenth-century French criminologist, Dr. Edmund Locard, formulated the foundation of forensic science based upon this fact. In simple terms, this means that every time two objects interact, some type of transfer occurs —something is taken and something is left behind.

Understand what is meant by Locard's exchange principle

7.1.4 Digital/Computer Forensics

CORE **CONCEPTS**

- Digital forensics is the scientific examination and analysis of data.
- Live evidence is data that is stored in a running system in places like random access memory (RAM), cache, buffers, and so on.
- Forensic copies refer to identical, bit-for-bit copies of a digital media source, like a hard drive.
- Digital forensics tools, tactics, and procedures facilitate proper and immediate response to live systems.
- Artifacts are remnants of breach or attempted breach and can act like breadcrumbs that point to the path followed or activities pursued by an attacker.

With computer security, the primary focus is computer, or digital, forensics. *Digital forensics* is the scientific examination and analysis of data from storage media in such a way that the information can be used as part of an investigation to identify the culprit or the root cause of an incident.

Understand the implications and challenges of working with live evidence

Live Evidence

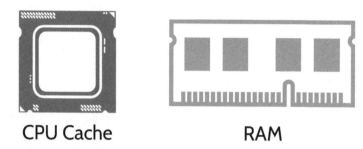

CPU Cache   RAM

With digital forensics, one of the primary considerations is what's referred to as live evidence. Live evidence is data that is stored in a running system in places like random access memory (RAM), CPU, cache, buffers, and so on. If the keyboard is tapped, if the mouse is moved, and certainly if the plug is pulled or the system is powered off, the live evidence changes or disappears completely. ***Examining a live system changes the the state of the evidence.*** This fact makes it immediately clear that examination of a live system requires expert knowledge and specialized tools to extract live evidence and minimize contamination. As noted, live evidence is often stored in locations like RAM, cache, and the CPU, and if power to the system is disrupted, the live evidence is gone.

Copy 1   Original   Copy 2

Forensic Copies

Another major source of digital evidence on a computer system is the hard drive. For example, imagine you're investigating a crime and have discovered a laptop that was likely used to commit the crime. The laptop is already turned off, so there are no concerns about contaminating live evidence. However, the hard drive might contain evidence, so you remove it to conduct forensic analysis. *Whenever a forensic investigation of a hard drive is conducted, two identical **bit-for-bit copies** of the original hard drive should be created first.* Then, the original hard drive should be placed in an evidence bag, the bag sealed, and the drive never touched again. Similarly, the first copy of the hard drive should be treated the same. The second copy of the drive is the working copy.

What does "bit-for-bit copy" mean? It simply means it is an exact copy, down to every bit on the original drive, and specialized tools are required to create bit-for-bit copies. After the bit-for-bit copies are created, the original drive and the two copies should be hashed. If the hash values match, the copies are exact, bit-for-bit copies. That ensures integrity is maintained.

> **Understand the importance of creating bit-for-bit copies of a hard drive**

Why is it harder to do forensic analysis of mobile devices?

- Manufacturers **frequently change** OS structure, file structure, services, and connectors

- No **single method or tool** can extract all the data

- Hibernation and suspension of apps

- Extensive new training required for examiners

> **Understand why forensic analysis of computers and mobile devices can be difficult**

Reporting and Documentation

The final phase of the forensic investigation process is reporting and documentation, though documentation should be an integral component of every step in the process. At this point, all evidence has been examined, and the most relevant evidence should be documented for the sake of use by all relevant stakeholders, including:

- Prosecution/Defense

- Judge/Jury

- Regulators

- Investors

- Insurers

Artifacts

Forensic artifacts are remnants of a breach or attempted breach of a system or network, and they may or may not be relevant to an investigation or response. They're breadcrumbs that can potentially lead back to an intruder or at least identify their actions and the path they followed while in the system or network. Artifacts can be found in numerous places, including:

> **Understand the importance and potential relevance of artifacts to an investigation**

- Computer systems

- Web browsers

- Mobile devices

- Hard drives

- Flash drives

Examples of artifacts include IP addresses, hashes, file name/type, registry keys (Windows), URLs, operating system information, as well as logged information, like account updates, profile changes, file changes, and so on, that point to malicious behavior. Undoubtedly with so many potential sources of artifacts available, identifying relevant artifacts can be akin to finding a needle in a haystack—a very large haystack—and the forensic investigator must be very skilled and careful in evaluating what is most pertinent and therefore most valuable for the sake of the investigation. Artifacts that support or refute a hypothesis related to an investigation or response can be used as evidence.

7.1.5 Chain of Custody

CORE CONCEPTS

- **The primary focus of chain of custody is control of evidence to maintain integrity for the sake of presentation in court**

Chain of Custody

One very important aspect of evidence collection is that the **chain of custody** must be established immediately and maintained. The *chain of custody is ultimately focused on having* **control** *of the evidence: who collected and handled what evidence, when, and where.* Crime scenes should always be thoroughly documented via photos and diagrams. Additionally, evidence should be collected in a manner that protects it from tampering, contamination, or other things such as corruption or deterioration. It's imperative that evidence be controlled from the moment of collection to the moment it might be presented in court, which could potentially be years later. Regardless of the time frame, if the chain of custody is maintained, evidence will have a better opportunity to be admissible.

> Understand the "chain of custody" and its importance

A useful way to think about establishing the chain of custody is to tag, bag, and carry the evidence as depicted in Figure 7-1. Tag the evidence to clearly note where the evidence was collected, on what date, and by whom. Bag the evidence—carefully store the evidence to minimize contamination. Carry the evidence back to a secured evidence storage location, such as an evidence locker.

Tag

Bag

Carry

Figure 7-1: **Chain of Custody**

7.1.6 Five Rules of Evidence

For any evidence to stand the best chance of surviving legal and other scrutiny, it should exhibit five characteristics, also known as the "five rules of evidence," described in Table 7-3.

Understand the five rules of evidence and their meaning	
Authentic	Evidence is not fabricated or planted and can be proven so through crime scene photos or things like bit-for-bit copies of hard drives. This points back to securing the scene, to ensure the best chance of preserving all critical pieces of evidence for the sake of an investigation and any legal proceedings.
Accurate	Evidence has not been changed or modified—it has *integrity*.
Complete	Evidence must be *complete,* and all parts presented. In other words, *all* pieces of evidence must be available and shared, whether they support or fail to support the case.
Convincing or Reliable	Evidence must be conveyed in a manner that allows anybody to understand what is being presented. Evidence must display a high degree of veracity—it must demonstrate a high degree of truth. Additionally, nontechnical people, including judges and juries, must be able to understand what is being presented.
Admissible	Evidence is accepted as part of a case and allowed into the court proceedings. Chain of custody can help, but it does not guarantee admissibility.

Table 7-3: **Five Rules of Evidence**

Investigative Techniques

Several investigative techniques can be used when conducting analysis.

One of them is media analysis. Media might include the analysis of things like hard drives, flash drives, tapes, CDs, USB drives, or anything similar. With media analysis, oftentimes the search is for what's not there as much as what is there. For example, when examining a hard drive, if someone has deleted a file, is that file gone from the hard drive? Oftentimes the pointer to the file has simply been deleted, but the file is still there. Media analysis examines the bits on a hard drive that may no longer have pointers, but the data is still there.

Software analysis focuses on an application, especially malware. With malware, the goal is to determine exactly how it works and what it is trying to do. An important facet of this relates to attribution and trying to determine who or where the software was created. Oftentimes, the source code can offer clues and pointers that help to pinpoint this information.

Network analysis attempts to understand how a network might have been penetrated, how the network was traversed, and what systems may have been breached. Typically, system log files provide the best source of information for network analysis.

7.1.7 Types of Investigations

Table 7-4 provides a summary of types of investigations, relating to an incident.

	Overview	Who drives the investigation?
Criminal	Deal with **crimes** and oftentimes with accompanying **legal punishment**. Convictions often lead to time in jail as well as a criminal record. These are conducted by law enforcement at the local, state, and federal levels, depending upon the nature and severity of the crime, and punishment can potentially be very harsh.	Primarily law enforcement with support from the organization
Civil	Deal with **disputes between individuals or organizations**, and whichever party is found guilty usually pays a fine or other monetary penalty as well as related court costs. Like criminal investigations, law enforcement conducts civil investigations too.	Law enforcement or the organization
Regulatory	Deals with **violations of regulated activities**	Associated regulatory body
Administrative	Focus on internal violations of organizational policies and incidents identified by an organization. Perhaps employee misconduct was involved, or policies or procedures were broken, or a hacker absconded with some credit card numbers. Unless it's determined that criminal activity resulted, administrative investigations are opened and closed by the organization itself.	The organization

Table 7-4: **Types of Investigations**

In the case of criminal and civil investigations in the context of an organization, the investigation might start internally. Once it becomes clear that criminal activity has taken place, law enforcement should be contacted, at which point the investigation would be handed over to them, and they would drive the investigation forward from there.

7.2 Conduct logging and monitoring activities

7.2.1 Security Information and Event Management (SIEM)

> CORE **CONCEPTS**
>
> - Security Information and Event Management (SIEM) systems ingest logs from multiple sources, compile and analyze log entries, and report relevant information.

The topic of logging and monitoring was first introduced in Domain 6, and now we're going to look at it more closely in the context of security information and event management (SIEM) systems. SIEM systems ingest logs from disparate devices throughout an organization, they aggregate and correlate the log entries and look for interesting activity. Relevant findings are reported, so additional action can be taken. At a high level, Figure 7-2 shows how a SIEM system operates.

Understand at a high level what a SIEM system is and its capabilities

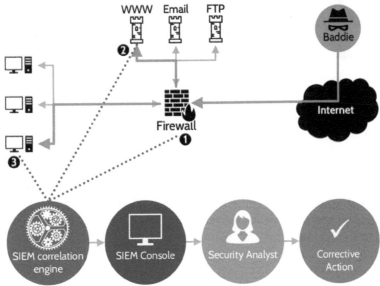

Figure 7-2: **SIEM Operation**

Let's examine a simple example of how this might work.

Imagine an attacker who starts poking at your network to determine what's where and what can be accessed. As this activity takes place, log events are being generated. A log event is simply a record of any event of interest. Most events that a SIEM ingests are meaningless, even some of the events being generated by the hacker, because the hacker is simply poking around. Now, let's further imagine that the hacker finds an entry point and successfully gains access to a web server, and from the web server they're able to locate a back channel that leads to internal systems. These additional activities, like before, continue to generate events, but now—when correlated to earlier events—they take on new meaning and, very likely, generate some type of alert that a security analyst would be tasked with examining further. Very quickly, the analyst is going to try and determine if this is a false-positive or if something malicious is really taking place, and this highlights an important point about SIEM systems in general and their installation and operation.

SIEM systems are much more than just technology. Yes, the technology is important and complicated and very hard to implement, but it's more than these facts. SIEM systems also require trained personnel. Let's look briefly at a real-life example to explain.

Company A (generic name used to protect the innocent) suffered two major breaches. After the first breach, they installed a number of expensive and sophisticated systems, which helped detect the second breach. In fact, two different teams—one in the United States and one in India—detected the breach. But there was a breakdown, and despite the technology that alerted about the breach, the alert was not properly escalated and was ultimately ignored. So, the technology was in place, it detected the hackers, and it even alerted the security team; then everything fell apart with the process of escalation and dealing with the situation. Again, this example highlights the fact that SIEM systems are complex and require expertise to install and tune properly, and they require a properly trained team that understands how to read and interpret what they're seeing as well as what escalation procedures to follow when a legitimate alert is raised. SIEM systems represent technology, process, and people, and each is relevant to overall effectiveness.

Figure 7-3 depicts another example.

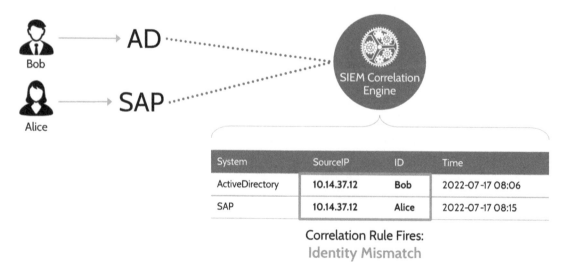

Figure 7-3: **SIEM Example**

Imagine two users, Bob and Alice, both working from home. Bob's an active user with a valid account, and he logs into Active Directory (AD). When Bob logs into Active Directory, an event is logged and captured by the SIEM system. Several minutes later, Alice logs into SAP. Alice is also a legitimate user with a valid account, and the event is similarly logged to the SIEM system. However, this time the SIEM system generates an alert because the IP address associated with Alice is the same as the IP address associated with Bob, which wouldn't make sense because they both live at different homes. This is not normal and may indicate a problem that needs to be further evaluated by an analyst. For example, an attacker may have compromised legitimate user accounts and is using those to access company systems. At the very least, this looks suspicious. Without the log events being correlated in the context of the SIEM system, this anomaly wouldn't have been identified because events logged in Active Directory and events logged in the SAP system are separate. However, once ingested and aggregated by the SIEM system, correlation took place, and the once disparate events now tell a different story. This functionality is one of the major advantages of SIEM systems.

Both examples point to the real power of SIEM systems. With traditional logging, where log files are only captured and maintained on individual systems, it would take enormous effort to access and analyze all the captured data and determine if anything out of the ordinary or malicious is taking place. It's like trying to find the proverbial needle in the haystack. With a SIEM system, significant intelligence is incorporated into their functionality, which allows significant amounts of logged events and analysis and correlation of the same to take place very quickly. And with the proper tuning, SIEM systems can identify and alert on even the least apparent telltale sign.

Figure 7-4: **SIEM Capabilities**

Let's look a bit deeper at SIEM system capabilities as also highlighted in Figure 7-4.

- SIEM systems allow for the **aggregation** of logged events from multiple systems. In other words, events logged in systems located throughout an organization's network can all be brought under one umbrella—the SIEM system.

- Once aggregated, logs typically need to be **normalized**, because different systems log events using different formats. For example, one system might log events using a twelve-hour clock, while another system might use a twenty-four-hour clock, or the dates might be in month/day/year format on one system and day/month/format on another. Events should be deduplicated, or simply deduped. This means that duplicate events are eliminated. Normalization helps clean up data, put it in the same format, and eliminate redundancy, so it can be easily analyzed and suspicious activity flagged, based upon rules that have been programmed into the system.

- After data has been normalized, **correlation** seeks to line up events and determine which of them alone and in combination might be important and indicative of problems.

- **Secure storage** is the concept where the SIEM system keeps a copy of all logged events from each device. The system is designed to store data for long periods of time, and ideally those log files are read-only, to prevent tampering or deletion.

- **Analysis** and **reporting** refer to the SIEM system rules that have been put in place, looking at data related to the same, and taking action when appropriate. As noted earlier, event log data can be collected from virtually every system within an organization. However, SIEM systems should be used to capture relevant logs, based on organizational risk, required budget, and regulatory obligations.

Example Sources of Event Data

As noted above, SIEM systems allow log data from multiple sources, such as those noted below, to be captured in one location.

- Security appliances
- Network devices
- DLP
- Data activity
- Applications
- Operating systems
- Servers
- IPS/IDS

Threat Intelligence

The term "threat intelligence" is an umbrella term encompassing threat research and analysis and emerging threat trends. It is an important element of any organization's digital security strategy that equips security professionals to proactively anticipate, recognize, and respond to threats. Many SIEM solutions offer threat intelligence subscriptions that add additional capabilities, strength, and value to already robust systems. However, actionable threat intelligence can also be gleaned from documents like vendor trend reports, public sector team reports (like US-CERT), related information sharing and analysis centers (ISACs), and more.

User and Entity Behavior Analytics (UEBA)

UEBA (also known as UBA) analysis engines are typically included with SIEM solutions or may be added via subscription. As the name implies, UEBA focuses on the analysis of user and entity behavior. At its core, UEBA monitors the behavior and patterns of users and entities, logs and correlates the underlying data, analyzes the data, and triggers alerts when necessary. The analytics component of a UEBA solution is based on machine learning, which allows a baseline for each user and entity to be created. If future behavior deviates from what is considered normal, an alert can be fired, and potential further action can be taken based upon the perceived or real threat. UEBA solutions can be used to address insider threats, hacked privileged accounts, or brute-force attacks, to name a few examples, and the sophisticated manner through which UEBA can detect behavioral shifts and anomalies and alert a security team before a breach occurs or progresses too far can potentially prove invaluable to an organization.

7.2.2 Continuous Monitoring

CORE CONCEPTS

- After a SIEM is set up, configured, tuned, and running, it must be routinely updated and continuously monitored to function most effectively.

- Effective continuous monitoring encompasses technology, processes, and people.

> Understand the concept of continuous monitoring
> and the value it provides to an organization

Figure 7-5: **Continuous Monitoring Steps**

Setting up a SIEM system can be a very long and arduous process, sometimes taking months or even longer, depending on the complexity of the environment and needs of the organization. However, once the system has been configured and is running, the work is not complete. In fact, the SIEM system must be updated and monitored continuously, because

- the threat environment is constantly changing,

- new vulnerabilities are constantly emerging,

- assets in the organization are changing,

- new monitoring rules need to be configured and programmed,

- the balance between false-positives and false-negatives must be closely monitored and responded to accordingly.

Finally, and perhaps most importantly, focus should be not only on the technology and related processes, but also on the people utilizing the technology and the escalation processes, so that timely and proper responses can take place before a breach can cause significant damage to the organization. The full continuous monitoring life cycle has been provided in Figure 7-5.

> Understand what continuous monitoring encompasses

In addition to the topics and subject matter covered here in 7.2, the Official CISSP Certification Exam Outline includes other topics in this section that are covered elsewhere in the book.

Please refer to Domain 4 for details on intrusion detection and prevention, and egress (and ingress) monitoring.

Please refer to Domain 6 for details on log management.

7.3 Perform configuration management (CM)

7.3.1 Asset Inventory

> CORE **CONCEPTS**
> - **Provisioning relates to the deployment of assets—hardware, software, devices, and so on—within an organization.**
> - **Part of provisioning should include maintaining and updating a related asset inventory database anytime an asset is added or removed.**
> - **Assets should be managed as part of an overall asset management life cycle.**

Figure 7-6: **Asset Management**

The full asset management life cycle can be seen in Figure 7-6.

Items can be requested to be procured after careful planning takes place about what's needed in the environment. However, they also need to be securely provisioned. That refers to how things like hardware, software, devices, and so on are provisioned or deployed. Secure provisioning is about the deployment process. For example, when a firewall is purchased, it's typically configured with default settings by the vendor. These default settings usually include default admin and user accounts and passwords as well as other configuration settings. It's not a best practice to deploy any device with default settings. In fact, a process already discussed—system hardening—should be used to ensure that the new system is properly secured and deployed according to policy and baselines established by the organization.

Additionally, whenever deploying a new asset—whether hardware or software—an associated asset inventory database should be updated. Assets represent an organization's attack surface. In other words, each asset is something of value that an attacker might target. Without a current asset inventory, including details about the asset owner, the assets have a very low chance of being patched, configured, scanned routinely, or otherwise kept up to date. It's easy to see that secure provisioning ties into the concept of asset management and the asset life cycle very closely.

7.3.2 Configuration Management

> CORE **CONCEPTS**
>
> - Configuration management is an integral part of secure provisioning.
> - Configuration management relates to the proper configuration of a device at the time of deployment.
> - Policies, standards, baselines, and procedures inform configuration management.
> - Hardening should be considered as part of the configuration management process.
> - Automated provisioning tools can help ensure consistency with the configuration and deployment process and save time.

A significant aspect of secure provisioning is configuration management. As the term implies, configuration management focuses on the proper configuration when a device is first deployed, and this is where tools like baselines, policies, and standards are utilized. Hardening—ensuring that only the necessary services and features of a given hardware device or piece of software are available—should be part of the configuration management process. Additionally—especially in large organizations—automated tools can be used for provisioning purposes. The use of automation can help ensure consistency with the provisioning process as well as save time.

Understand the value and key benefits of configuration management

Device configurations should be documented and reviewed on a periodic basis, and things like credentialed vulnerability scans can be used as a way to review hardware and software configurations. In fact, entire software suites exist for purposes of examining configurations of almost any type of system in an organization.

- Identify assets to keep under control
- Configure assets
- Document configuration
- Verify configuration

7.4 Apply foundational security operations concepts

7.4.1 Foundational Security Operations Concepts

CORE **CONCEPTS**

- Implementation of foundational security operations concepts can significantly improve security within an organization.

- Foundational security operations concepts include: need to know/least privilege, separation of duties (SoD) and responsibilities, privileged account management (PAM), job rotation, and service level agreements (SLA).

Privileged account management: Privileged accounts refers to system accounts that typically have significant power. System administrator accounts are one example of a privileged account, and they often give what's known as "root" or "admin" access to a system. In other words, the account can access and control every part of the system. In the wrong hands this type of control can obviously lead to significant problems. Therefore, privileged accounts should be very carefully managed. For one, access to them should be restricted as much as possible. For another, within an IT department, for example, personnel should have regular user accounts as well as accounts with increased privileges that are only used when needed. Additionally, privileged accounts should require additional authentication, like multifactor authentication. This should be the rule, not the exception. Finally, the use of privileged accounts should always be accompanied by increased logging and monitoring.

Understand foundational security operations concepts

Need to know and least privilege were discussed in 5.1.1, and Table 7-5 provides a summary of these terms.

Need to Know	Least Privilege
Restricting a user's **KNOWLEDGE** (access to data) to only the data required for them to perform their role	Restricting a user's **ACTIONS/PRIVILEGES** to only those required for them to perform their role

Table 7-5: **Need to Know and Least Privilege**

Job rotation: Another excellent fraud detection and deterrent technique is what's known as job rotation. When an organization employs job rotation, they're essentially telling employees that from time to time, another employee will assume their duties and they'll assume the duties of somebody else. Not only does this help prevent fraud and the perpetration of crimes, but it can also help ensure accurate processes as well as cross-training of employees to avoid a single point of failure.

Service Level Agreements (SLAs): SLAs are legal contracts and are part of the overall contract between a customer and vendor. They contain terms denoting related time frames against performance of specific operations that have been agreed upon. For example, an SLA could require a vendor to respond to a certain type of incident within one hour.

7.5 Apply resource protection techniques

7.5.1 Protecting Media

CORE CONCEPTS

- Media management should consider all types of media as well as short- and long-term needs.

- Mean Time Between Failure (MTBF) is an important criterion to consider when evaluating storage media, especially where valuable or sensitive information is concerned.

- Media protection techniques considers media and media management needs and incorporates several tools for the sake of protection of media.

Within any organization, data is one of the most important assets, and it follows that protection of data is critical for the ongoing success of the organization. This fact, therefore, presents some unique needs as well as some challenges. For one thing, data may be stored on a variety of media. For another, data may need to be kept for very long periods of time.

Media

Depending upon how data is being used, storage requirements, portability, and other factors, data storage media might include any of the following:

- Paper

- Microforms (microfilm and microfiche)

- Magnetic (HD, disks, and tapes)

- Flash memory (SSD and memory cards)

- Optical (CD and DVD)

The **Mean Time Between Failure** (**MTBF**) of media can help determine the best media to use for a given need, but no media is going to reliably last for significantly long periods of time. To best retain and protect data for very long periods of time, *processes* must be put in place that constantly move the data to new media, and *file formats should be updated in order to maintain compatibility* with applications that can manage the data. Additionally, and most importantly, the *protection of the data must be updated to reflect current cryptography standards* versus standards that may have been employed when the data was first created.

Media Management

When employing a media management process, some key considerations should include the items listed below, and they should try to look into the future as far as possible.

- Confidentiality

- Access speeds

- Portability

- Durability

- Media format

- Data format

For example, looking at confidentiality, perhaps a certain cryptographic algorithm would more than suffice to protect the data today, but will it suffice in ten years? If data needs to be protected that long, or longer, perhaps the strongest algorithm available should be used instead.

Media Protection Techniques

Associated with media management is protection of the media itself, which typically involves policies and procedures, access control mechanisms, labeling and marking, storage, transport, sanitization, use, and end of life. Which elements are involved and to what degree they are used points back to the value of the data stored on the media, relative to the goals and objectives and associated risk management process of the organization.

Hardware and Software Asset Management

Closely aligned with the information above is the management of hardware and software assets. To best manage either asset class, an inventory of all assets must exist, and it must be maintained. An owner should be assigned to each asset, with each owner accountable for protecting that asset, including things such as patching (software and firmware), maintaining proper licensing, and determining the most appropriate and secure configuration before deployment and on an ongoing basis. To summarize, the items noted below must be present.

- Asset management life cycle
- Inventories
- Patching
- Software licensing
- Secure configuration

7.6 Conduct incident management

7.6.1 Incident Response Process

> CORE **CONCEPTS**
> - Incident response is the process used to detect and respond to incidents.
> - Event = observable occurrence of something.
> - Incident = an adverse event.
> - Not all events are incidents.
> - Incident response process includes: preparation, detection, response, mitigation, reporting, recovery, remediation, and lessons learned.

Incident response is the process used to detect and respond to incidents and to reduce the impact when incidents occur. Incident response attempts to keep a business operating or to restore operations as quickly as possible in the wake of an incident. Furthermore, for the sake of ongoing operations, incident response seeks to learn from mistakes and strengthen the organization as a result.

Goals of Incident Response

- Provide an effective and efficient response to **reduce impact** to the organization
- Maintain or restore **business continuity**
- **Defend** against future attacks

Understand the difference between an event and an incident

Event
An observable occurrence

>

Incident
An adverse event

Events and Incidents

To know when an incident response process should be initiated, an important distinction needs to be made. Namely, what distinguishes an *incident* from an *event*. Events take place on a continual basis, and the vast majority of these are insignificant; however, events that lead to some type of adversity can be deemed incidents, which should then trigger an organization's incident response process.

Detection Examples

Organizations must have tools in place that can help detect and identify incidents. Most organizations use one or more of the tools noted below for detection purposes, and some of them—like IPS/IDS, DLP, and SIEM—require quite a bit of configuration and tuning to work optimally. Thus, a combination of automated and manual tools is usually the best and most effective approach.

- IPS/IDS

- DLP

- Anti-malware

- SIEM

- Administrative review

- Motion sensors

- Cameras

- Guards

Examples of Incidents

Incidents can take on many shapes and forms, and the examples below show a good mix of what might be called an incident. It's not important to memorize this list, as it's certainly not exhaustive; it simply serves to illustrate what types of incidents might be detected that require a formal response via the incident response process.

- Malware

- Hacker attack

- Insider attack

- Employee error

- System error

- Data corruption

- Workplace injury

Understand the incident response process and what happens at each step

Process Steps

The incident response process is outlined in Figure 7-7 and then further defined in Table 7-6.

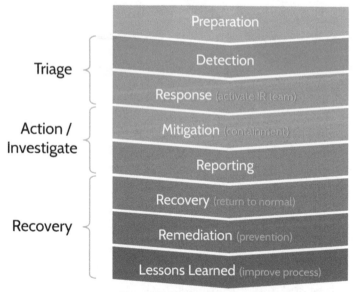

Figure 7-7: **Incident Response Process**

Preparation	Preparation is critical, as this will help anticipate all the steps to follow. Preparation would include things like developing the IR process, assigning IR team members, and everything related to what happens when an incident is identified.
Detection	Pointing back to the distinction between an event and an incident, ***the goal of detection is to identify an adverse event—an incident—and to begin dealing with it.***
Response (IR Team)	After an incident has been identified, the IR Team should be activated. Among the first steps taken by the IR Team will be an **impact assessment** to determine how big of a deal is the incident, how long might the impact be experienced, who else might need to be involved, and so on.
Mitigation (containment)	In addition to conducting an impact assessment, the IR Team will attempt to minimize—to contain—damage or impact from the incident. The IR Team's job at this point is not to fix the problem; it's simply to try and prevent further damage from taking place. For example, if a fire has broken out, the IR Team will focus on ensuring human safety, extinguishing the fire, and confirming that no hot spots exist that could flare up again.
Reporting	Reporting occurs throughout the incident response process. Once an incident is mitigated, formal reporting takes place, because there are often numerous stakeholders that need to understand what has happened. Especially in situations where a major incident has taken place, these stakeholders could include senior management, Board members, HR, Legal, IT, customers, vendors, PR, and even outside media outlets. As there are often numerous stakeholders seeking updates, this can quickly distract the IR Team from focusing on their role and responding to the incident, so it's important that one person be designated as the point person for purposes of reporting. Taking this approach helps keep the message consistent, and it allows those most directly involved with responding to the incident to stay focused on their jobs.
Recovery (return to normal)	At this point, the goal is to start returning things to normal, to getting back to business as usual. For example, looking back at the fire example, this is when cleanup of water and debris would take place, walls and ceilings replaced, systems put back in place, and so on.
Remediation (prevention)	In parallel with recovery, remediation is also taking place. The goal of remediation is to implement fixes and improvements to systems and processes to prevent a similar incident from occurring again.
Lessons Learned (improve process)	Lessons learned steps back and takes a more all-encompassing view of the situation related to an incident and asks questions like: ■ "What additional processes can be put in place?" ■ "How did our organization get here?" ■ "What can be done differently to improve how we run and protect our organization?" The findings from the lessons learned are used to further improve systems and processes to try to prevent future incidents from occurring.

Table 7-6: **Definitions of Incident Response Steps**

7.7 Operate and maintain detective and preventive measures

7.7.1 Malware

CORE **CONCEPTS**

- Malware is malicious software that negatively impacts a system.

- Many types of malware exist.

- Virus = malware that has to be triggered by a user.

- Worm = malware that can self-propagate and spread through a network on its own.

- Logic bomb = malware that executes based on logic embedded in the code.

- Trojan horse = malware that looks harmless but contains malicious code.

- Polymorphic = malware that can change multiple aspects of itself to evade detection.

- Ransomware = malware that encrypts a system or network of systems and then demands a ransom payment to gain access to the decryption key.

- Rootkit = malware that attempts to mask its presence on a system and is a collection of malware tools that can be used by an attacker to meet multiple needs.

- Zero-day = malware that has never been seen in the wild before, and therefore no detection or antivirus signatures exist for it.

Malware is malicious software that negatively impacts a system, and a number of different types of malware exist. It's very common that malware demonstrates multiple different personality traits. For example, a piece of malware can be considered a worm and it can be polymorphic. Table 7-7 describes different types of malware and their traits in more detail.

> **Understand different types of malware and characteristics of each**

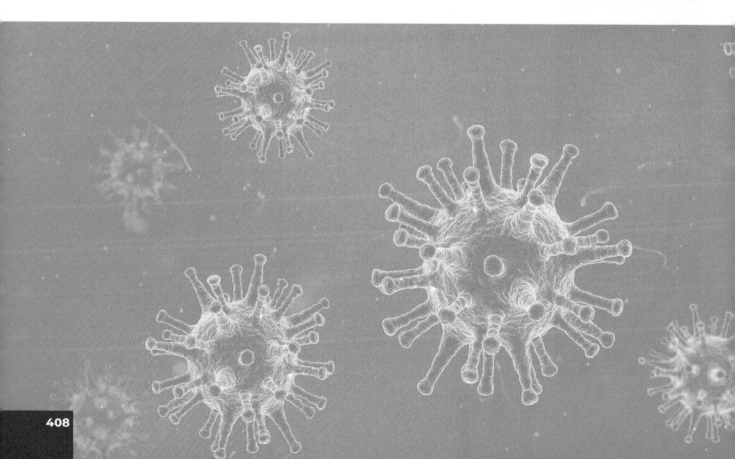

Types of Malware

Virus	The defining characteristic of a virus is it's a piece of malware that has to be **triggered in some way by the user**.
Worm	A worm is a piece of malware that is able to **self-propagate** and spread through a network or a series of systems on its own, **by exploiting a vulnerability** in those systems. Essentially, a worm can be much more dangerous than a virus.
Companion	Companion malware is **helper software**. It's not malicious on its own; rather, it could be something like a wrapper that accompanies the actual malware.
Macro	A macro is something often found in Microsoft Office products, like Excel, and is created using a very simple programming language to automate tasks. Because a programming language is involved, macros can be programmed to be malicious and harmful, and running macros automatically when opening an Excel or similar file—especially if the file originated elsewhere—is discouraged.
Multipartite	Multipartite means the malware **spreads in different ways**. Stuxnet is a perfect example of multipartite malware. Stuxnet was first introduced to and infected a system via the system's USB port. Once the system was compromised, it spread harmlessly to other systems until reaching the target systems—Iran's nuclear centrifuges—at which point it sped the centrifuges to the point of failure while indicating to plant workers that everything was working normally.
Polymorphic	This term is best understood by looking at its parts: *poly* and *morphic*. *Poly* means "many"; *morphic* means "having a form or shape." Put together, the word *polymorphic* means "many forms or shapes." Specifically, every time it replicates across a network, polymorphic malware **can change aspects of itself**, like file name, file size, code structure, and so on, in order **to evade detection**.
Trojan	A Trojan horse is malware that **looks harmless**, or even desirable, **but contains malicious code**. Trojans are often found in software that is easily and freely downloadable from the internet—audio and video codec files often harbor this type of malware.
Botnet	A botnet is **many infected systems that have been harnessed together and act in unison**. They're typically managed via some type of command and control structure created by the attacker. Botnets can be used for cryptocurrency mining, DDoS attacks, sending spam, and so on.
Boot sector infector	Boot sector infectors are pieces of malware that are able to **install themselves in the boot sector of a hard drive**. That allows it to run upon system boot up. Boot sector infectors are extraordinarily difficult to detect, and once installed, they're very difficult to remove. Most operating systems can't read the boot sector by default, so boot sector malware often stays very well hidden, almost as if invisible.
Hoaxes/ Pranks	Hoaxes and pranks are not actually software. Rather, they're typically **social engineering**—via email or other means—that intends harm (hoaxes) or just a good laugh (pranks). For example, a hoax could be something like telling a person they can speed up their system by going to a command prompt and typing DEL *.* In fact, following those instructions could potentially lead to the deletion of everything on a system. A prank could be something like editing the display settings of a system and flipping the screen upside down.

Table 7-7: **Malware Types**

Logic bomb	A logic bomb is a bit of code that, **based on some logic, will execute**. A classic example of this is a situation that involved a system administrator at a small/medium-size organization. He was the only IT person and had worked for the organization for years. Over time, he grew disgruntled and wrote a little logic bomb and planted it in a system. The logic bomb did one simple thing: it queried the HR database every morning and asked one simple question, "Am I still an employee?" One day, when the IT person was no longer an employee, the logic bomb continued to execute and deleted every bit of data from the systems. Think scorched earth—backups, files, email—everything was wiped out. As a result, the organization was seriously impacted. The former IT guy went to jail.
Stealth	Stealth malware is malware that uses various **active techniques to avoid detection**. Stealth malware will attempt to actively disable the security capabilities of the system (e.g., disable the antivirus software). Once a computer is infected with stealth malware, detection and removal can be a complex process.
Ransomware	Ransomware is gaining in popularity very rapidly. It is a type of malware that typically **encrypts a system or a network of systems**, effectively locking users out, and **then demands a ransom payment** (usually in the form of a digital currency, like Bitcoin) to gain access to the decryption key.
	Many ransomware attacks begin with the attacker gaining access to the target network and exfiltrating a significant amount of data from the organization. Once this is done, system and network encryption takes place. By threatening to release the exfiltrated data to the public and causing the organization reputational and other harm, the attacker increases the likelihood of receiving the ransom payment.
Rootkit	Similar to stealth malware, rootkit malware attempts to mask its presence on a system. As the name implies, a rootkit typically includes a collection of malware tools that an attacker can utilize according to specific goals. For example, one tool in a rootkit might be used to steal passwords, while another tool might be used to plant a backdoor or mask its presence by deleting critical system files and replacing them with fake ones.
Data diddler	A data diddler is a piece of malware that **makes very small changes over a long period of time** to evade detection. One example of this is known as a salami attack. How do you slice salami? Very thinly. A salami attack is specific to financial systems, with regards to calculating interest and taxes. Oftentimes these numbers are never calculated perfectly, thus allowing a salami attack to shave off fractions of amounts and put them in another account. Over time and with enough transactions, the shaved amounts can add up to quite a significant sum of money.
Zero day	A zero day is **any type of malware that's never been seen in the wild before**. The vendor of the impacted product is unaware, as are security companies that create antimalware software intended to protect systems. Certainly, customers are completely unaware of a zero day. The only person aware of a zero day is the creator of the malware; they're using it for the first time. Because this is day zero of the malware being "in the wild," no detection signatures yet exist, and this fact makes zero day malware potentially very dangerous.

Table 7-7 (continued): **Malware Types**

Third-Party Provided Security Services

As cloud technology and services have become more common, so too have phrases like "third-party provided security services." Third-party provided security services simply refer to the menu of security-related services that can be contracted. So, in addition to the many security-related practices and controls discussed in this section, SIEM, auditing, penetration testing, antivirus and malware, and forensic services can be provided by third-party providers.

7.7.2 Anti-malware

> CORE **CONCEPTS**
>
> - Anti-malware software designed to prevent malware from being triggered.
>
> - Policy and user training and awareness can help prevent malware outbreaks.
>
> - Signature-based anti-malware software can also help prevent malware outbreaks.
>
> - Heuristic anti-malware software looks at the behavior of code or a file to help identify malware.

Anti-malware, as the name suggests, is training or software designed to prevent malware from being triggered. One of the best anti-malware solutions is effective policy and providing user training and awareness to staff members. Considering that a virus requires human interaction—typically the click of a mouse on a link or opening of an attachment—to trigger it, it follows that providing a basic understanding of security and steps to follow can help prevent virus outbreaks.

> What is one of the most effective ways to prevent malware outbreaks?

More technical methods of detecting malware include using **signature-based antimalware** systems. These systems contain what are known as definition files—files that include signature characteristics of currently known malware—and scan systems using this information to detect suspicious and compromised files. These systems are **unable to detect zero-day malware**, and they're only accurate based upon accurate definition files, so they constantly need to be updated.

> Understand the difference between signature-based and heuristic malware detection software

Heuristic systems, on the other hand, do not look for malware based on a particular pattern or signature. Rather, they look at the underlying code or behavior of a file. For instance, if a heuristic system identified an executable file as suspicious, it might run the file in what's known as a sandbox, to see how the file behaves. Heuristic systems generally work one of two ways:

1. **Static** code scanning techniques: the scanner scans code in files, similar to white box testing
2. **Dynamic** techniques: the scanner runs executable files in a sandbox to observe their behavior.

Either way, by examining code or running in a sandbox, heuristic systems are attempting to determine what the code does or how the file behaves. If it detects something suspicious, it will block the file. Most malware is designed to know when it's being analyzed, especially in the context of a sandbox, and will behave normally (malicious operation will remain dormant). Then, once on a real system, it behaves maliciously. Also, heuristic systems tend to generate high numbers of false-positives; in other words, perfectly legitimate files and application programs are flagged as suspicious, which slows down productivity of staff members. The major advantage of heuristic scanners is they **can potentially detect zero day malware.**

Activity monitors monitor running systems to see what processes are active. If something suspicious is detected, an alert will be raised. Malware often installs itself on a system and runs in the background. Activity monitors are designed to detect the malware and send an alert.

Change detection (also known as file integrity monitoring), commonly found in Linux-based systems, focuses on modification of key system files. Change detection systems first create hashes of key operating system files and store the hashes in a secure location. Then, as frequently as necessary—every hour, every day, whatever interval makes sense—the tool will rehash the files and compare the new hashes against the stored hashes. If they match, everything is good; if they don't, something might be wrong and an alert is generated. Similar to other types of systems, especially signature-based antimalware systems, change detection systems require continual updating in order to be most effective.

Machine Learning and Artificial Intelligence (AI)-Based Tools

To understand what is meant by machine learning (ML) and artificial intelligence (AI)-based tools, it is important to have an understanding of each term. Of the two, artificial intelligence has been in use longer, and over the years its meaning has changed to reflect advances in technology and the goals trying to be achieved. In today's context, AI development has focused more on the use of human intelligence as a model and not as a goal unto itself.

With this understanding, machine learning (ML), which is often viewed as a subset of artificial intelligence, can be used for purposes of business growth, improving customer selection and satisfaction, and optimizing processes, logistics, speed of delivery, and quality, among others. In its simplest form, ML employs the strength of artificial intelligence, where a computer is used to learn from data inputs (the past) and make predictions (the future). In reality, ML systems are often networked computers that utilize very powerful processors to run complex algorithms in order to derive meaningful and actionable insights for the sake of future endeavors based upon data inputs generated by past events.

Together, ML and AI-based tools can:

- Empower systems to use data to learn and improve without being explicitly programmed
- Make predictions through the use of mathematical models to analyze patterns

ML/AI Security Application

Based upon the above information, in the context of security, ML/AI is specifically being leveraged to provide:

- Threat detection and classification
- Network risk scoring
- Automation of routine security tasks and optimization of human analysis
- Response to cybercrime:
  - Unauthorized access
  - Evasive malware
  - Spear phishing

In addition to the topics and subject matter covered here in section 7.7, the Official CISSP Certification Exam Outline includes other topics in this section that are covered elsewhere in the book. Please refer to Domain 4 for details on the following topics:

- Firewalls (e.g., next generation, web application, network)
- Intrusion Detection Systems (IDS) and Intrusion Prevention Systems (IPS)
- Whitelisting/blacklisting
- Sandboxing
- Honeypots/honeynets

7.8 Implement and support patch and vulnerability management

7.8.1 Patch Management

CORE **CONCEPTS**

- Patch management helps create a secure environment by fixing—patching—security flaws and vulnerabilities in systems.
- Patching only secures a system against known vulnerabilities.
- Change management should be part of a patch management program.
- Determining patch levels can be done via: agent, agentless, passive methods.
- Deploying patches can be done manually or automatically.

Patch management is a *proactive process to create a consistently configured environment that is secure against known vulnerabilities*. Patches fix security flaws and vulnerabilities in systems. Patches can also improve performance and add functionality.

Whenever deploying patches, it's important to do so in a manner that leaves the operating environment consistently configured. Patches should be deployed to the entire environment and verified that they were deployed properly and everything is consistently configured. Many patch management systems actually include the capability of knowing when new patches are available and specifically which ones need to be installed. For example, most

> **Understand why timely and consistent application of patches is beneficial and important**

Windows users are very familiar with the persistent notifications when a patch is available for installation. A number of other systems leave patching up to the system owner and do not indicate that a patch is available or needs to be installed. One other important aspect of patch management is the need for threat intelligence capabilities. Knowledge of new threats is imperative, along with up-to-date system inventories, including patching needs. Threat intelligence can be developed internally, through hardware and software vendor news feeds, email lists, and so on. The point is that patch management should be as proactive as possible to remain as secure as possible.

Once the need for an available patch has been identified, a change management process should be employed as part of the decision to move forward and install the patch. The full patch management life cycle can be seen in Figure 7-8.

Figure 7-8: **Patch Management Life Cycle**

Determining Patch Levels

As alluded to, it's important to be able to determine patch levels of systems, and several ways to do this exist. One way is agent-based. An agent is a small program installed on a host, and it monitors the host for patch needs. The agent knows what software/patches are installed on the host, and it routinely compares them to a master database to see if any needs exist. If patches are needed, the agent typically automatically initiates an update process.

> **Understand the methods used to determine patch levels and ramifications/ challenges of each method**

Agentless, as the name implies, means no agent is installed on the host system. Rather, monitoring software or a patch scanning system will routinely connect to the host and check patch levels.

Finally, there's what's known as passive detection. With this approach, a look back at vulnerability analysis is required—specifically with how operating system and software versions are detected on a system. This is done through fingerprinting, where activity on a system—network packets particularly—can identify system and software versions. Based upon this approach and data gathered, it can be possible to determine the patch level of systems and then respond accordingly.

Three methods for determining patch levels are summarized in Table 7-8.

Agent	Agentless	Passive
Update software (agent) installed on devices	Remotely connect to each device	Monitor traffic to infer patch levels

Table 7-8: **Patch Levels of Systems**

Deploying Patches

Once the need is identified, patches can be deployed via manual or automated means. With a manual approach, somebody actually logs into the target system and installs the software. With an automated approach, software is used to roll out the patches. A good example of the latter is Microsoft's Windows Server Update Services (WSUS), which helps maintain and update patches on Windows computers. With regards to high-value, high-priority production systems, automated patching shouldn't be used because patching sometimes breaks things. So, manual patching of these types of systems is often the best approach, as it allows for much better control and response if an issue arises. For rank-and-file systems, automated patching is the best approach and can help an organization maintain a consistently configured environment that was mentioned earlier.

> **Understand patch deployment methods and why it might make sense to use a manual method**

Manual versus automated patching are summarized in Table 7-9.

Manual	Automated
Somebody logs into the system and installs the software	Patching software automatically rolls out the software updates

Table 7-9: **Patch Deployment Methods**

7.9 Understand and participate in change management processes

7.9.1 Change Management

Change management is important in the context of security operations. In essence, **change management ensures that costs and benefits of changes are analyzed and changes are made in a controlled manner to reduce risks.** The actual change management process is described below.

Change Management Process

The first step is known as a change *request*. A change request can come from any part of an organization and pertain to just about any topic. A business owner might want new functionality. Someone in IT identified a misconfiguration that requires a change. A threat management application identified that a system is vulnerable and needs to be patched. Changes can come from everywhere. When a change request is made, the *impact of the change must be assessed*. How big of a deal is this change?

Understand the change management process and what happens at each step

If a vulnerable system requires a patch, should the change management process take the typical amount of time?

No, this is when emergency change management can be utilized. Related to the severity of the proposed change, the size of the change must be considered. If the change is minor and relates to a low-value system of secondary importance, how many levels of review and approval should be involved?

Common sense would dictate not many levels, but if this is a multimillion-dollar change that's going to affect multiple stakeholders and customers, how many levels of review and approval should now be involved? Probably quite a few.

After a change request has been assessed, *approval* should follow. Approval can take place at multiple stages, but if a significant and potentially costly change is being considered, it should definitely be approved first, Approval also takes place in the context of starting and designing a change as well as prior to implementation. Who approves change can vary significantly, but the owner of the system and potentially other relevant stakeholders should definitely be part of the approval process. This fact explains why **Change Advisory Boards (CAB)** are often utilized as part of the change management process, because they include key stakeholders from throughout an organization.

Once approved, the change should be *built and tested*, and key people should be *notified* before *implementing* the change. Testing might include things like regression testing, where changes can be tested to ensure that everything still works, including the new functionality. Other types of validation testing can also be conducted. Once a change has been built and tested, stakeholders notified, and the change implemented, management and other relevant parties should once again be notified to *validate* the change.

Finally, and perhaps most important, it's critical to update documentation and *versions and baselines*. In fact, documentation should take place throughout the process. The discipline and rigor that a company places upon change management is directly proportional to how well a company operates. In other words, if a company has terrible or nonexistent change management, their environment is most likely a mess, pointing toward disaster. It's undoubtedly reactive, and employees are probably constantly fighting fires. Without enough or proper change management, the environment is likely chaos. Contrarily, with too much change management, every change often requires too much time and too many layers of approval. In this context, people avoid and go around the process, which can lead to chaos as well. Proper change management strikes a balance between too much and too little oversight. All required change management steps have been depicted in Figure 7-9 and described in Table 7-10.

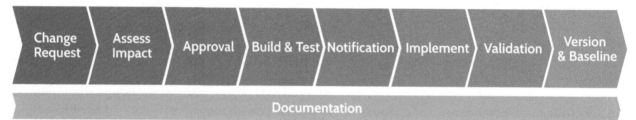

Figure 7-9: **Change Management Steps**

Change request	A change request can come from any part of an organization and pertain to almost any topic. Organizations typically use some type of change management software that includes a request portal, among other tools that help manage and track the overall process.
Assess Impact	After a change request is made, however small the request might be, the impact of the potential change must be assessed. Additionally, the size of the change should be included in this assessment.
Approval	Based upon the requested change and related impact assessment, common sense plays a big part in the approval process. If the requested change relates to a critical need, perhaps emergency change management protocols can be utilized. If the requested change relates to noncritical, lower-value items, the levels of review and approval should probably be minimal. However, if the change is significantly costly and going to impact multiple stakeholders, the levels of review and approval should likely be high.
Build and Test	After approval, any change should be developed and tested, ideally in a test environment. Testing should be thorough and include all steps necessary to ensure proper functionality of the change as well as viability of existing functionality.
Notification	Prior to implementing any change, key stakeholders should be notified.
Implement	After testing and notification of stakeholders, the change should be implemented.
Validation	Once implemented, senior management and stakeholders should again be notified to validate the change.
Version and Baseline	Documentation should take place at each of the steps noted, but at this point, it's critical to make sure all documentation is complete and to identify the version and baseline related to a given change. This last step is especially helpful, as maintaining discipline in this area can help an organization operate most effectively and efficiently in a proactive manner.

Table 7-10: **Detailed Description of Change Management Steps**

7.10 Implement recovery strategies

7.10.1 Failure Modes

CORE CONCEPTS

- Failure modes refers to what happens in an environment when something—component in a system, an entire system, facility—fails.
- Three failure modes: fail-soft (fail-open), fail-secure (fail-closed), fail-safe.
- Fail-safe prioritizes the safety of people.

> Understand the three types of failure modes and what each one prioritizes

Within any environment, consideration must be given to when things fail. Failure refers to components within a system, for example, disk drives or power supplies, as well as entire systems, like a firewall, or facilities, like an office or warehouse. Several failure modes exist, and they are explained in Table 7-11.

Fail-soft (Fail-open)	Fail into a state of *less* security, for example, a firewall **allowing all** traffic through if it fails. This could cause significant security problems.
Fail-secure (Fail-closed)	Fail into a state of the same or greater security, for example, a firewall **blocking all** traffic if it fails. Though this might block legitimate users, it would also **maintain security** by blocking all attackers.
Fail-safe	Fail into a state that **prioritizes the safety of people**, for example, the doors to a secure facility unlock automatically in the event of a fire alarm going off.

Table 7-11: **Failure Modes**

7.10.2 Backup Storage Strategies

CORE **CONCEPTS**

- Backup strategies are driven by organizational goals and objectives and typically focus on backup and restore time as well as storage needs.

- Archive bit is technical detail—metadata—that indicates the status of a backup relative to a given backup strategy; 0 = no changes to file or no backup required, and 1 = file has been modified or backup required.

- Backup strategies: incremental, differential, full, mirror

- Incremental backup: Changes since last incremental backup

- Differential backup: Changes since last *full* backup

- Full: All data

- Mirror backup = an exact copy of a data set is created, and no compression is used.

- Backup rotations refers to different types of tape backup strategies, like first in, first out (FIFO), grandfather-father-son, and Tower of Hanoi, to name a few. Each strategy dictates when a tape is used for backup, how long a tape is retained, and restoration requirements.

- Reasons for rotating backups include when a given tape is used, how long a tape is retained, and restoration requirements.

- A backup checksum is also known as a cyclic redundancy check or CRC. A CRC ensures the integrity of data through a bit of math and can be used anywhere data resides.

Recovery strategies focus on several key things, including bringing systems back online quickly, minimizing data loss, and architecting systems in a manner that precludes system downtime if a system failure occurs.

> **Understand different backup strategies and how a backup strategy fits into an overall recovery strategy**

An important component of recovery strategies is backup strategies, which focus on backing up data in such a manner that if the primary data store is lost, corrupted, stolen, or otherwise compromised, the data can be recovered and restored. Before diving in a bit deeper on this topic, it's important to understand a technical detail known as an *archive bit*. Within virtually every operating and associated file system, each file will have an associated bit. The bit is simply metadata, which is data about data.

Archive Bit

An archive bit, as depicted in Figure 7-10, can be set to zero (0) or one (1), and the setting indicates if the file needs to be backed up or not. If the archive bit is set to 0, the file does not need to be backed up; if the archive bit is set to 1, the file needs to be backed up. When a backup is performed, the archive bit is usually set to 0. After the backup, if any of those files are modified or if new files are created, the archive bit is set to 1, indicating that the file needs to be backed up.

0   1

No changes to file
No backup required

File has been modified
Backup required

Figure 7-10: **Archive Bit**

This is important to understand because different backup strategies deal with the archive bit differently. Incremental and differential backup strategies do not treat the archive bit in the same manner.

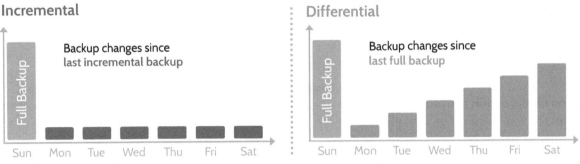

Figure 7-11: **incremental vs. Differential**

Figure 7-11, each diagram shows the days of the week on the horizontal line, because backup strategies are typically based on a seven-day calendar week. The varying height bars above each day represent the amount of data being backed up during each backup cycle.

Incremental Backup

An Incremental backup starts by performing a full backup, represented by the bar above Sunday. A **full backup** means that every file, regardless of the archive bit setting, is backed up, and the archive bit on each file is then set to 0. On Monday, the typical beginning of a work week, people show up and start creating or modifying files. The archive bit associated with every new or modified file is set to 1. On Monday evening, when the incremental backup is run, all of the files with an archive bit set to 1 are backed up, and the archive bit is reset to 0. On Tuesday, people once again come to work and create or modify files, and all of the files that have been created or changed since Monday are backed up during Tuesday's incremental backup. As the diagram depicts, incremental backups typically lead to a small amount of data being backed up each time. **Only the changes—new or modified files—since the last backup are backed up each evening**.

Differential Backup

A differential starts the same way, by performing a full backup, and the archive bit on each file is set to 0. On Monday, as before, people show up to work and create or modify files, and the archive bit on each new or modified file is set to 1. Here's where the difference exists: On Monday evening, when the differential backup is performed, the archive bit of backed up files is not reset to 0. All of the files whose archive bit is set to 1 are backed up, and the archive bit on each file remains set at 1. On Tuesday, people again create and modify files, and the archive bit on those files is set 1. Now, during Tuesday's differential backup, all of the new and changed files from Monday and Tuesday are backed up, and again, the archive bit on every backed up file stays set to 1. On Wednesday, Thursday, Friday, and Saturday, the same thing happens. As the graph depicts, differential backups result in more and more files being backed up each evening. In other words, **all of the changes since the last full backup** (on Sunday) are backed up each evening.

As one might imagine, each backup strategy comes with pros and cons.

One advantage of incremental backups is they're typically very fast, especially toward the end of the week when much less data is being backed up. However, a big disadvantage of incremental backups relates to recovery. Imagine a system has failed on a Saturday night, and we need to restore all of the data. First, Sunday's full backup would need to be restored, and then each incremental backup prior to Saturday (or including Saturday, if Saturday's backup took place prior to the failure) would need to be restored. This obviously represents quite a few backup tapes as well as time to recover.

Contrary to a longer recovery time with incremental backups, recovery with differential is much quicker. At most, only two backup tapes would ever need to be restored—the full backup and the most recent differential. This is a significant advantage relative to incremental backup. However, differential backup takes more time to perform, especially at the end of the week, and much more data storage is used.

Which strategy should be utilized? As with many decisions, the goals and objectives of the organization should drive this decision. What's the business trying to achieve? What are they willing to pay for? Similar questions will ultimately help drive the response to this question.

Mirror Backup

Another type of backup is known as a **mirror backup**, where **an exact copy of a data set is created, and no compression is used**. Mirror backups can often be created and restored quickly, but at the cost of significant amounts of data storage. Of the three types of backups mentioned, mirror is the fastest to backup and restore, but it requires a tremendous amount of data storage; incremental backups require the least amount of data storage. Table 7-12 contains a comparison of the prementioned back strategies.

Type	Data Backed Up	Backup Time	Restore Time	Storage
Mirror	Exact copy with no compression	Fastest	Fastest	High
Full	*ALL data*	Slowest	Fast	High
Differential	Full and then *changes since last full backup*	Moderate	Moderate	Moderate
Incremental	Full and then *changes since last backup*	Fast	Slow	Lowest

Table 7-12: **Summary of Backup Strategies**

Backup Storage Strategies

There is always a question about what locations are optimal to store backups. A good choice would be to store the backup media at a geographically remote location. Geographically remote means the backup location is far enough away from the primary location so a natural disaster, political uprising, or other significant event at the primary location won't impact the backup location. Some of the most common storage strategies are outlined below:

> **Understand backup storage strategies, including reasons for tape rotation**

- **Offsite storage:** This term refers to a place where, for example, backup tapes and copies of other important media can be stored. Typically, an offsite storage location is far from an organization's primary location.

- **Electronic vaulting:** This term usually implies some type of automated tape management system, like a tape jukebox. These systems contain numerous backup tapes, which are managed automatically by a robotic arm and backup scheduling software.

- **Tape rotation:** This refers to different types of tape backup strategies. Each strategy dictates when a tape is used for backup, how long a tape is retained, and restoration requirements.

Cyclic Redundancy Check (CRC)

In the context of backups and moving data around a network, a term known as cyclic redundancy check, or CRC, is often used. A CRC is a bit of math that is used to ensure the integrity of data, and CRC can be used anywhere data resides—hard drive, when moving data across a network, and even in RAM. Among other uses, a CRC can be used to validate backups in order to ensure the integrity of the backed up data. *A CRC is a method of detecting accidental changes to data at rest or in motion.*

Understand the purpose behind the use of checksums/CRC

7.10.3 Spare Parts

> CORE **CONCEPTS**
>
> - Spare parts strategies include: cold spare, warm spare, hot spare.
> - Which strategy is used is often dependent upon organizational goals and objectives.
> - Key considerations include: cost, criticality.

Oftentimes people take for granted that systems in a data center "just work" all the time. But what happens when those systems stop working due to a part failing? Business stops. So, with any critical systems, it's important to have spares of critical components for those systems on hand. Critical components include things like power supplies, cooling fans, hard drives, and so on. Then, if the primary part in a system fails, a spare part can be installed and up and running very quickly. Three types of spare parts exist, and the name points to the location. Table 7-13 contains a summary of all spare types.

Cold Spare	Warm Spare	Hot Spare
■ Parts sitting on a shelf, perhaps in a storage room. ■ If the primary part fails, the system will go offline until the needed spare part can be retrieved and installed. ■ Cold spares result in downtime, but they're also the least expensive.	■ Installed in a computer system, but not powered and available. ■ If the primary part fails, the system will go offline, but getting it back online quickly is often a simple matter of switching over to the spare part. ■ Warm spares lead to less downtime, but this benefit costs a bit more.	■ Installed in a system, powered, and available. ■ If the primary part fails, the spare part instantly takes over the primary part's function. ■ Hot spares are expensive, as are the systems within which they're used, but they also provide significant benefits to an organization.

Table 7-13: **Spare Types**

421

7.10.4 Redundant Array of Independent Disks (RAID)

> **CORE CONCEPTS**
>
> - Redundant array of independent disks (RAID) refers to multiple drives being used in unison in a system to achieve greater speed or availability.
>
> - RAID 0—also known as striping—provides significant speed data writing and reading advantages.
>
> - RAID 1—also known as mirroring—utilizes redundancy to provide reliable availability of data.
>
> - RAID 10—mirroring and striping—requires a minimum of four hard drives and provides benefits of striping (speed) and mirroring (availability) in one solution; this type of RAID is typically one of the most expensive.
>
> - RAID 5—parity protection—requires a minimum of three hard drives and provides a cost-effective balance between RAID 0 and RAID 1; RAID 5 utilizes a parity bit, computed from an XOR operation, for purposes of storing and restoring data.

Redundant array of independent discs, better known as RAID, is the concept that instead of one hard drive being utilized in a system, multiple drives are used in unison to achieve greater speed or availability. In this context, hard drives can be grouped in a number of different ways—called RAID levels—to achieve these goals. Three of the best-known RAID levels are RAID 0, RAID 1, and RAID 5. RAID 0 is also known as striping, RAID 1 as mirroring, and RAID 5 as parity protection. We are going to focus on the most well-known RAID levels.

> **Understand the primary types of RAID and pros and cons of each**

RAID 0—Striping

RAID 0 (shown in Figure 7-12), also known as striping, works as follows. Imagine a file is sent to the RAID controller on a system. The RAID controller is simply a piece of hardware (sometimes it's software) that manages the storage of data on connected hard drives. Depending upon the type of RAID configured, the controller will make the appropriate decision about how to best store the file. With RAID 0, the file is split into two pieces, and one piece is saved on one hard drive and the other on the other hard drive. RAID 0—striping—is all about speed of writing and reading data, because of the power of the RAID controller. If the file is split and written to two drives at the same time, write speed is effectively doubled. Similarly, when reading the file back from two drives at the same time, read speed is also doubled. RAID 0 is all about speed.

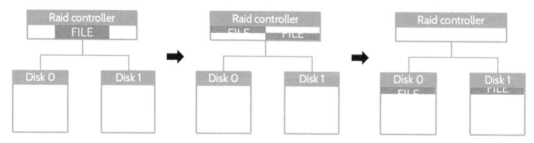

Figure 7-12: **RAID 0**

RAID 1—Mirroring

RAID 1 (shown in Figure 7-13), also known as mirroring, is set up exactly the same way as RAID 0. However, in this case, instead of splitting a file and putting a portion of each on separate drives, the file is written to each drive. In other words, the same file now resides on two different drives; thus the term mirroring. If one drive fails, the file can easily be recovered because it was written to two locations. RAID 1 is all about availability through redundancy.

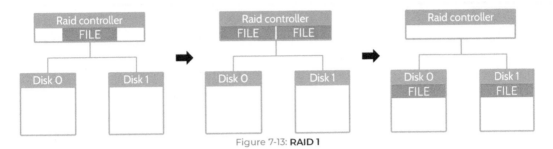

Figure 7-13: **RAID 1**

RAID 10—Mirroring and Striping

RAID 10 or RAID 1+0 or 0+1 (shown in Figure 7-14) is, in a sense, the best of both RAID 0 and RAID 1. With each of the latter approaches, a minimum of two hard drives is required. With RAID 10, a minimum of four drives is required, because you're treating data the way it is treated using RAID 0 and RAID 1. When a file is sent to the RAID controller, two copies are made, and then each copy is split, resulting in four chunks of data. RAID 10 offers the advantage of significant speed and redundancy, but these advantages come with the associated need for and cost of more hard drives.

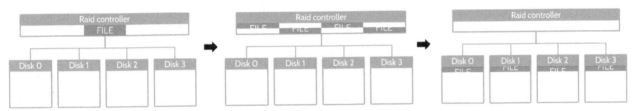

Figure 7-14: **RAID 10**

RAID 5—Parity Protection

RAID 5 (shown in Figure 7-15) attempts to strike a balance between RAID 0 and RAID 1 and provide availability in an efficient and cost-effective manner. Unlike RAID 0 and 1, where a minimum of two hard drives is required to work, RAID 5 requires a minimum of three hard drives. As before, a file is sent to the RAID controller, and the file is split into two parts, and one more piece of data—the **parity data**—is computed, using a binary mathematics operation known as XOR, or *exclusive or*. With the parity data in place, if either part of the file was lost, it could be reconstructed using the remaining part and the data contained in the parity data. So three pieces of data exist—the two file chunks and the parity data—and each is written to a separate hard drive. Additionally, to further provide protection against loss, the parity data is typically not written to only one drive. A round robin methodology is employed that varies the location of file chunks and parity data. RAID 5 offers very quick read/write speeds as well as redundancy.

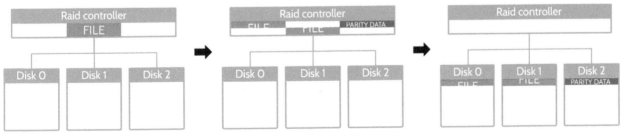

Figure 7-15: **RAID 5**

A comparison between the different RAID types is provided in Table 7-14.

RAID	Data Redundancy	Read/Write Performance	Min. # of Drives	
0 Striping	✗	Highest	2	▪ All about increasing read/write performance ▪ No data resiliency
1 Mirroring	✓	Moderate	2	▪ Great data resiliency ▪ No performance improvement
1+0 Striping + Mirroring	✓	Highest	4	▪ Performance and resiliency ▪ But requires a lot of hard drives
5 Parity Protection	✓	High	3	▪ Good balance of performance and resiliency and requires less hard drives than RAID 10

Table 7-14: **RAID Type Comparison**

7.10.5 Clustering and Redundancy

> CORE **CONCEPTS**
>
> ▪ **Clustering = a group of systems working together to handle a load.**
>
> ▪ **Redundancy = typically a primary system and secondary system, with the secondary system in standby mode and ready to take over if something goes wrong with the primary system.**
>
> ▪ **Clustering and redundancy both include high availability as a by-product of their configuration.**

Clustering and redundancy are two other important terms pertaining to recovery and protection of systems and data. Both concepts point to high availability (HA) of systems.

> **Understand the difference between clustering and redundancy and a primary by-product of each approach**

Clustering refers to a group of systems working together to handle a load. This is often seen in the context of web servers that support a website. Typically, incoming traffic will be managed by a load balancer that distributes requests to multiple web servers, the cluster. With clustering, if one system goes down, the amount of overall performance for the cluster drops by an equivalent amount.

Redundancy also involves a group of systems, but unlike a cluster, where all the members work together, redundancy typically involves a primary system and a secondary system. The primary system does all the work, while the secondary system is in standby mode. If the primary system fails, activity can fail over to the secondary. One or more secondary systems can exist, but there is always only one primary. With redundancy, if the primary system goes down, there is no loss in performance, because the secondary system takes over, and typically any secondary system will be configured exactly the same as the primary system.

Clustering and redundancy both include high availability (HA) as a by-product, which can help ensure ongoing operations in the face of planned/unplanned system outages, failure of components, or other disruptions to operations. Clustering is about systems working together, and redundancy is about one primary and one or more secondary systems.

Clustering and redundancy are summarized in Table 7-15.

Clustering	Redundancy
A cluster of **multiple systems work together** to support a workload	A **single primary system supporting the entire workload** and one or more and secondary systems that will take over if the primary one fails

Table 7-15: **Clustering and Redundancy**

7.10.6 Recovery Site Strategies

> **CORE CONCEPTS**
>
> - Recovery site strategies consider multiple elements of an organization—people, data, infrastructure, and cost, to name a few examples—as well as factors like availability and location.
>
> - Geographically remote and geographic disparity refer to where a recovery site is located relative to the primary site.
>
> - Internal recovery sites are owned by the organization; external recovery sites are owned by a service provider.
>
> - Multiple processing sites are more than one site where key business functionality is performed.
>
> - System resilience, high availability, quality of service (QOS), and fault tolerance are achieved using recovery site strategies as well as things like clustering, redundancy, replication, spare parts, and RAID.

Recovery to this point has been more focused on systems or components of systems. Recovery of sites is equally important. For example, what happens if an entire data center goes down?

Different recovery strategies exist, and elements like time to recover and money are important components of each. Something called a cold site is relatively inexpensive, but it takes a relatively long time to bring online. A mirrored or redundant site, on the other hand, can be brought online very quickly, but this type of site is also extremely expensive. Figure 7-16 illustrates this fact, and each type of strategy will be discussed in a bit more detail below.

> **Understand the time required to bring each type of recovery site online**

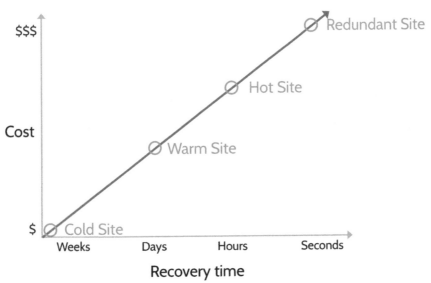

Figure 7-16: **Recovery Site Types**

Before looking more closely at different types of recovery sites, however, it's important to examine components related to each strategy.

Infrastructure and HVAC refer to the shell of a building and the heating, ventilation, and cooling equipment—pretty much the basic items that make up any building. It may also include equipment racks and basic cabling, but no computers or networking hardware. Racks and basic cabling are cheap; computer and networking hardware can be very expensive, potentially costing millions of dollars. Of course, data is the component that runs on the systems, and people are the component that run and manage the data center on a daily basis. As can be seen, a bare shell is much less expensive than a site that contains everything to run an organization. Recovery time, as noted above, can vary and is essentially the length of time to get back up and running.

The cheapest recovery option—**cold site**—is the least expensive for a reason. With this strategy, you essentially get a shell of a building that needs to be populated with equipment, data, and people. It usually takes weeks to bring a cold site online. The biggest advantage of a cold site is cost—it's cheap.

A **warm site** is better than a cold site, because in addition to the shell of a building, basic equipment is installed—racks are in place, cables are run, and so on. Servers, network, and other equipment as well as data and people are the missing components. Unlike a cold site, a warm site can be brought online in a matter of days.

Hot sites, compared to cold and warm sites, are significantly more expensive, because everything is ready to go except for the data and people. Servers, networking equipment, and so on are all in place, only waiting for data to be restored and people to operate the site. Hot sites can usually be brought online in a matter of hours.

A form of hot site is known as a **mobile site**. A mobile site is a hot site on wheels, and many companies use them in anticipation of emergency or severe business disruption. Essentially, a mini data center is built inside something like a shipping container, and then if something happens, the shipping container can be loaded onto a truck and moved where needed. The federal government uses these when hurricanes or other natural disasters strike. Similar to a stationary hot site, a mobile site can also be brought online quickly—in days, or even hours—with the time to move to location often being the biggest determining factor.

Finally, a **redundant site** is extremely expensive, because the basic infrastructure and equipment, expensive equipment, data, and people are in place and ready to go. A redundant site can be architected in such a manner that the primary site can automatically fail over to the redundant site if required. Thus, a redundant site can be online and running instantaneously or in a matter of seconds. Of course, this benefit comes at very high cost, and it is usually as much as the cost of the primary site.

The recovery sites are summarized in Table 7-16.

	Cold	Warm	Hot	Mobile	Redundant
People					✓
Data					✓
Computer Hardware			✓	✓	✓
Basic Equipment		✓	✓	✓	✓
Infrastructure/ HVAC	✓	✓	✓	✓	✓
Cost	$	$$	$$$	$$$	$$$$
Recovery	Weeks	Days	Hours	Days/Hours	Instant/Seconds

Table 7-16: **Recovery Site Type Comparison**

Understand the importance of geographic disparity to recovery site strategies

Geographically Remote/Geographic Disparity

Another topic of relevance is the notion of a recovery site being geographically remote. In other words, if an organization's primary site is on the East Coast of North America, perhaps the recovery site should be somewhere in the Midwest or West Coast of North America. The idea is that you don't want whatever may have brought a primary site down to also impact the recovery site.

Internal versus External Recovery Sites

The words internal and external refer to who owns the recovery site. Internal sites are owned by the organization; external sites are owned by a third party. A good example of an external site provider is Sungard. Companies like Sungard offer organizations a wide portfolio of colocation, data, and recovery centers around the globe. However, as the use of cloud services has continued to expand, many organizations use it as a significant part of their backup and recovery strategy.

Internal versus external recovery sites are summarized in Table 7-17.

Internal Recovery Site	External Recovery Site
Owned and operated by the organization	Provided by a service provider

Table 7-17: **Internal vs. External Recovery Sites**

Reciprocal Agreements

Another important concept is known as a reciprocal agreement, where two companies agree to support each other if either company suffers an outage. Each company essentially says to the other, "If you experience downtime, you can recover your key systems in our data center." In reality, reciprocal agreements are quite rare, especially in the context of private enterprise.

Multiple Processing Sites

Multiple, or multiprocessing, sites are more than one site where key business functionality is performed. A great example of where this is employed is in the credit card processing industry, where transactions are processed simultaneously at multiple sites located in different parts of the country. A primary record of the transaction is maintained, and the secondary records are there in case something happens at that site where the primary record is located. The premise of multiprocessing sites is geographically dispersed redundant processing, and this functionality is architected from the beginning, which makes it quite expensive but also very effective and reliable.

Disaster Recovery Solutions Summary

With the recovery site landscape described above, how does an organization decide which type makes the most sense? When considering this question, every organization should consider a couple of variables to help determine the answer. The two variables—RPO and RTO (shown in Figure 7-17)—point to data and time as relates to recovering from a disaster.

RPO stands for recovery point objective, and it refers to how much data an organization could afford to lose. The answer to this question specifically drives data backup and recovery strategies.

RTO stands for recovery time objective, and it refers to how long it takes an organization to move from the time of disaster to the time of operating at a defined service level. Defined service level does not mean back to business as usual but rather to some level of service that allows business to move forward.

The business impact analysis (BIA) is the process that helps an organization identify its most critical functions, services, assets, systems and processes, and RPO and RTO are subsequently determined to understand how much data and how quickly these systems and processes need to be recovered.

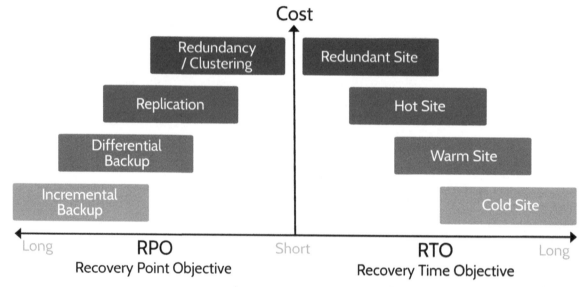

Figure 7-17: **RPO and RTO**

System Resilience, High Availability, Quality of Service (QoS), and Fault Tolerance

In addition to utilizing recovery site strategies, as noted above, system resilience, high availability, quality of service (QOS), and fault tolerance are achieved through the other means noted throughout this section:

- Clustering
- Redundancy
- Replication
- Spare parts
- RAID

As with most security- and cost-related considerations within an organization, goals and objectives ultimately drive decisions, including those related to utilization of one, a combination of, or all of the strategies and solutions noted here.

7.11 Implement disaster recovery (DR) processes

7.11.1 BCM, BCP, and DRP

CORE CONCEPTS

- A disaster is something that interrupts normal business operations

- BCM is the process and function by which an organization is responsible for creating, maintaining, and testing BCP and DRP plans

- BCP focuses on survival of the business processes when something unexpected impacts it

- DRP focuses on the recovery of vital technology infrastructure and systems

The processes described in this topic all help mitigate the effects of a disaster, preserving as much value as possible. Business Continuity Management (BCM), Business Continuity Planning (BCP), and Disaster Recovery Planning (DRP) are ultimately used to achieve the same goal—continuity of the business and its critical and essential functions, processes, services, and so on.

- BCP vs. DRP
- Understanding MTD, RTO, RPO, WRT

A disaster is defined as a sudden, unplanned event that brings about great damage or loss. In a business environment, it is any event that creates an inability on an organization's part to support critical business functions for some predetermined period of time.

Simply put, a disaster is something that interrupts critical and essential business processes. Related terms, like BCM, BCP and DRP, are all listed in Table 7-18.

BCM creates the structure necessary for BCP and DRP. Where BCP is primarily concerned with the components of the business that are truly critical and essential, DRP is primarily concerned with the technological components that support critical and essential business functions. BCP focuses on the processes; DRP focuses on the systems. One important thing to note is that not all business functions are critical or essential, and this should become very clear during the BCP process. Also, even when experiencing a disaster, an organization must still adhere to laws, regulations, privacy requirements, and so on.

Business Continuity Management (BCM)	
The business function and processes that provide the structure, policies, procedures, and systems to enable the creation and maintenance of BCP and DRP plans.	
Business Continuity Planning (BCP)	**Disaster Recovery Planning (DRP)**
Focuses on **survival of the business** and the capability for an effective response; **strategic**	Focuses on the recovery of vital **technology infrastructure and systems**; **tactical**

Table 7-18: **BCM, BCP, and DRP**

Steps in the BCP/DRP process

BCP is all about being able to continue performing work and delivering services at an acceptable level (often tied in with specific SLAs) after an impacting incident takes place at an organization. DRP aims at documenting a specific set of activities that will need to take place so an organization is able to recover from an incident and resume normal operations. It ultimately aims at allowing the organization to return to what is known as a Business As Usual (BAU) state of operation. The key BCP/DRP steps are included in Table 7-19.

1. Develop Contingency Planning Policy	This is a formal policy that provides the authority and guidance necessary to develop an effective contingency plan.
2. Conduct BIA	Conduct the business impact analysis, which helps identify and prioritize information systems and components critical to supporting the organization's mission/business processes.
3. Identify controls	Measures taken to reduce the effects of system disruptions can increase system availability and reduce contingency life cycle costs.
4. Create contingency strategies	Thorough recovery strategies ensure that the system may be recovered quickly and effectively following a disruption.
5. Develop contingency plan	Develop an information system contingency plan.
6. Ensure testing, training, and exercises	Thoroughly plan testing, training, and exercises. Testing validates recovery capabilities, whereas training prepares recovery personnel for plan activation, and exercising the plan identifies gaps.
7. Maintenance	Ensure plan maintenance takes place. The plan should be a living document that is updated regularly to remain current with system enhancements and organizational changes.

Table 7 19: **BCP/DRP Steps**

7.11.2 RPO, RTO, WRT, and MTD

CORE **CONCEPTS**

- **RPO, RTO, WRT, and MTD/MAD are all measurements of time.**

- **RPO = max tolerable data loss measured in time.**

- **RTO = max tolerable time to recover systems to a defined service level.**

- **WRT = max tolerable time to verify system and data integrity as part of resumption of normal ops**

- **MTD/MAD = max time critical system, function, or process can be disrupted before unacceptable/irrecoverable consequences to business.**

When dealing with BCP and DRP procedures, there are four key measurements of time to be aware of. Those are:

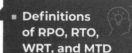
- **Definitions of RPO, RTO, WRT, and MTD**
- **Cost implications of RPO and RTO**
- **MTD = RTO + WRT**

Maximum Tolerable Downtime (MTD)/Maximum Allowable Downtime (MAD)

Refers to the maximum amount of time that an organization's critical process or processes can be impacted. MTD is sometimes referred to as maximum allowable downtime (MAD). If the MTD is reached or exceeded, the ongoing viability of the organization can be called into question, and in fact, the organization may have reached its end and will cease to operate. MTD is often considered relative to the recovery time objective (RTO). As a golden rule, the RTO should never exceed the MTD. In other words, MTD > RTO, or RTO < MTD should always be true.

Using a bank as an example, MTD measures how long their systems can be down before they're no longer in business. If the core banking systems go down and no one can access their money for any significant amount of time, the bank is likely to lose the trust of their clientele and go out of business. A bank's MTD is likely a matter of minutes.

Recovery Time Objective (RTO)

Refers to the amount of time expected to restore services or operations to a defined service level. For example, if a defined and reasonable service level during a period of disruption is 75 percent and it takes four hours to reach that percentage, the RTO is four hours. RTO is a component of MTD.

In the previously mentioned example, if the bank had a backup data center in a different city, the RTO might be a measure of how long it would take to get that backup data center up and running.

Recovery Point Objective (RPO)

Refers to the maximum amount of data that can be lost in terms of time. In other words, how much data is the organization willing to lose as a measurement of time: ten seconds worth of data, ten minutes, fifteen hours, two days, etc. The less data the organization is willing to lose, the more expensive the backup solution will need to be. If the organization is willing to lose up to twenty-four hours' worth of data, then a nightly backup is probably sufficient, but if the organization is only willing to lose a few seconds worth of data, then much more complicated and expensive solutions, like stream backups and/or replication, will be required.

For example, in the event of a massive earthquake, a bank would lose all of the information that wasn't backed up at the time of the disaster. If their maximum tolerable data loss was twenty-four hours, then a significant number of financial transactions would disappear, and the disaster would severely impact their reputation as well. As a result, banks usually have a much shorter RPO.

Work Recovery Time (WRT)

This is the time needed to verify the integrity of systems and data as they're being brought back online. Just bringing systems back online is not enough to ensure the viability and continuity of operations in an organization. There needs to be assurance that the systems are functioning properly. The WRT represents the time needed to perform this step, and it is also a component of MTD.

In order to get back to business as usual (BAU), the bank would need the information from that data center transferred to the original location. WRT would be the measure of how long it takes to ensure that the bank can return to conducting their day-to-day operations.

Figure 7-18 helps visualize how these measurements of time all fit together, while Table 7-20 provides their definitions. The horizontal axis is time, starting with business as usual, and then *kaboom!* Some sort of disaster occurs. The first measurement of time we can now look at is RPO, the maximum amount of data loss as a measurement of time. After the disaster has occurred, the next measurement of time is the RTO, the maximum amount of time to restore processes/systems to a defined service level. WRT is then the time required to validate systems as they are fully brought back online and return to business as usual. Finally, the MTD is the maximum amount of time processes/systems can be down before the business ceases to be a business. MTD is the most important measurement of time to consider when making the decision to declare a disaster.

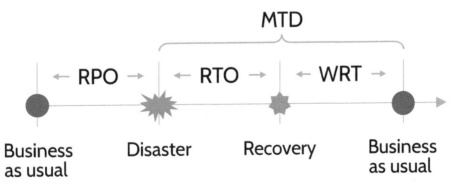

Figure 7 18: **MTD, RPO, RTO, and WRT Relationships**

RPO	**Recovery Point Objective:** Maximum tolerable data loss
RTO	**Recovery Time Objective:** Recovery time to defined service level
WRT	**Work Recovery Time:** Maximum time to verify integrity of systems and data
MTD	**Maximum Tolerable Downtime:** Maximum total time that a process can be disrupted

Table 7 20: **RPO, RTO, WRT, and MTD Definitions**

How to reduce the cost of BCP and DRP plans

When considering the cost related to implementing BCP and DRP plans, the more quickly a given process/function/system needs to be recovered, the more expensive the solution. In other words, the shorter the RPO and RTO requirements, the more significant the cost becomes. To extrapolate further, in order for an organization to make its BCP/DRP plan as cost efficient as possible, one of the goals should be to increase the RPO (more data can afford to be lost) and RTO (the time to recover can take longer) as much as it can tolerate within the acceptable bounds.

- Lower RPO/RTO = more expensive
- Higher RPO/RTO = less expensive

7.11.3 Business Impact Analysis (BIA)

CORE CONCEPTS

- BIA process identifies:
  - **the most critical/essential business functions, processes, and systems**
  - **potential impacts of an interruption as a result of disaster**
  - **the key measurements of time (RPO, RTO, WRT, and MTD) for each critical function, processes, and systems**

The Business Impact Assessment (BIA) is the most important step in Business Continuity Planning. Its purpose is to predict the consequences of a disaster or a disruption to business processes and functions and then identify them as time parameters for the whole purpose of gathering information to develop recovery strategies for each critical and essential function and process. The output of a BIA are key measurements of time: RPO, RTO, WRT, and MTD.

- **Purpose of the BIA process**
- **Steps in the BIA process**

The purpose of the BIA is to identify and prioritize system components by correlating them to the mission/business processes the system supports and then to use this information to characterize the impact on the processes if the system was unavailable. In the event of a disaster, having conducted a BIA ensures that security will make the right decisions about what assets to focus on and will choose the right resources for prioritization of their recovery efforts.

The BIA Process

Since many of the key systems in an organization are interdependent, creating the BIA is not a simple and quick process, and in some organizations it can take months to complete. Each critical business process and system will have its own RPO, RTO, WRT, and MTD measurements.

Identifying and assigning values to an organization's most critical and essential functions and assets is the first step in determining what processes to prioritize in an organization's recovery efforts. Financial records, workshops, questionnaires, interviews, and observation are typically used to determine and assign values, using quantitative and qualitative methods. A crucial part in this process is involving staff from the various company functions so input can be provided about critical systems and services to allow reaching the right decisions. Making these determinations is an iterative and team-oriented effort.

Once asset values are determined, priorities can be set, and processes to protect the most important assets can be identified. Table 7-21 denotes the steps included in the BIA process.

1. Determine mission/ business processes and recovery criticality	Business processes are identified, and the impact of disruption is determined, along with outage impacts and estimated downtime. The downtime should reflect the maximum that an organization can tolerate while still able to achieve the corporate mission. This downtime is reflected in the time-centric metrics discussed earlier: RPO, RTO, WRT, and MTD.
2. Identify resource requirements	Realistic recovery efforts require a thorough evaluation of the resources required to resume critical business processes and related interdependencies. Examples of critical resources may include business processes, facilities, personnel, equipment, software, data, and systems.
3. Identify recovery priorities for system resources	Based upon the results from the previous activities, system resources can be linked to critical business processes. Priority levels can be established for sequencing recovery activities and resources, typically by creating dependency.

Table 7 21: **BIA Steps**

7.11.4 Disaster Response Process

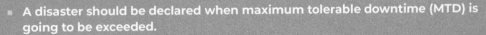

CORE **CONCEPTS**

- A disaster should be declared when maximum tolerable downtime (MTD) is going to be exceeded.

- Disaster response should include all personnel and resources necessary to quickly respond to the situation and restore normal operations.

- Disaster response team personnel should include stakeholders from throughout the organization.

- Disaster communications is critical and should include all relevant stakeholders.

As discussed, *a disaster is something that interrupts normal business operations.* Prior to a disaster being declared however, the incident response process should be followed. As review, the incident response process focuses on ongoing monitoring of events and determining which events are in fact incidents. Once an incident is identified, an assessment of its severity must be made. Is the data center in flames, or did a hard drive in one of the servers fail?

Understand the role maximum tolerable downtime (MTD) plays in the declaration of a disaster

During the assessment of an incident, one specific variable should be carefully considered—MTD, also known as Maximum Tolerable Downtime. MTD is the maximum amount of time that a business can sustain a loss of key functionality and remain viable. So, as part of the incident impact assessment, if it's clear that the MTD will be exceeded, a disaster should be declared and the disaster recovery plan immediately initiated. If the data center is burning and the MTD is four hours, will incident response activities have everything back to normal in less than four hours? No, so the DRP should be activated, which will enable the business to remain viable by bringing a hot, mobile, or redundant site online.

Declaring a Disaster

In the same vein used to discern an incident from an event, determining what is a disaster relative to an incident requires an understanding of what assets might be involved, how operations and processes might be impacted, and other factors that ultimately point to the risk to value and ongoing viability of an organization. The declaration of a disaster and therefore the activation of a business continuity plan needs to be done by an authoritative entity such as the CEO or a Business Continuity Board or Committee.

> **Understand what constitutes a disaster**

Assessment

As noted above, prior to a disaster being declared, the incident response process should be followed. Once an incident is identified, an assessment of its severity must be made. During the assessment of an incident, one specific variable should be carefully considered—MTD, also known as maximum tolerable downtime. *If the MTD is going to be exceeded, a disaster should be declared, and the response process and response team should be activated.* At this point, the response team will help manage an organization through the disaster until it is resolved. Through DR tests held as part of building a DRP, the response team should be able to quickly respond to the situation at hand and take all necessary steps to restore business operations to normal.

Personnel

The trained team—the emergency response team—should consist of stakeholders from throughout the organization. Examples might include personnel representing the following functional areas:

- Executive/senior management
- Legal
- HR
- IT
- PR

Training and Awareness

Success in any endeavor typically involves significant preparation and training, and this is certainly true where the disaster recovery process is concerned. As will be discussed in more detail later in this section, disaster recovery plans should be tested often—at least annually—to best familiarize staff members and members of the emergency response team with the proper steps to follow in the event of a disaster.

Lessons Learned

After a disaster has been handled and operations restored to normal, a review of everything that took place should be conducted. This "lessons learned" exercise should focus on every facet of a BCM and especially on the DRP to determine what worked well, what needs to be improved, and what needs to be added or eliminated from the plan. As planning goes, including a "lessons learned" element could prove to be invaluable for the sake of an organization's long-term success and viability.

Communications

As noted among the specific response components, when a disaster is occurring, communication is of critical importance and should include all relevant stakeholders, which can be a very large group of people.

Relevant stakeholders include people internal to the organization as well as people external to the organization.

- **Internal:** In the event of a disaster, internal communications are critical. Internal stakeholders could include senior management, Board members, business owners, legal, HR, and media and communications team members, among others.
- **External:** Equally critical in the event of a disaster is external communications. External stakeholders could include regulators, law enforcement, customers, the media, and others.

7.11.5 Restoration Order

> **CORE CONCEPTS**
> - The BIA determines restoration order when recovering systems—the most important and critical should be recovered first.
> - Dependency charts and mapping can help inform system restoration order.
> - After declaring a disaster, the most critical systems should be brought online at a recovery site.
> - When restoring systems/operations to the primary site, the least critical systems should be restored first, in order make sure the site is working properly.

How is the order determined for restoring systems?

With multiple systems and accompanying DR plans that make up the overall plan, how is the order of system recovery determined? Which systems are brought back first? Knowing that recovery resources are limited, the BIA helps determine which systems receive priority. The most critical systems, based upon the goals and objectives of the organization, should always be recovered first.

> Understand how a dependency chart informs restoration order of systems/applications

Dependency Charts

Another way to determine system/application restoration order is using dependency charts. For example, let's imagine we want to bring the primary website back online. Is this as simple as turning on the web server and then the site is up? No, because the web server might be part of a more complex architecture that includes a load balancer, a database server, and a cluster of web servers. So, to bring the website back up, each underlying component would first need to be online and available. Dependency charts, like the one shown in Figure 7-19, can map out exactly what components are required and even their initiation order.

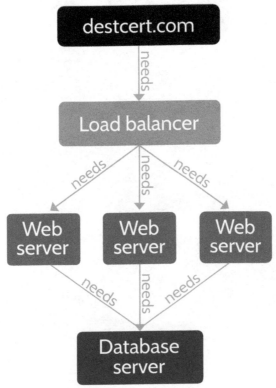

Figure 7-19: **Restoration Order Determination**

Understand the order when moving systems/operations to/from a DR site

What systems/operations should be moved first to the DR site?

After declaring a disaster, the first order of business should always be to get the most critical processes and elements of the business up and running at the recovery site.

Once the primary site is fixed, what systems/operations should be moved back first?

As time progresses, and the primary site is rebuilt and ready to once again host business operations, the processes and systems that should be restored first are the least critical. Why is this the case?

In essence, because the primary site is essentially new, it makes more sense to restore less critical processes and systems first to make sure the new site is working as expected. Once any kinks or issues are resolved, then the most critical processes and systems can be restored.

7.12 Test disaster recovery plans (DRP)

7.12.1 BCP and DRP Testing

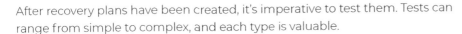

CORE **CONCEPTS**

- DRP testing is a critical component of plan creation and development.
- DRP tests include: read-through/checklist, walkthrough, simulation, parallel, full-interruption/full-scale.
- A full-interruption test should only be performed after management approval has been obtained.

After recovery plans have been created, it's imperative to test them. Tests can range from simple to complex, and each type is valuable.

> **Know the order of DRP testing and which test is least/most impactful**

The first type of test is the easiest and is known as a **read-through test**. This test simply ensures that the major components of the DRP are included, including first steps, accurate contact lists, and so on. Are all of the major pieces of information included in the plan?

The next test is what's known as a **walkthrough test**. The thinking behind a walkthrough is that all of the key stakeholders convene in a conference room and walk through the plan. Key stakeholders could include business owners, IT staff, senior management, legal, and so on. Each person receives a copy of the plan, and everybody walks through it together, thereby allowing problems and holes to be identified, so improvements can be made. The entire exercise is paper-based, but the outcome often proves very valuable.

A **simulation test** follows, and it too is paper-based. Key stakeholders are once again brought together, but this time a facilitator is also included for purposes of moderating a scenario that requires the stakeholders to respond according to what's happening. For example, the facilitator might present a scenario that includes a major fire at a production facility or a dangerous virus outbreak. Once the scenario is presented, the stakeholders must use the DRP to help guide their response. At the same time, the facilitator can continue to throw curveballs at the situation, which requires the stakeholders to think quickly and respond accordingly.

It's important to reiterate at this point that these tests are not an "IT-only business." Whether reviewing BCPs or DRPs, all relevant stakeholders should be at the table and part of the process.

Up to this point, all of the tests have been paper-based exercises. The following section describes tests that include working with systems.

The first is known as a **parallel test**. It's very similar to a simulation test, but in this case the scenario is responded to with people located where they'd be if it was an actual situation. People would touch systems, but only backup systems, not anything in production. This is why it's known as a parallel test—people are only working with systems parallel to production systems.

The last test is what's known as a **full-interruption** or **full-scale test**. With this test, backup and production, or primary, systems are used to respond to the scenario. That is a very important point—with a full-scale test, production systems will be impacted.

Based upon the descriptions above, it's clear that the riskiest type of test—full-scale—is also the best type of test for confirming whether a DRP is going to work. Otherwise, there's really no way to know for sure how the plan, including the response of personnel, is going to function. As risky as they can be, full-scale interruption tests will often reveal the tiniest of holes in a plan and therefore are extremely valuable.

When should a full-scale, full-interruption test be conducted? *Only after every other test has been successfully conducted and with management's approval should a full-interruption test be conducted.* Because a full-interruption test can potentially take production systems down, it's important that senior management be aware of and approve the possibility of this happening. Table 7-22 contains a summary of all prementioned DRP test types.

Type	Description	Affects backup / parallel systems	Affects production systems
Read-through/ Checklist	Author reviews DR plan against standard checklist for missing components/completeness		
Walkthrough	Relevant stakeholders walk through the plan and provide their input based on their expertise		
Simulation	Follow a plan based on a simulated disaster scenario. Stop short of affecting systems or data.		
Parallel	Test DR plan at recovery site/on parallel systems	✓	
Full-interruption/ Full-scale	Cause an actual disaster and follow DR plan to restore systems and data	✓	✓

Table 7-22: **DRP Test Types**

7.13 Participate in business continuity (BC) planning and exercises

7.13.1 Goals of Business Continuity Management (BCM)

> CORE **CONCEPTS**
>
> - BCP and DRP = Business Continuity Management (BCM).
>
> - BCM includes three primary goals: safety of people, minimization of damage, survival of business.
>
> - The number one goal of BCM is safety of people.

 Understand the three goals of business continuity management (BCM)

The goals of business continuity management (BCM), which is the overall BCP and DRP process, are simple, yet important. BCM includes three primary goals:

1. **Safety of people**

2. **Minimization of damage**

3. **Survival of business**

The number one goal of any component of BCM is safety of people. Next, the second goal is minimizing damage to facilities and the business. Finally, the third goal is ensuring the survival of the business. Within all of these goals, *BCM should focus on the most critical and essential functions of the business.*

 Understand the number one goal of BCM

In addition to the material covered in this domain, the (ISC)² Official Exam Outline lists:

7.14 Implement and manage physical security

- ▪ Perimeter security controls

- ▪ Internal security controls

All physical security concepts, including the specific bullet points noted above, have been covered in Domain 3.

7.15 Address personnel safety and security concerns

As already noted, safety of humans should be the paramount consideration within any organization's security plan. Security training and awareness programs, emergency response and management training, and physical security and access controls all help in this regard.

However, two additional subjects related to this topic also need to be touched upon:

- ▪ Travel

- ▪ Duress

Oftentimes employees must travel for work, and sometimes this may include visits to less safe or stable parts of the world. Even though an employee may not be physically present on a corporate campus, the organization is still responsible for ensuring the employee's safety, which might include providing additional medical coverage, travel and health insurance, and an action plan in the event of an emergency. In fact, due to the continued rise in global travel and associated security-related complexities, many organizations—especially large multinational corporations—outsource the travel logistics to companies like International SOS. International SOS acts as a single point of contact and helps design and implement integrated health and security policies and procedures that give access to 24/7 global health, security, travel, and emergency assistance to corporate subscribers.

Along with an understanding of travel-related considerations, security professionals should have a basic understanding of how to handle situations that involve employees under duress. Duress is defined as *"threats, violence, constraints, or other action brought to bear on someone to do something against their will or better judgment."* An example of duress is being held at gunpoint and forced to withdraw money from an ATM, or being threatened with violence unless some type of illegal action is taken. Regardless of the cause of duress, employees should be trained in how to respond in a pressured situation. Depending upon the context, this training might involve the use of code words to alert coworkers of a need for assistance, or perhaps it could involve pressing a silent alarm button that alerts security and other personnel. Most importantly, employees should be trained to respond with reason and to not react to the situation at hand.

MINDMAP REVIEW **VIDEOS**

Investigations
dcgo.ca/CISSPmm7-1

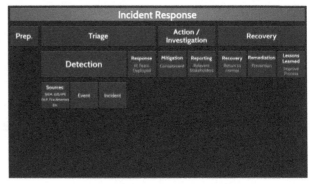

Incident Response
dcgo.ca/CISSPmm7-2

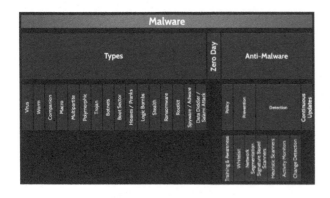

Malware
dcgo.ca/CISSPmm7-3

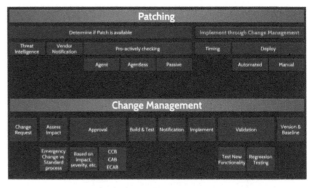

Patching & Change Management
dcgo.ca/CISSPmm7-4

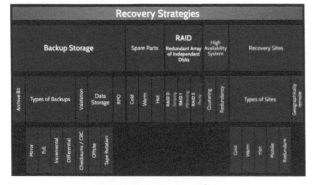

Recovery Strategies
dcgo.ca/CISSPmm7-5

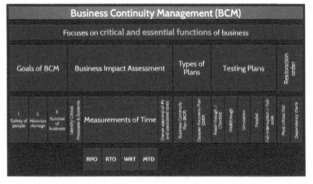

BCM
dcgo.ca/CISSPmm7-6

CISSP PRACTICE QUESTION APP

**Download the Destination CISSP Practice Question app
for Domain 7 practice questions**

dcgo.ca/PracQues

Software Development Security

DOMAIN 8
SOFTWARE DEVELOPMENT SECURITY

Domain 8 is focused on helping security professionals to understand, apply, and enforce software security, otherwise referred to as "application security." The application environment has become very complex, and organizations rely heavily on applications in every facet of the business. As applications have become more intelligent and functional, so have the challenges related to protecting and securing the application environment.

Even though this domain is titled "Software Development Security," it not only focuses on the development life cycle of applications and how security needs to be involved right from the start and throughout the development phases of applications and systems, but also during the entire life of the applications, including the operations phases and decommissioning and disposal phases.

8.1   Understand and integrate security in the software development life cycle (SDLC)

8.1.1 Security's Involvement in Development

> CORE **CONCEPTS**
>
> - **Security should be involved at every phase of the development life cycle.**

As mentioned above, security needs to be an integral part of the development process, and as we've mentioned many times in this book, the best type of security is what is designed into an architecture. This is especially true for applications. Security needs to be involved from the perspective of designing the right level of protection, based on requirements, and therefore needs to be involved at the early phases of software development and throughout each of the subsequent phases.

Similar to when a system reaches end of life and is retired, when an application reaches end of life, security must also be involved to ensure proper archival and disposal. Recall from Domain 4 that quite a lot of attacks take place at Layer 7, the Application layer. This is because so much functionality in the form of applications is available at this layer. Unfortunately, during the development process this functionality is often not considered from the perspective of an attacker, and unforeseen vulnerabilities and potential for exploit often result. Additionally, security is often not involved from inception and throughout the software development process. It typically is tacked on at the end, and this simply does not work. It's very cost inefficient for one thing, and oftentimes it fails to cover all the security needs or gaps. Security should be involved from the beginning, through the deployment and use phases, and all the way to the retirement phase. The entire life cycle should include security at each stage.

Many concepts covered in Domain 8 have already been covered in one manner or another in other domains. Security needs to be included as an integral part of the software development life cycle (SDLC) as well as the system life cycle (SLC). As the name suggests, the SDLC focuses on the development of an application; the SLC picks up at the point where an application is put into production and focuses on use and testing, changes, decommissioning, and disposal.

Understand when security should be considered as part of the SDLC

8.1.2 **SDLC and SLC**

> CORE **CONCEPTS**
>
> ■ Security should be considered at every phase of SDLC/SLC.
>
> ■ Risk analysis and threat modeling are very important components of the early phases of SDLC/SLC.
>
> ■ Testing should include static, dynamic, and fuzz (a form of dynamic testing) tests.
>
> ■ Certification and accreditation should be performed prior to release/deployment/implementation.

Figure 8-1 depicts the SDLC/SLC and how the two relate to each other.

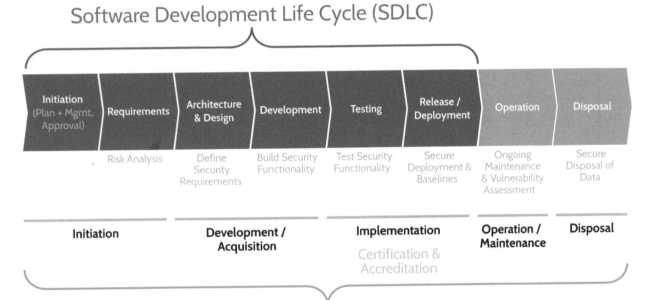

Figure 8-1: **SDLC Phases**

The key thing to focus on is the flow and what happens during each phase, because different methodologies use different names for the same essential steps. In fact, it's quite common for companies to mix and match software development methodologies—agile and structured development, for example, are two common approaches often used to save time and money. For similar reasons, *agile* is a term found in other contexts too, like internal audit and process development. Though the goals of agile are efficiency and cost-effectiveness, quality is not sacrificed in the process. Both goals are met through the utilization of skilled teams composed of subject matter experts, who can adapt and change quickly to meet specific needs immediately at hand. Regardless of the approach—agile or structured, or anything else—security needs to be considered, ideally as early as possible and throughout each of the phases

> **Understand the flow of the SDLC/SLC and what happens at each phase, specifically where security-related activities are concerned**

The SDLC/SLC include management involvement and approval as well as post-deployment activities related to operations, including decommissioning and disposal. Regardless of the phase, security should be involved. For example, during the operations phase, changes are often desired or necessary, and change management helps drive them in an orderly manner. Security in this context helps to ensure that the desired changes meet requirements from a security perspective, and security should ultimately be part of change approval. Unfortunately, many organizations fail to include security as part of change control committees, which should also include senior management, application owners, technology representatives, and so on.

> **Understand at which phase threat modeling should take place and how these results inform the following phase**

It's important to pay close attention to the text underlying each phase of the SDLC, especially where the requirements and architecture and design phases are concerned. During the requirements phase, security should be considered in the form of risk analysis related to the application being developed. Risk analysis continues through to the architecture and design phase, where the architecture of the application is considered in the context of existing infrastructure and systems. Also at this point, specifically where design is concerned, threat modeling is used to determine what security elements should be incorporated into the design of the application. At this point, the application is ready to be coded (development phase), and security can be built into it proactively. It should be noted that portions of the testing phase can overlap with the development phase—specifically static testing/code review can be conducted as units of code are completed. However, the bulk of testing—static (SAST), dynamic (DAST), and fuzz—will take place in the testing phase. This phase of the SDLC is critical and should be comprehensive to include all considerations—normal, error-prone, and malicious—related to usage of the application. Additionally, as part of the transition from testing to release/deployment (SDLC) or during the Implementation phase (SLC), certification/accreditation are performed.

Development and Maintenance Life Cycle

Historically, development methodology has typically followed what's known as a "waterfall" approach, which is simply a phased, step-by-step approach to software development. To move to the next phase, the previous phase must be completed. Sign-offs and approvals mark each phase. As seen in Figure 8-2, the process resembles a waterfall—moving from the top to the bottom in succession. This model includes an inherent flaw, however, in the fact that going backward is not possible. Similar to an actual waterfall, where water can only flow downwards, the waterfall development process only allows downward movement. To further illustrate this point, imagine an application owner wants to develop a new software application. Their first step is to contact technology. In order to best understand the application requirements and start translating those into technical and other specifications, most likely, business analysts will be engaged to effectively and efficiently facilitate the need to bridge technology and business requirements related to the application. The business analysts will spend time with the application owner, asking questions and trying to understand what the owner wants to accomplish with the application. Then the analysts will return to technology and begin the process of developing the application. Here's the problem: at this point, the owner is not involved anymore, but they're still interested in observing all phases of the development process because they're invested in the application. As this process unfolds, of course the owner is likely to come up with new ideas and other feedback.

How does the development team respond? If they're following a waterfall approach, the owner will likely be told that going backward is not possible. The design is frozen, and that's what will be built; however, all those requests can easily be accommodated later as part of change management, which costs more time and money. This is problematic, and the software development industry has attempted to develop new methodologies to address this and other issues.

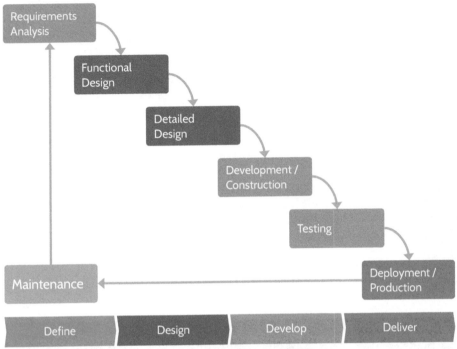

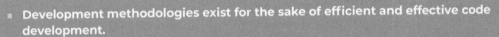

Figure 8-2: **Waterfall Model Phases**

8.1.3 Development Methodologies

CORE **CONCEPTS**

- **Development methodologies exist for the sake of efficient and effective code development.**
- **Many methodologies are a reflection of the waterfall methodology.**
- **Regardless of the methodology, security should be considered at every stage of the development process.**
- **Methodologies can be combined to utilize the best features of each of them.**
- **Agile scrum masters understand how all team efforts fit together and can therefore effectively and efficiently lead activities.**

As noted above, in response to structured and potentially timely and costly software development approaches like waterfall, the industry has developed innovative approaches to accelerate development and still produce quality code. Each of these methodologies reflects the waterfall model, simply with a variation in approach. For example, spiral is aptly named because it allows for the development process to circle back on itself to address an issue or functionality that was part of a previous phase. Similarly, agile refers to a smaller, team-based approach that allows for efficient and cost-effective parallel development. These different approaches have been summarized in Table 8-1.

The bottom line is this: *Whatever methodology or combination of methodologies is used for software development, security must be included throughout the process.*

Be familiar with various development methodologies and key characteristics of each

Waterfall	Complete each phase of development, before flowing—waterfalling—down to the next phase, until the process is complete. This model does not allow a previous phase to be revisited.
Structured Programming Development	A logical programming approach that is said to be foundational to object-oriented programming. Structured programming places heavy emphasis on structured control flow and aims to improve clarity, quality, and development time.
Agile	Divide the development process into multiple, rapid iterations of defining, developing, and deploying, with heavy customer interaction throughout the process.
Spiral Method	A risk-driven development process that follows an iterative model while also including elements of waterfall. The spiral model follows defined phases to completion and then repeats the process; this model resembles a spiral when mapped to paper.
Cleanroom	Development process intended to produce software with a certifiable level of reliability by focusing on defect prevention.

Table 8-1: **SDLC Methodologies**

Understand the different priorities of waterfall and agile methodologies

Waterfall versus Agile

Figure 8-3 depicts waterfall and agile methodologies. Don't focus as much on the phases of waterfall but rather that it's a phased approach. Agile, in comparison, adapts the waterfall methodology and approaches development from the perspective of smaller, highly skilled and motivated teams. Additionally, agile is more focused on early and often delivery of code via what are known as "sprints" led by an agile scrum master.

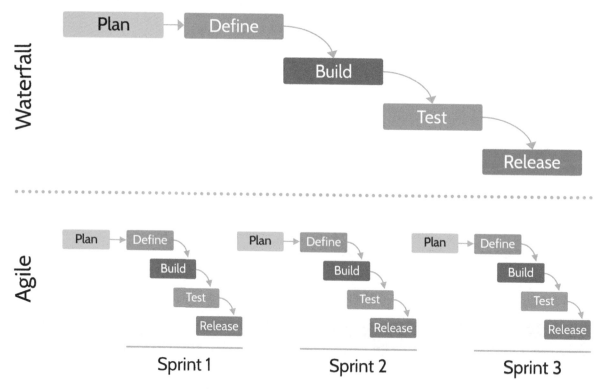

Figure 8-3: **Waterfall vs. Agile Methodology**

Agile Scrum Master

With agile, each team works very closely and in a very time efficient manner, while all of the team's efforts are coordinated by a person known as the scrum master. The scrum master understands how all the team efforts fit together and can therefore effectively and efficiently lead activities. Additionally, the scrum master shields team members from external interruptions, which further enhances productivity. Scrum masters are typically hyperfocused on completing tasks as quickly as possible and hopefully *not* at the expense of security. Other advantages of having a scrum master include the following:

> **Understand the role of a scrum master in agile development**

- Shields team from external interference
- Enforces scrum principles
- Facilitator and removes barriers
- Enables close cooperation
- Improves productivity

8.1.4 Maturity Models

> ### CORE **CONCEPTS**
>
> - Like development methodologies, maturity models also help improve the development process.
> - Capability Maturity Model (CMM) is one of the most popular models and includes five levels of maturity: initial, repeatable, defined, managed, optimized.
> - Each level of maturity of the CMM is defined by certain characteristics.

Other methodologies that improve the development process, even from a security perspective, are known as maturity models and include one known as the Capability Maturity Model (CMM). CMM, sometimes referred to as SW-CMM, offers a structured approach that allows an organization to measure processes and understand where strengths and room for improvements exist.

CMM, depicted in Figure 8-5, includes five phases or levels of measurement. Level 1—initial—is marked by new or unrefined processes that might be considered reactive or chaotic. Level 2—repeatable—is marked by the ability to consistently repeat certain processes for projects, but a reactive and chaotic approach still underscores activities at this level. Level 3—defined—is marked by well-defined and well-documented processes, and a shift from a reactive approach to a planned, proactive approach takes place. At Level 4—managed or quantitatively managed—in addition to the proactive approach seen at Level 3, the use of meaningful metrics is incorporated for the purpose of better process management and improvement. Finally, at Level 5—optimized or optimizing—processes are continually improved using multiple tools.

As noted, each higher level inherits the best aspects of the level below. Ideally, every organization reaches Level 5, but the reality is that most organizations are at Level 3 or below. Regardless, CMM provides an excellent basis for measuring the processes, including software development processes, within an organization and improving them as much as possible.

> **Know the name and characteristics of each level of the Capability Maturity Model**

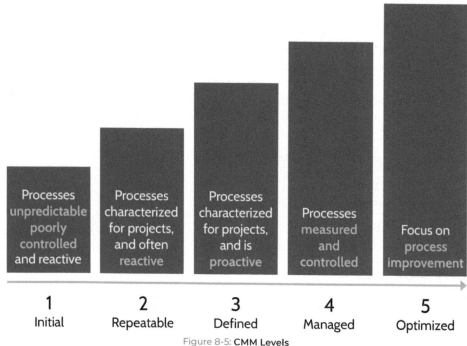

Figure 8-5: **CMM Levels**

Software Assurance Maturity Model

OWASP's Software Assurance Maturity Model (SAMM), is, in OWASP's words, *"to be the prime maturity model for software assurance that provides an effective and measurable way for all types of organizations to analyze and improve their software security posture. OWASP SAMM supports the complete software life cycle, including development and acquisition, and is technology and process agnostic. It is intentionally built to be evolutive and risk-driven in nature."* (https://owaspsamm.org/model/)

SAMM consists of three maturity levels:

- Level 1—Initial Implementation
- Level 2—Structured Realization
- Level 3—Optimized Operation

Maturity levels can be measured from a coverage and a quality perspective based upon quality criteria and a software assurance scoring model that can be referenced by auditors and organizations.

SAMM looks at software assurance from the high-level perspective of five business functions:

1. Governance
2. Design
3. Implementation
4. Verification
5. Operations

Operation and Maintenance

The success of software development is not pinned to the release of an application to production. In fact, it could be argued that long-term successful—and secure—software releases happen as a result of ongoing operation and maintenance that includes **monitoring, periodic evaluation, and patching.**

Individually and collectively, the three actions help ensure software that functions properly and is secure.

Proactive monitoring can uncover security-related problems before they become widespread. Likewise, periodic evaluation that dives deeper can, among other things, confirm that the best components and coding techniques are in place to ensure continued security of the application. When monitoring and periodic evaluations are performed diligently, patching typically follows. Patching may be done for any of several reasons, the most common being to secure a vulnerability in the code or to enhance the functionality of the application.

Change Management (Review)

Among the many topics covered in **Domain 7—Security Operations**, change management was covered in **7.9.1 Change management**. As a review, *change management ensures that costs and benefits of changes are analyzed and changes are made in a controlled manner to reduce risks*. This applies in the context of operations as well as in the context of software development. As Figure 8-6 shows, a change request might be initiated for one of several reasons. It might come in the form of a service request, as part of the incident management process, or as part of a service level agreement (SLA). Additionally, when considering software development-related changes, configuration management and release management must be integral components of the change management process to best assure stable and secure releases.

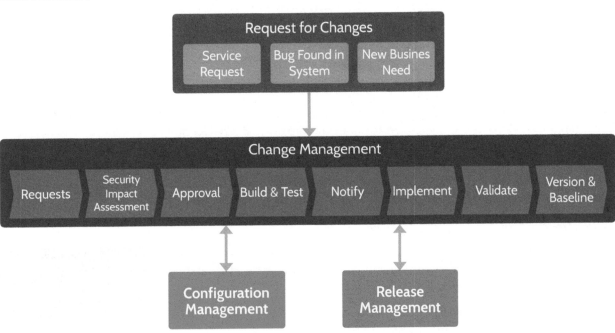

Figure 8-6: **Request for Change (RFC) Process**

8.1.5 DevOps

Integrated Product Team (IPT)

An integrated product team (IPT) is a team of skilled professionals who each bring specific expertise and skills to a development project. At any given point in time, one or numerous members of the team may be more fully engaged with the project, but collectively the entire team is committed and invested in delivering a secure and functional product as well as ensuring this remains the case throughout the product's life cycle.

At its core, the IPT is a fancy name for DevOps, depicted in Figure 8-4, which is a software development approach that aims to unify:

- Software development
- Operations
- Quality assurance

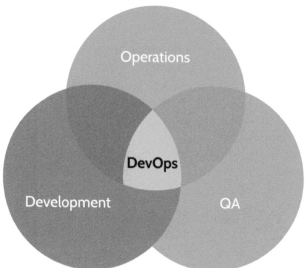

Figure 8-4: **DevOps**

DevOps refers to the integration and inclusion of team members from all relevant areas from the very beginning. The goal of this unification is to create a more agile and responsive environment, which is ultimately more efficient and desirable than having separate teams that must complete their work before passing the project along to the next team. Separate teams often leads to a lack of collaboration and aligned pursuit of common goals. It also often leads to security being tacked on at the end of the project instead of at the beginning and throughout the project.

DevOps Security

As noted above, many traditional security techniques, for example, items like penetration tests, security analysis, and so on are **too slow** for rapid iteration of DevOps.

> **Know when security should be involved with DevOps**

However, DevOps should ideally be referred to as DevSecOps, where security is an integral part of the development process.

Incorporating security into DevOps should include the following components and approach:

- Plan for security
- Strong engagement between developers, operations, and security
- Engage developers
- Develop using secure techniques and frameworks
- Automate security testing, for example, using a robust CI/CD pipeline
- Use traditional techniques sparingly

Combining Development Methodologies

Many organizations combine methodologies to suit their specific needs, and this approach can work with DevSecOps.

8.1.6 Canary Testing and Deployments

CORE **CONCEPTS**

- Canary testing and deployments refer to hyperfocused testing of new application code/features by pushing out the changes to a small subset of users versus pushing out to all users.

The phrase "canary in a coal mine" refers to a practice utilized by early miners to ensure the safety of mining teams deep underground. The teams would carry caged canaries into the tunnels, and if dangerous gases—such as carbon monoxide—collected in the mine, the canaries would die and thus act as an early warning system so the miners could escape a similar fate. In a similar vein, *canary testing and deployments* refers to a software deployment

> Understand what is meant by the term *canary testing and deployment*

approach where new code and features are pushed out to a small subset of users as an initial test, before release to all users. Taking this approach allows problems to be identified and resolved before a full release.

Smoke Testing

Smoke testing is another commonly used type of testing in software development. Smoke testing focuses on quick preliminary testing after a change is made to identify any simple failures of the most important existing functionality that worked before the change was made.

8.2 Identify and apply security controls in software development ecosystems

8.2.1 Software Development Overview

It is important to have a basic understanding of how applications are written. First of all, a programming language is used, and programming languages have evolved over time to become quite powerful and even intelligent. In fact, incorporating security into applications is much easier today because of advancements in programming languages and related tools.

Programming languages have evolved over the years as generations, as depicted in Table 8-2.

Generation 1 and 2 refers to low-level programming languages, like assembly language, which allowed programmers to write programs more easily, but ultimately the CPU would be tasked with translating everything into binary code, into 0s and 1s.

From early generation languages, high-level languages evolved. Generation 3 and 4 languages, structured and object-oriented languages like COBOL, PL/1, Fortran, and BASIC, became more commonplace, and now Generation 5 languages—natural programming languages like Prolog—are coming to the forefront. Even today, however, with newer languages becoming more prevalent, legacy applications written in languages like COBOL are still in production.

Generation		Type of Language	Examples
Low-level languages	1	Machine languages	Strings of numbers that CPU can process
	2	Assembly languages	Cryptic as they use symbolic representation
High-level languages	3	Structured languages	Pascal, C, Cobol, Fortran
	4	Object oriented languages	C++, Visual Basic, Java
	5	Natural language	Prolog

Table 8-2: **Programming Language Generations**

Libraries

By simple definition, a library is a collection of resources. The collection could be resources specific to one topic, or it could be resources that cover a vast array of topics. Code libraries are frequently used in application development and include resources such as documentation, code snippets, functions, and other elements necessary to develop and configure applications that function properly and, ideally, adhere to accepted standards. Why reinvent the wheel—recreate some code that someone else has already written—when it already exists in a library?

Like a public library that houses a myriad of books, publications, and other resources that can be utilized by anybody with a library card, a software library is typically organized in a manner that allows code to be used by disparate applications that have no relationship to each other. Additionally, libraries allow elements of programs and code to be reused again and again.

Two primary types of libraries exist: static and dynamic (runtime).

If code of the library is accessed while the invoking program is being built, the library is referred to as a static library. Alternatively, if the library is called after the program is executed, the library is referred to as a dynamic or runtime library.

Tool Sets

In the context of software and application development, a tool set is a compilation of development tools and utilities that aid the creation of applications. Tool sets are more often referred to as software development kits (SDK), and tools and utilities typically include a compiler and debugger as well as application programming interfaces (APIs), documentation, libraries, and perhaps a development framework. SDKs are often tailored to the development of applications for specific hardware—desktop, laptop, mobile device, for example—and operating system platforms, like iOS, Linux, or Windows. SDKs are typically utilized in the context of larger integrated development environments.

Integrated Development Environment (IDE)

An integrated development environment is a software application that serves as an umbrella for purposes of software development. It's essentially a one-stop shop that provides the tools programmers need to perform their development tasks. Typical IDEs include the following:

- Code editor
- Compiler
- Debugger
- Automation tools

By providing integrated components, an IDE allows programmers to work efficiently and effectively. Some examples of IDEs include Microsoft's Visual Studio, NetBeans, IntelliJ IDEA, Eclipse, and Code::Blocks. Factors that differentiate one IDE from another include: cost-free/open source or licenses (typically annual subscription), programming languages supported, and learning curve. Some IDEs are quite powerful but difficult to learn; others are very beginner-friendly. Determining which IDE is optimal for a given coding environment is really a matter of prioritizing required and desired features and then exploring the IDE landscape to identify the best solution.

Programming Language Translators

Even though better ways to program have evolved over time, computers have not evolved in a similar manner. In fact, computers today still only understand the language they understood fifty to sixty years ago—binary code or machine language. This explains why tools like assemblers, compilers, and interpreters exist. Their job is to take a given programming language and render it as machine language that the computer can understand.

- Assemblers read entire programs and then convert low-level assembly language into machine language.
- Compilers read entire programs and then convert high-level language into machine language.
- Interpreters convert high-level language one line at a time into machine language at runtime.

Runtime

In the context of computing and software, runtime refers to the time when code is being executed on a computer.

Continuous Integration, Delivery, and Deployment

Often referred to simply as *CI/CD or the CI/CD pipeline*, CI/CD is a highly respected practice and approach for DevOps teams to utilize. Additionally, as automation is such an integral part of CI/CD, security can be integrated at every step. Figure 8-7 shows the following components:

- **Continuous Integration (CI)** is a development mindset and set of practices that frequently pursues small code changes and updates to code libraries. Through automation, the process can lead to consistency with the building, packaging, and testing of applications, and it can ultimately lead to better software.

- **Continuous Delivery (CD),** also automated, picks up where CI leaves off, and delivers applications to production, user review, and testing environments. This helps ensure that code changes are delivered quickly and that the delivered code is consistent across all environments.

- **Continuous Deployment (CD),** like CD, ensures that tested and accepted code is deployed to production.

The testing aspect of this process is extremely important, as proper and thorough testing allows for the consistent delivery of quality applications and code to users.

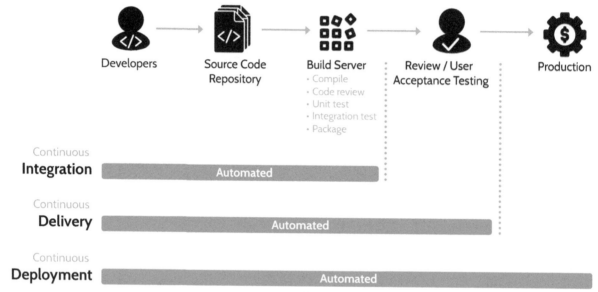

Figure 8-7: **CI/CD Process**

Security Orchestration, Automation, and Response (SOAR)

SOAR is a collection of compatible technologies that take input and data from disparate sources—such as other devices, email, Security Information Event Management (SIEM) systems, user submissions, and manual input—and apply rules and workflows aligned to organizational processes and procedures.

SOAR focuses on three key areas:

- Threat and vulnerability management

- Incident response

- Security operations automation

SOAR tools can be integrated with other technologies and automated to orchestrate a desired outcome and better visibility. SOAR tools typically include incident and threat intelligence management features, reporting, and data analytics. Additionally, through machine-learning and machine-powered assistance, SOC activities and threat detection and response by analysts can be efficiently and consistently improved.

Software Configuration Management (SCM)

As the name suggests, *software configuration management* specifically focuses on managing changes in software and is part of the overall configuration/change management. Like other configuration/change management activities, SCM best practices include baseline establishment and revision control, build and process management, and the facilitation of strong teamwork among the software development team. Though not comprehensive, a summary of some of the most notable benefits of SCM is below:

- Process to systematically manage, organize, and control the changes in the documents, codes, and so on during the SDLC
- Part of overall configuration management/change management
- Increased productivity while minimizing mistakes

Code Repositories

A code repository is, in its simplest form, a storage location for software and application source code. Popular code repositories include Github, SourceForge, Project Locker, and SourceRepo, among others. Most code repositories support public, open source projects as well as private projects, though some, like Project Locker, focus entirely on private, enterprise-grade repositories.

Most code repositories offer much more than simple storage. In addition to hosting project code, repositories typically provide project versioning and release control, support for code review, interaction with others through discussion forums, bug tracking, document management, and patches.

Application Security Testing

Domain 6—Security Assessment and Testing—covers application security testing, and specifically **6.2.1 Testing Techniques** covers static application security testing (SAST), dynamic application security testing (DAST), and fuzz testing. Recall that each method differs from the others, as noted in Table 8-3. Thus, the most effective application security testing incorporates all three techniques.

Static (SAST)	Dynamic (DAST)	Fuzzing
- White box - Examines code	- Black box - Examines application itself	- Form of dynamic testing - Premise is chaos

Table 8-3: **SAST, DAST and Fuzzing**

Secure Programming

Looking back at early programming methods, it's clear that encompassing and meeting security requirements was a difficult task. Over the years, programming methodologies have evolved—including security—and meeting related requirements has become much easier. In fact, most modern programming languages require an understanding of built-in security capabilities to code applications properly. If security requirements related to an application are understood, the inherent security capabilities of the programming language can be incorporated into the finished product.

By focusing on security from the beginning of a project that follows a SecDevOps approach, the right people can help define necessary security requirements. So, the information owners, the business people, the technology experts, and others can all help define, identify, and understand the needed security components.

This is what's important and points to security capabilities that should be incorporated into applications. As noted earlier, many newer programming tools facilitate the integration of these capabilities as part of the overall system. For example, many tools include **inheritance** capabilities. *Inheritance in this context refers to new objects—pieces of code—that automatically inherit characteristics of previously created objects.*

This capability serves several purposes:

- Eliminates the need to program the same characteristics into multiple objects
- Consistent programming and security can be easily propagated to new objects

This implies that the starting point must incorporate sound programming practices; otherwise, weak or missing security characteristics could result, leading to an overall very vulnerable application.

Encapsulation, discussed in the context of remote and VPN connections, is also found in programming. As a quick review, encapsulation means tunneling. In programming, encapsulation involves wrapping an object—a piece of code—to hide certain information or characteristics or to adapt to specific application needs. In a sense, today's code could almost be thought of as "smart code." The code itself can make determinations about actions to take based upon functionality built into the programming tools.

From a security perspective, code can adapt and exhibit characteristics of **polymorphism** and **polyinstantiation**. Like a polymorphic virus, polymorphic code can change. However, unlike polymorphic viruses, which are malicious, polymorphic code changes to meet certain needs or requirements, and it does so for the benefit of the application.

The bottom line is that addressing security to the level needed is much easier today because the tools used to create programs and applications include this functionality by default. A summary of some key terms is provided in Table 8-4.

Inheritance	The ability of an object—a piece of code—to inherit characteristics of previously created objects.
Encapsulation	The idea that an object—a piece of code—can be placed inside another. Other objects can be called by doing this, and objects can be protected by encapsulating or wrapping them in other objects.
Polymorphism	Like a polymorphic virus that can change its behavior to avoid detection, polymorphism in programming refers to code that can change based upon requirements. Think of it as "smart code" that can understand the environment and respond accordingly to meet the needs presented by objects in the environment.
Polyinstantiation	Polyinstantiation refers to something being instantiated into multiple separate or independent instances, and it is covered in **8.5.4 Secure Coding Practices** in detail.

Table 8-4: **Inheritance, Encapsulation, Polymorphism and Polyinstantiation**

8.2.2 Code Obfuscation

CORE CONCEPTS

- **Obfuscation refers to hiding or obscuring something; code obfuscation refers to hiding or obscuring code to protect it from unauthorized viewing.**
- **Three primary types of code obfuscation: lexical, data, control flow.**

The term *code obfuscation* refers to hiding or obscuring code to protect it from those who are unauthorized to view it. More specifically, **code obfuscation is *intentionally creating source code that is difficult for humans to understand,*** which makes it difficult to reverse engineer, or it conceals the purpose of the code. The three main types of obfuscation are outlined in Table 8-5.

Understand the term *code obfuscation* and the three primary types of obfuscation

Lexical Obfuscation	Modifies the **look of the code** (changing comments, removing debugging information, and changing the format of the code) Easiest but weakest form of obfuscation
Data Obfuscation	Modifies the **data structure**
Control Flow Obfuscation	Modifies the **flow of control** through the code (reordering statements, methods, loops, and creating irrelevant conditional statements

Table 8-5: **Types of Obfuscation**

One caveat with regards to code obfuscation relates to a disaster. Specifically, what recourse does an organization have if application code has been obfuscated using one of the techniques noted above? For example, if lexical obfuscation has been used, an organization may have little to no recourse to bringing an application back online quickly. With this in mind, a software vault should be used to securely store unaltered mission critical source code, and planning around the same should be incorporated into an organization's BCM plan.

> **Understand a significant potential disadvantage of using code obfuscation**

Security of the Software Environments

Within the software development environment, most organizations employ the "best practice" of separating specific components. As Figure 8-8 shows, separation of the development and production environments from each other as well as separation of the test and QA environments is prudent. In this same vein, security should be present as an advisor in each context.

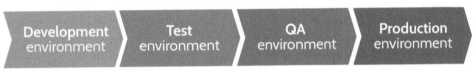

Figure 8-8: **Security of the Software Environments**

8.2.3 DBMS, Concurrency, and Locks

CORE **CONCEPTS**

- **Components of DBMS include: hardware, software, language (SQL, for example), users, data.**
- **Database terminology: columns/fields = attributes; records/rows = tuples.**
- **Foundation of a relational database is the concept of primary and foreign keys.**
- **Primary keys: one or more columns whose values uniquely identify a tuple (row) within a relational database.**
- **Foreign keys: one or more columns whose values in a table refer to the primary key in another table.**
- **Concurrency: ability for multiple processes to access or change shared data at the same time.**
- **Locks prevent data corruption when multiple users try to write to the database simultaneously.**
- **ACID: atomicity, consistency, isolation, durability.**

One of the most important environments driven by applications is a database environment. Databases have been in use for decades. They allow us to store sensitive and valuable information that can be accessed and drive business decisions. It follows that database environments require attention to security to protect the information and ensure only authorized users have access to it. Security needs to exist within the database itself as well as within the applications that access the database.

The architecture is broken down into components, and each component is secured. The underlying hardware and software need to be secured, the proper tools that allow access to the data need to be secured, and users need to understand usage policies related to the information, security responsibilities, as well as how to properly use the tools that allow access to the data. Of course, the data itself must be secured and protected.

Database Management Systems (DBMS)

A database architecture is composed of several components, typically including those noted in Table 8-6.

Hardware	Hardware refers to the computer—usually a dedicated server—upon which other DBMS components reside. DBMS hardware usually includes a dedicated RAID controller and associated storage as well as redundant power, cooling, and network components.
Software	Software refers to the operating system (OS) as well as the application that supports the database and allows users to interact with database contents. Application security is very important to protect the underlying data.
Language (e.g. SQL)	Language refers to the syntax and commands that make user interaction with database contents possible. Specifically, SQL stands for "Structured Query Language," and many dialects of SQL exist, including T-SQL, MySQL, PostgreSQL, and SQLite.
Users	Users refers to the people who need to work with data stored in a DBMS. Most often, users interact with data through a software interface; other times, super and admin users might work directly with data through a query feature built into the DBMS application.
Data	Data refers to all the important data stored in a DBMS that should be protected by a well-planned architecture that includes security in every component, including hardware, software, and user management.

Table 8-6: **DBMS Components**

Relational Database

Like most technology over time, databases have evolved too. In the past, databases were hierarchical, flat files stored on tapes. Today, relational database management systems (RDBMS) are the most frequently used database systems. As the name suggests, RDBMS allow objects and data to be stored and linked together—to be related—to drive better decision-making. Information can be related to other information and thereby drive inference and deeper understanding. A database can contain one or more tables of data as depicted in Figure 8-9.

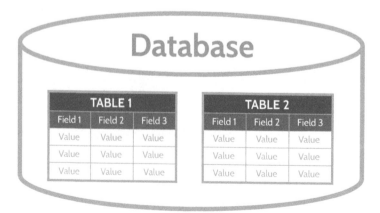

Figure 8-9: **Relational Database Table**

Attributes and Tuples

RDBMS are structured as two-dimensional tables composed of rows and columns as depicted in Figure 8-10. This structure allows tables of information to be linked together, which allows inference to take place. In addition to what might be viewed as traditional terminology, it's important to understand other words that mean the same thing as rows and columns. Columns or fields are called **attributes**, and records or rows are called **tuples**.

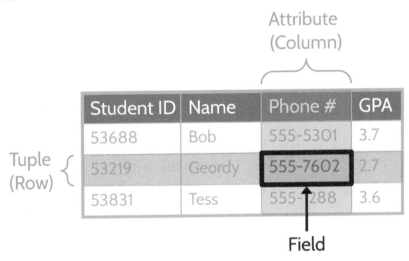

Attribute (Column)

Student ID	Name	Phone #	GPA
53688	Bob	555-5301	3.7
53219	Geordy	555-7602	2.7
53831	Tess	555-1288	3.6

Tuple (Row)

Field

Figure 8-10: **Database Table Structure**

Primary and Foreign Keys

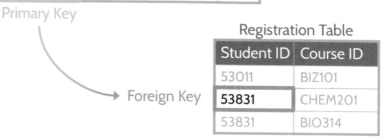

Student Table

Student ID	Name	Phone #	GPA
53688	Bob	555-5301	3.7
53219	Geordy	555-7602	2.7
53831	Tess	555-1288	3.6

Primary Key

Registration Table

Student ID	Course ID
53011	BIZ101
53831	CHEM201
53831	BIO314

Foreign Key

Figure 8-11: **Primary and Foreign Keys**

Figure 8-11 depicts two tables: a student table and a registration table. The student table contains information that would typically relate to a student; the registration table contains information about course registrations. To gain more information about a student and their courses, it makes sense to link the tables together. To do so, some type of common denominator must exist in each table. In this example, the common denominator is "StudentID," which functions as a unique identifier and is also known as the **primary key**. The entire purpose of a primary key is to make each row—each tuple—unique. In the registration table, StudentID also exists, which allows the two tables to be linked together. When the primary key from one table references the same key in another table, the referenced key is known as the **foreign key**. In this example, the primary key is StudentID in the student table; the foreign key is StudentID in the registration table.

> **Understand how primary & foreign keys function together to maintain referential integrity within a database**

Another important requirement related to primary keys is that they must be valid. In other words, validation of the primary key takes place when a record is added to a table. This typically means that the key is checked against rules to make sure the data conforms to requirements like length, data type, uniqueness, and so on. This validation process ensures what's known as referential integrity, which is a critical component of relational database systems. In this example, referential integrity ensures that every instance of StudentID in the student table is valid and that every instance of StudentID in the registration table exists in the student table.

> **Understand the meaning of common database terms**

A summary of key database terms has been included in Table 8-7.

Tuple	Single **row** of a two-dimensional table within a relational database
Attribute	Single **column** of a two-dimensional table within a relational database
Field	The intersection of a row (tuple) and a column (attribute) is a single field of data
Primary Key	One or more columns whose values uniquely identify a tuple (row) within a relational database. For example, AuthorID in the authors table.
Foreign Key	One or more columns whose values in a table refer to the primary key in another table. AuthorID would be the primary key in the authors table. Any books in the books table by an author would have a foreign key referring to the author in the authors table.

Table 8-7: **Key Database Terms**

Concurrency and Locks

Among security issues that exist within the context of database environments, concurrency, locking, and controls related to each are essential to consider. Databases are valuable for several reasons, including that they contain up-to-date and relevant information for purposes of decision-making. This means that multiple people may sometimes attempt to access or update the same database element at the same time. When this happens, integrity issues could arise. As a result, the logic and controls to handle **concurrency** (the ability for multiple processes to access or change shared data at the same time) and locks are standard within DBMS. Locks are used to protect the integrity of data elements. For example, when User A accesses an element and begins making changes, the element is **locked**. Thus, another User B is prevented from updating the element. User B can only view the element. Once the original User A is finished with their operation, the element is unlocked and released for other users to access and edit

> **Understand how concurrency and locks function to protect the integrity of databases**

Concurrency and locks are summarized in Table 8-8.

Concurrency	Locks
Ability for multiple processes to access or change shared data at the same time	**Prevent data corruption** when multiple users try to write to the database simultaneously. A record can be locked.

Table 8-8: **Concurrency and Locks**

ACID

Related to concurrency and locks controls is specific functionality represented by the acronym ACID. ACID stands for atomicity, consistency, isolation, and durability and relates to how information and transactions in an RDBMS environment should be treated. It is important to understand what each term means, and Table 8-9, breaks down ACID in more detail.

> **Understand the acronym ACID and what each term means**

A	**Atomicity – All** changes take effect or **None at all**
C	**Consistency –** Consistent with the **Rules**
I	**Isolation –** Transactions are **Invisible** to other users until complete
D	**Durability –** Completed changes will not be **Lost**

Table 8-9: **ACID**

8.2.4 Metadata

CORE **CONCEPTS**

- Metadata is data about other data

The term metadata refers to information that offers insights about other data. Essentially, it's data about data. For example, metadata about a file would include creation date, last modified date, file owner, file size, and so on.

8.2.5 Development Ecosystems

CORE CONCEPTS

- CI/CD, SOAR, and SCM are development ecosystems.
- Though the focus of each is different, they each share common characteristics.

Different types of development ecosystems exist, and several of them were noted at the beginning of section 8.2. They are: continuous integration; delivery and deployment (CI/CD); security orchestration, automation, and response (SOAR); and Software Configuration Management (SCM). Though each of these has a different focus, they share similar characteristics:

- The use of automation to ensure consistency and quality

- Efficient and effective delivery of product, results, and protection

- Protection of the organization and partners/customers through a proactive focus on security

8.3 Assess the effectiveness of software security

8.3.1 Software Security Assessment Methods

CORE **CONCEPTS**

■ Software security effectiveness can be determined through auditing and logging of changes and risk analysis and mitigation, among other methods

This section is really a short review of Domain 6, Security Assessment and Testing; for more details, refer to Domain 6.

In order to assess the effectiveness of application security, testing should be conducted, and logs should be reviewed, among other things. Testing could include white box testing and black box testing as well as items like threat modeling and penetration testing. Security should be involved with:

■ Risk analysis and mitigation

■ Auditing and logging of changes

■ Logging and monitoring

■ Internal and external audit

■ Procurement process

■ Certification and accreditation

■ Testing and verification

■ Code signing

As noted above, certification and accreditation are parts of this process.

Certification is the comprehensive and technical analysis of something—an application in this case—to make sure requirements and needs are met. Accreditation is management's official decision and sign-off to implement a solution. Both activities relate to security's goal of providing confidence and assurance.

As noted earlier, this topic is a quick review of Domain 6, Security Assessment and Testing, and it covers both bullet points noted in the Official CISSP Certification Exam Outline:

■ Auditing and logging of changes

■ Risk analysis and mitigation

8.4 Assess security impact of acquired software

Does purchasing software preclude the need for security to be assessed? Many organizations do not have the time or resources to develop their own software, so they contract the development to a third party, or they purchase the software from a vendor. Regardless of the source of software—internally developed or externally purchased—security should always be involved with the process. Whether testing functionality or assessing potential vulnerabilities, security must be included.

When purchasing software, oftentimes the seller will not provide the source code—only the finished product. In cases like this, the purchasing company might ask that the source code be stored in escrow to provide ongoing access, regardless of what may happen with the seller over time (e.g., going out of business).

8.4.1 Acquiring Software

> CORE **CONCEPTS**
>
> - Acquiring software should be taken as seriously as developing software, and security should be considered at every step in the process.
>
> - Software assurance phases for acquisition include: planning/requirements, contracting, acceptance, monitoring and follow-on.
>
> - Common ways to acquire software is via: COTS, open source, third party, managed services.

Software development should be underpinned by a strong focus on security from inception to deployment to retirement. The acquisition of software should require and receive the same level of attention and scrutiny. At a high level, the software acquisition process should follow a similar process as noted.

Software Assurance Phases for Acquisition

- Planning/requirements

- Contracting

- Acceptance

- Monitoring and follow-on

> Based upon Software Assurance Phases for Acquisition, understand what steps should be included first with ANY acquisition of software

Software may be acquired in a multitude of legal and illegal ways. Some of the more common legal means of acquiring software include COTS, open source, third party, and managed services.

Commercial-Off-the-Shelf (COTS)

Among most organizations, COTS software is typically used, because it is often readily available to the general public, and it is user friendly. Additionally, active user communities often develop around COTS software that allow user support, software use scenarios and examples, troubleshooting, and bug reports to become a dynamic and collective community-based effort versus isolated user dependence upon the COTS provider. Examples of COTS software include Microsoft 365, antivirus, and security software as well as numerous other types of software, including enterprise resource planning (ERP), customer relationship management (CRM), point of sale (POS), billing, accounting, and invoicing, among many other COTS solutions.

Use of COTS software offers pros and cons.

Pros include:

- Functionality of the product can be more easily verified/confirmed

- Comparisons of similar products can be made

- Third-party evaluation of the product can be made

- Existing customers can be contacted

- Software updates and patches are likely more readily available

Cons include:

- Inability to conduct white box testing, due to code base not being available for examination

- Possibility of the vendor going out of business

- Support and related issues

- Missing features and functionality

- Vulnerabilities being identified and taken advantage of by malicious users as widely used software is more likely to be probed for weaknesses due to larger user base

Like when software is developed in house, the acquisition of COTS software should result from a correspondingly rigorous application of the SDLC, despite things like white box testing not being possible.

> **Understand how COTS and open source are similar and different from each other and pros and cons of each method of procuring software**

Open Source Software

In many respects, open source software is very similar to COTS software, with one significant exception: unlike COTS, open source software is software with source code that anyone can inspect, modify, and enhance. As a general rule, open source software licenses invite collaboration among a user community. Furthermore, modification of code and incorporation of changes into projects can lead to enhanced functionality and new uses of the software. An organization may choose to use open source software for any of a number of reasons, including those noted below:

- **Control:** the organization can thoroughly examine the code to make sure it is safe, and they can choose to modify or omit parts of the software.

- **Training:** programming students can use open source software as a learning tool and invite feedback and scrutiny from a much wider audience.

- **Security:** due to the "open" nature of open source software, vulnerabilities and issues that may impact the stability of the software are typically identified and corrected much more quickly. Additionally, missing functionality can be added just as quickly.

Additionally, open source software typically provides a level of stability not always found with COTS or proprietary software, because the ongoing viability of open source software is not dependent on the original creators. Rather, open source software—like larger COTS platforms—typically leads to the growth of communities around it and these communities provide ongoing care, support, and upkeep.

With all of this in mind, however, prior to using open source software in an organization, the software should be examined and treated as if it was being developed in house. The SDLC, or a similar security-centric approach, should be applied, and the code confirmed to be safe for use. Otherwise, due to the community-based nature of open source software, vulnerabilities—accidental or malicious in origin—could exist. A classic example of this centered around a popular piece of software called OpenSSL. Due to a simple programming error, a security hole was opened and later exploited in what became known as Heartbleed. Due to widespread use of OpenSSL around the globe, Heartbleed affected millions of devices.

Third Party

In the context of software development and acquiring software, third-party code is code developed by programmers not employed by the organization. Whether acting as an independent contractor or as an employee of a software development company, third-party programmers and their code should be held to the same level of scrutiny as other vendors and their software products. The SDLC process should be applied to the extent possible, in order to ensure that the application is secure and functions as expected.

Managed Services (SaaS, IaaS, PaaS)

Managed services, such as Software as a Service (SaaS), Infrastructure as a Service (IaaS), and Platform as a Service (PaaS) are discussed in greater detail in Domain 3—Topic 3.5.9, Cloud Service and Deployment Models.

Regardless of the service model used, organizations should always properly assess the managed service provider to best ensure that organizational goals and objectives, especially where security and privacy are concerned, are met. Proper assessment would typically include:

- Evaluation of SOC reports prepared by an independent auditor
- Site visits by senior management and key stakeholders of the organization assessing the managed service provider
- Discussions with existing customers of the managed service provider
- If applicable, industry and regulatory assessments of the managed service provider for the sake of specific needs relevant to the organization

Additional assessment criteria may be used as well. Regardless of the assessment protocol followed, any organization that chooses to use a managed service provider always retains ultimate accountability for data and other information that may be stored or processed in a managed service provider's environment.

8.5 Define and apply secure coding guidelines and standards

8.5.1 Secure Coding Guidelines

To produce consistently secure software, it is important to define and apply secure coding guidelines and best practices. As noted earlier, programming tools today offer significant functionality, including the ability to include security as part of the process. This is what needs to be enforced. Several frameworks and sources exist to aid with these efforts, including Open Web Applications Security Project (OWASP). Every few years, OWASP publishes a Top 10 Web Application Security Risks document that includes a list of risks, their descriptions, and mitigation strategies. Similarly, other organizations, like NIST and CIS, also offer secure software development frameworks and resources devoted to best software development practices. Table 8-10 contains a list of the most common security weaknesses and vulnerabilities present at the source code level.

Covert Channels	***Unintentional*** communications path that has the opportunity of disclosing confidential or sensitive information. Two types of covert channels exist: timing and storage.
Buffer Overflows	Buffer overflows take place when application input information exceeds the storage space—the buffer—allocated to store that information. Buffer overflow conditions are not uncommon and typically can only be fixed through application of a software patch.
Memory/ Object Reuse	The ability to overwrite storage where secure and sensitive information has been written or stored. Most applications don't have the ability to overwrite storage where sensitive information has been written, which can lead to this information being available or viewable by other applications.
Executable Mobile Code	Executable mobile code is code that is downloaded to a system and then run on the system. This may happen because of clicking a link on a webpage or in an email. Once the link is clicked, the code downloads to the machine and runs locally, and therefore it is referred to as "mobile" code. If the code is malicious, serious harm could follow. A protective measure is to test the code in a sandbox environment first.
TOCTOU	TOCTOU refers to time-of-check time-of-use, and it may also be referred to as "race condition." This occurs when a time gap exists between when a value is checked/ enforced and when the value is used. This gap leaves room for malicious activity to occur.
Backdoors/ Trapdoors	Backdoors/trapdoors are intentionally put in place by developers so they can quickly access an application to perform legitimate work. They're sometimes also referred to as maintenance hooks. A problem arises, however, when these backdoors/trapdoors still exist after development is finished. Numerous examples of backdoors found in operating systems and applications exist, and oftentimes they can only be identified by examining the source code.
Malformed Input	Malformed input means exactly that—input that does not meet certain criteria or rules. Data or input validation functionality should exist in applications and check data before it is accepted. In fact, inadequate input validation is one of the leading causes of attacks on web applications, and it routinely shows up in OWASP's Top 10 vulnerabilities list.
Citizen Developers	Citizen developers is a term that politely refers to normal users having access to powerful programming and similar tools. A perfect example of this is giving users access to SQL query tools, so they can perform their own queries against the contents of a database instead of relying on somebody to do the work for them. As a result, these users often have access to very functional and powerful tools without commensurate security skills to protect their activities. Policies, security awareness, training, and education can help alleviate and bridge this gap.

Table 8-10: **Security Weaknesses and Vulnerabilities at the Source Code Level**

8.5.2 Buffer Overflow

> ### CORE **CONCEPTS**
>
> - Buffer overflow is a common problem with applications and happens when information sent to a storage buffer exceeds the capacity of the buffer.
> - Buffer overflow vulnerabilities can be exploited to elevate privileges or launch malicious code.
> - Address space layout randomization (ASLR) can be used to protect against buffer overflows.
> - Parameter/bounds checking is another way to protect against buffer overflows.

Let's examine the concept of buffer overflows more closely. As described above, a buffer overflow happens when information sent to a storage buffer exceeds the capacity of the buffer, especially in applications. At a high level, applications accept input, process it, and provide output. When designing applications, buffers—temporary memory storage areas—are included to handle the input, processing, and output functionality. Buffer sizes are often determined ahead of time and don't dynamically change. Thus, if an application somehow sends more information than a buffer can handle, an overflow condition results.

> **Understand what is meant by the term** *buffer overflow* **and how a buffer overflow works**

The inability of a buffer to dynamically change size points to the way an attacker could creatively use a buffer overflow to exploit a system. An attacker could create a situation where the overflow data that contains executable code is placed into a storage area where the code is then executed. For example, this could allow the attacker to elevate their system privileges.

Though the buffer overflow problem has been around for decades, ways to mitigate or prevent buffer overflows do exist. **Address Space Layout Randomization (ASLR)** is one of the best techniques to protect against buffer overflows. In essence, it works by randomizing the locations of where system executables are loaded into memory. In other words, without ASLR, an attacker could learn how a program operates and what parts of a buffer are utilized by a given program, and this knowledge can lead to the creation of an attack. With ASLR enabled, because the location of system executables is randomized, it makes it very difficult for the attacker to guess the locations and therefore launch a successful attack.

> **Understand how a buffer overflow situation can be mitigated through ASLR**

Another software development technique commonly used to prevent buffer overflows is **bounds checking.** The input to a variable should be checked to ensure it is within some bounds, before it is used. For example, that a string is of a certain length, a number fits into a given type, or an array index is within the bounds of the array.

> **In addition to ASLR, understand other ways to protect against buffer overflow situations**

In addition to ASLR & bounds checking, other ways to protect against buffer overflow situations include:

- Parameter/**bounds checking**
- Improve software development process, including thorough code review
- Runtime checking of array and buffer bounds
- Use safe programming languages and library functions

8.5.3 Application Programming Interfaces (APIs)

CORE CONCEPTS

- Application programming interfaces (APIs) provide a way for applications to communicate with each other; APIs act as translators.

- Two of the most common APIs are Representational State Transfer (REST) and Simple Object Access Protocol (SOAP).

- APIs should be secured along with other components of an application; security can include authentication and authorization mechanisms, TLS encryption for data traversing insecure channels, API gateways, and data validation, among others.

Due to the proliferation of use of the internet and the way applications are programmed and operate today, many of the programs in use today are disparate components that talk to and work with each other. A perfect example of this fact is web application environments, where many different components might exist and need to communicate with each other. This communication is facilitated by standards that allow components to understand each other. These standards are better known as application programming interfaces or APIs.

Here's an example to better illustrate: Imagine walking into a restaurant and sitting down at a table to order a meal. After looking at the menu, a server takes the order and relays it to the kitchen, where the cooking team will prepare the food. In this context, the server is like the API that relays information from the customer to the kitchen in such a way that a meal will be prepared as the customer specified. Like the language used to communicate between servers and kitchen staff, APIs provide a way for applications to communicate with each other. If the goal is for two applications to communicate, regardless of the language they speak, a translator must exist. APIs act as translators and facilitate this communication. The two most used API formats are REST and SOAP, and each format has strengths and weaknesses.

> Understand what the term *application programming interface* means and what function an API provides to applications

Application Programming Interfaces (APIs)

As noted above, how to access web services really boils down to the question of which API should be used, as both REST and SOAP are viable options. Table 8-11 outlines differences between the two standards.

> Understand the two most common API formats and characteristics of each

Representational State Transfer (REST)	Simple Object Access Protocol (SOAP)
▪ Representational State Transfer	▪ Simple Object Access Protocol
▪ Newer	▪ Older, originally developed by Microsoft
▪ More flexible and lighter weight alternative to SOAP	▪ More rigid and standardized
▪ HTTP based	▪ XML-based
▪ Easy to learn and use	▪ Extensible through use of WS standards
▪ Fast in processing	▪ Strong error handling
▪ Output can take several forms, including CSV, JSON, RSS, and XML	

Table 8-11: **REST vs SOAP**

Security of Application Programming Interfaces

Among ways to protect APIs, best industry recommendations include:

Understand techniques commonly used to secure APIs

- Authentication and authorization (access tokens/OAuth)
- Encryption (TLS)
- Data validation
- API gateways
- Quotas and throttling
- Testing and validation

8.5.4 Secure Coding Practices

CORE **CONCEPTS**

- **Secure programming can help prevent software vulnerabilities.**
- **Secure coding practices include: input validation, authentication and password management, session management, among others.**
- **Coupling and cohesion are relational terms that indicate the level of relatedness between units of a code base (coupling) and the level of relatedness between the code that makes up a unit of code (cohesion).**
- **Low coupling (meaning units of code can stand alone) and high cohesion (meaning the code that makes up a unit of code is highly related) are optimal.**
- **Polyinstantiation refers to something being instantiated into multiple separate or independent instances and can be used to prevent unauthorized inference.**

Secure coding practices refers to steps and techniques taken to minimize or eliminate vulnerabilities in software that could lead to exploitation. In addition to some that were mentioned earlier, other steps and techniques are noted below:

- Input validation
- Authentication and password management
- Session management
- Cryptographic practices
- Error handling and logging
- System configuration
- File/database security
- Memory management

Coupling and Cohesion

Coupling and cohesion are relational terms that indicate the level of relatedness between units of a code base (coupling) and the level of relatedness between the code that makes up a unit of code (cohesion). Low **coupling** (meaning units of code can stand alone and are not dependent on other units of code to function) and high **cohesion** (meaning the code that makes up a unit of software is highly related) are optimal, whereas high coupling and low cohesion is typically indicative of poorly written code.

> Understand the terms *cohesion* and *coupling* and which combination (low or high) is ideal for purposes of coding

Polyinstantiation

The word *poly* means many. The word *instantiation* refers to an instance or example of something. Put together, *polyinstantiation* refers to something being instantiated into multiple separate or independent instances. A better way to illustrate this is through an example.

> Understand the term *polyinstantiation* and what it can help prevent

Imagine a military environment—an army base—where one of the systems is used to track and manage military units. One day, a General requests that a new military unit—Charlie Company 6—be added to the system. Upon trying to enter information about this unit to the system, the system operator receives the error message: "Unable to add unit Charlie Company 6." Simply based upon this transaction and error message, unauthorized inferences can be made—that error message is essentially saying that a unit named "Charlie Company 6" already exists in the system.

If polyinstantiation techniques had been designed into the system, the system would have recognized that Charlie Company 6 already existed in the system at a higher classification level than what the operator was allowed to see. The system would then know that when anybody at the lower level refers to Charlie Company 6, it will be mapped to something else at that lower level. In other words, technology will handle the management of data using polyinstantiation techniques based upon classification and clearance levels, which will prevent unauthorized inference from taking place.

Unauthorized inference can be a particular issue where people and databases are concerned. Most of the time, inference is a good thing. This is why databases and similar repositories exist, to facilitate queries that can lead to the discovery of information valuable to an organization and thereby drive better decisions. However, some types of information should only be viewed by certain people. Otherwise, more unauthorized inference of more sensitive information might result.

Polyinstantiation can be used to **prevent unauthorized inference**, and it allows the same data to exist at different classification levels.

Software-Defined Security

As the name suggests, software-defined security is security in a computing environment that is implemented, controlled, and managed by software. As with other software-defined functions, the development and growth of software-defined security has coincided with continued growth of cloud and virtualization. Specific functionality of software-defined security can mimic that found with traditional hardware-based solutions; firewalls, intrusion detection and prevention, access control and management, among others, can all be instantiated, configured, and managed through software-defined security solutions. Furthermore, functionality of software-defined security is typically driven by policy that supports an organization's overall goals and objectives in a cost-effective manner.

8.5.5 Software Development Vulnerabilities

CORE **CONCEPTS**

- Insecure coding practices and citizen developers writing code usually leads to software development vulnerabilities.

- Backdoor/trapdoor attacks often result from software vulnerabilities.

- Between-the-lines attack = attacker intercepts/modifies communication between devices/people over a network; also known as a man-in-the-middle attack.

Software development vulnerabilities often arise because of:

- Use of insecure coding practices.

- Citizen developers writing code.

As noted earlier, **citizen developers** often have access to powerful programming tools, but they're typically self-taught and unskilled with regards to secure coding practices, which can lead to insecure and unreliable application development. Insecure coding practices can lead to backdoor or trapdoor situations, whereby an attacker is able to bypass normal authentication mechanisms as a result of installing remote access software on a computer as well as attacks like:

> Understand the primary reasons that lead to software development vulnerabilities

- **Between-the-lines attack,** where an attacker intercepts or modifies communication between devices/people communication over a network. This type of attack is also known as a man-in-the-middle attack.

- **Memory reuse (object reuse)**, where remnants of data that relate to a previous operation are accidentally or intentionally read, used, or otherwise disclosed. In practice, residual data should be cleared from memory before another operation is performed.

MINDMAP REVIEW **VIDEOS**

Secure Software Development
dcgo.ca/CISSPmm8-1

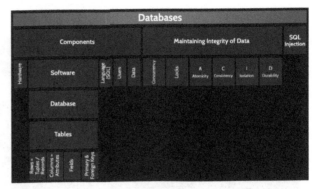

Databases
dcgo.ca/CISSPmm8-2

CISSP PRACTICE QUESTION APP

Download the Destination CISSP Practice Question app for Domain 8 practice questions

dcgo.ca/PracQues

REFERENCES AND FURTHER READING

Resource	Link
(ISC)2 Code of Ethics	https://www.isc2.org/Ethics
(ISC)2 CISSP Exam Outline (effective May 2, 2021)	https://www.isc2.org/CISSP-Exam-Outline
California Privacy Rights Act of 2020	https://iapp.org/resources/topics/ccpa-and-cpra/
COPPA	https://www.ftc.gov/legal-library/browse/rules/childrens-online-privacy-protection-rule-coppa
COBIT	https://www.isaca.org/resources/cobit
CVE	https://www.cve.org/
CVSS	https://www.first.org/cvss/
DMCA	https://www.gpo.gov/fdsys/pkg/PLAW-105publ304/pdf/PLAW-105publ304.pdf
DREAD	https://en.wikipedia.org/wiki/DREAD_%28risk_assessment_model%29
FedRAMP	https://www.fedramp.gov/
FIPS 140-2	https://csrc.nist.gov/publications/detail/fips/140/2/final
GDPR	https://gdpr.eu/tag/gdpr/
GLBA	https://www.govinfo.gov/link/plaw/106/public/102?link-type=pdf&.pdf
HIPAA	https://www.hhs.gov/hipaa/index.html
ISO 15408	https://standards.iso.org/ittf/PubliclyAvailableStandards/index.html
ISO 27001 & 27002	https://www.iso.org/isoiec-27001-information-security.html
ISO 29134:2017	https://www.iso.org/obp/ui/#iso:std:iso-iec:29134:ed-1:v1:en
ITIL	https://www.axelos.com/certifications/itil-service-management
ITSEC	https://op.europa.eu/en/publication-detail/-/publication/f06fe0df-1d9b-430e-bc82-f8c63ea1c394/language-en/format-PDF/source-search
Kerckhoff's Principle	https://en.wikipedia.org/wiki/Kerckhoffs%27s_principle
Locard's exchange principle	https://en.wikipedia.org/wiki/Locard%27s_exchange_principle
NIST Cloud Computing Forensic Science Challenges	https://csrc.nist.gov/publications/detail/nistir/8006/final
NIST SP 500-241	https://www.nist.gov/publications/quick-reference-list-organizations-and-standards-digital-rights-management
NIST SP 800-12 Rev 1	https://csrc.nist.gov/publications/detail/sp/800-12/rev-1/final
NIST SP 800-34 Rev 1	https://csrc.nist.gov/publications/detail/sp/800-34/rev-1/final
NIST SP 800-37 Rev 2	https://csrc.nist.gov/publications/detail/sp/800-37/rev-2/final
NIST SP 800-41 Rev 1	https://csrc.nist.gov/publications/detail/sp/800-41/rev-1/final

Resource	Link
NIST SP 800-53 Rev 5	https://csrc.nist.gov/publications/detail/sp/800-53/rev-5/final
NIST SP 800-61 Rev 2	https://csrc.nist.gov/publications/detail/sp/800-61/rev-2/final
NIST SP 800-63	https://pages.nist.gov/800-63-3/
NIST SP 800-88 Rev 1	https://csrc.nist.gov/publications/detail/sp/800-88/rev-1/final
NIST SP 800-115	https://csrc.nist.gov/publications/detail/sp/800-115/final
NIST SP 800-122	https://csrc.nist.gov/publications/detail/sp/800-122/final
NIST SP 800-124 Rev 1	https://csrc.nist.gov/publications/detail/sp/800-124/rev-1/final
NIST SP 800-125	https://csrc.nist.gov/publications/detail/sp/800-125/final
NIST SP 800-137A	https://csrc.nist.gov/publications/detail/sp/800-137a/final
NIST SP 800-153	https://csrc.nist.gov/publications/detail/sp/800-153/final
NIST SP 800-207	https://csrc.nist.gov/publications/detail/sp/800-207/final
OECD Privacy Guidelines	https://legalinstruments.oecd.org/en/instruments/OECD-LEGAL-0188
OWASP Mobile Security Testing Guide	https://owasp.org/www-project-mobile-security-testing-guide/
OWASP Mobile Top 10	https://owasp.org/www-project-mobile-top-10/
OWASP Software Assurance Maturity Model	https://owaspsamm.org/model/
PASTA	https://versprite.com/blog/what-is-pasta-threat-modeling/
PCI DSS	https://www.pcisecuritystandards.org/
Privacy by Design	https://iapp.org/resources/article/privacy-by-design-the-7-foundational-principles/
Sarbanes–Oxley Act (SOX)	https://www.govinfo.gov/link/plaw/107/public/204?link-type=pdf&.pdf
STRIDE	https://docs.microsoft.com/en-us/azure/security/develop/threat-modeling-tool-threats
TCSEC (Orange Book)	https://csrc.nist.gov/csrc/media/publications/conference-paper/1998/10/08/proceedings-of-the-21st-nissc-1998/documents/early-cs-papers/dod85.pdf
The Wassenaar Arrangement	https://www.wassenaar.org/
TPM Standard	https://www.iso.org/standard/66510.html
USML	https://www.ecfr.gov/current/title-22/chapter-I/subchapter-M/part-121

ACRONYMS

AAA	Authentication, Authorization and Accounting
AAL	Authentication Assurance Levels
AES	Advanced Encryption Standard
AH	Authentication Header
AICPA	American Institute of Certified Public Accountants
ALE	Annualized Loss Expectancy
API	Application Programming Interface
APPs	Australian Privacy Principles
APT	Advanced Persistent Threat
ARO	Annualized Rate of Occurrence
AS	Authentication Service
ASLR	Address Space Layout Randomization
ATM	Automated Teller Machine
ATM	Asynchronous Transfer Mode
AV	Asset Value
AV	Anti-Virus
BAU	Business as Usual
BC	Business Continuity
BCM	Business Continuity Management
BCP	Business Continuity Procedure
BCP	Business Continuity Plan
BGP	Border Gateway Protocol
BIA	Business Impact Analysis
CA	Certificate Authority
CaaS	Containers as a Service
CAB	Change Advisory Board
CAM	Content Addressable Memory
CAPTCHA	Completely Automated Public Turing test to tell Computers and Humans Apart
CBC	Cipher Block Chaining

CBK	Common Body of Knowledge
CCTV	Closed Circuit Television
CD	Compact Disc
CDMA	Code Division Multiple Access
CEO	Chief Executive Officer
CER	Cross over Error Rate
CFB	Cipher Feedback
CHAP	Challenge Handshake Authentication Protocol
CI/CD	Continuous Integration, Continuous Delivery
CIO	Chief Information Officer
CIP	Critical Infrastructure Protection
CISO	Chief Information Security Officer
CISSP	Certified Information Systems Security Professional
CMM	Capability Maturity Model
CORPA	Consumer Online Privacy Rights Act
COSO	Committee of Sponsoring Organizations of the Treadway Commission
COTS	Commercial-Off-The-Shelf
CPE	Continuing Professional Education
CPTED	Crime Prevention Through Environmental Design
CPU	Central Processing Unit
CRC	Cyclic Redundancy Check
CRL	Certificate Revocation List
CRM	Customer Relationship Management
CRT	Cathode-Ray Tube
CSMA	Carrier Sense Multiple Access
CSMA/CA	Carrier Sense Multiple Access (Collision Avoidance)
CSMA/CD	Carrier Sense Multiple Access (Collision Detection)
CSO	Chief Security Officer

CSP	Cloud Service Provider		**ECB**	Electronic Codebook
CSR	Certificate Signing Request		**ECC**	Elliptic Curve Cryptography
CSRF	Cross Site Request Forgery		**EF**	Exposure Factor
CTR	Counter		**ERP**	Enterprise Resource Planning
CVE	Common Vulnerability and Exposures		**ESP**	Encapsulating Security Payload
CVSS	Common Vulnerability Scoring System		**FaaS**	Function as a Service
CWE	Common Weakness Enumeration		**FAR**	False Acceptance Rate
DAC	Discretionary Access Control		**FCoE**	Fibre Channel over Ethernet
DAST	Dynamic Application Security Testing		**FERPA**	Family Educational Rights and Privacy Act
DBMS	Database Management System		**FIA**	Fault Injection Attack
DCS	Distributed Control System		**FIM**	Federated Identity Management
DDoS	Distributed Denial of Service		**FIM**	Federated Integrity Management
DES	Data Encryption Standard		**FIM**	File Integrity Monitoring
DFS	Distributed File Systems		**FISMA**	Federal Information Security Modernization Act
DLP	Data Loss Prevention		**FISMA**	Federal Information Security Management Act
DMCA	Digital Millennium Copyright Act		**FRR**	False Rejection Rate
DMZ	Demilitarized Zone		**FTP**	File Transfer Protocol
DNS	Domain Name System		**GDPR**	General Data Protection Regulation
DNSSEC	Domain Name System Secure		**GLBA**	Gramm–Leach–Bliley Act
DoS	Denial of Service		**GPS**	Global Positioning System
DPIA	Data Protection Impact Assessment		**GRE**	Generic Routing Encapsulation
DPO	Data Protection Officer		**GSM**	Global System for Mobiles
DR	Disaster Recovery		**HIPAA**	Health Insurance Portability and Accountability Act
DRM	Digital Rights Management		**HIPS**	Host Intrusion Prevention System
DRP	Disaster Recovery Protocol		**HMAC**	Hash Message Authentication Code
DRP	Digital Rights Protection		**HSM**	Hardware Security Module
DRP	Disaster Recovery Plan		**HTTP**	Hyper Text Transfer Protocol
DVD	Digital Versatile Disc		**HTTPS**	Hyper Text Transfer Protocol Secure
EAL	Evaluation Assurance Level		**HVAC**	Heating, Ventilation and Air Conditioning
EAP	Extensible Authentication Protocol			
EAR	Export Administration Regulations		**IaaS**	Infrastructure as a Service

IAM	Identity and Access Management		**MAM**	Mobile Application Management
IAM	Identity Access Management		**MASVS**	Mobile Application Security Verification Standard
IANA	Internet Assigned Numbers Authority		**MD5**	Message Digest 5
ICMP	Internet Control Message Protocol		**MDM**	Mobile Device Management
ICS	Industrial Control Systems		**MIC**	Message Integrity Check
IDaaS	Identity as a Service		**MOM**	Motive Opportunity Means
IDE	Integrated Development Environment		**MPLS**	Multi-Protocol Label Switching
IDS	Intrusion Detection System		**MSTG**	Mobile Security Testing Guide
IEEE	Institute of Electric and Electronic Engineers		**MTBF**	Mean Time Between Failures
			MTD	Maximum Tolerable Downtime
IGMP	Internet Group Management Protocol		**NAC**	Network Access Control
IKE	Internet Key Exchange		**NAT**	Network Address Translation
IoT	Internet of Things		**NCA**	Non-Compete Agreement
IP	Intellectual Property		**NDA**	Non Disclosure Agreement
IPSec	Internet Protocol Security		**NetBIOS**	Network Basic Input/Output System
IPT	Integrated Product Team		**NIDS**	Network Intrusion Detection System
iSCSI	Internet Small Computer Systems Interface		**NIPS**	Network Intrusion Prevention System
ISO	International Organization for Standardization		**NIST**	National Institute of Standards and Technology
IT	Information Technology		**NTP**	Network Time Protocol
ITAR	International Traffic in Arms		**OCSP**	Online Certificate Status Protocol
ITSEC	Information Technology Security Evaluation Criteria		**OECD**	Organization of Economic Cooperation and Development
IV	Initialization Vector		**OFB**	Output Feedback
JIT	Just In-Time		**OSI**	Open Systems Interconnection
KDC	Key Distribution Center		**OSPF**	Open Shortest Path First
KEK	Key Encrypting Keys		**OUI**	Organizational Unique Identifier
KPI	Key Performance Indicator		**PaaS**	Platform as a Service
KRI	Key Risk Indicator		**PAP**	Password Authentication Protocol
L2F	Layer 2 Forwarding		**PASTA**	Process for Attack Simulation and Threat Analysis
L2TP	Layer 2 Tunneling Protocol		**PAT**	Port Address Translation
MAC	Mandatory Access Control		**PbD**	Privacy by Design
MAD	Maximum Allowable Downtime		**PBX**	Private Branch Exchange

PCI DSS	Payment Card Industry Data Security Standard		**RPO**	Recovery Point Objective
PDPL	Personal Data Protection Law		**RSA**	Rivest–Shamir–Adleman
PEAP	Protected Extensible Authentication Protocol		**RTO**	Recovery Time Objective
PGP	Pretty Good Privacy		**RUM**	Real User Monitoring
PIA	Privacy Impact Assessment		**S/MIME**	Secure/Multipurpose Internet Mail Extensions
PII	Personally Identifiable Information		**SA**	Security Association
PIPA	Personal Information Protection Act		**SaaS**	Software as a Service
PIPEDA	Personal Information Protection and Electronic Documents Act		**SABSA**	Sherwood Applied Business Security Architecture
PKI	Public Key Infrastructure		**SAML**	Security Assertion Markup Language
PLC	Programmable Logic Controller		**SAMM**	Software Assurance Maturity Model
POA&M	Plan of Actions and Milestones		**SAST**	Static Application Security Testing
POS	Point of Sale		**SCADA**	Supervisory Control And Data Acquisition
PPTP	Point to Point Tunneling protocol		**SCM**	Software Configuration Management
PSTN	Public Switched Telephone Network		**SDK**	Software Development Kit
PSTN	Public Switched Telephone Network		**SDLC**	Software Development Life Cycle
PtH	Pass the Hash		**SDN**	Software Defined Network
PVC	Permanent Virtual Circuit		**SESAME**	Secure European System for Applications in a Multi-Vendor Environment
QA	Quality Assurance			
QoS	Quality of Service		**SETI**	Search for Extraterrestrial Intelligence
RA	Registration Authority		**SHA-1**	Secure Hash Algorithm 1
RADIUS	Remote Authentication Dial-In User Service		**SHA-3**	Secure Hash Algorithm 3
RAID	Redundant Array of Independent Disks		**SIEM**	Security Information and Event Management
RAM	Random Access Memory		**SIP**	Session Initiation Protocol
RBAC	Role Based Access Control		**SLA**	Service Level Agreement
RDBMS	Relational Database Management Systems		**SLC**	Software Life Cycle
REST	Representational State Transfer		**SLE**	Single Loss Expectancy
RFID	Radio Frequency Identification		**SLIP**	Serial Line Internet Protocol
RIP	Routing Internet Protocol		**SLR**	Service Level Requirements
RMC	Reference Monitor Concept		**SMART**	Specific, Measurable, Achievable, Relevant, Timely
RPC	Remote Procedure Call		**SMTP**	Simple Mail Transfer Protocol

SNMP	Simple Network Management Protocol
SOAP	Simple Object Access Protocol
SOAR	Security Orchestration, Automation, and Response
SOX	Sarbanes-Oxley
SPML	Services Provisioning Markup Language
SQL	Structured Query Language
SRTP	Secure Real-time Transport Protocol
SSD	Solid State Drive
SSH	Secure Shell
SSID	Service Set Identifier
SSL	Secure Sockets Layer
SSN	Social Security Number
SSO	Single Sign-On
STP	Shielded Twisted Pair
SVC	Switched Virtual Circuit
TACACS	Terminal Access Controller Access-Control System
TCB	Trusted Computing Base
TCP/IP	Transport Control Protocol/Internet Protocol
TCSEC	Trusted Computer System Evaluation Criteria
TGS	Ticket Granting Server
TGS	Ticket Granting Service
TGT	Ticket Granting Ticket
TKIP	Temporal Key Integrity Protocol
TLS	Transport Layer Security
TOCTOU	Time-of-check Time-of-use
TOGAF	The Open Group Architecture Framework
TOR	The Onion Router
TPM	Trusted Platform Module
UBA	User Behavior Analytics

UEBA	User Entity Behavior Analytics
UPS	Uninterrupted Power Supply
UTP	Unshielded Twisted Pair
VESDA	Very Early Smoke Detection Apparatus
VLAN	Virtual Local Area Network
VM	Virtual Machine
VMM	Virtual Machine Manager
VoIP	Voice over Internet Protocol
VPN	Virtual Private Network
WEP	Wired Equivalent Privacy
WRT	Work Recovery Time
WSUS	Windows Server Update Services
XACML	eXtensible Access Control Markup Language
XML	Extensible Markup Language
XSS	Cross Site Scripting

INDEX